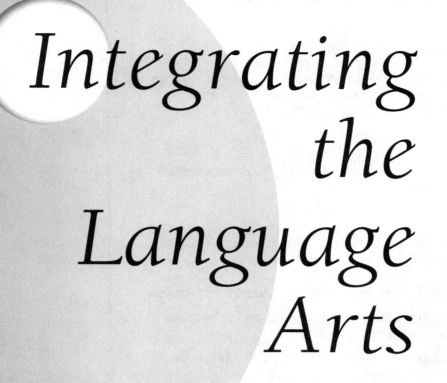

Integrating
the
Language
Arts

THIRD EDITION

DAVID YELLIN
OKLAHOMA STATE UNIVERSITY

MARY E. BLAKE
COLLEGE OF CHARLESTON

BEVERLY A. DEVRIES
SOUTHERN NAZARENE UNIVERSITY

Holcomb Hathaway, Publishers
Scottsdale, Arizona 85250

Library of Congress Cataloging-in-Publication Data

Yellin, David.
    Integrating the language arts / David Yellin, Mary E. Blake, Beverly
A. DeVries.— 3rd ed.
        p.   cm.
    Includes bibliographical references and index.
    ISBN 1-890871-51-6
    1. Language arts (Elementary)—United States. 2. Language experience
approach in education—United States. 3. Interdisciplinary approach in
education—United States. I. Blake, Mary E., 1949- II. DeVries, Beverly
A., 1947- III. Title.
LB1576.Y45 2004
372.6—dc22

                                        2003020243

Dedication

David Yellin: To my wife, Pamm, and daughters, Lindsay and Aubree.

Mary Blake: I dedicate this edition to my students and colleagues,
who have taught me so much.

Beverly DeVries: I dedicate this book to my husband, Merlyn,
who encouraged me through each step of this endeavor.

Copyright © 2004 by Holcomb Hathaway, Publishers, Inc.

Holcomb Hathaway, Publishers, Inc.
6207 North Cattletrack Road
Scottsdale, Arizona 85250
(480) 991-7881
www.hh-pub.com

10 9 8 7 6 5 4 3 2

ISBN 1-890871-51-6

Contents

Chapter 3

PLANNING AND DELIVERING LANGUAGE ARTS INSTRUCTION 64

Chapter 4

LANGUAGE ORIGINS, ACQUISITION, AND DEVELOPMENT 110

Chapter 5

LISTENING AND SPEAKING 144

Chapter 6

LANGUAGE AND LITERACY: THE READING FACTOR   194

Chapter 7

CHILDREN'S LITERATURE: THE CORNERSTONE OF A LANGUAGE ARTS PROGRAM   240

Chapter 8

THE PROCESS OF WRITING 274

Chapter 9

THE TOOLS OF WRITING 328

Chapter 10

READING AND WRITING ACROSS THE CURRICULUM   376

Chapter 11

WORKING WITH A DIVERSE POPULATION   424

Appendices

Preface

The third edition of *Integrating the Language Arts* reflects the latest research in the fields of literacy education, approaches to teaching, lesson planning, language acquisition, oral/aural development, reading, children's literature, student diversity, and technology. Direct instruction is balanced with integrated and comprehensive approaches. The importance of caregivers and community involvement in children's education is featured. Practical teaching ideas are found throughout each chapter. Special sections on visual literacy, reading and writing workshops, and the new legislation that affects the language arts are also highlighted.

Whether you teach all subjects (self-contained primary/elementary grades) or specialize in the language arts exclusively (departmentalized middle grades), this textbook is for you. Take a moment to peruse the table of contents to familiarize yourself with the different chapters and their subareas. Also note the new addition of helpful appendices.

Each chapter begins with an overview and objectives. These are followed by a K-T-W-L chart. The K-T-W-L stands for what I **K**now, what I **T**hink I know, what I **W**ant to know, and what I have **L**earned. Take a few minutes to complete the first three columns of the chart in your own notebooks before you read each chapter. This will get you more actively involved as you read the content of each chapter. After reading the chapter, discuss with your classmates what you have learned and enter this information in the last column.

The special features that characterize this third edition include

- K-T-W-L charts at the beginning of each chapter
- classroom vignettes of real children and teachers using specific techniques
- boxed features called "In and Beyond the Classroom" and "Beyond the Classroom" to give you ideas for activities and projects you may wish to do to further your understanding
- meaningful quotations in the margins to stimulate class discussions
- updated technology and websites at the end of each chapter to get your students using the Internet and creating PowerPoint displays, videos, and photo journals
- more practical and fun activities to do with children at the end of each chapter
- related readings at the end of each chapter

We hope readers will use this textbook in an interactive manner, as we have designed it to be used. Encourage your students to discuss each chapter openly in class and to complete as many of the "In & Beyond the Classroom" suggestions as possible. Have them access websites and do field observations of children and teachers in order to learn from others in the field. Encourage students to keep a journal of reflections about their readings, their observation experiences in classrooms, and other field experiences. Have them share journal reflections with you and with their peers. Each person gets something different out of a textbook and a college course. Teaching is truly a collaborative undertaking—through sharing with others we all grow in our understanding of how to teach.

Acknowledgments

We would like to thank the following reviewers, who read the manuscript for this new edition and offered constructive suggestions for its improvement. The book is better as a result of their efforts: M. Priscilla Myers, Plattsburgh State University of New York; Sherron Killingsworth Roberts, University of Central Florida; Gail J. Gerlach, Indiana University of Pennsylvania; Charles E. Matthews, College of Charleston; Elizabeth Day, Santa Clara University; Richard Ingram, Winthrop University; Rolland Menk, Martin Luther College; Fannye E. Love, The University of Mississippi; Rachael Hungerford, Lyoming College; and Carol Taylor, Southwestern College.

In addition, David Yellin would like to acknowledge the following people for their support and encouragement in this textbook project: his wife, Pamela Gold Yellin; his early mentors at Arizona State University; his colleagues at Oklahoma State University; and the many classroom teachers around the state of Oklahoma. A special thanks to Liliana Cardenas-Risley.

Mary Blake wishes to thank all her students, past and present. She also wishes to thank her former advisers at the University of Connecticut: Donald Protheroe, Judith Meagher, and the late William Page. A special thanks goes to Rebecca Shuler for gathering much of the research for this edition.

Beverly DeVries wishes to thank her students who willingly became partners in action research. Also, special thanks to Linda Jones, Tammy McGee, and Shari Kimbro for providing research on the gifted programs, to Jo Dorhout for providing information for the technology sections.

Integrating the Language Arts

THIRD EDITION

To the Student

At the beginning of each chapter, you will find a K-T-W-L chart. This chart was developed by Donna Ogle (1986) as an aid to help students become active readers of expository text. The K-T-W-L stands for What I **K**now, What I **T**hink I Know, What I **W**ant to learn, and What I **L**earned. Filling out the chart will give you the opportunity (1) to activate your prior knowledge of the concepts discussed in the chapter, (2) to reflect on what you would like to learn about the concepts, and (3) to personally reflect on the concepts you have learned after you have read the chapter.

Many teachers in all grades (1–12) use K-T-W-L charts at the beginning of units to activate students' prior knowledge. Teachers have students distinguish what they definitely know from what they think they know when they fill in the first two columns. We suggest that as you complete the first two columns, you draw from your own elementary school experiences and from observations that you have done as a preservice teacher. If you have no background knowledge of the topic, be honest and write this down.

In the "W" column, teachers build students' interest in the topic by having them write down what they would like to learn. You too should think about what you would like to learn about each of the topics. You can also use this information to guide your reading of the chapter.

After the unit, teachers have students review what they learned by writing down things they learned. As students discuss with classmates what they learned, they clarify in their minds each concept. We recommend that at the end of each chapter, you also reflect with classmates regarding what you learned. These discussions will help you clarify the concepts and help you remember the concepts for tests and for your future teaching.

1

Introduction to the Language Arts

I n this chapter, you will learn about the *Standards for the English Language Arts,* established by the International Reading Association and the National Council of Teachers of English, the six components of the language arts, two learning theories that support the teaching of the language arts, the different approaches to teaching the language arts, and the way politics influence schools.

CHAPTER OBJECTIVES

After reading this chapter, you should be able to accomplish the following objectives:

1. Name the six components of language arts.
2. Explain what the acronym IRA represents.
3. Explain what the acronym NCTE represents.
4. Discuss the eight conditions that Brian Cambourne believes must be present in order for learning to take place.
5. Discuss Jerome Bruner's Learning Experiences Ladder.
6. Explain what types of learning activities are best for children.
7. Discuss the four ways to teach the language arts.
8. Explain the content of the No Child Left Behind Act.

CHECK YOUR BACKGROUND KNOWLEDGE. Before reading the chapter, complete the K-T-W-L chart based on the chapter overview and objectives provided at left. In column "K," write what you know about the topics in the objectives. In column "T," write what you think you know. In column "W," write what you want to learn. Finally, after you have read the chapter, write what you have learned in column "L."

Know	Think you know	Want to learn	Learned

Teaching the Language Arts

Traditionally in the primary, elementary, and middle grades (kindergarten through grade 8), the term **language arts** is defined in terms of four curriculum areas: listening, speaking, reading, and writing. In some school districts, this is referred to as the communication arts block; in other districts, it is called the English curriculum, although the term *English* as a subject area is more often used at the high school level. In this text, we use the most common term, *language arts*, to refer to the English communication skills taught in grades K–8.

The two major professional organizations concerned with teaching the language arts, the **International Reading Association (IRA)** and the **National Council of Teachers of English (NCTE),** met together to create the *Standards for the English Language Arts* (1996). Classroom teachers from all over the United States working in small groups and large, over a number of years, pooled their expertise, their knowledge, and their experiences and were able to agree on certain fundamental concepts that should guide the teaching/learning of the language arts. It is their work and wisdom that form the foundation of this new edition, *Integrating the Language Arts.*

One of the significant contributions of the IRA and NCTE committees that created the new *Standards for the English Language Arts* was the addition of two components to the traditional four language arts components: viewing and visually representing have been added to listening, speaking, reading, and writing. **Viewing** refers to the communication processes involved when children view videos, computer simulations, and computer games; comprehend book illustrations; and interpret charts, tables, maps, and other print media. **Visually representing** is the other side of viewing, namely, illustrating books; producing home pages on the Internet; creating murals, dioramas, collages, and other works of art such as sculpture; dancing; and doing mime. Figure 1.1 depicts the six components of the language arts. Both the IRA and the NCTE acknowledge the importance of these two areas as we move forward in the twenty-first century by giving them equal weight with the more familiar listening, speaking, reading, and writing.

FIGURE 1.1

Integrated language arts wheel.

In addition, the NCTE/IRA *Standards for the English Language Arts* identifies 12 major tenets that should guide the teaching/learning process at all grade levels. Figure 1.2 presents these tenets for your discussion and reflection. As you read this chapter and the rest of the textbook, refer back to these 12 standards often. They are the structure that guides this textbook and should provide you with material to reflect on as you enter the teaching profession.

FIGURE 1.2

The NCTE/IRA Standards for the English Language Arts.

1. Students read a wide range of print and nonprint texts to build an understanding of texts, of themselves, and of the cultures of the United States and the world; to acquire new information; to respond to the needs and demands of society and the workplace; and for personal fulfillment. Among these texts are fiction and nonfiction, classic and contemporary works.

2. Students read a wide range of literature from many periods in many genres to build an understanding of the many dimensions (e.g., philosophical, ethical, aesthetic) of human experience.

3. Students apply a wide range of strategies to comprehend, interpret, evaluate, and appreciate texts. They draw on their prior experience, their interactions with other readers and writers, their knowledge of word meaning and other texts, their word identification strategies, and their understanding of textual features (e.g., sound–letter correspondence, sentence structure, context, graphics).

4. Students adjust their use of spoken, written, and visual language (e.g., conventions, style, vocabulary) to communicate effectively with a variety of audiences and for different purposes.

5. Students employ a wide range of strategies as they write and use different writing process elements appropriately to communicate with different audiences for a variety of purposes.

6. Students apply knowledge of language structure, language conventions (e.g., spelling and punctuation), media techniques, figurative language, and genre to create, critique, and discuss print and nonprint texts.

7. Students conduct research on issues and interests by generating ideas and questions, and by posing problems. They gather, evaluate, and synthesize data from a variety of sources (e.g., print and nonprint texts, artifacts, people) to communicate their discoveries in ways that suit their purpose and audience.

8. Students use a variety of technological and information resources (e.g., libraries, databases, computer networks, video) to gather and synthesize information and to create and communicate knowledge.

9. Students develop an understanding of and respect for diversity in language use, patterns, and dialects across cultures, ethnic groups, geographic regions, and social roles.

10. Students whose first language is not English make use of their first language to develop competency in the English language arts and to develop understanding of content across the curriculum.

11. Students participate as knowledgeable, reflective, creative, and critical members of a variety of literacy communities.

12. Students use spoken, written, and visual language to accomplish their own purposes (e.g., for learning, enjoyment, persuasion, and the exchange of information).

I believe we are here on planet earth to live, grow up, and do what we can to make this world a better place for all people to enjoy freedom.

ROSA PARKS

IRA and NCTE. (1996). Standards for the English Language Arts (p. 25). Newark, DE: International Reading Association, and Urbana, IL: National Council of Teachers of English. Reprinted with permission.

As you study, reflect on, and discuss the *Standards for the English Language Arts* in your class, pay attention to the following. First, note that these standards reflect the wisdom and consensus of veteran teachers throughout the nation regarding what is most important to know about the English language arts. Second, most of the standards are general and straightforward enough that you should feel comfortable with them as you prepare to teach the language arts in grades K–8. For example, standards 1, 2, and 3 refer to the need for students to read widely and apply their reading as they interact with other readers and writers. Standards 4 and 5 refer to the ability to use language flexibly in a variety of ways and to meet a variety of situations. Standard 6 addresses the notion of language structures, conventions, and genres. Standard 7 speaks to the relatively new notion of students (and teachers) as researchers; not only are you expected to be consumers of research, but teachers today are expected to do research in their classrooms and share their findings with other teachers. Standard 8 emphasizes the need for students to be familiar with and use advanced technology. Standards 9, 10, and 11 speak to the broad issue of diversity within and outside the classroom. It calls for respect and understanding of others who may be different from you. And, finally, standard 12 refers to the need for students to use language, in all its forms, to accomplish their own goals and needs.

> **Beyond the classroom**
>
> Write, phone, or email either the IRA (IRA, 800 Barksdale Road, P.O. Box 8139, Newark, DE 19714-8139; 1-800-336-7323; www.reading.org) or the NCTE (NCTE, 111 W. Kenyon Road, Urbana, IL 61801-1096; 1-800-369-6283; www.ncte.org) and request your own complete copy of the new *Standards for the English Language Arts.*

DEVELOPING A PHILOSOPHY OF EDUCATION

When the classroom teachers met to discuss and eventually formulate the new *Standards for the English Language Arts,* they were not only pooling their wisdom based on experience but were also collaborating and articulating their philosophies regarding children, the content and materials of the language arts, and the nature of the teaching/learning process. Successful teachers also act on the basis of a personal teaching philosophy, a set of beliefs that guides their practices with children.

You cannot teach a person anything—you can only help him find it in himself.

GALILEO

As you continue reading this text, you should gradually begin to shape your own philosophy of education, particularly as it relates to how you will teach students about the language arts. In 1916, the famous educator–philosopher John Dewey said that every teacher brings to the classroom a philosophy about education, about how children learn best. It is this philosophy that allows you to make decisions each day—from how you will arrange the furniture in the classroom to how you will evaluate your students' skills in reading or writing to which methods and materials you will use to teach spelling and handwriting to how you will maintain classroom control and discipline. In short, all of the choices regarding how, when, and what you teach are ultimately dependent on your personal philosophy.

Reflect on the following quote for a moment: "Teaching without developing one's own philosophy of education would be analogous to building a house on sand instead of on a firm foundation, or taking a trip without a road map" (Hessong & Weeks, 1987, p. 144).

Just as you would not embark on a long vacation trip without a road map, so too you need a map to guide you as you prepare to teach. The constant decisions you will be called upon to make throughout the school year must be based on a consistent set of beliefs if your students are to trust you as their guide in the learning process.

Acquiring such a philosophy is a slow and sometimes arduous process; it requires that you be open to the views of others but strong enough in your own convictions to resist being led by others. In *The Lonely Crowd* (1961), a classic sociological study of the American character, David Riesman describes two types of individuals: The **other-** or **outer-directed** person conforms, follows, and looks for the approval of others before acting; the **inner-directed** person follows an inner set of beliefs and values that guides his or her decision making. Psychologist Jerome Bruner (1962) saw individual mental growth and development in terms of how people move from a state of outer-directedness to one of inner-directedness. As you become more inner-directed as a person, your personal philosophy as a teacher will become more evident. Eventually you will see yourself as a decision maker whom others look to for advice and guidance.

To help you in this process, the remainder of this chapter describes some other learning theories that affect teachers and a number of different ways of viewing the language arts. Each language arts approach has its own strengths and possible weaknesses. Analyze them and reflect on them in conjunction with other learning theories that you have studied. Since every child is different and every child also possesses unique strengths and weaknesses, no one approach will be suitable for all students all of the time. For that reason, we ask you to pick and choose the best from many options to find your own way. Cunningham put it this way: "When a teacher provides more routes to the goal of literacy, more children will find a route that will take them there" (1995, p. 19).

Examine the following approaches to viewing the language arts critically. Compare them to your own experiences and observations in the classroom. Your ability to analyze this text, other research literature in the language arts, other learning theories, and your observations in the classroom is part of the process of becoming a reflective teacher with your own personal philosophy of education. As you reflect critically on what you see, hear, and read, you will become a more responsible decision maker in the classroom, which is the hallmark of the professional educator.

> *We don't see things as they are, we see them as we are.*
>
> **ANAÏS NIN**

Beyond the classroom

As you read this text in conjunction with the course you are taking, keep a weekly journal of your thoughts, observations, and experiences. Keeping a regular written journal is one of the best ways to clarify and develop your own philosophy of education.

RELATED LEARNING THEORIES

Before examining the various approaches to teaching the language arts, consider two learning theories that greatly affect teaching in general, and thus teaching of the language arts. One theory is Bruner's Learning Experiences Ladder and the other is Cambourne's Learning Theory.

Jerome Bruner's Learning Experiences Ladder

While researching children, Bruner (1966) found that children learn best from personal experiences and learn least from verbal explanations. See Figure 1.3 for Bruner's **Learning Experiences Ladder.** Just as the first rung of a ladder is the easiest to climb, the easiest way for students to learn is through direct experiences. And since this is the most effective way a student learns, a teacher should provide as many direct experiences as possible. Obviously, not all teaching can be through direct experiences; therefore, the teacher should provide many simulated experiences that demand students use more than one sense. Some of these experiences can be playing simulated games, constructing models, or role-playing. If direct or simulated experiences are not available, the next experience, though not as effective because it does not engage as many senses, is vicarious experiences. Many of these experiences, such as computer programs and videos, are readily available today. Visual experiences, which only include the visual sense, are better than just a verbal explanation, which is the least effective way to learn. Many textbooks provide pictures, charts, and graphs to explain a concept.

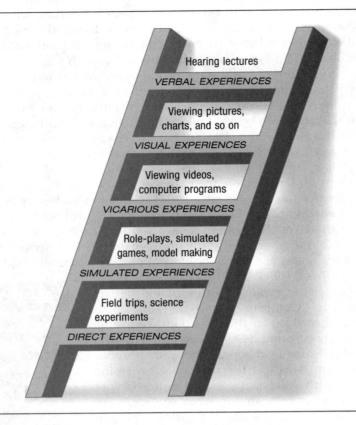

FIGURE 1.3

Bruner's Learning Experiences Ladder.

Source: Adapted from Bruner (1966), as cited in Kellough & Roberts (1991).

Teaching means helping a child realize his potential.

ERICH FROMM

An example of a teacher putting Bruner's theory into practice is Mr. Lopez. When he was preparing to study popular children's author Tomie dePaola with his second-graders, he decided that the least effective way for his students to learn about dePaola's life and books would be if he prepared a lecture about the author. He knew it was necessary to bring in pictures of Tomie dePaola and some of his books. He knew that an even more effective way for them to appreciate Tomie dePaola would be for him to show a video of Tomie dePaola working in his studio, explaining how he gets his ideas. Mr. Lopez also planned for his students to become actively involved by acting out some of their favorite stories they would be reading. The last and the best learning experience he planned for the students was for Tomie dePaola to visit the classroom and tell about himself, and then read some of his books out loud to the students. Mr. Lopez not only put Bruner's theory into practice but also integrated the six components of the language arts. Although not every teacher will be fortunate enough to have well-known authors visit the classroom, many other learning experiences are equally effective.

Brian Cambourne's Learning Theory

Another theory that emphasizes the importance of students' direct involvement for effective learning is Brian Cambourne's **Learning Theory.** Cambourne (1988) posits that eight conditions are necessary for learning to take place: immersion, demonstration, expectation, response, employment, responsibility, approximation, and engagement. Figure 1.4 shows how the eight conditions are interrelated, with student engagement being at the center of the learning process.

FIGURE   **1.4**

Cambourne's conditions necessary for learning.

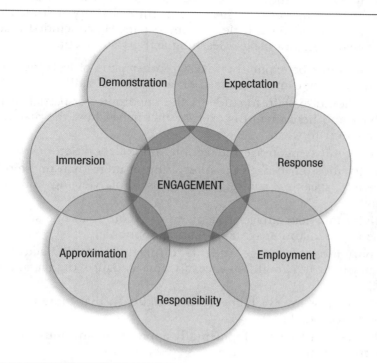

Immersion, demonstration, expectation, and response are led by the teacher. It should be the teacher's goal to set up a classroom that immerses students in worthwhile, authentic learning tasks. There should be (1) numerous opportunities to read about topics that interest the individual student; (2) varied opportunities to learn how to effectively articulate information, stories, poems, and so on, either verbally or in written communication; and (3) many opportunities for students to express themselves through the visual or performing arts. It is important that the teacher demonstrate the new concept to the students as well as how to use the information in real-life settings. Also, the teacher needs to set high but realistic standards for all students and expect all students to be successful in learning the concept or task. It is then the teacher's responsibility to respond to the students with encouraging feedback that praises the students' approximations or attempts and that does not criticize them. This feedback should be verbal and occur while students are engaged in the task.

Employment, responsibility, and approximation are the conditions that the students bring to the learning process. It is the responsibility of the students to apply themselves when given the opportunities to immerse themselves in reading, writing, and other learning activities; they cannot be mere spectators. Students must assume responsibility for their learning; therefore, they need to be willing to spend more time on tasks that are difficult for them. They also need to assume responsibility for the final results of their learning. As students learn, there will be times when their work is a mere approximation of their best work; the learning process does not always result in perfect understanding the first or second time students encounter a new idea or task. However, during the process, students should be encouraged to take risks and experiment with new ideas because that is when growth takes place.

Beyond the classroom

Interview a teacher, principal, or parent regarding theoretical orientation to learning and the language arts. See how different the viewpoints are within a school building, across a school district, and among districts.

After eight years of studies conducted in grades 1 through 5, Cambourne (2001) found that no matter how great the learning activity, if students are not engaged deeply in the activity, little learning occurs. He concluded that the following eight characteristics make a learning activity successful.

1. The activity must be explicitly linked to other parts of learning. In other words, the activity cannot be based on an "isolated" skill.
2. A teacher should explain to students the importance of participating in the activity and help them discover for themselves how the material is personally relevant to them.
3. The activity must encourage interaction and collaboration.
4. The activity must encourage the integration of more than one mode of language (e.g., speaking, reading, writing, listening, viewing, and visual representing).
5. The activity must encourage students to use more than one subsystem of language (e.g., semantics, syntax, and graphophonic).
6. The activity must encourage students to integrate meaning across different semiotic systems (e.g., oral language, art, music, dance, drama, and pantomime).
7. The activity must involve higher-level thinking so that more than one response is acceptable.
8. The activities must be developmentally appropriate and must not demand a lot of time or money to create.

When you read Chapter 8, you will see how Brian Cambourne's Learning Theory applies to writing.

Ideologies Underlying the Language Arts Curricula

Ideologies are personal views of how the social world ought to be (Galindo, 1997). Ideologies are not based on research, but rather on what an individual thinks is logical. Individuals view their ideology as "common sense"; therefore, they believe others should agree with their idea. Two basic ideologies influencing the language arts curricula in most elementary schools are functional literacy and progressive literacy (Cadiero-Kaplan, 2002).

FUNCTIONAL LITERACY

Functional literacy ideology focuses on learning to read and write instead of reading and writing to learn. This ideology does not encourage students to read critically or to relate reading passages to their lives, but instead encourages students to learn to read and write so that they can function in society. Schools based on this ideology stress cultural literacy by requiring students to read the "classics" so that all students learn to embrace the core values of the middle class. Schools based on this ideology mandate the teaching of skills as necessary in order to become literate. A vast amount of time is spent on learning to decode words and using the mechanics of writing correctly.

PROGRESSIVE LITERACY

The second ideology, **progressive literacy,** focuses on a student-centered curriculum that is based on students' interests, needs, and personal backgrounds.

This ideology is based on constructivism (the theory based on the premise that students construct knowledge based on what they already know) and on democratic ideals that embrace free interchange of ideas between teachers and students. Schools that embrace this ideology understand that emotional learning activities help students learn, use, and retain necessary information. Teachers in these schools are not considered "dispensers of knowledge, promoting only one canon or belief, but agents of change, assisting students in seeing themselves within the larger historical, political, cultural, and economic structures where student voices exists" (Cadiero-Kaplan, 2002, p. 379). Under this ideology, mastery of skills is not ignored but, rather, is learned in meaningful context while reading and writing whole texts.

Each of the four methodologies or approaches to teaching the language arts—separate skills approach, whole language approach, integrated approach, and comprehensive approach—is based on one of these ideologies.

Approaches to Teaching the Language Arts

There are many ways of looking at an entire curriculum area such as the language arts. In this section, four different approaches to teaching the language arts are presented for you to reflect on and discuss in your class: the separate skills approach, the whole language approach, the integrated approach, and the comprehensive approach. By clarifying some of the similarities and differences among these approaches, we hope you will avoid some of the confusion that occurs in education when similar terms are used interchangeably or without clear definitions. As we introduce each of the approaches to teaching the language arts, we will explain on which ideology each approach is based.

SEPARATE SKILLS APPROACH

The separate skills approach, based on the functional literacy ideology, is one of the approaches observed in the elementary grades due to the way most schools are presently organized. In the **separate skills approach,** each language arts subskill area (reading, spelling, handwriting, grammar) is viewed as a unique entity, separate from other subject areas. Often these separate skills are taught during distinct times of the day. The school day is divided into specific subject areas and regulated according to strict time periods.

Daily Schedule
8:00–8:15   Opening activities
8:15–8:35   Spelling test
8:35–9:05   Grammar
9:05–10:05   Reading

Within these time periods, each subject area is further broken down into smaller and smaller subskills, such as a lesson on the long vowel sound of /a/ in reading, the adding of "ing" to words in spelling, and contrasting nouns and pronouns in grammar. Such an approach is based on behavioristic principles of part-to-whole learning (Goodman, 1986).

By emphasizing separate skills in isolation from one another, teaching becomes a dissection process; that is, listening, speaking, reading, writing, viewing, and visual representing are all broken down and divided into myriad subskills, following an elaborate predesignated scope and sequence. Textbooks and curriculum guides further support this dissection process. By implication, the teacher is to follow the chapters in the textbook, in sequential order, teaching one subskill after another. Again we see here the part-to-whole sequencing of instruction and learning most characteristic of behavioral psychology. Figure 1.5 shows the separate skills approach in diagram fashion.

Note in this diagram that each language arts subject area and the subskills within each area are isolated from one another. This is a major characteristic of the separate skills approach. Learning is compartmentalized; course content in one area is taught separately from all other areas. Since a certain amount of subject matter must be covered within each specific time block, the class tends to be teacher-dominated, relying on whole-group lecture. Direct, intensive, systematic instruction controlled by the teacher is another characteristic of this approach (Allington, 2002b). This approach emphasizes covering content by learning separate skills. Critics of the separate skills approach (Goodman, 1986; Kohl, 1967; Kozol, 1967; Weaver, 2002) have argued that such an approach treats teachers and children as things to be manipulated, leaves little room for active student involvement, and assumes that knowledge of the separate parts will eventually lead the student to an understanding of the greater whole of literacy.

If the separate skills approach has so many drawbacks, why is it still widely employed in the K–8 curriculum? There are several reasons. First, the separate skills approach is an old and time-honored view of what school should be like. This is the way it has been for many years, and many people seem satisfied with it. The schools are basically a conservative institution in our society; change occurs very slowly, as John Goodlad (1997) noted in his study of American education.

Second, the separate skills approach, from a principal's view, serves administrative purposes well. For example, it allows the school principal to know exactly what children and teachers are working on at a particular time of the day. The entire school can be organized around subject areas, fitting into specific time slots and specific rooms. This makes for an efficient use of people, building, and material resources. It is also relatively easy to evaluate such an approach. Evaluation can be done on a mass scale, periodically, through group-administered standardized tests, and is further encouraged by the current "testing" atmosphere in many states.

Third, the powerful influence of commercial textbook publishers leads to the longevity of the separate skills approach. Many schools rely heavily on basal readers and other standardized textbooks to teach subject matter. Since these

A great teacher makes hard things easy.

RALPH WALDO EMERSON

Separate skills approach charts.

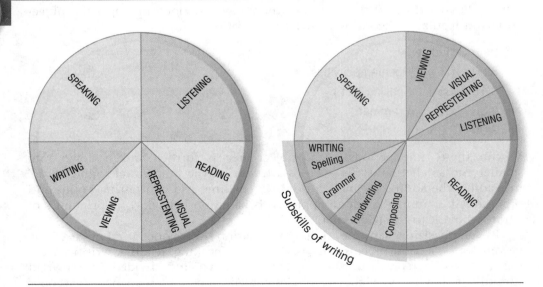

are organized into chapters and subheadings along separate subskills, teachers are encouraged to instruct in a similar manner. Joel Spring (1988), another critic of American education, has argued that the primary purpose of the textbook industry is to make a profit; therefore, innovation and creativity in the industry are discouraged.

Finally, another support for the separate skills approach relates to the public's concerns about schools in general. A widely held belief, according to public opinion polls, is that classroom management or discipline should be a primary objective of the schools (Rose & Gallup, 1998). Therefore, for some people the use of bell systems, separate time periods for separate subjects, direct lecture, and systematic instruction implies a more managed, orderly approach to schooling.

Today, among the strongest advocates of the separate skills approach are G. Reid Lyon (1998) of the National Institutes of Health in Washington, D.C.; Marilyn Adams, author of *Beginning to Read: Thinking and Learning About Text* (1990b); and Lisa Delpit (1995), an authority on minority education. To learn more about the separate skills approach you might wish to read any one of these three authors' works.

WHOLE LANGUAGE APPROACH

Standing in contrast to the separate skills approach is the whole language approach, based on the progressive literacy ideology. Advocates, such as Ken Goodman and Yetta Goodman (1992, 1996), Carol Edelsky (Edelsky, Altwerger, & Flores, 1991), and Constance Weaver (2002) contend, first, that the **whole language approach** is a philosophy of language education that looks at the whole child learning language within the natural environment of the home, community, and school. Second, it is a child-centered philosophy that favors giving students choices as to what they will read and write. Third, language arts subjects, such as reading and writing, are not taught separately but instead are inextricably linked together. Finally, whole language advocates argue that the skills of language arts are best learned through indirect means by authentic reading, writing, listening, speaking, viewing, and visually representing activities, based on children's interests (Goodman, 1996; Veatch, 1992; Watson, 1989).

Let's elaborate briefly on some of the major points associated with the whole language approach, remembering that this and other approaches will be addressed more specifically in the chapters on reading and writing.

The whole language approach to teaching is based on students' needs, interests, and experiences as opposed to a predetermined curriculum or teacher-controlled scope and sequence of skills. It believes in intrinsic motivation rather than extrinsic rewards. The language arts are viewed as a whole. Children are encouraged to choose entire books to read, to write complete stories, and to discuss their reading and writing with the teacher and their peers. Figure 1.6 represents the whole language approach. Note that a slice from the whole language "pie" includes all aspects of the language arts.

In the whole language classroom, children use language to learn about language. This means that the teacher begins at whatever point in learning the student feels comfortable. For most young children, this means starting with listening and speaking activities. Listening either to the teacher read books aloud or at the listening center, engaging in discussions about picture books, chatting with one another over their drawings at the art centers, and conducting puppet shows help give young children confidence in using language that later they will apply as they learn to read and write.

Such classrooms look different from separate skills classrooms in that much in-class time is devoted to free reading and writing. Whole language teachers believe that only by reading and writing can students become readers and writers. Children's literature books rather than basal readers are at the heart of these

FIGURE **1.6**

The whole language "pie."

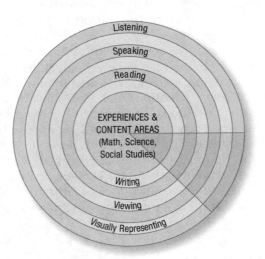

Teaching is the art

of assisting discovery.

MARK VAN DOREN

classrooms. The students are treated as authors themselves and encouraged to talk about books they have read and share stories they have written.

Authentic literacy is another term applied to the whole language classroom (Krashen, 1993). This means first that children get to choose what they read and write. Second, they are encouraged to talk about their reading and writing. Using language freely, exploring with language, and experimenting as part of the learning experience are other aspects of authenticity (Goodman, 1996). Examples of authentic literacy activities include reading; writing; and sharing songs, letters, recipes, jokes, lists, directions for playing games, food labels, and cartoons.

The following two classroom examples exemplify the child-centered, indirect instructional approach characteristic of whole language:

A young child is writing her first story. She does not know how to spell most of the words she wants to use. "How do you spell *house*?" she asks her teacher. Depending on the nature of the writing activity or the teacher's understanding of the child's needs at the time, the teacher might simply spell the word for her or else say something like: "What do you think it begins with? Now sound out the rest. That's a good spelling of *house*." Note that while the student may not have spelled the word correctly, her attempt to invent or construct a spelling based on her knowledge of sounds and symbols is important. Children use their temporary self-constructed spellings as they gradually attain spelling awareness through much reading and writing. The work of Donald Graves (1994) in the area of process writing expands on this notion and will be discussed further in the chapter on writing.

In another classroom, a student is reading silently. He moves his finger along the page slowly; his lips keep moving. When he comes to a really difficult word, he raises his hand and waits for the teacher to help him. There are other hands raised in the classroom. The teacher is moving about the room rapidly, but it is obvious she cannot get to every single child immediately. Finally she stops and says, "Boys and girls, listen to me. If you come to a really hard word in your book, take a guess at it and see if it makes sense as you read further. Another thing you can do is ask a friend for help. You don't have to wait for me to continue reading." This indirect approach to reading

VIGNETTE in the classroom

Miss Allison teaches second grade in a small town in eastern Oklahoma. Her students are interested in studying about animals, so this becomes the first unit of the year. She begins by reading some simple fiction books about animals. However, she quickly discovers that the children are more interested in facts, so she introduces them to nonfiction. She brings three books to class: *Elephants* by Anthony Fredericks (1998), *Wild Cats: Cougars, Bobcats and Lynx* by Deborah Hodge (1996), and *Llamas* by Emilie Lepthien (1996). Some students begin drawing and writing about their favorite animals; they use the three reference books. Some decide to make clay figures of the animals. Others go to the library to find still more books about animals. As the children's enthusiasm builds, the teacher decides that this would be an ideal opportunity to take a field trip to the zoo in Oklahoma City. She enlists the help of a few parent volunteers. The students write letters home explaining when the trip will be and what they will need to bring (paper bag lunch).

Miss Allison: Today I want to read you a book that has something to do with our field trip tomorrow.

June: I know, it's about the zoo.

Miss Allison: That's right. This book is called *One Day at the Zoo* (1968) by Dick Snyder. Let's listen and look at the photographs of the animals. (She reads aloud from the book.) Now that we've heard this story, what do you think we will see at the zoo tomorrow?

Hands fly up all over the room; many responses are given. A lively discussion about zoo babies begins and continues throughout the period. Miss Allison writes the children's responses on the board.

The field trip proves to be a great success. For many of the students, this is their first visit to a real zoo. During follow-up discussion of what they saw and did at the zoo, Miss Allison draws three columns on the board and asks, "What do you remember hearing, seeing, and doing at the zoo?" She writes their brainstorming responses in the three columns.

Next, Miss Allison asks, "How many of you would like to write your own stories about a visit to the zoo?" A few hands go up. "Perhaps the rest of you would like to draw your stories first and then write about them later." More hands go up. The writers go to the writers' corner to get paper and pencils. They occasionally glance at the three columns on the board. The artists work hard on their drawings of animals at the zoo. Some of them put titles at the top or bottom of their drawings. As she walks about the room, Miss Allison encourages each of them to write a sentence about the drawing.

A few of the parent volunteers come to visit the room while the students are working on their stories. Miss Allison decides to enlist the volunteers' help in making bound books of the children's stories. As the students finish writing their books, the parent volunteers help create hard covers for them. For these young authors, seeing their own writings bound like real books is as exciting as the trip to the zoo!

instruction is consistent with the philosophy of whole language as described by Frank Smith (1997).

Using temporary or experimental or invented spelling in writing and making predictions (taking guesses) in reading are encouraged in whole language classrooms and will be discussed further in later chapters. Both of these concepts reflect the central focus of the whole language approach on meaning and understanding as well as the use of an indirect approach toward skill instruction. If you would like to read more about the history and background of whole language, see Julia DeCarlo's *Perspectives in Whole Language* (1995).

The classroom vignette that appears above exemplifies the whole language approach, which emphasizes the teaching of communication skills in a natural manner, in keeping with the interests of the students.

INTEGRATED APPROACH

The term *integrated curriculum* or *integrated approach*, also based on the progressive literacy ideology, is often associated with the whole language approach (Tompkins, 2002). In fact, some authors use the terms interchangeably or include the integrated approach under the whole language philosophy. There are many similarities between the whole language and integrated approaches; however, for the sake of clarification, we will distinguish between the two as follows.

The focus of an integrated approach is on content; it attempts to combine or integrate various subject areas within a single class period. As such, it views all subject matter disciplines (listening, speaking, reading, writing, viewing, and visually representing as well as math, science, social studies, etc.) as related in terms of the way students approach learning. Historically, the concept of integration can be traced back to John Dewey in the 1930s, who argued for linking children's experiences with the new knowledge they were acquiring in the classroom; Dewey also believed in incorporating real-life activities in the classroom. The term *integration* appeared in the 1980s when literacy scholars began linking reading and writing instruction (Tierney & Pearson, 1983). This then led to the linking of oral language with reading and writing as literacy researchers sought a broader view of their field (Au, Mason, & Scheu, 1995). This linkage among the various subject matter disciplines is also in keeping with what has come to be known as **brain-based learning;** brain-based theories of learning argue that the human brain naturally seeks to make connections among the various pieces of information provided by the environment (Caine & Caine, 1994).

This linking or integrating among aspects of the communication arts content reflects the **social constructivist** perspective toward language. This view holds that learners use language as a primary means to construct their knowledge of the world. Learning to read and write involves higher mental processes than mere skill memorization and cuts across all the subject content areas. For instance, students read and write in social studies class as a way of learning about history and geography. Through talking and sharing with their teachers and peers, children gradually construct anew their understanding of specific content.

One of the primary ways that teachers attempt to integrate subject matter content across the various disciplines is through thematic literature units. By having children read books (across all genres) on a particular theme (say, animals) and doing a variety of activities related to that theme (e.g., research writing, mural construction, graphing of facts learned), the concept of integration is achieved.

Another type of integration, found most often in the upper elementary, middle, and secondary school grades, is the notion of **reading and writing across the curriculum** (Lapp, Flood, & Farnan, 1996). This is the specific use of reading and writing activities in subject discipline areas (such as history, math, earth science) to aid the student in learning the specific content of that subject. Teaching students how to peruse a textbook in terms of an author's purpose, how to use subheadings, how to outline and take notes—these all fall under the heading of reading and writing across the curriculum. Expanding students' reading beyond the textbook in biology by encouraging them to read a biography of Charles Darwin is another use of reading across the curriculum. Having students in a middle-grade American history class write a diary entry from the point of view of Meriwether Lewis incorporates writing across the curriculum. Figure 1.7 depicts the comprehensive approach and demonstrates how the six components of the language arts are woven into the study of all subject areas as one theme is studied.

COMPREHENSIVE APPROACH

The newest among the four terms discussed here is the **comprehensive approach.** Why a new term in the field of literacy? This new term was intro-

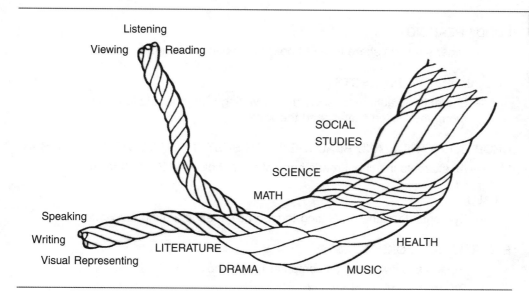

FIGURE **1.7**

In the integrated approach, the six components of the language arts are woven into the study of all subject areas.

duced because there was a misunderstanding among educators and researchers about a term that became popular in the midnineties. That term was the *balanced* approach. Educators and researchers interpreted the term in many different ways. Some used *balanced* to indicate that phonics and whole language were both given "equal" time in the curriculum (Baumann, Hoffman, Moon, & Duffy-Hester, 1998; Wharton-McDonald et al., 1997). Others used the term to refer to the practice used in New Zealand since 1960, which was also called "reading to, with and by" children (Reutzel, 1999a, 1999b). Still another group defined *balanced* to mean an eclectic literacy program that teachers use, based on children's needs. Because of this confusion, some educators and researchers have abandoned the term *balanced* and now use the term *comprehensive*, which focuses on the needs of individual learners (Reutzel & Cooter, 2003). To understand both terms, one must see language arts from a political perspective.

Since the 1980s, literacy educators and researchers have disagreed on the "best" approach to teaching reading. Some support Jeanne Chall's separate skills approach, whereas others support Ken Goodman's whole language approach. In 1995, California's superintendent of public instruction, Bill Honig, contended that whole language was not meeting the needs of elementary students and that a "balanced" approach to reading was needed. As stated previously, because educators and researchers began to define the term *balanced* differently, the term *comprehensive* is now used.

Beyond the classroom

Research your state's legislation or interview a state legislator regarding the phonics/whole language controversy. Verify which theory the stance is based on.

The comprehensive approach, based on the progressive literacy ideology, is broad and flexible to accommodate the needs of individual learners who benefit from both holistic teaching and the teaching of skills (Kaufman, 2002). Teachers who use the comprehensive approach stress holistic teaching to literacy and teach skills explicitly when students need them. For example, teachers use the reading workshop (see Chapter 6) and writing workshop (see Chapter 8), which emphasize students reading and writing authentic texts of their choice. Within each workshop, teachers teach needed skills to the whole class during the daily mini-lessons and teach needed skills to individual students during the conferences. Within each workshop, students also share favorite books as well as their compositions, poems, essays, and other writings with classmates. Figure 1.8 gives an overview of classroom strategies with a description of their purpose and

FIGURE 1.8

Classroom strategies used in the comprehensive approach.

BUDDY READING
— Older students share love of books with younger students.

COLLABORATIVE PROJECTS
— Students do authentic research and writing with other students in the class-room, the United States, and the world.

DROP EVERYTHING AND READ (DEAR) OR SUSTAINED SILENT READING (SSR)
— All students in school reads book of their choice for 15 to 30 minutes.

E-PALS
— Students do authentic writing to form new friends around the world.

ELECTRONIC BOOKS
— Students follow along as computer reads books.
— Students hear fluent reading.
— Students are introduced to new vocabulary words.

ELECTRONIC RESEARCH PROJECT
— Students share research projects with other students around the world.

GUIDED READING
— Teachers work with homogeneous groups to teach reading skills.
— Teachers teach phonics, word analysis, vocabulary, etc.
— Students read under teacher's supervision.
— Students read graded books on their instructional level.

GUIDED WRITING
— Teachers work with homogeneous groups to teach writing skills.
— Teachers teach phonics, word analysis, vocabulary, etc.
— Students practice skills under teacher's supervision.

INTERACTIVE WRITING (e.g., MORNING MESSAGE)
— Teachers do majority of writing, and students "share the pen" when they know letters/words.
— Teachers explicitly teach phonics, word patterns, and other spelling skills.

JOURNAL WRITING
— Students express themselves personally.
— Students write for authentic purposes.

LANGUAGE EXPERIENCE APPROACH (LEA)
— Students express themselves while teacher acts as scribe.
— Students recognize words in print they use in their speech.

LITERACY CLUB
— Students who share interest in same book/author read and discuss books.

(continued)

FIGURE   **1.8**

Continued.

PUPPET SHOW
- — Students work in small groups.
- — Students improve expression and fluency.
- — Students perform for audience.

READERS THEATRE
- — Students work in small groups.
- — Students improve expression and fluency.
- — Students perform for audience.

READING WORKSHOP
- — Students choose genre and topics.
- — Students share favorite books with peers.

Mini-lessons
- — Teachers share with class information about authors and genres.
- — Teachers instruct class on reading skills.

Conferences
- — Peers read to each other.
- — Teachers give explicit instruction on skills to individuals.

Share time
- — Students share favorite sections or passages.
- — Students share new vocabulary words.

SHARED READING
- — Teachers share good literature that is at higher reading level.
- — Students hear advanced vocabulary.
- — Teachers and students discuss elements of stories.
- — Teachers and students discuss information given in passage.

THINK-ALOUDS
- — Teachers model reading strategies.
- — Teachers teach metacognition skills.

WORD WALLS
- — Teachers display words in categories to help students automatically recognize words.
- — Students learn patterns within words.
- — Students increase their vocabulary.

WRITING WORKSHOP
- — Students choose genre and topics.
- — Students share writing with peers.

Mini-lessons
- — Teachers give explicit instruction on writing skills to class.
- — Teachers share types of writing with class.

Conferences
- — Peers help with revising and editing.
- — Teachers give explicit instruction on writing skills to individuals.

Share Time
- — Students share finished product with class.

activities that teachers who embrace the comprehensive approach use. Figure 1.9 is a graphic depiction of the comprehensive approach.

It is obvious that approaches to teaching the language arts changed throughout the twentieth century. If one were to visit classrooms throughout the United States, virtually every conceivable approach would be encountered. Some teachers who are slow to embrace change may still use the same method in which they were taught. Other teachers may embrace new trends quickly, making frequent changes without really understanding the theories behind new approaches. All teachers must study theories and become reflective, flexible teachers. We must remember that we are teaching students, and not teaching a particular method. One approach to teaching language arts may work with some students; however, another group of students may need a different approach. A good teacher always meets the needs of individual students and understands why he or she uses a particular approach.

Teachers and Schools Undergo Change

STANDARDS, INCLUSION, DIFFERENTIATION

No matter which approach to teaching language arts teachers embrace, they are challenged to meet the demands of state standards in an inclusive classroom. **Standards,** also called **benchmarks** or **competencies,** are skills and concepts that students must master by the end of each grade level in each subject area. The standards are written by and issued from each state's Department of Education. The standards are written as objectives. For example, in Oklahoma one standard for fifth-grade students is: "The student will analyze media as sources of information, entertainment, persuasion, interpretation of events, and trans-

> You may be disappointed if you fail, but you are doomed if you don't try.
>
> **BEVERLY SILLS**

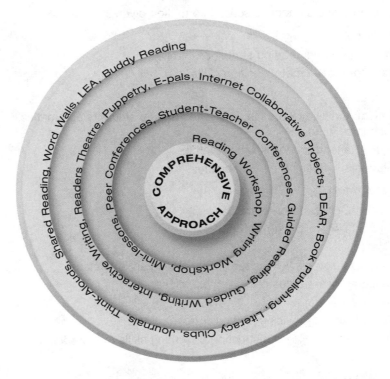

FIGURE 1.9

Comprehensive approach model.

mission of culture" (Oklahoma State Department of Education, 2003, p. 60). All the standards in each subject area become the core curriculum for each grade. The goal is for all students to meet those standards.

To ensure that all students do meet the standards, **high-stakes tests** are given each year. High-stakes tests are designed by a state's Department of Education and given to all students to ensure that they know the information stated in each standard. The tests are referred to as high-stakes tests because they are used to evaluate teachers' ability to teach, to determine which schools are "doing their job," and to retain students. Teachers can lose their jobs if their students do not perform well on the tests, and schools can lose state and federal funding if the majority of their students do poorly on the tests. If all students had the same abilities and learned at the same pace and had the same learning styles, the task would be challenging, but not as challenging as what teachers encounter when teaching in classrooms with diverse populations.

Beyond the classroom

Call your state education department for a copy of your state's standards. Most states now have them available on their website.

Inclusion is a term that evolved from the **Individuals with Disabilities Act (IDEA) of 1997,** which requires a free, appropriate public education in the least restrictive environment for individuals with disabilities identified by the Act. These students have an **individualized education program (IEP).** IEPs are educational plans that must be prepared for any child with a disability in a public school. IEPs are agreed upon by parents, classroom teachers, special education teachers, and administrators who set long- and short-term goals for the student with a plan of action that will help the student reach the state standards. As teachers prepare daily lessons, they need to differentiate the learning experience in order to meet the needs of students who have IEPs and any other students who need modifications.

Differentiation is the modification teachers make for individual students so that they may reach their potential. Some of these students may have IEPs, whereas others may not. For example, in Mr. Green's classroom, one student needs additional time to complete assignments while another student needs an adult to sit alongside him so that he remains focused. The student who is blind needs all texts on tape, and the student with a hearing loss needs to sit close to Mr. Green so that she can hear him and read his lips. The student who is totally deaf needs someone to sign during instructional times. All the differentiations or modifications are necessary in order for Mr. Green's students to complete lessons successfully.

"(D)ifferentiation is not a recipe for teaching. It is not an instructional strategy. It is not what a teacher does when he or she has time. . . . It is a philosophy" (Tomlinson, 2000, p. 6). According to Tomlinson, teachers who practice differentiation believe that

- same-age students differ in their readiness to learn.
- students have different abilities.
- students have different interests.
- students have different learning styles.
- students have different background experiences.
- students learn at different paces.
- students learn best in a community of learners who support them.
- students learn best when they can connect school learning to their personal lives.
- students need accommodations in order to reach their potential.

As you read this text and learn about different activities to use while teaching the language arts, reflect on how you can differentiate your teaching to meet the needs of students who face various challenges, of students who have limited

English skills, of students who have hearing disabilities, and so on. Chapter 3 gives you an opportunity to learn how to differentiate units and lessons, based on state standards so that all students can reach their potential. Chapter 11 addresses each of the needs of diverse learners in greater detail; however, it is never too early to reflect on how you will meet the needs of all students.

THE VOICES OF POLITICIANS AND PUBLISHING COMPANIES IN EDUCATION

It is important that preservice teachers become familiar with the political arena of education by understanding how and why politicians and publishers of school textbooks continue to "monitor" and use the media's reports on standardized tests scores and any other "report" about schools. Legislators often use education and, in particular, standardized test scores as one of their platforms when running for office. For example, if the media reports a "drop in standardized reading scores," reading reforms become a major issue for candidates. Candidates give voice to how they will reform the present system to ensure that all students in their state will read above the national average. In their zeal to get elected or reelected, they often get the "facts" wrong.

In recent years, politicians proclaimed that 40 percent of fourth graders could not read independently, even though the National Assessment of Educational Progress reported that reading achievement has remained relatively stable over the past 30 years (Allington, 2002c). In fact, when standardized test publishers renormed tests, the average reading ability actually rose. Fourth graders in the United States rank second in the world; Finland, which has no mandatory testing, nor state-mandated curriculum, is number one.

How do politicians become misinformed? Partly by not understanding the way the three levels of reading are reported. The three levels of reading are "basic," "proficient," and "advanced." The basic level means readers have literal comprehension of grade-appropriate texts. However, politicians misinterpret this to mean "minimal" competence.

Publishers of school textbooks also benefit from standardized testing and changes in curriculum materials. These companies benefit from annual and biannual testing because they sell more tests and services used to score the tests. Textbook publishers also benefit when the three largest states—California, Texas, and Florida—mandate curriculum changes. In the 1990s, when California mandated reading texts with decodable text, publishers were happy to accommodate the need because it required schools to buy their reading texts that had decodable stories. Publishers also benefit when all states mandate their schools to use "scientifically proven" materials that are required by the No Child Left Behind Act of 2002. Publishers create scripted materials and package them as products that are based on scientific research. Most scripted phonetics programs have materials that students write on, so schools must purchase new materials each year.

LEGISLATIVE INVOLVEMENT IN EDUCATION

National Reading Panel

In 1997, the U. S. Congress asked the director of the National Institute of Child Health and Human Development and the U. S. Secretary of Education to form the National Reading Panel (NRP), a 14-person panel, of whom most were reading researchers. The NRP was charged with reviewing and assessing the research on teaching reading over the past 30 years, with implications for classroom practice and further research (Cunningham, 2002). In essence, the NRP was to find out what effective reading practices were being used in school and then to mandate those effective practices to be used in all schools.

The panel released a two-volume report titled "Teaching Children to Read: An Evidence-Based Assessment of the Scientific Research Literature on Reading and Its Implications for Reading Instruction." This report carries much clout because it was backed by the U. S. Congress (Garan, 2002).

Educators and researchers, however, criticized the panel's findings, arguing that the panel distorted research by choosing some studies over others in order to get the results it desired; the panel aimed to fit politicians' agendas—to prove that students need explicit, systematic phonics instruction (Allington, 2002a; Cunningham, 2002; Garan, 2002). The same critics state that the report is not based on scientific evidence, even though the report used that phrase more than a hundred times (Allington, 2002c). Figure 1.10 lists some of the reasons why literacy educators and researchers disagree with the NRP's report.

The panel presented its research findings to the U. S. Congress with a "guide for scientifically based reading instruction" (Coles, 2001, p. 206). Based on the panel's findings, President Bush passed the Reading First Legislation of 2002, often referred to as the No Child Left Behind Act (PL 107–110). According to Rose and Gallup (2002, p. 42), this act "represents the greatest federal incursion into K–12 education to date" and has put state departments of education and school districts in a tailspin. This act specifies that in order for schools to qualify for Title I monies, they must use "scientific evidence–based" educational plans and document student growth in six areas of reading: phonemic awareness, systematic phonics, spelling and writing, fluency, text comprehension, and vocabulary. The beginning reading program that supposedly is scientific evidence–based is direct, explicit, and systematic instruction in skills (Coles, 2001);

FIGURE 1.10

Critical review of the NRP's findings.

1. The phonics subgroup examined only 38 studies even though the panel stated that the study was scientifically rigorous. Nine of these 38 studies were done in foreign countries. Twenty-nine of the 38 studies assessed isolated skills instead of requiring students to apply skills to actual reading of text.

2. The phonics subgroup studied three groups of problem readers—kindergarten and first graders who were at risk, disabled readers, and low-achieving readers—yet the results were generalized to all students.

3. The panel did not show how intense phonemic awareness and phonics instruction in kindergarten helped reading comprehension in later grades.

4. The panel failed to show that playing with sounds, using inventive spelling, and working with onset and rimes do not help students develop phonemic awareness and phonics skills.

5. The panel did not show what instruction each controlled group received.

6. The panel gave mixed results. It said that phonemic awareness should begin in pre-K and kindergarten, which is before phonics, yet it stated that phonemic awareness should be done with letters, which is considered phonics instruction.

7. The subgroup on reading comprehension did not perform any meta-analyses; it merely summarized the research that fit its criteria.

8. The subgroup on teacher education and reading instruction could not conduct a meta-analysis because there were too many different kinds of treatment.

9. The subgroup on computer technology and reading instruction could not conduct a meta-analysis because not enough studies met the panel's criteria. It concluded that some students benefit from computer technology in reading instruction.

Sources: Adapted from Cunningham (2002) and Garan (2002).

in other words, phonics instruction. Therefore, in many states, state funds can only be used for phonics programs that use scripted instructions for teachers to ensure that all students receive the same instruction and that state funds only be used to buy decodable reading texts for young readers.

What are the negative aspects of scripted phonics programs? Scripted, systematic phonics programs are designed for large-group instruction. In large groups, some students get lost in the process. For example, a teacher asks the students "If "bug" begins with a /b/ sound, echo the word." A group of students who know the answer respond immediately; those who are not sure only respond after they hear the first group respond. There may be another group of students who never respond and never are detected as not knowing the answer. Most commercial, scripted phonics programs demand a long period of time each day, 60 to 90 minutes. This time takes away from independent reading time. Another negative aspect of these programs is that all children get the same instruction even though some students do not need it. *No one method of teaching reading has ever been effective for all students.* Many students often become bored with the repetition, which results in behavioral problems. Scripted programs view teachers as incapable (Meyers, 2002); professional teachers resent this but feel if they are noncompliant, they may be fired.

Richard Allington, one of the preeminent literacy researchers in America, takes issue with the panel's report and the movement toward legislating early reading instruction based on "questionable" research techniques. In his book *Big Brother and the National Reading Curriculum: How Ideology Trumped Evidence* (2002b), Allington states that these new educational reforms are merely "recycled bad ideas" (p. vi) and that "dumbing down the curriculum and curriculum materials through narrowly conceived accountability schemes and scripted materials didn't work in the 1970s and it won't work now" (p. vii).

It is important for readers of this textbook to be aware of the various sides in the reading debate. It is also important to keep up with the latest legislation in your own state as it affects reading instruction, particularly when one method is mandated over another method. However, the position taken here is that language arts instruction must be based on *all* research findings, as well as a respect for different learning styles. We agree with the International Reading Association's position statement on phonemic awareness, which states that "phonemic awareness should not be overemphasized to the point that other important aspects of balanced literacy curriculum are left out or abandoned" (International Reading Association, 1998, p. 8).

In this book, you will find methods and strategies that reflect the separate skills, whole language, integrated, and comprehensive approaches. Teachers need to develop a repertoire of teaching techniques based on the multiple approaches to teaching the language arts in order to adapt their teaching to the individual needs of their students. The primary focus of this textbook, however, is the integrated approach. The book advocates not only the integration of the six communication arts areas but also holds that these areas serve as foundation blocks for learning about other content areas such as math, social studies, and science. For example, in the upper elementary, middle, and senior high grades, all students are required to listen to class lectures, take written notes, engage in oral discussions, read from their subject matter textbooks, and view videos and computer screens. The higher the grade level, the greater is the demand placed on the communication skills for mastering content matter. This idea is developed further in later chapters.

High-Stakes Testing

We are a nation obsessed with testing, rating, and ranking children, teachers, and schools. This obsession is based on the belief that more testing will help children learn more and that rating and ranking schools will push them to high standards of achievement (Stiggins, 2002). This is as true for reading, math, science, and social studies as it is for writing. But do children learn more if they are tested more?

In the 1960s, the buzzword was accountability, which led to each school district creating its own standardized tests to ensure that teachers were doing their job based on how children performed. In the 1970s, still dissatisfied with student scores, we moved to statewide standardized tests. By the 1980s and 1990s, national assessments were used to rank schools, with the lowest schools threatened with sanctions and even closings. In 2002, President George W. Bush's No Child Left Behind act mandated standardized testing at all grades, in all years and tied student promotion and graduation to test scores (Lewis, 2002). Educators call this high-stakes testing, and, as stated earlier, the pressure on students and teachers alike is enormous.

Today high-stakes standardized testing dominates our nation's schools. Standardized tests are developed by professional test-making companies, working in conjunction with state departments of education that solicit "wish lists" of questions from teachers, academicians, and others of the "things they believe all children should know . . . at particular ages or grades" (Meier, 2002, p. 192). Each state has its own name for such tests. For example, in Massachusetts, it is called the Massachusetts Comprehensive Assessment System (MCAS), in New York it is the Regents Examinations, in Texas it is the Texas Academic Assessment System (TAAS), and in Virginia it is the Standards of Learning (SOL). But just because it is popular does not mean standardized testing is good for children.

Critics of high-stakes testing are many and vocal. Stiggins (2002) sees the single-minded focus on standardized testing to assess learning as part of the crisis in American education. He notes that falsely equating test results with learning may be detrimental. For example, for many years we have known that the minority poor in America do not do as well on tests as middle- and upper-class white children. Should we penalize the poor for being poor? In Alaska, native students fail the statewide tests in reading, writing, and mathematics at double the rate of white students (Jones & Ongtooguk, 2002). And what about students with learning disabilities? Should we deny diplomas to students who have successfully passed their subjects over the course of 12 years but cannot pass the high school exit exam? Alfie Kohn (2000) and Susan Ohanian (1999), two longtime critics of standardized testing, have argued that trying to fit all students into one mold does more harm than good and undermines the true meaning of education.

Who dares to teach must never cease to learn.

JOHN COTTON DANA

TECHNOLOGY AND WEBSITES

THE INTERNET AS A RESOURCE FOR TEACHERS

Each chapter in this book includes a section called Technology and Websites. Throughout the past two decades, technology, both in general and in schools, has changed and with it the educational paradigm. The Internet has become a great tool for teachers; many websites offer lesson plans, information about recent research, and other interactive activities for students. Two websites that are very helpful to teachers are the following:

1. http://marcopolo.worldcom.com is an excellent search engine created for education. Partners for this site are The John F. Kennedy Center for the Performing

Arts; ArtsEdge; the American Association for the Advancement of Science; Science NetLinks; the National Council of Teachers of Mathematics; Illuminations; the National Endowment for the Humanities; EdSitement; the National Council on Economic Education; the National Geographic Society; Xepeditins; and the International Reading Association, read-write-think.

2. http://rubistar.4teachers.org is a particularly helpful website for beginning teachers as they create scoring rubrics. One aspect of teaching that becomes overwhelming for many beginning teachers is fairly and accurately assessing students' work. Scoring rubrics help teachers to do this, using the same criteria for every student. Students appreciate scoring rubrics because they see that all students are assessed in the same manner. Scoring rubrics are particularly beneficial to students when teachers give them when they assign students' work.

This website has many types of scoring rubrics for many different subjects. Some of the main subjects are oral presentations, research/writing projects, science, math, music, art, multimedia, and work skills. Once teachers select the subject area, they are given many categories to choose from within that main area. For example, under oral presentations, there are rubrics for puppet shows, class debates, interviews, storytelling, video–talk shows, and many others. Teachers select a rubric and then the categories they wish to assess. Teachers can create rubrics that give a numerical score or a descriptive score. This site also permits teachers to personalize a rubric and save it for later use. Using this website can save teachers hours of work as they create scoring rubrics. Appendix C has a small example of two rubrics, one for puppet shows, using numerical scoring, and one for storytelling, using descriptive scoring.

OTHER USEFUL WEBSITES

http://nces.ed.gov/pubsearch
The National Center for Education Statistics releases the statistical reports for education in the United States. It includes such topics as academic achievement and assessment, elementary education, parental involvement, students at risk, and technology and access to the Internet.

www.negp.gov/Reports/20nelson.htm
This is the home page for National Education Goals Benchmarks and Standards as Tools for Science Education Reform.

www.nctm.org
This is the home page for National Council of Teachers of Mathematics.

http://school.discovery.com/schrockguide/edref.htm
This is the DiscoverySchool home page.

www.edbriefs.com
The U. S. Ed.Net Briefs and Washington Ed.Net Briefs are free weekly newsletters sent to subscribers via email. They summarize interesting education news stories.

www.edbriefs.com/resource.html
This site lists the newest and most useful online resources pertaining to education.

www.edcen.ehhs.cmich.edu
This site is a resource center for educators to exchange views and experiences.

http://clearinghouse.com

This site reviews and supplies purchasing information for numerous software titles for K–12 language arts application.

www.uni.edu/currtech/teach.html

This site links teachers to lesson plans and telecommunication projects.

www.eduplace.com.rdg/index.html

This is Houghton Mifflin's site for reading and language arts lesson plans.

www.scholastic.com

The "Write with the Authors" section of this site has take-home materials in Spanish, and lots of teacher resources and teaching ideas.

www.aea2.k12.ia.us/tutorials/Copyright/Copyright_html

This site gives information about copyright issues.

www.classroom.com

This site encourages interactive learning.

www.classroom.net

This site offers collaborative projects with students in other classrooms around the world.

www.kidlink.org:80/KIDPROJ

This site permits teachers either to post a topic that interests their students or to check out different postings by other teachers.

www.reading.org

This is the International Reading Association's site.

www.ncte.org

This is the National Council of Teachers of English's site.

www.ciera.org

This is the Center for the Improvement of Early Reading Achievements' site, which has publications online.

www.eric.ed.gov/searchdb/index.html

This site permits users to conduct online searches of the ERIC database.

www.ncrel.org

This site has information regarding early childhood education and critical issues dealing with assessment.

www.education-world.com

This site has a large database of information addressing education issues.

Summary

Good teaching involves constant and continuous decision making. This is at the heart of what it means to be a reflective teacher. To achieve this, a teacher must possess a philosophy of education in general, as it relates to children, teaching, and learning, and must apply this philosophy specifically to the teaching of language arts.

There are at least four main approaches to teaching the language arts. In the separate skills approach, the language arts curriculum is broken down into many separate subskills, which are taught in isolation from one another. This is more of a managerial system than an instructional approach, with the teacher as the prime manager and students assuming passive roles. The whole language approach is more student centered because students are given a choice of which books to read and what types of genre to write in. The whole language approach integrates all six of the language arts areas. It focuses on the needs, experiences, and interests of the individual child; uses authentic texts to develop literacy awareness; and tries to make learning language a natural extension of using language. In the integrated approach, the six areas of the language arts are used as the students study broad themes that encompass other content areas such as math, science, social studies, and the arts. The comprehensive approach, a relatively new term, uses the whole language approach with a balance of teacher-taught skills that are part of the reading and writing activities.

ACTIVITIES *with children*

These activities are designed to be used with students in an elementary classroom. They reflect the variety of approaches—separate skills, whole language, integrated, and comprehensive—discussed in this chapter. It is important that you get a chance to work with students in real classroom learning situations so you can determine for yourself what does and does not work. Such experience also gives you an opportunity to reflect on how children learn.

Brainstorming

Teach a group of students the rudiments of brainstorming. Select a topic with which they are familiar, such as school or sports or favorite foods. Then brainstorm in a small group, recording the children's ideas. Your list should form the basis for a later writing lesson.

Group Experience

The following activity is one way to use the Language Experience Approach in the classroom. After returning from a field trip, encourage your students to talk about it. Record their statements on a large language-experience chart and have them read the chart. Then encourage them to illustrate some of the sentences or develop their own stories.

Spelling Hunt

In the whole language and comprehensive approaches, peers help each other with the mechanics of writing. As part of the students' ongoing writing activities, have them pair off and become peer editors for spelling. One of their jobs is to hunt for misspelled words, circle them, and help write them correctly.

The Journal

Share with your students the journal you are keeping; perhaps read them an entry or two. Then discuss with them why people keep journals. Suggest that they begin to keep a journal for the school year to record their experiences. Try to give students some time each day to write in their journal.

RELATED READINGS

Select one or more of the articles and books listed here. Find the work in the library or on the Internet, read it, and write a brief summary. Share your summary with other members of your class. Becoming a reader of research will help you become a more reflective practitioner in the language arts.

Allington, R. (2002). *Big brother and the national reading curriculum.* Portsmouth, NH: Heinemann.

Coles, G. (2003). *Reading the naked truth: Literacy, legislation, and lies.* Portsmouth, NH: Heinemann.

Flurkey, A. D., & Xu, J. (2003). *On the revolution of reading: The selected writings of Kenneth S. Goodman.* Portsmouth, NH: Heinemann.

This is a collection of Kenneth Goodman's provocative past writings.

Goodman, K. (1996). *Ken Goodman on reading: A common-sense look at the nature of language and the science of reading.* Portsmouth, NH: Heinemann.

This book is an easy-to-understand text about the characteristics of language and how it works. It explains how proficient reading works and how written texts are organized. It also discusses the reading process and how to teach reading and writing.

Graves, D. H. (2002). *Testing is not teaching.* Portsmouth, NH: Heinemann.

This is a collection of 22 essays that emphasize how testing encroaches on teachers' freedom and how narrow standards can reduce student achievement.

Guthrie, J. T., & Wigfield, A. (1997). *Reading engagement: Motivating readers through integrated instruction.* Newark, DE: International Reading Association.

This book is a collection of works by reading experts. Each chapter emphasizes a different way to motivate students to read by engaging them in meaningful activities. The goal is self-efficacy in literacy.

Smith, F. (1997). *Reading without nonsense* (3rd ed.). New York: Teacher's College Press.

This is an excellent text on the reading process. Smith looks at what happens when the eye meets the page and how the brain plays an integral part in the reading process. He believes that using whole texts makes reading easy; separating it into parts makes reading very difficult. In Chapter 11 of his book, he gives some rules teachers should never follow and some rules all teachers should follow if they want to help students as they begin to read.

Trussell-Cullen, A. (1996). *Inside New Zealand classrooms.* Katonah, NY: Richard C. Owen Publishers.

This book explains how the New Zealand schools are organized. A child enters school on his or her fifth birthday. The levels of progression are different from those of the United States. Classroom organization is also discussed, based on a child-centered philosophy.

2

Language Arts Integration Beyond the Classroom

In this chapter, you will learn about the importance of home and community influences on children's language arts abilities. Teachers need to understand the significance of caregiver–child interaction, the influence of the home, the role of play, and the influence of the community if they are to work with children as individuals.

CHAPTER OBJECTIVES

After reading this chapter, you should be able to accomplish the following objectives:

1. Explain how caregivers influence students' oral language.
2. Explain how caregivers can help their child develop reading skills.
3. Explain what caregivers can do to help their child develop writing skills.
4. Explain what teachers can do to better communicate with caregivers.
5. Explain what community organizations can do to assists students' education.

CHECK YOUR BACKGROUND KNOWLEDGE. Before reading the chapter, complete the K-T-W-L chart based on the chapter overview and objectives provided at left. In column "K," write what you know about the topics in the objectives. In column "T," write what you think you know. In column "W," write what you want to learn. Finally, after you have read the chapter, write what you have learned in column "L."

Know	Think you know	Want to learn	Learned

Caregiver Influence and the Language Arts

Caregivers are the first and primary language model an infant encounters. Young children, for example, often unconsciously imitate the speech and mannerisms of their caregivers. In fact, all aspects of oral language acquisition and development are influenced enormously by caregivers. Not only the actual language spoken (such as French, Spanish, English) but also the form of that language (standard or nonstandard) is the result of neighborhood and community influence. The language skills of reading and writing are also tremendously affected by caregivers' behaviors (Dickinson & McCabe, 2001; Rush, 1999). The social interaction between caregiver and child and the attitudes generated about oral language and literacy form the basis of teachers' concerns for much closer cooperation between school and home (Faires, Nichols, & Rickelman, 2000).

Many researchers, beginning with Lev Vygotsky (1976), have stressed the importance of caregiver–child talk in the home for the child's later cognitive development and success in socialization with peers. Vygotsky's theory about the importance of social interaction for specific language growth and general cognitive development is one of the foundations upon which whole language philosophy is based. Vygotsky believed that two important things occur when caregivers and children interact verbally in social settings. First, children learn to express ideas in words. All of the stimuli and experiences of childhood need the outlet of language. The feedback children receive confirms their notions of themselves as persons. Second, words help children clarify their thinking. According to Vygotsky's theory, language and thought are closely linked. Children use language to solve real-world problems, assisted by adult learners. Eventually adults give less and less assistance as children begin to learn and discover on their own.

Scholars have also linked this early caregiver–child talk and cognitive growth to later achievement in school learning (Dickinson & McCabe, 2001; Finn, 1998; Zellman & Waterman, 1998). Both the quantity and the quality of oral language and print experiences in young children's environments affect their level of attainment in reading and writing.

CAREGIVERS AND LANGUAGE

One of the first things teachers need to know is that language learning in the home occurs easily and naturally because it is part of the normal social interaction between caregiver and child. This confirms Vygotsky's belief in the importance of social interaction for learning. Research on the interaction of preschool children with caregivers and siblings at home (Dickinson & McCabe, 2001) concluded that three main factors make this a most positive beginning for the child:

1. Language in the home is always situation specific.
2. Home language focuses on meaning rather than form.
3. Caregiver–child language is based on mutual trust.

Language is situation specific. Observations of children interacting with their caregivers and siblings at home show that language is always used in a purposeful manner that is comprehensible to the child. This is because the language relates to objects, events, and actions in the immediate environment of the youngster. For example, a caregiver may tell her child, "Stop climbing on that sofa." Another time she might say, "You can have only one cookie before dinner."

In *Piagetian* terms (see Chapter 4 for a discussion of Piaget), this environment is said to be highly concrete. Abstract language, if used at all, is always clarified by reference to the physical environment so familiar to the child. For example, a caregiver may tell his child, "You have to be careful with electrical appliances. If we plug too many into one outlet . . . there, did you see that spark?" One result of this use of situation-specific language is that the child begins using language with a sense of its place in her or his real world.

Language focuses on meaning rather than form.
In caregiver–child interaction, language is always used for some meaningful purpose. As long as meaning is conveyed, the language flow is not interrupted. Corrections of a child's pronunciation and grammar do occur in the home, but infrequently and generally only when a caregiver cannot comprehend what the child is saying. More often than not, however, caregivers respond to the content of their children's speech. If it is meaningful—that is, if the caregiver can understand the message—the dialogue continues.

> ## Beyond the classroom
>
> With a small group of your peers, make a list of all the ways you can think of in which a teacher can acquire information about a student's home and community life. Select one of these ways and try it. For example, you might visit a playground or some other area in the community after school and observe children to learn about other influences on learning language arts in your classroom.

Contrast this situation with one that can occur in school. Individual students sometimes find their speech interrupted by a teacher more concerned with the grammar the child is using than the message he or she is trying to convey.

Language in the classroom should always focus on meaning rather than correct grammar. However, when teachers and students come from different cultural backgrounds, meaning may be interrupted because teachers and students do not understand each other's way of interacting with other speakers (Brice Heath, 1983; Viadero, 1996). Viadero (1996) gives the example of a white teacher teaching first graders how to tell time. She points to a clock and tells the children, "It is 10 o'clock because the little hand is on the 10 and the big hand is on the 12." She then asks, "What time is it?" The white students raise their hands, but the African American children do not. The white teacher may interpret this to mean that the white students know the answer while the African American children do not. However, in the African American culture, such a question would only be asked if the students knew that the teacher did not know the correct time. Brice Heath (1983) also found that members of the African American community in which she lived for 10 years had the same interaction with their children; adults never asked children questions if the adults knew the answer.

Today, the majority of teachers come from white middle-class backgrounds and are slow to understand the differences between how they communicate meaning and how their students are accustomed to communicating meaning. This lack of knowledge causes roadblocks in children's learning. Viadero (1996) encourages all teachers to "find ways to recognize the culture of their students, to acknowledge it in their teaching, and to make clear to students from different backgrounds the previously unstated expectations that the mainstream culture—and the school—has for them" (p. 2).

Language is built on trust. Language is one of the primary ways in which caregiver and child are bonded to each other. The language they use is both purposeful and meaningful; therefore, it is carefully attended to by both parties. Language is also the primary way in which children share with their caregivers and receive important information. Without the proper information regarding what is expected of each member of the household, misunderstandings arise. Finally, children use language to express their deepest feelings and emotions. This actually begins with an infant's first cries and the attention received from the child's caregivers as a result.

Language Development in the Home

Observational studies of caregiver–child interaction have helped teachers understand ways in which oral language is developed in the home (Snow, 1983). Teachers must understand the impact that the family and/or community culture has on oral language development. Shirley Brice Heath (1983) in *Ways with Words,* describes how the community culture influences how children acquire language in two different communities. The culture in both communities affects how caregivers communicate with babies and preschool children. In both communities, it is through oral communication that children learn the "ways of acting, believing, and valuing" of those about them (p. 6). The two communities, although they are close in proximity and of the same socioeconomic status, have very different cultures. For example, in one community, a baby is passed to anyone old enough to hold the baby; however, no one ever talks directly to the child, whereas in the other community, the baby is left to lie in his crib until he cries, indicating hunger. Then it is the mother or one older relative who handles the baby, talking all the time directly to the baby.

Snow (1983) also studied caregiver–child interactions and found three specific ways in which oral language is developed in the home. Caregivers spend a great deal of time answering children's questions: "How long before we get to Grandma's?" "Why can't I go to Janey's house?" "When will Daddy be home?" Even noncaregivers are familiar with this "Why?" stage of child language. Furthermore, when children talk, caregivers don't just give simple responses. Almost automatically, adults add on to or expand the child's speech, sometimes with grammatical elaboration, other times with additional information or facts. This is how dialogue between caregiver and child is sustained over long periods of time. Snow termed this the semantic contingency of language. **Semantic contingency** refers to adults focusing on the meaningful intent of a child's statements rather than on the form it takes (i.e., grammatical or limited vocabulary).

A second characteristic of caregiver–child language interaction is **scaffolding,** a term used by Jerome Bruner (1983) to describe how adults structure dialogues with children to ensure communicative success. That is, caregivers subtly lead a child's talk back and forth in a way that maintains a sense of meaningful direction. The adult provides the scaffolding, or structure, upon which the child builds language competence. This is particularly important for young children, whose minds and speech tend to flit from topic to topic. Scaffolding is thus a gentle way of supporting young children's early attempts to sustain dialogue with their caregivers in significant ways.

Accountability is a third term associated with caregiver–child interaction; it too enhances language growth (Snow, 1983). Here are some examples: A caregiver insists that her child answer the question asked before going on to another topic; a child old enough to speak properly lapses into baby talk, and her caregiver tells her to speak correctly; a child begins a lengthy explanation of something and switches in midsentence to another topic, so the caregiver brings him back to the original topic with a question or two. In each of these instances, the child is held accountable to the sole standard of meaningful communication.

Beyond the classroom

Identify one student in an elementary classroom. Record a sample of the child's language in school using either a tape recorder or written notes. Then visit the child's home and make a similar language-sample recording either in the home or in the community. What similarities and what differences can you discover between the two samples?

CAREGIVERS AND READING

As with oral language, it is important that teachers know about the reading environment in their students' homes. Teachers' childhood experiences with reading may differ greatly from those of their students. In their childhood, many teachers may have experienced their caregivers taking them to the library and reading to them during the day and at bedtime. They saw their caregivers reading and were encouraged to "read" books by themselves. Teachers need to understand that not all families value reading like they do, and not all families have positive reading habits in the home. It is prudent for teachers to understand the literacy culture of the community of their students.

In school, reading is probably the most important subject in terms of caregiver, teacher, and child concerns, and the most time is devoted to this area. Frank Smith (1997) has argued that caregiver–child interaction involving print exerts enormous influence on the later development and interest of children in school-based reading activities. As with oral language, therefore, the more teachers of young children know about the home as a reading environment, the better they are able to help children in their classes (Burgess, 2003; Koskinen et al., 1999).

Burgess (2003) found that the characteristics that contribute to positive reading outcomes in a child are the following:

1. access to children's books
2. frequently being read to
3. special areas for reading
4. parents' positive attitude toward reading
5. frequent visits to the library
6. conversations with caregiver about books

Rush (1999) states that if caregivers cannot read, they should be encouraged to view the pictures with the child and ask higher-level questions such as "Why?" while they discuss the pictures.

In her study of children who learn to read at a very early age, Karen Thomas (1985) applied the concepts of semantic contingency, scaffolding, and accountability to understand the influence of caregivers and home environment on reading. In comparing the homes of children who learned to read early with those of children who did not, Thomas noted that the significant difference lay in the *type* of social interaction between adult and child. For example, caregivers and older siblings who answer a child's questions regarding the print or pictures in books and magazines provide examples of the concept of semantic contingency as applied to reading. Other examples of semantic contingency come from adults who read aloud often to young children, reread a child's favorite story over and over again, and tell stories from memory. In all cases it is the quality of the adult–child interaction involving print that makes the difference in the child's later reading interests and abilities.

When caregivers structure conversations with children around the books they have read, they become examples of the notion of scaffolding as applied to reading. The back-and-forth dialogue between child and adult, in which the adult offers support when needed by providing information or asking questions, focuses the child on the meaning of print in a most positive way. Thomas also found that children living in such an environment eventually begin to model the verbal behaviors of their caregivers; that is, they ask and answer questions about stories in a way that reveals an internalized sense of what a story is and what books are all about. In kindergarten and first grade, teachers often spend weeks trying to teach these same concepts under the heading of general readiness for reading. Imagine the head start that the children described by Thomas have when they first enter school!

Other researchers have echoed the importance of the earliest caregiver–child interaction as preparation for school (Rush, 1999). Stephen Burgess (2003), Marie Clay (1979), and Don Holdaway (1979), all leading authorities on early literacy acquisition, stressed the importance of having caregivers read aloud to their preschoolers. Children whose caregivers read aloud to them on a regular basis are better prepared to deal with the processes of reading and writing when they arrive in school. They can relate print to sound, have a grasp of the structure of language, understand the concept of story, and have been exposed to adults as reading models. In short, they are motivated to want to read and write upon entering the school building for the first time.

The significance of parents reading to and with young children cannot be overemphasized. Federal research studies, such as the National Indicators of Well Being and the National Household Education Survey, done as early as 1996, clearly showed a correlation between preschool children who were read to by their caregivers and their later reading achievement. Children whose caregivers read to them did better in reading than children whose caregivers did not read to them (International Reading Association, 1997/1998). The National Center for Family Literacy (2002) found, for instance, that 54 percent of children in the United States ages three to five were read aloud to every day. Other interesting statistical findings from federal research indicate that as caregivers' education level rises, the more likely they are to read to their child on a daily basis: sixty-one percent of children whose caregivers had less than a high school education were read to three or more times a week, compared with greater than 90 percent of children whose caregivers' had graduated from college or a professional school. A breakdown of the data regarding reading and the home reveals the following:

- Thirty-eight percent of children in families below the poverty line were read to every day compared with 58 percent above the poverty line in 1999.
- Fifty-eight percent of children living in two-parent homes were read to every day compared with 43 percent of children living with one or no parent (National Center for Family Literacy, 2002).

These statistics clearly show the relationship between caregiver availability and children's literacy development. Caregivers living below the poverty line and caregivers who are the sole providers often work two or more jobs in order to provide for their families. When they are at home, they must tend to common household chores, which does not always leave them enough energy or time to read to their children. Teachers should not interpret this to mean that these caregivers do not care about their children's education; teachers need to understand the importance of the home situation.

Statistics such as these confirm something teachers probably intuitively know—that learning to read is an active social process. Simply creating a pleasant environment with a variety of print samples is important, but more important is the positive social interaction that must take place between adult and child within that environment. The implication of these studies for the classroom teacher of language arts is clear: Literacy instruction should take place in a warm social setting in which children feel comfortable and have easy access to adults as models, guides, and resources for the reading process.

CAREGIVERS AND WRITING

In the past, not as much attention was paid to writing as to reading. Today educators do not separate the two literacy skills. For example, it has already been noted that children whose caregivers read to them and talk about books with them tend to also be more successful in writing activities in school. This is true because the underlying principles of language (the sound–symbol relationship, syntactic rules, focus on meaning) apply equally well to both reading and writing. The two are twin aspects of communication.

One educator who has stressed caregiver involvement in preschoolers' writing experiences is Linda Lamme of the University of Florida. Lamme bemoans the fact that writing in the home has been ignored and argues that the consequences are serious. In her book *Growing Up Writing* (1984), she states:

There are both educational and social reasons for the decline in writing ability. Writing at home is less common than it was in the days before the telephone. Today, fewer family members keep journals or diaries than in the days before television. (p. 15)

To correct this problem, Lamme makes specific suggestions for caregivers in order to encourage them to write in the home with their children. First, caregivers too often dismiss the scribblings of their youngsters as unimportant. Scribbling, however, is the foundation for writing. Therefore, caregivers should value their children's scribbles and talk about them. Lamme urges caregivers to tell their children what they like about their writing rather than asking them, "What is it?"

To further encourage home writing, Lamme suggests providing time, space, and materials for writing. Designating some time during the day for encouraging writing also implies monitoring the amount of time spent watching television. Space for writing can be created in a number of ways. Stand-up writing places can be created with newsprint or butcher-block paper taped to a refrigerator, door, or wall. With sturdy cardboard and chalkboard paint, caregivers can create their own chalkboards. Sit-down places can include a small desk, a dining table, or the floor. Finally, materials for writing can include any type of inexpensive paper, lined or unlined: newsprint, butcher-block paper, paper bags, old magazines—literally anything will work. To write or draw, children need a variety of pencils, pens, crayons, magic markers, paints, and brushes.

> ## Beyond the classroom
>
> Interview the caregivers of a young child. Determine what, if any, activities they engage in with their child that relate to reading and writing. Also, see if you can determine the attitudes of these caregivers toward reading and writing at home. Finally, ask them how they remember learning to read and write.

The key element, according to Lamme, is to get families to spend time writing together. For instance, in the Lamme household, notes are continually exchanged between caregivers and children. There is also a memo board on which family members can write messages to one another as they come and go throughout the day. All family members keep scrapbooks and diaries. Older children write stories and learn how to do simple bookbinding. And all of this takes place in the natural social setting of the home, where the child feels most comfortable. Figure 2.1 gives some suggestions for writing activities at home.

When families do engage in various writing activities, the benefits for children are enormous. Youngsters begin to recognize print in the environment beyond their homes, such as the O in the stop sign on the corner. They recognize other letters on food packages in the grocery store, such as the D in *Doritos*. Eventually they begin to recognize whole words in print, such as *Wal-Mart* and *McDonald's*. This is called **environmental print**. Denny Taylor's (1983) studies of young children demonstrated that many youngsters are aware of print in their

Scribbling on large paper	Posting a home memo board
Writing on slate boards	Using sticky notes
Water painting on newsprint	Writing holiday cards
Drawing with pencils and crayons	Writing about vacations
Finger painting	Keeping scrapbooks
Creating collage cutouts and written words	Writing in journals
Labeling family photographs	Keeping diaries
Writing or drawing notes to grandparents	Labeling trip photographs
Exchanging family notes	Using the Internet to write to favorite authors

FIGURE 2.1

Suggestions for writing at home.

homes and communities and begin to associate words with meaning before they enter school. These environmental-print experiences and this print awareness are what teachers should build upon when young children enter school.

The Importance of Play

Child psychologists and educators agree that play serves an important role in human development. Vygotsky (1976) and Piaget (1983) recognized that cognitive abilities are nurtured through play. Researchers today recognize that play not only nurtures cognitive abilities, but also builds social and literacy skills (DeKroon, Kyte, & Johnson, 2002; Jones, 2002; O'Gorman & Carter, 2002). For example, cognitive abilities are nurtured when children play with alphabet blocks; they learn about the properties of blocks and other objects. Play gives them opportunities to explore spatial relationships, speed, weight, size, shape, and sequence.

Playing together in a social setting also leads to another important type of learning. Rule learning, so crucial to later success in school, is almost always developed first through the preschool child's engagement in play. When children play cooperatively, one of the first requirements is that certain rules or guidelines be established. This is done quickly and the rules are followed literally. Violations of the rules of a game lead to quarrels but also to revisions of the rules. Such a revision can be both a powerful learning experience and an excellent vehicle for verbal and cognitive development (O'Gorman-Hughes & Carter, 2002).

In addition to rule learning, play among young children utilizes extensive *symbolic representation*, which is another excellent example of creativity developed through play. As the term implies, symbolic representation occurs when, for example, children agree to call a stick a horse, to be ridden in a particular game. Such representation also follows carefully designated rules, which children are quick to point out to one another when violated. The large amount of time children spend utilizing symbolic representation in these make-believe games forms the foundation for the development of abstract thinking and problem-solving skills, again so crucial for later success in school (Jones, 2002).

STAGES OF PLAY

Other educators have stressed the importance of child play for social development (Davie & Kemp, 2002). With very young children, there appears to be a progression in the social involvement of early play experiences. At first, the child plays alone; this is known as *solitary play*. In some instances, young children create imaginary playmates with whom they carry on lengthy conversations. Singer (1973) contended that this type of imaginative play is very stimulating for cognitive growth and the development of creativity in young children. Next the child engages in *parallel play*, in which two children play independently in the same room. Later comes *associative play*, in which children share toys but continue playing on their own. Eventually comes *cooperative play*, in which two or more children engage in a common task. Although every type of play is important, associative and cooperative play provide the best opportunities for children to learn through social interaction by using language in purposeful settings. Figure 2.2 outlines the stages of play.

DRAMATIC PLAY

Perhaps the best example of play that brings together cooperative activity, social skills, symbolic representation, and verbal abilities is dramatic play. It is one of the primary ways in which young children communicate with their caregivers

FIGURE   **2.2**

Stages of play.

TYPE	DESCRIPTION
Solitary play	Single child and a toy or imaginary playmate
Parallel play	Two or more children engaged in separate activities
Associative play	Two or more children sharing toys but without real interaction
Cooperative play	Joint task pursued; sharing; following rules

and peers about their environment, their culture, and themselves. Piaget believed that it is the most natural way for young children to communicate, since it allows for sound, gesture, and movement to complement speech. **Dramatic play,** also known as social pretend play, occurs when children with playmates or caregivers play "house," "cooking," doctor's office," "store," and so on. When children engage in dramatic play with adults, it increases oral language even more than play with peers because adults extend conversation (DeKroon, Kyte, & Johnson, 2002). Through quality conversation with an adult, the child learns technical terms for objects and actions. Here is a conversation that takes place as a child and adult play with a cooking center:

CHILD: I'm making a cake.

ADULT: What kind of cake are you making?

CHILD: A birthday cake.

ADULT: What flavor do you want your cake to be? Vanilla? Chocolate? Strawberry? Lemon? Cherry?

CHILD: A chocolate birthday cake.

ADULT: What ingredients are you putting in your cake?

CHILD: What's an ingredient?

ADULT: It's what you put in your cake, such as flour or sugar.

CHILD: I'm going to put in sugar, lots of sugar, flour, chocolate, lots of chocolate (as she begins to pretend to add ingredients to the bowl).

ADULT: Maybe you need to add an egg too.

CHILD: (pretends to crack open an egg and mixes) There, now it goes in the oven.

ADULT: Let's first put it in a cake pan.

CHILD: Yes, a round cake pan (as she picks up a round pan and pours the mixture into the pan).

ADULT: Let's put it in the oven.

CHILD: (puts pan in the oven and turns oven dial) Turn the oven on.

ADULT: (picks up pretend recipe card) Let's see. The recipe says it must bake at 350 degrees for 45 minutes. Don't forget to set the timer.

CHILD: (punching the "timer") It's set for 350 degrees for 45 minutes.

Notice how the adult encourages the child to extend her thinking and vocabulary by asking what kind of cake and what flavor. The adult was using the technical terms when naming flavors, giving the number of degrees and exact time. When the child did not understand the term *ingredient*, the adult gave a definition that the child understood.

Jones (2002) found that when children are engaged in dramatic play, the interaction is greater when two children who are friends play together.

LANGUAGE PLAY

There is another realm of play called **language play.** Children of all ages delight in playing with or using language in creative, often humorous ways. There are silly rhymes—actually poems taken from playground games—that all children can recite: "I scream, you scream, we all scream for ice cream." There are also challenging tongue twisters such as "Peter Piper picked a peck of pickled peppers." And who doesn't have a favorite "knock, knock" joke based on a play on words? Then there are the hundreds of children's jump-rope rhymes, such as "My name is Alice and I come from Alabama; my husband's name is Allan and we sell apples." In a classic work entitled *A Rocket in My Pocket* (1948), Carl Withers collected hundreds of such rhymes and playground games. Don and Alleen Nilsen (1978) have even written a college text on linguistics that incorporates the notion of using word play, games, advertising jingles, and place names as a means of teaching about the creative nature of language.

In summary, children's play is much more than mere play: It is a learning experience; it is a social experience; it is a language experience. The discerning teacher capitalizes on all the students' social and language experiences in the classroom.

Beyond the classroom

Observe some preschool children on a playground or at a park. Better yet, volunteer to supervise some neighbor's or relative's children in a play situation. Record their language and actions. What kinds of play can you identify? What skills, verbal and nonverbal, are being learned and practiced? Reflect on how this observation experience could be applied to a learning experience for older students in a language arts classroom.

Home Differences and the Hidden Curriculum

Sociologists have long known that there are significant differences in the home life and child-rearing practices among different cultures, races, and ethnic groups. Research has shown that children's attitudes toward schooling and school achievement are affected by many social, cultural, and economic factors (Burgess, 2003; Dickinson & McCabe, 2001; Mendelsohn et al., 2001; Rush, 1999).

Discrepancies in reading achievement between children from low socioeconomic (SES) environments and those from middle to upper SES environments begins before children enter school. The caregiver is a child's first and primary teacher, and the literacy opportunities a child has in the home affects the child's literacy attainment in school (Burgess, 2003; Dickinson & McCabe, 2001). The effect of home–community life on students' academic achievement or the social dimension of schooling is also known as the **hidden curriculum**—what students are taught by inference or learn indirectly (McInerney & McInerney, 1998). For example, daily conversation with adults affects oral language skills. Some of the activities in the home that are natural settings for conversation include the following:

- conversing during mealtime about the day's activities instead of watching TV
- using correct terms while playing with toys
- taking trips to grocery and department stores
- visiting zoos, museums, and other places of interest
- watching educational TV programs together and discussing them
- playing board games that demand strategic thinking
- engaging in pretend play together

- acting out stories
- playing outdoor games
- taking nature walks
- reading environmental print when walking around the neighborhood
- working in a garden together

Natural conversation is important; however, the greatest quantity and quality of language interaction occurs when a caregiver reads to a child (Davie & Kemp, 2002; Mendelsohn et al., 2001; Morrow, 1999). The amount of time the caregiver reads to a child is important, but the quality of language experiences during the shared reading contributes to the discrepancy in literacy achievement. As a child hears the rich language of stories, she learns the pronunciation and meaning of words. Then when the child encounters those words in books, she can verify the pronunciation and meaning (Morrow, 1999). As the caregiver discusses the illustrations, using the correct terms, the child begins to use the words, which builds her oral vocabulary. As caregivers read stories, they need to take time to have the child ask questions and discuss unknown concepts so that the child comprehends the information.

Certain books are especially good for children. Predictable books and poems that have repetitive and cumulative structure permit children to become familiar with the words in context. Young children tend to enjoy books and poems with rhyme and rhythm especially when caregivers draw attention to the sounds and rhythm. Books with illustrations that support the text are helpful as caregivers discuss the new concepts with the children.

CHILDREN FROM IMPOVERISHED VOCABULARY BACKGROUNDS

Some children from less economically advantaged homes, some children from homes where caregivers are too busy to interact with them, or some children from homes where family members do not speak English may be at a disadvantage in English literacy. They come to school with an impoverished vocabulary, which greatly affects their literacy attainment (Anderson & Roit, 1996; Dickinson & McCabe, 2001; Mendelsohn et al., 2001).

In working with these students, teachers should first validate the language and literacy experiences the students bring with them and then extend and enrich them. Teachers are responsible for providing many language activities in school to help students who do not have a rich oral language background. There are many ways to increase oral language. The following list gives the teacher some ideas to use with children who lack language skills (Anderson & Roit, 1996):

- engaging in shared reading to hear vocabulary words in context
- constructing vocabulary webs to show the relationship of words
- drawing pictures to depict the meaning of words
- predicting before reading
- discussing illustrations
- explaining the text structure of concept books
- permitting children to ask questions
- having children explain text instead of merely asking them to summarize the plot verbatim
- using culturally familiar informational books
- conversing with children about everyday events

Chapters 6 and 7 provide more information on each of these strategies that help develop students' vocabulary.

Language Arts and the Community

Caregivers and the home environment thus exert powerful influences on children's language development and literacy attainment. But there are still other influences beyond the home that must be taken into account in order to truly make school a place where each child's individual potential is developed. One of these influences is the community in which the child lives.

Frank Smith (1975), a psycholinguist and reading authority, has argued that children learn about the world through three primary modes: experience, observation, and language. In the home, language is primarily developed through social interaction between caregiver and child. What the child sees and does in the home is crucial to his or her development as a learner. In the broader environment of the community and neighborhood, experience, observation, and language are enormously expanded and influenced by various forces, many of which cannot be controlled by the caregiver. These forces, too, exert a powerful influence on the child as a learner.

ORAL LANGUAGE DEVELOPMENT AND THE COMMUNITY

Next to the caregiver and home, the neighborhood community is the most important influence in a child's early life as it relates to later school achievement (McQuillan & Au, 2001). The clearest example of this influence is in oral language usage. Although most people in the United States speak English, there are different forms, or dialects, of English. Courtney Cazden (1981) found that many myths are associated with dialects. For example, some people believe that a dialect is a substandard language. Not so: Everyone speaks a dialect. In the United States, people refer to the Southern drawl, the Midwest twang, and the New England clipped tongue, to name just three of the larger dialect regions. Furthermore, within each of these large dialect regions, there are hundreds of subdialects, such as the Bostonian ("pahk the cah") and Brooklynese ("toity-toird street"). A **dialect,** therefore, is simply a language variation influenced by communal and geographic factors. No one dialect is superior or inferior to another.

The dialects spoken by other children and adults in the community partially shape every child's language long before he or she enters the classroom. And this shaping affects more than mere language usage: It also serves, in Jerome Bruner's (1983) view, as "a linguistic model of reality" that the child carries to school. This means that the child's language, influenced by the community, has major implications for how the child performs in school. To better understand this notion of a linguistic model of reality, it is important to consider a bit of language history, beginning with the Whorfian hypothesis.

Whorfian Hypothesis

Benjamin Whorf was an anthropologist and linguist who worked in the early part of the twentieth century. Some of

Beyond the classroom

Visit a neighborhood different from your own. Shop in some of the stores. Observe children in the parks or on the playgrounds. Record your observations in your journal. As a teacher, what aspects of this community life could you build on to develop in your students a more positive attitude toward school and literacy attainment? Share your findings with other members of the class.

Beyond the classroom

Interview some minority college students about their early schooling experiences. Do they recall any conflicts between school and community? How did they deal with these conflicts? What have been their experiences at college? Also, try to read some articles in the *Journal of Negro Education* or a popular magazine such as *Ebony* to learn more about a culture that you will encounter when you teach and that may be foreign to you. The classic text in this area is J. L. Dillard's *Black English* (1973, New York: Random House).

his observational research was carried out among the Hopi and other Native American tribes in the southwestern United States. Whorf noted that in comparison with English, the Hopi language has restricted concepts of time and space. He also noted that the Hopi have a view of the world quite different from that of other peoples. Whorf (1956) suggested that the structure of the Hopi language influenced their worldview and cultural values. That is, the language of the community influences the individual's cognitive processing of experiences. Although linguists and educators have argued about the degree of influence that language exerts over the way people view the world, most agree that Whorf was correct. Each person's language is not neutral; rather it shapes, to some extent, the way that person experiences and sees the world, which in turn affects the way that person learns.

> ### Beyond the classroom
>
> Make an analysis of your own community similar to the one in this chapter's Classroom Vignette. List potential resources in the Yellow Pages that relate to the language arts. Then brainstorm ideas for each resource. Next, share your list with a classroom teacher. What is the teacher's reaction? Does he or she see any impediments to implementing these ideas? If so, how can you work around these?

Dialect and Academic Achievement

For many years educators, linguists, sociologists, and politicians have argued about the relationship between dialect and academic achievement. This debate has centered around the high failure rate of youngsters from minority backgrounds who do not speak standard English.

The significance of Benjamin Whorf's theory for educators becomes clear when looking at language differences (dialects) within the same culture. In the 1960s, Basil Bernstein (1971) collected language samples from working-class and middle-class children in England. He noted that the linguistic differences between these two groups were specific enough to constitute two different language dialects, or codes: the restricted code spoken by working-class children and the elaborated code spoken by middle-class children. Bernstein concluded that children from the lower classes speak a form of the language substantially different from that spoken in school. These differences between children's language and school language might partially explain the poor academic performance of children of lower socioeconomic status (Ogbu & Simons, 1994).

In the United States, Bernstein's writings and their implications for schools refocused attention on the issue of nonstandard dialect and academic achievement during the late 1960s and early 1970s. Since most poor minority children in the schools who were experiencing serious academic difficulties were also nonstandard-dialect speakers, some educators jumped to the conclusion that nonstandard dialect must be the culprit. The reasoning went something like this: Compared to standard English (the language of schools), nonstandard English appears to be deficient in its ability to communicate thoughts and ideas. Thus, the linguistically different child who speaks nonstandard English in the classroom is at a great disadvantage. The implied solution is to change the child's language to meet the standards of the school. This belief is referred to in the literature as the **Deficit Theory of Language** (Blank & Solomon, 1972).

In the United States, perhaps the strongest critic of the Deficit Theory is William Labov, the linguist from the University of Pennsylvania who in 1985

> ### Beyond the classroom
>
> Get together with a fellow student and take a walk through your community. Note the aspects of community life (signs, billboards, window displays, and so on) that could be utilized to teach about functional literacy. Make a list of all the potential functional literacy materials you find. Discuss your findings in class and relate them to the language arts. Then visit some classrooms in your community to discover which teachers are incorporating this type of information into their lessons.

VIGNETTE *in the classroom*

Mrs. Boltman, a fifth-grade teacher in a medium-size rural community, is dissatisfied with the way some of her lessons are going. Her students seem less than enthused with the language arts textbook. Furthermore, they complain that they cannot see the point in what they are being asked to study. Many of the students say they already know what they want to be once they finish school (which for many will be when they turn 16 and can legally drop out).

In search of a new approach to teaching the language arts, Mrs. Boltman turns to the Yellow Pages of the telephone book. She begins by listing the names and addresses of businesses and organizations that might relate to her language arts curriculum for the year. Then she contacts these resources. After doing field research in her community and interviewing some key people, she decides what to do. With the permission of her principal, she arranges for a series of mini–field trips, interviews, guest speakers, and other educational experiences in her community. The field trips will be ongoing, conducted throughout the school year, and related to the course content taught in class. Figure 2.3 shows a partial sample of her list.

first showed that nonstandard speech, though different, is nevertheless a viable speech form. Labov's central argument is that dialect speech is logical and systematic, contains its own grammar, and is fully capable of meaningful communication. The problem is that most white, middle-class teachers do not understand it and therefore label it as inferior, deficient, or something requiring remediation.

Joan Tough (1985) is another well-known linguist and educator who is sharply critical of the Deficit Theory and the negative approaches taken toward speakers of nonstandard English in the classroom. She has argued that language is not a mere set of skills to be memorized through extensive drills. In real language situations, there are no prescribed answers. Instead, language must be used, experienced, and recognized as a primary means of expression. Above all,

FIGURE 2.3

Community resources for the language arts.

YELLOW PAGES LISTINGS	LANGUAGE ARTS IDEAS
Antique Repairing and Restoring	Examine old objects, relate to history, stimulate creative writing from unusual object.
Aquarium and Pet Shop	Choose a pet, name it, describe it.
Cessna Pilot Center	Interview pilots, read about planes from the past, create instructional manual.
Farm Animal Auction Center	Visit and later act out auction scene.
Holiday Travel Agency	Use dozens of colorful brochures to stimulate imagination about faraway places, acting, reading, writing.
Lie Detection and Security Service	Initiate mystery reading, writing, play acting.
South Community Hospital	Interview doctors and nurses, follow-up reading, writing (compare with soap operas about hospitals), discussion.

language must be accepted as long as it communicates meaning effectively, regardless of its style or form.

Salinger (1988) has suggested the following five guidelines for working with linguistically different students:

1. In the early grades, children should be encouraged to acquire standard English in addition to their own dialect.
2. The process of acquiring a second "language code" is difficult and requires practice over long periods of time.
3. Modeling standard English construction, rather than overcorrecting, is the preferred teaching strategy.
4. Oral reading miscues caused by dialect differences should not be corrected as long as the deviations do not change the meaning of the text.
5. Dialect speakers should be encouraged to write extensively and to work out their own sense of grammar. In time, with more exposure to standard English forms in books, their writing will approximate standard grammar.

Education takes place in the combination of the home, the community, the school, and the receptive mind.

HARRY EDWARDS

Teachers Involving Caregivers

Teachers must understand that students benefit in a number of ways—academically, physically, socially, and emotionally—when their caregivers are involved in their education at home and/or at school. Studies indicate that students from all economic levels and races who are more successful academically have caregivers who are involved in their education (Henderson, 1988; Ho, 2002; Love, 1996; Rasinski & Padak, 2000; Sheldon, 2002; Sullivan, 1998). Their academic success is reflected in the daily grades and test scores. Students whose caregivers are involved in their education have a positive attitude toward learning as well as a positive perception of the effectiveness of their school (Henderson, 1988; Ho, 2002; Sheldon, 2002).

There are two types of involvement: school involvement and home involvement. School involvement includes volunteering in the child's classroom or in the school library, accompanying classes on field trips, holding positions on the local school board or parent–teacher organization (PTO), and attending parent–teacher conferences, open houses, and other school events. Home involvement includes caring for the child's physical needs, monitoring homework, and showing interest in school by discussing the school day with the child.

Because caregiver involvement affects the child's success in school, the National Parent–Teacher Association (PTA) developed national standards for caregiver/family involvement programs (Sullivan, 1998). The six standards give general ideas for fostering positive school/caregiver relationships:

1. There must be regular communication between home and school.
2. Schools must provide support in caregiver skills.
3. Schools must provide information on how caregivers can assist student learning.
4. Schools must encourage caregivers to volunteer at school, and caregivers need to volunteer.
5. Caregivers must be involved in school decision making.
6. There must be collaboration with the community to provide resources in schools.

REGULAR COMMUNICATION BETWEEN HOME AND SCHOOL

It is important that teachers regularly communicate with caregivers about events that are happening in school. Effective communication increases caregivers' level of interest in school activities. There are numerous ways teachers can communicate with caregivers.

Letters of introduction. At the beginning of the year, teachers can write a letter of introduction, telling who they are, explaining what their goals are for the year, and giving vital information about how caregivers can contact teachers. Figure 2.4 is an example of such a letter.

If teachers know that a caregiver cannot read, they should personally call each home, giving some of the same information as in the letter. If a teacher does not speak the caregivers' language, he or she should then find someone in the community who can relate the information to them. The purpose of the home contact is to build rapport with the students' caregivers. Making sure each home is contacted may be time-consuming, but the effort is rewarding. All caregivers should know they are a part of their child's education and classroom.

FIGURE 2.4

Example of a letter of introduction.

Dear Parents and Caregivers:

I am excited to be a new member of this community and to become a partner in your child's learning! This summer I moved to Edmond from Kalamazoo, where I also taught second grade. I already have enjoyed Edmond's new library and Shakespeare in the Park. Besides reading and going to plays, I love country music and long walks.

It is my goal that every one of my students will become a successful reader and that he or she will spend some spare time reading materials that interest him or her. I hope that is also your goal for your child.

Central Elementary is embracing a new reading program this year called "Taking Flight with Books." The school's goal is to have each child read at least 100 pages each week at home. Our school is encouraging caregivers to listen to their child when possible and to discuss the material with him or her. At Open House I will further explain this new program and answer any questions you may have.

Central Elementary Open House is September 1, 2005, at 7 P.M. I am eager to meet each one of you and to personally encourage you to become involved at school if you can. At Open House I will have sign-up sheets for different activities—reading with students, playing word activities with students, binding students' books, organizing our classroom library, recording our "Taking Flight with Books" pages, and many other activities. Meanwhile, please save your old candles, scraps of material, and any broken appliances. Our class will need all these materials for art, science, and social studies projects. I am looking forward to meeting you at Open House on September 1. Please note that if you need to contact me, you can email me at jbarryman@centralelementary.edmond.edu or call me at school between 8:00 and 8:20 any morning.

Sincerely,

Jan Barryman

Open houses. If the school or class has a reading initiative program, teachers can introduce it and the reading log that will be used for the program during Open House. Caregivers should understand that the goal of the program is to get students to read at home, and that the caregivers are the cheerleaders for this project. Figure 2.5 is an example of a reading log.

At the beginning of the year, teachers may invite caregivers to share some information about their child that will help the teacher better understand the child. At Open House, teachers may invite caregivers to complete a "Getting to Know Your Child" card. On this card teachers ask for information such as the child's learning style, personality, family arrangement, extracurricular activities, and any other information the caregiver would like to share. Teachers need to make clear that sharing the information is optional because not all caregivers want to share personal information. Teachers need to be sensitive to all caregivers' feelings! Figure 2.6 is an example of a "Getting to Know Your Child" card.

The ideal scenario would be that all caregivers attend Open House and home–school conferences. However, that is never the case. Teachers should be

FIGURE 2.5

Example of a reading log.

READING LOG

Taking Flight with Books

Child's Name _____   *Grade* _____

DATE	TITLE/AUTHOR	PAGES	CAREGIVER'S SIGNATURE

FIGURE   2.6

Example of a "Getting to Know Your Child" card.

Getting to Know Your Child

Child's name _____

Child's best subject _____

Child's least favorite subject _____

Child's favorite way to learn _____

Child's personality _____

Child's extracurricular activities _____

_____

Other information you want the teacher to know _____

_____

_____

Thank you for sharing this information; it will remain confidential.

_____

Caregiver's signature

prepared to contact the home through a telephone call or through an inter-preter for English-as-second-language students and invite caregivers to share information about their child that will help the teacher better understand that child.

Your children need your presence more than your presents.

JESSE JACKSON

Monthly newsletters. Another form of school–home communication is a monthly newsletter that explains special events that are taking place in the class. In the newsletter, teachers can give specific learning activities for caregivers to do with their child to help the child understand concepts. Teachers can also recognize caregivers who volunteer in the school or classroom. Samples of children's artwork or writings can be included; however, it is important that teachers receive permission from caregivers to print their child's work. Figure 2.7 is an example of a permission request. Also in the newsletter teachers can give caregivers ideas for read alouds, or inform them of upcoming educational TV programs and family events in the community. Figure 2.8 is an example of part of a newsletter.

Good news telephone calls/emails. Teachers should get into the habit of giving caregivers "Good News Telephone Calls/Emails" to let them know that their child improved in some subject, reached a goal, or did an act of kindness. Too often teachers contact caregivers only to inform them of something the child did wrong. "Good News Telephone Calls/Emails" open communication between teachers and caregivers so that when caregivers need advice, they feel they can contact the teacher for help. Happy Grams are also ways to commu-

FIGURE   **2.7**

Example of a permission request.

Dear _____,

Our class has enjoyed _____ (child's name)
poem/story/essay _____ (title of composition). I
would like to include it in our next monthly newsletter, but I need your
permission to publish it. Please complete the permission slip at the bottom of this note and return it with _____ (child's
name) by _____ (date).

Sincerely,

Jan Barryman

Dear Ms. Barryman,

_____ I give you permission to publish my child's work in the newsletter.

_____ At this time I do *not* want you to publish my child's work.

_____
Caregiver's signature

nicate a success story to caregivers. They are written notes to let caregivers
know what success their child has had in school. Figure 2.9 is an example of a
Happy Gram.

Weekly assignment sheets. Most caregivers are concerned about homework
assignments. Teachers can create weekly assignment sheets that go home each
evening with the child. Caregivers then can monitor the child's homework and
sign the sheet to inform the teacher that they have done so. Figure 2.10 is an
example of an assignment sheet. Teachers should create sheets that fit their needs.

Again, teachers *need to know their students' community*. For example, many
caregivers may be single and/or working nights or more than one job. And in
some affluent communities, caregivers are not available because they are away
on business trips or may encourage their children to participate in extracurricular activities, such as piano, dance, karate, tennis, golf, or gymnastics. For
these reasons, teachers may consider adjusting the number of daily homework
assignments.

Technology. Schools can also effectively communicate with caregivers
through the use of technology (Borelli, 2001). Many schools have their own Web
page, which includes information of interest to caregivers. It is important for
schools to remember that not all caregivers have access to the Internet; therefore,
they need to make the information on their Web page available to those caregivers as well. Many schools create an analog phone system so that these

FIGURE **2.8**

Example of part of a monthly newsletter.

Second-Grade Monthly Newsletter

NOVEMBER 2, 2005   CENTRAL ELEMENTARY

CONGRATULATIONS!

In the month of October, our class read an average of 116 pages a week! That is 16 pages higher than our goal. We thank you for encouraging us at home, giving us quiet time to read, and for discussing great books with us. We understand that you are turning off the TV and also reading! Keep up the good work!

Activity for the Family

We are learning probability in math. We take two minutes each morning to first predict how many heads and tails we will get when we toss a coin 20 times. Then we see how close we get to our prediction. You can also do this at home as a family activity.

Field Trip

On Friday, November 15, our class is going to see the play *The True Story of the Three Pigs* at 12:00 at the State Fair Ground Theatre. The buses will leave at 11:00 and return at the end of the school day. Our class needs five or six adults who will come with us. Your ticket, like the students' tickets, is free! Please call me if you can help us! When you see one of the Allied Art Council members, thank them for giving us this opportunity! They are providing the free tickets.

Acrostic Poem

Footballs flying through the air,
Apples ripening to bright red,
Leaves turning orange and yellow,
Leaves crunching under feet.

by Juan Garcia

FIGURE **2.9**

Example of a Happy Gram.

Hear Ye! Hear Ye!

I am happy to inform you that today _____ did the following:

_____

_____

_____

_____

Teacher's signature

FIGURE 2.10

Example of an assignment sheet.

Assignment(s) Not Completed in School or Other Homework

For Week of _____

DAY	ASSIGNMENTS	CAREGIVER'S COMMENT
Mon.		
Tues.		
Wed.		
Thurs.		

Note: I will not assign homework on Friday; I want to encourage the family to do other activities together.

_____

Teacher's signature

caregivers can punch in their child's personal identification number to get class assignments, grades, and attendance. Figure 2.11 provides ways schools can use technology.

Entertainment nights. Schools can provide entertainment nights, which are free to the family. Teachers should consider the community when they plan activities for these nights. The goal of an entertainment night is to get caregivers, students, teachers, administrators, and staff to interact in a relaxed, enjoyable setting. Some activities that would be appropriate for most communities include the following:

- Invite an entertaining local children's author/illustrator to come share his or her personal life and work. Ask a local business to donate money so that each child receives an autographed book. Ask a local photographer or someone else to donate a camera and film so that each student with his or her caregiver can have a picture with the author/illustrator.
- Teachers can perform a one-act play, a puppet show, a readers theatre, or sets of poems.
- Children can read books that they have prepared to their caregivers. A photographer who will donate camera and film can take pictures of the caregiver with the child reading.

FIGURE **2.11**

Using technology to communicate with caregivers.

1. Create a school website to inform caregivers of the following:
   a. Child's attendance and grades, which only the caregiver can access.
   b. Class activities.
   c. Community events.
   d. Homework assignments.
   e. Upcoming school events.
   f. Need for volunteers for particular activities.
   g. Need for supplies, such as plastic containers, potting soil for science experiments, and shoe boxes to create dioramas.

2. Share websites that caregivers can explore with their child:
   a. **www.afterschool.gov** gives tips for after-school activities, has links to reinforce reading and writing skills, and has links to information about the world.
   b. **www.whitehouse.gov** permits viewers to "tour" the White House and gives historical information about the White House.
   c. **Authors' websites.** Appendix A includes a list of children's literature author websites.
   d. **www.yahoo.com** allows users to provide an author's name as the search word in order to locate other authors.

- Children can demonstrate to caregivers their keyboarding skills and how to use a word processor, such as the copy/paste function and using different fonts.
- Invite a local storyteller to read to small groups in a circle while enjoying some refreshments.
- Invite a magician to entertain. Ask local businesses to donate the funds to pay the magician. A word of caution: Some communities with strict religious beliefs may not approve of a magician.
- Provide a carnival night with games such as tossing rings on bottle tops, penny toss, dunking tanks, and clowns who make animal balloons.

The purpose of these nights is to get teachers, caregivers, and students to interact in a relaxed environment. Caregivers enjoy seeing the different personalities of the teachers. It is also great for teachers to see how caregivers interact with their children.

SCHOOLS PROVIDING SUPPORT IN CAREGIVER SKILLS

No credentials are needed to become a caregiver, yet it is the most difficult task adults do. Ruby Payne (2001) believes that poverty is a cycle. Many caregivers living in poverty grew up in poverty and never received the nurturing needed to become a nurturing caregiver. Schools need to recognize that not all caregivers know how to provide the emotional and social nurturing that will aid their child's education. There are a number of activities schools can provide to help with these caregiver skills. Schools can provide opportunities for caregivers to hear professionals who understand good caregiver skills. They can also provide time for caregivers to get together to informally share ideas that work for them or to discuss concerns they have. Most schools find that caregivers who need to hear professional speakers or need to become a part of informal discussion groups are the ones who do not attend these meetings. One of the most efficient ways schools can share caregiver tips is through a newsletter sent to caregivers right before parent–teacher conferences. Teachers then can discuss some of the tips with caregivers at these conferences. Figure 2.12 is an example of a newsletter providing tips on caregiving.

WAYS CAREGIVERS CAN ASSIST STUDENT LEARNING

The Goals 2000 Education America Act states: "Every school will promote partnerships that will increase parental involvement and participation in promoting social, emotional and academic growth of children." There are many ways schools can encourage caregivers to aid the academic growth, and in particular,

FIGURE 2.12

Example of a newsletter providing tips for caregivers.

Central Elementary Newsletter
100 S. Edgewood
Edmond, OK 73034

Dear Caregivers,

Occasionally, especially as we begin a new school year, it is prudent for all caregivers (including me) to be reminded of some of the responsibilities we have to our children. Many responsibilities we caregivers have at home help our children become successful in school. The items listed below are some of these responsibilities:

1. Care for the child's physical needs by providing breakfast. (If the child qualifies for free breakfasts, caregivers need to get the child to school in time for breakfast.)
2. Insist on a consistent bedtime so that the child gets proper rest.
3. Provide healthy snacks, such as a piece of fresh fruit or carrot sticks, and plenty of water instead of sugary drinks.
4. Provide time for physical activity outdoors.
5. Teach good hygiene, such as brushing teeth, washing hair, and bathing daily.
6. Discuss school happenings with the child, thus showing the child that you value education.
7. Monitor homework by providing a quiet time and place. Turn off the TV!
8. Model reading and writing in front of the child.
9. Establish prosocial behavior: Respect others and their property, be patient, be kind, use appropriate language, and so on.

Personally, I am going to post this list on my refrigerator so I am reminded each day of my responsibilities to my two children.

We at Central Elementary wish you well as you work with your child. If you have any questions, please call the school counselor or discuss the issue with your child's teachers during the upcoming conference.

Sincerely,

Dr. J. Rush, Principal

the literacy growth of their child. This information can be given during a PTO meeting, open house, parent–teacher conference, or through a newsletter. Figure 2.13 lists a variety of activities caregivers can do at home to aid the literacy development of their child. Again, teachers need to remember the community of their students; not all suggestions are appropriate for all communities.

The First-Start Program, developed at Kent state, is a program that gives specific hints to caregivers on effective reading with their child. First the caregiver reads the passage to the child and talks about the passage. Then the caregiver and child read the passage in unison. Next, the caregiver listens as the child reads the passage. The caregiver and child then choose one or two words from the passage that the child wants to remember and the child writes it on an index card. The cards become the child's personal set of flashcards.

Faires, Nichols, and Rickelman (2000) found that training caregivers in selected components of the Reading Recovery model, which the caregivers implemented at home three times a week, was an effective way to increase students' reading ability. The teacher provided the appropriate trade books for rereading and instructional reading, magnetic letters, and sentence strips. The caregivers were trained to use the following lesson structure:

- The child rereads two or more familiar books.
- Using magnetic letters, the child works with letter identification.
- The child writes a sentence of a short story with caregivers, and then the caregivers help the child listen for letters in unknown words.
- Caregivers write the child's sentence or story on a sentence strip, cut it apart, and ask the child to reassemble the sentence.
- Caregivers introduce a new book by talking about illustrations and then have the child read it.

These same caregivers were also trained to use the Helping Hand strategy during these lessons. The Helping Hand strategy follows these steps:

- Think about the story.
- Read the story.

FIGURE 2.13

Things caregivers can do at home to aid their child's literacy development.

1. Read engaging books that are above their child's reading level so that the child is introduced to an advanced vocabulary.
2. Read in unison with their child.
3. If caregivers cannot read, they can listen with their child to books on tape, or view and discuss wordless books.
4. Model reading in front of their child.
5. Write with their child.
6. Help with spelling by helping their child see patterns within words.
7. Watch and discuss educational TV programs with their child.
8. If caregivers have access to the Internet at home, they can research a topic together with their child. (A child should not be allowed to use the Internet without supervision. It is wise to have the computer in a room other than the child's bedroom.)
9. Make regular visits to the local library with their child.
10. Do word puzzles with their child.

- Reread the story.
- With unknown words, get the mouth ready for the initial sound of the word.
- Make a guess at unknown words and check if that guess fits the meaning of the sentence.

It takes time for teachers to train caregivers to use the Reading Recovery model, but the benefits make it worthwhile. Not only does students' reading ability increase, but caregivers' interest in their children's education increases (Faires et al., 2000).

CAREGIVERS VOLUNTEERING AT SCHOOL

Caregivers who are engaged in the child's education at home may not always be engaged at school. For example, in 1996, the National Center for Education Statistics estimated that in two-caregiver families, only 15 percent of fathers and 41 percent of mothers volunteered at their child's school, while in single-caregiver families, only 23 percent of fathers and 29 percent of mothers volunteered (NCES, 1998).

Who are the caregivers who are involved in their children's school? Caregivers volunteer at school when they believe that they can affect children's education, they are important to children's development, their school wants their help, they feel comfortable helping at school, and they can be successful in helping with their children's learning (Hoover-Dempsey & Sandler, 1997).

Teachers can encourage caregivers who have the time to volunteer for a wide array of tasks at school. Volunteerism includes holding positions in the local PTO or PTA, serving on the local school board, chaperoning class field trips, doing clerical jobs in the classroom and school, and participating on a regular basis in the classroom.

The clerical jobs that teachers give caregivers should not allow access to confidential records. Some appropriate clerical jobs include the following:

- typing class newsletters or other general letters that go home to all parents if caregivers have keyboarding skills
- hanging individual certificates of the class book chain
- changing bulletin boards
- photocopying certificates, Happy Grams, and newsletters
- organizing the classroom library
- repairing books and games
- making posters announcing a new class project
- assisting students with bookbinding
- repairing puppets and games
- keeping records for any schoolwide reading program (e.g., Just Read or Pizza Hut Read).

Some caregivers would rather help students than do clerical work. There are a wide variety of activities they can do to aid student learning:

- Tutor a student in reading if properly trained.
- Listen to a child read.
- Read to a child.
- Assist a group of students as they prepare a puppet show.
- Assist a group of students as they practice a readers theatre script.
- Assist a student with editing the final copy of his composition.
- Assist a student as she tapes a passage she reads aloud.
- Participate in an activity (e.g., Word, Scrabble) that reinforces skills.

- Assist a student on the computer as he researches a topic.
- Assist a student with spelling words.
- Read with a group of advanced readers while the teacher works with the less advanced readers.

Because volunteerism at school improves caregivers' perception of school effectiveness (Henderson, 1988; Ho, 2002), teachers should embrace caregivers who desire to volunteer at school.

CAREGIVER INVOLVEMENT IN SCHOOL DECISION MAKING

Not only should caregivers be encouraged to volunteer at school, but they should also be part of making decisions that effect policies. Too often caregivers battle their local school board over major issues of change. To avoid conflict, schools should invite caregivers to be members of committees that instigate changes for the school. Caregivers can serve in their area of interest or expertise. For example, caregivers who are former educators have the expertise to serve on committees that select new textbooks and curriculum. Other caregivers may have an interest in selecting new playground equipment. Still other caregivers may have the expertise and/or interest to organize after-school programs or new reading initiatives. When caregivers serve on decision-making committees, they support the school and get other caregivers to support the school as well.

COMMUNITY RESOURCES

Communities concerned about education collaborate with schools in providing resources. Often community libraries, civic organizations, and church groups offer after-school, summer, and weekend enrichment programs and free tutoring services.

After-School Programs

Many communities recognize after-school programs as a necessity instead of a luxury (Feinstein, 2003). In 2001, the After-School Alliance found that 94 percent of voters believed after-school supervision for students was a necessity, and 93 percent of those voters believed the school was the best place for supervision because students were already there. After-school programs, which occur at school, usually run from the time school is out to about 6:30 P.M. These programs are free to all students, and all participants come on a volunteer basis. The goal of these programs is to provide a safe, fun place where students "develop positive peer relationships, create a sense of identity, encourage positive self-esteem and enhance good decision making skill" (Feinstein, 2003, p. 35).

After-school activities are enrichment activities and intervention programs structured to help individual students. Enrichment activities include games such as foosball, Ping-Pong, checkers, and chess; video games; computer activities; a variety of sports; weekly field trips; tennis lessons; and cooking classes (Feinstein, 2003).

Public Libraries

Access to reading materials influences the amount of reading that students do, regardless of their ability, and more free reading is associated with higher reading scores (Halle, Kurt-Costes, & Mahoney, 1997; McQuillan & Au, 2001). Community libraries with a large collection of children's books, magazines, and computer programs on a variety of topics can influence the amount of reading children do. Many libraries understand the importance of providing a large selection of books on tapes so that caregivers who are not proficient in English can still "read" with their children.

Some communities that understand that access to books affects reading achievement provide Libraries on Wheels, which are large charter buses converted into libraries that move from neighborhood to neighborhood so that children and adults who do not have personal transportation to public libraries can have access to books and books on tape.

Many community libraries provide after-school, weekend, and summer library activities for children because they understand that these programs build children's reading skills. Some activities for younger children are storytelling, shared reading, and puppet activities. For older children, the library may feature an author or a theme for a month so children can become involved in topics that are not studied in school. Forming a literacy club for students gives them the opportunity to discuss and critique books while they form a sense of belonging. Some libraries also arrange for authors from their area to give presentations about their life and work.

Community Programs

There are other community groups that understand the importance of providing literacy activities for children after school. For caregivers who do not have the means to pay for reading tutors, many churches, synagogues, mosques, and civic groups organize after-school tutoring programs for neighborhood children. Religious and civic groups seek volunteers from the community or from a nearby university to read with children or help with other homework. The meeting places are in safe places such as community centers or neighborhood religious facilities. Some civic and religious groups also provide a meal or snack for the children and transportation to and from the meeting center so that all children who desire the help can receive it. Sometimes a coordinator from the school will work with the civic or religious group to provide information about the child's reading level and particular literacy need. This communication between the school and civic or religious groups makes these tutoring programs effective. These programs not only help children develop literacy skills, but also help build self-esteem and a sense of belonging (Bross, 2003; King, 2003).

Volunteerism or Service Learning in the Schools

"Service learning is a way to help our young people grow individually and as members of society. It is about helping our young people grow up to understand the connection between living and learning, what it means to be an adult, what it means to live as a citizen in a free and 'civil' society, and what it means to live as a truly compassionate and caring human being" (Carol Kinsley, executive director of the Community Service Center, Springfield, MA).

More and more communities are involving adults and school-age children in the concept of service learning. Service learning benefits the students who provide the service as well as the people in the community who are directly affected by the service. Although service learning has been focused at the high school level, it is also prevalent in many middle and elementary schools. In Springfield, MA, for example, teachers utilize service experiences at every grade level and in every curriculum area (Kinsley, 1997).

The service-learning concept has been around for many years on an informal basis under the heading of volunteerism. For example, individual classroom teachers or school clubs ask their students to volunteer for a particular service project, such as cleaning up around the school grounds, reading books to younger children, or visiting with the elderly in nursing homes. But such projects were dependent on individual teachers and small groups of motivated students. Today the term *service learning* is conceived more broadly, encompasses more students, and has taken on a more formal structure.

In the past decade, both Presidents Bill Clinton and George W. Bush have promoted service-learning projects in their speeches and have allocated federal funds for initiatives. Each year $43 million has been budgeted for service-learning projects.

Service-learning projects are more than volunteerism. Volunteerism focuses on service, while **service learning** focuses on connecting students' academic learning with civic life (Allen, 2003). For example, schools may ask students to volunteer to plant trees, shrubs, and flowers in their playground, while a service-learning project includes students studying where trees and shrubs are needed in their community, what types of trees and shrubs flourish best in that environment and soil, and how they will keep soil from eroding.

The goal of service-learning projects is to give students the opportunity to "gain the ability to critically examine and respond to social issues" (Allen, 2003, p. 52). Students examine current social issues that affect the community, analyze them, "envision an improvement to which they can actively—and collectively—contribute" (Allen, 2003, p. 52), and then reflect on the end results.

Service-learning projects reveal students' civic capacity—their ability to be responsible citizens. Joseph Kahne, a professor at Mills College in Oakland, CA, identified three types of citizens: *personally responsible citizens*, who work, pay taxes, vote, and obey the laws; *participatory citizens*, who get involved in civic organizations and projects; and *social reformers*, who advocate social change for a fairer, democratic society.

For service-learning projects to be successful, they must be connected to state standards, student centered, based on constructivist theory, and beneficial for classroom practice (Allen, 2003). They include projects that give students the opportunity to become personally responsible citizens, participatory citizens, and social reformers.

Being an integral part of the school curriculum is another one of the things that makes service learning different from mere volunteerism. Service-learning programs engage young people in community activities that show how skills acquired in school can be used to solve real-life problems. At the same time, these program activities help students understand their ability to address the quality of life as well as real needs in their communities (Alt, 1997).

For example, students might visit a homeless shelter on a weekly basis and read and write with the children there. Visiting with these children, they establish relationships with people different from themselves and gain an understanding of the conditions that lead to homelessness. A good program design or framework can help students act out of a desire to meet a genuine human need. Conscious planning and purposeful thinking can maximize the potential outcomes of the service-learning experience.

Service-learning planning includes several phases (Berkas & Maland, 1993). The first phase, *preparation*, consists of the learning activities that take place prior to the service learning itself. Students must first understand what is expected of them as well as what they can expect from the service-learning project. Preparation components include the following:

- Identify and analyze the problem to be addressed.
- Select and plan the project.
- Conduct training and orientation sessions with the students.

The next phase of service learning is the *action* phase. This is the actual service itself, and it too must meet certain criteria. Primarily these are the criteria:

- Be meaningful.
- Have academic integrity.
- Have adequate supervision.
- Provide for student ownership.
- Be developmentally appropriate.

Reflection is the third phase of service learning. Reflection enables students to think critically about their service-learning experience. When students reflect on their experiences, they think about them, read about them, write about them, discuss them with others, and learn from their experiences. Reflection time is structured time, built into the overall plan of service learning and is a real learning experience for children. Reflections can be enhanced through the following:

- discussion
- reading
- writing
- projects

The final phase is the *celebration* component of service learning. Celebration is the way in which students are recognized for their service contributions. It also provides closure to a sometimes lengthy (a full semester) ongoing service activity. Celebration is one way adults let children know that their service efforts are valued. The following are examples:

- school assemblies
- certificates
- special media coverage
- pizza parties
- joint party celebration with the service recipients (e.g., cookies and punch with preschoolers)

If you would like to learn more about service learning in the schools and communities, contact the University of Minnesota at 1-800-808-SERVE.

TECHNOLOGY AND WEBSITES

PROTECTIVE PROGRAMS AND SEARCH ENGINES

When connecting to the Internet, one concern of caregivers and educators is the accessibility of information that is objectionable for elementary students. The Children's Internet Protection Act (CIPA-HR4577) requires measures to be taken to ensure children's safety while using the Internet. Several means are available, one of which is filtering software. School districts can use districtwide solutions such as N2H2. Caregivers and educators can purchase and install on their computers software programs designed to protect youngsters from offensive material. Following is a list of sample programs with the Web address so one can download the program and receive additional information on how the particular program works:

Cyber Patrol
www.cyberpatrol.com

CYBERSitter
www.solidoak.com

Net Nanny
www.netnanny.com

Pearl Software
www.thepsef.org/beta

Often caregivers and teachers search the Internet for information but do not get the information they desire because they do not use the correct search engine. Following is a list of various search engines:

www.infoseek.com
This site is sponsored by GO Network, which is ESPN, ABC, and Disney.

www.excite.com
This is one of the major search engines.

www.yahoo.com
This search engine is well organized with headings and subheadings. It links the viewer to many publishers, organizations, and companies.

www.google.com
This search engine is written by Stanford and permits the viewer to search the Web and U. S. government documents.

www.hotbot.com
This search engine is well organized with headings and subheadings and is not cluttered.

www.gogettem.com
This site features all the search engines and directories.

www.yahooligans.com
This search engine is the Web guide for kids.

OTHER USEFUL WEBSITES

www.pbs.org/rogers
This is Mister Rogers' website, which includes articles for caregivers and a list of stories that correlate with the TV program's themes.

www.parentsplace.com/sorry.html
This site is a newsletter that has resources for parents to work with the children.

www.kn.pacbell.com/wired/bluewebn/index.html
This site promotes Internet projects and is a terrific general resource that is sorted by topic.

www.nieonline.com
This site is a browsing place for lesson ideas. It is sorted by grade level and subjects.

www.gsh.org
This is a publishing center and forum about using technology successfully. It is geared for teachers and caregivers.

http://npin.org

This site gives caregivers suggestions on helping their child.

http://scholastic.com/inschool

This is the site for the *Instructor* magazine.

www.eric.indiana.edu/www/indexfr.htm

This site contains stories for caregivers to read to their children. They are arranged by grade level.

www.puzzlemaker.com

This site permits you to create mazes, word searches, crosswords, math squares, etc., for any lesson.

www.pta.org

This site gives the national standards for caregiver and family involvement in schools. It gives tips on helping with homework.

www.americaspromise.org

This site gives information on how to become one of Colin Powell's Schools of Promise.

www.ctw.org

This site has the alphabet according to Sesame Street.

http://discoveryschool.com/schrockguide

This site is sponsored by Discovery Channel. It has a Quick Search feature for resources by subject area.

www.nida.nih.gov

This site provides caregivers and teachers with information about issues related to drug abuse.

www.ncsu.edu/cpsv

This site provides research about prevention of school violence.

www.ed.gov/pubs/parents

This U. S. Department of Education's site offers brochures for caregivers on pertinent family issues.

www.ncel.org

This site analyzes caregiver involvement practices.

www.family.com

This is Disney's family site.

Summary

Teachers need to acquaint themselves with the educational environment beyond the classroom if they are to help their students more effectively. This means meeting caregivers, learning about home environments, and visiting the community. It also means that teachers should incorporate into their classroom instruction the new knowledge they glean from interacting with caregivers and experiencing firsthand students' homes and communities.

Social interaction is an important learning force for children. Caregivers who interact with their children in the areas of oral language, reading, and writing are preparing their children for the world of school. The nature of social interaction, however, varies considerably in both the home and the community, particularly according to socioeconomic level. Children from low-income backgrounds do not have the same types of home and community experiences to draw upon as middle-class children. This fact must be taken into consideration by the teacher, and certain adjustments must be made.

A close working relationship between school and community, between teachers and caregivers, is also crucial. Home and community must be understood by teachers as learning environments and utilized in the classroom. The first step in this process involves gaining knowledge of these environments; the second demands reassessment of the working relationship between school and home—or the lack of such a relationship. The powerful potential of schools working closely with caregivers and the community has yet to be tapped.

ACTIVITIES *with children*

These activities are designed to be used with students in an elementary classroom. They reflect the variety of approaches discussed in this chapter. It is important that you get a chance to work with children in real classroom learning situations so you can determine for yourself what does and does not work. Such experience also gives you an opportunity to reflect on how children learn.

Community Interview

Teach the children about interviewing, and then role-play an interview in class. Have each student select a person in the community whom he or she knows well and interview that person about the job she or he does. Students should try to find out specifically what types of reading and writing skills the job requires.

Community Literacy Hunt

Have each student in your classroom spend a half hour on a main local street examining signs, store windows, advertisements, and the like. Ask students to make a list of the different types of reading materials people encounter daily on this street.

Daily Schedule

Most young people do not know how to schedule their time. Ask each student to keep an account of his or her after-school activities on an hourly basis. Students should do this for one week. Then have them make charts to determine the best time for them to schedule their daily homework.

Survey Your Home

Ask students to survey their homes. What kinds of books, magazines, and newspapers can they find? Have them make a list of their findings and share it with the rest of the class.

Brainstorming

Teach a group of children the rudiments of brainstorming. Select a topic with which they are familiar, such as school or sports or favorite foods. Then brainstorm in a small group, recording the children's ideas. Your list should form the basis for a later writing lesson.

RELATED READINGS

Educational Leadership (1998), 55(8).

This entire issue, titled Engaging Parents and the Community in Schools, has articles on involving caregivers in their child's education. The articles give practical programs that have been tested in a number of schools across the United States.

Emergent literacy: The role of parents and teachers (video). Produced by Magna Systems, Barrington, IL.

This video shows parents and children interacting in a variety of tasks that affect children's level of attainment in reading and writing.

Fox, B., & Wright, M. (1997). Connecting school and home literacy experiences through cross-age reading. *The Reading Teacher*, 50(5), 396–403.

This article describes Storymates, a cross-age reading program that connects school and home literacy experiences for 9- to 11-year-olds through storybook reading to younger children.

Heath, S. B. (1983). *Way with Words*. New York: Cambridge University Press.

This book gives insight on the importance of teachers understanding the influence of community's culture on children's language.

Lazar, A., & Weisberg, R. (1996). Inviting parents' perspective: Building home–school partnerships to support children who struggle with literacy. *The Reading Teacher*, 50(3), 228–237.

This study explains how children's reading improved when the parents were asked to share their knowledge and insight about their children's reading habits.

Payne, R. (2001). *A framework for understanding poverty* (new revised ed.). Highlands, TX: aha! Process, Inc.

This book describes the cycle of poverty and how poverty affects students in schools.

Search Institute. (2003). *Your family: Using simple wisdom in raising your children*. Minneapolis, MN: Search Institute.

This compact booklet gives practical suggestions to caregivers on how to bring good things into the lives of their children.

3

Planning and Delivering Language Arts Instruction

This chapter covers some of the general concepts regarding the nature of learning, the principles of effective teaching, the importance of planning, and the relationship between children's learning styles and various teaching strategies.

CHAPTER OBJECTIVES

After reading this chapter, you should be able to accomplish the following objectives:

1. Name some of the general principles of learning.
2. Explain the concept of extrinsic and intrinsic motivation.
3. Name the general principles of teaching.
4. Describe the different types of plans teachers use.
5. Discuss the four learning domains.
6. Identify who the at-risk students are in a school.
7. Explain the term *kidwatching*.
8. Describe the different teaching styles.
9. Explain the theory of multiple intelligences.
10. List some different types of mini-lessons.

CHECK YOUR BACKGROUND KNOWLEDGE. Before reading the chapter, complete the K-T-W-L chart based on the chapter overview and objectives provided at left. In column "K," write what you know about the topics in the objectives. In column "T," write what you think you know. In column "W," write what you want to learn. Finally, after you have read the chapter, write what you have learned in column "L."

Know	**T**hink you know	**W**ant to learn	**L**earned

Planning for Learning

Teachers bring many different philosophical perspectives to teaching. Some focus on conveying specific skills to their students. Others focus on motivating a broad-based love of knowledge in their students. Many teachers today consider themselves "balanced" or comprehensive in the sense that they teach skills and are concerned about improving their students' test scores but, at the same time, wish to respect their students' interests and provide meaningful learning choices for them. But one thing all teachers have in common is their commitment to planning for instruction. Effective teaching/learning does not happen by accident or because of the individual teacher's charisma; it happens because good teachers plan carefully. Planning involves hours spent creating daily lesson plans for each subject, a weekly plan to guide student activities, unit plans for long-term projects, and so on. Planning also means finding time to grade student papers in a timely manner, prepare meaningful homework assignments, evaluate student journals and portfolios, and reflect on class and individual student needs based on careful observation and record keeping.

GENERAL PRINCIPLES FOR TEACHING AND LEARNING

Teachers approach their job with certain beliefs or principles regarding children, learning, and teaching. Gardner (1993) described different ways of looking at and evaluating intelligence with specific implications for classroom learning. Marzano (1992) described five dimensions of learning that focus on the learner. Gee (2001) analyzed children's fascination with video games and argued for their cultural relevance in terms of the learning principles they exemplified. Cambourne (2002b) argued for the importance of the proper conditions for learning to take place. The following is a brief summary of these principles and their importance for educators:

- *Positive attitudes toward learning are essential:* For both teacher and student alike, having a positive attitude is crucial for success. The classroom should be a safe, friendly, positive environment, but not all children view it that way. Each day a teacher's behavior in the classroom, the way he talks to and looks at his students, influences their attitudes toward him, the classroom, and learning in general. Wong and Wong (1991) found that the emotional tone of a classroom is measured by the quality of the positive human interactions.

- *Learning is constructive and meaningful:* For children to make learning their own, they must construct for themselves the rules that a teacher passes out daily in lectures. That is, understanding comes through personal meaning and identification. The first-grade student in rural North Dakota who is trying to understand her teacher's explanation of a New York City skyscraper must connect it first to something known, a large wheat silo or 36 grocery stores stacked on top of each other. Fourth graders in Mesa, AZ, pay careful attention to the lesson on poisonous snakes as they prepare for a field trip to the desert.

- *Learning is a habit of the mind:* Children are naturally curious and creative. In school, teachers create classroom environments that build on that curiosity and creativity while also demanding discipline and responsibility. Learners need to be engaged, make a commitment to learning, and be willing to take risks. Risk taking and divergent thinking should be encouraged and rewarded if good learning habits are to be developed.

- *The curriculum should be developmentally appropriate:* Just as children grow physically from one year to the next so, too, their cognitive and affective skills develop gradually over time. Teachers need to design activities that are appropriate for their classes and for individual students. Complex activities can be broken down and taught based on their simpler subsets (Gee, 2001). A teacher's effectiveness is not measured by how many chapters in the textbook he covers or how many worksheets he assigns in a day but, rather, by his students' enthusiasm for learning and the individual growth they show over time.

- *High academic standards for all students should be maintained:* Research in learning achievement shows that when teachers set high expectations for their students, both personally and academically, they get better results (Wong & Wong, 1991). Teachers need to let students know what they expect: proper headings on all papers, neatness, punctuality, pride in their work, and so on. Although we all recognize that not all students learn at the same rate, teachers must believe that all students can learn. Some students will simply need more practice and different instructional strategies than others (Gee, 2001).

- *Planning should be cooperative:* Children need to have a say in their own learning, feel that the class is as much theirs as it is the teacher's. Allowing students to help plan out future lessons, design bulletin boards, gather materials for long-term units, have choices in the activities they do all help to instill in students the idea that it is their class too and motivates them to do their best. During free-reading time students should be allowed to choose their own books. Learning centers can be discussed and created through joint planning and cooperation; caregivers can be invited to help also.

- *Alternative assessments should be implemented:* Most schools today are driven by the need to raise their students' standardized test scores (Appleman & Thompson, 2002). Most classrooms are dominated by tests: end-of-the-week tests, spelling retests, grammar quizzes, unit tests, basal reader chapter tests, and so on. There are alternative means of evaluating children's learning: teacher observations and anecdotal record keeping, oral reports and panel discussions, written portfolios, informal reading inventories, unit projects, checklists, and rubrics. These and others will be discussed further in later chapters.

- *Multimodal learning enhances the learning experience:* Gee (2001), Gardner (1993), Baker, (2000), and others have argued that meaningful learning takes place in various modalities. Students need to not only read books but to explore the World Wide Web on the Internet. They should not only write stories by hand, but they should compose on computers and create PowerPoint presentations to share with others. After viewing a video on insects, students may wish to use the school's video recorder and digital camera to make their own videos and computer images. Art and music should become integral parts of the math, science, and social studies classrooms and, of course, the literacy classroom.

- *Learning about multiculturalism and diversity widens the students' view of the world:* In the twenty-first century, recognizing the fact that we live in a multicultural world and valuing the diversity that fact implies is not something teachers can leave to chance. In class, children should read books about people of different economic groups, races, religions, cultures, and viewpoints. They should do projects on cultures and countries other than their own. Teachers should show videos and films of faraway lands where people look and live differently than we do. In this sense, teaching is a global act that expands the students' world.

- *Motivation drives learning and achievement:* All students want to learn, to succeed, to experience the intrinsic rewards of skill/knowledge mastery that derives from effort (Gee, 2001). However, some children may need guidance to discover what they want or need to learn and what the school has to offer. Teachers use extrinsic rewards (grades, praise, and so forth) to initiate motivation, but, ultimately, the reward in learning should be success in learning. Paralleling the child's achievement in school is growth in self-concept, self-esteem, self-worth, and perceived competence as a learner and person.

AT-RISK STUDENTS: YOUR RESPONSIBILITY

Today's schools are different from the schools your parents attended and probably different from the schools you attended. The primary reason is demographic: The population of the United States continues to grow at an incredible rate. There are now more than 53 million children enrolled in our public schools. More than one-fourth of them live in poverty. More than one-third have limited English proficiency (LEP). About 35 percent represent racial and ethnic minorities. Projections are that by the year 2010, 20 percent of our school-age population will be Hispanic, 17 percent African American, 5 percent Asian American, and 2 percent Native American (Futrell, Gomez, & Bedden, 2003).

Even now, many African American and Hispanic children attend schools that have more than 90 percent minority enrollment. Often such schools are understaffed; are in need of structural repairs; and lack basic textbooks, computers, and other materials. In his book *Savage Inequalities*, Jonathan Kozol (1991) paints a disturbing picture of what life is like in many minority inner-city schools. Our diversity does, however, represent a great mixture of races, cultures, social classes, and languages, which present today's teachers with both enormous potential and great challenges.

In the past the subject of school failure among children of the poor, LEP children, and minority children has been given only peripheral attention in teacher education programs. Today our multicultural, diverse society demands that all teachers be prepared to teach children from different cultures, who speak different languages and may have different understandings of school expectations (Villegas & Lucas, 2002).

In and beyond the classroom

Observe one at-risk child over a period of three weeks. Describe in as much detail as possible the child's actual behaviors in class. What characteristics do you notice? What evidence of the self-fulfilling prophecy can you identify in the classroom or school?

Who are the **at-risk children?** Although they have been given many labels for many reasons, the term *at risk* is used because these are the children who face the greatest risk of dropping out of school without the necessary skills, knowledge, and attitudes to function successfully in society. In school they make up a disproportionately high percentage of the students in special education classes and remedial reading programs. Often they are the children of the poor, of recent immigrants who speak little English, or of minorities who have been discriminated against. They already may have been held back one year in school, are reading and writing two or more years below grade level, have poor attendance records, and are labeled as discipline problems.

Despite the many strikes against these at-risk children, they can be taught and they can learn. And the individual teacher is the key. Years ago, research confirmed the notion of the **self-fulfilling prophecy** (Rosenthal & Jacobson, 1968). What teachers expect from children they often get. If teachers expect children to fail in school, then they are likely to fail. However, if teachers treat at-risk children with respect, dignity, and the expectation that they will succeed, then success is possible. It is the teacher's attitude toward children that makes the difference.

Language arts teachers in particular have an added responsibility in working with at-risk children because typically it is the language arts skills, or lack thereof, that doom such children to failure. The ability to speak clearly and effectively, the ability to read and write will determine the success of these children not only in language arts class but also in math, science, social studies, music, and art classes. Researchers have documented the things that at-risk children need to be successful:

- smaller class size
- direct explicit instruction when needed

- a supportive, positive classroom environment
- additional time to complete tasks
- one-to-one help from the teacher throughout the day following group lessons (Slavin, 2002)

PRINCIPLES FOR EFFECTIVE INSTRUCTION

Whatever your philosophy of education or preferred approach to teaching the language arts, all teachers plan and prepare carefully for effective instruction. Here are some general principles to keep in mind.

Get to Know Your Students

Effective teachers begin with children in mind: their experiences, their abilities, their interests, their needs. With children as the focus of your planning, you must first spend time getting to know your students. Four ways to do so are show-and-tell activities, autobiographies, interest inventories, and kidwatching.

Show-and-tell is one of the oldest and most popular activities in the primary grades. It is also used successfully with older students, who call it "sharing." In either case, show-and-tell consists of a student bringing some object from home and preparing a brief talk about it to present to the whole class or to a small group. The teacher questions the child about the object and thereby perhaps learns more pertinent information about the student's home, parents, siblings, and interests. All of this information eventually helps the astute language arts teacher prepare more personalized and motivating lessons.

A second means of acquiring information about your students is by having them write their own life stories, or **autobiographies.** To get the students started on this, write your own autobiography and share it with them. This helps them to better understand what an autobiography consists of, while giving you a chance to demonstrate your openness and thereby to start creating links between yourself and the children. Once your students get the idea, they will be excited about telling their stories. Even young children can write autobiographies. Often they rely on pictures as much as words. Combining pictures and words is a good creative activity even for older students. Other types of autobiographies include photographic exhibits, collages, and three-dimensional displays. Show or model a few of these options and then let your students choose.

A third popular way to get to know your students is through the use of **interest inventories.** These are written forms completed by the students. They are teacher-made and generally utilize a fill-in-the-blank format, a checklist, or a combination of the two. They can be administered early in the school year, even on the first day, to give you some idea of the children's interests regarding home, school, particular subjects, sports, television, books, travel, and so on. Appendix C contains an example of one type of inventory suitable for use with upper elementary and intermediate students.

The term **kidwatching** was coined by Yetta Goodman in 1978. Since that time, it has been widely discussed and associated with the whole language approach to the language arts. Goodman, like so many other educators, argued against the proliferation of standardized testing and the dominance of commercial textbooks and learning kits in education. She contended that a professionally trained teacher possesses skills of observation that, when applied properly, are an alternative form of evaluating teacher instruction and pupil learning. It is through time spent watching children in learning situations that teachers can best evaluate the successes and failures of previously taught lessons and can plan appropriately for upcoming lessons. Without such *kidwatching* time, teachers either operate in the dark or blindly follow the dictates of the basal reader manual or some other prepackaged curriculum material.

All teachers spend some time during class simply watching their students work. These periods of casual observation subtly confirm or refute the standardized test results of individual children, influence teacher planning of future lessons, and serve as a major source of information for conferences with caregivers. Observing students is respected as a valuable part of what teachers do to learn about the individual needs of all their students.

For example, at The Awakening Seed, an alternative elementary school in Tempe, AZ, teachers spend a good deal of time watching kids. Observation is part of their professional duties. They know that what they observe influences their beliefs about learning and their practices as teachers. These teachers are learning from watching their students. By reflecting on what they have observed, these teachers can adapt their teaching to the needs of their children (Mersereau, Glover, & Cherland, 1989).

If you are to become an effective teacher, you will have to spend some time each day in class really looking at and listening to children. Some of your kid-watching time will be brief and informal and utilize mental note taking. At other times, however, you may wish to sit at length with notebook by your side, carefully observing a single child or group of children.

Plan for In-Class Reading Time

Teachers need to have large blocks of reading time during the day—not time for teaching reading skills but time for children to read in school. In *Becoming a Nation of Readers*, Anderson, Hiebert, Scott, and Wilkerson (1985) found that in the primary grades the average daily amount of time that children actually spent reading was only 7 minutes. Instead, most reading classes consisted of the teacher talking about reading and the children filling in worksheets.

Mrs. Bowker, a second-grade teacher who has been teaching for a number of years, tries to have as much free reading as possible. Her classroom is a **print-rich environment.** There are books, hardback and paperback, everywhere: on bookshelves, lining the windowsills, in children's cubbyholes. There are also magazines, newspapers, maps, brochures, and posters. The room is saturated with reading materials of all kinds. Real reading is in evidence throughout the daily routine.

The day's activities begin with quiet time for journal writing; each child writes in his or her personal journal and then reads it silently. For the next 15 minutes, the teacher reads aloud to the class from a lengthy book, one that not all of the children might tackle on their own: *From the Mixed-Up Files of Mrs. Basil E. Frankweiler* by E. L. Konigsburg. When she finishes reading, the children all take out their own books and begin reading; their reading period lasts for 1 hour, a technique called **sustained silent reading (SSR).**

Despite the variety of activities going on, the room seems quiet and calm. The teacher is seated at a table surrounded by a group of children. These are her slowest readers. Each child has selected her or his own book from a list of books by Bernard Waber: *An Anteater Named Arthur; Ira Sleeps Over; Lyle Finds His Mother; Lyle, Lyle, Crocodile;* and *A Firefly Named Torchy.* The class theme for this month, Author Study, involves reading a number of books by the same author. One child at a time reads aloud as Mrs. Bowker listens. Undisturbed, the other children in the group continue their silent reading in their own books until they are called on to read aloud.

Some of the other children in the class are stretched out on a rug reading. Four little girls are seated around a small table; occasionally they whisper to each other about parts of their books. They are all reading different books by Beverly Cleary, the second author selected by the class for intensive study. The list of books by this author includes *Beezus and Ramona, Ellen Tibbits, Henry and the Clubhouse, Henry and Ribsy, Dear Mr. Henshaw, Henry and Beezus, Henry and the Paper Route,* and *Henry Huggins.*

The reading group around the teacher breaks up. One boy goes to the tape recorder and puts on a headset. Then he opens his book and reads silently as he listens to the tape. Another boy takes out drawing paper and begins to copy an illustration from his book. Other members of the group return to their desks or favorite corners of the room to continue their reading, this time silently. While the Waber group is dispersing, the Cleary group gathers around one child who has brought a special pen/pencil case from home. These students put their reading books aside to talk about it. The teacher notices this but does not say anything. A few moments later they break up, giggling, and go back to their reading.

Over in the corner, two girls are sitting by themselves softly reading aloud to each other. They have both selected Beverly Cleary's *Ramona the Pest.* They hold hands as they enjoy the book together.

The teacher now calls one little girl to her desk. They begin conferencing about the book she is reading: *Little House on the Prairie* by Laura Ingalls Wilder, the third author chosen as part of the theme. Wilder's books also include *Little House in the Big Woods, Little Town on the Prairie,* and *On the Banks of Plum Creek.* This literature conference lasts about 10 minutes. The child is obviously enthused by the book as she explains a favorite passage. The teacher, too, listens with interest; she asks the child questions, trying to draw out still more information about the book.

Still other students go to the class library to use the large dictionary or work on activities in their reading folders. There is a pleasant hum in the room, but it is not so loud as to interfere with the conference or small-group activities.

Later in the same day, after lunch, the class engages in SSR for 20 minutes: Some of the children continue reading their books from the morning during this free-reading time; others select different free-reading books; still others thumb through favorite magazines. By the end of the day, the children in this class have read or listened to someone else read for a total of 95 minutes!

Plan for In-Class Writing Time

Effective teachers also plan for large blocks of time devoted specifically to writing. Additional writing activities are incorporated into mathematics, social studies, and science lessons.

Recall that in Mrs. Bowker's class the very first activity in the morning is journal writing. Every child keeps a journal in a spiral-bound notebook. Journal writing is a time for putting thoughts down quickly. Some children want to share their journals with the teacher immediately; others do not. Later in the day, the children may refer to their journals as a source of creative writing ideas. Journal writing is discussed later in this text.

In addition to journals, all of the children in Mrs. Bowker's class keep writing folders in which they place their creative writings. They work on writing for one hour a day, following the hour of reading: Some of the children are writing short stories; others continue longer works begun the previous week; a few are involved in collaborative group creations. Again, the teacher spends part of this time conferencing with individual students about the progress of their writing.

Although in theory this teacher spends one hour on reading and another on writing, in actual practice reading, writing, and talking about literature flow naturally back and forth throughout the two-hour period. Research indicates that reading, writing, and literature are all part of literacy and cannot be separated by artificial time periods or separate subject designations (Fisher & Frey, 2003; Routman, 1996).

Include Visual Literacy and Technology

Literacy, defined as the ability to read and write, has been expanded in recent years to include the term **visual literacy.** The latter term includes the ability to interpret and create visual forms of media including art, video, animated graphics, PowerPoint displays, and Web pages. According to the National Council of Teachers of English statement of support, "To participate in a global society, we continue to extend our ways of communicating. Viewing and visually representing are part of our growing consciousness of how people gather and share information. Teachers and students need to expand their appreciation of the power of print and non-print texts. Teachers should guide students in constructing meaning through creating and viewing non-print texts" (Bianchini, 2003, p. 1).

Today the presence of computers in schools and in many individual classrooms, plus the existence of separate library–media–technology centers make the concept of visual literacy along with the use of technology a reality. Students can do research in every imaginable subject by using the World Wide Web. There are even specially designed search engines for children, such as Yahooligans (www.yahooligans.com) and Ask Jeeves for Kids (www.ajkids.com). Leu (2001, 2002) recommends using specific research assignments to teach children how to conduct an Internet workshop. The steps, which involve all forms of literacy, include the following:

1. Ask students to select a topic or create research questions they wish to investigate.
2. Have students use a search engine to begin their research.
3. Have students branch to other Internet sites for more research, take notes, and create an outline of their report.
4. Have students write the report and present it orally to the class using a PowerPoint presentation.

Additional projects could include the following: viewing and interpreting art via the Internet or actually visiting a museum; interpreting videos and film in specific content areas and comparing information learned with more traditional textbooks; having students create specific school documentaries (i.e., a day in the life of the secretary) using still cameras, digital cameras, and videocam recorders. In the latter, as with print media, students need to be taught to organize their materials, revise, and edit before producing a final product to share with others.

Create an Environment Conducive to Language Development

Earlier we discussed the importance of creating a positive, supportive learning environment. In the language arts, this means creating and sustaining an atmosphere conducive to language use and development. Children need to be encouraged to use language in both oral and written form.

Effective teachers place oral language use at the heart of all lessons. During reading and writing activities, children converse with the teacher, ask for help from friends, and share their work in small groups. There is usually a low hum in the room, but it is not so loud as to be distracting to other students engaged in silent work.

Children must be taught to converse in low tones while working in small groups. In fact, training children to work cooperatively, to modify their voice levels, and to monitor their own movement around the classroom is a crucial part of the teacher's job. Language arts teachers need to take time at the beginning of the school year to teach children the behaviors necessary to work independently, to cooperate in small groups, to make choices, and to ask for help from other students when the teacher is busy.

The real voyage of discovery consists not in seeking new landscapes, but in having new eyes.

MARCEL PROUST

When students are permitted and encouraged to converse naturally as a part of the learning process, their talk is not aimless but meaning focused. That is, children talk about the meaningful activities they are engaged in. For example, one study found that before and during writing activities children talk to one another in order to clarify their ideas and test new techniques (Wells, 1986). Another study found that children use oral conferencing with both teachers and peers to further clarify their own thought processes before writing (Graves, 1994). Finally, Savage (1998) found that children use language to reflect on the significance of literature read in class for their personal lives. Relating events in one's own life to stories read in class sometimes results in overly exuberant students and a too-noisy classroom. However, the increased appreciation for literature and the enthusiasm for reading are well worth it.

Educators have long known that language develops and improves only through regular use in a variety of settings and for a variety of purposes. The more children use oral language and interact with print, the more confident they become of their language abilities. It is thus a major responsibility of the language arts teacher to plan for and provide a literate environment in which students flourish as language users and learners.

Facilitate Independent Working and Learning

Finally, it is important to develop in children the skills necessary to work independently. If children are to grow as readers, writers, and oral language users, they must develop a sense of competence in their own communication abilities. This can only happen when teachers trust children as learners (Comber, 1987). This is another benefit of kidwatching because it forces the teacher to stand back and observe from a distance. When teachers do this, they observe some children getting started on their own almost immediately, others requiring teacher assistance, and still others going to their friends for help or feedback about work they have completed. Teachers also witness how children reflect over a choice of activities, ponder which book to read for free reading, or chew on a pencil while trying to resolve a writing problem. These things only happen when teachers provide time and choices for students. In this manner, competence ultimately develops from independence.

Facilitating the development of this sense of competence in independent work again necessitates careful teacher planning. Reutzel and Hollingsworth (1988) have suggested three ways in which teachers can lead children to learn both independent work habits and decision-making skills: learning centers, units of study, and in-class projects. All three of these topics are discussed in greater detail later in this text, so for now it will suffice to briefly define and describe them.

A **learning center** is a place in a classroom containing the materials and directions for completing a series of related activities, usually in a brief period of time. Generally the center provides children with a choice of activities and a means of self-checking before moving on to the next activity. Small groups may work at the center together, or students may perform their tasks independently of one another.

A **unit** is a series of related activities focused on a single topic or theme; it is usually completed over a longer period of time, perhaps a few days or weeks. Although a unit may center on a specific content area, such as dinosaurs, it always includes listening, speaking, reading, writing, and art activities. Children are required to share their expertise, work cooperatively on a joint venture, and work independently of others.

A **project** is a physical creation related to a curriculum area. It can result from a lengthy unit or stand alone. Small projects (such as book reports) can be completed individually, but most larger projects require a small group of students, working cooperatively, to create something (e.g., a class newspaper or puppet show). Projects contain separate parts, which require a division of labor. Children can contribute to the project in the area in which they are most skilled or have a particular interest. In a newspaper project, for example, one student might focus on illustrations, a second child might interview classmates, and a third could be responsible for editing the written work.

Types of Plans Teachers Use

Effective teachers of the language arts rely on a variety of plans. Careful and consistent planning is also one of the marks of the reflective teacher. Keep this in mind as you read about the following types of plans: yearly or semester, unit, weekly, daily, and mini-lessons.

THE YEARLY OR SEMESTER PLAN

The new school year is only a few weeks away. You have many things on your mind: What will the children be like? Who are their caregivers? How should you arrange the classroom? What materials do you need to order from the school? These and many other questions are swirling around in your mind as the excitement builds. But this is also the time to give some thought to your long-range goals for the coming year or semester. Take some time to reflect on what you expect from your students and yourself over the course of the year. Now make one list of all the questions you have and another of your general goals and expectations. This is how you further the process of reflection and make it something concrete.

Using your lists, you can begin to sketch out a long-range plan. Keep in mind that you are creating a broad outline, a general plan of goals to be achieved later with the help of more specific unit, weekly, and daily plans. There are a number of ways to approach long-range planning. Such plans usually do not contain many specific details; often there are spaces left to be filled in as the year progresses. Figure 3.1 is one teacher's yearly plan.

In this particular plan, the teacher begins by thinking about the children and their caregivers. She knows she will be having individual conferences with them, but what else can she do to establish the kind of relationship and atmosphere she wants? She also realizes that she will need to create group and individual projects if the students are to learn cooperation and independence. She thinks of possible field trips and in-class activities that could further help the class come together as a group. She sees that such activities allow some of the caregivers to involve themselves with the class as well.

One of the first things this teacher should do is get caregivers' addresses and phone numbers and make early contact with the families of the students she is teaching. She may inquire about their home and work schedules and learn about their particular interests in helping in the class. Since it is just the beginning of the school year, her plans in this area remain open and heavily dependent on the children and caregivers themselves.

In her plan, this teacher has resisted the temptation to list a scope and sequence of skills, giving instead just major headings. School-provided textbooks and curriculum guides are just that—guides. They cannot be allowed to totally dictate what and how a teacher teaches. Planning, instead, should also be

Beyond the classroom

Visit one school and examine its calendar. Discuss it with the secretary, the principal, and a classroom teacher. What valuable information does it provide? List some ways the calendar might influence your planning for the coming school year.

MY GOALS	ACTIONS I TOOK TO ACHIEVE GOALS	HOW SUCCESSFUL WAS I?
Children		
Establish rapport		
Establish trust		
Establish cooperation		
Establish independence		
Encourage creativity		
Caregivers		
Make contacts	Letters sent home	
Recruit aides	Phone calls made	
Encourage support with homework		
Subjects		
Listening	Tape recordings	
Speaking		
Reading	SSR	
Writing		
Math		
Science		
Social Studies		
Resources		
Other classroom teachers		
Reading/speech specialists		
Librarian	Once-a-week visits	
Principal		
Audiovisual equipment		
Community		

FIGURE 3.1

Sample yearly plan.

guided by diagnostic testing, student classroom inventories, the children's writing folders, and hours of careful student observation.

The final section of this sample plan, Resources, is crucial to effective teaching yet often ignored in teachers' plans. There are many resources that teachers utilize. For example, at the beginning of the school year, the teacher may inventory the available audiovisual equipment in the school in order to plan future units and projects. These are material resources. People are also resources: teachers, administrators, staff, and members of the community who can contribute a wealth of information, abilities, ideas, and support.

Another way of viewing a yearly or semester plan is in terms of the school calendar. Most schools publish a calendar that lists special events on a month-by-month basis. The school secretary can provide you with the dates of field trips, special auditorium programs, holidays, early dismissal, open house, standardized testing, and so on. Noting important school dates on your own calendar in September can assist you in your planning throughout the school year.

THE UNIT PLAN

According to Jerome Bruner (1961a, 1983), knowledge is structured and ordered into large concepts or patterns. A unit is one way of concretely structuring new knowledge and skills for children. Although the teacher should begin the year with some general themes in mind, units often arise naturally from the needs and interests of students. For example, students in one second-grade classroom became enthralled with dinosaurs because of a few books they had read. This led the teacher and her pupils to search the library and Internet for more information about dinosaurs and to plan some art activities and an original dramatization around the single theme of dinosaurs. Another class decided to design a series of activities around a study of weather following a visit by a local meteorologist. In both cases, the teacher and pupils jointly planned the unit and the related activities. And in the course of each unit, there was ample opportunity to integrate other subject areas—such as social studies, science, art, and music—with the language arts.

Creating units through integrated planning is not easy. One common mistake that teachers make is assuming that units automatically correspond to chapters in a textbook that can be used in their entirety. Another mistake is believing that all theme units should be given equal time and emphasis; this happens because typically textbook chapters are of approximately the same length, implying that equal amounts of time should be devoted to each.

How, then, should a unit be created? To begin, the teacher must recognize that units do not exist in books; they must be created. This means starting with textbooks but also using additional reading and reference materials related to the unit topic. Materials that may not be present in the school building should be collected. Finally, the teacher must assess the skill needs and abilities of the students in determining the kinds of listening, speaking, reading, and writing activities to organize. Clearly unit planning requires a teacher to make many decisions. Here are 10 questions to keep in mind to help you venture into unit planning:

1. What is the major concept I wish to develop?
2. What are the related subsidiary concepts?
3. What background information and experiences should I provide for my students?
4. Where can the students go to find additional information?
5. Are there sufficient resources within the classroom and school, or must I provide supplementary materials?
6. What resources are available in the community?
7. What specific activities will the children engage in? Individual? Small group?
8. How will I integrate listening, speaking, reading, viewing, visual representing, and writing into this unit?
9. How will I evaluate the unit? A test? A class project? Group or individual reports? Portfolios? PowerPoint presentations? WebQuest?
10. How much time does this unit warrant?

For example, one teacher initiated a unit on poetry suitable for fifth or sixth grade intended to last two to three weeks. The teacher's literature book contained a few good poems, and the grammar textbook suggested some poetry-writing assignments. A few students brought in favorite poems from previous classes; other students suggested activities involving poetry. The unit began to take shape. Figure 3.2 shows the teacher's initial outline for the poetry unit; more detailed planning was reserved for the weekly and daily lesson plans.

RESOURCES	ACTIVITIES	EVALUATION
Class library	Reading aloud	Individual poetry
School library	Choral speaking	Group reports
Home resources	Illustrating poems	PowerPoint presentations
Public library	Writing original poems	
Recordings of poems	Researching the lives of poets	
Internet	Doing searches of websites	
	Dance, plays	

FIGURE 3.2

Sample unit outline: poetry.

A unit plan can also be conceptualized with a schematic diagram. A **schematic diagram** is a visual means of organizing vocabulary terms related to a unit. It also helps students to better conceptualize the overall content of the unit. Although originally designed to support vocabulary development within content-area reading lessons (Early & Barron, 1969), the schematic diagram can be used to introduce key terms and concepts in any unit. To construct a schematic diagram, a teacher must first decide on the major concepts to be taught in a unit and identify the important related terms. This material is presented to the class in the form of a diagram on an overhead transparency or ditto handout. Figure 3.3, for example, compares poetry with prose.

Another type of unit can be created around a single book. Study the Classroom Vignette and Figure 3.4 that follow describing how one fifth-grade teacher responded to the needs and interests of her class and created an integrated unit.

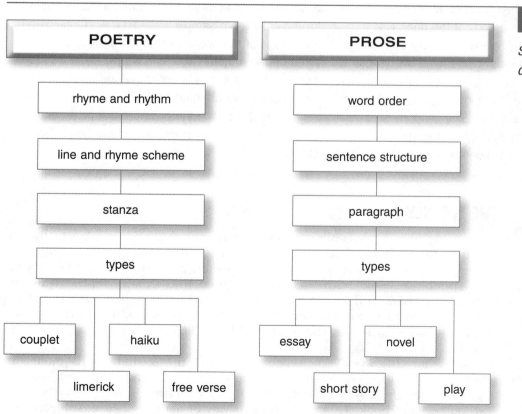

FIGURE 3.3

Sample schematic diagram: poetry unit.

VIGNETTE *in the classroom*

One day an impromptu discussion about fear begins among a group of fifth-grade children.

"I know someone who won't walk in the woods because he's afraid of snakes," Bobby says.

"Heck, I once saw a water moccasin jump into a boat," Paul says.

"I'd be scared of snakes too if it had been my boat," Ralph says.

"Yeah, but you wouldn't be afraid of going out in a boat again, would you?" Bobby asks.

"Snakes aren't that scary, but I know someone who's afraid of crowds and small rooms. He won't even ride in an elevator," Margie says.

The talk continues like this, with students sharing about other fears they or people they know have: fear of heights, fear of spiders, fear of the dark.

"What about comic book heroes like Superman and Batman?" Lindsay asks. "They are so powerful they probably aren't afraid of anything."

"How would you like to read a book about a boy who had a fear of the water and discovered his own source of courage?" their teacher, Ms. Whitecloud, asks. She shows them a copy of the book *Call It Courage* by Armstrong Sperry, the story of a young boy in Polynesia who must prove his bravery against many odds and overcome his fear of the sea.

Once the actual unit begins, it grows; it stretches from two weeks into a month. The children read the novel in and out of class. They also spend hours making toothpick constructions of traps and huts and balsa wood carvings of canoes as well as doing library research reports. From paper and other art supplies, they make replicas of South Sea islands, huts, and canoes. An entire scene of Polynesia is painted on butcher-block paper and then placed on the classroom walls as a background mural. As the unit comes to an end, the student committees share their reports and posters.

Finally, all of the constructions are combined to make one gigantic scene that the students share with the primary grades. As the younger children are escorted into the room, they marvel at the mural and replicas. Then the fifth-graders begin a dramatic retelling of the entire story. As they speak, they point to the places where specific events have occurred. The primary-grade children are spellbound by the story and also by the three-dimensional illustrations.

Afterward some of the caregivers wish to see this extravaganza for themselves; they agree to help put on a little Polynesian celebration for the children. Fruit punch, bananas, breadfruit pudding, mangoes, coconut milk, and other exotic foods are brought in for the children to sample while Hawaiian music and recordings of the ocean play in the background. What began a month ago as a simple class discussion has become a gala event that the children will remember for years to come.

Figure 3.4 shows the outline this teacher and her students created for the unit on the book *Call It Courage.*

THE WEEKLY PLAN

The weekly plan is probably the most commonly used type of plan in the elementary grades. It is also the one you are most likely familiar with from your school days. Generally it is contained in a plan book that looks like an ordinary spiral notebook, with each page divided into squares representing the days of the week and the subject periods within each day. Traditionally a teacher lists in each box the period, the subject, the subskill, and the chapter or page number in the textbook or workbook. Figure 3.5 shows one teacher's plan book.

Note that this weekly plan book illustrates the separate skills model, in which time periods correspond to separate subjects, and these subjects are approached as skills to be taught, usually in conjunction with chapters in a textbook or workbook. This is an efficient way of managing time, subjects, and

FIGURE 3.4

Sample unit outline: Call It Courage.

CONCEPTS TAUGHT

1. Legends
2. Fiction vs. nonfiction
3. Characteristics of the novel
4. How fears develop
5. The nature of courage
6. Survival skills

BACKGROUND INFORMATION

1. Other legends read aloud
2. Map study of Pacific and Polynesia
3. History of Polynesia

MATERIALS

1. 30 copies of the book
2. Other library books by Armstrong Sperry
3. Maps and books on Polynesia
4. Glue
5. Toothpicks
6. Balsa wood
7. Construction paper

ACTIVITIES

1. In-class reading
2. Home reading
3. Chapter discussion
4. Projects:
    A. Individual paper-and-toothpick construction
    B. Small-group boat and village making
    C. Whole-class wall mural
5. Group reports on food, clothing, shelter of Polynesia
6. Dramatization and celebration

materials, but it is also unnaturally fragmented and ignores opportunities for unit integration. Contrast this weekly plan with the one shown in Figure 3.6, which was taken from the plan book of a second-grade teacher from Gainesville, FL, who was moving toward a more comprehensive approach.

This is an interesting weekly plan from a number of perspectives. This school relies heavily on the textbooks and curriculum guides of a major publishing company. Every language arts teacher is required to provide the skill lessons contained in the guides—primarily phonics lessons. The teachers are also required to give the end-of-term tests contained in the basal reader series, and to prepare students for the FCAT and Florida Writes assessments administered in third grade. (Florida is not alone among states in using multiple standardized tests.) The pressures on this second-grade teacher are therefore enormous.

In her classroom, the day begins with dialogue journals: children's personal writings, to which the teacher responds. This is followed by the Morning Challenge, a few short quiz questions over skill areas she knows the students will be tested on. For instance, she includes a decoding question on the long vowel sound of /a/, a coin-recognition math problem, and a clock-reading problem.

FIGURE 3.5

Sample traditional weekly plan.

	1	2	3	4	5	6	7
	Reading Ginn Ch. 3	Spelling Pretest	Grammar Nouns & pronouns (Ch. 6)	Lunch Recess	Math Fractions (Ch. 5)	Soc. Studies The First Colonies (Ch. 4)	Science The Cell (Ch. 10)
Monday	bring pictures	correct in class				bring maps	borrow charts
Tuesday							
Wednesday							
Thursday							
Friday							

These skills are not taught as whole-class, full-period skill lessons; instead they are group checked at the end of the day. The teacher then decides which students need more practice in a particular area for the next day or week. Three times during the day, she devotes time to reading aloud to the class: once from a short picture book, then from a resource book related to the weekly or monthly theme, and finally from a longer chapter book. Thus, the bulk of the morning is spent on independent work related to an integrated theme, in this case an environmental science/social studies exchange project with a second-grade class in Salem, OR. Every day includes free reading, writing folders, and math work.

THE DAILY LESSON PLAN

Although the weekly plan may look thorough, it is more of a guide or outline. The details underlying each subject lesson are omitted. Unless you have taught the same subject and grade for many years, it is difficult to teach directly from such a plan. Determining the structure, sequence, and materials you need for each subject lesson requires a daily lesson plan. A daily lesson plan is a detailed, written explanation of what a teacher will do and what students are expected to learn during a single subject period. As you plan your lessons, keep in mind your state standards. The plans shown in Figures 3.7 and 3.8 describe and give an example of a skill lesson for a 45-minute period.

FIGURE 3.6

Sample integrated plan.

Monday
- 7:50–8:05 — Dialogue Journal / Morning Challenge / Independent Work
- 8:10–8:40 — Music
- 8:45–9:20 — Read Aloud: Book _____ Poem _____ Song _____ Poetry Person _____
- 9:25–10:30 — Theme Study Ch. 1—Ki, Byron ESL—Gabriel
- 10:30–11:00 — Independent Reading
- 11:00–11:30 — Process—Writing Block
- 11:30–12:00 — Math: Ch. 2 Enrichment
- 12:00–12:30 — Lunch
- 12:30–1:00 — Media
- 1:00–1:15 — Free Play
- 1:15–1:30 — Read Aloud Chapter Book
- 1:30–2:00 — Check Morning Challenge / Take-Home Folders Ready

Tuesday
- 7:50–8:05 — Dialogue Journal / Morning Challenge / Independent Work
- 8:10–8:40 — P. E.
- 8:45–9:20 — Read Aloud: Book _____ Poem _____ Song _____ Poetry Person _____
- 9:25–10:30 — Theme Study Ch. 1—Ki, Byron ESL—Gabriel
- 10:30–11:00 — Independent Reading
- 11:00–11:30 — Process—Writing Block—Gifted
- 11:30–12:00 — Math
- 12:00–12:30 — Lunch
- 12:30–12:45 — Free Play
- 12:45–1:00 — Read Aloud Chapter Book
- 1:00–1:30 — Check Morning Challenge
- 1:30–2:00 — Sharing _____ Old Story _____ Old Poem _____ Old Song _____

Wednesday
- 7:50–8:20 — Dialogue Journal / Morning Challenge / Independent Work
- 8:25–9:10 — Art
- 9:10–9:30 — Read Aloud: Ch. 1—Krystal Book _____ Poem _____ Song _____ Poetry Person _____
- 9:30–10:30 — Theme Study Ch. 1—Ki, Byron ESL—Gabriel
- 10:30–11:00 — Independent Reading
- 11:00–11:30 — Process—Writing Block
- 11:30–12:00 — Math Enrichment
- 12:00–12:30 — Lunch
- 12:30–12:40 — Free Play
- 12:45 — Early Dismissal

Thursday
- 7:50–8:05 — Dialogue Journal / Morning Challenge / Independent Work
- 8:10–8:40 — Music
- 8:45–9:10 — Read Aloud: Book _____ Poem _____ Song _____ Poetry Person _____
- 9:10–9:25 — Ch. 1—Krystal Finish: Dialogue Journals Morning Challenge Independent Work
- 9:25–10:30 — Theme Study Ch. 1—Ki, Byron ESL—Gabriel
- 10:30–11:00 — Independent Reading—Gifted
- 11:00–11:30 — Process—Writing Block
- 11:30–12:00 — Math
- 12:00–12:30 — Lunch
- 12:30–1:00 — Computer Lab
- 1:00–1:15 — Free Play
- 1:15–1:30 — Read Aloud Chapter Book
- 1:30–2:00 — Check Morning Challenge Sharing

Friday
- 7:50–8:05 — Dialogue Journal / Morning Challenge / Independent Work
- 8:10–8:40 — P. E.
- 8:45–9:20 — Read Aloud: Ch. 1—Krystal Book _____ Poem _____ Song _____ Poetry Person _____
- 9:25–9:40 — Finish: Dialogue Journals Morning Challenge Independent Work Theme Study Ch. 1—Ki, Byron ESL—Gabriel
- 9:40–10:30 — Theme Study
- 10:30–11:00 — Independent Reading
- 11:00–11:30 — Process—Writing Block
- 11:30–12:00 — Math Enrichment
- 12:00–12:30 — Lunch
- 12:40–1:00 — Process—Writing Block
- 1:00–1:15 — Free Play
- 1:15–1:30 — Read Aloud Chapter Book
- 1:30–2:00 — Check Morning Challenge

THE MINI-LESSON

The daily lesson plan is an example of a traditional lesson plan. However, it has a serious drawback: It can take too much time to complete all the activities outlined, and consequently students do not have enough time to practice on their own. This is especially true for students who are anxious to get started on their work while other students hold up the class asking questions. For this reason, many teachers are shifting to the mini-lesson (5–10 minutes) as an alternative approach to daily lesson planning.

The mini-lesson was originally described by Lucy Calkins (1994, 2001). Calkins was looking for an alternative to the "maxi-lesson" (45-minute skill period) that would allow more time for students to actually write during class yet still provide them with the skills knowledge they need. Nancie Atwell (1998), another well-known process-writing advocate, also uses the mini-lesson each day to get the

FIGURE **3.7**

Components of a full-form daily lesson plan.

1. **Curriculum Area**
   The curriculum area is a brief identification or title for the subject area being taught and the specific subskill within the subject. The teacher must therefore decide which concept within each subject area to teach that day. Your specific state's standards can be listed here, also.

2. **Aim or Goal**
   The aim or goal is the introduction to any lesson. It may be written on the chalkboard in explicit terms. A question related to the aim should be placed on the board, as in the guided discovery approach.

3. **Motivation**
   Motivation is whatever the teacher does to stimulate student interest in the topic before beginning formal instruction. This might mean asking a provocative question, beginning a discussion, showing a film, reading a passage from a book, or playing a tape recording. Regardless of the nature of the motivational technique employed, it must be clearly understood that motivation comes before, and is separate from but related to, the actual teaching steps.

4. **Materials Needed**
   Each separate lesson requires the teacher to identify the materials needed for that lesson and to acquire them beforehand.

5. **Teaching Procedures/Steps**
   In this section of the plan are listed the actual things involved in teaching the lesson. This includes giving oral directions, writing examples on the chalkboard, questioning students, and distributing handouts.

6. **Practice Activity**
   The teaching steps should not take the entire class period. If they do, then the teacher has dominated the lesson. Some time must be allowed for student practice to ensure learning.

7. **Follow-Up Activity**
   First, the follow-up or conclusion of the lesson should adequately summarize the teaching and learning that took place during the period. The teacher might provide the summary or call on a child to do so. Second, follow-up includes assigning a related activity, generally done at home, to reinforce classroom learning.

Source: D. Yellin (1985), *Integrating the Elementary Language Arts.*

writer's workshop started with her middle school students. When carefully planned, the mini-lesson is a viable alternative to the full-period daily lesson plan. Furthermore, a lesson plan such as one combining a writer's workshop with a mini-lesson reflects the comprehensive approach to teaching. It is authentic and contextually driven yet provides direct instruction on a specific, needed skill.

The mini-lesson can be applied to any subject area. It first requires that the teacher understand the immediate needs of the students. Next, the teacher should analyze the skill or behavior to be taught. Finally, the lesson derived from this analysis must be presented without lengthy explanation or theoretical justification, no more than 10 minutes.

As an observant, reflective, kidwatching teacher, you will soon get a sense of your students' interests, strengths, weaknesses, and needs. From this knowledge,

1. **Curriculum Area:** Listening, speaking, writing

2. **Aim or Goal**
   A. Cognitive: The children will be able to improve listening skills while listening to the teacher read a story and while listening to descriptions given by their classmates.
   B. Affective: The children will enjoy using their mind's eye as they listen to a story.
   C. Physical: The children will use their senses to enrich their learning.
   D. Intuitive: The children will use guided fantasy to enrich their learning.
   E. Social: The children will respect their classmates as they in turn describe the "hidden treasure" they found.

3. **Motivation:** Questions/discussion
   A. "When we read a story, what do we use?"
   B. "When we listen to a story, what do we use?"
   C. "Today we are going to use only our ears, so let's close our mouths and eyes and listen carefully to the story I'm going to read. As I read it, try to imagine the story in your mind."

4. **Materials Needed**
   A. *Show and Tell* by Elvira Woodruff (1991), New York: Holiday House.
   B. One hidden treasure (small object, such as old potato masher, meat thermometer, pot holder, salt/pepper shaker, or broken small toy) wrapped as a present for each child with his or her name on it. The teacher hides the treasures around the room while the children are at recess.

5. **Teaching Procedures/Steps**
   A. Direct students to close their eyes and mouths and listen carefully.
   B. Read *Show and Tell* with as much expression as possible.
   C. After the reading, ask the students to imagine what would happen next if the story continued.

6. **Practice Activity** (whole class or small groups)
   A. Tell the children to look around the room and find the package with their name on it. They are not to open the treasure until everyone is back in the circle on the floor.
   B. When everyone returns to the circle, have all the children but one close their eyes while the one student opens the treasure.
   C. Ask the child who unwraps the treasure to explain the object without telling what it is. The children get three guesses. If no one can guess what it is, have the children open their eyes to see the treasure. (If the teacher is concerned about children peeking, have the child who is opening and describing his or her treasure hide behind some object.)
   D. Permit all children to open and explain their treasure, with the classmates guessing.
   E. After everyone has had a turn, ask the children to write a sequel to the story *Show and Tell* using their new treasure as the item used for show-and-tell.

7. **Follow-Up Activity**
   A. Discuss the importance of carefully listening to the story and the descriptions of others.
   B. Share the stories that the students wrote.

FIGURE 3.8

Sample daily lesson plan for grade 1 or 2.

your own mini-lessons will emerge naturally. Basically there are three types of mini-lessons: classroom management, specific skills, and techniques or tips.

Classroom Management Mini-Lessons

Early in the school year, one third-grade teacher creates a number of interesting learning centers for her students. She hopes these will liven up some lessons and also teach the children how to work responsibly without constant teacher supervision. A few weeks into the semester, however, problems arise over how one of the centers should be used. The teacher therefore calls the class together for a mini-lesson on how to use a learning center.

She restates the specific instructions for using the listening center with a **brief lecture:** "Class, we are having some difficulties using the listening center properly. I want to review the rules with you again so we won't have to stop in the middle of the lesson. I'll demonstrate this with the Orange Group. Everyone in the Orange Group take your seats at the listening center table and put on your headsets."

She waits until the children are seated and ready. Allowing time for children to get settled is important. "Everyone ready? Now Brenda will pass out the paper you will need to write your responses. Carlos will be in charge of turning on the tape recorder. Good. Did everyone see how they did it? Let's let the Blue Group try." Again she waits while the two groups trade places. Learning how to get organized takes time, particularly with young children.

"See if they remember the rules for using the center. Watch to see how the helpers do their jobs so there is no arguing or wasted time at the center. Watch carefully as they demonstrate how to adjust the headsets, distribute the papers, and turn on the tape recorder."

The class observes the Blue Group go through a mock version of the center. The children are now paying attention. "Does everyone understand how we work at the listening center? Good. Now let's get back to work, and I'll watch to see how you do." The mini-lesson is over.

A second example of a classroom management mini-lesson occurs later in the week. This one centers around how to choose a book for free-reading time. Again the mini-lesson takes the form of a brief lecture and demonstration.

The teacher uses the **think aloud** technique to show the students how she solves problems in her head. "Class, today I want to talk to you about how I go about choosing a book for free-reading time. First, let's walk over here to the class library. There are lots of good books. How shall I decide? Well, here's an interesting title, *The Witch of Blackbird Pond*. The paper cover on the book is called the book jacket. On the inside of the book jacket, there is a brief summary of the story." She reads silently for a few moments. "Hum, this sounds interesting. Here's another book with an interesting title, *James and the Giant Peach*, but it doesn't have a book jacket. I'll just sit here and read the first two pages to see how I like the beginning of the story." She sits and reads for a minute. "I'm not sure about this book. I think I'll put it back. You know it is okay to choose a book, start reading it, and then later decide to put it back on the shelf and try another. It's your choice. Now, let's all practice for a few minutes selecting a book from the library that we might want to read later."

The point of this mini-lesson is to help children get started in their free reading. Some children like to read but just cannot seem to find a book. They choose books to read on the basis of their size. Perhaps their caregivers or teachers always selected books for them in the past; now they must choose for themselves. This is hard. As they procrastinate in choosing a book, such children may wind up disrupting the free-reading time of other students in the class. This mini-lesson on how to select a book is important if free-reading time is to be successful.

Specific Skills Mini-Lessons

The students in one fourth-grade class have been writing reviews of their favorite books. The reviews are to be published in the school newspaper. In reviewing the rough drafts, the teacher notices that there seems to be some confusion over how book titles should be written in the narrative of a report. Therefore, the teacher decides to conduct a mini-lesson on underlining titles and capitalizing important words in a book title.

Her lesson takes the form of a brief lecture with examples. "I've prepared an overhead transparency with some of the book titles you've used in your writing. First, notice that titles of books are always underlined. I know that in the books you read, you may see titles written with a funny kind of print, known as italics. But since we can't do this in our handwriting, we simply underline the words in the title. This tells the reader that this is the name of the book and not part of the discussion. Are there any questions?" A few students raise their hands. "Now study the different examples of book titles on this poster:"

Book Titles Underlined

Anne Frank: The Diary of a Young Girl

Julie of the Wolves

The Wind in the Willows

And Then What Happened, Paul Revere?

To Kill a Mockingbird

A Wrinkle in Time

Ira Sleeps Over

"Now we need to talk about capitalization in book titles. Do you see that not every single word is capitalized? Little words like *a, of,* and *the* are usually not capitalized because they are not the most important words in the title. However, we always capitalize the first word of a book title even if it is *a, the,* or *to,* as the examples show. In short titles, every single word may be capitalized. Now let's look at a few more titles from the books you are reading."

Another mini-lesson focuses on the different uses of the comma and the period in writing. Again, this lesson originates when the teacher reviews the children's story writing and notices the same types of errors appearing on a number of different students' papers. One way to teach skill mini-lessons about punctuation is to show the children paragraphs taken from their favorite books and reproduced on overhead transparencies. The teacher and students can discuss how the periods and commas are used by referring to the example on the overhead transparency. Then the students can copy the example into their notebooks for future reference. Having an actual example to refer to is often more helpful than memorizing a complicated rule. The final step is for the students to take out a rough copy of their own writing and reexamine how they used commas and periods. The teacher then can move about the room helping individual children edit their stories.

Techniques and Tips Mini-Lessons

Another kind of mini-lesson can be even briefer than the ones already described. For example, one teacher notices from the students' writings that certain words are often misspelled: *receive, piece, believe, deceive, achieve.*

Her mini-lesson consists of a brief spelling tip to help the children in the future. "Class, let me have your attention. I've noticed that many of you have made a particular kind of spelling error involving the letters *i* and *e.* Here is a little rhyme you can remember that may help you in your spelling: '*i* comes before *e* unless after *c* or when it sounds like *a* as in *neighbor* and *weigh.*'" The rhyme is written on the board, and the students copy it into their notebooks. They spend a few minutes brainstorming other words that fit the rule. Then the children go back to their writing.

The teacher is well aware that there are some common exceptions to this little rule, but those will come later. Identifying all the examples that fit the rule plus all of the exceptions would take half the period. Also, she wisely does not attempt to teach any other spelling rules in this mini-lesson because that would leave no time for actual writing.

Two weeks later in this same classroom, the teacher notices another common spelling error in the children's writing. This time it concerns words ending with the (/uh/ + r) sound. She decides to give them another little spelling tip rather than teaching a full-blown lesson. It is brief and to the point. "Boys and girls, when I have to decide how to spell a word with the /ur/ ending sound, I remember this rule: Most two-syllable words in English with that ending sound are spelled *-er*. Therefore, when in doubt, use *-er*. Only a few words are spelled with *-ar* or *-or*. Can you think of some *-ar* or *-or* examples?" The class comes up with *dollar, collar, doctor,* and *tractor*. They also discover many more *-er* endings. After a brief discussion, the children return to their writing.

Shelly Harwayne, a master teacher, teaches her sixth-graders a technique to get started quickly in their writing folders each day instead of staring into space, waiting for inspiration (Calkins, 1994). Harwayne explains that many writers, even professionals, have trouble gearing up to write. She then suggests a way to help her students get the writing period off to a good start. Her mini-lesson technique consists of three steps:

1. Reread what you've written the day before.
2. Ask yourself how you feel about it.
3. Decide where you can make it better.

By beginning with what they have done previously, the students are able to get back into the flow of writing.

Although most mini-lessons are directed at the entire class, the teacher may decide to do one for just a few students. Language arts teachers know that the skill or information covered in such a small-group mini-lesson will eventually spread to the rest of the class. This is because the children are encouraged to conference together, to share and help one another as a regular part of the learning process. Lucy Calkins (1994) views small-group mini-lessons as a way of adding new information "to the class pot" without spending a lot of valuable time repeating instruction to every student in the class individually.

When you use mini-lessons, keep these points in mind:

- Teach what is most immediately relevant.
- Make it useful and generalizable to students' work.
- Keep the session brief—10 minutes maximum.
- Allow time for questions.
- Do not expect mastery of the skill immediately; that will come later, after considerable practice.

Meeting Learning Objectives

When teachers plan for learning experiences, they must keep several factors in mind: the abilities and interests of their students, the materials available, and the nature of learning. The last of these is probably the most misunderstood. This section discusses four domains of learning: cognitive, affective, psychomotor, and socialization.

Often school curriculums, and particularly standardized tests, artificially separate these equally important aspects of learning. Even worse, the affective, psychomotor, and socialization aspects of learning may be omitted entirely from the curriculum because they are not as frequently tested by standardized instruments. The result is a curriculum based exclusively on one type of learning: cognitive. However, studies in child psychology, brain development, and academic achievement have demonstrated that all four learning domains are equally important for the complete development of young people (Sarafino & Armstrong, 1986). Figure 3.9 summarizes the four learning domains.

COGNITIVE LEARNING

Almost all schools in the United States emphasize the **cognitive learning** domain, the area of learning that stresses the mental or intellectual processes. Jean Piaget's theory of the stages of cognitive development (sensorimotor, preoperational, concrete operations, formal operations) provides one way of describing the mental development of children and is probably the most influential theory in the schools today. In his *Taxonomy of Educational Objectives Handbook 1: The Cognitive Domain* (1956), Benjamin Bloom delineated the cognitive domain as a hierarchical arrangement, from low-level memorization to higher-level reasoning abilities. Bloom's taxonomy has also had enormous impact on the curriculum, particularly on the scope and sequence of skills found in basal reader series and curriculum guides.

The emphasis on cognitive learning in the schools can be attributed in part to teachers' overreliance on textbooks. Textbooks generally present factual material, which requires student memorization rather than discussion or inquiry. Teachers using textbooks as their primary instructional resource usually require students to listen to lengthy lectures (which are particularly inappropriate for young children), define specific terms, recall the names of people and places, and memorize dates and specific rules. In part, this instructional approach is a response to the increasing pressures on teachers to prepare students for **standardized tests** at the national, state, and district levels, all of which emphasize cognitive abilities and are evaluated with multiple-choice, machine-graded instruments (Clay, 1990).

Today most educators agree that the stress placed on cognitive learning to the exclusion of other types of learning in the elementary grades is too narrow and inappropriate for educating the whole child (Brandt, 1997; McCarthy, 1997; Pool, 1997). First of all, learning is complex and multifaceted; it includes more than IQ scores and test-taking abilities. Research on how the brain operates and

	COGNITIVE	AFFECTIVE	PSYCHOMOTOR	SOCIALIZATION
Type	Intellectual	Emotional	Physical	Interactive
Activities	Memorizing phonics rules	Observing the class gerbil	Pantomiming	Preparing a class newscast
			Hitting a baseball	
	Defining parts of speech	Listening to poetry	Writing and illustrating poetry	Creating a group social studies mural
	Correcting punctuation errors in workbooks	Displaying *all* children's work in the classroom	Drawing, cutting, pasting, and sewing bookbindings (publishing)	Preparing a readers theatre presentation

FIGURE 3.9

Four learning domains.

how learning occurs has also shown that all learning is holistic: It requires both halves of the brain, analytic/logical reasoning as well as intuitive/emotional responses (Clark, 1986). In short, cognitive learning cannot be truly separated from the other learning domains. To exclude the affective, psychomotor, and socialization aspects of learning is to ignore the reality of how children learn and to hamper the very cognitive abilities teachers try so hard to develop.

AFFECTIVE LEARNING

The **affective learning** domain includes feelings, emotions, attitudes, and appreciation of aesthetics (sense of beauty). For example, teachers know that if a student does not like school, she or he will not do well in it, regardless of how high the child's IQ may be. Furthermore, all children like certain subjects and activities more than others. These preferences are reflected in achievement: Students perform better in subjects they enjoy. Finally, children's attitudes toward school in general and toward particular subjects very often reflect their caregivers' attitudes (Draper, Ganong, & Goodell, 1987). Caregivers who express negative attitudes about school or speak disparagingly of a teacher in front of their children make it much more difficult for those children to adjust to the school environment.

Of greater concern is what teachers do to create positive attitudes toward school and learning in their students. An overemphasis on basic skills, drill exercises, and memorization of facts has resulted in a neglect of the affective domain of learning in many classrooms (Sternberg, 1997). This imbalance has created some serious negative consequences. For example, students often leave school without having attained any appreciation of art, music, literature, or history (Jarolimek & Foster, 1985). Despite 12 years in supposedly integrated school systems, many high school graduates also remain closed-minded to views that differ from their own and to people who talk, look, or act differently.

In the integrated, whole language, and comprehensive approaches to language arts, the affective domain is inextricably tied to cognitive learning. The language arts teacher has the opportunity to create an atmosphere, design activities, and encourage active student participation in learning that links the affective to the cognitive. This is done in part by building lessons and units based on students' interests as well as their needs. For example, reading conferences and small-group discussions of books focus on students' emotional reactions to and feelings about what they have read rather than on the facts they remember. In a reading conference, a teacher might begin by asking a child, "Why did you choose this book to read?" Follow-up questions could include "What was your favorite part?" "Is there anything about the book you didn't like?" "How did the book make you feel?"

Teachers can include the affective learning domain in the curriculum in the following ways:

- Relate school subjects to students' lives by personalizing the curriculum.
- Give students a choice of subjects to read and write about.
- Encourage small-group discussions about the content of lessons.
- Build on the honest feelings of students toward the material they are asked to learn.
- Incorporate student suggestions for making subject-matter lessons more interesting (e.g., after expressing dislike for labeling the parts of speech for each word within a sentence, one fifth-grade class came up with several alternative games to learn the parts of speech).

PSYCHOMOTOR LEARNING

Psychomotor learning is defined as the use of physical movement to enhance general understanding of school concepts. It includes such varied activities as facial expressions used in pantomime; tactile and manipulative skills required for constructing, drawing, cutting, pasting, and sewing; and bodily movements used in dramatics and play activities. Unfortunately, for a long time psychomotor learning was associated only with the very young child and with the learning-disabled child. Today it is recognized as equally important as and supportive of the other learning domains, and it should be an integral part of the school day (Carbo, Dunn, & Dunn, 1986). Even older students learn best when they have a chance to participate physically in the learning experience.

Basic to all child development theories since the 1950s and the publication of Jean Piaget's works in the United States, this concept is not always practiced in the classroom. Often in primary, intermediate, and middle school classrooms, too much emphasis is still placed on long periods of silent listening and seatwork. This reflects the still-prevalent view that talk and movement are disruptive to intellectual pursuits.

The work of William Glasser (1984), among others, has shown that higher levels of cognitive growth occur when psychomotor aspects of learning are incorporated into the classroom. Allowing children to move around the room, to manipulate objects, and to use their bodies as well as their minds actually increases learning. For example, formal grammar lessons in the elementary grades are among the most abstract and obtuse for young children to learn. Here are three psychomotor activities that serve as alternatives to rote memorization:

1. Teach children to pantomime the meaning of certain phrases within sentences, such as *under the bed, above the ground, around the tree,* and *into the barn.*

2. Ask children to act out the difference between a *blind Venetian* and a *venetian blind.*

3. Have students work in small groups to arrange word and phrase cards demonstrating the relationship between sentence structure and meaning.

Other psychomotor activities in the language arts classroom include illustrating, cutting, pasting, stapling, and sewing as part of bookmaking to share written work. Presentations of finished research projects or theme units can incorporate songs, dances, posters, dramatic acting, and the use of original props.

Another important aspect of the psychomotor domain of learning is *attention span,* the ability to concentrate on a task. In general, the younger the child, the shorter is the attention span (Sarafino & Armstrong, 1986). For example, while a fifth-grader may sit and work on a composition for 30 minutes without getting up, a first-grader may need to walk around after 5 minutes of intense, concentrated writing. Teachers should try to break up longer lessons with special time-outs for stretching, water breaks, peer discussions, or rounds of Simon Says. It makes little sense for a teacher to plow along in a lecture, even the best lecture, when students' heads are drooping and yawns fill the room. Such signs mean the children need a break. Physical activities can be used to make any lesson more enjoyable and appropriate to the attention-span limitations of the students.

SOCIALIZATION LEARNING

Socialization learning is defined as the physical and verbal communication skills needed to sustain human relations and to function effectively in our society. The process of socialization begins at home and is furthered in the community. However, it is in school that this process really broadens to include contact with diverse religious, racial, and ethnic groups. The notion of the school as a melting pot, a place for broadening horizons and relationships, is an old one. However, the socialization process is too often taken for granted; this is a mistake because, like any other important aspect of learning, it must be planned.

According to Jarolimek and Foster (1985), there are actually three aspects to socialization learning: social interaction skills, cooperative group skills, and conflict resolution skills. *Social interaction* skills begin with the establishment of a positive self-image in each individual student. A teacher can foster this development by designing activities that allow students to experience success and a sense of competence in the classroom. Success and competence are the key ingredients to a positive self-image. Only when children feel good about themselves and believe they are worthy of respect and praise can they be taught the appropriate behaviors for interacting with others in different situations. Some simple activities that promote social interaction through success and competence include the following:

- appointing students to distribute and collect class papers
- appointing monitors to assist with attendance taking
- rotating leadership roles during group activities
- allowing students to help with bulletin board preparations

Using *cooperative groups* allows children to experience specific situations that require them to use their individual social skills. Johnson and Johnson (1987) have written extensively on the topic of cooperative learning. Their central argument is that too many classrooms are organized around either a competitive or an individualistic model. The result is that many children pass through years of schooling without having developed the cooperative social skills required for participation in society. Since the classroom is the one place where diverse groups of children are brought together on a regular basis, it is also the ideal place for cooperative learning.

One way to teach cooperative learning skills is through role-playing and dramatics. Through play acting, children have a chance to act out the skills they will need later to function in a group. These important skills include taking turns speaking and listening, sharing materials among the group members, dividing various tasks so that all contribute, and ensuring that all children can assume leadership roles when appropriate. Another strategy for improving children's cooperative learning skills is the use of *literature response groups*, in which small groups of children discuss a book they have read and their reactions to it (see Chapter 6). Such important behaviors cannot be learned working alone in a corner of the room (Johnson & Johnson, 1987).

The final aspect of socialization learning is *conflict resolution*. Young children typically resolve conflicts by physical means: the fight-or-flight response. For example, two children want the same ball during recess. Instead of fighting, the teacher would have the children discuss their feelings and work out an agreeable solution. In school, they learn the rules of behavior and how to communicate their feelings, desires, and needs verbally rather than physically. Here are three positive alternatives for conflict resolution that teachers can give students:

1. *Chatter groups.* Informal talk sessions about topics of immediate concern to a particular group of children or the entire class. These groups can meet early in the morning or late in the afternoon.
2. *Brainstorming.* The technique of generating ideas through brainstorming that can be applied to social as well as academic problems.
3. *Role-playing.* Simple skits in which children act out their feelings regarding problems that have arisen in class, on the playground, between friends, and so on.

Beyond the classroom

Survey students in an elementary classroom about their likes and dislikes about school in general and certain subjects in particular. Chart or graph your findings. Are there any patterns? If so, what do you think explains the patterns? Compare your results with those of your fellow students.

Language arts teachers recognize that all these activities involve the use of oral language ability. Thus, they not only help in resolving potential classroom conflicts but also enhance students' verbal skills by giving them an opportunity to practice communication about real-life issues.

Learning Styles

Each child has a unique or preferred manner for approaching a learning situation, called a **learning style.** (Similarly, every teacher has a preferred way or method of teaching certain concepts, called a teaching method or strategy.) A teacher who can identify a child's preferred learning style also understands that child's strengths in learning and can teach to those strengths.

For example, traditional whole-class instruction is generally not successful with children with specific learning disabilities. Instead, special education teachers try to match their instructional approaches to the specific learning styles and strengths of their students (Hodgin & Wooliscroft, 1997). In recent years, more and more educators have taken the position that all teachers should be able to identify the learning styles of their students and then teach using the most appropriate instructional techniques (Dunn, 1996). This is a complex and controversial area; the purpose of this section is merely to acquaint you with the idea of student learning styles and to get you thinking about utilizing a variety of teaching strategies. This section should also help you reflect on your kidwatching experiences in classroom or laboratory settings.

Everyone has a learning style. Some people learn best in highly structured settings, guided by written directions, moving step-by-step in a logical, analytical fashion. Such people have been called left-brain oriented because the left hemisphere of the brain is associated with visual and analytic information processing. Other people take a more global approach to learning, making intuitive guesses, utilizing tactile methods, and preferring more informal settings; these people are called right-brain oriented (Dunn, Cavanaugh, Eberle, & Zenhauser, 1982; Levy, 1982). During the 1980s, many educators became enamored of brain research as it applied to instruction. However, merely labeling people as right- or left-brain thinkers is misleading. Research clearly shows that although individuals have preferred learning styles, both the right and left hemispheres of the brain are involved in all aspects of learning (Yellin, 1983b).

The more one investigates the topic of learning style, the more complex it appears. For instance, an individual's preferred learning style is affected by such variables as temperature and time of day. Are you a morning person who prefers a cool room or a night owl who likes a warmer setting for studying? Do you learn best in an absolutely quiet setting, or do you need music in the background? Does snacking help you concentrate, or is it a distraction? These factors are also part of learning style. Interestingly enough, some evidence suggests that while most teachers have their big burst of intellectual energy early in the morning, more than half of elementary-age children concentrate best in the late morning or early afternoon (Dunn, Beaudry, & Klavas, 1989). Figure 3.10 summarizes some of the factors that affect learning style.

There are many ways to classify learning styles. This section identifies just a few of the most common and presents them in a dichotomous model based on the work of Claxton and Ralston (1978). A dichotomous approach contrasts two opposite learning style descriptions along a continuum. Although some children may appear to fit one of the two extremes, most children exhibit some of the characteristics of both learning styles and thus fall somewhere along the continuum between the two extremes. Figure 3.11 lists some common learning styles.

FIGURE 3.10	
Learning style factors.	Environment: sound, light, temperature, room arrangement Emotionality: interest, persistence, responsibility Sociological needs: learning alone, learning with others, learning with media aids Physical characteristics: child growth rates, perceptual strengths, mobility needs Psychological inclinations: hemispheric preference, inductive/deductive preference, impulsive/reflective preference

Source: Adapted from M. Carbo, R. Dunn, & K. Dunn (1986), *Teaching Students to Read Through Individual Learning Styles.*

FIGURE 3.11	
Student learning styles.	IMPULSIVE ——— REFLECTIVE GLOBAL ——— ANALYTIC VISUAL ——— AUDITORY VISUAL-AUDITORY ——— KINESTHETIC

IMPULSIVE–REFLECTIVE

The learning style dimension characterized by impulsivity or reflectivity is associated with the work of Jerome Kagan (1965, 1987; Kagan & Kagan, 1970). Kagan's Matching Familiar Figures Test is still used to assess this dimension of learning.

In the classroom, the impulsive learner is most easily recognized. This is the child whose hand always flies up even before the teacher has finished asking the question. Such children have little fear of failure and appear to be more concerned with responding than with giving the correct answer. Often they are easily distracted by irrelevant material and miss the main idea or central theme of a book. On spelling and grammar tests, they rush to finish but often make many careless errors. Speed rather than accuracy drives the impulsive student.

The reflective child is slow and deliberate. Such children consider all alternatives before responding and approach problem solving in a highly systematic, critical way. This is the little perfectionist in your classroom. A favorite of teachers, the reflective child may nonetheless be one who is overly inhibited and anxious about schoolwork. These children may freeze up during test situations. They also respond very negatively when their written assignments are returned with red marks for grammar, punctuation, and spelling errors. In short, these are the students who need to be taught that making mistakes is part of learning, that taking risks is allowed.

GLOBAL–ANALYTIC

Carbo and colleagues (1986) have done extensive work in applying the notion of learning styles to reading behavior and instruction. They contend that despite the many approaches to teaching reading, "every reading method emphasizes either an essentially global or analytic approach to reading" (p. 60).

A global reading style is one in which the student learns best when presented with whole texts. These children respond to the story itself rather than to individual details. They learn as they read, processing information in large patterns despite making individual errors. Though they enjoy reading stories, such children often dislike memorizing dates, places, and names. Analytic readers, on the other hand, learn information best when it is presented in bits and pieces. They are more concerned with remembering individual details than with subjectively responding to the story as a whole.

According to Carbo (1997), most primary-grade children are global learners; that is, they learn to read best when given the opportunity to listen to and read entire stories.

VISUAL–AUDITORY

Visual and *auditory* are the two most common terms applied in the teaching of reading. Although children utilize both auditory and visual processing while learning to read, it is nonetheless possible to identify individual children who appear to process information more readily when it is presented auditorily in a teacher lecture or on a listening tape. Phonics instruction, which predominates in the primary grades, is an auditory approach to teaching reading because it stresses the learning of isolated sounds and symbols. Recent research suggests that young children, who have very limited attention spans, are less likely to be successful learners using a strictly auditory approach. Thus, teachers who utilize auditory approaches should supplement their lessons with visuals on the chalkboard or on overhead transparencies (Carbo et al., 1986).

Visual learners, on the other hand, learn best when material is presented in a format they can see: on the chalkboard, on large charts, on overhead transparencies, and in books. Such students respond to whole texts, sight-word vocabulary, and other global reading activities. Since young children are more likely to have visual acuity skills superior to their auditory discrimination abilities, whole-text and sight-word approaches are more likely to be successful (Carbo et al., 1986).

VISUAL–AUDITORY–KINESTHETIC

Most approaches to reading today combine aspects of auditory and visual learning. The teacher usually spends some time teaching phonics as well as sight-word vocabulary. This eclectic approach seems appropriate because most children utilize both auditory and visual styles in learning to read. However, for primary-grade children, even this combined approach leaves much to be desired. In a summary of the research on reading styles, Carbo and colleagues (1986) concluded that "many students do not develop full visual acuity until third grade and full auditory acuity until fifth grade."

The implications of these findings are important for all teachers of reading. Because perceptual strengths (visual and auditory) mature more slowly than other physical abilities, many primary-grade students are frustrated by their inability to remember the material taught. The problems such young children encounter suggest the need for an alternative approach to teaching reading.

The kinesthetic learning style utilizes all of the senses, not just sight and hearing. It incorporates tactile and bodily movement along with the manipulation of materials. Learning by physically doing characterizes this approach. Research has shown that most young children, as well as underachieving older children, tend to be kinesthetic learners. In the language arts classroom, these youngsters learn best when given opportunities to manipulate letters and words and to engage in reading games, pantomiming, tracing, book illustrations, and dramatics. Ironically, many remedial reading programs, which are designed for poor readers, focus on students' weaknesses in the visual and auditory areas rather than capitalize on learning style strengths in the tactile/kinesthetic area (Carbo et al., 1986).

Multiple Intelligences Theory

In recent years, researchers and educators have studied Howard Gardner's **Multiple Intelligences Theory.** Even though it was not written as an educational theory, the theory has greatly impacted education. While studying the human brains of stroke victims, Gardner became interested in the various parts of the human brain that controlled different physical functions. He realized that even though a person lost his speech after a stroke, that same person might still be able to sing. In *Frames of Mind*, Gardner (1993) described his theory of seven intelligences. Later he recognized an eighth intelligence (Checkley, 1997). See Figure 3.12 for a description of the eight intelligences.

Gardner believes that all humans possess some degree of all eight intelligences, but each human does not have the same strength in each intelligence. It is the nurturing and the importance of a single intelligence within one's culture that will develop that one intelligence over the others. Gardner posits that each intelligence must be nurtured in order for it to develop properly and more fully and that many people have a dominant intelligence at birth.

How does this theory relate to the teaching of language arts? Teachers need to recognize that each child's mind is different and that any subject material can be taught in more than one way. Study Figure 3.12 to understand the personality traits that accompany each intelligence. Reflect on how the personality traits would affect a student's approach to the reading, writing, listening, speaking, viewing, and visual representing activities that you would

---

FIGURE 3.12

Howard Gardner's Multiple Intelligences Theory.

INTELLIGENCE	DEFINITION	PERSONALITY TRAITS
Linguistic	Mastery of language	Loves to read, writes well, enjoys jokes, has well-developed vocabulary, speaks well
Musical	Superb musical competence	Sings well, plays instruments well, has ability to compose and hear environmental sounds as music
Logical–Mathematical	Ability to calculate easily and think abstractly	Computes complicated problems in head, enjoys brainteasers, enjoys games such as chess
Spatial	Ability to form spatial images	Is able to create models and sculptures and use maps and compasses
Bodily–Kinesthetic	Ability to use one's body for expressive or athletic goals	Excels in sports and drama, enjoys tactile materials
Intrapersonal	Ability to understand oneself	Is able to express oneself well, possesses high self-esteem
Interpersonal	Ability to understand and "read" others	Loves to socialize, is a natural leader, possesses empathy for others
Naturalist	Ability to classify plants, minerals, and rocks	Loves to study the outdoors, quickly sees things in nature that others do not see

Source: Adapted from Gardner (1993) and Checkley (1997).

do in your classroom. The Classroom Vignette that follows explains the activities that Mrs. Bee does with her class in order for her to understand her students. Notice how Mrs. Bee uses Gardner's Multiple Intelligences Theory to help provide a wide variety of language arts activities through the use of learning centers and activity cards. See Figure 3.13 for the activity cards for each center.

VIGNETTE *in the classroom*

After studying Gardner's Multiple Intelligences Theory, Mrs. Bee, a fourth-grade teacher, decides to set up centers based on the eight intelligences in order to do a little classroom research. She wants to find out which type of activity each of her students prefers in order to see if that activity might correlate with his or her dominant intelligence.

She sets up eight centers with the activity cards found in Figure 3.13. She gives the students three and a half weeks to complete all the centers. They are instructed to write in their journals after they have completed each center. They are to explain if they liked or disliked the activity and give their reasons. After the centers are completed, Mrs. Bee collects the journals and reads them. She makes a list of children who enjoyed each center. Then in small groups, she discusses the activities in each center and asks which center they enjoyed most and why. She finds it interesting that all the students state their likes and dislikes just as they did in the journal; however, as they discuss the activities with their classmates, they elaborate more on the reasons for their likes and dislikes. Because of her findings, Mrs. Bee attempts throughout the year to give a large variety of activities for each thematic unit she teaches. She wants to give each student an opportunity to learn in his or her dominant intelligence.

FIGURE 3.13

Activity cards Mrs. Bee used for each of the eight learning centers.

1. *Linguistic.* You remember the familiar song "Old MacDonald Had a Farm." Your task is to write a poem about Old MacDonald. You may imagine new information about him that the rest of us do not know. Your poem can be any type; it does not have to rhyme or have rhythm. After you have revised it, edited it, and have it ready for publication, share it with a small group.

2. *Musical.* Compose a new version of the song "Old MacDonald Had a Farm." When you are ready, sing it into the tape recorder that is provided. Be very creative with a new tune and a new text!

(continued)

FIGURE 3.13

Continued.

3. *Logical–Mathematical.* Following is a list of livestock that Old MacDonald has to sell. Each day that the market is open, the prices change. Each day that he goes to market, it costs him $250 (gas, meals, rent of truck, etc.). You must decide which day he should sell his livestock. Of course, he desires the greatest profit possible. His livestock that are ready for market are listed, and the prices are given for each day that the market is open.

OLD MACDONALD'S LIVESTOCK
   7 cows, 15 sheep, 10 pigs, and 20 ducks

MARKET DAY

Livestock	Monday's Price	Friday's Price
Cows	$950 each	$900 each
Sheep	$800 each	$975 each
Pigs	$800 each	$825 each
Ducks	$45 each	$40 each

4. *Bodily–Kinesthetic.* You may do one of the following activities:
   A. Create a dance that fits your rendition of "Old MacDonald" or the original song of "Old MacDonald." Be sure to practice it so you can perform it for the entire class at the end of the three weeks.
   B. Create a new game that Old MacDonald or his children would enjoy playing on the farm during the day or during the long winter evenings. It can be a game that is played with a ball or some other object, or it may be a new board game. Be creative!

5. *Intrapersonal.* By yourself, do one of the following activities:
   A. Write about the type of farm and animals you would have if you lived on a farm. Describe your farm, explaining where it would be located and what your main source of income would be.
   B. Draw a mural or a diagram of the type of farm you would like to have. Include the surroundings, buildings, animals, etc.

FIGURE **3.13**

Continued.

6. *Interpersonal.* Do this activity with six other classmates. When you find six other classmates, each of you must become one of the following people—Old MacDonald, George, Tom, Joe, Hank, Al, and Jim. When you have decided who each of you will be, do the following activity.

Old MacDonald and his neighbors are planning a neighborhood park. Presently the land is a grassy area with no sidewalks or streetlights. All the neighbors have donated equal amounts of money except Old MacDonald, who donated a larger amount of money and all the land. There is $50,000 to spend on the equipment, lighting, and sidewalks for the park. Your group must decide what equipment to purchase and then draw a plan. All the neighbors want it to be a beautiful, safe place during the day and night.

Following is a list of possible equipment with the price of each, and a list of the neighbors with their preferences.

EQUIPMENT	PRICE
Wading pool	$9,000
Swimming pool	$35,000
1-mile jogging trail	$20,000
Swing set	$500
Tennis court	$35,000
Streetlight	$300 each
Slide	$200
Bench	$65 each
Shuffleboard court	$1,700
Basketball court	$1,000
Basketball hoop	$250 each

NEIGHBORS

A. Old MacDonald and his wife are retired and are too old for jogging. They love to swim and play shuffleboard. Their grandchildren, who visit often, are toddlers.

B. George and his wife are young with two toddlers. They cannot swim but love to play tennis.

C. Tom and his wife have three teenage daughters, who are on the swim team but who pay big dollars to use the city pool during the summer. Tom is willing to donate $2,000 extra for the swimming pool.

D. Joe and his wife have three teenage sons, who are basketball stars. Joe's wife loves to jog.

E. Hank and his wife have one teenage daughter and a toddler. The teenage daughter is on the track team and the swim team.

F. Al and his wife have three teenage sons. One is on the track team and the other two play tennis. Al is willing to donate $2,000 extra for the tennis court.

G. Jim and his wife are also retired. Jim's wife jogs to maintain her health; Jim loves to play shuffleboard with his brother, Old MacDonald.

(continued)

7. *Naturalist.* Go outside to the back playground. If this was Old MacDonald's land, what do you think he would do with it? Be creative as you write or draw your plan!

8. *Spatial.* In the ziplock bags, you will find toothpicks, straws, noodles, labels, rubber bands, Q-tips, craft sticks, waxed paper, and clear contact paper. Using any of these materials, construct something that would be useful to Old MacDonald. Display your project on the shelf in the back of the room.

Teaching Strategies

A **teaching strategy** is a specific set of organized teacher behaviors designed to facilitate student learning. Though the goal for the student remains the same—learning new material—the strategy or strategies employed by a teacher to reach that goal vary considerably. The plural term *strategies* is perhaps more appropriate because it reflects the actual classroom practice of teachers who rarely use a single approach for all children in all learning situations. And this is as it should be. Good teachers are eclectic strategists: They pick, choose, and adapt various methods to meet specific conditions and students' specific learning needs. Similarly, the research on teaching methods does not support any one teaching strategy for all children at all times. Rather, it shows that good teachers adapt methods to their personal style and the idiosyncrasies of the teaching/learning situation (Jarolimek & Foster, 1985; Joyce & Weil, 1980).

Three teaching strategies—direct lecture, guided discovery, and learning centers—are general approaches to teaching. More specific teaching strategies related to language arts content are discussed in later chapters.

In and beyond the classroom

Analyze the materials in an elementary-grade classroom. What evidence can you find that these materials are geared to a particular style of learning? Next observe some students in this same room. What evidence can you find that these children exhibit a particular learning style preference? Record your observations and share them with your peers.

DIRECT LECTURE

The direct lecture, a form of direct instruction, is the most traditional and still the most popular of teaching strategies. Separate surveys of kindergarten teachers, graduate students, elementary teachers, and preservice teachers revealed that most preferred the whole-group direct lecture approach (Kagan, 1987). Why is this so?

One reason is that many teachers believe that the direct lecture approach is the most efficient way to get information across to students in a clear, concise, and relatively rapid manner. Given the fact that most school systems are dominated by fixed time periods during which specific subject matter must be covered, it is not surprising that so many teachers rely on the direct lecture strategy.

A second major reason for the popularity of direct lectures relates to teacher control. In the direct lecture approach, almost all the learning variables can be controlled: the amount of information presented, the manner of presentation, the time allotted for the lesson, the questions and answers. Furthermore, the direct lecture allows a teacher to face the entire class all the time, which at least theoretically ensures a certain amount of classroom control.

The biggest disadvantage of direct lecture is that it tends to make students passive listeners rather than active learners. Without active student involvement, it is also difficult for the teacher to assess student progress. Since lengthy lectures allow little time for discussion, student understanding is tested almost exclusively by written exams. Finally, the teacher-dominated lecture allows little time in class for children to interact with one another concerning the material to be learned; thus, the affective domain and the development of social learning skills are largely ignored.

GUIDED DISCOVERY

The guided discovery strategy, or inquiry-based learning, is most often observed in the science and social studies areas, yet it is equally applicable to the language arts (Rotherman, 1987). It begins with the presentation of a problem or question. Facts are gathered, past experiences are recalled, and discussion ensues. Then the data are organized and hypotheses formulated. The latter are tested and either accepted, rejected, or revised. Finally, conclusions are drawn that relate to the original question or problem. Throughout this process, the teacher serves as a guide and resource when needed, but the discussion and investigation are student led; instruction is thus more indirect.

The obvious advantage of guided discovery is the active involvement of students in the learning process. There are constant peer interaction, small-group discussion, questions and answers. Social interaction skills and sharing of information characterize this strategy, which focuses on children "learning how to learn" (Morine & Morine, 1975). The guided discovery approach also allows the teacher to evaluate student progress and learning through kidwatching in addition to the standardized test instruments that the school system may require. Evaluation through observation allows the teacher to identify those students who are having difficulty mastering a new concept or utilizing critical thought processes or who lack vocabulary knowledge to express themselves effectively. Once these students are identified, mini-lessons or personal conferences can be arranged to help them immediately.

The major criticism of the guided discovery strategy concerns the effective use of time. Since the lesson is dependent on student involvement, there is no guarantee that the teacher's intended goal can be met within the time limits of a single period. What if the students develop unusual hypotheses that lead them down false trails? Is this a valuable use of class time? This is one of the risks of the guided discovery strategy. Teachers must constantly make decisions regarding the quality of the student discussion and investigation. Then, if necessary, they can always step in and redirect the lesson.

Another possible disadvantage of this strategy relates to classroom control. By its very nature, the guided discovery lesson results in more student movement and talking than the direct lecture approach. Obviously, excessive amounts of movement and noise by a class of 30 or more children can be potentially chaotic. In this sense, the guided discovery strategy places great demands on the teacher's organizational skills and ability to teach children to work independently and cooperatively.

In terms of the actual content learned in a lesson, research has shown that the direct lecture and guided discovery strategies are equally effective (Jacka, 1985). The Classroom Vignette on the following page is an example of how a specific third-grade skill lesson in the language arts might be taught using each of these approaches.

VIGNETTE *in the classroom*

Direct Lecture Example

A teacher writes on the chalkboard the following definition: *A noun is the name of a person, place, or thing.* Then he says, "Today we are going to learn about nouns. Copy this definition into your notebooks." The class copies.

When all the students are finished, the teacher continues. "Here are some examples of nouns," he says. He writes on the board the words *man, New York,* and *apple.* Then he makes three columns on the board: *People, Places,* and *Things.* Next he writes the nouns in the appropriate columns and asks the students to copy the chart into their notebooks.

"Nouns are all around us," he says. "Can anyone think of a noun you see in this room?" A few hands go up, and the teacher calls on one student.

Student: I see pencils, books, and chairs.

Teacher: Good, Bobby. Let's write those on our list.

As the list grows, the teacher explains, "Some nouns are always written with a capital letter. These are called proper nouns." He writes some proper nouns on the board and directs the students to copy them into their notebooks. The lesson continues in this manner, with the teacher lecturing and the students copying.

Guided Discovery Example

A teacher writes on the chalkboard *The _____ raced across the street.* She then turns to the class and asks, "Who can read this sentence?" Hands go up to volunteer. After calling on one student, the teacher asks, "What's wrong with this sentence?"

Student: There's a word missing.

Teacher: Okay, who can give us the missing word?

Student: Car.

Teacher: Good. Is there another word we could use?

Student: Dog.

Student: How about camel? (The class laughs, but the teacher writes down all the responses.)

Teacher: Now I want you to work in your groups and see how many more words you can come up with.

The students begin whispering among themselves and writing down their ideas. The brainstorming gets lively. Some of the students notice that some words can be used as nouns in certain sentences but as verbs in others. Their lists grow as each group tries to outdo the others. The teacher walks around the room observing the groups.

Teacher: Okay, let's add all your words to our list. Now study the list on the board. What do these words have in common?

Students: There are some people. There are some animals. Most of the words begin with consonants. And they're all one- or two-syllable words.

Teacher: That's very good.

The teacher did not anticipate the last two responses; nevertheless, she writes them on the board, even though they are not characteristics of nouns. To get students back on track, she asks, "Can anyone think of a three-syllable word that begins with a vowel but would still fit in our sentence?"

Student: Elephant.

Teacher: Good. Now let's try some more sentences in our groups.

The students work in their groups, filling in the blanks in the new sentences with nouns. As they brainstorm, more and more of the groups discover that the same word can be either a verb or a noun, depending on how it is used in a sentence. For example: Don't *toy* with your food./My brother brought me a *toy.* The lesson continues in this manner until the teacher feels the children are ready to generate their own definition of a noun based on their discoveries.

LEARNING CENTERS

The use of learning centers is a third teaching strategy. Unlike a direct lecture or even a guided discovery strategy, both of which begin with whole-group activities, a learning centers strategy is based on the philosophy that children learn best in small groups working with their peers (Vermette, 1998). Many elementary-grade teachers utilize a learning centers strategy to some extent.

There are four major components to a learning centers strategy:

1. physical rearrangement of the room
2. control of student movement
3. teacher as resource person
4. evaluation of individual student progress

The physical rearrangement of the room is an important step of the learning centers strategy. Chairs and desks can be moved to form separate learning areas. Bookcases and cardboard partitions can also divide the room into special centers. The new space arrangement is one that allows children to sit face-to-face rather than in rows, looking at the backs of heads. Figure 3.14 shows a sample room arrangement.

Another aspect of the learning centers strategy is student movement. How can you get students to move from one center to another in an orderly fashion? How long should a group remain at a particular center? Do the children move as groups or individuals? These are some things you must think through before sending students to the centers. Here are three ways to manage movement in the learning centers approach:

1. Make a bulletin board display showing the various learning centers and their locations. Next, place colored tags on this display to represent your

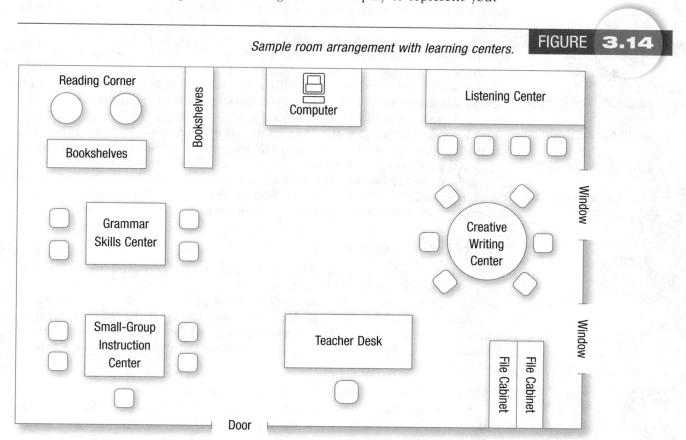

Sample room arrangement with learning centers.   **FIGURE 3.14**

different student groups. When you move the tags from one center to another, the children know that they should move as well.

2. Each day create a schedule for the use of the learning centers. Post this schedule for the groups to read, and go over it in class. The schedule tells the class groups how to move throughout the day.

3. Use a "post office" delivery system. Every child has a cubbyhole in which to store personal books. Each morning deliver a short letter telling the child what to do during the day and stressing the sequence of movement from center to center. Such a procedure also reinforces the functional nature of reading skills, as each child must read his or her own schedule.

In the learning centers strategy, the teacher assumes a variety of roles, which require the teacher to do the following:

- Conduct mini-lessons for groups of children.
- Tutor individual students in skill areas.
- Answer questions from individual students at the centers.
- Observe and evaluate individual children at work.
- Direct the movement between centers.
- Serve as a resource for students.

The learning centers strategy can employ many traditional ways of evaluating students. These include end-of-the-week tests, unit exams, and standardized tests. In addition, other types of evaluation are associated with the learning centers strategy; two of the most common are observation and work portfolios.

Kidwatching, or careful observation of individual students, is one of the most important forms of evaluation a teacher can perform in the classroom (Goodman & Goodman, 1989). The teacher observes in order to accurately describe a child's actual behaviors. How well does the student work in a small group? What kinds of cooperative learning skills does the student exhibit? How well does the student perform a task when left alone? Does the student show initiative? Can the student handle responsibility? In this way teachers individualize instruction.

The use of portfolios to evaluate students' performance during the course of a school year is growing in popularity (Farr & Tone, 1998). Portfolios (or folders for younger students) can also be used in conjunction with the learning centers strategy as a record of the child's work during a period of time. The portfolio or folder contains work samples that the student has completed at each center during the course of a week or more. Some children's folders will contain more than others. But over the course of a few months, every child will accumulate work that is representative of her or his accomplishments during that time; the teacher can assess the work accordingly. The portfolio or folder should contain evidence of what the student has accomplished and in which skill areas the child has grown.

There is always one moment in childhood when the door opens and lets the future in.

GRAHAM GREENE

Types of Learning Centers

Learning centers take on many different looks, depending on the physical setup of the classroom and the teacher's preferences. Many teachers who use learning centers on a regular basis like to create large, colorful posters that display the rules for using various centers. At the beginning of the day or before the children break to go into their centers, the teacher reviews the rules so that the centers will operate smoothly. For example, at the learning center you might see the following rules:

1. Only six children at a time.
2. Only the leader gets to operate the tape recorder.
3. Adjust your listening headsets and get out your worksheets before turning on the tape recorder.
4. No talking while the tape recorder is running.

Several types of learning centers and the necessary equipment and materials are as follows:

- *Reading center:* comfortable chairs; pillows; plenty of magazines, books, newspapers
- *Listening center:* a table with a tape recorder, headsets, worksheets to write on
- *Grammar center:* teacher-made or commercial worksheets to practice grammar concepts
- *Creative-writing center:* table, chairs, extra paper, pencils, a picture file, plus physical props like an old tennis shoe or candy bar to stimulate ideas
- *Publishing center:* cardboard, stapler, sewing materials for simple bookbinding of finished works
- *Report-writing center:* reference materials, note-taking suggestions, computer for Internet website research
- *Arts/projects center:* materials for murals, collages, science experiments, and so on

Teaching Strategies and At-Risk Students

Earlier in this chapter, we discussed the unique problems of at-risk children, the potential dropouts who without special attention are not likely to survive in the present school system. This chapter concludes with a discussion of the special teaching strategies required to meet the needs of these students. Special strategies are needed because the traditional practices just have not worked with at-risk students in the past (Slavin, Kerweitt, & Madden, 1989). The sad conclusion of recent research is that "even the best instructional programs cannot ensure success for every child" (Slavin, 1996, p. 5).

In short, research has shown that at-risk students require a radically different approach to schooling and the use of much more innovative teaching strategies than those currently being practiced. Ironically, these radical approaches are often the hallmark of the most effective schools in the United States, which have few at-risk students. They focus on motivating individual students, not groups, and they stress learning how to learn rather than the memorization of facts in isolation from application. The key concepts associated with motivating and teaching the at-risk student in the language arts are summarized in the following paragraphs.

SELF-MONITORING

The slowest or academically weakest students are often the ones who do not recognize their own difficulties in learning. They tend to plod along, period after period, absorbing little but somehow believing that learning is magically taking place. Such students need to be taught to monitor their own learning and specifically to recognize when learning breaks down (Brandt, 1997). **Self-monitoring** is a term describing the ability of a student to recognize when learning is not taking place, to identify the cause of the problem, and to make the proper adjustments.

Self-monitoring strategies are most easily taught in the area of reading. Reading is a search for meaning, a problem to be solved, an answer to be discovered, a concept to be understood. The act of reading, either for pleasure or for information, is the reconstruction of the author's intended meaning in light of the reader's experience. Therefore, when understanding is blocked or meaning interfered with, the reader must stop and adjust his or her reading behavior. Some adjustment strategies include **rereading** a difficult passage, seeking key or clue words (nouns or adjectives), reading beyond the difficult passage in search of more clues to meaning and then returning to the passage, formulating questions while reading and trying to answer those questions, and asking help of the teacher or a friend.

These self-monitoring strategies are used almost automatically by good readers. However, the weakest readers in a classroom—those ultimately at risk of dropping out—do not utilize such strategies because they do not recognize when the comprehension process has broken down. The errors they make and the confusion they encounter while reading are not seen as signals to alter their reading strategies. Instead, such readers passively read on, expecting understanding to come to them miraculously.

Thus, the teaching strategy for such students should be twofold. The teacher must first *explain the notion of self-monitoring*, particularly how to recognize when the comprehension process has broken down. Once students grasp the notion of reading as an active, meaning-focused process, they are no longer satisfied with mere word calling or page turning. Then the teacher can instruct students about some of the specific strategies to help them focus on comprehension and understanding.

RISK TAKING AND LEARNING

There is a strong correlation between school achievement and motivation to learn. Typically, the at-risk student is not motivated in school and subsequently experiences failure, which discourages effort toward achievement. It is a predictable pattern. One of the best theoretical models to address this issue is known as the Risk Taking Theory, first described by John W. Atkinson (1974; Atkinson & Birch, 1978). In summary, Atkinson has argued that in all learning situations there are two separate and contending forces to be dealt with. On the one hand, there is the *need to achieve success* in order to receive praise, rewards, and recognition; on the other is the real *fear of failure* as well as the ridicule, condemnation, and punishment it may bring. There is thus a psychological dilemma facing the child, who must weigh the chances of success against the chances of failure. Risk taking is therefore an integral part of learning and must be taught as such (Gee, 2001).

SUCCESS BREEDS SUCCESS

The most successful students are those who have experienced the most success in the past and therefore are willing to take more risks in difficult learning situations. The weakest students, the potential dropouts, have years of failure behind them. Their school experiences have often taught them not to try, not to take chances, because they will meet failure anyway. Thus, they are not willing to risk failure, which is a prerequisite for achieving success (Cambourne, 2002a).

Teachers who work with at-risk students therefore need to create situations in which these students will experience success. They can shorten work activities so that students can complete assignments; provide study guides and vocabulary sheets to make reading assignments easier; and document small successes with graphs, written comments, and letters to caregivers. All these activities are necessary to encourage students to take risks in the more difficult learning situations ahead.

THE IMPORTANCE OF SUBGOALS

For the weakest students in the classroom, most school tasks seem insurmountable; these students see only an interminable string of activities ahead. One way to help them is to model how to analyze a task into smaller, more attainable subgoals. In this way, students encounter small successes on the way toward accomplishing the larger task of a project (Gee, 2001; Levin, 1986).

In the language arts, this can be accomplished in a number of ways. For example, students can be taught how to make outlines or graphic organizers for each of their assignments. A reading assignment might include the following tasks: identify the purpose for reading; formulate questions to guide your reading; read the passage while keeping these questions in mind; and write an answer for each question formulated. In a writing assignment, an outline of subtasks might include the following: brainstorm with a friend for ideas to write about; jot down ideas and select one you like; complete an outline or rough idea of what you want to write about; and get together with a friend to discuss your rough idea before making changes. In both of these examples, the focus is on several small subtasks. The larger task—reading the book or writing the composition—is completed gradually in a series of small steps; thus, it does not seem so overwhelming to the student with a history of failure or incomplete assignments.

COOPERATIVE LEARNING STRATEGIES

Some researchers suggest that the dominant models in school, competitive and individualistic, work against the poorest students (Johnson & Johnson, 1987). For example, in a classroom set up to emphasize competition through spelling bees, timed exercises, and handwriting awards, the weakest students invariably fail. An alternative model is one that emphasizes cooperative learning activities that require individuals to work in groups toward a single group goal. Cooperative learning thus provides a chance for success for students who may not achieve it on their own. Following are the six characteristics of such a learning model:

1. A group goal means all share the success attained.
2. Achieving a mutual goal requires a division of labor.
3. Interdependence among group members is positive and supportive.
4. Rewards are linked to interdependence and cooperation.
5. Individual accountability is reduced but still important.
6. Interpersonal and socialization skills are learned and practiced along with content knowledge.

Changing Teacher Roles

According to some research studies, teachers relate to students in one of two ways: They either exercise control over student behavior or support student autonomy (Ryan, Connell, & Deci, 1985). Controlling student behavior makes for orderly classrooms but also results in passive students who lack the incentive to do independent creative work. As discussed earlier in this chapter, research shows that students perceive themselves as most competent when given some autonomy in a learning experience. This is particularly true of at-risk students who have experienced much control, little autonomy, and still less success in school, to the extent that their self-esteem is at rock bottom.

To change this attitude, teachers need to reassess their own roles. First, they must relinquish some of their controlling behaviors. For example, instead of lecturing to students, some teachers now see themselves as leading and encouraging students in independent and group work. Serving as a resource, answering questions, and coaching students on a one-to-one basis allow teachers to maintain order and discipline while permitting greater student autonomy. This additional autonomy leads the at-risk student with low self-esteem to take more risks, exercise choices, and tolerate uncertainty in learning situations without frustration. Only in such a free atmosphere can students come to believe in their own abilities and become motivated to exert the effort necessary for academic success (Brophy, 1982; Cambourne, 1995).

One-to-One Tutoring

Perhaps the most controversial conclusion regarding at-risk children is that for them to be successful in the traditional classroom, some time each day must be spent in one-to-one tutoring. Individual tutoring is not a new idea. However, in the past most educators rejected the notion of individual tutoring as a solution to the high dropout rate among at-risk students because it was unrealistic: Too much money and too many people would be required to implement such a program on a large scale in most schools.

Despite the cost and difficulty of implementation, experts in this field, such as Robert Slavin (Slavin, 1996; Slavin & Madden, 1989; Slavin, Kerweitt, & Madden, 1989) and Benjamin Bloom (1981, 1984) have concluded that only one-to-one tutoring makes a difference with at-risk students. This means that schools must make a serious commitment to recruiting the volunteers and hiring the paraprofessionals necessary for such a large-scale tutoring program.

Approximately 1,000 school districts in the United States have approached the problem of potential dropouts among at-risk students by adopting Communities in Schools (CIS), which was founded in 1977. CIS is committed to connecting community resources with schools and their students and families in order to help students who are at risk of dropping out of school. It begins in the elementary school and continues through high school.

This program has been highly successful in Charlotte-Mecklenburg, NC, where CIS is now in 21 of its public schools, serving more than 6,000 students. These 21 schools use a wide variety of programs. Volunteers from the community and civic organizations become tutors and mentors for at-risk students; dentists provide free dental exams; and volunteers from the Junior League become involved with service projects with these students to help them learn the joy of giving to others. One of Charlotte-Mecklenburg's elementary schools is open year-round and for extended hours during the school year in order to provide classes in dance, art, and computers (Lewis & Morris, 1998).

The new electronic interdependence re-creates the world in the image of a global village.

MARSHALL MCLUHAN

In El Paso, TX, one of its 53 CIS sites works with former gang members. The focus of this CIS is to provide these students who have dropped out of school with strategies to resolve conflict without fighting. These students may also attend classes so they can earn a GED. Another CIS site in El Paso provides summer programs for younger students on a college campus, while other sites provide literacy classes for adults who speak Spanish (Lewis & Morris, 1998).

The CIS program has been successful in providing at-risk students personal attention from a caring adult, a safe learning environment, lifelong skills, and opportunities to serve others. The primary mission of the CIS program is to keep at-risk students from dropping out of school.

No educator likes to admit that the schools have failed to educate some children. Yet for many at-risk children, this is the reality. Such students thus require a radically different approach and new strategies (Slavin, 1996). This is why programs such as CIS should be examined carefully and considered seriously as alternatives to the present educational system when working with at-risk children.

TECHNOLOGY AND WEBSITES

While teachers plan for the delivery of language arts and other subjects, they must also think about the rules that students must follow in the classroom, in the halls, and on the playground to provide a safe environment for all. Today teachers and administrators must also post the rules that students will follow while in the computer lab and while using any classroom computer. Many schools have an Acceptable Use Policy (AUP) that must be signed by a legal guardian before the child is permitted to use the computers (Kehoe & Mixon, 1997). Kehoe and Mixon (1997) give the following sets of rules concerning courtesy, safety, and general basics:

RULES CONCERNING COURTESY

1. Save only on floppy disks.
2. Do not waste paper.
3. Log off when leaving the computer.
4. Speak softly in the lab.
5. Remember that your email can be read by others.
6. Do not be a "pig" and take too much time on the computer.

RULES CONCERNING SAFETY

1. Do not give your real name, home address, or telephone number on the Internet.
2. Do not meet privately with someone you met on the Internet.
3. Do not share your password with anyone.
4. If you have "strange" feelings about someone you meet on the Internet, tell an adult.

BASIC RULES

1. Do not sell or exchange or buy illegal items on the Internet.
2. Do not exchange sexually explicit material on the Internet.
3. Do not send threatening messages on the Internet.
4. Do not plagiarize; give credit to the source.
5. Do not forge any email.
6. Do not post defaming messages.

Teachers and administrators can download a variety of templates for AUPs by contacting www.gsn.org. In addition, a good resource on Internet use is *Complete and Easy Guide to the Internet* by Heide and Stillborne (1999).

www.ed.gov/free

This site has hundreds of free educational resources from federally sponsored programs.

http://educate.si.edu

This site contains lessons, activities, and nearly 500 educational products.

www.col-ed.org/cur

This site has lesson plans for elementary language arts, math, science, and social studies.

www.sreb.org

This is the site for the Southern Regional Education Board, which includes a broad range of information and links to educational sites from early childhood through college.

www.sreb.org/main/Goals/goals.asp

This is a great link, state by state, to legislative changes that affect education, including major educational reports.

www.ivla.org

This is the site for the International Visual Literacy Association, useful for educators, artists, and researchers. The site provides good teacher ideas for using visual literacy.

www.crayola.com

This is a great educational activities site for teachers produced by the Crayola Crayon company. Many suggestions are provided for activities, projects, and crafts to do with children.

www.selfgrowth.com/reading.html

This site provides teacher articles on reading comprehension, speed reading, and much more.

Summary

Planning for a successful language arts program takes time, but it is time well spent. Among the various types of plans used by teachers are the yearly or semester plan, the unit plan for a single book or subject area, the weekly plan book, the individual daily plan, and the mini-lesson plan.

Related to planning are the concepts of students' diverse learning styles, multiple intelligences, and teachers' varied instructional strategies. All students exhibit varied learning styles, including visual, auditory, tactile, and kinesthetic. All students possess the eight intelligences—linguistic, musical, logical–mathematical, bodily–kinesthetic, intrapersonal, interpersonal, naturalist, and spatial—with one intelligence being dominant. Teacher knowledge of both students' learning styles and the multiple intelligences helps in the task of individualizing lessons. Teachers' instructional strategies include the direct lecture, guided discovery, and learning centers. The strengths and weaknesses of these various strategies should be considered before being employed in a given teaching situation.

Finally, at-risk children pose unique problems for the classroom teacher. Such children, often from disadvantaged backgrounds and lacking in basic academic skills, require alternative teaching strategies if they are to acquire the skills of literacy. Placing such children in traditional classroom settings is not the answer: Programs such as CIS should be considered.

ACTIVITIES *with children*

Learning Styles Lesson

Create a reading comprehension lesson. Tape-record a short story. Have students read the story while they listen to it through headsets. Use kinesthetic activities involving paper, paint, yarn, cardboard, and miscellaneous objects to create a three-dimensional representation of a scene from the book.

Map Making

Teach the whole class the rudiments of map making using the classroom as your subject. After each student has created a map of the classroom, discuss the alternative uses of learning space. Then let students create a map of their ideal classroom.

Class Calendar

Show the class a copy of the school calendar and discuss the importance of planning in school. Then create your own class calendar. List important class activities such as students' birthdays, holidays, tests, parties, and field trips.

RELATED READINGS

Educational Leadership (December 1994/January 1995) 52(4).

This issue, titled "The Inclusive School," discusses the various types of special needs.

Educational Leadership (February 1996) 53(5).

This issue, titled "Students with Special Needs," discusses topics such as attention deficit, ESL, and the gifted.

Educational Leadership (March 1997) 54(6).

This issue, titled "How Children Learn," discusses the brain, learning styles, multiple intelligences, and neural branching.

Guthrie, J., & Wigfield, A. (eds.). (1997). *Reading engagement: Motivating readers through integrated instruction.* Newark, DE: International Reading Association.

This book is a collection of essays from reading experts on how to teach reading so children are actively engaged instead of passive learners.

Ohanian, S. (1999). *One size fits few: The folly of educational standards.* Portsmouth, NH: Heinemann.

This book is a must read to understand the controversy surrounding state-mandated standards and standardized tests.

Phi Delta Kappan (May 2002) 83(9).

This issue contains interesting articles on accountability, the Department of Education, standards, and school discipline.

Roller, C. (1996). *Variability not disability: Struggling readers in a workshop classroom.* Newark, DE: International Reading Association.

This book is especially helpful for teachers who desire to use the reading workshop. Roller explains how to ensure that readers of all abilities and learning styles succeed.

Sailor, W. (2002). *Whole-school success and inclusive education: Building partnerships for learning, achievement, and accountability.* New York: Teachers College Press.

This book provides an optimistic look at improving America's schools.

4

Language Origins, Acquisition, and Development

This chapter introduces you to the field of linguistics, the scientific study of language. You will learn about how children first learn a language, the conditions for language development, the impact of nonstandard English, and the role of language in the classroom.

CHAPTER OBJECTIVES

After reading this chapter, you should be able to accomplish the following objectives:

1. Explain how children acquire language.

2. Describe the factors that influence language development.

3. Give your definition of language.

4. Describe the different functions of language.

5. Describe the relationship between language and cognition.

6. Describe the contributions of Vygotsky, Bruner, and Piaget to language theory.

7. Describe three contrasting theories of language acquisition.

8. Describe a developmentally appropriate language curriculum.

9. Explain the notion of the critical period of language.

10. List the steps for evaluating quality education software programs.

CHECK YOUR BACKGROUND KNOWLEDGE. Before reading the chapter, complete the K-T-W-L chart based on the chapter overview and objectives provided at left. In column "K," write what you know about the topics in the objectives. In column "T," write what you think you know. In column "W," write what you want to learn. Finally, after you have read the chapter, write what you have learned in column "L."

Know	**T**hink you know	**W**ant to learn	**L**earned

Language Study

The study of language has fascinated humans for hundreds of years. Scholars throughout the world have sought to trace the origins of words in their own particular language. Some have even sought to identify the single perfect language. One bizarre experiment even involved placing an infant in an isolated environment devoid of language in an attempt to discover which, if any, language the child would produce naturally. Sadly, the child died and the project was abandoned. Today it is recognized that all languages are equally perfect for their own communicative purposes.

Linguists and teachers alike are interested in the relationship between thought and language. Does speech influence the thought processes? Can thinking be improved through verbal activities? Or are the two entities immune to each other's influence? This relationship is important because the newest research contends that listening, speaking, and especially reading and writing enhance learning in all content areas (Calkins, 2001).

The study of language is also one of the keys to understanding various teaching practices, such as author's chair, literature conferences, reciprocal questioning, and process writing. Teachers need to be aware of how children use language for learning. Chapter 3 described the role of the teacher as kidwatcher; this chapter stresses the importance of observing children particularly as language users. The information you gain from watching and listening to students in turn influences the kinds of materials you use and the manner in which you teach. This is how teachers individualize instruction. This is also the key to becoming a reflective teacher.

DEFINITION OF LANGUAGE

There are many ways of defining language. The definition used in this text comes from the linguist Ronald Wardhaugh (1972): "Language is a system of arbitrary vocal symbols used for human communication" (p. 14). Breaking this definition down into its component parts provides a better understanding of the nature of language.

Language Is Systematic

Anyone who has ever heard a nonsense rhyme and chuckled, seen a sign with a word intentionally misspelled (such as *Kountry Kitchen*), or corrected a child who said "That mines" intuitively recognizes that language has an organization. It is governed by certain rules. Language is also systematic. When a person violates the system or breaks the rules, language begins to dissolve; it no longer communicates clearly.

Language actually contains three systems: The phonological system deals with sounds; the semantic system deals with meaning; and the syntactic system deals with word order in sentences. It is important to note that in speaking, reading, and writing, all three systems interact to produce meaningful communication.

Language is a system of sounds.   **Phonology** is a systematic study of speech sounds. It is a broad field that encompasses many aspects related to the sounds of a language (Lass, 1984). When linguists study a language, one of the first things they do is analyze the speech sounds of that language. For example, some linguists want to know exactly how certain sounds in a language are produced by the vocal chords and the placement of the tongue, teeth, and lips.

Such knowledge is helpful in learning a foreign language or correcting a speech impediment. This particular branch of phonology is known as *phonetics*. The speech therapist in your school or district has studied phonetics intensively and can help you work with children who have speech difficulties. Articulation problems are one common example of a childhood speech problem. A student in your class may pronounce the /th/ sound as /d/. Through specific speech exercises, the speech therapist can help the child correct this problem.

Any language can be broken down phonetically into the distinct, separate sounds that make up words; such an individual sound is known as a phoneme. A *phoneme* is the smallest significant unit of sound in a language. To represent the significant sounds in a word, linguists place each symbol for a sound between two slash marks like this: /c/ /a/ /t/. This tells people to pronounce the sounds "cuh," "ah," and "tuh" rather than the names of the letters. Although the human voice is capable of making many different sounds, the English language is based on only about 44 phonemes.

These 44 sounds in turn are represented by 26 letters, or graphemes. *Graphemes* are written symbols that represent phonemes or sounds. As a teacher of reading, you can easily see that one of the first problems all young children face in learning to read is how to decide which sound a particular letter or combination of letters makes in a given word. If there were the same number of letters in the alphabet as there are sounds in the English language, reading could be taught as the mere memorization of the match between sound (phoneme) and symbol (grapheme). However, approaching the sound system of English in isolation from its system of word arrangement and meaning is contrary to the way people communicate.

Although there is not a perfect one-to-one match between the sounds and symbols of the English language, it is nonetheless important for students to understand that there are certain conventions or rules they must follow as speakers, readers, and writers. In writing, for example, *fl, th, cr, ab, ot,* and *er* are systematic arrangements of letters that form parts of English words; however, combinations such as *bc, pk, qr, uu,* and *tp* are not. As children use language orally; experiment with writing; and see print in books, on posters, and on signs, they gradually become accustomed to and internalize the common patterns in English. Thus, four-year-old Aubree can tell her sister "I'll help you with that after I've finished my pudding" long before she hears about dependent clauses and prepositions.

The notion that internalized language patterns follow systematic rules is the foundation on which classroom instruction should be based. This is implied by the hierarchical description of the functions of language given by Halliday (1982), as well as by research showing that young children learn and acquire knowledge through active participation and manipulation of concrete materials in language-rich settings (Kantrowitz & Wingert, 1985).

Language is a system of meaning.   **Semantics** is the general term given to the study of meaning in a language (Miller, 1985). A person who is speaking does not use sounds randomly; such talk would sound nonsensical and would serve no purpose. Even very young children recognize this. Nor do people use sounds in isolation; instead, they string phonemes together into meaningful patterns to form words. Words are not used randomly either. They are strung together in meaningful units to build sentences. Finally, sentences must be arranged in meaningful patterns to form paragraphs and extended discourse (speeches, novels, plays, and so on). All these levels are included under the heading semantics.

Linguists generally begin their study of meaning at the word level; they use the term *morphology* for the study of word meanings. When a group of phonemes is arranged to produce a meaningful unit, that unit is called a *mor-*

pheme. Any word in the English language can be considered a morpheme: *ball*, *house*, *run*, *blue*, and so on. Some words, however, contain more than one morpheme. In the compound word *baseball*, there are two distinct units of meaning, *base* and *ball*; therefore, there are two morphemes in this one word. Compound words are easily recognized, but what about the word *uncovering*? There are actually three separate morphemes in this word: the prefix *un-*, the root or base word *cover*, and the suffix *-ing*. Prefixes and suffixes are known as *bound morphemes* because they only take on meaning when they are bound or attached to words. Words such as *cover* are *free morphemes* because they contain meaning even when they are free, or standing alone. Identify the free and bound morphemes in the following words: *boys, softly, rebuild, unfriendly*.

Vocabulary lessons about root words, prefixes, and suffixes are examples of lessons in morphology. Studying about synonyms (words that have the same meaning), antonyms (words that have opposite meanings), and homonyms (words that sound alike but are spelled differently and have different meanings) is also part of morphology lessons.

Language is a system of arrangement.   *Syntax* provides the rules or system for arranging words into orderly and meaningful sentences (Miller, 1985). This is true in both written and spoken language. To understand the importance of the syntactic system, consider the following example:

The dog bit the man.
The man bit the dog.

Although the two sentences contain the same words, the new arrangement of words in the second sentence obviously alters its meaning. Other times the words in a sentence can be rearranged without altering its underlying meaning. Though the word order is different, the following sentences express the same meaning:

The girl gathered the flowers.
The flowers were gathered by the girl.

If there were no rules for the ordering of words, any random arrangement could constitute language. But this is not the case. *The by gathered flowers girl* is clearly nonsense or a nonsentence. In school, the rules of syntax are taught under the heading of *grammar;* sentences that do not make sense or are missing a word are considered *ungrammatical.*

It should be apparent by now that the semantic system for meaning is related to the syntactic system of word order. The two are parallel and dependent on one another. Children simply and naturally use language in meaningful ways. Even very young children who are just acquiring language do not go around creating nonsensical sentences, at least not for long. And even though they may not be able to define the terms *adverb* and *preposition*, they still can recognize what is and is not a meaningful sentence.

The systematic nature of language at the phonological, semantic, and syntactic levels is also what makes language predictable. When presented with an oral sentence such as "The young _____ ran across the street," very young children can make meaningful predictions based on their intuitive knowledge of language. Similarly, when shown the letter *q* followed by a blurred mark (perhaps a printing error), school-age children who have had a few years of experience with print can predict what letter will follow. All readers predict on the basis of their desire to make sense out of what they

VIGNETTE *in the classroom*

Joan Warren is a teacher consultant in South Brunswick, NJ. She believes that young children learn best through "active, hands-on teaching methods like games and dramatic play," that "youngsters' social growth is as essential as their academic achievement," and that teaching "should fit the child instead of making the child fit the school" (Kantrowitz & Wingert, 1985, p. 50).

Observers of the Greenbrook school in South Brunswick see youngsters scattered throughout the room, working in small groups on cooperative projects of their own choosing. The children talk as they work. They use language to interact with their peers, to ask questions, to request things, to direct others. As they play with geometric puzzles, shape blocks, dolls, and trucks, they continue to talk. They also use language to learn about language. Every day for about a half hour, they listen to a story read by their teacher. During story time, they ask questions about the words they see in print; later they act out parts of the book. Their knowledge of print grows as they

begin to recognize familiar words in other books and magazines and on boxes and candy wrappers. Print is as natural to the learning environment as talking. Children also ask about words and use words in their writing as naturally as they speak to one another. Their focus is on meaningful communication; the teacher serves as a guide, resource, and helper as needed.

In another school, children are seated at separate desks. The desks are arranged in rows, one child behind the other, with the teacher at the front of the room. All eyes are on the teacher. The students chant in unison a rule from their workbook; then they bend their heads over their papers and carefully copy the rule into their notebooks. There is no talking in the class. The teacher walks up and down the aisle to check that everyone has copied the rule correctly. Some children are having difficulty and must start over again; others have finished early and look toward the clock on the wall, waiting for recess.

see on the printed page. Making sense out of print is what drives the reading comprehension process. Reading authority Robert Tierney (1990) has put it this way:

> Readers use their background knowledge in conjunction with their expectations to develop meanings by continuously relating their views and experiences to the ideas, characters, and events suggested by the text. They visualize people and events, tie together ideas, anticipate outcomes, ask themselves questions, assess the plausibility of understandings, and revise their ideas as they mentally revise the text or replace it with others. (p. 38)

Language Is Arbitrary and Symbolic

Though the three systems of language can be used to predict certain word spellings and word arrangements, the individual meanings of words cannot be predicted from the sound or appearance of those words. This is because meaning must be assigned, and each language assigns meaning in a slightly different way, using different sounds and different symbols. For example, there is no inherent connection among the sounds /d/ /o/ /g/, the symbols d-o-g, and the furry, tail-wagging animal that barks. This is what is meant by the idea that language is arbitrary. Figure 4.1 shows some common words written in five different languages.

It is obvious that objects and ideas can be represented in many different ways through language. But no one way is more effective than another. This means that no single language is either superior or inferior to any other lan-

FIGURE 4.1

Common words in five languages.

ENGLISH	FRENCH	SPANISH	GERMAN	CHINESE	
dog	chien	perro	Hund	狗	gǒu
cat	chat	gato	Katze	猫	mūo
one	un	uno	eins	一	yī
two	deux	dos	zwei	二	èr
boy	garçon	muchacho, niño	Junge	男孩	nán hái
girl	fille	muchacha, niña	Mädchen	女孩	nǚ hái
book	livre	libro	Buch	書	shū
green	vert(e)	verde	grün	綠	lǜ
apple	pomme	manzana	Apfel	苹果	píng guǒ

guage. However, throughout history people have believed—and fought bloody wars over their belief—that their own language was superior to that of their neighbors. The language issue becomes even more complex because of the multiple variations, or dialects, within a single language. For example, the New England dialect, the Southern dialect, and the Midwestern dialect are just a few of the speech variations used in the United States. Again, as with separate languages, no one dialect is superior or inferior to another; they are all merely variations within a language.

When spoken languages take on written form, the use of symbols also comes into play; in this sense language is also symbolic. The phonological system must be represented graphically for there to be a written system of language. Once again, every language has its own symbols. Thus, speakers of English use an alphabet of 26 letters to represent their language, while the Chinese employ 3,000 characters (Bromley, 1988). Written languages differ in other ways. Israeli children learning Hebrew read and write from right to left; Chinese children read their language from top to bottom. Thus, the symbols and arrangement of symbols can vary greatly from one language to another. This is another example of the arbitrary nature of language.

Beyond the classroom

Symbols that represent meaning do not have to be letters or words. In advertising, for example, symbols are used to represent entire products. Collect examples of symbols used on television, in magazines and newspapers, on billboards, and on T-shirts. How can these symbols be used to teach children about the symbolic nature of language?

Language Is Vocal

For linguists, speech is primary. In all societies, speech precedes the written form of language development. This is not to minimize the importance of writing but, rather, to put it in its historical perspective. Writing systems developed only as a means to give permanence to spoken sounds; not all societies, even in modern times, have a written language. Therefore, oral language forms the foundation for later literacy instruction.

One way of understanding the importance of speech for later literacy development involves studying the vocal patterns or rhythmic nature of speech. *Intonation* is a term describing how a speaker expresses emotion and feeling with words. This is a primary way of conveying a message with words. The three main aspects of intonation are *stress*, *pitch*, and *juncture*, which are also aspects of the phonological system.

Stress is a term meaning "accent." It refers to the degree of emphasis placed on certain syllables, words, or phrases within sentences. Stress influences meaning, as the following examples demonstrate:

> Will John *really* be at the party?
> Will *John* really be at the party?

By emphasizing one word more than another in a sentence, a speaker conveys a slightly different meaning. Accenting different syllables within the same word can even produce new words with different meanings:

> Margie was *present* at the concert.
> Margie will *present* the award to the winner.

The term *pitch* refers to the rise-and-fall patterns in voices, particularly at the ends of sentences. By altering the level of his or her voice, a person can also slightly alter the meaning of the sentence. Pitch is represented in print with punctuation, as in the following examples:

> Alice is beautiful.
> Alice is beautiful!
> Alice is beautiful?

The first sentence is read in a normal tone of voice. The second sentence causes a speaker to raise the pitch of her or his voice. And the third sentence alters the pitch still more to ask a question. Skilled writers use punctuation, varied spellings (such as *we gonna go*), and slang expressions to mimic different speech patterns. When children are encouraged to do the same in their writing, they begin to see some of the relationships between spoken and written language.

The term *juncture* refers to the way speakers pause or terminate the flow of speech, particularly within and between sentences. Notice how the varying use of punctuation causes you to pause at different places in the following sentences and subsequently to alter the meaning of the sentences, though the words are exactly the same:

> Yolanda likes to eat ketchup, macaroni, and cheese.
> Samantha likes to eat ketchup and macaroni and cheese.

Understanding the vocal intonation patterns of the English language provides a better appreciation of punctuation. It is not uncommon for two different writers to punctuate the same sentence differently depending on the emphasis and meaning they are striving for. Although there are certain restrictions on the use of punctuation, there is also a great degree of literary license. Children learn this by experimenting when they write.

There are certain aspects of vocal language that cannot be represented by punctuation. These are the nonverbal gestures, or body language, that often accompany speech; linguists call these *paralinguistic* features of language. Body language is important, particularly in dramatic presentation, because it too conveys meaning. Among the more common examples of body language that accompany vocal speech are postures, hand gestures, and facial expressions. Squared shoulders, a chest thrust forward, a pointed finger gesture, and eyes narrowed into a glare imply something about a speaker.

Beyond the classroom

Tape-record some speech samples of children and adults. Listen to the intonation patterns and try to represent them in writing. Transcribing vocal speech into written form is a good way to understand the importance and function of punctuation. What differences do you notice between the patterns in adult and child language?

VIGNETTE *in the classroom*

Mr. Baron's third-grade classroom is located in a large city in the Southwest. The school population is a mixture of white; African American; Hispanic; Native American; and, most recently, Vietnamese and Cambodian children. In Mr. Baron's class alone, there are children who speak English, Spanish, Navajo, Apache, French, Vietnamese, and Cambodian. On the walls of the room are posters and signs that reflect all the different languages spoken. Throughout the day, children use their native tongues as well as English. Mr. Baron regularly asks the students, "How do you say that in English?" If the child does not know, he or she goes to one of the many bilingual paraprofessionals in the building to get the translation. These students are learning English, but there is no stigma attached to the use of their native language. In fact, being bilingual or even trilingual in this school is valued and seen as something very positive.

Language Is Used for Human Communication

Language exists for the purpose of communication: The content of the message is more important than the style of the delivery. This is true of spoken as well as written language. Language also distinguishes humans from other species. Though they may communicate in various ways—lion's roar, whale's sing, bee's dance—their communication abilities cannot compare with those of humans.

HALLIDAY'S SEVEN FUNCTIONS OF LANGUAGE

The purpose of language is communication. A well-known description of language by the British linguist Michael Halliday is enlightening on this point. Halliday's study of the language used by his son Nigel and his writings on grammar, the social significance of language, and the role of language and meaning have influenced the work of many scholars in the fields of linguistics and language teaching (Halliday, 1975, 1976, 1977, 1978, 1982).

Halliday proposed that a child defines language in terms of its meaning potential and its usefulness. The more the child hears and uses language, the more she or he becomes aware of the power of language. Halliday described the child's growing awareness of the significance of language as a series of stages leading to adult language. The stages are described in terms of the different functions that language serves. This is similar to the sociolinguistic view that children's language functions develop through a process of interaction with others, primarily adult language users. Study Figure 4.2 and consider the same three questions that Halliday asked himself in formulating his model: How is language used by the young child? What purposes does language serve? How are these purposes achieved through listening, speaking, reading, and writing? Following is a more detailed description of Halliday's seven functions.

1. Instrumental. The *instrumental function* is seen quite early in life when a child discovers that language is a way of satisfying basic needs. When a child is hungry and cries, his mother nurses him. When he falls and screams in pain, someone comforts him. When he actually begins to use meaningful words, he further discovers that language can be a tool or an instrument to satisfy a need; state a wish; or obtain some basic object, such as food. The child has discovered that language can be useful.

2. Regulatory. The *regulatory function* occurs once a child realizes the power of language to control others. There is no end to the demands that this child

FIGURE **4.2**

Halliday's seven functions of language.

FUNCTION	CHILD'S LANGUAGE EXAMPLE	ENHANCING EXPERIENCES
1. Instrumental (satisfy needs)	"I want that cookie."	Simple problem solving; business letters
2. Regulatory (provide instrument of control)	"Do this first."	Role-playing; games
3. Interactional (provide social maintenance)	"Let's do this together."	Conversational play; friendly letters; chatter groups
4. Personal (express individuality)	"I like this the best."	Journals; discussions; tape recordings; show-and-tell
5. Heuristic (explore outside environment)	"Why is it snowing?"	Interviews; discussions; question-and-answer games
6. Imaginative (create own environment)	"Let's pretend that we're lost and . . ."	Make-believe; dress-up; dramatic acting
7. Representational/Informative (convey information to others)	"This is my new Barbie."	Show-and-tell; sharing discussions

Source: Adapted from M. Halliday (1977), *Explorations in the Functions of Language.* Copyright © Elsevier Science Publishers BV.

makes of adults and peers: "Pick me up." "Tie my shoe." "Give me that toy." The discovery of the regulatory function of language leads the child to give instructions and orders. This is particularly evident in the play of young children, especially when they are learning and then changing the rules of a new game. Halliday calls this the "do as I tell you" stage.

3. Interactional. The *interactional function* occurs as a result of an awareness of the regulatory function of language and opportunities to play with other children. It eventually leads the child to understand that language is the way people maintain relationships with others. Halliday refers to this as the "me and you" or "let's do this together" function. It is the way in which young children form friendships and adolescents bond into close-knit groups. Teenager cliques are defined by their way of talking among themselves; newcomers are automatically outsiders until they learn the language of the group.

4. Personal. The *personal function* is closely tied to the interactional function. In addition to being a way to bond with a group, language is the way to stand out. It is a way to form and express individuality: "I like vanilla fudge ripple the best." "I love to swim, but I'm afraid of water snakes." "I think fast cars are great." Through language, people express their opinions, feelings, attitudes, and emotions. In responding to others, a child is also becoming a unique individual. Thus, language also serves a very important role in the development of personality and in answering the question, "Who am I?"

5. Heuristic. The *heuristic function* literally concerns seeking information. Halliday terms this the "tell me why" function of language. "Why is the sky blue?" "Why do I have to go to bed at eight o'clock?" "Why do I have to eat my vegetables?" Through the heuristic function of language, the child grows intellectually by acquiring new knowledge. Growing awareness of the larger environment leads to growing appreciation of the value of language in asking questions of others.

Not the school, nor the teachers, but the student is the preponderant factor in education.

JAMES WELDON JOHNSON

Without language as a guide, everything would have to be experienced firsthand, often with disastrous consequences. ("Why can't I touch the stove, Mommy?")

6. Imaginative. The *imaginative function* occurs when children discover that language can also be used to create one's own environment. This is the world of make-believe, or "let's pretend that   . . ." It is the basis of solitary and eventually group play. Imaginative language can also function to maintain an internal world, carried around by talking to oneself, humming a favorite sound, or smiling over a riddle. Through language, the child creates a unique world, a world of fantasy, of princesses and dragons, of dreams and poetry. Words such as *make-believe* and *pretend* enter the vocabulary. The imaginative function is thus also a primary way for the child to express creativity.

7. Representational/Informative. The *representational/informative function* is the function of language in which information is conveyed to others. In one sense, it completes the communication cycle that begins with the child using language to satisfy basic needs. Sending messages, giving reports, describing objects, and helping others are all part of the representational or informative function of language. This more complex and sophisticated use of language characterizes adult language. No longer is language used just to satisfy basic needs, ask questions of others, or socialize. These are all very important functions in themselves, but now language takes on the role of conveying important information to others who require it. The child is becoming an adult. Furthermore, the representational function of language is most often called upon in school settings. Without question, the school is a language environment that demands much of a youngster's language ability.

Halliday's seven functions of language have influenced many scholars because they provide a useful way for grouping and talking about language. This model can also be used to describe some of the ways in which children learn about language in school. For example, Frank Smith (1977) and Gay Pinnell (1985) have developed approaches to language instruction in the schools based upon Halliday's original model.

Halliday's model can also be considered as a description of how language develops. The four major conclusions that can be drawn from this model are as follows:

1. Learning to talk is inextricably tied to meaning.
2. Language develops primarily in a social setting.
3. Language is both a personal tool and a social instrument.
4. Language development from childhood to adulthood is dependent on social interaction with other language users.

In and beyond the classroom

After studying and discussing Halliday's seven language functions, observe a classroom of young children. Listen and tape-record their language. Try categorizing the language samples according to Halliday's seven functions. What implications for instruction does this model have?

A Brief History of the English Language

All languages are continually changing over time; American English is no exception. Nearly 5,000 years ago, hundreds of small nomadic tribes roamed the plains of central Europe and Asia. Oftentimes they fought one another. One such tribe, the Teutons, migrated to the area that today includes Germany and parts of Scandinavia. From a single Teutonic dialect grew the modern languages of German and Dutch, which later greatly influenced modern English (Yellin, 1983b).

Linguists and historians alike divide the history of the English language into three major periods: Old English, Middle English, and Modern English. Old English (449–1066) includes the language influences of the Celtic tribes that invaded the British Isles around 600 B.C. and were later, in turn, themselves conquered by the Romans under Julius Caesar in 55 B.C. The Roman influence and particularly the Latin language had an enormous impact on life and language in the British Isles. Later, following the withdrawal of the Romans, Germanic tribes such as the Saxons, Angles, and Jutes again crossed the English Channel. They adopted many of the Latin words (*colony, village, inch, mile, street*) but also added their own terms. This process of word changes and exchanges among various languages, called **borrowing,** is a fundamental concept of language development. Finally, this period gave us the most significant early written work, the epic poem *Beowulf.*

The Middle English period (1066–1500) began when William the Conqueror, duke of Normandy, successfully invaded England and brought with him the French language from the province of Normandy. For the next 400 years, French remained the language of government and the courts although the masses continued to speak their Anglo-Saxon dialect. French words were borrowed, altered, and eventually Anglicized; examples of such words are *peach, beef, baron,* and *crime.* Chaucer's *Canterbury Tales* was written during this time and reveals how the English spelling system had changed.

The Modern English period (1500 to the present) begins with one of the most prolific writers of all time, William Shakespeare (1564–1616). This was the time of the Renaissance, or cultural rebirth, when literature, art, and music were supported by all the monarchies of Europe. Shakespeare was revered in his own country not only as a writer but also as an inventor of words, more than

VIGNETTE *in the classroom*

Mrs. Hightower teaches language arts and social studies to the fifth-graders in a small, rural school in eastern Oklahoma. In the past, she has used separate textbooks for each subject and has taught them during separate times of the day. This year she has decided to experiment with a unit approach that encompasses content and skills from both the language arts and social studies curriculums. First she combines the periods to give her one large block of time for language arts and social studies. Then she asks her students what they would like to study that combines these two subject areas. The students decide to study their own state, from settlement to statehood.

They begin their unit by studying the map of Oklahoma and identifying specific place-names that they recognize. Many of the names are of Native American origin, as this part of the Midwest was once designated by the government as Indian Territory, an area of settlement for the tribes displaced from the eastern portion of the United States. Some of the students in Mrs. Hightower's room are Native Americans and have heard family stories of the Trail of Tears and the Oklahoma Land Run. They share their grandparents' exciting firsthand accounts of life in the early Oklahoma settlements. From studying the map further, the students discover place-names, such as *Stroud,* whose origins can be traced back to cities in Europe. The study of word origins is also a lesson in geography and history.

As the unit grows, the students clamor for visits to the school and public libraries to do research to supplement the firsthand interviews with members of the community. Mrs. Hightower is amazed at how rapidly her students' research skills improve through using the Internet, encyclopedia, dictionary, atlas, and other reference materials. Classroom textbook lessons on how to do research have always met with great resistance in the past; now the students cannot wait to get to the library to look up unusual place-names.

1,700 in fact! During this period, too, the widespread use of the printing press led to a greater consistency in spelling the written language; previously hand-written documents were often spelled as the copier saw fit.

When the Pilgrims crossed the Atlantic Ocean to America, they brought with them their English language. Other immigrants from many different countries followed. European place-names such as Hamburg, Frankfurt, Tangiers, and Turkey were associated with foods such as hamburger, frankfurter, tangerines, and turkey. Contact with Native Americans resulted in the use of new words such as *raccoon, squaw, pecan, chipmunk, moose, skunk, canoe,* and *moccasin.* French fur trappers added such words as *chowder, rapids, pioneer,* and *prairie.* In the Southwest, settlers adopted such Spanish terms as *fiesta, parade, siesta, rodeo, lasso,* and *ranch.*

Today the English language reflects its borrowings from Native American languages as well as from the languages of immigrant groups. Example place-name borrowings include Tallahassee, FL; Shawnee, OK; Moscow, ID; Florence, AL; Baton Rouge, LA; El Paso, TX; and San Diego, CA.

Language and Cognition

How does the brain actually work? What is the role of language in thought? For example, does the way people speak influence the way they think? The question of the relationship between thought and language is an old one. Aristotle believed that a person's perception of the world was transmitted as sensations throughout the body as well as the mind. The cognitive processes were viewed as intrinsic to the brain and immune from environmental influences such as language. Thus, Aristotle concluded that there was no connection between thought and language. This classical Greek view persisted unaltered until the seventeenth century, when the philosopher John Locke theorized that internal mental activities were composed of individual ideas, which in turn had been derived from external sensations. Therefore, Locke argued, internal thought must be related to external stimuli such as language. But the nature of this relationship remained to be determined by later scholars (Carroll, 1972; Vinacke, 1974).

Eventually psychologists also began to investigate observable body movements as a clue to understanding the mechanism of thought. Early behavioral psychologists, such as J. B. Watson, believed that movements of the tongue, lips, and vocal chords responded to the thought processes in some manner. For Watson, thought was inseparable from speech. The physical movements of the speech mechanism he viewed as the overt manifestation of covert thinking (Carroll, 1972; Vinacke, 1974).

The purpose of education is to awaken joy in creative expression and knowledge.

ALBERT EINSTEIN

THREE COGNITIVE THEORISTS

The nature of the relationship between language and thought has been crystallized through the work of three psychologists: Lev Vygotsky, Jerome Bruner, and Jean Piaget. The research and theories of these individuals have contributed to knowledge about language and thought, which in turn has greatly affected the latest developments in language arts instruction.

Lev Vygotsky

Lev Vygotsky (1962) observed young children in Russia as they used language in play and other social situations. Based on these observations, Vygotsky argued that thought development was partly determined by language development. According to his theory, when children talk, either to themselves or to others, they are shaping their internal thought patterns. The development of the child's ability to think out loud is thus the key to the development of complex thought processes (Hennings, 1989). One significant aspect of this development is the notion of **egocentric speech:** talk not directed to another object or person. Egocentric speech, Vygotsky argued, is the key transition period leading toward true thought as characterized by inner speech. Inner thought processes, he believed, are structured by inner speech and later by overt speech. Viewing speech and thought in this deterministic manner, Vygotsky argued that improving the linguistic abilities of children also improves their overall cognitive abilities.

Central to Vygotsky's views is the influence of adults on children. His observations led him to conclude that children's interactions with adults not only shape their language patterns but also influence their thought patterns. At first, children can understand adult language but cannot reproduce it or generate complex ideas. Later, as speech is internalized, it is used to control thinking. In this sense Vygotsky, like Halliday, believed that verbal interactions between children and adults help children "learn how to mean." Meaningful social interactions with adults spur cognitive as well as verbal development in the child. This theory, called the **Social Interaction Theory of Development,** has greatly influenced the current whole language movement (Bayer, 1990).

Another key concept of Vygotsky's theory is the notion of the **zone of proximal development.** This refers to the gap between what the child knows and can express on her or his own and what the adult must provide in terms of information and language structures. Children need adults to grow linguistically and cognitively. In a sense, the child is always one step behind the adult, straining to keep up. With the proper adult role models, the child's language and thought continue to develop; without them, the child's thought processes are severely limited.

Jerome Bruner

Jerome Bruner (1961b, 1962, 1978) saw language as a tool of the intellect and a cognitive instrument capable of transforming experience. Language, in Bruner's view, aids reasoning powers by freeing the mind from total dependence on the appearance of reality. For example, the child who can verbalize a situation is not easily fooled by a parent who hides a ball and claims it has disappeared. Thus, according to Bruner, one role of language is to activate thought and concept development. Concept development involves the creation of **schemata,** or models in the brain, which store information necessary for higher-level thinking. The older the child, the greater the role language plays in the creation of these schemata. In one experiment, children were asked to sort pictures into categories. The experimenter noted that children ages two to six categorize only on the basis of color, shape, or size. Around age seven, there is a shift from reliance on perceptual appearances to reliance on symbolic representation. Consequently, older children can explain their grouping strategy by saying, "They're all tools." The term *tools* permits a form of classification higher than color, shape, or size, all of which are grounded on physical perception.

Bruner also believed in the importance of social interaction for a child's linguistic and cognitive growth. Building on Vygotsky's earlier work, Bruner argued that the child uses the language of adults to move from one stage of language development to another; thus, the child's language leans and builds upon the adult's. This process Bruner termed **scaffolding** (1978, 1987). The linguistic scaffold, or structure provided by the adult, allows the child to construct language and internalize the rules of language through experience.

Bruner's theories on thought development and schema formation can be seen in the classroom when teachers use schematic diagrams, semantic maps, and web diagrams. Though these terms are used slightly differently, the processes they represent all include similar steps: A verbal brainstorming session leads to a visual representation, which eventually creates a mental picture that the student uses to store information suitable for later problem solving. In the elementary classroom, diagramming, mapping, and webbing are used to help children better comprehend text structures they have read, lectures they will hear, and written work they wish to produce (Pearson & Johnson, 1985).

Jean Piaget

Jean Piaget (1952, 1959, 1964, 1965, 1967) observed children in Geneva, Switzerland, over a period of many years, during which time he formulated his theories on learning and development. Piaget's central theory is that a human is a biological system, structured by laws of growth and development that can only be modified within limits. Thought and language are also rooted in this sequential development. Though Piaget granted that language may reflect and to an extent facilitate cognitive development, he stressed that language cannot account for thought. Unlike Vygotsky, Piaget argued that thought precedes and is separate from language.

Recall from Chapter 2 that Piaget took a developmental view of cognitive growth and language development. He saw mental growth occurring parallel to physical growth. It begins with the newborn infant listening to the sounds of the environment and continues as the child imitates sounds and creates new sounds while exploring language. With increased age also comes vocabulary growth. Joan Tough (1984) found that children on average use about 3 words at 12 months, 20 words at 18 months, 300 words at 24 months, 900–1,000 words at 36 months, at least 2,000 words by the age of 5, and 4,000 words by the age of 7.

Piaget described child language in terms of egocentric speech and socialized language. Egocentric speech only takes into account the child's view. In communication settings, this means failing to listen to others or respond to others effectively. Egocentricity also helps explain young children's limitations in projecting beyond immediate, concrete situations (Tough, 1984). Both language and thought are constrained by egocentricity initially, but as children grow older and become more aware of others, they need to give and receive information; peers become more important. Children's speech and thought therefore adapt through interactions with other speakers and thinkers. Eventually this leads to the socialized speech so important for Vygotsky's view of cognitive growth.

Three terms are associated with Piaget's view of language development: assimilation, accommodation, and equilibrium. **Assimilation** occurs when new information and perceptions are organized into already existing schemata. Assimilation is therefore a continuous process through which an individual integrates new information into older or established patterns of thought. But what happens when the child encounters a new piece of information or engages in a new experience unrelated to previous ones? Since this new information cannot be structured into an existing pattern, a new pattern must be created. This process Piaget called **accommodation,** a continuous process through which new informational patterns are created in the mind to store and utilize new objects, facts, or experiences. **Equilibrium** is a continuous process involving the harmonious interplay between assimilation and accommodation.

Beyond the classroom

Find out more about Piaget's theories by consulting Hans Furth's *Piaget for Teachers* (1970), P. Richmond's *An Introduction to Piaget* (1970), or other references mentioned in this chapter. From these sources, develop a list of oral and written language activities that you consider appropriate for students in the various stages of mental development. Observe children at play with other children and interacting with adults. What evidence can you find to support Vygotsky's notions of the zone of proximal development and the importance of social interaction?

STAGE	CHARACTERISTICS
Sensorimotor (birth to 18 months)	Children act upon real objects to learn about the world. By learning through the five senses, concepts of cause and effect and of object permanence develop.
Preoperational (18 months to 7 years plus)	Children use words as symbols to represent objects and ideas. Learning through play becomes more important; real and imaginary objects are incorporated into activities. As the concept of "word" develops, the power of egocentrism declines. Egocentrism must again be overcome when learning to read and write in school.
Concrete operations (7 to 11 years plus)	Children begin to use logical reasoning and are able to classify and perform simple operations. Concrete, manipulable objects are important for learning abstract concepts. Mental processes, in addition to trial and error, are utilized in problem solving. Learning becomes internalized.
Formal operations (12 years plus)	Children's verbal and logical reasoning is not restricted to physical objects or concrete situations. As language abilities develop, abstract reasoning becomes easier. Wide reading, extensive writing, and small-group oral language activities expand children's cognitive growth.

FIGURE 4.3

Piaget's stages of cognitive development.

Source: Adapted from J. Piaget (1965), *The Language and Thought of the Child;* E. Sarafino & J. Armstrong (1986), *Child and Adolescent Development;* J. Tough (1984), "How Young Children Develop and Use Language"; L. Calkins (1983), *Lessons from a Child.*

Another of Jean Piaget's famous theories contends that the interaction among assimilation, accommodation, and equilibrium, in combination with environmental forces, leads children to pass through a series of distinct stages of mental development. These stages in turn are influenced by and correspond to stages of language development. Figure 4.3 summarizes Piaget's stages of mental growth.

Piaget's theory of mental development and its relationship to language can be useful to a teacher if viewed judiciously. Piaget never meant to suggest that the age levels are fixed and absolute. For example, the concrete operations stage of learning persists long into adulthood as a primary way of learning new things. Imagine trying to understand the workings of an automobile engine without having an actual engine to study and greasy parts to handle!

PSYCHOLINGUISTIC VIEW OF LANGUAGE AND THOUGHT

The most recent views concerning the relationship between language and thought come from the psycholinguists. The psycholinguists in turn built their theories on the constructivist views of Piaget and Vygotsky. Essentially **Psycholinguistic Theory** states that the sound system (phonology), the system for word meanings (morphology), and the system for arranging words into sentences (syntax) cannot be separated from the larger system of meaning (Norton, 1989).

Goodman and Burke (1988) have described the development of the psycholinguistic position as follows:

VIGNETTE *in the classroom*

Ralph, a fifth-grader, is studying about plants and flowers. He comes across a new word, *chrysanthemum,* which he cannot pronounce. His teacher helps him with the pronunciation; together they look up the word in the dictionary. Ralph discovers that a chrysanthemum is a type of brightly colored flower. He is already familiar with roses, so he can easily assimilate this new piece of information into his existing concept of flowers. In a later science lesson about the root system of plants, Ralph is confused about how water and minerals travel through a plant. His teacher takes time to briefly explain the concept of plant vessels. Ralph must develop a new schema in his cognitive system to accommodate this information, which he will later use in assimilating higher-level information about the physical properties of matter.

Ralph thus maintains a healthy balance between assimilation and accommodation. However, if Ralph had an imbalance in favor of assimilation, he would know only a few broad categories, so crammed with facts as to be cognitively useless. If he had an imbalance in favor of accommodation, he would know too many narrow categories without establishing clear relationships among them, which would also inhibit problem solving. The key, in Piagetian terms, is to maintain equilibrium between assimilation and accommodation.

Psychologists have emphasized the use that people make of language, the ways that language relates to learning and thinking, and how language controls people's behavior. Linguists have analyzed the structural components of language, explored the meaning of words and sentences in different settings, and described how language changes are based on historic, economic, age, geographic, or racial differences. (p. 93)

In the 1960s and 1970s, the fields of psychology and linguistics came together. Communication theory, the sociology of group interaction, brain research, and the grammatical theories of Noam Chomsky all combined into psycholinguistic research, which attempted to show the "interrelationship between thought and language processes . . . how people use language, how language affects human behavior and how language is learned" (Goodman & Burke, 1988, p. 94).

Today the impact of the psycholinguistic view can be seen most clearly in the area of reading. Psycholinguists such as Frank Smith (1988) have argued that reading is not a passive act but, rather, one that involves an active, complex interaction among experiences, thought processes, and language. This theory of reading is termed **meaning centered.**

The psycholinguistic view states that reading involves the use of three separate cue systems: graphophonic, semantic, and syntactic. The **graphophonic system** allows the reader to pick up visual symbols (graphic system) and translate them into sounds (phonological system). The **semantic system** draws on the cognitive schemata of the reader, which are stored in the brain as meaningful units relating words, clauses, and sentences to functions and ideas. Finally, the **syntactic system** links the graphophonic and semantic systems through a system of grammatical rules (Goodman & Burke, 1988). Figure 4.4 shows the relationship among the three cue systems.

The Whole Language Theory of the 1980s and 1990s takes the Psycholinguistic Theory one step further by stating that just as reading development cannot be separated from language and experience, so writing cannot be separated from reading (Flower & Hayes, 1980; Tierney, 1990).

FIGURE   **4.4**

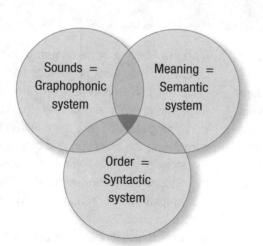

Cue systems linking thought and language.

BRAIN RESEARCH AND LANGUAGE AND THOUGHT

The phenomenal breakthroughs in brain research that allow neurobiologists and neurosurgeons to study the living brain with microscopic cameras have altered our view of learning. Educators particularly are gaining a greater appreciation for the incredible amount of learning that takes place in the first few years of life. At birth, a baby's brain is a bundle of millions of neurons, each emitting an electrical impulse to other neurons. Every time a neuron is used, activated by an experience in the environment, it becomes part of the giant electric circuitry that is the human brain. If not used, the neurons may die and permanently affect future learning (Begley, 1996).

The relationship between language and thought can also be examined in terms of the functioning of the brain. Most of the current knowledge about the brain comes from neurological reports of brain-injured persons. The portion of the brain studied most during these medical operations is the cerebral cortex. The cerebral cortex is divided into twin hemispheres—left and right—which are joined by the corpus callosum, a bundle of interconnecting fibers. The hemispheric, or lateral, specialization of the brain is unique to the human species and accounts in part for the unique evolutionary development of language in humans (Ornstein, 1977).

The concept of lateral specialization of the brain has been the subject of extensive study, much speculation, and still more controversy. Research has found that the left side of the brain controls the right side of the body, and the right side of the brain controls the left side of the body. It is more difficult to pinpoint the locus of specific functions such as analytic reasoning, spatial processing, musical talent, and verbal abilities.

In the late 1970s and early 1980s, a dichotomous view of the brain's functions was popularized by many educators. For example, Lee and Rubin (1979) stated:

> Now we know that left brain thinking is logical and symbolic, the right comparative and relational; the left verbal and mechanical, the right spatial, musical and integrative; the left analytic, sequential, logical and linear, the right, imaginative, holistic and intuitive. (pp. 32–33)

In general, the left-brain/right-brain dichotomy was a simplistic attempt to subdivide complex thought processes; it contributed more myth than fact to knowledge about how children learn. Today most educators take a whole-brain

VIGNETTE

in the classroom

Mrs. Brown is preparing a reading skill lesson. In years past, she has chosen this lesson from the teacher's manual accompanying her basal reader. It showed her how to set a purpose for reading, suggested questions for her to ask the children to test their comprehension, and gave her suggestions for follow-up activities. This approach was satisfactory for Mrs. Brown, but she was concerned that her students were passively awaiting her directions. Then the reading specialist in her school suggested that she read an article by Garner in *The Reading Teacher* (1984). This made her start thinking of reading as a problem-solving process, one that should call for more active participation by her students.

Now Mrs. Brown begins her reading lesson by having her students browse through the book or selection they will read; she calls this *sampling.* Through sampling, the students get a feel for the work they will read. Next Mrs. Brown asks them to read the first line or paragraph of the story and discuss what they think is going to happen later. This is the *prediction* step in reading. Then the students read further to check some of their predictions. This is the *confirming* step. Finally, the children pause before completing the selection and discuss how they think the story ends. This is the *anticipating* step.

Students are allowed to work through these various steps in small groups or individually, moving at their own pace. Reading as problem solving allows students to utilize their own experiences and refer to other books they have read. Predicting as part of reading comes naturally to Mrs. Brown's students, mainly because it is fun. Mrs. Brown believes it makes them better problem solvers in general because it causes them to think rather than be dependent on her for answers and direction. Many teachers (like Mrs. Brown) are reading professional journals to find new ideas to help them in their teaching.

view. Learners may prefer a particular way of processing information (e.g., visual or spatial), but as tasks become more complex, the left and right sides of the brain interact. The whole brain is involved both in solving a mathematical problem and in writing a poem (Yellin, 1983c).

The position taken in this text therefore is that both the left and right hemispheres of the brain play distinctive and interactive roles in all learning situations. Listening, speaking, reading, writing, viewing, and visual representing all affect the thought processes of the individual. Furthermore, oral language activities, such as discussing and explaining, enhance critical or higher-level thinking regardless of the task. In one study involving 300 schools in 21 different states, students were given specific instruction in higher-order thinking skills (HOTS). Each day, for 35 minutes, these students were encouraged to talk to one another about their own thought processes: how they solved problems, how they reasoned. Talking about thinking in this way helps people to develop **metacognition,** awareness of thought processes. At the end of the project, standardized tests revealed that students enrolled in the HOTS program improved in reading and mathematics skills as a result of the specific attempts to link language and thought (Pogrow, 1990).

Language Acquisition

Many teachers, particularly in the upper elementary and middle school grades, focus their efforts on teaching a specific content subject, such as science or geography. They assume that their students already possess the necessary skills to learn these subjects. However, to be really effective, teachers need to know where students have come from and what they can do in a particular subject area. This is especially true in the language arts, for the various communication abilities build on one another over time.

The two areas of study that address language backgrounds of students are language acquisition and language development. **Language acquisition** is the way in which newborn infants begin the process of acquiring language. **Language development** includes the various factors that influence and shape the growth of language prior to and during school.

Language acquisition and language development are also influenced by various social and economic factors. The research of the anthropological linguist Shirley Brice Heath of Stanford University has shown a link between how children and adolescents acquire and use oral language and their later development. In her classic 1983 work, *Ways with Words: Language, Life and Work in Communities and Classrooms*, and in her 1993 book *Identity and Inner-City Youth: Beyond Ethnicity and Gender*, Heath shows how language influences race relations, employment and social skill learning. Teachers at all subject and grade levels therefore need to have some background knowledge of the underlying theories of language acquisition, which influences the later language development of children.

LANGUAGE ACQUISITION THEORIES

Three theories of language acquisition—behaviorist, innatist, and pragmatic— represent the major contrasting views among linguists today. Teachers familiar with these language acquisition theories can work more effectively in developing the oral language abilities of their students.

The Behaviorist Theory

The **Behaviorist Theory** that B. F. Skinner argued in his book *Verbal Behavior* (1957) states that language is like any other physical behavior: It can be controlled and shaped by altering the environment in which an organism lives. The behaviorist argument dominated scholarship in the 1950s and 1960s because of the immense popularity of Skinner. Learning experiments using stimulus– response conditioning techniques to teach pigeons, mice, and rats how to manipulate mazes and obtain food flourished. It was a next logical step for Skinner to propose that the same stimulus–response conditioning could explain how human infants acquire language.

According to Skinner, an infant's brain is blank at the moment of birth. Immediately afterward, forces in the environment begin to imprint themselves on the child's brain. Most important of all, the caregivers' language provides the stimulus that starts the conditioning chain reaction in motion. Later, at that wondrous moment when the child responds by saying, for example, "Mama" or "Dada," the acquisition process begins in earnest. Mommy and Daddy support the child's efforts (response) by repeating the words, by smiling, and by hugging the child for appropriate language use (the rewards). In effect, the caregivers create a controlled environment for language, in which they reward and respond positively to the child's appropriate imitation of their language.

The notion that language is acquired through imitation, rewards, and reinforcement is a powerful one that makes good common sense. A child raised in a home in which only Chinese is spoken naturally grows up speaking Chinese; a Chinese infant raised in a home in which the caregivers speak only French probably speaks French. However, linguists have long had a problem with the Behaviorist Theory. Menyuk (1988) has noted that assuming that language acquisition is mere imitation is also assuming that the young child has enormous powers of memorization. Yet to memorize all the possible language structures and variations within those structures is virtually impossible. Stoodt (1988) has also noted that young children acquire language in their early years at an extremely rapid rate, much too quickly to allow for constant reinforcement by caregivers (as the behaviorists have argued). Finally, linguists and caregivers alike have noted literally hundreds of examples of young children producing language that they almost surely did not hear any adult produce: "Grandpa, higher the swing, my feet are dragging." "I'm puttin' on my two pantses." "We breaked the toy." "I digged in the sandbox." Clearly something more than mere imitation is operating in the language acquisition process.

The Innatist Theory

In contrast to the behaviorist view, the **Innatist** (or Nativistic) **Theory** asserts that language acquisition in young children is a creative process that is more than mere imitation. Innatists such as Noam Chomsky (1974) and David McNeil (1970) have further argued that language, or the ability to acquire language, is innate to all human beings: The brain is not blank at birth, as the behaviorists claim, but rather is biologically programmed to learn language. Chomsky has gone so far as to argue for the existence in the brain of a language acquisition device, which is activated by a language environment to begin the acquisition process.

The evidence to support the innatist position comes from a number of sources. For example, as noted previously, young children produce words and sentences that sound strange and often humorous to adults—language that is obviously not mere imitation. For example, in studies at Harvard University, young children were tape-recorded using terms such as *sheeps, deers, peoples, firemans, pantses, digged,* and *ringed.* Linguists call these terms *overgeneralizations* because the child overapplies a common rule, such as adding *-s* to make words plural or *-ed* to indicate past action. Figure 4.5 provides some examples of common childhood overgeneralizations. Earlier theories dismissed these as mere language errors, but the innatists have argued that they provide proof that language is creative. Innatists view young children as little linguists, testing hypotheses and creating new language forms.

A second argument of the innatists centers on the fact that only humans possess language. Without formal instruction, the average infant acquires language automatically. Chomsky has argued that this is because only the human brain is predisposed to acquire language. Animals are intelligent, but intelligence is not the necessary requirement for language; innate capacity is. Witness the fact that even severely retarded children acquire language. How could this be possible unless all humans are predisposed for language?

A third argument to support the innatist position comes from linguists such as Courtney Cazden, who has studied the grammatical development of children. Cazden showed that despite attempts to get children to imitate adult language structures, children's oral production often remains uniquely creative. For example, a child asked to repeat the sentence "Give me the ball" produced "Give ball." When told to produce the sentence "Here's mommy's dirty socks," the child said, "Mommy sock" (Cazden, 1972). Earlier research by Jean Berko Gleason (1967) found similar results: A child who was asked "Did you say your teacher

FIGURE 4.5		
Overgeneralizations in child language.	Nouns:	peoples, sheeps, fishes (no plural forms); mans, snowmans, mouses, knifes, toothes, feets (irregular plural form); pantses, sockses (double plural)
	Adjectives:	greens, pinks
	Verbs:	comed, drinked, goed, waked up, runned

held the rabbits?" replied "Yes, she holded the baby rabbits." If language acquisition were strictly imitation, such common errors would not occur.

A fourth argument advanced by the innatists is the existence of *language universals* (Lenneberg, 1967). These are characteristics of language present in all languages throughout the world, regardless of the environment. For instance, all languages contain semantic, syntactic, and phonological features. All languages contain terms for describing people, places, things, and actions. These universals make it possible for a speaker of one language to learn other languages. If language were dependent only upon the immediate environment and upon rewards and reinforcement, such universals would be superfluous and foreign language learning next to impossible.

The Pragmatic Theory

Some theorists and many teachers feel that the true nature of language acquisition lies somewhere midway between the behaviorist and the innatist positions. These people believe that language is indeed unique to the human species and that therefore it must be innate, but they also argue that it needs to be triggered by an appropriate language environment (Norton, 1989). This position is known as the **Pragmatic** (or Sociocultural) **Theory** because of its emphasis upon the environment and social controls. Pragmatists believe that language is learned through caregiver–child interaction and the controlling nature of language through requesting, receiving, commanding, and so on (McCormick & Schiefelbusch, 1984).

The Pragmatic Theory represents the middle position in the debate over language acquisition, and it reflects the work of Michael Halliday described earlier in this chapter. Recall Halliday's seven functions of language and their importance for meeting the child's needs in the real world. Language is indeed highly practical. The interaction between infants and their caregivers also demonstrates the social nature of language learning. Caregivers continually adjust their language to carry on dialogues with their children (Wells, 1981). Infants, in turn, struggle with their truncated baby talk to converse with their caregivers. In short, language acquisition appears to be both highly functional and social.

Occasionally the functional and social aspects of language take a bizarre twist for which Behaviorist Theory cannot account. Innatists and pragmatists argue that such unusual language occurrences are difficult to explain but nevertheless proof of the inborn nature of language. The case of twins Grace and Virginia Kennedy is one such example (Wilwerth, 1979). In 1977, at the age of seven, they were taken from a school for the mentally retarded and brought to the San Diego Children's Hospital for examination. Their language sounded like this:

> "Pinit, putahtraletungay."
>
> "Nis, Poto?"
>
> "Liba Cabingoat, it."
>
> "Ya."

The twins spoke an original language, referred to by linguists as *idioglossia*. Idioglossia is extremely rare, but it does occur occasionally and always in twins. Grace and Virginia could talk to and understand each other, but neither their parents nor the linguists, speech pathologists, and psychologists who observed them could understand or explain this phenomenon. For hours the two girls would play and converse, oblivious to the grown-ups observing and tape-recording their mysterious tongue. Eventually, after much intensive remedial language therapy, the twins were taught to speak a halting form of English, but their strange original speech continues to puzzle scientists.

One of the most difficult tasks we face as human beings is communicating meaning across our individual differences, a task confounded immeasurably when we attempt to communicate across social lines, racial lines, cultural lines, or lines of unequal power.

LISA DELPIT

Brain Research Theory

The latest information on language acquisition, both first and second languages, comes from the field of brain research, or neurobiology. We know that at birth the newborn infant's brain is already a complex maze of neurons and electrical impulses, like the circuit wiring in a computer. Each connection from neuron to neuron, triggered by an environmental stimulus, means another piece of learning is taking place. By adulthood, the brain has 100 trillion connections (Begley, 1996).

Researcher Patricia Kuhl of the University of Washington has mapped the brains of infants in terms of how neurons respond to heard phonemes in the child's environment. At a much earlier age than previously recognized, infant brains are responding to language. By age 1, infant brains distinguish sounds in their environment as significant or not significant in terms of their own language. The more often a particular phoneme is heard, the more connections are made in the auditory cortex of the brain. From sounds, the infant's brain moves toward words, already programmed by the initial electrical connections. At the same time, the brain is continually filtering out other phonemes and words that differ from the established language pattern. That, according to Kuhl, is why after age 10 it is so difficult to acquire a second language with the proficiency of a native speaker (Begley, 1996).

Further evidence for the early development of the brain and its impact on later learning goes beyond language acquisition. For example, at the University of California at Irvine, researchers are examining higher-order thinking and spatial reasoning in terms of early neuron electrical activity. They discovered that preschoolers who were taught to play the piano and given singing lessons were later found to have increased abilities to work mazes, draw geometric figures, and copy intricate patterns using two-color blocks. There seemed to be a connection between the brain's activity involving music and mathematical tasks (Begley, 1996).

Other researchers at Rutgers University and the University of California at San Francisco have studied language-based learning disabilities in children, namely, reading problems. Their theory is that reading problems in school-age children stem from earlier auditory distinction problems, the ability to hear the difference between /b/ and /d/, for example. In the auditory cortex of the brain, neurons respond to such differences in microseconds. Among learning-disabled children, the neuron response is 10 times as long as that of normal children. Researchers are working on developing computer-produced sounds that can be used to drill such children in the areas in which they are lacking (Hancock, 1996).

STAGES OF LANGUAGE ACQUISITION

Although it is not absolutely clear how language is acquired, there is agreement on the stages of language acquisition. Roger Brown of Harvard University is among the most well-known scholars in the field of early-childhood language acquisition. Brown and his colleagues conducted a classic longitudinal study of three children, nicknamed Adam, Eve, and Sarah. Tape recorders were placed in the homes of these children; their language was recorded and then analyzed. The methods used by Brown and his colleagues have since become the model for language acquisition research (Brown, 1974; Cazden, 1972). Further studies have confirmed the existence of the following four stages of language acquisition.

Stage 1: Babbling (birth to 12 months). Newborn infants emit a variety of undifferentiated sounds, almost as if they are testing the language spectrum. This form of vocal play is labeled *babbling*. To adults, older siblings, or other language users present, the undifferentiated sounds may eventually become recognizable as phonemes in a particular language. In English, these early significant sounds include both consonants and vowels ("ma ma"). Researcher Patricia Kuhl has measured the electrical impulses of neurons in babies and found that by age 6 months infants have already established "auditory maps" for their own language; by 12 months, the maps are complete (Begley, 1996).

But if the infant is capable of producing a great variety of sounds, why doesn't this variety persist into childhood language? The answer lies in the important role of adults. At some point, the infant begins to reproduce only those sounds to which the adult responds. Donoghue (1990) has called this process "rewarding selective responses." Since only certain sounds or meaningful words receive responses, meaningless language eventually ceases.

Stage 2: Holophrase (12 to 18 months). Around the end of the first year, the child may utter a single recognizable word, called a *holophrase*. In English, common first words are *Mama*, *Daddy*, *cookie*, *bye*, *no*, and *yes*. However, the most significant aspect of such speech is the fact that the child is using this single word to represent an entire sentence. "Mama" may mean "Mama, please pick me up." "Dada" may mean "I want my Daddy now." Holophrases are generally nouns, verbs, or adjectives. Since the child cannot express the entire sentence, the meaning of the holophrase is conveyed by volume, intonation, facial expression, bodily gesture, and the specific situation. Caregivers can thus interpret the meaning of the single word and carry on a conversation with the child.

Stage 3: Pivot–open (18 to 24 months). *Pivot–open* refers to the two-word stage of language acquisition. Like the holophrase, the two words uttered by the child represent an entire sentence in baby talk. The pivot word is derived from a limited grammatical class, such as the personal pronouns *my*, *your*, and *me*. The open word is usually a noun, an almost infinite class of words. Combining the two words results in simple sentences such as "My ball" and "Your cookie." Again, remember that the child is probably trying to say, "Where is my ball?" or "I want your cookie." The meaning of the complete sentence must be inferred from the situational context and the child's facial and body language.

Stage 4: Telegraphic (24 to 40 months). The use of three or more words in the child's language to represent adult speech patterns begins in the *telegraphic* stage. Unlike adult speech, which is generally complete both semantically and syntactically, the telegraphic speech of children retains appropriate semantic elements but omits terms that serve a grammatical function only, terms that linguists call *functors*. Functors include prepositions, conjunctions, and articles. The child in the telegraphic stage of language acquisition might use sentences such as "Me feet cold, Mommy," or "Doggie go home." Like a telegram, the child's speech is missing certain words but retains the most important meaning-bearing terms. Also, as with the earlier stages, meaning is still highly dependent upon context and intonation. During the telegraphic stage, word order becomes important; thus begins the development of syntax (Bloom, 1991).

The telegraphic stage provides important evidence that children can recognize that the purpose of language is to communicate meaning. It also provides evidence that even very young children test hypotheses and revise their speech based on the feedback they get from caregivers. Though such language contains obvious grammatical errors and still sounds like baby talk, the telegraphic stage clearly leads toward the development of adult-sounding speech.

Factors Leading to Adult Language

Over time and with practice, a child's language grows and develops. By age four, many children have a speaking vocabulary of 1,000 words or more and can create an infinite number of sentences. Kantrowitz and Wingert (1985) have noted that these early years of social and language growth are perhaps the most important in a person's life, and they go a long way toward explaining later academic success or failure.

Four factors in particular help explain how a child's language progresses during this period until it becomes similar to the language patterns of adults. These factors are reduction, expansion, extension, and environment.

Reduction is what the child does to the caregiver's language. When the child tries to reproduce what an adult has said, the result is often a reduced version of the adult sentence. For example, father might say to Adam, "Goodbye, Adam. I'm going to work now." Adam might repeat the sentence as "Going work now." Although the sentence itself is reduced, the important meaning is retained. Even at a very early age, the child thus recognizes which are the meaning-bearing words.

Expansion refers to the common phenomenon recorded by Roger Brown and others in which caregivers almost automatically supply missing words in a child's speech patterns. For example, Adam might say, "My cookie gone." His mother would expand the sentence by saying, "Oh, your cookie is gone. Would you like another?" By adding the function word *is*, she expands the child's sentence and unconsciously demonstrates the role of grammar. Expansion is thus one way of stretching the child's speech and modeling standard grammatical sentences.

Extension goes a step further than expansion. In this process, the caregiver expands the child's sentence by adding function words but also extends the dialogue by adding new information. For example, little Eve might tug at her mother's apron and say, "Mommy, dindin good?" Her mother might reply, "Yes, dear, dinner is almost ready. We're having potatoes and chicken. You like that, don't you?" Note that this caregiver is not intentionally trying to teach a specific language pattern; rather, the language learning occurs naturally. What would you predict about a child's language growth if his or her caregivers continually responded with baby talk because they thought it was cute?

When taken together, expansion and extension go a long way toward explaining how children's language develops. They serve to support and encourage language in the young child. As discussed earlier, the verbal interactions between caregiver and child provide the scaffolding, or support network, that the child needs to grow as a language user. Thus, in a very natural manner, scaffolding leads the child forward, encouraging language use and development.

Although some linguists have argued that the most significant unit of language is the word, language acquisition studies suggest that it is a still larger unit. The linguist David McNeil (1970) has argued that ultimately the acquisition of language comes down to the development of sentences. Conversations take place by employing sentences; meaning is conveyed through sentences. According to McNeil, when children struggle to reproduce or create their own sentences, they are engaged in hypothesis testing of the language based on their innate sense of the sentence. Thus, McNeil, like Chomsky, subscribes to the belief in innate language abilities. McNeil's view about the centrality of the sentence for language development is particularly ironic considering that primary-grade instruction often focuses on the sound and word levels, as in phonics lessons.

The **environment** influences the way in which speech develops. All physically normal children acquire language automatically as long as their environment includes language. The ideal language environment is nonetheless difficult to define. Research studies conducted with young children have concluded that certain aspects of the environment are positive reinforcers of language whereas others are not (Lindfors, 1987). *Positive* environmental reinforcers of language include the following:

- the number of caregiver–child trips into the community
- the number of adults present around children
- caregiver acceptance of the child's communication efforts
- caregiver response to meaning rather than correct form

Negative environmental factors include the following:

- few exposures to community language experiences, such as visits to the grocery store or department store
- greater amount of time spent with other children than with adult language users
- greater amount of time spent watching television than engaging in conversations
- caregiver focus on form rather than meaning during conversation

Language acquisition is an ongoing process. However, educators generally use the term *acquisition* in relationship to the child from ages 1 through 6. This is not to say that the language acquisition process is complete by age 6; some English grammatical structures are not fully acquired until age 10 or 11. Some phonetic combinations, such as the triblend /thr/, are not even developed until the end of the primary grades. Figure 4.6 summarizes aspects of early language and cognitive development.

FIGURE 4.6

Summary of early language and cognitive development.

INFANTS AND TODDLERS

A. Importance of trust

B. Exploring and experimenting

C. Gross motor skills developed through crawling and walking

D. Fine motor skills developed through picking up objects

E. Egocentric; no sharing or waiting

F. Repetitious babbling (leads to speaking)

18-MONTH- TO 3-YEAR-OLDS

A. Major language development

B. Large muscle development (jungle gyms)

C. Lengthened attention span; carry on conversations

D. Vocabulary expands; listen to stories

E. Play with another child or small groups

3-YEAR-OLDS

A. Doing things for themselves

B. Competing with older siblings

4-YEAR-OLDS

A. Small motor skills developing (cutting, painting)

B. Scribbling; listening to others read

5-YEAR-OLDS

A. Improved memory; recognize words

B. Fine motor skills improving (write own names)

6-YEAR-OLDS

A. Interact with peers

B. Comparing to others

C. Speech developed; firsthand experiences

D. Learning by doing

7-YEAR-OLDS

A. Think and solve problems in their heads

B. Reliance on real objects to direct thinking

C. Lengthened attention span

Source: Adapted from B. Kantrowitz & P. Wingert (1985), "How Kids Learn." From *Newsweek*, 4/17/89, © Newsweek Inc. All rights reserved. Reprinted by permission.

Is There a Critical Period for Language Acquisition?

All developmentally normal children acquire language; however, the rate of acquisition and degree of facility with language vary considerably from child to child. In some cases, children even enter school without sufficient language skills to begin reading and writing. This has caused scholars in the field to ask: If a child has never been exposed to language, is there a critical period, an age beyond which language acquisition will not occur?

Obviously this is a difficult area to investigate because all children are exposed to language of some sort. However, there are some documented cases of young children raised in nonhuman speech environments. In 1970, a so-called wild child was discovered in California by a social welfare worker. The child, estimated age 13, was partially crippled, malnourished, and filthy. She could not speak, and she constantly salivated and spat. Obviously she had been severely abused. "Genie," as she is called in the literature, to protect her true identity, was taken by police to the Los Angeles Children's Hospital for what would become years of rehabilitation and special training. There she was studied and befriended by Susan Curtiss, a graduate student in psycholinguistics at UCLA. Over time, Curtiss eventually uncovered the facts behind Genie's early years and wrote a book about her life (Pines, 1981).

Genie was tested, studied, and worked with for years; her progress was videotaped. Curtiss focused her efforts on teaching Genie language. In listening tests, Genie's left ear functioned with 100 percent accuracy, but she had little consistent hearing in her right ear. Tests done on Genie's brain waves also suggested that the right hemisphere of her brain was functioning better than the left. Her tested IQ increased from 38 to 74 over a period of six years. However, on tests of auditory memory (a left-brain function), she still performed like a 3-year-old at the age of nearly 20.

Genie's unusual case raised anew the question of a critical period for language acquisition. Curtiss concluded in the affirmative. She hypothesized that normal hemispheric brain specialization is triggered by language acquisition. Because Genie had not been exposed to language, the left hemisphere of her brain began to atrophy. This meant she became overly dependent on the right side of her brain for all tasks. For example, Genie did learn to communicate by gesture, primarily by pointing. She also acquired some words that she could string in simple telegraphic fashion. However, she never acquired the grammatical principles that, according to Chomsky, underlie language use and are innate to all humans.

The issues of language acquisition and the critical period are still not resolved. Genie's display of nonverbal intelligence, despite her severe linguistic limitations, also raised new questions regarding the relationship between thought and language.

In the 1990s, the most important research done in the area of language acquisition and the existence of a critical period came from the area of neurobiology, or brain research. We now know for certain that the nine months when a child is developing in the mother's uterine environment and the first year of life outside the womb are among the most crucial periods for the individual's later linguistic and intellectual development (Begley, 1996, 1997). Apparently there are "windows of opportunity" when the brain is literally creating itself neuron by neuron, connection by connection. Those "windows" are open for only a short time and then close forever. The proper environment, the proper stimulus at the right moment means that extraordinary learning takes place; conversely, if that opportunity is missed, the language stimulus is not present and crucial learning may be lost forever. Research in the area of language learning, done by Patricia Kuhl of the University of Washington, suggests that the auditory mapping of the brain through heard language in the child's environment is nearly complete by age one (Begley, 1996).

Language Development at Home and at School

The elementary school years are one of the most important periods for language development. During this period, children acquire an enormous speaking vocabulary that will continue to expand rapidly into the middle school years. Researchers believe that this time forms the foundation on which academic subjects (particularly reading and writing) rest (Dickinson & Tabors, 2000). Teachers, too, recognize that it is easier to provide a strong oral language development program in the early grades than to engage in the difficult process of remediation in the middle grades.

The first point to remember is that listening, speaking, reading, graphic interpretations, media, and writing are interdependent on one another. This means that having children listen to tapes and teacher explanations as well as other language interactions leads to improved vocabulary knowledge used in speaking and writing. Reading books, listening to others read books, and discussing them helps children to develop a feel for sentence structure and grammar, which aids the children's writing.

The second point to remember is that all communication needs to be meaningful both at home and in school. When caregivers explain to their child why it is important for him to pick up his room before leaving the house, they expect their child to listen, understand, and perform. While on walks, caregivers point out signs that are important to read for safety's sake, such as Stop, Railroad Crossing, or Do Not Walk. Similarly, in school teachers ask children to read labels such as Boy's Room, Principal's Office, and Supply Closet. Children label their desks and supply kits with their own names to make it easier to find things.

Improving language development early to assist later literacy acquisition is crucial for all students regardless of ethnicity, cultural background, or socioeconomic status. In Brownsville, TX, teachers initiated a successful language development program among the Hispanic children to improve their reading and writing skills. More than 100 children's books were brought into kindergarten and first- and second-grade classrooms to be read aloud by the teachers and shared with the students in unique ways. For example, the children ate bread and jam while they listened to their teacher read *Bread and Jam for Francis*. To develop fluency, the teachers read aloud from Big Books and then asked the children to model their reading. Charts were kept of the books listened to and read. Finally, the children were encouraged to write their own books (Roser, Hoffman, & Farest, 1990).

The work of Shirley Brice Heath and her colleagues at Stanford University also stresses the importance of language development in adolescents in order for them to engage in nonviolent conflict resolutions and for later successful participation as adults in community projects and organizations (Heath, 1998; Heath et al., 1998; Wolf & Heath, 1999). Thus, language development during the early grades is crucial for later achievement in life beyond the classroom.

Understanding how children grow and learn is key for teachers who wish to create a **developmentally appropriate curriculum.** This means recognizing that children learn at different rates even though they are all in the same grade. Thus, effective teachers continually adjust their listening, speaking, reading, and writing activities to meet the needs of the individual students in their classes.

Creating a developmentally appropriate curriculum in which listening, speaking, reading, writing, as well as computer and other technology skills are required is equally important in the middle grades (Finders & Hynds, 2003). Teachers often integrate these areas by teaching through units of study spread out over a few weeks that allow older students to do research in the library, work in cooperative groups, and present their findings in both oral and written form to the entire class. For more middle school ideas, see the Middle School Teaching Institute website at www.scu.edu/education/msti/index.html.

Here are some classroom activities that can be used to enhance language development as well as literacy skills:

- *Word walls:* Cover one wall in the classroom with butcher-block or chart paper. Add words on a daily basis. Encourage students to write a favorite word. Add key vocabulary terms from subject areas. Elementary teachers often organize the word wall alphabetically, but words can also be organized by units.
- *Classroom congress:* Organize the class into committees responsible for different aspects of class governance: supplies, room arrangement, group projects, study skills and test preparation, disruptive behaviors. Each day have a different committee report on its findings to the class.
- *Dramatic role-playing:* Divide the students into groups based on the different books they are reading. Allow time in class for the groups to get together to talk about the books (called reader response or literature groups). Periodically have each group perform a brief dramatic reading or recitation (similar to readers theatre) in front of the class.
- *KWL activity:* To introduce units of study on any topic at any grade level, create KWL charts: What do we Know? What do we Want to know? What have we Learned? Display these charts in the class and add to them as the unit progresses.

Halliday and Language Development

One way to conceptualize the role of language development is to refer again to the work of the British linguist Michael Halliday. According to Halliday (1982), language development includes three interrelated aspects:

1. *Learning language.* Children interact with adults and other children to construct their own language system using the symbols and functions of oral speech. The same process occurs in learning written language through modeling, experimentation, and trial and error, with the focus on meaning.
2. *Learning through language.* Children use language in school and in their communities to learn about the world and to acquire new knowledge and information. Through speaking, reading, and writing in content-area subjects, they discover that language is a tool to enhance thinking and understanding.
3. *Learning about language.* As they use language, children become aware of its nature and the various forms it can assume. They appreciate language jokes, puns, riddles, and advertisements that utilize plays on words. They recognize irregular spellings in advertisements that are used to catch a customer's attention, as in *Kountry Kitchen.* They use the language of grammar (nouns, verbs, subjects, clauses, and so on) to talk about their writing with other writers.

Halliday stressed that these three aspects of language development occur simultaneously and often subconsciously. They occur most naturally when children participate in a classroom social environment in which language is used in positive and meaningful ways.

It should be clear by now that children's language develops greatly during the early school years. By the end of this period, the phonological system is nearly complete. Syntactic development continues through exposure to reading and practice in writing. Morphological development, particularly vocabulary in content areas, also expands greatly during this period. However, in every classroom there are some children who experience difficulties using language. This may be because these youngsters come from homes in which English is not spoken, in which adults believe children should be seen and not heard, or in which there is little printed material. These students can be recognized by their inability to express themselves verbally and by the concomitant problems they encounter in learning to read and write.

TECHNOLOGY AND WEBSITES

Just as teachers must understand the uniqueness of the English language, they also need to be knowledgeable about some of the generic factors that earmark high-quality software, such as written documentation or instruction, adequate graphics and print, and a certain amount of user-friendliness. Teachers also need to be very clear about what they want the software to accomplish for their students and how well particular software complements their views about reading and writing. If teachers are emphasizing an integrated or comprehensive approach to reading and writing, it is likely they will concentrate more on word processing and computer tools than on drill-and-practice software, which is more appropriate for a separate skills orientation to the language arts. In other words, teachers need to set their goals first; then they need to search for high-quality software to facilitate meeting those goals.

One way of initiating the search for software is to review articles about and critiques of software in computer magazines, educational computing magazines and journals, and specific software directories. Teachers may want to consult some of the following resources:

EDUCATIONAL COMPUTING MAGAZINES AND JOURNALS

Classroom Computer Learning

Computers in Schools

Electronic Learning

Teaching and Computers

Computers and Education

Computing Teacher

Education Computer News

SOFTWARE DIRECTORIES

Microcomputers in the Classroom: A Compendium of Courseware Reviews
Pro-Ed, 5341 Industrial Oaks Boulevard, Austin, TX 78735

Software Evaluation Exchange Dissemination (SEED)
200 Park Offices/Suite 204, Research Triangle Park, NC 27709

Only the Best
Education News Service, P.O. Box 1789, Carmichael, CA 95609

TESS: The Educational Software Selector
Epie Institute and Teacher's College Press, Box 839, Water Mill, NY 11976

MAGAZINES AND JOURNALS

Instructor

Language Arts

Learning

The Reading Teacher

However, teachers should not rely on someone else's review to decide whether a piece of software is appropriate for their students. To make a software evaluation uniform and efficient, teachers may want to use the form found in Figure 4.7.

FIGURE **4.7**

Software evaluation form.

Name of program _____

Publisher _____

Copyright _____ Cost _____

Computer and memory required _____

Grade level(s) _____

Type of computer program (check as many as are applicable):

☐ Drill-and-practice   ☐ Test development

☐ Tutorial   ☐ Programming

☐ Simulation   ☐ Management

☐ Information processing or retrieval   ☐ Creativity

☐ Problem solving   ☐ Gradebook

☐ Teacher utility   ☐ Game format (graphics, music)

Other _____

PROGRAM ANALYSIS

1. Is the content of the program accurate as well as relevant to language learning?

   _____

2. Are the program's stated objectives compatible with your curriculum objectives?

   _____

3. Does the program reflect the current research on language learning?

   _____

4. Is the program skills oriented?

   _____

5. Does the program involve extended reading and writing?

   _____

6. Will the program be motivational for your students?

   _____

7. Does the program make provisions for special-needs students in your class?

   _____

8. Does the program have adequate documentation?

   _____

FIGURE   **4.7**

Continued.

9. Does the program have features that will make it easy for you and your students to use?

Appropriate difficulty level

Proper print size

Appropriate graphics

Effective feedback

User control of the pace of the program

Ability to save

Ability to self-correct any mistakes

Help commands

Teacher utility package

Management options

10. Are there guides for both the teacher and the students?

11. Is this computer program the best way to achieve the desired learning?

12. Is the program cost-effective for your classroom program?

Source: Based on questions raised by E. Balajthy (1986), *Microcomputers in Reading and Language Arts.*

www.slanguage.com

This site gives the various dialects for the regions of the United States.

www.exploratorium.org/memory/index.html

This site permits one to explore a museum and to play games that expand the brain.

www.newhorizons.org

This site hosts a compendium of full-text articles and resources, including articles about brain research.

www.cnbc.cmu.edu/OtherTrain

This site links to many centers, research groups, laboratories, and institutes studying how the brain works.

www.musica.uci.edu/index.html

This site helps answer questions like these: What effect does music have on learning? Should I play Mozart to my unborn baby? How does music affect emotion?

www.billnye.com

Bill Nye the Science Guy provides teachers with excellent ideas and suggestions for integrating science activities into all other subject areas including the language arts.

www.ctw.org

This is the home page for the Sesame Street workshop. It provides many activities and ideas for preschool and early elementary grades.

www.pbskids.org

This is the home page for public television's educational programs such as "Arthur" and "Clifford the Big Red Dog." Good elementary grade ideas are formed here.

www.disney.com

This is the home page of Walt Disney Company. It provides general and specific classroom ideas for all grades.

Summary

Many of the major issues in the field of linguistics have implications for the language arts classroom. Teachers must have some working definition of language. Knowing something about the history of the English language can also give students a greater appreciation for how language has changed over time and is continually changing.

The work of Vygotsky, Bruner, and Piaget has also had an impact on classroom practices in the language arts, particularly in pointing out the significance of oral language development and social interaction. Similarly, the Behaviorist, Innatist, and Pragmatist Theories of language acquisition are important for teachers to remember. Knowledge of these theories, as well as an understanding of language development and the issues surrounding nonstandard English, should also influence instructional practices.

ACTIVITIES *with children*

Picture Writing

The letters on a page are symbolic representations to which people have assigned meaning. Other languages use different symbols; for example, the Egyptians used pictures to present words and ideas. Create your own language combining pictures and letters to spell out secret messages; for example, a picture of an eye could stand for the pronoun *I*.

Mapping Language

Identify some common English words that have been derived from other languages, such as *patio, rodeo, pretzel,* and *boulevard.* Then draw a map of Europe and identify the countries from which these words came. Have your students work in groups to come up with as many foreign word borrowings and their countries of origin as possible.

Language Recordings

Discuss with your students the various language differences or dialects that people use. Then tape-record the speech of the children. Have them analyze their own speech. Tape-record speech samples from students and teachers in other classes. How many different dialects do you notice?

Language Development

With permission from caregivers and/or teachers, go to day care centers, preschools, and kindergarten classrooms and record the children's speech as they play with you and with their peers: 1-year-olds, 18-month-olds, 2-year-olds, 3-year-olds, 4-year-olds, 5-year-olds, and a kindergarten class. Take note of how language develops. Also note how they use language as described by Halliday.

RELATED READINGS

Allington, R. (2001). *What matters for struggling readers.* New York: Longman.

Brandt, R. (1997). On using knowledge about our brain: A conversation with Bob Sylwester. *Educational Leadership, 54*(6), 16–19.

This article explains how magnetic resonance imaging gives mankind the ability to see inside the human brain. It discusses which part of the brain is used for various functions.

Dixon-Krauss, L. (ed.). (1996). *Vygotsky in the classroom: Mediated literacy instruction and assessment.* White Plains, NY: Longman.

This book, written by various researchers, gives a biographical sketch of Vygotsky and explains how his theory of learning applies to Western literacy instruction. Chapter 6 explains how children use language to learn.

Leu, D. (2000). Literacy and technology: Deitic consequences for literacy education in an information age. In M. Kamil, P. Mosenthal, P. Pearson, & R. Barr (eds.), *Handbook of reading research.* Mahwah, NJ: Erlbaum.

Savage, J. (2001). *Sound it out: Phonics in a balanced reading program.* Boston: McGraw-Hill.

Schunk, D. (1996). Cognitive learning and complex processes. In D. Schunk, *Learning theories: An educational perspective.* Upper Saddle River, NJ: Prentice Hall.

This chapter explains the concept of learning based on constructivism. It also explains metacognition and how it affects the child's learning.

Stull, A., & Ryder, R. (1999). *Education on the Internet: A student's guide.* Upper Saddle River, NJ: Merrill/Prentice Hall.

Trelease, J. (2001). *The read-aloud handbook* (4th ed.). New York: Penguin Books.

Trelease explains the importance of reading aloud to young children. He posits that a child's vocabulary is enhanced by a caregiver reading to children and talking about books. He provides lists of books that are good for each age.

Listening and Speaking

This chapter discusses the major components of listening and speaking and the importance of giving students the opportunity to develop these skills. Specific teaching strategies and activities are provided.

CHAPTER OBJECTIVES

After reading this chapter, you should be able to accomplish the following objectives:

1. Discuss the different types of listening.

2. Describe the four levels of questioning.

3. Describe some strategies to help develop students' listening skills.

4. Explain how teachers can help students develop their speaking skills.

5. Discuss some strategies to help develop students' vocabulary.

CHECK YOUR BACKGROUND KNOWLEDGE. Before reading the chapter, complete the K-T-W-L chart based on the chapter overview and objectives provided at left. In column "K," write what you know about the topics in the objectives. In column "T," write what you think you know. In column "W," write what you want to learn. Finally, after you have read the chapter, write what you have learned in column "L."

Know	**T**hink you know	**W**ant to learn	**L**earned

Developing Listening Skills

This discussion begins with listening because listening comes first: It is the first skill exercised by an infant. The child hears and begins to understand language before he or she can speak, read, or write. Thus, listening is really the starting point for all the other communication skills.

LISTENING DEFINED

Most people tend to take listening for granted because it is something everyone does unconsciously. Yet despite its universal nature, listening is often misunderstood. For example, many teachers make the assumption that a child who hears well is a good listener and therefore does not require instruction in listening. This is a false assumption because hearing and listening are not the same. Hearing is a physical act that involves the reception of sound waves through minute vibrations in the outer, middle, and inner portions of the ear. **Listening,** on the other hand, is a mental process; it involves the active conversion of sound waves into meaningful information by the brain.

This definition of listening should be examined in a bit more detail. As a mental process, listening depends more on the brain than on the ear. A person must have good hearing to initiate the listening process, but unless the brain is actively engaged, the sounds heard remain mere sounds. Bauman (1987) has suggested that listening involves the brain in a search for meaning amid all the sounds that the ear picks up. How many college students have sat through an hour-long lecture and left the room without understanding a thing? They heard the words, but they were not listening.

The other major point to remember is that listening cannot be separated from speaking. Listeners and speakers are interdependent: They rely on each other for the creation and exchange of information. Listening and speaking are also the twin pillars of language that lead children toward literacy.

BACKGROUND RESEARCH IN LISTENING

There has not been a great deal of research in listening skills in recent years. However, today's educators agree that active involvement following a listening activity is more effective than a passive activity (Hoyt, 2000; Miller, 2000; Pinnell & Jaggar, 1992). Miller (2000) found that the typical person listens to only about 50 percent of what he or she receives, and comprehends only 25 percent of that information.

LISTENING AS PROCESS

Many researchers have described the steps that a person goes through from the time sounds are heard in the environment to the conversion of those sounds into meaningful information by the brain (Jalongo, 2000). Freshour and Bartholomew (1989) reviewed the earlier literature on listening and came up with the following six steps in the listening process: receiving, attending, understanding, analyzing, evaluating, and reacting.

Receiving. The listening process begins when a person receives sounds from the environment. This is basically the act of hearing. Picture a group of graders listening to the teacher read Beatrix Potter's classic *The Tale of Peter*. They receive the words of the story, but they also hear other sounds: the sounds of a car horn in the street, the banging of a classroom door, children laughing in the halls, chairs scraping as their occupants fidget.

2. Attending. As the story of Peter's adventures continues, the children begin to pick up on certain details, such as the names of the other rabbits and the description of the farmer's garden. The students now choose from the many sounds in their environment and attend to the voice of their teacher. They try to focus their attention on the story. But from time to time, they still become distracted by the other sounds of the environment. Attending is an ongoing process that must be checked by the teacher periodically. Eventually, however, attending means self-monitoring, paying careful attention to the task at hand.

3. Understanding. The purpose of listening is to understand the message heard. Pictures or mental images of the activities of the little rabbits, Mr. Mac-Gregor's garden, Peter's escape, and so on should all be forming in the minds of the listeners. The words should be shaping themselves into thought. Understanding occurs gradually as the brain receives more and more information. As understanding increases, it becomes easier for the listener to attend, to focus, to block out extraneous noises. But attention does continue to wander, even in older students, which is why people must continually monitor their listening if they want to understand. Understanding requires self-discipline.

4. Analyzing. Meaningful listening requires thinking about what is heard. Analysis is an aspect of understanding that involves raising questions about the validity of the information received. The first-graders in this classroom are familiar with Peter Rabbit. They know what is supposed to happen next and are already predicting the sequence in their minds. If their teacher changes a scene or misreads a sentence, they recognize it because the alteration does not fit their analysis and expectations.

5. Evaluating. As the teacher reads aloud, she is communicating a message, in this case, the events of a particular story. The student listeners either accept or reject that message. If they are interested in the story, have focused their attention on it, and are not easily distracted, they can evaluate the actions of the characters and cheer for Peter's escape or question whether going into the garden without permission was the right thing to do. Evaluative understanding demands concentrated involvement.

6. Reacting. True understanding only comes when the listener reacts or responds to the message in some way. Emotional response, such as clapping at the end of a happy story or booing the entrance of a villain (such as the Big Bad Wolf in *Little Red Riding Hood*), is one type of reaction. Engaging in a discussion about the story after it has been read is another. Doing a creative follow-up activity, such as writing a sequel to the story or making a drawing featuring Peter Rabbit and his family, is still another way of reacting to content heard. Reacting can also include physical activity, such as role-playing a story heard. In each of these cases, the children must be able to remember the details of the story in order to react to it; thus, memory is also a crucial part of the understanding process.

CREATING A POSITIVE ENVIRONMENT FOR LISTENING

Teachers want their students to be active, responsive listeners but often are not sure how to accomplish this objective. It is important that they begin by creating an *emotional environment*, or positive climate, in which children see a purpose for and feel comfortable with exercising their listening skills. The Classroom Vignette that follows illustrates how one teacher changed her approach to listening.

VIGNETTE in the classroom

Linda Paul has been teaching in the same school for five years, the last three years in second grade. Her students like her, her colleagues respect her, and she receives favorable ratings from her principal. But Linda is dissatisfied with her performance. Too often she comes home frustrated and disappointed.

"There's something wrong with my teaching," she tells a colleague one day over coffee in the teachers' lounge. "I know it, but I can't put my finger on the problem. Maybe I'm just burned out after five years."

"No way, Linda. You're one of our best teachers. I think you're being too hard on yourself. But if you like, I'll observe in your class this week. I've got a break period on Wednesday afternoon."

Wednesday arrives. Linda is a bit nervous, but once she starts her lesson, she forgets about her colleague sitting quietly in the back. The lesson goes well. Linda introduces a story and then reads part of it aloud to the class. She leads the class in a brief discussion and then helps the students get started in the follow-up activities. Linda is satisfied that the lesson was a success. After school, she waits outside the building to catch up with her friend.

"Linda, that was a great lesson," says the colleague, "but I think I know what the problem is that you couldn't quite identify."

"Go ahead; I'm waiting."

"Well, it's just that you don't listen to the kids."

"I what?"

"You don't listen to them. You talk to them, you direct them, you guide them, but you rarely listen to what they have to say. Or else you listen for a brief while and then cut them off because there's something more important you must do."

"Maybe you're right. I think what gets me most frustrated is when I'm reading or speaking to the children and they aren't listening to me. Perhaps I've taught them not to listen. You've really given me something to think about."

Linda is actually more upset than she appears. She tells her husband what happened, what her friend observed. They talk late into the evening, and Linda is unable to sleep. Instead she gets up, fixes herself some hot cocoa, and sits down at the kitchen table to ponder the issue of listening. An hour later, she has created a self-checking listening list, shown in Figure 5.1.

The teacher in this Classroom Vignette is engaging in reflective teaching. She has taken time out to stop and think about her own performance in the classroom. She has analyzed the problem areas and even asked the help of a colleague. She has formulated a plan to check her own teaching behavior, a form of teacher self-monitoring. In so doing, she has begun to model for her students the practices of a good listener.

FIGURE 5.1

Linda's listening list.

	Yes	No
Did I listen to my students today?	☐	☐
Did I interrupt student talk?	☐	☐
Did I dominate class discussions?	☐	☐
Do I look at the children when they speak?	☐	☐
Do I listen to all children, those with special needs and others?	☐	☐
Do I remember what they've told me?	☐	☐
Do I think about (reflect on) what the students say?	☐	☐
Do I face my body to the child who's speaking?	☐	☐
Do I show by my facial expression that I am listening?	☐	☐

TYPES OF LISTENING

Children listen for a variety of purposes and in a variety of situations. Teachers who recognize this try to identify the different types or kinds of listening activities that go on during the school day. When teachers can categorize the different types of listening, they can better integrate listening instruction within the entire curriculum. Miller (2000) classified listening into five categories:

1. **Discriminative listening** is listening in order to differentiate sounds in the environment and speech sounds.
2. **Purposeful listening** is when the listener attends to information and directions given by the speaker and then responds to the information.
3. **Creative listening** stimulates the listener's emotions and imagination.
4. **Critical listening** involves the listener's ability to understand the information presented by the speaker, evaluate the information, and formulate opinions about the information.
5. **Appreciative listening** is listening for pleasure. It may be listening to music, the rhyme and rhythm in poems, and the humor or suspense in a story.

In and beyond the classroom

Using Linda's list in Figure 5.1, observe a classroom teacher's listening behaviors. Add other listening behaviors as you see them. Does the teacher create a good classroom climate for listening? If so, how? Is there evidence that the teacher's listening behaviors carry over to the students' listening behaviors?

INTEGRATING LISTENING INTO THE CURRICULUM

A good listening program is integrated throughout the curriculum, and understanding the relationships between listening and reading, listening and speaking, and listening and writing is a good place to start that integration.

Listening and Reading

Recall that listening and reading are dual aspects of the receptive process, the way in which people receive information. Data received through listening or reading must be converted by the brain into meaningful information. Thus, both listening and reading are active, cognitive processes because both involve thinking in the search for meaning.

Constructing meaning from sounds (listening) or print (reading) requires that the listener or reader be familiar with language. For example, not knowing the meaning of the term *parallelogram* places the geometry student at a severe disadvantage in solving word problems. An inability to remember larger units of meaning, such as phrases, sentences, and paragraphs (either orally or in writing), further handicaps the student. Reflect on the following example. A student hears or reads a sign proclaiming *We are in support of striking Afghan hemp workers* and is confused. Do the creators of the sign support people refusing to work, or do they favor hitting these workers for poor performance? If the student cannot recall the context of the sentence, he or she is lost.

When comparing listening and reading, teachers remark that poor listening abilities often lead to problems in reading. For example, children who cannot comprehend a sentence that is read to them will likely also fail to comprehend it when they read it silently. Some educators have even argued that remedial readers are also remedial listeners and that both receptive areas need to be addressed.

Listening and Speaking

The most obvious way in which listening and speaking are related is that they both share a *common code*. The same sounds or phonemes used by the speaker are heard by the listener, and both must convert those sounds into meaningful units or words in order to communicate. Occasionally students may mishear similar-sounding words, such as *cup* for *cut* or *pen* for *pin*. The latter example may also be a matter of dialect, since some dialects consider *pen* and *pin* to be homonyms. Speakers of nonstandard English who omit the final consonant sounds /t/, /d/, /r/, and /l/ may further confuse the listener by pronouncing the words *fat*, *fad*, *far*, and *fall* all like "fa." The ability to hear fine distinctions among similar but not identical words is known as **auditory discrimination** and is often taught as a readiness skill in kindergarten and the primary grades.

Most children develop a listening/speaking vocabulary that exceeds their reading/writing vocabulary. This is only natural. Every day students hear and use words and expressions that they may not recognize easily when they read or be able to recall when they write. The common vocabulary of listening and speaking must later be transferred to the realm of print. This process is described later in the chapter.

Listening and Writing

Listening is part of the receptive process; writing is part of the productive process. Thus at first glance, it appears that the two are not closely related. But listening and writing are associated and actually support one another. For example, young writers often have difficulty recalling ideas and words they wish to use in writing. They then engage in **internal listening,** a process similar to speaking to themselves, to stimulate thought and memory. Some children even mouth the words they hear inside their heads before putting them down on paper. Even adults often listen to an inner voice to aid comprehension, especially when trying to write or read a particularly difficult passage. Finally, professional writers often read their own writing aloud, just to hear if it sounds the way they imagined it would.

Teaching Listening in the Classroom

Some educators are divided over whether or not listening should be taught as a separate skills lesson or as part of integrated content lessons. This text takes the position that listening instruction should be an integral part of content areas and should always be related to speaking, reading, and writing. This does not exclude direct instruction in listening skills but places such instruction in proper perspective: Listening is always done for a purpose, not just for the sake of listening.

Before considering specific teaching strategies related to listening, keep in mind some general guidelines. First, as with all lessons, you should have a specific purpose as you begin instruction, and that purpose should be communicated clearly to the class. The purpose or aim can be stated verbally or written on the chalkboard. For example, a teacher who reads a story aloud or plays a recording of a children's book might give the following mini-lesson: "Today I want you to listen carefully as you hear about the adventures of three characters. See if you can detect clues as to who the hero of the story will be. Later we will discuss and write our own hero stories."

In addition to setting a purpose for listening, keep the following five tips in mind:

1. Model good listening habits yourself: Listen to your students; maintain eye contact with the speaker; nod or show some facial expression to indicate you understand what the student is saying.
2. Before speaking, make sure you have everyone's attention. Stop speaking if you think the students are not listening attentively.

CHECK YOUR BACKGROUND KNOWLEDGE. Before reading the chapter, complete the K-T-W-L chart based on the chapter overview and objectives provided at left. In column "K," write what you know about the topics in the objectives. In column "T," write what you think you know. In column "W," write what you want to learn. Finally, after you have read the chapter, write what you have learned in column "L."

Know	Think you know	Want to learn	Learned

Developing Listening Skills

This discussion begins with listening because listening comes first: It is the first skill exercised by an infant. The child hears and begins to understand language before he or she can speak, read, or write. Thus, listening is really the starting point for all the other communication skills.

LISTENING DEFINED

Most people tend to take listening for granted because it is something everyone does unconsciously. Yet despite its universal nature, listening is often misunderstood. For example, many teachers make the assumption that a child who hears well is a good listener and therefore does not require instruction in listening. This is a false assumption because hearing and listening are not the same. Hearing is a physical act that involves the reception of sound waves through minute vibrations in the outer, middle, and inner portions of the ear. **Listening,** on the other hand, is a mental process; it involves the active conversion of sound waves into meaningful information by the brain.

This definition of listening should be examined in a bit more detail. As a mental process, listening depends more on the brain than on the ear. A person must have good hearing to initiate the listening process, but unless the brain is actively engaged, the sounds heard remain mere sounds. Bauman (1987) has suggested that listening involves the brain in a search for meaning amid all the sounds that the ear picks up. How many college students have sat through an hour-long lecture and left the room without understanding a thing? They heard the words, but they were not listening.

The other major point to remember is that listening cannot be separated from speaking. Listeners and speakers are interdependent: They rely on each other for the creation and exchange of information. Listening and speaking are also the twin pillars of language that lead children toward literacy.

BACKGROUND RESEARCH IN LISTENING

There has not been a great deal of research in listening skills in recent years. However, today's educators agree that active involvement following a listening activity is more effective than a passive activity (Hoyt, 2000; Miller, 2000; Pinnell & Jaggar, 1992). Miller (2000) found that the typical person listens to only about 50 percent of what he or she receives, and comprehends only 25 percent of that information.

LISTENING AS PROCESS

Many researchers have described the steps that a person goes through from the time sounds are heard in the environment to the conversion of those sounds into meaningful information by the brain (Jalongo, 2000). Freshour and Bartholomew (1989) reviewed the earlier literature on listening and came up with the following six steps in the listening process: receiving, attending, understanding, analyzing, evaluating, and reacting.

1. Receiving. The listening process begins when a person receives sounds from the environment. This is basically the act of hearing. Picture a group of first-graders listening to the teacher read Beatrix Potter's classic *The Tale of Peter Rabbit.* They receive the words of the story, but they also hear other sounds: the sounds of a car horn in the street, the banging of a classroom door, children laughing in the halls, chairs scraping as their occupants fidget.

2. Attending. As the story of Peter's adventures continues, the children begin to pick up on certain details, such as the names of the other rabbits and the description of the farmer's garden. The students now choose from the many sounds in their environment and attend to the voice of their teacher. They try to focus their attention on the story. But from time to time, they still become distracted by the other sounds of the environment. Attending is an ongoing process that must be checked by the teacher periodically. Eventually, however, attending means self-monitoring, paying careful attention to the task at hand.

3. Understanding. The purpose of listening is to understand the message heard. Pictures or mental images of the activities of the little rabbits, Mr. MacGregor's garden, Peter's escape, and so on should all be forming in the minds of the listeners. The words should be shaping themselves into thought. Understanding occurs gradually as the brain receives more and more information. As understanding increases, it becomes easier for the listener to attend, to focus, to block out extraneous noises. But attention does continue to wander, even in older students, which is why people must continually monitor their listening if they want to understand. Understanding requires self-discipline.

4. Analyzing. Meaningful listening requires thinking about what is heard. Analysis is an aspect of understanding that involves raising questions about the validity of the information received. The first-graders in this classroom are familiar with Peter Rabbit. They know what is supposed to happen next and are already predicting the sequence in their minds. If their teacher changes a scene or misreads a sentence, they recognize it because the alteration does not fit their analysis and expectations.

5. Evaluating. As the teacher reads aloud, she is communicating a message, in this case, the events of a particular story. The student listeners either accept or reject that message. If they are interested in the story, have focused their attention on it, and are not easily distracted, they can evaluate the actions of the characters and cheer for Peter's escape or question whether going into the garden without permission was the right thing to do. Evaluative understanding demands concentrated involvement.

6. Reacting. True understanding only comes when the listener reacts or responds to the message in some way. Emotional response, such as clapping at the end of a happy story or booing the entrance of a villain (such as the Big Bad Wolf in *Little Red Riding Hood*), is one type of reaction. Engaging in a discussion about the story after it has been read is another. Doing a creative follow-up activity, such as writing a sequel to the story or making a drawing featuring Peter Rabbit and his family, is still another way of reacting to content heard. Reacting can also include physical activity, such as role-playing a story heard. In each of these cases, the children must be able to remember the details of the story in order to react to it; thus, memory is also a crucial part of the understanding process.

CREATING A POSITIVE ENVIRONMENT FOR LISTENING

Teachers want their students to be active, responsive listeners but often are not sure how to accomplish this objective. It is important that they begin by creating an *emotional environment*, or positive climate, in which children see a purpose for and feel comfortable with exercising their listening skills. The Classroom Vignette that follows illustrates how one teacher changed her approach to listening.

VIGNETTE
in the classroom

Linda Paul has been teaching in the same school for five years, the last three years in second grade. Her students like her, her colleagues respect her, and she receives favorable ratings from her principal. But Linda is dissatisfied with her performance. Too often she comes home frustrated and disappointed.

"There's something wrong with my teaching," she tells a colleague one day over coffee in the teachers' lounge. "I know it, but I can't put my finger on the problem. Maybe I'm just burned out after five years."

"No way, Linda. You're one of our best teachers. I think you're being too hard on yourself. But if you like, I'll observe in your class this week. I've got a break period on Wednesday afternoon."

Wednesday arrives. Linda is a bit nervous, but once she starts her lesson, she forgets about her colleague sitting quietly in the back. The lesson goes well. Linda introduces a story and then reads part of it aloud to the class. She leads the class in a brief discussion and then helps the students get started in the follow-up activities. Linda is satisfied that the lesson was a success. After school, she waits outside the building to catch up with her friend.

"Linda, that was a great lesson," says the colleague, "but I think I know what the problem is that you couldn't quite identify."

"Go ahead; I'm waiting."

"Well, it's just that you don't listen to the kids."

"I what?"

"You don't listen to them. You talk to them, you direct them, you guide them, but you rarely listen to what they have to say. Or else you listen for a brief while and then cut them off because there's something more important you must do."

"Maybe you're right. I think what gets me most frustrated is when I'm reading or speaking to the children and they aren't listening to me. Perhaps I've taught them not to listen. You've really given me something to think about."

Linda is actually more upset than she appears. She tells her husband what happened, what her friend observed. They talk late into the evening, and Linda is unable to sleep. Instead she gets up, fixes herself some hot cocoa, and sits down at the kitchen table to ponder the issue of listening. An hour later, she has created a self-checking listening list, shown in Figure 5.1.

The teacher in this Classroom Vignette is engaging in reflective teaching. She has taken time out to stop and think about her own performance in the classroom. She has analyzed the problem areas and even asked the help of a colleague. She has formulated a plan to check her own teaching behavior, a form of teacher self-monitoring. In so doing, she has begun to model for her students the practices of a good listener.

FIGURE 5.1

Linda's listening list.

	Yes	No
Did I listen to my students today?	☐	☐
Did I interrupt student talk?	☐	☐
Did I dominate class discussions?	☐	☐
Do I look at the children when they speak?	☐	☐
Do I listen to all children, those with special needs and others?	☐	☐
Do I remember what they've told me?	☐	☐
Do I think about (reflect on) what the students say?	☐	☐
Do I face my body to the child who's speaking?	☐	☐
Do I show by my facial expression that I am listening?	☐	☐

3. Try not to repeat a child's response in class. Instead, encourage students to listen to each other and to paraphrase what others have said.

4. During lengthy listening periods, encourage children to take written notes to help them remember what a speaker said.

5. Be aware of how the physical arrangement of your room affects listening comprehension. Are chairs arranged so that students speak face-to-face, or are children continually turning their heads to see the speaker?

Good listening lessons can be taught with a variety of materials. Teachers may tape-record educational programs from the television and then play those tapes in class for students to listen to. A radio can be brought to class when there are special programs of interest for children, such as those regularly featured on National Public Radio. Commercial listening tapes can also be purchased that direct students to listen for specific skill areas such as identifying main characters, inferring details, and drawing conclusions. But most teachers see listening lessons as an ideal vehicle to bring children's literature into the classroom on a regular basis. Particularly for young children, listening to an exciting story read aloud by the teacher is an excellent way to acquire the skills that are needed when reading on their own.

LISTENING ACTIVITIES

It has been argued that many classroom teachers do not stress listening skills or feel comfortable teaching listening. Often such teachers assume that listening skills develop automatically over time. Still others believe that it is sufficient for students to engage in listening practice activities. But research has demonstrated that some systematic instruction is necessary for improvement in listening skills (Miller, 2000). Furthermore, the teaching of listening should not be confined solely to language arts classes. Listening lessons should also be integrated into other content areas, such as math, science, and social studies.

The following listening activities are applicable for any grade. *Creating Competent Communicators: Activities for Teaching Speaking, Listening and Media Literacy in K–6 Classrooms* (Cooper & Morreale, 2003) is an excellent resource for additional listening activities.

Singing Songs and Finger Plays

Listening to songs on audiotapes and then inviting students to sing them is a useful strategy to improve students' listening skills. Listening skills are best developed when students listen to the songs without seeing the words. Songs for young children have repetition or repeated phrases so that they are easy to learn. After listening to the song one or two times, students begin to sing along. One song that is particularly good for developing young children's listening ability is "Little Peter Rabbit Had a Fly upon His Ear" (Beall & Nipp, 1979) because one word is omitted from the song during repeated singing of each verse. Students need to listen carefully as the words are skipped. The song goes as follows:

Verse 1: "Little Peter Rabbit had a fly upon his ear." (Repeat two times.)
"And he flicked it 'til it flew away."

Verse 2: "Little Peter (rest) had a fly upon his ear." (Repeat two times.)
"And he flicked it 'til it flew away."

Verse 3: "Little Peter (rest) had a (rest) upon his ear." (Repeat two times.)
"And he flicked it 'til it flew away."

Verse 4: "Little Peter (rest) had a (rest) upon his (rest)." (Repeat two times.)
"And he flicked it 'til it flew away." (Beall & Nipp, 1979, p. 20)

Figure 5.2 lists resources for children's songs.

FIGURE **5.2**

Resources for children's songs.

Wee Sing: Children's Songs and Finger Plays by P. C. Beall and S. H. Nipp (1979) has 73 classic children's songs and an audiotape.

Eye Winker, Tom Tinker, Chin Chopper by T. Glazer (1973) is a collection of 50 musical finger plays with piano arrangements and guitar chords.

Children's Favorites is an audiotape produced by Music Little People (1987).

Sing Me a Story! Tell Me a Song! by H. Jackman (1999) includes creative curriculum activities for many songs for young children.

Finger Frolics by L. Crowell and D. Hibner (1994) includes songs with finger plays.

Fingerplays for Young Children produced by Scholastic (1996) is a selection of songs with finger plays.

Favorite Fingerplays by G. Kable (1979) has songs with finger plays.

Improvisations

Improvisations are spontaneous "plays" for which students have had no time to prepare. They are given roles and situations and must react immediately. The fewer the details the students are given, the better. Improvisations are good activities for teaching listening because they require students to listen to each other and to react to what the others say. Improvisations also allow students to use their imaginations.

Improvisations can be done in pairs or in small groups. An example of a pair improvisation for older students is to tell Student A that he is a hypochondriac who wants pills and to tell Student B that she is a doctor who opposes medication, but favors therapy. Student A only knows that Student B is a doctor, while Student B only knows that Student A is a patient. An example of a group improvisation is to have Student A be a detective on the scene of a theft. Student B is the thief, while other students are witnesses who think they saw the robbery. No witness knows that Student B is the thief.

More examples of paired and group improvisations can be found at www.tefl.net/lessonplans/imp_group.htm. One book that has appropriate improvisations for elementary students is Marsh Gary Cassidy's *Acting Games: Improvisations and Exercises: A Textbook of Theatre Games and Improvisations*.

Directed Listening–Thinking Activity

Directed Listening–Thinking Activity (DL-TA) is designed to help students develop meaning from stories and to develop story structure as the teacher shares a book with the students. DL-TA follows this format:

1. The teacher reads the title of the book and asks the students to predict what will happen in the story.
2. Students pose questions that they think they will be able to answer after hearing the story.
3. The teacher reads the story, stopping when appropriate to have the students verify their predictions and answer their questions or formulate new ones.

Visualizing the Story

Today, with television, videos, computer screens, and delightful picture books, students are not given many opportunities to visualize settings, characters, and the action of a story. Using a read-along tape without using the book, have the students listen closely to the story on tape. After listening to the tape, invite younger children to draw a scene or character from the story and older students to create a windsock (see Figure 5.3) by drawing a scene or character from the story on the top of the windsock and providing the basic elements of the story on the four streamers. On the first streamer, have students write the title, author, and illustrator; on the second streamer, list the main characters; on the third streamer, give the setting; and on the fourth streamer, give a short synopsis of the plot or list the sequence of events. Appendix A has a list of listening tapes for some stories.

Listening Centers

A good listening center is equipped with cassette tape recorders, headphones, and a variety of read-along tapes with the books. Instruct students to listen to different books on tape and respond to the books by having them write about their favorite part in their journal or draw a picture or respond to a list of teacher-made prompts. If a small group of children listens to the same tape, have the group share their favorite part or character or discuss a set of teacher-made questions.

Teachers can create their own read-along tapes of the class's favorite stories, or they can use commercial tapes. Scholastic (1-800-724-6527 or www.scholastic.com) has a wide selection of books on tape that are suited for beginning readers, and Sundance Publishers, Department 0502 (1-800-343-8204 or www.sundancepub.com) has a wide selection of books on tape that are suited for grades 1–8.

Whose Voice Am I on the Tape?

For this activity, first collect photographs of different school personnel such as the principal, secretaries, cafeteria workers, librarian, physical education teacher, music teacher, computer teacher, art teacher, and custodians. Then ask each of these people to record a short poem on a tape. Encourage each reader to be as expressive as possible. Display the photographs on the chalkboard ledge and write the name of each person over his or her photograph. Have students listen to the tape and match the photograph with the voice. This activity can also be placed in the listening center.

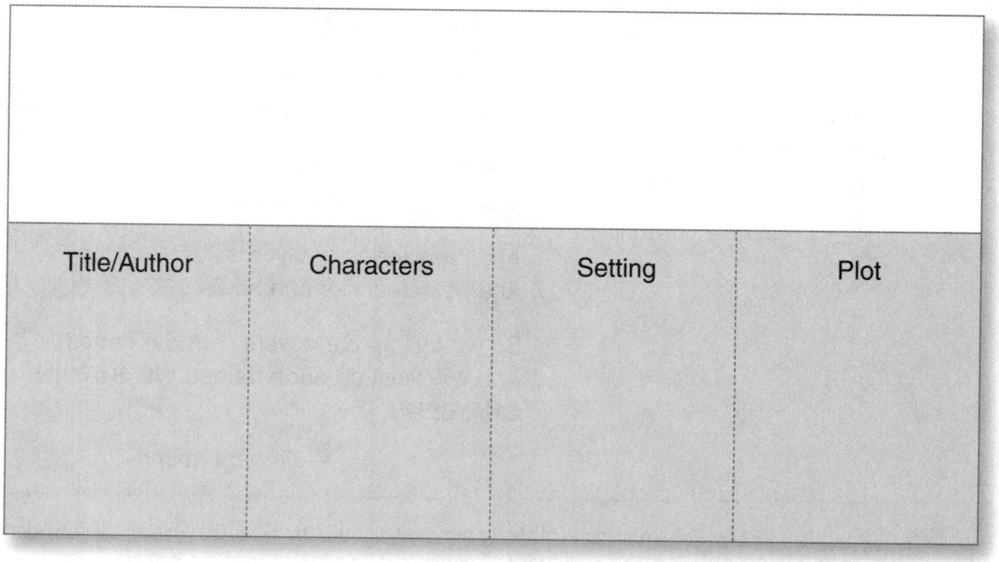

FIGURE 5.3

Windsock template.

Title/Author	Characters	Setting	Plot

Poetry and Music

This activity encourages students to listen for the mood of a poem and then create background sound effects that augment that mood. Working in small groups, have the students first construct "musical" instruments and experiment with various materials to create specific sounds. To make instruments, instruct students to use plastic containers of various sizes and different materials (salt, rice, beans, sand, and so on) to put inside the containers. Different materials in different-size containers create different sounds. For example, by putting salt in a small plastic container, students can create a swishing sound, or by putting lima beans in a larger container, they can create a castanet sound. Students can also crumple plastic bags, aluminum foil, and wax paper to create different sounds.

As a warm-up activity, instruct each group to experiment with the materials by having them create specific sounds. See Figure 5.4 for some examples. Allow the class to vote on which group had the best imitation of the sound, and then have those students explain how they created the sound.

After the groups have had some time experimenting with the instruments, give each group a short poem that includes onomatopoeia and instruct them to use their "instruments" to create background "music" for the poem. Then have them perform the poem for the class by reading the poem and playing the background "music." Figure 5.5 has two poems that work well for this activity. Appendix C has an assessment rubric to use with this activity. Note the assessment is over the process and product.

FIGURE 5.4

Creating sounds with student-made "musical" instruments.

1. Thunder
2. Lightning
3. Running water
4. Galloping horses
5. Snake
6. Airplane

FIGURE 5.5

"Musical" poems.

"Engineers"

Pistons, valves and wheels and gears
That's the life of engineers
Thumping, chunking engines going
Hissing steam and whistles blowing.

There's not a place I'd rather be
Than working round machinery
Listening to that clanking sound
Watching all the wheels go round.

—*Jimmy Garthwaite*

"The Small Ghostie"

When it's late and it's dark
And everyone sleeps . . . shh shh shh,
Into our kitchen
A small ghostie creeps . . . shh shh shh.

We hear knocking and raps
And then rattles and taps,

Then he clatters and clangs
And he batters and bangs,

And he whistles and yowls
And he screeches and howls . . .

So we pull up our covers over our heads
And we block up our ears and WE STAY IN OUR BEDS.

—*Barbara Ireson*

Draw the Design

Throughout all levels of school, students need to follow oral instructions. In this activity, students need to listen carefully to instructions, given by a peer, so that they can duplicate a drawing. This activity also helps develop oral skills because one student must give explicit directions. It is best if the two students are sitting back to back. Have one student explain how to draw a simple design that is on a piece of paper, while the other student listens carefully to the instructions and draws the design. The student who is explaining the design must give the instructions clearly. After all the instructions are given and the partner has drawn the design, have the students compare the design to the original. Figure 5.6 has two examples, one for older students and one for younger students. You can also tape the directions and place the activity in the listening center.

Creating a Junk Box

This is another activity in which students need to carefully listen to instructions. Students should be seated so that they cannot follow their neighbor's folds. Give each student one piece of construction paper or colored paper. Read the directions on how to make a junk box, having the students carefully listen to the instructions and construct the box. Give ample time between steps so that the students have time to complete the folds. Figure 5.7 has the instructions that you will read. You can also tape the instructions and place the tape in the listening center. As you tape the instructions, be sure to give a "stop" signal after each step so that students will stop the tape recorder and complete the step.

Activity for Older Students

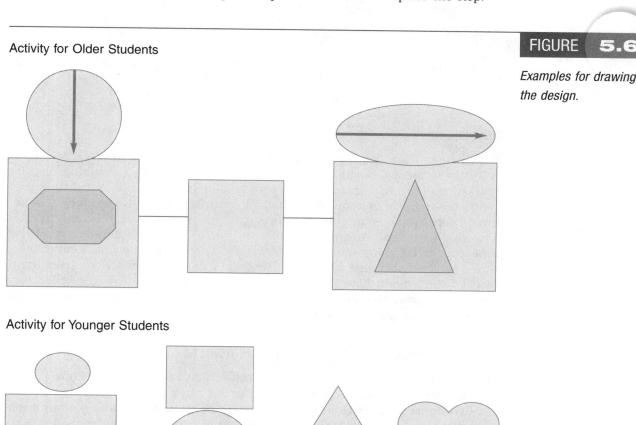

FIGURE 5.6

Examples for drawing the design.

Activity for Younger Students

FIGURE   5.7

Directions for making a junk box.

Each student needs one piece of 8 1/2-by-11-in. construction paper. Read each direction once and pause long enough for the students to complete the folds:

1. Fold paper in half the long way.
2. Unfold.
3. Fold the two long edges to the crease you just made.
4. Unfold.
5. Fold the paper in half the short way.
6. Unfold.
7. Fold the two short edges to the middle.
8. Do not unfold.
9. Look at your paper and see that the two raw edges are in the middle. Three creases go across. Fold in each of the four corners, to line up with the first crease that goes across—not all the way to the middle.
10. The strips of paper in the middle of the paper will not be covered by the corners. Fold the two strips of paper back to hold down the four corners.
11. Put your hands behind the strips in the center of the paper. Gently pull your hands away from each other. Your junk box is now complete.

Two books of origami with easy-to-follow instructions are *Origami Magic* by Florence Temko (1993), published by Scholastic, and *50 Nifty Origami Crafts* by Andrea Urton (1992), published by Lowell House Juvenile.

Advertising

Students are bombarded by advertisements any time they watch television. Advertisers use persuasion to change the viewer's mind or thinking. Because they are so prevalent in advertisements, readers need to understand the propaganda techniques that networks use. First explain and give examples of the seven propaganda techniques listed in Figure 5.8. For younger children, tape the advertisements used during children's programs. For older students, tape advertisements used during sporting events. During national, state, and local election times, you can also tape the advertisements of the politicians. After listening to each advertisement, have students discuss which techniques were used, which ones were persuasive, and why they were so compelling. To assess student's listening, you can use the scoring rubric in Appendix C.

Teacher Questioning for Listening Development

The primary way to teach listening comprehension skills is through questioning. Asking questions after children listen to a recording or hear a passage read to them is a traditional practice. However, the mere asking of questions does not mean that instruction is taking place. In fact, questioning students often resembles assessment, an oral test that students resent. In order to make questioning in the classroom part of the instructional process and not just another means of evaluation, teachers need to know something about the nature of questions.

There are different ways of classifying questions, most of them derived from the taxonomies referred to earlier. But questioning lists, like skill lists, can become lengthy and burdensome. The following hierarchy is intentionally short

Name calling	The use of derogatory labels to denounce, put down, or condemn a person or product. The purpose is to make the listener or reader pull back from the negative image created rather than evaluate the merits of the person or product. Words such as *pinko, commie,* and *cheat* are used in this manner.
Card stacking	Telling one side of the story or presenting only half-truths on an issue. The only information presented paints a favorable picture while omitting unfavorable points. For example, a TV commercial for a popular cereal talks about the vitamins and minerals it contains to give you energy and strong bones. Omitted are the amounts of sugar, preservatives, and food coloring, which weaken muscle tone and rot teeth.
Plain folks	Approach used by many politicians to curry favor, approval, and support by portraying themselves as ordinary people; the "good old boy" approach. Such commercials often feature politicians with their shirt-sleeves rolled up, wearing hardhats; picking crops; and, of course, kissing babies. One former president portrayed himself as an ordinary peanut farmer from Georgia; another had his picture taken chopping wood for the family fire.
Glittering generalities	The use of vague, general, but attractive expressions to paint a positive picture of a person or product without giving specific details or facts. For example, politician Smith begins his speech by introducing his lovely wife, Beth (president of the ladies' club), and his handsome son, Tom (captain of the football team); he then proceeds to describe his own activities as a Boy Scout leader, church deacon, and so on. All this is impressive but may have little to do with the office for which he is running.
Testimonial	A direct assertion by a well-known personality regarding the favorable characteristics of a product or an organization. Movie stars and athletes are used particularly because of their appeal to young people. The power of the technique lies not in what is being sold but in who is doing the selling. Bill Cosby tells kids to get their mothers to buy pudding; Michael Jordan sells sneakers.
Transfer	Similar to testimonial technique but more subtle. A man or woman, usually attractive, is shown using a particular product; then all sorts of positive things happen to that person, generally revolving around the opposite sex. Beer and perfume commercials often use this approach.
Bandwagon	Approach that emphasizes going along with the crowd or being a part of the group; the herd mentality. The appeal is to sameness and conformity, through such expressions as "Everyone who's anyone . . ."

FIGURE 5.8

Some advertising propaganda techniques.

and simple. It contains four different types of questions: literal, inferential, evaluative, and applied.

Literal question. This type of question calls for a response directly found in the material heard or read. This is also called *on-the-line reading* because the answer to the literal question is in the book. Taffy Raphael (1982) called this type the *right there question* because the answer is "right there" in the book. Probably because it is the easiest type of question to ask and answer, most teachers tend to overuse it. Basal reader manuals have also been heavily weighted toward questions focusing on factual information directly stated in the text.

Inferential question. This is a question whose answer must be inferred from the facts given in a story or lecture. The answer is not directly stated and instead must be discovered by examining the literal information. Raphael (1982) called this *think and search*. Inferential questions are considered more difficult than literal questions because they require the student to use and analyze previous information. Often teachers expect students to respond to questions immediately; Gambrell (1983) found that teachers wait about one second for a child to respond. Giving a child an extra few moments to think before responding usually results in a longer and more thoughtful response. This is known as *wait time* or *think time*. As a teacher, you should train yourself to give students this time and avoid the tendency to call on another student if the first student does not respond quickly enough. Research has also shown that most teachers allow less wait time for remedial students than for brighter students (Bromley, 1988). So take time to wait while students think before answering.

> ## Beyond the classroom
>
> Select one of the propaganda techniques and see how many examples of it you can find in a single day. Use newspapers, magazines, radio, television, lectures, and conversations. How might you teach this technique to elementary or middle school students? Record your ideas in your journal and try them out in a classroom.

Evaluative question. This type of question calls for the student to make a judgment about the material heard or read. It is not enough to know what happened in a story or even why it happened. Now the students must also assess the significance of the material in light of their own life experiences. Raphael (1982) called this *on my own*. For instance, a character in a story borrows a friend's bicycle in an emergency without asking permission. It is easy to tell what the character did and why he or she did it, but was this action right? Was it justifiable under the circumstances? Each student must judge this individually by evaluating the information, applying previous knowledge about related situations, and supporting his or her answer.

> *The mediocre teacher tells. The good teacher explains. The superior teacher demonstrates. The great teacher inspires.*
>
> **WILLIAM ARTHUR WARD**

Applied question. This type of question calls for the student to apply the information heard or read to a totally different situation. In most taxonomies, the applied level is the highest level. Students must first remember the literal facts and then infer additional details and make judgments. Finally, they must recall personal experiences and see a connection between what they have experienced and what they have heard or read. Raphael called this *writer and me questions*. For example, after a month-long social studies unit on early explorers and discoverers, a fifth-grade teacher asked his students to write an essay showing the similarities and differences between exploration and discovery in the fifteenth and sixteenth centuries and space exploration in the twentieth century. This final step, making the cognitive connection between two separate experiences, is what makes the applied question so difficult for many students.

To help you better understand the importance of questioning as a teaching strategy, keep the following in mind. Your primary goal as a teacher, regardless of the content you are teaching, is to make children think. Any question that requires a single-word response ("What do you call a word that names a person, place, or thing?"), a yes-or-no answer ("In *The Yearling*, was Jody right in keeping his pet fawn in the yard?"), or only one correct answer ("Who was the first president of the United States?") does not promote in-depth thinking. Such limiting questions are called *closed questions*. They focus on single correct answers, usually at the literal level. A better type of question is the *open question*, which usually has more than one right answer and requires more thinking and support to justify the answer. A closed question may also be opened up through the addition of "Why or why not?"

Asking questions at the various levels is a key part of any teacher's repertoire. In addition, students should be encouraged to ask questions of the teacher and their peers. An activity that involves back-and-forth questioning between teacher and student or among students over common material heard or read is known as *reciprocal questioning*.

Structured Listening Activity

The structured listening activity is an example of the direct, systematic approach to listening recommended by Devine (1982), Pearson and Fielding (1982), and others. It includes concept building, purpose setting, reading or telling, questioning, and recitation (Choate & Rakes, 1987). The following Classroom Vignette exemplifies a structured listening activity.

LISTENING ASSESSMENT

The listening ability of students can be evaluated in a number of ways. Many standardized tests, such as the Durrell Listening-Reading Series or the Stanford Achievement Tests, have a listening subtest. Generally the test requires the teacher or some other examiner to read aloud from printed material. The students listen and then answer multiple-choice literal, inferential, and applied

VIGNETTE *in the classroom*

At the front of Mrs. Lopez's classroom is a large map of Canada. During the previous days, her class has studied the map and brainstormed what they know about Canada. The students made lists of cities and discovered that Canada is divided into large provinces. They listed geographic features such as mountains, rivers, and bays. They also saw a film about animal life in Canada. Then the teacher began reading aloud from E. B. White's *The Trumpet of the Swan*. The story begins with young Sam Beaver and his father on a camping trip in the north woods of Canada. One day Sam discovers a secret pond hidden beyond the swamp. There a pair of swans have chosen to make their nest.

Now Mrs. Lopez picks up the story again. "Today, class, I want you to listen carefully as I read the further adventures of Sam Beaver. If you're good listeners, you might learn some interesting facts about birds." She begins reading: "In the spring of the year, nest-building is uppermost in a bird's mind: it is the most important thing there is. If she picks a good place, she stands a good chance of hatching her eggs and rearing her young. If she picks a poor place, she may fail to raise a family. The female

swan knew this; she knew the decision she was making was extremely important. . . ."

From time to time, the teacher pauses to ask the children a question to keep their attention focused: "What season of the year is it?" (literal). "Why do you think birds and other animals give birth in the spring?" (inferential). "Do you think Sam is doing the right thing by spying on the swans while they build their nest?" (evaluative). "What other things do you think Sam might do on his camping trip? Think of trips you've taken with your family" (applied). "What do you think a *marsh* is?" (vocabulary).

The lesson continues with Mrs. Lopez reading and the students listening. When Mrs. Lopez stops reading, the children get into small groups and begin writing the facts they have learned. On their tables are dictionaries and other science and social studies reference books. Afterward, some of the groups decide to illustrate what they have heard so far. Other students are at the map trying to find the exact location that E. B. White may have used for this story.

In and beyond the classroom

Observe a classroom teacher. What examples of indirect and direct listening instruction do you see? Describe a strategy or an activity that relates to listening. What other opportunities exist in the classroom to relate listening skills to reading, writing, and speaking?

comprehension questions related to the material. There are also vocabulary questions related to specific terms mentioned in the sentence or paragraph.

As an alternative to standardized reading tests, some teachers use informal reading inventories (described in Chapter 6). These tests are administered by one teacher to one student and allow for more accurate assessment. The *Classroom Reading Inventory* by N. Silvaroli (2001) is one popular example of an easy-to-use assessment instrument. This inventory is designed to assess independent, instructional, and frustration reading levels of elementary and middle school students. To determine whether the student can comprehend material at a higher level by listening than by reading, the *Classroom Reading Inventory* includes graded paragraphs as a listening assessment. The teacher reads the passage aloud and then asks the student questions. If the student answers correctly, the teacher reads the passage at the next level of difficulty. This continues until the student cannot answer the questions correctly. The listening capacity level of an individual student is determined in this way (Silvaroli, 2001).

Rubrics are effective ways to assess particular listening activities and to show growth in listening skills. (See Appendix C for some examples.) To create appropriate rubrics, teachers need to consider the specific criterion for each assignment and consider what weight each item has in comparison to the total score. For example, on the rubric for "Musical Poems," the teacher believed that a student contributing ideas and listening to classmates' ideas were of equal importance, but were more important than respecting materials and using indoor or soft-spoken voices. Another teacher may need to give more points for respecting materials and using indoor voices because his or her students have a tendency not to respect materials and they begin to shout when they work in small groups.

Rubrics used to show growth would be more general statements, often based on the state's standards. Teachers use the same rubric from one grading period to the next to indicate student growth. Appendix C contains a listening rubric for fifth grade (Rubric for Indicating Growth in Listening Skills). It is based on Oklahoma's Priority Academic Student Skills (P.A.S.S.), the state's core curriculum.

Developing Speaking Skills

Speaking skills, like listening skills, are often neglected in the classroom or assumed to be an area that does not require instruction or facilitation. Some teachers believe that because children can talk, they can automatically communicate their thoughts. Research has shown this not to be the case (Miller, 2000). In order to communicate effectively through speaking, children must exhibit fluency, clarity, and an awareness of audience. Such verbal communication skills are learned through practice and observation of an effective speaker, such as the teacher.

In addition to the fact that most teachers do not place a high priority on oral language instruction, many teachers feel ill prepared to teach specific speaking activities. The result is that students pass through their elementary years without instruction in or opportunity to practice oral communication skills.

To understand further the importance of speaking activities in the classroom, consider the following: Children with good oral language skills tend to learn to read more easily and to become better readers than other students. This was one of the conclusions reached by Walter Loban (1963) in his classic longitudinal study of children over a six-year period. Similarly, Cox (1984) reviewed the literature on the relationship between reading and oral language and concluded that speaking helps to develop knowledge of word meanings, word parts, and syntax, which are important cues in learning to read.

In addition to reading, writing ability is enhanced through oral language activities. Stoodt (1988) noted that children with strong, effective speaking skills later become good writers. This is because the same language elements used in speaking are found in writing: For every oral construction, there is a written counterpart. Donald Graves (2003), a leading authority on children's writing, also stressed the significant role of oral language, particularly as it is used in the primary school grades, in preparing for or rehearsing written activities. And in her observations of young writers at the Mast Way School in New Hampshire, Jane Hansen (1987) found that children use oral language to learn about their subject, to rehearse aloud what they want to say in their writing, and to develop their ideas through oral conferencing. In short, Hansen concluded that encouraging classroom talk among students has a positive influence on "children's writing, reading and attitude toward learning" (p. 190).

It is generally believed that speech facilitates thought, particularly the higher-level thinking required in problem-solving situations. Vygotsky (1962) argued that talking is one way children come to know things. Psycholinguist Frank Smith (1982b) has contended that when children talk to themselves (inner speech), they are actually facilitating their own thought processes. These researchers have recommended that teachers utilize more small-group activities that permit children to speak to one another as a natural part of the learning process in school.

Finally, the teacher plays a key role—either positive or negative—in the oral language development of students. As far back as 1970, Flanders noted that most classrooms are dominated by teacher talk; nearly two-thirds of the talk in these classrooms is done by the teacher. The message is clear: Teachers talk too much in class and don't listen enough to their students.

Education is a kind of continuing dialogue, and a dialogue assumes different points of view.

ROBERT HUTCHINS

CREATING A POSITIVE ENVIRONMENT FOR SPEAKING SKILLS

For the teacher, the key to encouraging speaking skills in the classroom is creating the proper environment. In a good oral language environment, children feel relaxed, social interaction with peers is encouraged, and cognitive growth occurs. To create a positive oral language environment, set some goals for your speaking skills program. One teacher stated four overall goals for her fourth-grade classroom:

1. to speak clearly with proper pronunciation and enunciation in order to communicate with others
2. to speak expressively with feeling and emotion and avoid the monotone
3. to speak effectively in different situations: with individuals, small groups, and the whole class
4. to utilize speaking in all the communication arts and content areas to further learning

To meet these goals, the teacher organized her instructional program around two requisite criteria: a positive, receptive teacher attitude and a physical environment conducive to language use (Kear & Yellin, 1978; Yellin, 1983a).

Develop a Positive, Receptive Teacher Attitude

Teachers must demonstrate by their behaviors that language use is important, that children should speak in class, and that what they have to say is valuable. Examine the Classroom Vignette that follows and identify the many ways this teacher demonstrates a positive, receptive attitude toward language.

VIGNETTE *in the classroom*

It's 8:15 A.M. in the second-grade classroom of Mrs. Majors. She is at her desk preparing for the day, which does not officially start for another 15 minutes, but already a few students are in the room.

"Hi, Charlie. How was soccer practice yesterday?" she asks one of them.

"It was great, Mrs. Majors. I scored a goal—my first one. And tomorrow we play the Ramblers."

"That's neat. I hope your team wins, Charlie."

"Mrs. Majors, look what I brought," says a girl holding up a jar with a spider inside.

"Wow! Where did you get that spider? It's a beauty."

"I—I mean we, me and my brother—caught it in the garden, with a jar."

More of the students have entered the classroom. Many of them stop by Mrs. Majors's desk to chat with her, to share something, or just to say hi. Whenever a child comes to her, Mrs. Majors puts aside her attendance book or bus forms or whatever she is working on. There will be other times during the day—a few minutes here, a few minutes there—to work on these forms, but when her students speak, Mrs. Majors listens.

Jasmine and her best friend, Aretha, have gone to the bulletin board and are stapling up word cards they brought from home. The bulletin board is entitled "New Words We've Learned." Everyone gets to add a new word each week. The board is already half full, and the students have suggested they should make it larger because they are learning so many new words.

Later in the day, several children talk about a rocket launch they recently saw on TV. Jack says the rocket is called a capsule, but the other students are not sure. "Why, Jack," Mrs. Majors says, "that's a great word. Let's add it to our list." Jack beams as Mrs. Majors prints the word on a card and gives it to him to place on the board. Any time a child uses an unusual word, phrase, or sentence, either orally or in writing, Mrs. Majors calls attention to it and praises the student's originality. Words are valuable in this classroom.

In addition to the bulletin board, there are mobiles hanging from the ceiling containing small cards with spelling words for the students to study. There is also a student-made chart of synonyms, antonyms, and homonyms the children have learned. Yet another chart details the history of some common place-names in the community.

Organize a Physical Environment Conducive to Language Use

The physical arrangement of a classroom that is most conducive to oral language development is organized around learning centers or small-group settings. A center can be a table, a workbench, or just a designated corner of the room. Each center should contain appropriate materials and poster-size instructions for using the center. Key words in the instructions can be highlighted or underlined for easier reading. Centers should be flexible and changed often enough to meet the needs of the students. Through learning centers or small-group activities, each child has the opportunity to participate, to interact with peers in a social learning situation, and to use oral language.

Traditionally classrooms have been whole-group oriented: The teacher is the primary lecturer or questioner, and only a few students have a chance to respond. While whole-class activities may be beneficial in some circumstances, they limit, by their very nature and structure, the amount and freedom of language use by children. Small groups encourage more students to participate, while large groups inevitably become listening situations in which only one person (usually the teacher) has the chance to speak (Kear & Yellin, 1978). Thus, to best encourage the development of speaking skills in young people, a classroom arranged around small groups is always superior to a large-group arrangement.

Small groups can be formed in many ways and are a valuable vehicle not only for enhancing academic learning but also for improving children's social skills. Moffett and Wagner (1991) have suggested five ways in which teachers can organize students into small groups:

1. *Self-selection.* Allow children to form their own groups by peer preference.
2. *Mixed ability.* Create groups of students with varying skill abilities in different areas to cooperate on a single project. This means selecting good readers as well as poor readers, children with artistic talents and those with organizational skills, and so on.
3. *Short-term.* Groups can be self-selected or teacher created for short-term projects, such as making and maintaining a weekly class bulletin board. Once the goal has been achieved or the project completed, the group disbands.
4. *Long-term.* Some projects (such as social studies reports and dramatizations) require the formation of long-term groups that work together on a single project for weeks or even months.
5. *Random.* For brief activities, one way to ensure a heterogeneous mixing of students is through random grouping. For example, have children call off the numbers 1 through 5. Then all the 1s form a group, the 2s another, and so on.

A teacher's ability to organize children into effective learning groups is one of the keys to a successful classroom. One thing for teachers to remember is to change groups throughout the day for different activities. David and Roger Johnson, in their text *Learning Together and Alone: Cooperative, Competitive and Individualistic Learning* (1987), have made a strong research-based case for using cooperative groups in the classroom. Hauchildt and McMahon (1996) found that small discussion groups changed resistant learners into enthusiastic learners when they were given a voice in the learning process. Spiegel (1996) found that when teachers trusted their students during small-group discussion, the students began to have "constructive transactions with the text" (p. 337). Ferguson and Young (1996) found small discussion groups useful with second-language learners as they acquired English. In short, research evidence supports the use of small groups to enhance academic success in reluctant learners, second-language learners, and all learners in general.

SPEAKING SKILLS: STRATEGIES AND ACTIVITIES

Once you have practiced forming groups, arranged your room, and acquired some materials, you are ready to begin instruction in speaking skills. Most oral language instruction takes place indirectly; that is, the teacher creates the positive climate and the motivational activity, and the students do the rest. Creating the climate is accomplished through strategies that the teacher explains to the children. Within each strategy are many activities through which the students practice their oral expression (Yellin, 1983a). An excellent resource for additional activities that enhance oral communication is *Creating Competent Communicators: Activities for Teaching Speaking, Listening and Media Literacy in K–6 Classrooms* (Cooper & Morreale, 2003).

Conversation/Discussion

The conversation/discussion strategy simply seeks to engage children in talk with other children in a relaxed atmosphere. The classroom is the primary place where a child interacts socially with his or her peers; as such, it is the ideal environment in which to prepare each individual to enter the larger society. Socialization skills as well as language are enhanced when students engage in the conversation/discussion strategy.

In and beyond the classroom

In an elementary classroom, gather some children around you in a circle. Explain the guidelines for the conversation strategy and then join the circle as a member. To get the group started, suggest topics such as pets, favorite TV programs, weekend or vacation activities, and favorite sports or hobbies. Remember that once the talk starts, the children do not have to stick to the initial topic. Conversations are intentionally free and open-ended.

Although conversation and discussion are presented as a single strategy, there are some significant differences between them. Conversation is informal, general talk, whereas discussion is more formal, topic-centered talk. The former is often spontaneous and relatively unstructured, whereas the latter focuses on a specific topic or purpose. Conversation and discussion are alike, however, in that they build on the student's home-learned experiences and serve to give practice in pronunciation, fluency, expression, and vocabulary. In addition, because it is nonthreatening, conversation/discussion helps young children build confidence to express themselves orally.

To begin, develop some guidelines for conducting conversation or discussion. Guidelines are most effective when developed cooperatively between teacher and students. One classroom came up with the following four basic rules, which they displayed on a poster:

1. Speak loud enough to be heard in your group but not so loud as to disturb others.
2. Only one person speaks at a time.
3. While one person is speaking, the other members of the group must actively listen to the speaker.
4. No one insults or offends any other member of the group.

A *conversation* is a verbal exchange of diverse ideas; wandering from one topic to another is acceptable as long as a thread of continuity is maintained from one speaker to the next. Conversation flourishes in an atmosphere in which children feel free to speak. Stoodt (1988) has described one second-grade teacher who has three different "talking times" each week. During these times, several students get in a circle and talk about whatever interests them. This is the "inner circle." Sitting around them in the "outer circle" are the rest of the students, who listen and observe. During the next talking time, the groups switch roles as talkers and observers. In this way, the students have the chance both to observe and to practice the skills of speaking in a group.

In the discussion strategy, sticking to the point is essential. The goal of a *discussion* is to reach a conclusion or solve a problem. Moffett and Wagner (1991) have referred to discussion as *task* or *topic talk*. According to them:

> Small group discussion should be a staple, significant classroom process given the same kind of importance and commitment afforded reading or writing activities. It is through discussing that learners face the challenge of defining, clarifying, qualifying, elaborating, analyzing, and ordering experiences, concepts, opinions, or ideas, thereby developing their thinking and verbalizing skills for reading and writing. (p. 85)

Before beginning a discussion, the topic should be clearly defined and understood by all. Usually it is stated in the form of a question such as: Should children have to do chores in order to earn an allowance? Other questions suitable for small discussion groups may arise from children's reading, particularly if they are organized into literature groups in which several children are reading the same book. Often students want to discuss the motives behind a character's actions in a particular story. After reading a book together, each member of the group can write down what she or he thinks lies behind the actions of a particular character. Then they can share and discuss their views with the group.

Additional sources for discussion topics include school events or experiences (How can the cafeteria food be improved?), current events (What can kids do to prevent crimes from occurring in the neighborhood?), and personal problems (How can a youngster learn to get along with a stepparent?). The last of these categories is particularly good for stimulating discussion among young people because all children have problems: problems with schoolwork, parents, siblings, and peers; concerns about their physical appearance; feelings of inadequacy in athletics or in relationships with the opposite sex. One way to initiate this kind of discussion experience is to have the students write their problems in the form of a letter addressed to a confidant. In Stillwater, OK, 12-year-old Shabana Kazi began her own school newspaper column, modeled on "Dear Abby" but aimed strictly at children her own age and younger. A classroom version of "Dear Shabana" can easily be set up, with different students taking turns answering the letters from their peers. The best letters then form the topic for small-group discussions during the week. Figure 5.9 shows an example of Shabana's column.

Dear Shabana

DEAR SHABANA: I'm having a problem on the bus. I like to ride the bus because I have a lot of friends on the bus. But there's this one big high school kid who always makes sure he sits behind me. Then when I'm beginning to enjoy the ride, and am having a chit-chat with my friends, he hits me on the brain. And he does it every day, too. The next time he hits me on the brain, I'm going to punch him on the heart. He gets on my nerves. If I go tell the bus driver on him, he'll probably start laughing at me for being a tattle-tale and a chicken. Should I punch that kid on the heart? — Bullied

DEAR BULLIED: I know what it must be like to have a kid like that on your bus. He probably gives you the shivers. But never fear. I have an idea for you. When you get on the bus with your friends, don't let them sit in the same seat you are in. Have one of your friends sit behind you, another one in front of you and one beside you and so on. That way you will be surrounded by your friends and there will be no room for that high school kid. He will have to sit far away from you. That will keep him from hitting your brain and it will keep you from wanting to punch him on the heart. This should solve the problem.

DEAR SHABANA: I have a problem. I have bad handwriting. All summer, I've been trying my best to improve my handwriting. But I just can't. I can't help it. Nobody likes my handwriting except my little brother who is fascinated with cursive. My older sister says my writing is sloppy. My mom and dad say I need to improve very badly on it. My teacher last year even said it was illegible—I don't want to give my new teachers a bad impression. What should I do?
P.S. help me soon! — Illegible

DEAR ILLEGIBLE: When you are ready to give up, please remember that nothing is impossible. To improve your handwriting, you must take it slow and easy. In the beginning, you must do each letter slowly and carefully. Once that gets easy for you, try doing them a little bit faster. In no time, your writing will have improved immensely. You will feel proud of yourself. It may take time to improve your writing, but you can do it if you try.

Dear Shabana
P.O. Box 967
Stillwater, OK 74076

Source: Stillwater News Press. Reprinted with permission of Shabana Kazi and the *Stillwater News Press.*

FIGURE 5.9

Sample "Dear Shabana" column.

A variation of the discussion strategy was developed by NASA as part of its space education program for upper elementary and middle school students. In this exercise, students are given a survival-type situation to discuss and a form to complete. The form lists various objects important to the survival of the group. The students discuss each item and then try to reach some sort of consensus regarding its importance to their imaginary situation. As they move down the list of objects, the number system changes and consensus becomes more difficult to reach, but the quality of the discussion improves greatly. Figure 5.10 offers a sample situation for this activity.

A more formal approach to discussion is through a **panel discussion;** generally panel members prepare themselves as experts on a particular topic and present various views or aspects of a topic too large for a single child to handle. The other key difference between the panel discussion and other discussion groups is that the panel members address their remarks to an audience. The concept of audience is important because effective speakers always keep their audience in mind: They talk to the audience and adjust their tone and delivery to appeal to the audience. This is true of writers as well as speakers. Moffett and Wagner (1991) have contended that the benefits of having an audience include the fact that "the participants in the discussion have the advantage of feedback on their ideas from the other panelists and feedback on the quality of their interaction from the audience." Teachers who employ unit activities and group projects often use panel discussions to conclude or summarize a unit.

For older students, a debate is another activity. An enjoyable **debate** focuses on a question or issue that involves conflicting views or opposing sides and follows specific rules that must be taught beforehand to the children. Both sides

In and beyond the classroom

During your classroom observation experience, gather a few children and teach them about the debate or panel discussion format. Brainstorm some topics the students are interested in, and help them prepare a short debate or panel discussion. Observe the students and note changes you might make the next time you use this strategy.

FIGURE 5.10

Sample NASA survival activity.

SPACE TRIP TO THE MOON

Instructions: You are a member of a space crew originally scheduled to rendezvous with the mother ship on the lighted surface of the moon. Because of mechanical difficulties, however, your ship was forced to land at a spot some 200 miles from the rendezvous point. During the landing, much of the ship and the equipment aboard were damaged; since survival depends on reaching the mother ship, the most critical items still available must be chosen for the 200-mile trip. Below are listed the 15 items intact and undamaged after landing. Your task is to rank them in order of their importance in allowing your crew to reach the rendezvous point. Place the number 1 by the most important item, the number 2 by the second most important, and so on through number 15, the least important.

_____ Box of matches

_____ Food concentrate

_____ Fifty feet of nylon rope

_____ Parachute silk

_____ Portable heating unit

_____ Two 45-caliber pistols

_____ Life raft

_____ Magnetic compass

_____ Five gallons of water

_____ One case of dehydrated milk

_____ Two 100-pound tanks of oxygen

_____ Map of the stars as seen from the moon

_____ Signal flares

_____ First-aid kit containing injection needles

_____ Solar-powered FM receiver-transmitter

or teams prepare themselves by researching the issue, rehearsing their arguments, and deciding on their debate strategy. Often the teacher serves as moderator, keeping time and directing the back-and-forth presentations. As with panel discussions, the rest of the students serve as the audience in a debate and can actually vote at the end for the team they think presented the most effective arguments.

For both panel discussions and debates, students should keep in mind the following five guidelines (Pinnell, 1984):

1. Research your topic thoroughly using the library and community resources.
2. Remember to support your opinions with facts.
3. Organize your thoughts before you speak and stick to the topic.
4. Use notecards to recall important points but do not read to the audience.
5. Listen carefully to others and react to their remarks.

Making a poster to display these guidelines in the room prevents the teacher from having to repeat them in class.

Transactional Literature Discussions

Dugan (1997) describes transactional literature discussions (TLDs) as an integrated talking, reading, and writing strategy. The TLD is a process that encourages students to discuss their ideas, listen to other opinions, and reflect on what they learned. Following are the six steps with a brief description:

1. *Get ready.* This step includes skimming a number of books to see which one the group would like to read and discuss. Once the book is selected, the group members skim through pictures of picture books or skim chapter titles of chapter books and make oral predictions about the story. They spend time analyzing each other's predictions and test the reasons for each prediction.
2. *Read and stop to think aloud.* The teacher models what he or she is thinking as the group reads in order for students to learn how to think about the text as they read.
3. *Write a response.* Time is given to students to write short responses to the reading on Post-its. These are self-selected responses, not responses to a set of teacher-directed questions.
4. *Engage in a discussion.* Students spend 15 to 30 minutes discussing their responses using the RQL2 strategy (Respond about likes or dislikes; Question aspects of the story they did not understand; Listen to classmates; Link story to one's life).
5. *Write.* Based on the discussion, students are given time to write in their journals.
6. *Review.* As a group, the students review what they learned about human nature, about things in nature, about themselves, or about any concepts in the reading.

Brainstorming

One of the best ways to generate a number of ideas in a short amount of time is through the brainstorming strategy. **Brainstorming** helps to stretch a student's imagination, encourages group cooperation, and leads to creative thinking through spontaneous contributions by all group members. James Moffett, an early advocate of the brainstorming strategy as a regular classroom activity, argued that it not only stimulates oral discussion but also is an excel-

True happiness . . .

is not attained through

self-gratification but

through fidelity to a

worthy purpose.

HELEN KELLER

lent source for gathering ideas for writing (Moffett & Wagner, 1991). Key principles of brainstorming include the following:

- Select a problem or topic and react to it quickly.
- Designate one person in the group as the recorder of ideas.
- Accept and record all ideas or suggestions.
- Build on other people's ideas.
- Do not criticize anyone else's ideas.
- Remember that, initially, quantity of ideas is more important than quality.

Many teachers are familiar with brainstorming but do not utilize it effectively or frequently enough. If you plan to make the brainstorming strategy part of your teaching practices, there are some procedures you should follow. First, begin with a whole-class brainstorming session during which each student records his or her own ideas. Provide a problem question as a stimulus and a time limit to eliminate frivolous ideas and daydreaming. When time is called, let each student share his or her list. Second, open up the brainstorming session to everyone. You can record the ideas for the whole class at the chalkboard, modeling the role of the recorder. Finally, you may begin to evaluate some of the ideas in terms of their effectiveness in leading the class to a solution of the initial problem.

One fifth-grade teacher gave her class the following assignment: "While on a trip, your car breaks down and you are stuck for the day on a desolate country road. In the backseat, you find some old magazines. What are all the possible uses of a magazine you can think of?" The teacher then passed out copies of real magazines to the class. Figure 5.11 is part of the list this class brainstormed.

The brainstorming strategy can also be used to help students expand their vocabularies, particularly for writing. The teacher begins by presenting a common word, such as *walk*. The class is then asked to think of other, more descriptive words that could replace this one. One group that did this exercise came up with the following list: *stroll, glide, stumble, amble, shuffle, stomp, strut.* The teacher suggested that this group make a poster entitled "Walking Words" to display for the rest of the class. To reinforce the meaning of these terms, the teacher asked for volunteer students to briefly pantomime each of them. Other groups later came up with their own posters listing "Funny Words" (*laugh, giggle, hilarious*) and "Soft Words" (*cuddly, fuzzy, tender*).

The brainstorming strategy can be further extended by turning the list of brainstormed terms or ideas into schematic clusters. Webs or clusters have the advantage of showing relationships or connections among ideas rather than merely listing the ideas. Figure 5.12 shows the cluster diagram that emerged from a fifth-grade class discussion of prejudice after students listened to their teacher read Florence Heide's *Sound of Sunshine, Sound of Rain*, which is about a blind African American boy.

FIGURE 5.11

Sample brainstorming list.

Problem: What can you do with a magazine?

Read it.	Fold it into a sun hat.
Look at pictures.	Make a megaphone.
Clip out coupons.	Use it for toilet paper.
Use it as a flyswatter.	Arrange the pages into the letters *SOS*.
Make paper airplanes.	
Burn it for fuel.	

FIGURE 5.12

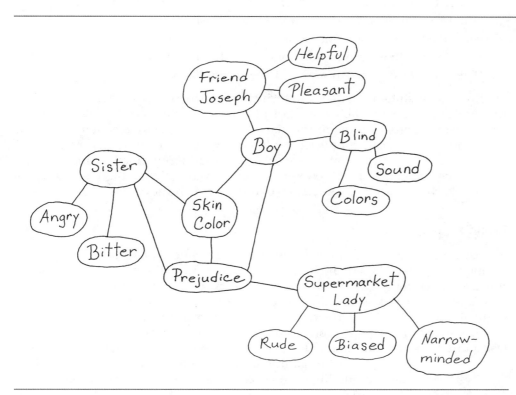

Sample schematic cluster: Sound of Sunshine, Sound of Rain.

Interviewing

Most information that is gathered by students for school projects comes from traditional resources: a dictionary, an encyclopedia, other library reference sources. Students need to learn that another way of gathering information is through *interviewing* (Moffett & Wagner, 1991), or asking someone for information or opinions. For example, when a student has been to the library in search of information regarding the proper soil, water, and sunlight conditions for growing a particular plant and is still not clear about what to do, it is time to ask for expert advice. Finding a specialist (a botanist, the owner of a nursery, an expert gardener) to interview would be a valuable shortcut to acquiring technical information. This is why knowing how to use the interview strategy as a research tool is so important.

Donald Graves (2003) recommends teaching young children about interviewing by having them poll their fellow classmates for information. In this simple polling technique, students choose a different interview or polling question to ask their classmates each day. Questions could include the following: Which is your favorite meal—breakfast, lunch, or dinner? Which is your favorite sport—baseball, football, or basketball? Which is your favorite color—red, green, or yellow? When the polling process is completed, a chart or graph can be prepared to show the class data.

Many older students are already familiar with the mechanics of an interview from having watched television stars such as Oprah Winfrey, who utilizes guest interviews as the basis of her show. Good interviewers keep in mind the following six points:

1. Gather background information on the subject.

In and beyond the classroom

Lead a group of students in a brainstorming session on any topic of their choice. You serve as the recorder. Remember to accept all responses and encourage children to build on one another's ideas. When you are finished, reflect on what you can do with the information you have brainstormed (e.g., record it as a cluster diagram).

2. Learn something about the interviewee (person being interviewed).

3. Decide ahead of time on the information desired.

4. Formulate appropriate questions.

5. Anticipate follow-up questions based on the interviewee's responses.

6. Determine how to begin and end the interview politely.

Eventually students will want to interview actual experts rather than continue role-playing with their peers. For primary-grade students, the teacher might invite these experts to come to the classroom, while upper elementary and middle school students can conduct their interviews in the community after school.

Interviewing is an important strategy for gathering information and conducting research on many topics. However, you must eventually tie interviewing to real projects so that children see a relevance to the research they are doing.

Group Projects

A great deal of classroom talk is stimulated when children engage in real projects in small-group settings. When children get together to build, make, or create something, they naturally talk about it as they work; this **incidental talk** associated with a particular task is actually the foundation for all other talk experiences. To facilitate such talk in class, the teacher needs to assess students' interests and then decide with them on some projects that can be done in class. The key is that the task must be a real one if real language is to be generated (Moffett & Wagner, 1991). In addition, small-group projects involve reading; doing library research; note taking; organizing information; writing an outline; listening; and, of course, speaking.

The following Classroom Vignette shows how one teacher utilizes the group projects strategy.

In and beyond the classroom

With a small group of students, brainstorm a subject for a group project. Decide on what you will do and how you will do it. Then identify someone in the community to interview in relationship to the project. Help the students to arrange and conduct the interview. Evaluate what you learned as a teacher from this experience.

Creating a newscast. A group project to develop students' communication skills is to create a complete newscast. The focus should be on fluent, distinct speaking so that each speaker is clearly understood. The teacher divides the class into groups. Each group is responsible for one of the various segments of the news: local news, state news, national news, global news, advertising, weather, and sports. The groups research some newspaper articles to gather information. Then, each group collaboratively writes the script for its segment. The various groups should be encouraged to interview caregivers or adults in the school for information for their segment. Next, the groups practice their segment of the newscast so that it is clear and fluent. It is important that each student have a speaking part. The teacher then videotapes each segment in the media center or some other quiet spot so that the other class members cannot see the taping. Later, all the students can view and critique their work. Appendix C has a rubric that can be used for the newscast.

Campaigning. Students learn the power of oral persuasion through campaigning for a change within the school. The change can be for more reading time in the media center, more time in the computer lab, a school mascot, a new sport during recess, or any other change the students would like to see in their school. After studying the propaganda techniques listed earlier in Figure 5.8, students can divide into teams to write and create a campaign slogan and a 30-second campaign advertisement for the change. As with the newscast, the students should practice it so that it is clear and fluent. The teacher then videotapes each one in the media center and plays them for the class. The class can critique each one, deciding why it was persuasive. When students critique others, teachers must

VIGNETTE *in the classroom*

Mr. McGuffee's fourth-grade classroom is buzzing with excitement this morning. Today is the day the students meet in small groups to begin planning their group projects.

"Okay, class," says Mr. McGuffee, "you all know what to do in your groups, so I'm going to give you 15 minutes to brainstorm about the projects that you'll be working on for the next two weeks. If there are no questions, go to work."

One of the groups has decided to make a small motor. In science class, the students learned about magnets; now they want to apply this knowledge to a motor. They've already contacted the electricity shop teacher at the high school and arranged for a meeting after school.

"David and I will go to the library and check out some books on electricity, magnets, and stuff about motors," says Randy.

"I'll see if there are any filmstrips on motors or electricity we can use," says Margie.

"My dad has a whole garage full of stuff like wire, switches, and wood blocks," says Philip.

Another group has decided to build kites. Working in pairs, the students are going to build three kites with different designs and materials and then see which one flies the best. Some of the members of the group have already gone to the library and found books and filmstrips about kites. They are all going to interview the owner of a hobby shop in town, who has said he can give them some tips on building their kites.

"Me and Delores are going to build a box kite," says Felicia. "We'll use sticks for the frame and butcher-block paper."

"We're using balsa wood for our frame," says Mike. "It's lighter and works better. We're also getting cellophane instead of paper."

"Don't forget to attach a cloth tail," says Ann. "This book I read said that kites fly better with a tail."

The students agree that they will also make practice kites and then meet with Mr. Barker, the hobby shop owner, to get his suggestions for improving them before the final test.

---

teach them first to name one or two things they really liked about the ad and why, and then to suggest one or two things the group could do to make it even better. Appendix C has a rubric teachers can use to assess students' understanding of propaganda techniques. Teachers can train students to do peer assessments by using the rubric or modifying it to fit the needs of the class.

Intellectual Kits

An **intellectual kit** is a collection of real materials or objects organized around a single category or sharing a common attribute, such as objects related to a farm or a collection of buttons. The purpose of the intellectual kits strategy is to encourage students' use of language to describe, categorize, and brainstorm uses of the objects and to role-play with the kit. Marie Clay was one of the early educators to suggest the use of real objects (as opposed to abstract or imaginary ones) to generate language and thought in young children. Preschool and primary-grade teachers use the kits to help children define similarities and differences among objects. Eventually this leads to development of the skills of comparing, contrasting, and classifying (Inhelder & Piaget, 1964).

The teacher first prepares a kit suitable for the age level and interests of the children. Then the students are free to discover what the objects all have in common and to determine various ways of categorizing or dividing the objects, such as by size, color, shape, texture, or function. Through the manipulation of concrete objects, the children learn to label objects; to describe their attributes in relation to other objects; and to compare, group, and predict. The teacher's role is to build on students' responses, model new vocabulary terms when appropriate, and relate the materials in the kit to other learning situations and subjects. Finally, the children are encouraged to think of additional uses for the objects in the kit.

In Tucson, AZ, the Tucson Early Education Model (TEEM) utilizes intellectual kits extensively to develop young children's language, thinking, and social skills. Teachers in the TEEM program develop their own kits from ordinary materials found around the home: beauty aids, bottles, boxes, brushes, clothing, combs, containers, fabric, footwear, gloves, hats, jars, jewelry, magazines, measuring devices, nails, rocks, seeds, shells, shoes, socks, soft objects, tools, and vegetables. One teacher designed an intellectual shape kit around the concept of *round*. She began with a dictionary definition of the word *round* and had the children add their own definitions ("it rolls," "it forms a circle"). Next she showed the children the objects in her kit: washers, corks, coins, balls, a rolling pin, an embroidery hoop, a spool, a ring, a coaster, checkers, pencils, hair rollers, a hatbox, buttons, wheels, an orange, cups, dishes, and bottle tops. She asked the children, "How is this object round? Is it round in the same way this object is?" "Which is more round—an orange or an egg?"

> ## In and beyond the classroom
>
> Create an intellectual kit and bring it into an elementary classroom. Observe as the children categorize and manipulate the objects. Record your observations in your journal. What kinds of language-learning experiences did you observe? How could you extend these experiences into reading or writing?

From there, the children took over and began discussing and grouping the objects. Later in the period, they went on a "round walk" in the room, collecting more round objects for their kit. Other extension activities included listening to the teacher read *Round as a Pancake* and *Moon Man* by Tomi Ungerer, making round collage designs at the art center, and learning circle games and dances.

Some teachers like to introduce an intellectual kit by reading a book. Mrs. Murphy, a first-grade teacher, read *There Are Rocks in My Socks (Said the Ox)* by Pat Thomas. After the children had enjoyed the book and talked about it, Mrs. Murphy brought out a large box containing . . . socks, of course! There were long, red Christmas stockings; little baby socks; athletic socks; women's nylons; wool socks; cotton socks; tennis booties; leg warmers; and so on. The children categorized the socks by size, color, material, and use. Then they talked about the different people who might wear these socks. Later the teacher brought markers, yarn, buttons, glue, needles, and thread and showed the children how to construct hand puppets out of socks.

Figure 5.13 outlines some guidelines for using intellectual kits.

Dialogue Improvisation and Patterned Conversation

Ferguson and Young (1996) explain how they use dialogue improvisation and patterned conversation with second-language learners to provide these students with opportunities to use English in a safe, meaningful way. Both activities permit the students to use prior experiences as they learn the structure of the English language; both are also good to use for all learners.

In **dialogue improvisation,** students (with the teacher's help) create new dialogue for the characters in a familiar story as they act out a part of the story. For example, after reading *Annie and the Wild Animals* (Brett, 1985), the teacher passes out various animal puppets, such as a crocodile, giraffe, monkey, and raccoon, to the students. The teacher begins the improvisation by acting like Annie, who wants a new pet after losing Taffy, her cat. The teacher puts out cornflakes on a plate on the floor and begins to wonder aloud about who will come to eat the food. The children in turn come to the plate and respond to Annie's question, "Will you make a good pet?" The children respond by explaining why they would not be a good pet. The dialogue is patterned after Brett's phrase: "I wouldn't be a good pet because . . ." This type of improvisation gives

BEFORE THE ACTIVITY

1. Decide on the type of kit.
2. List the different objects to include.
3. List your objectives.
4. List the new vocabulary to be learned.
5. Prepare questions to ask.

DURING THE ACTIVITY

You:

1. Model language patterns.
2. Use labels.
3. Ask questions.
4. Listen to children.
5. Observe children.
6. Evaluate.

Children:

1. Manipulate objects.
2. Label objects.
3. Categorize objects.
4. Ask questions.
5. Role-play.
6. Discuss with peers.

FIGURE 5.13

Instructions for using an intellectual kit.

students an opportunity to pattern the English phrase while adding their own reason for not being a good pet. Other books that Ferguson and Young suggest using for dialogue improvisation are *Pigs' Picnic* (Kasza, 1988), *"You Look Ridiculous," Said the Rhinoceros to the Hippopotamus* (Waber, 1966), *A Bag Full of Pups* (Gackenbac, 1981), and *I Wish I Were a Butterfly* (Howe, 1987).

In **patterned conversation,** the teacher chooses literature with predictable texts such as *I Went Walking* (Williams, 1989); after numerous readings, the students, again with the use of puppets or props, become one of the characters. The students read the statement "I went walking," followed by the teacher asking, "What did you see?" followed by the child's response, "I saw a . . ."

Other books to use for patterned conversation are *Hattie and the Fox* (Mem Fox, 1986), *Who Is Tapping at My Window?* (Demming, 1988), and *Polar Bear, Polar Bear, What Do You Hear?* (Martin, 1991).

Good teaching is one-fourth preparation and three-fourths theater.

GAIL GODWIN

Show-and-Tell/Sharing

Show-and-tell is one of the oldest and most popular oral language activities used in the primary grades. Generally it consists of a brief talk by a student describing a favorite object brought from home. Moffett and Wagner (1991) called this *topic talk* because the topic for the child's monologue depends on the object brought from home.

Although show-and-tell is a familiar and widely used activity in the primary grades, it is not a particularly effective oral language activity. This is because show-and-tell traditionally involves one child at a time getting up in front of the rest of the class. The rest of the students are expected to listen attentively. Try to picture this scene: Juan stands in front of the room holding up a toy robot he received for his birthday. He looks down and mumbles about his toy and who gave it to him. The children in the front can see the object, but they are also examining their show-and-tell objects in anticipation of their turns. Children farther back can neither hear Juan nor see the object clearly. They soon lose interest, fidget in their seats, and begin talking to their neighbors.

To make show-and-tell a truly meaningful oral language activity, divide the students into small groups. Then set aside time a few mornings a week for show-

and-tell. To teach the strategy to young children, bring something from your own home that is meaningful to you. Show it to a small group of children and talk about it. Allow the children to handle the object and to ask you questions about it. In this way, they learn how to conduct the small-group show-and-tell activity in which everyone gets a chance to talk and share about his or her object. Small groups are also less intimidating to young children, particularly to those who are shy about getting up in front of a large group to speak.

Ewards (1996) suggests that another way to make show-and-tell a truly meaningful oral language activity is to ask caregivers to help their child prepare for show-and-tell. Ewards also suggests that the topic be based on an experience or a small item found on a nature hike instead of an expensive toy or object belonging to the child.

From the teacher's point of view, show-and-tell is an excellent opportunity for young children to use language to describe, to explain, and to elaborate. For the students, it is a chance to talk about favorite things from home and to connect home and family experiences with school learning. As the children become more and more familiar with show-and-tell, their presentations improve and their talks are more organized.

This common form of the activity is considered "free choice" show-and-tell because the children can bring any object of their choice from home to talk about. Another use of show-and-tell involves "structured choices." The teacher may wish to relate the show-and-tell period to other school activities. For example, one primary-grade teacher created a science unit about various animals, domestic and wild, found in North America. For show-and-tell, he asked each student to bring an object from home that represented an animal she or he had or would like to have as a pet. The next day the children brought in dog bones, rubber toys, catnip, a leash, photographs of pets, pictures cut out of magazines, a tuft of fur, a carved antler bone pendant, and so on. The same teacher asked his students to bring in objects from home to represent the various geometric shapes they were studying in math class: square, rectangle, circle, and triangle. Another teacher asked her class to bring in objects that represented their caregivers' occupations. Students brought such things as a Bible, a stethoscope, a calculator, a chef's hat, farm tools, and file cards. Any unit in any content area can lead to a fun and interesting show-and-tell activity.

For older students (grades 4–8), the show-and-tell strategy is altered slightly and called *sharing* (Kear & Yellin, 1978). The primary difference is that in sharing, the object talked about must be a part of a demonstration. The student brings in an object and demonstrates its use while also providing a verbal explanation of the activity. In one seventh-grade language arts classroom, for example, a boy brought in a deck of cards, a box, and a scarf and demonstrated some magic tricks. A girl brought in her violin and demonstrated the fingering and bowing technique used in playing the instrument. Another boy set up a chess set and demonstrated the opening moves in chess; another student demonstrated a stitch in her needlepoint display. Sharing is more sophisticated than show-and-tell and requires the students to plan and practice before performing for the group. But like show-and-tell, it is essentially an exercise in clear communication, and it begins with the teacher sharing (demonstrating) something from his or her background and experiences.

DRAMA AND ORAL LANGUAGE DEVELOPMENT

Television has made us a nation of spectators. Children view it from infancy and surveys reveal that they spend more hours in front of the screen each week than they spend in school. The current craze for video games has intensified this situation; therefore, it is more important than ever that we make opportunities available for children to experience participation in the arts.

Creative drama is an ideal form for this participation, with its inclusion of the physical, mental, emotional, and social abilities of the participant. (p. 11)

Nellie McCaslin (1996) thus has summed up the thoughts of many childhood educators about the importance of drama in the language arts curriculum. Drama is included in this section on oral language development because it truly is one of the great oral communication forms. Morgan and Saxon (1988) argued that dramatic presentations are also one of the best ways to develop children's oral communication skills. But drama is much more than oral communication, for through drama children learn about life, experience the emotions of characters they are portraying, and learn a greater appreciation of literature (Cottrell, 1987).

Drama can take many forms in the classroom, from the simple dress-up play of preschoolers to full-blown theatrical productions with costumes, scenery, and memorized scripts. Whatever the form, the objectives of drama in the classroom, according to McCaslin (1996), remain the same:

- to encourage creative and aesthetic development
- to improve children's abilities to think critically
- to create an environment in which social and cooperative skills flourish
- to improve the general communication skills of students
- to enhance the individual child's knowledge of self

Dramatic Play in the Primary Grades

Probably the first dramatics activity that young children encounter in school is the make-believe center, where children have a chance to dress up in simple costumes, play with blocks and toys, and use their imaginations to create simple stories. In kindergarten and first grade, such centers are among the most popular and sought after by children. With simple props and actions, students imitate the world around them and create strange and wonderful characters to amuse their friends. Some dramatic play activities may become very complex, involve many children, and last nearly the entire period, whereas other play dramas may span only a few minutes (McCaslin, 1996).

Creating a center to facilitate dramatic play is relatively simple: A few old hats, scarves, simple makeup, a toy car, a stuffed doll, and some cardboard boxes and away you go. With very little prompting, young children join with a few friends and create imaginative dress-up plays. A more formal approach to dramatic or dress-up play utilizes prop kits. *Prop kits* are play centers focused on a single theme and similar to the intellectual kits described earlier.

Observing young children involved in dramatic play is an important part of a teacher's learning experience. Children's play is not mere play; it is serious. Through dress-up and dramatic play, students learn to take on other roles and to imitate important figures in their lives, such as mommy and daddy. According to noted child psychologist Bruno Bettelheim (1976), it is also a primary way in which young children learn to control their environment and deal with common situations and problems. Through observing children involved in dramatic play, you will soon realize why Virginia Koste, in her book *Dramatic Play in Childhood* (1988), called it "a rehearsal for life."

Movement or Warm-Up Exercises

Professional actors and actresses know the importance of "warming up" before a performance; it is similar to the stretching that an athlete does before going on the playing field. Young children should be introduced to simple warm-up or movement exercises to get them ready for more complicated aspects of drama. The Classroom Vignette that follows offers a few examples of how different teachers use warm-up or movement exercises.

VIGNETTE *in the classroom*

Teacher 1:

As part of a language arts unit on drama, the teacher has explained and demonstrated the notion of free movement to music. The desks and tables have been moved back against the walls of the room to create an open space in the center. "Now, children," says Mrs. Chang, "when I start the tape, I want you to move about the room using your arms, legs, and bodies to show how the music makes you feel." The tape begins with some slow classical music selections, moves into lively folk-dance tunes, and ends with some somber march music.

Teacher 2:

"Good morning, boys and girls," says Mrs. Birdsong. "Let's begin this beautiful day by singing our 'Good Morning Song.'" As the teacher and children sing the song together, they move their arms and bodies to imitate the little bird in the song.

> Way up in the sky
> (stretch way up on your tiptoes)
> The little birds fly
> (move your hands like you're flying)
> While down in the nest
> (crouch down on the ground)
> The little birds rest.
> (fold your head in your arms)
> With a wing on the left
> (raise your left elbow)
> And a wing on the right
> (raise your right elbow)
> The little birds sleep all through the night.
> (rest your head)
> The bright sun comes up
> (look up with your eyes wide open)
> The dew falls away
> (flutter your fingers)
> "Good morning, good morning,"
> (raise your arms to the sun)
> The little birds say.
> (turn to your partner and shake his or her hand)

Teacher 3:

"Okay, everyone," begins Mr. Johnson, "let's get real quiet and form a big circle. Shhh. Close your eyes. Listen carefully and you can hear it beginning to rain." The teacher rubs his hands together gently and the students imitate him. They rub harder. Then the teacher begins to snap his fingers—first one, then the other. The students do the same (it's raining harder now). The teacher slaps his legs. The students slap their legs, faster and faster (the rain is coming down very hard now). They stomp their feet (you can hear the thunder). Then the movements are repeated in reverse order as the rain gradually slows down and finally stops.

Teacher 4:

"Class, let's go on a bear hunt," says Ms. Aliota (slaps her legs to imitate walking). The children repeat her actions and chant, "Let's go on a bear hunt." As the teacher leads the hunt, the students repeat what she says and imitate her actions.

"I see a wheat field" (places her hand above her eyes and moves her head back and forth). "Can't go over it. Can't go under it. Let's go through it" (moves her arms through the field).

"I see a fence" (repeats looking gesture). "Can't go around it. Can't go under it. Let's go over it" (hands and arms climbing).

"I see a lake. Can't go over it. Can't go around it. Let's swim across it" (arms swimming).

"I see a tree. Can't go over it. Can't go under it. Let's climb up it" (wraps her arms around the tree and climbs, leg over leg; when she gets to the top of the tree, she looks for bears).

"I see a cave. Can't go over it. Can't go under it. Let's go in" (tiptoes in slowly). "I see two eyes" (touches her eyes). "I see two ears" (touches her ears). "I see a nose" (touches her nose). "I see a mouth" (touches her mouth). *"It's a bear! Run for it!"* (She repeats the actions in reverse order very quickly.)

Pantomime

The next step up from movement exercises is pantomime. **Pantomime** is defined by McCaslin (1990) as "the art of conveying ideas without words" (p. 73) and incorporates the gestures and expressions from movement exercises but is more intricate and longer than warm-up exercises. Pantomime is also more like theatre acting in the sense that an entire story can be told through the movements of the characters. Props and simple costumes can also be used, but no speaking is allowed. The most famous pantomimists, or *mimes* (such as the Frenchman Marcel Marceau), work alone on a bare stage. However, in introducing young children to the art of pantomime, it is best to start with small-group skits.

In preparing for their skit, the members of each group plan and talk among themselves. They choose parts; decide on the movements they will use to convey their story; and make simple props, signs, or costumes, if necessary. This aspect of the preparation involves verbal communication. But once the group gets onstage (the front of the class), no talking is allowed; this is the real challenge of pantomime. Figure 5.14 contains some simple group pantomime skits that can be adapted for various grade levels.

Another kind of group pantomime skit can be based on a familiar story that the class has heard or read. Some favorite stories that can be easily adapted to pantomime skits include *The Three Bears* by Paul Galdone, *Where the Wild Things Are* by Maurice Sendak, *Strega Nona* by Tomie dePaola, *The Three Billy Goats Gruff* by Paul Galdone, *Charlotte's Web* by E. B. White, and *Homer Price and the Doughnut Machine* by Robert McCloskey.

In and beyond the classroom

One way to get older students involved with pantomime activities is to teach them the game charades. In charades, a famous person's name; a title of a book, movie, or song; or a well-known quotation is acted out using hand, body, and facial expressions. To play charades, (1) establish common cues or signals, (2) show the number of words being acted out by holding up the same number of fingers, and (3) show the number of syllables in a word by placing the same number of fingers against your inner wrist. While one person acts out the charade, the rest of the group guesses.

---

1. Wake Up: Waking up in the morning, washing up, getting dressed. Mom calls you to breakfast. Dad's already having his coffee. Uh oh, Dad's late for work and you're late for school. Hurry up and grab your books.

2. Play Ball: What a great day for a game! You're with your friends, the sun is shining, everyone has the gloves, bats, and balls. The game starts, but then . . .

3. Dinnertime: It's your turn to fix dinner for the whole family. What will you fix? Will they like it?

4. Dentist/Patient: What a toothache! Lean back. Relax. This won't hurt a bit. Let me out of here!

5. Go Fly a Kite: It's a windy day, just right for you and a friend to go kite flying. Careful, don't let it go too high. Watch out for those trees. Careful!

6. Homework Excuses: What? Forgot your homework again? Tell me about it, but remember—no words.

7. First Dance: Your shoes hurt. Your shirt/blouse won't stay buttoned. The music is too fast/slow. You really don't know how but . . .

8. First Date: You're nervous. The car won't start. You have to walk. You forgot the tickets to the concert. But . . . it turns out okay.

9. Job Interview: The first questions are easy. Your resume is in order. But then your stomach begins to rumble. (You should have had your breakfast!)

10. Plane Ride: Buckle yourself in. Here comes the flight attendant. Here comes lunch. Careful, don't spill anything. Uh oh, your neighbor needs to get out.

FIGURE 5.14

Pantomime suggestions.

Choral Speaking

When considering the use of choral speaking with your class, you need to decide which form of the activity is most appropriate. There are several types of **choral speaking** from which to choose:

1. *Antiphonal or dialogue.* Poems with two parts or a question-and-answer format are appropriate for this type of speaking activity. Often the deep voices take one part while the light voices take the other; this usually translates into a dialogue between a group of boys and a group of girls. Some poems for which this approach is effective are "Who Has Seen the Wind?" by Christina Rossetti and the American folk song "Buffalo Gals."

2. *Line-a-group or line-a-child.* In this approach, individuals or small groups read one line of a poem at a time. They work to keep in harmony and tempo. Some appropriate poems are "The Sun Is Stuck" by Myra Cohn Livingston, "Let's Marry! Said the Cherry" by N. M. Bodecker, and "The ABC Bunny" by Wanda Gag.

3. *Refrain.* Narrative poems with a chorus are good candidates for refrain. A teacher or student can recite the story, with the other children in the class joining in on the chorus. Examples of poems with refrains are "The Green Grass Growing All Around" and "The Old Woman and the Pig."

4. *Unison.* Although unison speaking appears simple, it really requires skill for the students to keep together. Since everyone speaks every line, the rhythm and timing have to be perfect. Almost every poem is appropriate for unison speaking. Some particularly good poems are "My Name" by Lee Bennett Hopkins, "Dreams" by Langston Hughes, and "Mr. Skinner" by Bodecker.

5. *Cumulative speaking.* In cumulative speaking, one speaker begins with other speakers, one by one, joining the first speaker. This type of speaking helps the student who may be nervous or shy in front of classmates to gain confidence by speaking with others. Stories such as *I Know an Old Lady Who Swallowed a Fly*, retold by Nadine Bernard Westcott, and *Shoes from Grandpa* by Mem Fox can be used for cumulative speaking. Following is an example of the first part of *Shoes from Grandpa* to illustrate how this book can be used for cumulative speaking:

Grandpa:	My, Jessie, how you've grown! You'll need a new pair of shoes this winter, and I'll buy them.
Dad:	I'll buy you some socks from the local shops,
Grandpa & Dad:	to go with the shoes from Grandpa.
Mom:	I'll buy you a skirt that won't show the dirt,
Grandpa, Dad, & Mom:	to go with the socks from the local shops, to go with the shoes from Grandpa.

You may want to start choral speaking by just repeating some favorite poems to the children and having them join in with you. With longer poems, you may want the students to have copies of the text for reference. One pitfall you need to guard against is allowing this activity to become merely a test of oral fluency. The true goal is to help children understand the meaning of poems and to interpret that meaning through oral expression. For more information about using poems and stories for choral speaking and choral reading, check Tashjian's (1974) *With a Deep Sea Smile* and Pennock's (1984) "Choral Reading of Poetry Improves Reading Fluency."

Storytelling

Storytelling is one of the oldest forms of entertainment. Long before there was television, long before there was radio, families sat around the dinner table or gathered in front of the fireplace and told stories: funny stories about simpletons

It is far easier to start something than to finish it.

AMELIA EARHART

getting into trouble; scary stories with ghosts and goblins; legends and tales from faraway countries; and classic family stories that everyone knew by heart but wanted to hear again and again. Today the art of storytelling has been revitalized in the United States. Professional storytellers are appearing at festivals, in concerts, and in elementary and secondary classrooms to share their art form. In OK, for example, Lynn Moroney has revived many of the Native American stories, such as the star legends, coyote tales, and sky lore. In Portland, OR, Susan Strauss takes her tales of witches, queens, and goddesses into the classroom for students of all ages. In Pennsylvania, Linda Kumbaya Goss is the official storyteller of Philadelphia, where she tells African and African American tales. Dave Kristy of Pittsburgh, Pennsylvania, uses his fiddle, banjo, and guitar to tell tall tales and regional stories of Appalachia. (For a complete listing of storytellers in your state, contact the National Association of Professional Storytellers, P.O. Box 309, Jonesborough, TN 37659.)

Teaching children to tell stories to their classmates is one of the most effective ways to develop speaking skills in young children. Trousdale (1990) has recounted how one teacher used storytelling to develop the oral communication abilities of a child. Piazza (1999) has also noted that storytelling in the classroom develops students' listening skills, improves their reading comprehension, and stimulates their interest in writing stories.

To teach storytelling to young children, it is not necessary to be a great storyteller. It is helpful, however, if you can demonstrate to children some of the characteristics of an effective storyteller. A good storyteller should do the following things (Trelease, 1995):

- Select a story that he or she really enjoys and that is appropriate for the audience.
- Be thoroughly familiar with the story; memorize only key phrases, not the entire story.
- Be imaginative and include gestures and facial expressions to convey meaning.
- Speak with expression, feeling, and emotion.
- Look directly at the audience; gaze about so that everyone feels involved in the story.

Appendix C has three storytelling rubrics to use for assessing the students. In Chapter 1, we introduced the website http://rubistar.4teachers.org to the reader. Appendix C contains the storytelling rubric found on the website as well as a modification of this rubric. You will also find a rubric for voice inflection. Teachers always need to construct scoring rubrics based on the criteria they give to the students. Notice in the modified rubric that the speaking aspect of storytelling is emphasized by assigning more points for it. The modified rubric also emphasizes body movement.

After you have demonstrated storytelling techniques, divide your class into small groups and have students practice telling stories to one another. Storytelling is an art form that develops only through practice. When ready, the children can share their stories with the entire class. Here are some activities to involve your students in the art of storytelling.

Talk boxes. Provide the group with three boxes containing 5 × 8 index cards. The cards in the first box contain brief descriptions of characters (a nurse, a football player, a train conductor). Those in the next box contain brief plot descriptions ("You are on a trip and have lost your luggage"), and those in the third box contain descriptions of settings (a busy street in downtown Chicago, a lonely forest in Vermont, a sunny beach in Florida). Each child in the group chooses one card from each box. The children should study their cards for a few minutes and then make up a story that incorporates the character, plot, and setting listed (Kear & Yellin, 1978).

Story boxes. Teachers collect plenty of miscellaneous objects in their closets; here is an opportunity to use them. Into a box or large bag, put a variety of unusual objects (clothing, pictures, mementos from trips, old toys). Each child closes her or his eyes, reaches into the box or bag, and pulls out one object. After the children examine the object and think about it for a while, they should each make up a story that includes the object in some manner. Have them take turns telling their stories to the rest of the group (Kear & Yellin, 1978).

Wordless books. A wordless book tells a story through pictures alone. Unlike easy-to-read books or picture storybooks, wordless books contain no print at all. While turning the pages slowly, the "reader" adds the narration and dialogue to create a complete story with beginning, middle, and end. Once children see the wordless book strategy modeled by the teacher, they quickly pick up on it and begin telling stories themselves. Students can first dictate a story based on a wordless book. After the teacher has recorded the story, the children can read it back to one another. Even older students enjoy creating and reading their own stories based on wordless books. Figure 5.15 lists some wordless books for use in the classroom.

FIGURE 5.15

Wordless books.

The Lady and the Strawberry Snatcher (M. Bang, 1980)

The Grey Lady and the Strawberry Snatcher (M. Bang, 1996)

Zoom (I. Banyai, 1995)

ReZoom (I. Banyai, 1995)

Just in Passing (S. Bonners, 1989)

The Snowman (R. Briggs, 1978)

The Patchwork Farmer (C. Brown, 1989)

Do You Want to Be My Friend? (E. Carle, 1971)

In the Pond (E. Cristini, 1984)

Good Dog, Carl (A. Day, 1985)

Paddy's Pay-Day (A. Day, 1989)

Carl's Afternoon in the Park (A. Day, 1991)

The Yellow Umbrella (H. Drescher, 1987)

Paddy Under Water (J. S. Goodall, 1984)

Amanda and the Mysterious Carpet (F. Krahn, 1985)

On Top (M. MacGregor, 1988)

The Swan (V. Mayo, 1994)

The Gift (J. Prater, 1985)

Mouse Around (P. Schories, 1991)

Where's My Monkey? (D. Schubert, not dated)

Junglewalk (N. Tafuri, 1988)

Follow Me (N. Tafuri, 1990)

Free Fall (D. Wiesner, 1988)

Tuesday (D. Wiesner, 1991)

Sector 7 (D. Wiesner, 1999)

The Three Pigs (D. Wiesner, 2001)

Liar's goblet. Most children have heard of the lumberjack Paul Bunyan and his blue ox, Babe. Similarly, many children recognize the name of Pecos Bill, the cowboy. The stories of Paul Bunyan and Pecos Bill are examples of tall tales. Children love to expand on and embellish their own adventures. The liar's goblet activity builds on the idea of the tall tale and on children's enjoyment of exaggeration. It can be taught in the form of a game. First you need a goblet (a cup, glass, or mug will do). One person in the group takes the liar's goblet and makes up a short but exaggerated tall tale. The next person in the group takes the goblet and says, "That's nothing; why I remember . . ." Each student tries to top the previous story; each story, though different, grows more exaggerated. Figure 5.16 lists examples of tall-tale books.

Serial stories. This storytelling activity is also based on a game that many children are already familiar with. One person, usually the teacher or designated group leader, begins a story. At any point, the person stops and the next person in the group continues the story. A variation on this activity utilizes a ball of yarn. When the first storyteller stops, he or she tosses the yarn to any other person in the group, who must then continue the story. The ball of yarn is tossed back and forth, making a web design. Finally, one person tosses the ball of yarn back to the person who originally began the story; this is the signal that the story is about to end. The final storyteller concludes by saying, "And that's the end of this yarn."

Chalk or draw-along stories. In this activity, the storyteller begins the tale by drawing a circle or line on the board. As the story continues, the storyteller adds more details to the drawing. Eventually, when the story is completed, there is a finished drawing on the chalkboard. To teach this activity, draw and tell the entire story to a small group of children. When the students have learned the story and the picture drawing, they can tell it to another group of children who have not heard it yet. Figure 5.17 shows a chalk story version of "The Circus" as told by Rene Wojnoski, who teaches kindergarten in Ponca City, OK, and tells stories to her students as a regular part of her instruction.

New versions and new endings. Yet another storytelling activity involves changing elements in the story plot and/or altering the endings of familiar stories. It works particularly well with folktales and fairy tales. To start this activity,

---

John Tabor's Ride (E. C. Day, 1989)

John Henry: An American Legend (E. J. Keats, 1965)

Paul Bunyan (S. Kellogg, 1984)

Pecos Bill (S. Kellogg, 1986)

Johnny Appleseed (S. Kellogg, 1988)

Mike Fink (S. Kellogg, 1992)

I Was Born Ten Thousand Years Ago (S. Kellogg, 1996)

Sally and Thunder and Whirlwind (S. Kellogg, 1996)

The Song of Paul Bunyan and Tony Beaver (E. Rees, 1964)

Windwagon Smith (E. Rees, 1966)

Tall Tales of America (I. Shapiro, 1958)

Heroes in American Folklore (I. Shapiro, 1962)

American Tall Tale Animals (A. Stoutenburg, 1968)

FIGURE 5.16

Tall-tale books.

FIGURE 5.17

Sample chalk story: "The Circus."

 Let's go to a circus. Here is the circus ring inside the tent.

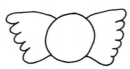 We'll need some seats for the audience.

 Inside the big ring are two small rings for the performing seals and dogs.

 Another small ring in the center contains a cage where the lions perform.

 Look! There's the high wire and net for the trapeze artists.

 At the end of the tent is a big cage for the elephants. But who's that funny-looking man running all around?

read a number of different versions of the same story to your students. For example, use a few different versions of *The Three Little Pigs.*

For a real change of pace, read to your class *The True Story of the Three Little Pigs* by A. Wolf (as told to Jon Scieszka). The story begins, "I'm the Wolf. Alexander T. Wolf. You can call me Al. I don't know how this whole Big Bad Wolf thing got started, but it's all wrong." Al Wolf then proceeds to explain how a great misunderstanding occurred between him and the three little pigs all because of a sneeze and a cup of sugar. This story is also a great vehicle for discussing point of view with the children. Explain that when a story is told from the point of view of a different character, it is quite different.

Puppetry and Storytelling

Like storytelling, puppets and masks have traditionally been associated with oral dramatic presentations. As with so many other activities, creating the proper environment is the essential ingredient to a successful puppetry experience. Begin by creating a simple puppet stage in one corner of your classroom. This can be easily done by draping an ordinary table with an old tablecloth or with decorated butcher-block paper. Another way to create a stage is to cut out the bottom of a large cardboard box, cover the box with colorful paper, and make a simple cloth curtain to hang over the front. Once your puppet stage is in order, the students naturally gravitate toward it.

The next step is to gather some simple materials for creating easy-to-make puppets. Linderman and Linderman (1984) have suggested the following list of materials: cardboard tubing, boxes, paper cups, paper plates, egg cartons, gift wrapping, various colored and textured pieces of cloth, tongue depressors, pipe cleaners, wooden dowels, old gloves, feathers, string, ribbons, cellophane, socks, tissue paper, paper bags, sticks, plastic foam cups, cardboard, construction paper, scissors, tape, paste, glue, washable markers or paints, crayons, buttons, thread, yarn, and felt. Piazza (1999) also suggests matchboxes, whisk brooms, and floor mops. Literally any scrap material can be used in the construction of puppets. There are several different kinds of puppets that young students can make.

Sock puppets. Begin by having each child bring an old sock from home. Demonstrate that by placing your hand inside the sock—your fingers in the toe, your thumb in the heel—you can make the puppet come alive simply by opening and closing your hand. Next add some cloth, felt, buttons, beads, yarn, and so on to make the eyes, mouth, nose, and ears. Additional cloth or felt can be used to construct clothing for the puppet to extend over the puppeteer's arm.

Finger puppets. The simplest way to make a finger puppet is with an old glove. On each finger, draw, color, or paint facial features of different characters. You can add tiny bits of yarn, sequins, or buttons. Each finger should contain a face with a different expression or look. In this way, you have large groups of tiny character puppets who can talk back and forth. You can even create a puppet family on one hand.

Paper-bag puppets. Paper-bag puppets are another easy and inexpensive way to introduce children to puppetry. Depending on the size of the paper bag used, you can create all types of puppets. Large paper (*never plastic*) bags, for example, can be placed over children's heads and worn as full masks. Holes for the eyes, nose, and mouth can be cut and the bags decorated with crayon, magic marker, felt, cloth scraps, and bits of string. Ears, hair, even hats made from colored construction paper can be added onto the bag with glue, paste, or tape. Smaller paper bags lend themselves as hand puppets.

Stick-and-ball puppets. With a wooden dowel, tongue depressor, or bent coat hanger plus a plastic foam ball or old tennis ball, you can teach children to construct stick-and-ball puppets. First cover the ball with felt or cloth and draw in the facial features. Then decorate with string, small buttons, and so on. Next insert the stick to support the head. (With the tennis ball, you have to cut a small hole to insert the stick.) Finally, cover the stick with a loose cloth, decorated to form a distinctive costume for your puppet. Insert your hand beneath the cloth and grasp the stick. Your puppet is ready.

Shadow puppets. Shadow puppets are particularly popular in Asian countries. To create a shadow puppet, you will use stiff cardboard or oak tag. Cut your puppet shape from the flat pattern in profile because only this outline is seen by the audience. Intricate facial features are not necessary; the unique characteristics of the puppet come from the cut outline. Next, attach the cutout to a stick to be held by the student puppeteer. The unique effect created by the shadow puppet depends on the special stage that you create by stretching a sheet of translucent cloth tightly in a frame. Stand behind the frame and place a bright light behind the shadow puppet and the screen. The audience sees a dark silhouette or shadow against the light screen. Bring out other shadow puppets to create a captivating form of entertainment.

Appendix C has two rubrics to use for puppet shows: the rubric found on the http://rubistar.4teachers.org website as well as a modification of it. Teachers always need to construct scoring rubrics based on the criteria they give to students. The emphasis of the modified rubric is the speaking aspect.

Improvisation

After children understand how bodily and facial gestures can suggest emotions and even tell a story, the next step is to add spoken dialogue. Using such free form dialogue along with pantomimed gestures to tell a story is known as **improvisation.** This improvisation is different from dialogue improvisation, which was discussed earlier in this chapter. This type of improvisation does not have any structure to the dialogue; dialogue improvisation does. In improvisation, the dialogue of the various characters is improvised by the actors as the story unfolds; however, an improvisation is not totally unplanned. Generally the story is known in advance, and the actors alter the dialogue as they see fit. In improvisation, unlike theatre acting, a script does not have to be memorized. However, simple props, costumes, and even scenery can be used, and students enjoy creating these in class.

One recommended way to lead into improvisation is through the use of children's literature (McCaslin, 1996). First, identify some stories familiar to the class. If you are reading aloud to the students on a regular basis and giving them free time during the school day to read books of their own choice, this should not be a problem. Let the class divide into groups with each group selecting a favorite story. Figure 5.18 lists books that can be easily improvised in dramatic presentations.

As with puppetry, improvisations based on children's literature books eventually lead children to want to write and create their own improvisational plays. McCaslin (1996) has noted that improvisational drama often lends itself to dealing with real problems that affect students in their daily lives.

Readers Theatre

Another form of dramatic presentation that increases children's comprehension of literature as well as develops oral language and pantomime abilities is readers theatre, sometimes called story theatre (Forsythe, 1995; Martinez, Roser, & Strecker, 1998/1999). **Readers theatre** has been defined by Laughlin

---

FIGURE 5.18

Books for improvisation.

Atnold, T. (1987). *No Jumping on the Bed.* New York: Dial.

Freeman, D. (1968). *Corduroy.* New York: Viking.

Galdone, P. (1973). *The Little Red Hen.* New York: Seabury Press.

Galdone, P. (1975). *The Gingerbread Boy.* New York: Houghton Mifflin.

Galdone, P. (1984). *The Three Pigs.* New York: Clarion.

Howe, J. (1988). *Rip Van Winkle.* Boston: Little, Brown.

Hyman, T. (1983). *Little Red Riding Hood.* New York: Holiday House.

Jungman, A. (1989). *The Day Teddy Wanted Grandpa to Notice Him.* New York: Barron's.

Kamerman, S. (ed.). (1987). *Plays from Favorite Folk Tales.* Boston: Plays, Inc.

Piper, W. (1980). *The Little Engine That Could.* New York: Grosset and Dunlap.

Scieszka, J. (1989). *The True Story of the Three Little Pigs.* New York: Viking Kestrel.

Sendak, M. (1963). *Where the Wild Things Are.* New York: Harper & Row.

and Latrobe (1990) as "a presentation by two or more participants who read from scripts and interpret a literary work in such a way that the audience imaginatively senses characterization, setting and action" (p. 3). Vocal intonation, facial expressions, and pantomime gestures can also be used to enhance the quality of the presentation. A narrator is often used to direct the various reader-actors on and off the stage and to communicate scene changes to the audience. Occasionally simple props and costumes are used to further suggest characters and setting.

Typically readers theatre utilizes the literature of folktales such as *Arrow to the Sun: A Pueblo Indian Tale* by Gerald McDermott, fairy tales, plays written especially for children, and short prose selections. However, McCaslin (1996) found that professional readers theatre productions also utilize historical works such as *Feast of Thanksgiving: The First American Holiday* by June Behrens, biographies, letters, news, articles, and even comic strips. Using literature that was not originally intended to be dramatized often requires that students write additional scenes, characters, and dialogue to ensure that the audience follows the story. Figure 5.19 lists sources for readers theatre, and Figure 5.20 lists books to use for readers theatre. Figure 5.21 is an example of simply taking a story such as *Wind Says Good Night* by Katy Rydell, which has repetitive text, and writing it for readers theatre.

Cheathem, V. (1977). *Skits and Spoofs for Young Actors.* Boston: Plays, Inc.

Durell, D. (1957). *Thirty Plays for Classroom Reading.* Boston: Plays, Inc.

Kamerman, S. (ed.). (1987). *Patriotic and Historical Plays for Young People.* Boston: Plays, Inc.

Kamerman, S. (ed.). (1987). *Plays of Black Americans.* Boston: Plays, Inc.

Laughlin, M., & Latrobe, K. (1990). *Reader's Theatre for Children: Scripts and Script Development.* Englewood, CO: Litran's Unlimited.

Scott, L. (1961). *Fairy Tale Plays in Rhymes.* Los Angeles: F. A. Owen Publishing.

Sloyer, S. (1982). *Reader's Theatre: Story Dramatization in the Classroom.* Urbana, IL: NCTE.

FIGURE 5.19

Sources for readers theatre.

A Most Unusual Lunch (R. Benders, 1994)

Jack's Garden (H. Cole, 1995)

Shoes from Grandpa (M. Fox, 1989)

Good-Night Owl! (P. Hutchins, 1972)

The Old Woman Who Lived in a Vinegar Bottle (M. MacDonald, 1995)

Too Much Noise (A. McGovern, 1967)

The Bag I'm Taking to Grandma's (S. Neitze, 1995)

"Not Now!" Said the Cow (J. Oppenheim, 1989)

Wind Says Good Night (K. Rydell, 1994)

The Little Old Lady Who Was Not Afraid of Anything (L. Williams, 1986)

The Napping House (A. Wood, 1984)

"Stop, Stop, You Big Old Bull!" (H. Zieffer, 1995)

FIGURE 5.20

Cumulative books to use in readers theatre.

Wind Says Good Night

by Katy Rydell

Nar #1:	It was late at night. All little children were in their beds, fast asleep. All except one. The night wind brushed against a window.
Wind:	Shh-h-h. Go to sleep. (Whispering)
Child:	I cannot fall asleep because outside, on the branch of a tree, Mockingbird is singing.
Wind:	Mockingbird, will you stop singing so the child can go to sleep?
Nar #2:	But Mockingbird loved to sing. Music spilled from deep in his throat, as he sang of green woods, bright flowers, and warm summer nights.
Mockingbird:	No! I can't stop singing until Cricket stops playing.
Nar #3:	From the tall grass by the back steps came the cheerful ring of Cricket's tune.
Wind:	Cricket, will you stop playing so Mockingbird will stop singing so the child can go to sleep?
Nar #4:	But Cricket didn't want to stop playing. His toes were tapping, his coat-tails flapping, as the melody flowed from his fiddle string.

Source: Adapted from *Wind Says Good Night* by Katy Rydell. Text copyright © 1994 by Katy Rydell. Reprinted by permission of Houghton Mifflin Co. All rights reserved.

Theatre Acting

Theatre acting includes all of the previously described oral language activities: movement exercises, pantomime, improvisation, speaking with feeling and expression, discussion and interpretation of scripts, and rehearsing. It also includes what for some children is the most difficult aspect of acting: the memorization of a script. Because of this requirement and the additional pressures that it places on young children, it is recommended that theatre acting come after students are already familiar with the other forms of oral expression. However, even very young children can be taught the rudiments of play acting.

Too often teachers are required by school administrators to have their class perform a play (the traditional Thanksgiving or Christmas auditorium performance) without any prior preparation in oral communication or acting. This is a mistake. Theatre acting should be part of the learning process that leads children to a greater appreciation of literature; builds confidence in oral communication abilities; and enhances social growth, including cooperative learning skills. Children's drama authority Nellie McCaslin (1996) has argued correctly that theatre acting is a vital part of the aesthetic education of children, which too often is missing or minimized in elementary curriculums.

To introduce theater acting in the elementary classroom, Dorothy Heathcote (Heathcote & Bolton, 1995) has recommended that teachers begin with discussion. Talk about the work to be performed. Encourage the children to make suggestions and decisions about the characters, the setting, the staging, and so on. Then improvise the play or story until everyone has a sense of the action, the movement of characters, and the overall theme of the play or story. Do not be afraid to revise lines, to change parts, or to recast characters. Depending on the nature of the work selected, older students may wish to do library research about the subject matter of the play or the specific time period depicted. Figure 5.22 suggests sources for theatre acting in the elementary grades.

> *Education is not filling a pail, but the lighting of a fire.*
>
> **WILLIAM BUTLER YEATS**

Burack, S. (1970). *One Hundred Plays for Children.* Boston: Plays, Inc.

Burack, S. (1990). *Plays: The Drama Magazine for Young People.* Boston: Plays, Inc.

Hugher, T. (1974). *The Tiger's Bones and Other Plays for Children.* New York: Viking.

Murray, F. (1984). *Mystery Plays for Young Actors.* Boston: Plays, Inc.

FIGURE 5.22

Plays for theatre acting.

Theatre acting represents the culmination of a dramatics unit. It brings together and integrates listening, speaking, reading, and writing skills like no other single activity. It gives students a heightened awareness of the power of literature to evoke emotions from an audience. It engages youngsters in critical thinking and discussion. However, choosing to do a full-scale play production in your class means a commitment of time and energy. You cannot squeeze it between spelling tests, ditto worksheets, and basal reader lessons. The sacrifices you make, however, are more than made up for by the excitement, enthusiasm, and genuine learning that take place when students discover their talents as actors.

SPEAKING ASSESSMENT

When a teacher wishes to assess the students' speaking abilities using a specific assignment, she should discuss with students from the beginning which areas will be assessed. This allows students to work on those skills while they prepare their assignment. It is then crucial that the teacher assess those specific skills during the assignment. At the beginning of the year, a teacher may want to emphasize only adequate coverage of content or volume and eye contact, in which case the rubric should include only those areas. However, toward the end of the year, the teacher may also require visual aids. In this case, it is important that she also assess the speaker's use of the visual aids. Appendix C has an example of a rubric a teacher used for research presentations that were given toward the end of the year. Take note that on this rubric each aspect of the presentation is of equal importance. However, the rubric used for storytelling is scored differently: the emphasis is on voice inflection, with each aspect of voice inflection given a different value. Appendix C also has rubrics for other speaking activities.

When a teacher uses a rubric, a student can see the specific strengths and weaknesses of his or her presentation. It is important, too, that a teacher (1) write general comments to encourage the student and (2) discuss the rubric with the student.

Vocabulary Development

In an integrated approach to the language arts, vocabulary development is a natural byproduct of listening and speaking. Jim Trelease (2001) in *The Read-Aloud Handbook* explains that reading aloud to children of all ages (from birth through middle school) is the most effective way to help them enlarge their vocabulary. Evans (1992) found that reading to seventh-graders each day was not only a pleasant experience but also a great way to increase the average/low-average seventh-graders' vocabulary and reading ability. There is debate among researchers, however, as to whether or not direct instruction is necessary for learning specific vocabulary terms.

The position of this textbook is that vocabulary knowledge develops in the normal course of engaging young children in listening, speaking, reading, and writing activities. However, at times teachers should use mini-lessons to teach vocabulary directly. In these cases, the following guidelines should be kept in mind (Rupley, Logan, & Nichols, 1998/1999):

- Always relate new vocabulary terms to students' prior knowledge and background.
- Focus on elaborating children's use of new terms rather than merely having them memorize definitions.
- Utilize activities that demand active student involvement in vocabulary learning, such as vocabulary games, dramatics, or writing activities, rather than passive fill-in-the-blank exercises.
- Help students develop strategies for acquiring new vocabulary independently, such as constructing concept wheels, semantic word maps, webs, and semantic feature analysis graphs.
- Build a conceptual base for the new vocabulary word.

VOCABULARY MINI-LESSONS

The following activities lend themselves to mini-lessons that reinforce specific aspects of vocabulary development.

Synonyms

Synonyms are words that have the same or almost the same meaning, such as *gigantic* and *enormous*. Knowledge of synonyms makes speech and writing more varied and interesting. Often young children rely on the same tired words over and over again because they lack synonym knowledge. Some synonym lessons can be tied to teaching students to use a dictionary or thesaurus. Other activities include having small groups brainstorm lists of synonym alternatives for commonly used words such as *said* or *talk*. These lists can later be displayed around the room as charts for easy reference when writing or reading (see Figure 5.23).

FIGURE 5.23

Synonym chart.

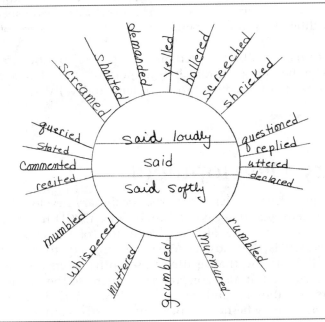

Antonyms

Antonyms are words that have opposite meanings, such as *hot/cold* and *fat/slender*. Teach a few common pairs of antonyms; then get students into small groups to brainstorm pairs of antonyms. Encourage them to use their dictionaries to find new words and their opposites. Charts of the antonym pairs can be made to reinforce vocabulary learning.

Homonyms

Homonyms are words that sound alike but are spelled differently and have different meanings. Homonyms are often confused by children and appear as errors in their writing. Identify common homonym errors by analyzing students' writing. For example, *to/too/two*, *there/their/they're*, *which/witch*, *wood/would*, *deer/dear*, and *bear/bare* are often misused in children's writing. Review the spelling and meanings of these common homonyms with your class, but remember they will only be learned as students use them in their writing over time. The isolated mini-lesson is only a first step toward vocabulary development.

Multiple Meanings

Common words sometimes take on new meanings depending on the context. For example, many words can be used as both a noun (a playing *card*) and a verb (to *card* wool). The key to teaching multiple meanings of words is to focus on the contexts of sentences. Contextual clues are the most powerful of the reading strategies for determining meanings of commonly used words. In how many different contexts can you use the ordinary word *run*? (Clue: You can *run* around the block and get a *run* in your stocking.)

Neologisms

Neologisms are new words that have entered the language through extensive usage or as labels for new discoveries, inventions, products, fashions, and so on. Children need to understand that words are created by people and that language is continually changing. Identifying new words that have entered the English language is one way of demonstrating language change over time. For example, find a dictionary from around 1945 and compare it with a dictionary printed in the 1990s. Note how many new words have been created in that roughly 50-year period. Words associated with space exploration, computers, discoveries in chemistry and physics, new fashion designs, and inventions are all neologisms. Some examples are *astronaut*, *laser*, *microwave*, *silicon*, *carcinogen*, *arthroscope*, and *bell-bottoms*.

Portmanteaus

A *portmanteau* is a new word formed by combining two existing words and omitting some of their letters. Lewis Carroll, the author of *Alice in Wonderland*, provided many early portmanteaus, such as "*chuckle* + *snort* = *chortle*." A common portmanteau students might recognize is the word *smog*, which weather forecasters used to describe certain very cloudy days made up of *smoke* and *fog*. A type of *motor hotel* is referred to as a *motel*; a light meal that comes after *breakfast* and before *lunch* is called *brunch*. See how many other portmanteaus your class can think of. The students may even wish to create their own portmanteaus. For example, one fourth-grade boy created a comic book character that was part *man* and part *bear* and called him *Bearan*.

Acronyms

An *acronym* is a word formed from the initials of an organization or phrase. This is a shortened way of saying something; over time, through wide usage, such acronyms have become accepted as actual words. For example, the military uses many acronyms. Children might recognize the word *M.A.S.H.* (from the TV show) as standing for Mobile Army Surgical Hospital. A soldier who is absent without leave is *AWOL*. The North Atlantic Treaty Organization is referred to as *NATO*. Many other groups and organizations employ acronyms: *NOW* stands for the National Organization for Women; *AIM* stands for the American Indian Movement. Brainstorm together additional acronyms.

Euphemisms

A *euphemism* literally is a "more pleasant sounding" word used instead of a term with negative connotations. Some euphemisms originate from social pressures of groups offended by certain inaccurate or inadequate terms. For example, the term *Native American* can be used instead of *Indian* since Christopher Columbus applied the latter term in the mistaken belief that he had landed in India. Recently the term *sanitation engineer* has replaced *garbage collector* although the job remains the same. Other euphemisms are created to hide the true meaning of terms. The military refers to *defoliation programs* rather than *chemical warfare*. Other common euphemisms are *senior citizen*, *retirement village*, and the *dearly departed*.

Regionalisms

Regionalisms are expressions associated with particular geographic regions of the country. As such, they are closely related to dialects, the unique pronunciation characteristics of specific areas of a country. Lessons on identifying regional expressions integrate nicely with geography lessons. For example, in the Northeast, people carry their groceries in a *bag*; in the Midwest, people use a *sack*. In the Deep South, you may hear the term *poke*. All three terms refer to the same object. Similarly, depending on the region in which you happen to live or travel, you may hear different terms all referring to the same food: *pancakes, flapjacks, griddle cakes, johnny cakes, a stack*. How many different terms can you think of for a large seat generally found in a living room?

TECHNOLOGY AND WEBSITES

The video camera, now available in many schools, is a useful tool to promote speaking skills and to integrate the language arts with the entire curriculum. One activity that can be done by the entire class is to plan and produce a newscast.

Following are a few of the activities that take place as the students plan and rehearse for the production:

- They research (read) for information.
- They write the news pieces.

- They practice speaking and listening skills as they interview people for the newscast. The video camera can also be used in the interviews.
- The student who does the weather may need to review weather terms and geographic locations.
- Students who read the news will need to be sure about the correct pronunciations of places and people's names.
- Students who produce the advertisement spots will have a chance to write and sing jingles and then act out the advertisements.
- As the students polish for the final production, they will listen, view, and self-critique their contributions to the newscast.

Another way to use the video camera in the classroom is to have groups of children practice and tape readers theatre, puppet shows, and skits. The students should be encouraged to view the presentation, work on fluency, and later show it to other classes and caregivers. As you can see, the video camera is a great tool to use as children become fluent speakers.

www.videomaker.com

This site is an outstanding magazine (print and electronic) for people interested in video production.

www.puppetresources.com

This site has free puppet scripts and other puppet resources.

www.aaronshep.com/rt

This is Aaron Shepard's home page, which has many scripts for readers theatre.

www.sitesforteachers.com

This site has many resources for language arts teachers, including those for speaking and listening skills.

www.geocities.com/enchantedforest/tower/3235

This site has many scripts for readers theatre.

www.stemnet.nf.ca/CITE/langrt.htm

This site explains how to write scripts for puppet shows and readers theatre.

Summary

Listening and speaking skills are two of the important foundation blocks for literacy instruction. Students' listening abilities can be developed through listening centers, listening/reading transfer lessons, and critical listening activities, such as recognizing propaganda devices. Because students spend the majority of their time listening, it is important that their skills in this area be developed and related to the other language arts.

Speaking skills develop through the creation of a positive learning environment in the classroom and through practicing speaking in a variety of settings and activities. There are many oral language activities that teachers can use to engage their students: conversation, show-and-tell, and storytelling are but a few. Dramatic play, improvisation, and readers theatre further develop speaking and acting abilities in a cooperative group setting. Theatre acting, which culminates in the performance of a play before a live audience, brings together all the communication skills in an exciting learning experience for teachers, children, and caregivers.

Vocabulary mini-lessons can also be taught to reinforce students' knowledge of synonyms, antonyms, homonyms, and other vocabulary constructs. However, such lessons are most effective when they originate from children's questions or appear in the reading and writing activities that the students have selected.

ACTIVITIES *with children*

The following activities can be presented in a game format and are helpful in developing the vocabulary and general speaking skills of young children. Work with a small group of students and explain or model the game. Then let them play the game while you observe how they use language and learn new vocabulary terms.

Going on a Picnic

Begin by saying, "We are going on a picnic and Ann is bringing apples." Then have each child think of an object to bring that begins with the same initial sound as his or her own name. Later they can think of objects that begin with the same sound as a friend's name. Once the students understand the pattern, begin the game, with each child introducing as many children as possible using the pattern "We are going on a picnic . . ." A more challenging version of the game for older students includes the insertion of a descriptive adjective with the same initial sound before the noun. For example, "We are going on a picnic and Donald is bringing delicious doughnuts."

In Your Own Voice

First teach children how to give a brief talk on a topic of their choice. Then have them tape-record their voice. Teach them to analyze their own speech. Is it clear? Too fast? Interesting? Tape the speech a second time and have students try to improve from the first effort.

Categories

Name a category (such as "vehicles") and then continue naming members of the category (car, bus, train, and so on). At any point, another person may say "category" and start over with a new category (such as "vegetables"). This game is played to a rhythm as follows: clap, clap, snap, snap, [category/example] (clap, clap, snap, snap, *vehicles*; clap, clap, snap, snap, *car*; clap, clap, snap, snap, *bus*; and so on).

Alphabet Game

Tell what you see inside or outside the classroom beginning with the letter *a*. Have the next person repeat your sentence and add an object beginning with the letter *b*. Then have the third person repeat the two previous sentences and add an object beginning with the letter *c*, and so on. For example, "I see an apple, a box, and a crayon." Encourage the children to use complete sentences.

Geography Train

This game combines knowledge of geographic place-names, spelling, and vocabulary. The first person names a country, a city, a state, or some other place. The next person uses the last letter of the place-name to begin the next term. The game continues until someone cannot think of a name beginning with the last letter of the previous word. For example, "Ethiopia, Alaska, Arkansas, Switzerland, Denver, . . ."

Noun Train

This game is played using the same rules as Geography Train except that any nouns can be used, for example, "Book, kitchen, napkin, noodle . . ." Another variation on this would be a Verb Train.

Context Challenge

This game emphasizes careful listening skills and particularly context clues. Write a challenge word on the board, one the students probably do not know, and then read aloud a passage containing that word. The children can only use the context clues heard in the passage to determine the unknown word.

Oral/Aural Math

One child dictates a simple addition, subtraction, multiplication, or division problem. The next student solves the problem aloud without using paper or pencil. Later, these oral word problems can combine addition, subtraction, multiplication, and other steps.

Oral Cloze

The cloze technique (discussed in Chapters 9 and 10) involves omitting words from a passage in a reading exercise. The reader must then fill in the blank with an accurate word or phrase. Oral Cloze utilizes the same skill but is done strictly at the listening and speaking levels. This exercise requires careful attention and listening.

Homonym Hop

First have students think of as many homonym pairs as possible. Next have them come up with a silly definition for the word formed by the combination of each pair. See if their classmates can guess the homonyms from their definition, for example: "A naked grizzly is a *bare bear*." "An unemployed rock star is an *idle idol*." "An ordinary jet is a *plain plane*."

RELATED READINGS

Cooper, P., & Morreale, S. (2003). *Creating competent communicators: Activities for teaching speaking, listening and media literacy in K–6 classrooms.* Scottsdale, AZ: Holcomb Hathaway.

This book gives a wide array of speaking and listening activities for elementary grades.

Cottrell, J. (1987). *Creative drama in the classroom grades 4–6: Teacher's resource book for theatre arts.* Lincolnwood, IL: National Textbook Company.

This book explains how to include creative drama as an educational tool. The author explains how to do sidecoaching, role-playing, pantomime, readers theatre, puppetry, and improvisation with literature as well as other subjects such as social studies and science. Included are scripts that are ready to be used in the classroom.

Holt, L. (2000). *Snapshots: Literacy minilessons up close.* Portsmouth, NH: Heinemann.

This book has mini-lessons to help students' listening and speaking skills.

Martinez, M., Roser, N., & Strecker, S. (1998/1999). "I never thought I could be a star": A reader's theatre ticket to fluency. *The Reading Teacher, 52*(4), 326–334.

McCaslin, N. (1996). *Creative drama in the classroom and beyond* (6th ed.). New York: Longman.

This book is a great starting point for teachers who have no experience in any of the creative dramatic activities. Included are scripts to be used in the various activities.

Miller, W. (2000). *Strategies for developing emergent literacy.* Boston: McGraw-Hill.

This book focuses on all types of emergent literacy activities, including listening and speaking, that are appropriate for young children.

Trelease, J. (2001). *The read-aloud handbook* (5th ed.). New York: Penguin Books.

Trelease offers a theory for reading aloud to students of all ages. He explains what makes a book a great read-aloud book and gives lists for all ages.

Language and Literacy: The Reading Factor

This chapter focuses on the role that reading plays in language development and learning. You will examine the major approaches to reading instruction: basal readers, literature, language experience, and the comprehensive approach. You will also learn about holistic approaches to evaluation and informal diagnostic strategies. Finally, you will explore ways to help struggling readers.

CHAPTER OBJECTIVES

After reading this chapter, you should be able to accomplish the following objectives:

1. Explain the three models of reading.
2. Identify the components of the basal reader approach.
3. Explain the language experience approach.
4. Identify the elements in a literature-based approach.
5. Define the comprehensive reading approach.
6. Explain how the 4-Blocks Literacy Model works.
7. Name the components of a reading/writing workshop.
8. Explain how to do a running record.
9. Explain how Accelerated Reader works.
10. Identify how to promote visual and technological literacy.

CHECK YOUR BACKGROUND KNOWLEDGE. Before reading the chapter, complete the K-T-W-L chart based on the chapter overview and objectives provided at left. In column "K," write what you know about the topics in the objectives. In column "T," write what you think you know. In column "W," write what you want to learn. Finally, after you have read the chapter, write what you have learned in column "L."

Know	**T**hink you know	**W**ant to learn	**L**earned

Language and Literacy

Literacy is one of the most important accomplishments of any society: It is the hallmark of civilization. However, coming up with an exact description of literacy can be difficult, and over the years the definition has changed. At one time, a person who could write and read his or her own name was considered literate. In more recent years, an individual's literacy level has been gauged by the highest school grade she or he has completed—a standard that is not always accurate. Currently, literacy is seen by many in terms of an individual's ability to function well in the workplace and in our surrounding society. This definition has grown out of the national concern about having people read and write well enough to create an effective workforce and democracy.

However, literacy really is much more than this. As Benjamin DeMott (1990) has written, literacy—reading and writing—is what helps people to understand each other, to connect with each other, and to know the truth for themselves. Literacy empowers people; it gives them the ability to acquire information for themselves. It makes them independent learners who are able to connect with and communicate with whomever they choose. Literacy helps individuals engage with technology and the Internet as the Information Highway becomes more and more electronic (Leu, 2000).

The mirror processes of reading and writing are also inseparable. Reading requires the written word; any writing requires a reader. The writer and the reader need each other; each is incomplete without the other. Therefore, it is essential that each individual develop both processes of literacy.

Of course, the reading aspect of literacy has its own special type of magic. A reader can unlock the code of those little black squiggles on paper and can make sense of someone else's words. A reader can visit other places and times, can give free rein to his or her imagination, and can create a special world of personal knowledge.

On the more practical, daily level, reading is needed in order to follow the directions for baking a cake, assembling a bicycle, completing a job application, or giving someone the proper dose of medicine. It helps people to find their way in strange cities by allowing them to follow a road map and read street signs. It also helps people read the labels and buy the right products in stores. Without reading, an individual is lost and helpless in a literate world. It is disturbing that the United States, compared with other countries, has had a greater concentration of adults at the lowest levels of literacy on prose, document, and quantitative materials (Organization for Economic Co-operation and Development and Statistics Canada, 1998).

Apparently, the number of people in the United States not truly engaged in reading may be growing. The National Assessment of Educational Progress (NAEP, 2000) found that between 1992 and 2000 there were declines in average reading proficiency in certain cultural groups across the nation. Our society cannot afford to let any more of its members be uninvolved with reading; the teaching profession needs to help all people enjoy reading.

Reading Explored

Reading, like literacy, has often been difficult to describe. Many people have their own ideas about the process, ideas based on their experiences both in and out of school. An activity completed by one group of college-level methods students has illustrated this point (Blake, 2000). Each semester the incoming students conducted a small survey to find out how individuals define reading. The students interviewed people of different ages and backgrounds and received some surprisingly varied responses.

Children interviewed in this survey often described reading as completing a workbook, sounding out letters, or reciting the alphabet. A certain number believed that reading was listening to a storybook or figuring out a story for themselves. The ideas of these young readers echoed the research of Johns and Ellis (1976), who found that children's views of reading generally reflect how they learn to read in school. Students also indicated that they saw reading as something that girls did more than boys (McKenna, 1997), and older students frequently reported negative attitudes about reading, which research links to poor reading ability in the upper grades (McKenna, Kear, & Ellsworth, 1995). These negative attitudes are particularly disturbing because we now know that attitude toward reading is a major factor affecting reading achievement and performance (Wixson & Lipson, 2000). Adults also gave some interesting responses, many of which were related to the ways in which they used reading in their schooling and work. However, most of their answers focused on reading as an attempt to comprehend information.

Research has now shown that real reading takes place only when meaning and understanding are present. Over the years, educators have definitely moved beyond the notion that reading is "a precise process" that involves "exact, detailed, sequential perception and identification of letters, words, spelling patterns and larger language units" (Goodman, 1967, p. 126). Beginning with Goodman's work, which viewed reading as a type of "psycholinguistic guessing game" (p. 127), an interaction between thought and language, specialists began to see that reading is much more than the exact perception of simple parts of language.

Later researchers have demonstrated that reading is actually a constructive process of obtaining meaning from text. This construction process is social, dependent on the learner's goals, and firmly tied to the context in which the reading and learning take place (Cambourne, 2002b). Good readers use their prior life experiences and their knowledge about books and language to help themselves construct meaning from the written page. They also try to monitor themselves as they read to see if what they are reading actually makes sense. In other words, reading is a very individual process in which what the reader already knows greatly affects what he or she learns from a text.

For example, consider what happens when you read the following sentence:

> As the storm approached, the people in the town stored provisions to make sure that they would survive.

Depending on what part of the world you are from, the storm might mean a snowstorm, a blizzard, a hurricane, a tornado, a monsoon, or a typhoon. Your ideas about provisions might vary from canned tuna and potato chips to dried meat or sacks of rice. Survival might mean "How do we get through a week without electricity?" or "Where can we get brush and wood to make a fire to keep us warm?" Your prior life experiences and the context of the reading situation affect your interpretation of the words in the sentence (Nagy & Scott, 1990).

In reading these words, you are also making use of your knowledge of both oral and written language. After years of speaking and listening, you do not have any trouble associating the letters with the sounds and figuring out the words. You also have some idea about the right intonation to use as you say the sentence. Your previous experiences with writing, grammar, and punctuation enable you to spot the subject and verb of the sentence without any trouble and to decide where the sentence begins and ends. In reading the sentence,

Beyond the classroom

There have been many community efforts throughout the United States to combat the problem of illiteracy (e.g., Literacy Volunteers of America). Find out what people in your community are doing to promote literacy for adults as well as children. You might even give some thought to volunteering time to help them.

your mind interacts with the text (writing) to construct meaning. The reading is not done in isolation; it is integrated with your prior knowledge and all the language arts, especially writing.

MODELS OF READING

This view of reading as an active, constructive process is the result of theories and research models of the reading process. To date, documented models of reading include the bottom-up model, the top-down model, and the interactive model (Weaver, 1994).

Bottom-Up Model

The **bottom-up model of reading** has its origins in theories and approaches that emphasize precise identification, or *decoding*, of the individual parts of language; it follows a sequential or serial path that begins with an understanding of the sounds of language and their corresponding letters and moves word by word through sentences, paragraphs, and larger selections of text (LaBerge & Samuels, 1985; Pressley, 2002). Through the perception and discrimination of these unique elements, the reader obtains meaning. Essentially, says this model, the language of the text holds the key to meaning. It is a commonsense approach (Weaver, 1994).

Since decoding, or "cracking the written code of the text," is of prime importance in this model, emphasis is placed on mastering the subskills of reading—those concerned with comprehension (such as identifying the main idea and details, following directions, making inferences, and predicting outcomes) as well as those that reflect the rules of language related to letters and sounds (such as phonics, structural analysis, spelling patterns, and syllabication). Proponents of the bottom-up approach believe that when readers have learned the various subskills well enough, reading becomes an automatic process of obtaining meaning from the text.

Although a body of research does support the belief that reading contains a hierarchy of subskills, there are some concerns about this approach to teaching reading. First, it is difficult to get reading specialists to agree on which subskills should definitely be learned by all readers (Burns, Roe, & Smith, 2002). Some suggested lists emphasize certain skills at the expense of others. Also, many reading educators are convinced that meaning lies not within the text but in the reader's mind and in the reader's ability to integrate that knowledge with learned strategies for decoding language.

Top-Down Model

Emphasis on the critical role that the reader's mind plays in comprehension is the cornerstone of the **top-down model of reading,** in which understanding, the key objective, takes place through the use of information in the mind rather than through the text itself.

Research in psycholinguistics (Goodman, 1967, 1976) has shown that in processing language a person makes use of three cue systems:

1. *Graphophonic:* the relationship between the sounds of oral language and the letters in the text
2. *Semantic:* the actual meaning of the words and the context in which they are used
3. *Syntactic:* grammar; the rules that govern the organization of the language

According to the top-down model, the reader uses these cue systems to make predictions or educated guesses about the meaning of what she or he is reading.

What the reader expects or anticipates has a profound effect on how he or she actually perceives the textual material.

Suppose you are reading a passage about dolphins and come across a phrase that you read as *the silvery dolphins*, a description that you frequently associate with the mammals. However, further reading shows that the passage is referring to dolphins caught in an oil slick and that your interpretation of the phrase does not really make sense. Upon rereading the phrase, you see that it actually says *the slimy dolphins*. You have tested your original hypothesis for the meaning of the phrase and found that it does not work, that there is a mismatch (a *miscue*, in psycholinguistic terminology) between what you perceived and what is actually in the text. You looked for an overall meaning first; when you realized that your first attempt at understanding did not make sense, you then consulted the individual units of language for clarification. This process of attempting to grasp meaning first has caused proponents of the top-down model to view reading as a holistic experience rather than a series of language subskills (Pressley, 2002).

In accordance with the top-down view, children should be given opportunities to use their minds in reading. They should have experiences with meaningful stories, literature, and **big books** rather than concentrate on specific language models or rules. However, this emphasis gives some educators cause for concern. They believe that in addition to meaningful experiences, many children truly need to learn specific strategies for processing language. In light of the success of the Reading Recovery program for at-risk first-grade students (an approach discussed later in this chapter), these concerns must be taken seriously.

Interactive Model

The **interactive model of reading** is an attempt to reconcile top-down and bottom-up processing; reading is viewed as a continual interaction between reader and text in which the reader brings meaning to and derives meaning from the page (Kintsch, 1998). In this construction of knowledge, the reader attempts to achieve understanding by using prior knowledge stored in mental units of information called *schemata* (Rumelhart, 1980) as well as specific learned strategies for decoding the language of the text.

Reading is thus a highly individualized and personal activity because each person's schemata and ability to use them are unique. How a person interprets a text depends a great deal on the schemata he or she has developed and how effectively they are used. Therefore, it is possible for two individuals to come to some very different conclusions about the same passage.

Many reading specialists agree with the theory behind the interactive model. However, some questions have been raised concerning the specific ways in which the model functions. Are both forms of processing equally important, and do all readers use the processes simultaneously? So far, research has indicated that readers in the stage of emerging literacy may concentrate more on decoding the specific elements in the text than on recalling information in the mind; more mature, efficient readers appear to do the opposite. As more knowledge is gained through research, reading educators may have to modify these views. However, the essential point is that both top-down and bottom-up processing are essential components of reading comprehension. Reading educators need to recognize this when planning instruction for children.

Figure 6.1 offers a visual representation of how these models work. Although each model has its merits, the interactive view provides the most comprehensive and effective description of the reading process, especially when combined with

Beyond the classroom

Interview three or four people about their definitions of the reading process. Be sure to include children of varying ages as well as adults in your sample. Make notes about their responses in your journal, and reflect on how their ideas relate to those presented in this chapter.

FIGURE 6.1

Three models of reading.

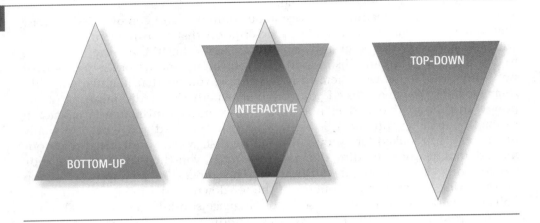

a personal, *transactional relationship* to the world around us (Rosenblatt, 1978). In such a system, each student is part of a dynamic construction of meaning when engaging with text—a process in which cultural, social, and environmental factors influence his or her unique interpretation of the words on the page (Rosenblatt, 1994). While reading continues to be seen as a holistic construction of knowledge, it also requires specific strategies for understanding textual language; there should be a balance (Pressley, 2002). Many approaches for engaging with text are encouraged: experiences with real books and literature, use of specific strategies to facilitate understanding of text, development of story structure, use of questioning strategies, experiences with differing language patterns—basically the use of any technique for making reading an active, constructive undertaking.

Reading Research

Over the years, much research has been conducted about the many complex factors involved in reading. Prominent research topics have included cognitive functioning, schema theory, metacognition, the proper role of phonics, characteristics of successful readers, and the effects of particular strategies to enhance reading comprehension. As a result, reports have emerged describing everything from students' achievement on national reading assessments to how students monitor their own cognitive processes. These research results constitute a significant body of knowledge concerning issues with a direct impact on learning to read and the type of instruction needed to facilitate this process.

Reading research is valuable to teachers in that it allows them to make a difference in the real world. In general, the research most helpful to educators is that which has provided information about how readers function, the impact of text upon comprehension, and the effects of classroom instruction. Therefore, for the purposes of this chapter, the research data from reading studies are presented in three categories, focusing on the reader, the text, and the instruction.

THE READER

A child does not become a reader in a vacuum. She or he comes from a home and a family; as discussed in Chapter 2, the home environment is one of the greatest influences on how well any reader functions. Just as caregivers support and help a child in taking his or her first few steps, they also provide the child's first encounters with the essentials of reading and writing. It is only natural that children look to their primary caregivers and protectors for role models and for encouragement in these important components of the communication process.

According to *Becoming a Nation of Readers* (Anderson, Hiebert, Scott, & Wilkinson, 1985), caregivers who expose their children to a wide variety of experiences—such as trips to stores, parks, zoos, and museums—and who then communicate carefully with the children about these experiences tend to produce more successful readers. Prior knowledge abut print is also related to the frequency that caregivers focus their children on print during the activities of writing their names, playing cards, or reading stories (Purcell-Gates, 2000). Caregivers can also increase children's chances for reading success by using daily read-aloud sessions to show children that adults truly enjoy and value reading (Wigfield & Asher, 1984). Reading aloud to children has been shown to be the most important activity for fostering reading success (Anderson et al., 1985). In addition, the act of reading aloud together, each reader taking a turn, has the added benefit of evolving into a lifelong habit of successful social interaction and collaboration (Burns et al., 2002).

The importance of the home in supporting reading and writing does not decrease once a child enters school. Caregivers should support classroom literacy instruction by attending school meetings and being well informed about school programs. It has been suggested that greater involvement and empowerment of caregivers results in more successful readers. According to *The Nation's Report Card: Fourth-Grade Reading 2000* (National Assessment of Educational Progress [NAEP], 2000), students who indicated that they had received home support in the form of home reading materials and caregiver interest in their schoolwork were more proficient readers. These were the same children who read often, visited libraries, watched only a small amount of TV, and completed homework assignments.

From the child's experiences at home and at school, he or she develops a body of background knowledge that can be assessed and used in reading comprehension. This information that the reader already possesses is called *prior knowledge*. Readers use such knowledge to help them make sense of what they are reading, much as you did when reading the brief references to the storm and the dolphins. Of course the idea of the importance of prior knowledge in constructing meaning can be traced back to the work of Goodman (1967, 1976) and Smith (1982a) on psycholinguistics. Recall that in the psycholinguistic system, the reader's expectations—related to the graphophonic, semantic, and syntactic cues in the text—are the driving factor in obtaining meaning from the text. These expectations arise from the reader's store of background knowledge, which in turn has been built on that individual's previous experiences.

Prior knowledge has proved to be a better predictor of recall from reading than verbal intelligence, word recognition, overall reading ability, or vocabulary knowledge (Anderson & Pearson, 1984). Such knowledge, said Tierney, "guides the reader through the text and allows him or her to suggest scenarios, make predictions, identify and empathize with characters, and relate to events or settings and their interplay" (1990, p. 38). Readers use background knowledge and expectations to construct meanings; they consciously access information that relates to what they are preparing to read or are actually reading. Use of prior knowledge makes engaging with text an extremely purposeful activity (Graves, Juel, & Graves, 1998).

Prior knowledge is also organized into schemata, which, according to the interactive model, play an important role in the development of reading skills. These schemata, "the building blocks of cognition" (Rumelhart, 1980, p. 33), are acquired through experiences: They are the generic theories individuals form about the world and the way it runs. Through the years, schemata shape people's expectations of what will or should happen; they are necessary in processing any new information learned through individual comprehension strategies (Vacca, 2002b).

By drawing upon the "grocery-shopping schemata" that they already had in their heads, the children in the Classroom Vignette that follows are better able to comprehend the story. They have the ability to access a huge store of knowledge about shopping through their rich, internalized networks of schemata (Graves et al., 1998). However, imagine what the case would have been had Mrs. Blackmon asked the same question of a child who had never seen a supermarket. How might this child have reacted to a story involving grocery shopping? Since meaning is constructed by comparing prior knowledge (knowledge driven) with new text information (text driven) (Bransford & Johnson, 1973; Goldman & Rakestraw, 2000), the child's lack of a particular schema—in this case, for grocery shopping—would have greatly limited his or her ability to obtain meaning from the story. The same would be true for any child who had not had opportunities to develop a storehouse of particular schemata.

Another area of research into cognitive functioning that has had a tremendous impact on reading instruction is that of metacognition. **Metacognition** is defined as people's awareness of their own activities when they are reading, solving problems, and studying, as well as being an active learner capable of monitoring these processes. Basically, metacognition is what a child knows about his or her own thinking and how the child is able to monitor that thinking. It is what enables a child to become a strategic reader, capable of deciding when comprehension is or is not occurring and what to do when things do not make sense. Such readers are able to use their prior knowledge, identify purposes for reading, make predictions, focus on the content, reread any confusing parts, visualize the images in the text, and summarize information (Paris, Lipson, & Wixson, 1983).

An adage for metacognition might be "Reader, know thyself." Children who employ metacognition know both their strengths and their weaknesses as readers. One child might know that she or he is quite good at reading a passage and answering some simple questions about it but not so good at reading the same passage and writing an alternative ending for it. The child (or maybe the teacher) might then realize that it would be wise to spend some time practicing brainstorming and predicting strategies as well as rehearsing and drafting summaries. Realizing what you need to do is as important as realizing what you already do. Currently, metacognition is considered to be so important to the reading process that a study on how readers use it within reading strategies is being considered by the NAEP (2001).

One activity for developing metacognitive knowledge that has received much attention is *reciprocal teaching* (Palincsar & Brown, 1986). In this approach, the teacher and students take turns at teaching. Initially the teacher models the needed behaviors and strategies, such as previewing, predicting, summarizing, and questioning. Then the process is gradually transferred to the students. Reciprocal teaching has been shown to be not only interactive but also a very effective and direct way of using teacher modeling to promote student understanding. According to Carter (1997), the use of reciprocal teaching has the ability to raise students' achievement scores after only one year of implementation. Now that is something worth trying.

To be successful, today's reader must be an active participant in reading, a participant equipped with knowledge of the world, knowledge of self as a reader, and knowledge of the strategies needed for successful reading.

THE TEXT

Obviously, the text is no longer the only determinant of successful reading comprehension; instead it has become what Pearson has termed a "blueprint for meaning" (1985, p. 726); a reader constructs his or her own interpretation or

VIGNETTE
in the classroom

Mrs. Blackmon, a second-grade teacher, plans to have some of the students in her class read a story involving grocery shopping. In order to find out about their schemata and to prepare them for the reading experience, she says to them, "Tell me what you know abut grocery shopping." The children's answers are random at first, but then it becomes apparent that the children have very individual inter-pretations of generally similar concepts. After some discussion, Mrs. Blackmon helps the students cate-gorize their ideas.

GROCERY SHOPPING

Goal: To get the groceries and go home.

People Involved:	You, your mother and/or father, other shoppers, the store people or clerks, the cash register person, the bagger.
Objects:	Cart, shelves, aisles, place for meats and frozen food, different kinds of food, stuff to clean the house, flowers, things to drink, bags (plastic and paper), cash register, money.
Sequence of Events:	Get to the store (walk, bicycle, car), get a cart, check your list, get what you need, get in line at register, pay, get your bags, put them in the car (if you have one), go home, unpack.

meaning from it (Collins, Brown, & Larkin, 1980). It is a basic guide or sugges-tion for meaning rather than the meaning itself. As mentioned earlier, it is quite possible for two readers to develop entirely different interpretations as they work their way through the same passage or text. The meaning is created through a multitude of interactions: the reader, the text, the classroom influ-ences, and the environment (Ruddell & Unrau, 1994).

However, some aspects of the text still have an important impact on reading. It is easier for students to read texts for which they have prior knowledge and schemata; it is also easier for them to read materials with plenty of illustrations and less print on the page. Everyone has seen a poor reader go to the library and only look for thin books with lots of pictures and very little print.

Because textual difficulty affects children's comprehension, it is very important for teachers and schools to choose texts of appropriate difficulty lev-els. Many schools thus use **readability formulas,** which gauge the difficulty of a text by averaging the number of syllables and number of sentences for three 100-word passages and then assigning the text an approximate grade level (see Chapter 10 for a complete description of this process). However, there is controversy about the use of these formulas because they do not tell whether books have literary quality, interest for children, clear and accurate writing, or logical organization—factors that contribute to textual difficulty. Even the cur-rent and popular Lexile system, which is based on the same measures as prior readability formulas—semantic difficulty (the presence of a text's words on a word list) and syntactic difficulty (sentence length)—has not been able to resolve the problem (Hiebert, 2002).

It is very important that stories for early readers be well organized and have a definite structure. Typical story elements include a setting, characters, a theme, a plot related to the goals of the characters, and an orderly sequence that makes sense to the reader. Through listening to well-formed stories, young chil-dren develop a sense of story structure, which later helps them to comprehend stories in print. The closer a story fits the format, the easier it is for young read-ers to comprehend it (Burns et al., 2002).

Books that have a *repeating verse* or sentence pattern are ideal for beginning readers (McMackin, 1993). Such books can have repetitive language patterns;

The elementary school must assume as its sub-lime and most solemn responsibility the task of teaching every child how to read. Any school that does not accomplish this has failed.

JACQUES BARZUM

story patterns; or familiar sequences of numbers, days of the week, or months (Huck, Hepler, & Hickman, 1993). The *repetition* provides a reliable and consistent verbal scaffolding or support for the child (Bruner, 1973), thus freeing him or her to focus on other parts of the text. Alphabet books, counting books, cumulative tales, and books with *predictable plots* can all help young children become confident, joyful readers and writers (Saccardi, 1996). Their very *predictability* allows children to attend to meaning, syntax, graphophonics, and the overall context or direction of the story. Some books with predictable stories and repetitive phrases are *Brown Bear, Brown Bear, What Do You See?* by Bill Martin Jr., *The House That Jack Built* by Rodney Peppe, and *Chicken Soup with Rice* by Maurice Sendak (Trelease, 2001). Experiences with such books help emergent readers develop positive feelings about the reading process as well as increased vocabulary knowledge and practice in using context to construct meaning.

The transition from the stories of early reading to nonfiction or expository text has often been difficult for young readers. Since this type of text generally is organized differently from stories, the reader has less to use as a guide in the construction of meaning. Research has indicated that when expository materials are clearly written and possess a logical organization, students tend to understand much more (Herman, 1984). Therefore, it is crucial that expository texts be more than just lists of facts; these books need to be especially well-organized texts containing adequate explanations, appropriate concepts, and accurate facts, all of which better enable children to understand them.

Because text has an impact on reading, you, as a future teacher, need to make sure that you have many print resources in the classroom—more than just the school textbooks or basal readers. You need to use books that are accurate, interesting, clearly written, and organized in such a way that they can be easily understood by students. The books you use for reading instruction should contain variety and be real literacy events (Goodman, 1986). They should be worth reading.

THE INSTRUCTION

In recent years, much research has been concentrated on defining the type of instruction needed to promote reading comprehension. The successful strategies that have emerged from that research can and should make a difference in every classroom (Tierney & Readence, 2000).

Phonics

If reading is viewed as the construction of meaning, all aspects of reading instruction should be seen as ways to facilitate comprehension, including the teaching of phonics. The real value of phonics, and the subsequent knowledge of letters and sounds, is that it allows readers to automatically process print, freeing them to think about what the language is saying and to construct meaning from the text (Adams, 1990a).

Research has shown that it is no longer a question of whether phonics instruction is needed but of how to implement it in order to promote successful reading. The key issue is one of helping children develop awareness of phonological relationships in a meaningful context, such as those found in literature books. Children need to see that the end product of the use of phonics is the construction of meaning; teachers must help students realize this fact in their period of emergent literacy. To help young children acquire literacy, remember that teachers must facilitate each reader's individual progress of particular skills (Strickland & Cullinan, 1990). Phonics is discussed in more detail later in this chapter.

Working Toward Comprehension

Research has identified some specific comprehension competencies that students need to acquire: using prior knowledge, creating and answering questions, making predictions, evaluating what is important, summarizing, interpreting graphic information, visualizing and imaging, and monitoring understanding (Pearson, Roehler, Dole, & Duffy, 1992). Because certain children may have difficulty developing these abilities, teachers often need to use direct instruction in explaining thinking, problem-solving, and metacognitive processes. Such tactics may include the think aloud strategy as well as modeling and several types of questioning (Rosenshine, Meister, & Chapman, 1996).

Think alouds. The think aloud strategy is a type of direct instruction that can aid children with reading comprehension (Davey, 1983). In using *think alouds,* the teacher reads a passage that might pose some comprehension problems; when confusion arises, the teacher shows students what to do to resolve it: Make a prediction of what might happen; describe how to visualize or picture what has been read; make connections through analogies; clarify confusing points by talking about them; or use self-help strategies such as rereading, asking questions, or trying to change the way the story is viewed (Monahan & Hinson, 1988).

Modeling. Of course, a basic method of direct instruction is *modeling,* specifically teacher modeling of the reading behaviors children need. However, modeling alone will not work; it is important to provide a means of gradually turning over responsibility to students. Gordon (1985) has proposed a method that can be used in the modeling and transfer of any technique to students. First, the teacher asks questions about the technique, answers those questions, finds evidence for using the technique, and provides a line of reasoning. Through a series of practice sessions, students assume responsibility for each of the steps until they take ownership and become independent learners. Figure 6.2 illustrates Gordon's method.

Some teachers like to bring a book that they have read to class and to talk about it in the following manner:

> When I first picked up this book and looked at the title, I asked myself, "Is this something that interests me?" Since I knew that [subject of book] is something that I love, I felt that I would probably enjoy the book.
> Then I started to look at the cover, the headings of the chapters [if any], and the illustrations. I tried to figure out what I would find out from the

FIGURE 6.2

Gordon's method for modeling strategies.

STAGES	ASKS QUESTIONS	ANSWERS QUESTIONS	FINDS EVIDENCE	LINE OF REASONING
I. Modeling	T	T	T	T
II. Guided Practice	T	T	S	S
III. Guided Practice	T	S	T	S
IV. Practice/Application	T	S	S	S
V. Student Control	S	S	S	S

T: Teacher
S: Student

Source: From Gordon, C. (1988). Modeling teaching strategies. *New Directions in Reading Instruction.* Copyright © 1988 by the International Reading Association. (Originally published in *Journal of Reading, 28,* Feb. 1985.) Reprinted with permission of Christine Gordon and the International Reading Association. All rights reserved.

book and even made a list of predictions or possibilities in my head. In this particular book, I really liked the illustrations because they went along well with the text. I also liked the way that the headings of each chapter gave me an idea of what was going to happen. So I decided that I definitely did want to read this book.

As I read the book, I helped my comprehension by always noting what was happening, the time and location, and who or what was involved. I did this so I would be sure to remember the important parts. Sometimes I would put a bookmark in a section that I really found interesting.

After I finished the book, I summarized it for myself and tried to figure out what it was really about. Then I tried to remember some similar books and to decide how the books were the same or different. Finally, I settled on why I [liked/disliked] the book and why I [would/would not] recommend it to my friends.

Questioning. One important outgrowth of much of the current research is that it has really changed the way teachers look at questions and questioning strategies. Questions are no longer the "who, what, when, where, why, and how" of literal information. Research has demonstrated that one of the most important aspects of questioning is the relationship between the question and the location of its answer, and that it is empowering to help students understand where to search for answers to questions (Raphael, 1984, 1986).

Raphael has outlined the four basic question–answer relationships (QARs), which were explained in Chapter 5.

1. right there questions
2. think and search questions
3. on my own questions
4. writer and me questions

Children who understand these relationships comprehend more and have higher levels of achievement (Raphael, 1986).

Another way of viewing the use of questions with texts has emerged: *Questioning the Author (QtA)* (Beck, McKeown, Hamilton, & Kucan, 1997). This QtA strategy is based on the idea of students constructing meaning as they proceed through a text. QtA supports immediate construction of meaning through discussion; students actively formulate their ideas while reading. The approach can be used with either expository, informational texts or narrative stories and involves the teacher interacting with the students as they try to build understanding of a text they are reading for the first time. The focus of QtA in the classroom is the use of queries that are posed by the teacher. The following list is a sample of different types of queries (Beck et al., 1997, p. 45):

INITIATING QUERIES

- What is the author trying to say here?
- What is the author's message?
- What is the author talking about?

FOLLOW-UP QUERIES

- What does the author mean here?
- Did the author explain this clearly?
- Does this make sense with what the author told us before?
- How does this connect with what the author told us before?
- Does the author tell us why?
- Why do you think the author tells us this now?

NARRATIVE QUERIES

- How do things look for this character now?
- How has the author let you know that something has changed?
- How has the author settled this for us?
- Given what the author has already told us about this character, what do you think he's up to?

Source: Excerpt from Beck, I. L., McKeown, M. G., Hamilton, R. L., & Kucan, L. (1997), *Questioning the Author: An Approach for Enhancing Student Engagement with Text.* Reprinted with permission of Isabel L. Beck and the International Reading Association. All rights reserved.

While queries are an important aspect of this process, the benefits of constructivism in creating meaning lie in the ensuing discussion and interaction among the students and the teacher.

Connecting Reading and Writing

In the past decades, educators have come to realize more and more that reading is intricately tied to all the language arts, especially writing. One of the most exciting changes in reading instruction is the practice of combining reading with writing instruction (Tierney, 1990). This results in a more integrated, holistic approach to helping students become literate.

Writing is a good partner to reading because it helps children add to and clarify meaning for themselves—to make a book and the language of the book their own (Jensen & Roser, 1990). Both reading and writing are forms of communication; both are active thinking processes that get at meaning. Observations of language development in classes have shown that "in order to write, writers read. In order to learn from reading or respond to reading, readers often write" (Jensen & Roser, 1990, p. 11). Often, using writing to summarize information or restate what the author has said in a more concise format (Burns, Roe, & Ross, 1996) is what helps students truly get at the heart of what they have read. Therefore, it seems natural to make no real distinction between reading and writing in the classroom.

Students who see the connection between reading and writing actually are more perceptive about both processes. Having class opportunities to write helps students to learn reading and writing in meaningful ways. Allowing children to use process writing—to write and read letters and lists, to keep and share journals—helps them to see the problems and complexities of each process from both sides. They see reading as an author would; they see writing from the reader's point of view. In the end, they arrive at a clearer notion of what they need to do to make each process work for them. Combining class writing and reading instruction also serves as a meaningful way of helping students acquire the mechanics—grammar, punctuation, spelling—of writing.

Teachers now appreciate that reading is an active, constructive process; writing is also an active way to construct meaning. It is important to implement these research findings and thereby empower children.

Beyond the classroom

Explore some of the research issues raised in this section a bit further. Read one (or more) of the texts cited in this section, or ask your instructor for other suggestions. Write in your journal a summary of your findings and their relationship to the material in this chapter.

READING/WRITING WORKSHOP

Perhaps the best way to connect reading and writing is through a reading/writing workshop. This strategy organizes reading instruction to promote balanced literacy (Searfoss, Readence, & Mallette, 2001). In the workshop children can choose their own materials as they are engaged in periods of extended reading and writing. Searfoss and colleagues (2001, compiled from pp. 115–119) suggest the following format:

1. *Opening/teacher share time.* This is a time period in which the teacher might read a book aloud or promote a particular text through a book talk. For example, a teacher of the second or third grade might read a nonfiction book such as *Fly Traps! Plants That Bite Back* by Martin Jenkins.

2. *Brief lesson.* This is a time period in which skills and various strategies are taught with the whole group. Since there are many cause/effect situations in *Fly Traps!* this would be an ideal time to teach children how to recognize cause/effect in context. For example, a teacher could ask the children how a bladderwort sets its traps or makes its trap door open.

3. *Student-selected reading/writing and response.* This is the major part of the workshop. During this section students must be reading and writing. Options vary from writing in a journal to tape-recording an interesting part of a book to writing a sequel to a book that a student has read. It is common for teachers to hold individual reading or writing conferences while the students are engaged in this part of the workshop. During this period students might read other books about plants that eat insects, plan and act out a retelling of the text, or write a response to it in their journal. All the while the teacher monitors what they do.

4. *Closing/student share time.* This period allows students to share both the texts that they have been reading and the products of their writing responses.

What Makes a Successful Reader? Competencies to Support Reading

In order to become successful, effective, and efficient readers, children need to acquire a number of *competencies*, mastery over certain types of reading behavior. Although there is not always a rigid order in how these competencies should be acquired, the process is not random either. Children need to develop particular competencies during the period of emergent literacy, others while they are acquiring word recognition and vocabulary strategies, and still others as they continue to build comprehension.

EMERGENT LITERACY COMPETENCIES

Learning to read is not something that happens overnight for children. Nor does it occur in the same specific sequence of events and accomplishments for each child. However, in the years between birth and age eight, certain conditions are needed to support children's literacy development, specifically an environment that is both print rich and language rich (International Reading Association & National Association for the Education of Young Children [IRA & NAEYC], 1998). As an example of the powerful impact print in the environment can have on young children, Goodman (1989) has cited the fact that when children first come to school, many of them only print in capital letters. They do this because in their interaction with their environments, they have seen primarily capital letters on street signs, billboards, and advertisements.

As discussed earlier in this text, a print-rich environment begins with the home and with caregivers who not only read to their children but also talk to them and provide them with a wide variety of experiences. Teachers need to recognize the home–school connection in fostering literacy. They need to get and keep caregivers involved in informal, supportive activities and then build on that naturalistic learning in the classroom. Teachers also need to heed the work of Shirley Brice Heath (2002) in recognizing that different families and cultures surround their children with different types of talk. Therefore, children need to be in classrooms that focus on all kinds of talk. They need to practice language uses that they may not have acquired at home, such as labeling items, telling stories, describing experiences, acting in plays or skits, narrating puppet shows, describing pictures, and answering questions about what they are saying. They need to talk about talk (Heath, 2002).

In the acquisition of literacy, cognitive development is certainly important. However, equally important is each child's knowledge about the "purpose and process of language" (Weir, 1989, p. 458). Because literacy and language learning have strong social and psychological bases (Teale & Sulzby, 1989), it makes sense to think of acquiring literacy as a type of "apprenticeship" (Wells, 1990, p. 15) in which children learn about language functions through meaningful activities guided by more competent language users (Rogoff, 1990; Tharp & Gallimore, 1989). In such an approach, the teacher is seen as a facilitator and model rather than an instructor.

Citing the work of a large number of researchers—including Clay (1979, 1991), K. S. Goodman (1980), Y. M. Goodman (1980), Lomax and McGee (1987), and Stein and Glenn (1979)—Searfoss et al. (2001) have outlined competencies basic to the emerging literacy of the young child:

1. *Awareness of print.* Sensitivity to print in the environment, such as ads, signs, and billboards; the informational print of maps, recipes, and directions; job-related reading of caregivers; and fun reading of comics and pictures.
2. *Concepts about book print.* Ideas about what the print in books looks like and how it differs from other types of print.
3. *Story sense.* Ability to recognize the structure of a story; to develop the schemata for story structure; and to internalize the story elements of setting, characters, theme, plot, and resolution.
4. *Oral language development.* Communication competencies built on the development evident when the child enters school; developed in connection with beginning reading and writing since acquiring literacy is an interdependent process in which all the language skills support each other.
5. *Emergent writing.* Recognizing that scribbles, anything written down, needs to mean something and contain a message.

Children's emerging literacy can best be accommodated in classrooms in which reading and writing reflect the reading of the real world (White, Vaughn, & Rorie, 1986). In such environments, print dominates daily activities. Children and teachers are involved in book experiences in which they share books, read and tell stories, scribble and write about stories and experiences (often with invented spellings), and discuss the varied aspects of all that is happening in the class. Most of all, reading aloud to children is the single most important activity to build literacy in such classrooms (Bus, Van Izendoorn, & Pellegrini, 1995).

It is through literature-based activities that children learn how to handle a book, to differentiate the front cover from the back, to recognize the title page and author credits. Even more important, youngsters learn about the *directionality* of print: They see that it moves from left to right on the page and from the beginning to the middle to the end of a book. They begin to see the structural sequence in this progression. From their earliest experiences with books, children also move beyond their basic concepts about language and print to a visual and sound awareness of letters. They develop an alphabetic principle and an initial understanding of the pattern of the relationship between letters and sounds (Adams, 1990a). Through rhyming and word games, they become linguistically aware of language sounds, which leads to phonemic awareness (IRA

& NAEYC, 1998). Eventually, they become able to discriminate among letters, words, and sentences.

One final (and perhaps most important) competency that emerging readers and writers exhibit is a sincere interest and delight in books. They come to recognize that books are not only informative but fun and that people need to interact with them on a daily basis.

WORD RECOGNITION AND VOCABULARY DEVELOPMENT COMPETENCIES

In order to become automatic, efficient readers who can construct meaning from text, youngsters need to decode printed symbols into meaning very rapidly. They need to become competent in word recognition strategies that enable them to be fast and accurate readers. As with emerging literacy, the competencies related to word recognition and vocabulary development do not always develop in a rigidly specific order. In fact, it now appears to be most beneficial for teachers to help students develop the competencies as needed to construct meaning from text.

Although different reading situations demand different word competencies, they generally all work together to facilitate understanding of the text. Four fundamental areas in which readers need to develop competencies are the following:

1. *Sight vocabulary.* A store of words that the child recognizes on sight, which makes the reading process rapid and automatic and facilitates comprehension. Without a store of sight words, children must struggle to analyze print, a tactic that slows them down and can impede comprehension. Sight-word knowledge can be developed in conjunction with meaningful activities in the classroom.

2. *Phonics.* The structured relationship between phonemes (sounds) and graphemes (letters). For example, some facsimile of the sound "buh" is normally associated with the letter *b*. Because phonics is a way to get at meaning quickly, it is an area that receives much attention in the primary grades. In fact, Durkin (1988) reported that in kindergarten classes the most apparent type of reading instruction was phonics. Teachers do need to heed the advice of *Becoming a Nation of Readers* (Anderson et al., 1985)—it recommends that phonics be started early, worked on intensely, and concluded by the end of second grade. However, while the teaching of phonics is an important aspect of beginning reading instruction (International Reading Association, 1997), it is wise to remember that phonics is only one factor, or cue system, in helping children construct meaning from text. Figure 6.3 lists the basic components of phonics.

3. *Structural analysis.* The ability to use meaningful word parts to decode an unknown word. By knowing the meaning of specific parts of the word, a child can figure out the meaning of the complete word. For example, the child who knows that the prefix *un-* generally means "not" or "to undo" has a head start in unlocking the meaning of words such as *unhappy, unfriendly,* and *untie.* Common elements inherent in structural analysis are illustrated in Figure 6.4.

4. *Context clues.* The surrounding textual cues that a reader uses to decode an unknown word. For example, in the following sentence a child would figure out the unknown word *wagged* by using known words and prior knowledge about dogs: *The happy dog wagged his tail.* The child would scrutinize the context of the print on the page to unlock the word's meaning by focusing on the way it is used. In general, proficiency in the use of context clues is tied to vocabulary development, which is initiated through the oral activities of Chapter 5 and refined as children engage in their own reading and writing.

Although there is not total agreement on a particular sequence of instruction to develop word recognition competencies, it is widely acknowledged that

FIGURE 6.3

Components of phonics.

Consonants are all letters other than *a, e, i, o,* and *u*. Consonants may be consistent (stand for a single sound) or inconsistent (stand for more than one sound, depending on the influence of adjacent vowels). Some inconsistent consonants include *c, g,* and *s*.

Consonant blends occur when two or three adjacent consonants are combined in a word but each consonant retains some of its original sound. For instance, in the word *play* the sounds of /p/ and /l/ are heard in the *pl* blend.

Consonant digraphs occur when two adjacent consonants are combined to form a single new sound. The most common digraphs are *ch, th, wh, sh,* and *ng,* as in the words *church, thin, when, ship,* and *ring.*

Vowels are the letters *a, e, i, o,* and *u,* each of which represents both a long and a short sound. The letters *y* and *w* may also exhibit vowel characteristics.

Long vowels		Short vowels	
cake	rope	cat	rot
Pete	mute	pet	nut
rice		pit	

Vowel digraphs occur when two adjacent vowels represent a single sound. Usually one of the vowels is sounded. Note the sound that you hear in the vowel digraphs in the following words: *boat, heat, pain.*

Diphthongs occur when two adjacent vowels are blended together to produce a single new sound. The most common are *ou* as in *about, oi* as in *toil, oy* as in *coy,* and *ow* as in *howl.*

FIGURE 6.4

Elements of structural analysis.

A **prefix** is a group of letters that when attached to the front of a root word modifies the meaning of that word.

Prefix	Meaning	Word
un-	not, undo	unhappy
bi-	two	bicycle
pre-	before	prepay
sub-	under	submarine

A **suffix** is a group of letters that when attached to the end of a root word also alters the meaning of that word.

Suffix	Meaning	Word
-less	without	penniless
-ous	full of	famous
-able	capable of being	acceptable

An **inflectional ending** is a letter or group of letters that when added to the end of a root word changes number, case, or gender (nouns); tense or person (verbs); or degree (adjectives). Some examples are *toys, witches* (nouns); *walks, walking, walked* (verbs); *older, oldest* (adjectives); and *Mary's* (possessive).

A **contraction** occurs when two words are combined into one word and some of the letters are omitted. The omitted letters are indicated by an apostrophe. Examples: *wasn't, what's, I'll, they're, I'd, I'm, we've.*

A **compound** is a new word formed when two existing words are joined. The pronunciation of the original words is usually retained in the new word, but the meaning of the compound may be altered in the process of combining. Examples: *workbook, cowboy, baseball, postcard, doghouse.*

embedding phonological awareness activities into a meaningful language arts program can greatly assist students in developing into successful readers and writers (Ericson & Juliebo, 1998). Word recognition and decoding strategies should be done in ways that actively involve each child working with words. Such instruction can be accomplished through chants, nursery rhymes, literature, poetry, storytelling, drama, writing, and alphabet songs and books. Cunningham and Hall (1997, 1998) recommend the use of a word wall with words categorized according to initial letter and sound as well as the creation of tongue twisters (Cleo the clown cleaned the closet). When children have become proficient in the basics of word recognition strategies, much of their continued vocabulary development can and should be related to the content areas in which the words most frequently occur.

One of the most promising developments in the successful teaching of word recognition strategies has been the advent of **Reading Rods** available through ETA/Cuisenaire®, the creators of the Cuisenaire Math Rods. Just as the Math Rods have provided a hands-on approach to developing mathematical thought, the Reading Rods now allow children to physically manipulate letters and their corresponding sounds as they make new words. Through the use of three-dimensional snap-together blocks, children can see and feel how words and sentences are formed as they begin to understand the underlying concepts of language use. The following are some of the Reading Rod kits available: Alphabet and Phonemic Awareness; Short Vowel Word Families; Phonics Word-Building; Prefixes, Suffixes, and Root Words; and Sentence Construction. For more information and activities, visit the ETA/Cuisenaire website at www.etacuisenaire.com.

COMPREHENSION COMPETENCIES

Reading comprehension is one specialized aspect of general language comprehension. As children use oral language to communicate with others through meaningful speech and perceptive listening, they employ comprehension strategies. When teachers question students in class, encourage discussions, and promote activities involving listening, they facilitate development of these strategies. All that remains is to encourage children to apply the same type of strategies to printed materials.

As with the other language arts, students learn to read by practicing their reading strategies with real books. When teachers provide children with the opportunity to read real texts, to use their prior knowledge, and to make predictions and judgments about what they are reading, they are handing their students the keys to reading comprehension.

It is generally recognized that there are several types, or levels, of comprehension for which students need to develop competencies: literal and interpretive as well as the higher levels of critical and creative comprehension (Burns et al., 2002). However, these levels do not operate in isolation from one another. In successful reading, they most often operate together to help the reader obtain a thorough understanding of the text.

Literal Comprehension

Literal comprehension involves getting meaning straight from the text; usually, the information is directly and plainly stated on the page. Students who are competent in this type of comprehension are able to get information from pictures, to find main ideas and details in text, to identify the sequence of events, and to comprehend the vocabulary used in the selection. Literal comprehension is generally considered the most easily achieved level of comprehension and includes the who, what, when, where, why, and how information.

Interpretive Comprehension

Interpretive comprehension involves obtaining meaning implied by statements in the text. The reader has to search for information, think about it, and interpret it. For example, a teacher might say to students, "Explain the differences between Cinderella and her sisters." In order to do this, the students have to review some information in the text and think about it before they can come up with an answer. It is a lot like reading between the lines.

A reader proficient in interpretive comprehension is able to detect theme and author's purpose; infer cause-and-effect relationships; predict events, outcomes, and results; make comparisons; and draw conclusions. Once children achieve this level, they are able to put information in their own words through paraphrasing and summarizing the main idea. The overall pattern of inferential processes activated during reading may have an impact on how much text is actually remembered (van den Broek, Risden, Fletcher, & Thurlow, 1996).

Critical Comprehension

The third level of comprehension is known as *critical comprehension*, which occurs when the reader is able to integrate her or his own thinking with the information from the text. That is, the reader moves beyond the information mentioned on the page to make judgments about the content and the style of the text.

Individuals who comprehend at this level are able to differentiate among fact, fantasy, and opinion. They not only know what is relevant or irrelevant but can provide evidence to support their views. They respond emotionally to what they are reading. In addition, competent readers are able to visualize information from the text, to form mental pictures of what they have read. This ability often enables them to respond creatively through art, music, drama, and writing.

VIGNETTE *in the classroom*

In her class, Mrs. Oliwa is reading a series of fairy tales with her young students. Among the tales included in the series is "Jack and the Beanstalk." Because giants play such an important role in this and many other tales, both teacher and children want to make sure that everyone can recognize the word *giant* automatically. To help **individual** children internalize the word, the teacher conducts several **individual** sessions using the five-step teaching plan for sight vocabulary advocated by Johnson and Pearson (1984):

1. *Seeing.* The teacher writes the word *giant* on the chalkboard. Then she says, "A *giant* is much, much bigger than an ordinary person. The *giant* in 'Jack and the Beanstalk' was 10 times larger than Jack." She also shows each child several illustrations of giants from various tales.

2. *Discussing.* The teacher encourages each student to tell what he or she knows about giants. Mrs. Oliwa adds her own observations and tries to clarify any misunderstandings that the children express.

3. *Using.* Then each child uses the word *giant* in a sentence or sometimes two sentences.

4. *Defining.* Because *giant* is a concrete word with pictures to go with it, and because the children have heard many stories about giants, most of the students do not have too much trouble defining it.

5. *Writing.* As a final step, each child writes the word on a word card and adds it to **individual** word banks. Many children also illustrate their cards.

Creative Comprehension

The readers then move on to *creative comprehension* as the authors and communicators of new information. For example, a teacher can stop at the climax of a story and ask the students to write an ending. Or a teacher can finish reading a story or book and ask the students to provide ideas for a sequel.

Beyond the classroom

Interview several teachers in your field experience school or reading educators at your college, and in your journal summarize their thoughts on what makes a successful reader. You can then reflect on how these views compare and contrast with the information in this chapter.

How and when teachers should work with students to develop these competencies depend a great deal on the type of classroom, the demands of the activities in which the children are engaged, and the needs of the individual pupils. However, when it is necessary to help and support students in becoming strategic readers, there are many techniques that teachers can use. Some have already been mentioned, such as direct explanation lessons, modeling, think alouds, questioning, QARs, QtA, and summarizing information.

Questioning is probably the most frequently used method for helping students develop proficiency in comprehension. Some questions are directed at the literal level, while others requiring more thought relate to the inferential and evaluative levels. Knowing where to find the answers to particular questions reduces the confusion that some students feel when faced with different types of questions. It certainly helps to know that literal questions can be answered directly from the text, inferential questions require a bit more searching, and evaluative questions require thought from each individual.

Of course there are many other strategies that teachers can use to help their students become competent readers: anticipation guides, story grammars and maps, semantic maps, dialogue journals and letters, and techniques to develop self-questioning. These and other comprehension strategies are discussed in Chapter 10.

Major Approaches to Reading Instruction

There are many ways to approach reading instruction, none of which is considered the only solution to the problem of making sure every child becomes literate. How you approach reading instruction is based partly on your own philosophy of reading and partly on the philosophy of the school district in which you teach. You can be sure that as you grow as a teacher, not only your views but also those of the school district will change. Therefore, it is very important for you to be receptive to a variety of ideas about teaching reading and for you to consider them carefully before deciding which ones really make sense to you and deserve a place in your classroom.

This chapter presents major aspects of several approaches to reading and writing: the basal reader approach, which over the years and in many different forms has been the predominant teaching method in many schools in the United States; the more child-centered literature-based approach, which involves thematic units and the content areas; the language experience approach, which uses children's experiences and language; and the eclectic comprehensive approach, which is currently being used. It is important to remember that there is no magic formula for teaching reading and that each approach has its own merits.

As you read through this section of the chapter, try to keep the different models of reading (described earlier) in mind. See which of the approaches most closely reflects the theories behind each particular model. By doing this, you will be able to formulate your own reading philosophy more clearly and to make more careful decisions about which overall approach and specific strategies you would prefer to use in your own classroom.

BASAL READER APPROACH

The basic idea behind the use of the **basal reader approach** is that a student must master a series of competencies or discrete skills as he or she progresses through reading. Reflecting the ideas of the bottom-up model, these published reading series have evolved over time; they tend to help students move from the part to the whole by prescribing the acquisition of skills and competencies in a systematic order and fashion (Mickelson, 1989). For many years, basal readers have been the most widely used reading program in American schools. Some or all aspects of the approach are still used in a great number of elementary classrooms.

Basal Reader Materials

The major component in the basal reader approach is the collection of materials that are used for teaching reading in the elementary grades. In general, these materials include the following:

- There is a series of graded children's readers, which generally range from K–8. The books are carefully graded between and within each grade level and get progressively more difficult through the use of controlled vocabularies. Only a certain number of new words are introduced per story; each story builds on the vocabulary of the previous one. Along with vocabulary development, each story tries to build word recognition and comprehension competencies.

- In addition to the children's readers, there are accompanying workbooks with ready-made activities for developing phonics, word recognition, and comprehension competencies and skills.

- A teacher's manual for each series contains detailed lesson plans for instruction in vocabulary, word recognition, and comprehension. These lesson plans follow a formula known as the directed reading activity, which is discussed later.

- Supplementary materials, such as duplicating masters, cassette tapes, filmstrips, tests, computer software, and video programs, accompany each series. Over the years, the tests associated with basal readers have continued their importance as a way of determining whether or not students have mastered particular competencies or skills.

Traditional vs. Literature-Based Basal Series

Not all basal reader programs are the same. Some of the more traditional basal series that are still in use focus specifically on reading instruction that has sequenced, isolated skills work. They have very carefully controlled vocabulary instruction and are primarily teacher centered. In addition, some may emphasize a single method, such as a linguistics (emphasizing the oral aspects of language and reading) or an intensive phonics approach (stressing the isolated sounds).

What has emerged is a trend toward including more literature in the basal readers as well as suggestions for activities that will promote integration among the language arts that can be extended to other areas of the curriculum. Some basals are promoted as literature-based reading series. This type of series includes actual literature selections (often unchanged) that are organized into units reflecting an underlying theme that flows through the stories. Activities are suggested that help the students use strategies to decode words and unlock deeper comprehension. Ideas are provided for incorporating subject areas such

Reading books contains two different delights, both definable as learning. One is the pleasure of apprehending the unexpected: when one meets a new author who has a new vision of the world. The other is the pleasure of deepening one's knowledge of a special field.

GILBERT HIGHET

as science, math, music, and art into the lessons associated with the particular theme. Magazines, trade books, and journals are often included to promote comprehension-extending activities. Recent research indicates that these new basals are having a positive effect on students and are helping them to be more independent as readers (Hoffman et al., 1998).

Directed Reading Activity

The major instructional strategy associated with basal readers is the **directed reading activity (DRA),** which is a special session for the specific purpose of teaching reading; separate sessions related to a single story or lesson often are spread out over a series of days.

Traditionally, a typical DRA has included the following five steps (adapted from Tierney & Readence, 2000):

1. *Readiness.* Involves discussing previous experiences and activating prior knowledge to develop a conceptual background for the material. This also includes getting students interested in and excited about the reading material. During this readiness phase, the teacher introduces new vocabulary and reviews any strategies that might be needed in the lesson. The last step of the phase is to establish a purpose for reading—something that can be accomplished by either the teacher or the students. Teachers generally set purposes through questioning, while students can do this by predicting what the material may be about.

2. *Directed silent reading.* Is a type of guided reading in which the students silently read the story as the teacher guides them with appropriate questions and comments.

3. *Comprehension check and discussion.* Generally begins with the teacher asking the students comprehension questions and can evolve into a discussion, a debate, or even a dramatization with a bit of oral rereading.

4. *Oral rereading.* Consists of the students rereading selected passages of the text. This may be done as part of the discussion. It is important that the oral rereading have a purpose and not degenerate into a session in which students simply take turns reading selected passages aloud.

5. *Follow-up activities.* Are designed to extend knowledge. These may take the form of specialized strategy lessons on vocabulary or comprehension. The activities may also involve workbooks and skill sheets to build and strengthen specific competencies, or they may be projects related to the arts and the other content areas.

Basal Reader Controversy

There has been and probably will continue to be criticism or controversy about the use of all types of basal readers. Most of this is related to the perception that in the underlying basal philosophy, reading tends to go from smaller to larger units of understanding and can be accomplished through a sequence of skills or competencies learned in some type of order.

However, basal readers have been a tradition in reading instruction and will probably continue to have some impact on American education. The National Council of Teachers of English has recommended using basals flexibly or finding alternatives and supplements to them. Teachers are encouraged to be more involved with decision making and not to use information in the basal reader teacher's manual blindly. Teachers need to remember the importance of their role in the classroom reading situation.

If you do decide to use basal readers, you need to do it with intelligence and wisdom. You need to make sure that you have enough information about reading so that you become a knowledgeable professional who can make decisions about what is and what is not appropriate instruction for your students. If you find that some aspect of the basal program fits the needs of your classroom instruction, then you should use it. It is not the basal readers but your own philosophy and teaching sensitivity that will determine the quality of reading instruction in your class (Reutzel, 1989).

Basal Reader Supplements

There are many ways to supplement the activities of the basal program. Some activities that have worked well for teachers we know are the following:

- *Keeping a journal.* This activity allows children to reflect on what they have read and to unite the reading and writing processes. Particularly effective are dialogue journals, which enable a student to share ideas confidentially with a teacher or peer. The children begin to see that they have achieved something of value in their reading when they share it with others. The letters that appear in the Classroom Vignette (p. 220) on more holistic approaches are an example of the format a dialogue journal might take.

- *Sustained silent reading (SSR).* SSR gives children the opportunity to choose their own reading materials, to practice real reading with real books, and to become independent daily readers. One benefit of SSR is that students see their own teachers reading with them and conclude that daily reading is an important adult activity, something to which they should aspire. Also, having the freedom to choose their own books helps children develop literary tastes and preferences. (See Chapter 7 for further discussion.)

- *Sharing books.* This activity can provide students with the opportunity to read aloud or to orally express their ideas about a particular book they have been reading. They are able to unite speaking and listening with reading and writing. The activity also helps children see themselves as real readers. Ford (1989–1990) cites a study (Mundi, 1989) in which intermediate students advertised themselves as readers, and primary teachers rented them for oral reading sessions. The program eventually became known as Rent-a-Reader.

- *Directed reading–thinking activity (DRTA).* The DRTA is an alternative that may be used instead of the DRA with certain selections from the basal reader. In fact, it may be used with any selection of informational text. Stauffer (1969) outlined the format for the DRTA in two basic phases: The first promotes thinking and predicting; the second builds competencies or reading skills. In the first phase, the readers predict what they will learn, read to prove their predictions, and then evaluate and revise their original ideas. They continue this procedure with each segment of text until the selection is completed. The second phase of the activity varies according to the needs of the students. The teacher might use the opportunity to conduct a strategy lesson related to word knowledge, using context clues or monitoring metacognition. Tierney and Readence (2000) find it suitable for almost any reading selection. (See Chapter 10 for further discussion.)

> *Not wanting to reread a good book is like saying, "Paris? I've already been there."*
>
> **FAYE MOSKOWITZ**

In and beyond the classroom

Try to view a class in which the teacher uses the basal reader approach. Note the materials that are used and how the DRA is conducted. Inquire about any strategies or techniques that the teacher uses to supplement the basals. You will probably want to include a summary of this observation in your journal.

Use of these strategies helps broaden the basal reader approach and allows it to encompass a variety of language activities that integrate the language arts. These strategies provide a more holistic perspective to the approach in that they give the reader some purposeful and thought-provoking activities that incorporate the type of reading the student will encounter in real life. As with all new techniques, you will need to model these strategies for your students.

LITERATURE-BASED APPROACH

Over the years, there have been many changes in literacy education; one change that has had a tremendous impact on how schools approach the teaching of reading has been the advent of whole language. While whole language is difficult to define, Watson's (1989) succinct words tackle the complexities quite well: "Whole language is a perspective on education that is supported by beliefs about learners and learning, teachers and teaching, language and curriculum" (p. 133). Thus stated, *whole language* crystallizes as a philosophical view about literacy education that says reading and writing progress from recognizing the whole of language to an understanding of the specific parts (Reutzel & Hollingsworth, 1988). Teachers subscribing to such a holistic viewpoint know how important it is to help young children understand about books and the purposes of reading and writing and believe that the best way to do this is to surround students with print, to read and tell stories to them, to encourage children to write and read their own stories, and to promote social and collaborative learning, using a **literature-based approach.** By involving students in learning choices and decisions, these teachers hope to develop each child's "ownership" of reading and writing. Their ultimate goal is to produce readers who are thoughtful and accomplished rather than merely skilled.

> *Reading helps you think about things, it helps you imagine what it feels like to be somebody else . . . even somebody you don't like!*
>
> PAULA FOX

Guidelines for a Literature-Based Approach

For many teachers, a holistic view of literacy has evolved into using literature and children's responses to literature as the starting place for reading and writing instruction. These activities, most often associated with the interactive model of reading, can and do play a central, unifying role in the language arts curriculum. However, for such a program to be successful, several important guidelines need to be followed. Many teachers have found the following suggestions helpful (Smith, 1988):

- Students need to have access to a wide variety of trade (story) books that they can choose for reading.
- Class time should be set aside for SSR so that students can read in class. Giving the children this class time for individual reading is crucial because some of them do not read outside of school.
- Reading aloud by the teacher needs to be a daily event. This activity introduces books to children and shows them that the teacher really values reading.
- Students and teachers should share their ideas, likes, and dislikes about books with each other. Book sharing will increase students' curiosity about books.
- Children need to be encouraged to respond to books in a variety of ways, including retelling, art, drama, and cooking.
- Reading and writing activities related to books should be integrated. Writing activities must have a real purpose.
- Books can and should become integrated into other subject areas within the curriculum.

Literature-based activities and ways of obtaining books are discussed in Chapter 7.

Strategies Used in the Literature-Based Approach

One way of helping you better understand how literature-based reading works in the classroom is to share aspects of various teachers' methods of implementing this approach.

Whole-class reading. Many teachers have always used some literature in their classrooms. It then becomes easy for them to expand what they do to a *whole-class reading* of a core text in which each student has a personal copy of the book (Zarillo, 1989); there may be both oral and silent reading followed by student responses in the format of retellings, creative dramatics, art projects, and individual writing activities. Other teachers, rather than using a core book, tend to focus on children's *individualized reading*, which is guided by students' self-selection of books, self-pacing, independent work, sharing of what has been read, as well as an ample supply of materials and flexible needs grouping (Tierney & Readence, 2000). Teachers keep track of children's progress through conferences and develop strategy and skills lessons as needed (Tierney & Readence, 2000).

Literature response groups/literature circles. Teachers can also foster participation in *literature response groups* or *literature circles* (Short & Kauffman, 1995; Short & Klassen, 1993) in which there must be a sense of community in the classroom to support the intense and high-level talk that goes on among the students. Characteristics of such classrooms include the use of multiple texts with multiple copies, whole-group and small-group discussions, response journals, and literature logs (Strickland, Dillon, Funkhouser, Glick, & Rogers, 1989).

Themes/thematic units. A significant number of teachers decide to use *themes* and *thematic units* as a way of organizing books and book experiences for the children and integrating them with other aspects of the curriculum. Such an integrated program is more structured, with more emphasis on content and skills development. For example, if a primary class decided to explore themes related to animals, typical units might be Pets and Their Families, Wildlife Is Wonderful, Jungle Animals Far Away, and Fairy Tale Animals of Long Ago. Such a classroom would start the day with a read-aloud session, a serial reading of a book that the children enjoy and that reflects the theme of the current unit. As a response to the session, the teacher may use a writing activity, such as the dialogue letters featured in the following Classroom Vignette, or class discussions about the book. These discussions can take a variety of forms. During one period, a teacher might want to stimulate further thinking about what has been read by asking particular comprehension questions and encouraging the students to summarize the information or make predictions about what might happen next in the story. On some of these occasions, the teacher might realize that many of his or her students are having difficulty recognizing cause–effect relationships or drawing conclusions and take the opportunity to model a strategy lesson in which she or he demonstrates how to figure out relationships and draw conclusions about stories.

> ### In and beyond the classroom
>
> Check with schools in your area and find a teacher who uses a literature-based approach in class. If possible, obtain permission to observe in the classroom and make notes on the activities that are in progress. Decide how these activities relate to the ideas this chapter has presented on literature-based reading. You may even want to try some of these activities yourself, such as reading aloud to the children or participating in a book-sharing session.

Book sharing. Other times a class might progress from talking about the read-aloud book to sharing information about individual books they are reading. In the *book-sharing* time, the children might retell parts of the stories they have read, explain why they chose certain books, describe what they like or dislike about any book, and even exchange books with one another. If the students are studying about cats, some stories they might mention are *Sam, Bangs, and Moonshine; Millions of Cats; The Owl and the Pussycat; A Cat's Tale; Cat and Canary;* or *Socks and the Tenth Good Thing About Barney.* Book sharing is particularly important because it encourages children to keep trying out new books.

VIGNETTE *in the classroom*

This morning Mrs. Jackson has already started her daily read-aloud session with the class. She is doing a serial reading of the book *Bunnicula,* which is the rather lively story of the Monroe family and its pets—Harold the dog, Chester the cat, and a new pet rabbit whom Chester suspects of being a vampire. Through Harold's eyes, the children are learning about Chester's hysterical accusations and Harold's own valiant attempts to calm him. Many of the children are commenting about the two animal friends in their letters to Mrs. Jackson, who decided to incorporate letter-writing activities after reading research (Smith, 1982a; Strickland, 1987) that pointed out the benefits of purposeful communication between teachers and students. Following are two letters representing a typical exchange in this classroom:

Dear Mrs. Jackson,

This book is neat. I really love mysteries. This is one. But I'm worried about Chester. He was acting crazy in the part read this morning. Where he used the towel and dressed up like a vampire and bit Harold on the neck. That's weird. You think Chester is right about Bunnicula? I can't wait to find out.

Your Student,

Alice

Dear Alice,

I am very pleased that you are enjoying the book so much. One of my goals is to help the class see that reading is really fun for you to do.

Mysteries are my favorite stories, too. If you really like this book, you might want to read the sequel *The Celery Stalks at Midnight* during SSR time.

You know I think you are right to worry about Chester. Even though cats can do some pretty unusual things, Chester's behavior seems to surprise everyone. I guess we'll have to see what he does tomorrow.

Mrs. Jackson

Sustained silent reading. *SSR* would be another daily occurrence. Students select their own books and join their teacher in reading silently for 20 to 30 minutes. Everyone reads, and interruptions are not tolerated. SSR is important because it helps children gain self-direction and independence in selecting and reading books. Often the books selected for SSR will reflect the current theme in the classroom. (See Chapter 7 on children's literature for further discussion.)

Literature response charts. In some classrooms, children refine their language competencies through *literature response charts* and bookmaking activities. For example, the class featured in the Classroom Vignette created the Why We Like Cats chart that is pictured in Figure 6.5.

Several children in the Classroom Vignette have enjoyed reading the chart both silently and aloud. Sometimes Mrs. Jackson has caught one or two students standing in front of it and repeating the lines to themselves. Mrs. Jackson encourages the children to use charts because she believes that it helps them appreciate the pattern and structure of language. She has used this chart to help some of the students understand the use of independent and dependent clauses (and cause–effect relationships) in reading and writing.

Learning centers. Throughout the day, children in integrated literature programs continue to engage in language activities that enhance both language and content learning. During project time students rotate through a variety of

WHY WE LIKE CATS

FIGURE 6.5

Literature response chart.

Mrs. Jackson likes cats because they purr.

Sonia likes cats because they like to play.

Ramona likes cats because they stretch and roll over.

Demont likes cats because they jump and climb.

Nicholas likes cats because they catch mice and bugs.

Sammie likes cats because they snuggle up to you.

Cassie likes cats because they are furry and warm.

Alex likes cats because they are curious and smart.

We all like cats because they are our friends and playmates.

---

learning centers that have been established. One group might be working at an arts center to get ready for a storytelling production, while others might be at the writing center either completing required log entries to keep track of books they are reading or writing ads for books they have finished. Sometimes students get the opportunity to write letters to a favorite author. If the room has a listening, language, and literature center, class members would have the opportunity to listen to book tapes. Many teachers find that it really helps some of the less capable readers to hear the tape as they follow along in the book. Very often, these students will tape themselves retelling a story they have just completed.

Projects are also a major part of the science and community centers that are established in many classrooms. These centers provide students with the opportunity to integrate language with other content areas and to gather information from actual observations, experiments, encyclopedias, databases, and nonfiction books. One class we know of was writing a report containing facts about local South Carolina fish and the fishing industry. Their teacher arranged a class visit from several marine biologists. The students spent several days of center time researching information about fish and developing a set of questions to ask the biologists. Eventually, they published a book containing much data about local fish.

Each day a teacher in a literature class needs to check on the progress of each child. She or he may decide to use center time to conference with individual students and to check on the proficiency of their language learning. Usually a conference does not last more than seven minutes and generally includes the following five steps:

1. having the child share and discuss a story
2. asking the child comprehension questions to help the teacher determine the child's ability to think about the story
3. having the child perform an oral reading of a story passage
4. giving the child suggestions for activities to build language competencies, project work, and future book selection
5. conducting a conference summary in which the teacher checks the child's log entries to assess how much reading is actually being done and notes the child's specific competencies and needs

Although literature-based classrooms are active and noisy, no one would call them disorganized. In fact, many teachers find they must take time to carefully structure and sequence the experiences for their classes; however, the children's success and continued enjoyment of reading make it all worthwhile.

LANGUAGE EXPERIENCE APPROACH

The **language experience approach (LEA)** is one that uses the child's own language and experiences in developing literacy. Language experience, which also reflects the top-down model, is not new; however, in recent years it has gained support through research related to emergent literacy, invented spelling, and the impact of children's early writing on the acquisition of literacy (Tierney & Readence, 2000). While a number of people are associated with the LEA (Ashton-Warner, 1958, 1963; Stauffer, 1970), the words of Roach Van Allen (1973) appear to express the basic LEA philosophy best:

What I can think about, I can talk about.

What I can say, I can write—or someone can write for me.

What I can write, I can read.

I can read what I write, and what other people can write for me to read. (p. 158)

In the implementation of this approach, recommended for students of varying ages and abilities, there are a number of ways for a classroom to evolve. Within the class, there may be whole-class activities, group activities, or individual activities. To present a concise and comprehensible sample of how LEA works, we have adapted Stauffer's (1970) recommendations from Tierney & Readence (2000).

Strategies Used in the LEA

Although a teacher may use many other types of literacy and hands-on experiences with his or her students, the following three activities—dictated experience stories, word banks, and creative writing—represent the basics of LEA.

Dictated experience stories. Whole-class-dictated stories are a way for students to become familiar with the LEA procedure and to begin to see reading as similar to talking. Every story must be generated by a stimulus in experience, which can be an event or a concrete object. Having the experience (e.g., making popcorn) or interacting with the object (e.g., creating pinwheels and going outside to test them) should generate a good bit of talk among the students. When the teacher feels they are ready, the students can begin dictating their ideas about what has transpired. The teacher will then record them on lined chart paper. Once the story is completed, the teacher will read it aloud first; then the teacher and the students will read it together. All during this time, the teacher will be pointing to each word as it is read. Art activities or the identification of known words may be used to bring closure to this initial session.

On the second day, the teacher may divide the class into groups and start by having them follow along as the story is read again. Then both teacher and students read in unison, while the teacher points to the words. Later selected children may read the whole story or just small portions of it. At this point, the children begin to name and locate words they recognize. Words that are known are underlined. A final step on the second day is to reread the dictated story, emphasizing the identification of underlined words. Any underlined word that is missed gets its underlining crossed over to show that it is not yet known.

On the third day, the teacher reproduces the story and distributes it to the students, who read it over and underline known words. The stories are kept in both class and individual portfolios. In addition to being done with a whole class, dictated stories may be created by small groups within the class or by individuals.

Word banks. Each student generates a word bank from the dictated stories. This bank only includes words that are recognized consistently and underlined in the story. These known words are written or typed on small cards (i.e., index cards) and filed in an alphabetic system. They become a dictionary resource for categorization activities, decoding activities, or the actual writing of stories.

Creative writing. Children begin creative writing with sentences constructed from the word banks. They can even start by laying out the word cards and then writing in words not in the bank. Students should be encouraged to write about anything they wish. Word processing can aid this process and encourage children to create their own books, which then become the reading materials for the class.

Teacher variations on this approach make it quite flexible and compatible with either basal readers or literature-based strategies. Rarely is LEA used in isolation. However, because of its merit of using the students' own language and experiences, it is recommended not only for very young and emergent readers (Collins & Shaeffer, 1997) but also for older students in the upper grades who are moving into content-area instruction (Burns et al., 2002). At this level, they can keep logs of what they have read, describe projects they have completed, or document results of scientific inquiry activities. This approach is also beneficial for modeling the basic framework and construction of stories and helping students to evolve as authors.

COMPREHENSIVE APPROACH

Over the years, there has been much debate about the merits of skills-based versus more holistic instruction. One solution has been the emergence of whole-part-whole instruction, which provides a **comprehensive approach** to literacy by focusing on the needs of individual learners instead of a method (Reutzel & Cooter, 2003). Such a framework would generally involve the initial use of whole texts, either a book or a language experience chart, to promote the development of comprehension. This might then be followed by a specific skills or strategy activity (such as locating the *ch* sound in words) that would help students work toward developing phonemic awareness. Then students would have the opportunity to engage with whole texts again to apply what they have learned (Kaufman, 2002).

A comprehensive program is one that focuses on reading and writing for meaning while recognizing that systematic instruction to meet the needs of individual learners is essential. It is also a program in which the teacher is knowledgeable about the competencies and literacy strategies that his or her students need to develop and is able to document progress through the use of running records and analysis of writings and invented spellings (Reutzel & Cooter, 2003).

In two position statements, the International Reading Association (IRA) has provided support for the use of a comprehensive approach. The first statement, *Using Multiple Methods of Beginning Reading Instruction* (April 1999), indicates that no single method or single combination of methods can teach children to read. Therefore, teachers must know a variety of methods and various ways of combining them. They must know what is available and how to use it effectively. In June 2002, the IRA added another statement—*What Is Evidence-Based Reading Instruction?*—as the way to promote reading success in diverse classrooms, providing further evidence that teachers must be able to make decisions about how to provide a balance of instruction in their classrooms.

Strategies Used in the Comprehensive Approach

Classrooms that practice comprehensive reading instruction appear to use a variety of strategies: reading and writing workshops, rereading for comprehension and fluency, reading aloud, buddy reading, reading responses, journal writing, guided reading, and a daily message for practicing skills and strategies (Reutzel & Cooter, 2003). (See Chapter 1 for a complete list of strategies.) Often the *daily message*, which provides the important news of the school day, is a major vehicle for teaching phonics and other decoding skills. For example, the *ch* sound might first be noted in the message's comments about the first *chilly* weather of the fall. References to that *ch* sound might then be made during the teacher-directed or guided reading time, journal time, reading response, or book-sharing time (Fowler, 1998). By applying this new awareness to meaningful texts and activities, the students are able to make this knowledge their own.

The **4-Blocks Literacy Model** developed by Cunningham, Hall, and Defee (1991) provides a framework for visualizing a comprehensive approach (Sigmon, 1997). The model, which is intended for the primary level, is an outline of what needs to happen in the two hours devoted to literacy learning each school day. The four blocks are entitled Guided Reading, Self-Selected Reading, Working with Words, and Writing. In Guided Reading the major focus is building comprehension by exposing students to an extensive array of literature and mini-lessons on skills. Self-Selected Reading helps students with fluency and confidence by allowing them to work on literature texts that are on their independent reading levels. In the Working with Words block, children read, spell, and use high-frequency words. They also learn word patterns necessary for decoding and spelling. Finally, a major purpose of the Writing block is to help the children build confidence as writers. This is accomplished through using the writing process and applying knowledge of phonics. School districts employing this method provide their teacher with initial training and follow-up support. For more detailed information about this approach, refer to *Implementing the 4-Blocks Literacy Model* by Cheryl Mahaffey Sigmon.

Beyond the classroom

Interview teachers from the school district to determine who might be utilizing a comprehensive approach to literacy. If possible, obtain permission to observe in their classrooms and make notes on the activities that are in progress. Then compare what you have seen to the information in *Implementing the 4-Blocks Literacy Model* by Cheryl Mahaffey Sigmon (1997). Decide how these activities support a comprehensive approach to literacy in an entry in your journal.

The guided reading component of any literacy program based on the comprehensive approach deserves more attention. Although it is but one component of a comprehensive literacy program, guided reading is its core, for this is where teachers show children how to read and support their growth as readers (Fountas & Pinnell, 1996). Generally, in **guided reading** a teacher works with a small group of children and helps them learn how to use specific reading strategies independently; while doing this, the teacher must continually observe the students and assess how well they are learning each strategy and its applications. It also requires that the teacher know quite well the specific needs of the children and the processes involved in reading. Fountas and Pinnell (1996, p. 4) have identified the essential components of guided reading:

- A teacher works with a small group.
- Children in the group are similar in their reading development and are able to read about the same level of text.
- Teachers introduce the stories and assist students' reading in ways that help to develop independent reading strategies.
- Each child reads the whole text.
- The goal is for students to read independently and silently.
- The emphasis is on reading increasingly challenging books over time.

- Children are grouped and regrouped in a dynamic process that involves ongoing observation and assessment.

Because literature books, carefully grouped according to developmental difficulty, provide the texts for guided reading lessons, the newly learned strategies can readily be applied to the other balanced literacy reading components: reading aloud, shared reading, and independent reading. In turn, the literature can support as well as be a model and stimulus for the framework's writing components: shared writing, interactive writing, guided writing/writing workshop, and independent writing (Fountas & Pinnell, 1996).

Overall, the emergence of a comprehensive approach to literacy bodes well for reading instruction and for our children. The comprehensive approach is broad and flexible, and it focuses on the teacher using appropriate strategies that his or her students need at a particular point in time.

The Classroom Vignette on the following page illustrates a teacher's individual literacy strategy using newspaper articles in her version of a comprehensive program.

HOW SUCCESSFUL ARE THE APPROACHES?

Research can be found to support all the approaches and to show that they can and do work. Basal readers have been a tradition in American classrooms; many people have learned to read with them and have learned to like reading. Tunnell and Jacobs (1989) cited an earlier report by Thompson (1971), who examined studies comparing the success of basal readers with that of individualized literature-based reading (one of our holistic approaches). Thompson found that of the 40 studies he reviewed, 15 were tied (the results of each approach were about equal), 24 studies favored the individualized literature approach, and 1 supported the basal system.

Tunnell and Jacobs (1989) have also cited a number of later studies reviewing the results of literature-based reading. Research by Eldredge and Butterfield (1986) compared the basal approach to five other reading methods, two of which contained a literature component. The overall results favored using literature combined with a series of strategy lessons on decoding, a method that sounds very much like the comprehensive approach to literacy.

There may not be a real answer to the question of which is the most successful approach for teaching children how to read. Perhaps the solution lies with teachers who have knowledge about reading, a commitment to their students, and the insight and courage to make educationally sound decisions about instruction. As a teacher, you hold the key to helping your students unlock the code of literacy. You, combined with appropriate materials and strategies, make the difference.

Assessing Reading

No matter which method you choose for your classroom reading instruction, you will want to keep track of the progress your students are making. Evaluation is integral to the whole process of instruction. Every time you implement a strategy or an activity in your classroom, you should be keeping an eye on how it is working and how the children are responding to it.

INFORMAL READING INVENTORIES

A way for teachers to get more information about children's reading progress is to use an **informal reading inventory** (IRI), an informal evaluation technique designed to help diagnose a child's reading strengths or weaknesses through the

VIGNETTE *in the classroom*

To help her students keep abreast of current events, Ms. Irwin has been having her class read articles in local newspapers. They are exploring the differing viewpoints about the involvement in Iraq by U. S. troops. Today the class's assignment is to read "Air Base Ready" from *The News and Courier* in Charleston, SC.

1. *Preparing.* Prior to actually reading the article, Ms. Irwin activates her students' prior knowledge about the information by asking them to tell her what they know about the troops and their homecoming from the war in Iraq. She organizes the children's responses on a chart similar to the one pictured in Figure 6.5 (seen earlier). She also asks the children to predict what they will learn in the news story and to use these predictions to guide their reading. Finally, she reminds them to read the story carefully so that they remember as much about it as they can. In this way she really helps them set a purpose for their reading.

2. *Reading.* Students read the material silently and indicate when they are finished.

3. *Recalling the facts.* The children recall as much information as they can about the article. Each remembered idea is recorded exactly as the child states it, even if it is not totally accurate. To assist with the recording process, Ms. Irwin has several student volunteers help write the recalls on the board. Right now the idea is to get the information down.

4. *Rereading to make corrections and additions.* After all the information is recorded, Ms. Irwin directs the class to reread the passages for any corrections or additional information. She indicates this by getting students to examine the ideas on the board to check for any mistakes or gaps in information. Then, with the help of the students, she corrects the inaccuracies and adds the new ideas that they find.

5. *Organizing the information.* The children and Ms. Irwin decide that the best way to organize the information from this article is to draw a timeline and to list the facts in chronological order to reflect the pattern of the text.

6. *Applying the information.* Ms. Irwin tries to get the students to see the relevance of this new information to their own lives. She asks them what impact this war and homecoming have on their own lives and on their views of their country.

7. *Testing.* As a way of gaining closure on the information, Ms. Irwin gives the class a brief short-answer quiz about the article. They then discuss the results as a way of seeing how well the strategy has worked for them. The children are encouraged to present their own ideas about the strategy and how they think it has helped them. Because this strategy is quite demanding, Ms. Irwin uses it no more than once a week.

---

oral reading of a series of graded word lists or sentences and text selections. The word lists or sentences are designed to give the teacher an idea of the child's approximate grade level of reading; the selections of text and accompanying comprehension questions help the teacher to determine which strategies the child uses to decode information and how much of the information the student actually comprehends. IRIs can be bought commercially. Well-known commercially prepared IRIs include the following:

- Bader, L. (2002). *Bader Reading and Language Inventory* (4th ed.). Columbus, OH: Merrill.
- Flynt, S. and Cooter, R. B. (2001). *Flynt–Cooter Reading Inventory for the Classroom* (4th ed.). Columbus, OH: Merrill.

- Johns, J. (2001). *Basic Reading Inventory—Preprimer through Grade 12 and Early Assessments* (8th ed.). Dubuque, IA: Kendall/Hunt.
- Roe, B. (2002). *Burns/Roe Informal Reading Inventory* (6th ed.). Boston: Houghton Mifflin.
- Silvaroli, N., and Wheelock, W. H. (2001). *Classroom Reading Inventory* (9th ed.). Boston: McGraw-Hill.

Through the use of an IRI, a teacher can assess each child's independent, instructional, and frustration levels of reading. The teacher can also determine a student's potential for reading by analyzing the child's ability to comprehend a passage that has been read aloud. The four levels of reading comprehension are as follows:

1. *Independent level.* Indicates the grade level of materials a child can read on his or her own. This level is determined by the child's ability to recognize 99 percent of the words in the word list and to answer 95 percent of the reading comprehension questions correctly.

2. *Instructional level.* Signifies the level of materials that should be used for reading instruction. At this level, the child can recognize 95 percent of the words and answer 75 percent of the passage comprehension questions.

3. *Frustration level.* Occurs when a child begins to encounter great difficulty in reading and does not really comprehend much of what is happening. At this point, the child is able to answer less than 50 percent of the comprehension questions and to recognize less than 90 percent of the words from the word list. The child should not be required to read materials at the frustration level.

4. *Listening level.* Helps to determine a child's potential for reading. A child's ability to answer 75 percent of the questions about a passage that has been read aloud by the teacher is considered adequate in designating this level.

RUNNING RECORDS

An informal technique that is similar to an IRI and gaining in popularity is the running record. It has been advocated by Clay (1979, 1985, 1991) as a way of indicating how well a child is processing text. In a **running record,** the child reads a selection from a book or books with which he or she is quite familiar while both the teacher and the student are looking at the same text; as the child reads, the teacher codes the behaviors on a separate piece of paper while maintaining a position of neutrality. Checks are given for correct words; miscues that occur are noted with as much accuracy as possible. Types of miscues that are noted are substitutions, multiple attempts at a word, omissions and insertions, and the need to provide a word for the child. Substitutions are written directly over the text, with multiple attempts also being noted but not counted. If a child is told a word, a *T* is written below the line. With an omission a dash or line is placed above the word in text. An insertion of a word is placed above the line and a dash is placed below. Repetitions are coded with a check—one for each attempt. Self-corrections, which are a vital component of the record, are not considered errors and are noted by an *SC.* See Fountas and Pinnell (1996) for more variations on doing running records.

In addition to quantitatively analyzing the records, a teacher needs to look at them qualitatively. The teacher needs to note whether or not a student is using letter/sound cues, syntactic cues, or semantic cues when trying to comprehend the meaning of the text. Then the teacher can use the information from the running record to make informed and continuing decisions about future instruction. Running records are an important part of the guided reading component of a comprehensive literacy program (Fountas & Pinnell, 1996). See Figure 6.6 for a visual representation of the coding system in a running record.

FIGURE 6.6

The coding system in a running record.

READING ACTIVITY	TEACHER'S CODE
Correct Reading	✓ ✓ ✓ ✓ ✓ for each correct word
Substitution	$\dfrac{\text{attempt}}{\text{text}}$
Told a word	$\dfrac{-}{\text{text}}$ | T
Omission	$\dfrac{-}{\text{text}}$
Repetitions	✓ R ✓ R ✓ ✓ Checks indicate correct words ✓ R 2 R indicates repetition ✓ R 3 Number indicates amount
Insertion	$\dfrac{\text{word}}{-}$
Self-Correction	$\dfrac{\text{attempt}}{\text{text}}$ | SC

Source: Adapted from Fountas and Pinnell (1996).

OTHER INFORMAL ASSESSMENT TECHNIQUES

IRIs and running records provide only a sampling of what a child is able to do in reading, a sampling that can easily be affected by a child's anxiety or response to distractions during the test period. These inventories too must be supplemented with other types of data, such as the teacher's own knowledge of the student's ability and information about the child's daily progress. Informal assessment, which can be conducted on a daily basis, includes observation; the use of conferences, checklists, and rubrics; and the examination of students' portfolios (their written responses to reading). These techniques embody the ideas of observation, interaction, and analysis put forth by Y. M. Goodman (1989).

Observation

Observation can take place during all types of reading activities. For example, you might note that during silent reading, one child is always pointing to the individual words. This might give you a clue that the student is having some difficulty with word recognition and fluency, something you might want to question the child about later. Your goal is to document language development in a variety of literacy situations.

There are several ways you can keep track of your observations. You may simply want to jot your ideas down in a small notebook. However, it may be more efficient to keep more formal anecdotal records, which you can use for sharing information with administrators and caregivers. This type of record allows you to monitor both the entire class and individual children; it helps you to know where progress is occurring and where changes need to be made. A typical format of an anecdotal record is shown in Figure 6.7.

DATE	STUDENT	ACTIVITY	COMMENTS
4/30	Alice M.	Reading aloud	Alice hesitates frequently—stumbles over words. Possibly book is too difficult. Suggest using a cloze activity to determine independent, instructional, and frustration levels. In the meantime use The Great Kapok Tree (a simpler picture book) as an alternative for reading.

SUMMARY

FIGURE 6.7

Anecdotal record form.

Conferences and Checklists

Conferences are a way of interacting with students that allows you to learn specific information about individuals and to clarify any confusion you may have about a particular child's progress. Conferences can take a variety of forms. Although it may be informal, the conference has a specific structure. An excellent example is the one outlined in the Strategies Used in the Literature-Based Approach section of this chapter. The teacher in this example knows what to look for and uses questions and comments to get that information. She is also able to give future direction to the activities of each student. Frequently she uses checklists, such as the Reading Conference Checklist in Appendix C to document specific information.

Rubrics

Rubrics provide specific criteria for evaluating student performance at differing proficiency levels. Students receive specific credit for minimal work, average work, or high-quality work. Some areas have developed statewide standards and train teachers in how to be consistent in their scoring (Garcia & Verville, 1994).

Rubrics are very helpful in that they give students information about what is really expected of them. Appendix C has an example of what a teacher might use for a reading rubric.

Portfolio Assessment: Analysis of Children's Responses

Yet another way of assessing progress is to review and analyze children's written responses to reading, usually kept in writing *portfolios.* Among other things, these responses might include a journal, a written summary of a story, several drafts of a poem, a letter to a character in a story, a description of a character accompanied by a portrait, a completely new ending for a story, and some self-appraisal forms. Many educators advocate using portfolio models or checklists as a means of selecting what should go into each child's folder (Vizyak, 1997).

Teachers and students can work together to keep portfolios of selected writing projects. This not only provides information for the teacher but also encourages the students to engage in self-monitoring, an activity that empowers students by allowing them to take some responsibility for their own progress (Rief, 1990). In reviewing the various writings of the children, teachers can begin to make judgments not only about the students' reading comprehension but also about the increased sophistication of their written work. More specific information on how to maintain and evaluate children's writing portfolios as well as how to conduct individual conferences specifically related to evaluating writing can be found in Chapter 8.

STANDARDIZED TESTS

In public schools, there has been a tendency to confine reading evaluation to the separate assessment periods associated with **standardized tests,** commercially available tests that measure a child's level of achievement. Some tests also give more specific information by diagnosing a child's individual reading strengths and weaknesses.

Achievement tests provide information about how well a child is functioning in selected aspects of reading. The two basic types of achievement tests are norm-referenced tests and criterion-referenced tests. *Norm-referenced tests* are used to compare each child's achievement level to national *norms*, or standards of performance. These norms are established by giving the tests to large groups of children around the United States and then using the normal distribution of the children's test scores to come up with a standard of achievement. Generally, these tests are used to record and compare the progress of groups of children as well as that of individuals. Comparing an individual child's score with this national standard provides information about how well the child is performing in comparison with others in similar conditions. Information from these tests is usually reported in percentiles and stanines.

On the other hand, *criterion-referenced tests* compare the child's achievement level not with that of other children but with a certain standard that has been set for demonstrating mastery of a specific type of learning. A criterion-referenced test might be used to demonstrate that a child has achieved a satisfactory level of competency in the ability to comprehend the overall idea of a story. Such testing only provides information about a particular child's progress in developing needed competencies; it does not compare that child with other students in any way.

A **diagnostic test** can be used to demonstrate where a child's reading strengths and weaknesses lie by identifying which competencies a child does or does not have. Diagnostic tests usually have specific criteria for determining levels of competency. The results of this type of test are often used to plan instruction and remediation.

However, while standardized tests provide general information about the success of reading instruction, they do not yield all the information teachers need to know about students' progress (Anderson et al., 1985). For example, they do not always measure a child's unique reading competencies or weaknesses, how well a student understands and differentiates between stories and expository text, or even a child's attitudes toward reading. Nor do these tests reflect the collaboration and interaction that are so often a part of real-life assessment (Wineburg, 1997). *Becoming a Nation of Readers* (Anderson et al., 1985) has cautioned that, at best, standardized tests are a partial assessment that should be combined with observation of children's reading proficiency and habits as well as a review of children's responses to reading and interactions with others.

Reaching At-Risk Readers

As with all areas of education, reading and writing are continually being influenced by new developments. Today some encouraging breakthroughs are occurring in various areas of instruction for at-risk students. Following is a brief synopsis of three programs: Reading Recovery, Success for All, and Accelerated Reader. While none of these provides *the* answer for reading education, they do provide *some* answers, even though many educators may be hesitant to provide unconditional endorsement for those answers.

READING RECOVERY PROGRAM

Reading Recovery is a short-term, early intervention program that seeks to prevent reading failure rather than treat it through remediation. The target audience for the program is at-risk first-graders who traditionally would fail to learn to read by the end of the year. The idea is to reach these children before they experience failure, to help them develop strategies that will make them readers rather than nonreaders.

The program was developed in New Zealand by Marie Clay (1979). Through her work with children, Clay had become convinced that children can and do develop concepts about letters and print, about reading and writing, and about how they all work together. When this happens, children can take charge of their own reading. These successful readers learn a system of behaviors that continues to operate on its own and allows them to be independent learners. Clay saw Reading Recovery as a way to help all children develop these specific reading strategies and to become independent readers who are involved with real books.

The at-risk first-graders chosen for the program receive specialized one-on-one instruction for 30 minutes each day. Pinnell (1988) described the typical cycle of instruction as one in which the child first reads short, predictable stories and then writes stories. During this time, there is discussion and interaction with the teacher in an "intimate process" (Pinnell, Fried, & Estice, 1990, p. 283) that builds an attentive relationship while providing needed instruction and insights. At the end of the lesson, the child is introduced to a more difficult book that he or she is expected to reread the following day. When the student has developed enough strategies to read on her or his own, the intervention ends. The child is then able to function without assistance in the regular classroom.

The original research and several follow-up studies in New Zealand by Clay (1985) appear to demonstrate the effectiveness of Reading Recovery. Children who have completed the program have returned to the regular classroom and have not needed further assistance. Studies in Ohio (Pinnell, 1988; Pinnell, DeFord, & Lyons, 1988) have also indicated that Reading Recovery is an effective program for first-graders in the United States who may be in danger of failing to learn to read. The program, which is based on the importance of helping children make connections between reading and writing (Pinnell, 1988), provides hope for children, caregivers, and especially reading teachers who have had to deal with the frustration of reading failure despite the use of myriad materials and countless hours of instruction. However, some districts have begun to rethink the cost of the program; with a one-teacher-to-one-student format, Reading Recovery can add considerable expense to a district's instructional budget (Collins & Stevens, 1997; Pressley, 2002). Some school districts are scaling back and looking for other options, such as having a Reading Recovery teacher spend half of the school day in a classroom and the other half of the day in a Reading Recovery room (Collins & Stevens, 1997).

SUCCESS FOR ALL PROGRAM

Success for All is a program that targets early instruction for at-risk and low-achieving learners using a unique, comprehensive reading strategy. It has been used in schools that serve inner-city populations in high-poverty neighborhoods (Slavin, Madden, Dolan, & Wasik, 1996). While Success for All can be a vehicle for comprehensive school reform, its basic core is the innovative reading curriculum, which demands a school schedule allowing a 90-minute reading period. During this time, students are regrouped (from regular classes) into ability-level reading groups of no more than 20 students. During each 90-minute period, there is intensive whole-group instruction, which focuses on language skills as well as reading and writing activities with whatever basal reader a particular school is using. Students work in cooperative groups as they develop strategies for understanding a story. Students also read trade books and share information on a weekly basis. As students progress, a systematic writing program is introduced, usually implemented in the second year of school (Tierney & Readence, 2000).

If students are not successful in the structured reading groups, they are then tutored by qualified teachers in one-on-one situations. These tutors support what the regular reading group is doing, identify reading problems, and work with the teachers to make instructional decisions about the children. Generally, systematic assessments are done every eight weeks to support the quality of the program.

One key to the success of the program is the teacher who acts as the program facilitator at each school site (Madden, Livingston, & Cummings, 1995). This person coordinates the all-important staff development for the teachers, works with them to solve problems, handles scheduling, and facilitates getting support for the families. The facilitator also organizes intensive classroom follow-up for the teachers.

The evaluations of Success for All indicate that its method can be replicated and that systemic school change can take place that gives each child an opportunity to succeed in school (Slavin et al., 1997). While the program is not a magic wand for reading problems, it most certainly is a comprehensive approach that combines early intervention, small class size, regrouping, tutoring, cooperative learning, and family support with a balanced variety of workable reading practices. The combination has the potential to work (Ross, Smith, Madden, & Slavin, 1997). However, reanalysis of Success for All data by Venezky (1998) revealed that in the upper grades many students in Success for All schools slipped behind expectations, thus illustrating that nothing works for everyone.

ACCELERATED READER PROGRAM

Technology, both in and out of education, continues to be a fast-developing area. However, teachers need to be cautious about the ways they use it; they need to avoid falling into the habit of using computers or other electronic equipment for its own sake. Whatever is used in the classroom must satisfy a particular need, fulfill a specific purpose, or convey some aspect of instruction that might not be possible through other means. Technology is a tool or an aid, not an end in itself.

For teachers who want systematic formal assessment of books students have read, there is the **Accelerated Reader program,** a computerized reading management system for K–12 that manages and tracks literature-based reading. It has computerized tests for more than 14,000 books that are found in most school libraries. After students read self-selected trade books, they take a quiz on the computer. A student selects the title and takes the short-answer quiz; the computer immediately reports the points the student earns. The points are based on the length of the book, the book's reading level, and the number of correct responses. Peek (1998) believes the program motivates students because they receive their results immediately and can track the number of total points they earn. The program also gives the teacher the student's grade-equivalent score, national percentile rank, and instructional level. The computer provides a letter with all this information, which can be shared with the student's caregiver.

With this program, there is no social interaction or discussion about each book with others. Also, the program does not encourage any writing extensions or creative responses. Recent research (Pavonetti, Brimmer, & Cipielewski, 2002–2003) has indicated that the overall goal of Accelerated Reader to create lifelong readers has not been supported. Middle school students who have used Accelerated Reader in the elementary school do not necessarily continue to read independently. However, as a technology tool, the Accelerated Reader program works by helping the teacher manage the record keeping of the books read by all the students within a particular time frame.

> ### Beyond the classroom
>
> Depending on your particular interests, you may want to continue investigating one of the programs presented in this section. You can begin by reading any article related to the topic in the Related Readings. Then, if sample classrooms are available, you might want to visit one and keep a record of your thoughts about the specific program and your observations concerning the way in which it functions.

ESL READERS

ESL students (English as a second language) are those who live in an English-speaking environment but whose primary language is not English (Burns et al., 2002). Many schools serving ESL students seek to immerse the children in the English language; teachers in such schools need to keep the following principles in mind:

- The student's first language plays an essential role in the acquisition of a second language.
- Educational programs need to include what students bring with them.
- Learning a second language is a long and difficult process.
- Fluency in the hallway does not necessarily mean proficiency in the classroom.
- Learners acquire a second language in different ways.
- Errors can indicate progress.
- Language develops in a variety of settings that promote talk and interaction.
- Literacy is part of language; thus, reading and writing develop alongside speaking and listening.
- Schools should demonstrate appreciation and respect for cultural diversity (Ernst-Slavit, Moore, & Maloney, 2002, pp. 118–119).

Strategies intended to help ESL students in their acquisition of literacy include creating a stress-free environment, using anticipation guides, employing graphic organizers and other visual aids, encouraging the use of books on tape, and supporting participation in book clubs (Kong & Fitch, 2002–2003). Absolutely critical for ESL students is their active participation and even risk taking in classroom instruction that focuses on reading and writing as meaning-making processes (Burns et al., 2002).

TECHNOLOGY AND STRUGGLING READERS

Technology has the potential to help all readers, especially those who are struggling with the literacy process. Being literate in technology implies that a student can use technology to enhance his or her academic performance. In this type of

FIGURE 6.8

Example of an STW chart.

WHAT DO I SEE?	WHAT DO I THINK?	WHAT DO I WONDER?
In Slide 6 I see Mrs. Wishy Washy washing a very dirty elephant.	I think that the elephant won't like it when Mrs. Wishy Washy tries to do his ears.	I wonder if it tickles when elephants get their ears washed.
In Slide 10 I see Mrs. Wishy Washy squirting a zebra with a hose.	I think that just getting squirted with a hose might be fun if the water isn't too cold.	I wonder if the stripes will wash off of a zebra.

literacy, students can use word processing, the Internet, digital cameras, video cameras, and tape recorders (Smolin & Lawless, 2003). One group of first-graders has demonstrated their technological expertise in the production of Techno Books (Micklos, 2002–2003). The children used digital images in a PowerPoint slide show along with Kid Pix illustrations to create several different Techno Books. Among them was *Mrs. Wishy Washy Goes to the Zoo*, their rendition of *Mrs. Wishy Washy* by Joy Cowley; the final computer-generated product was videotaped for sharing with caregivers and also printed out and published as a class book.

Survival in the technological age also requires that students acquire visual literacy, which is the ability to comprehend and create visual images and messages (Smolin & Lawless, 2003). One strategy that can help students with both digital images and story illustrations is the What do I See? What do I Think? What do I Wonder? (STW) framework (Richards & Anderson, 2003). Because visual images are so powerful, their use in this framework provides an impetus for class discussion and the development of critical thinking. Figure 6.8 provides an example of an STW chart. As can be seen, STW provides some colorful options for creative thinking and for enhancing visual literacy, whether it is on the computer or with storybook illustrations.

In today's technological world, information literacy or navigating the World Wide Web has great potential as a literacy tool. Teachers can use Filamentality (www.kn.pacbell.com/wired/fil) to create templates that allow students to engage in controlled learning environments. One such activity is a website sampler in which a teacher can select and organize a number of websites around a particular topic or theme (Smolin & Lawless, 2003). This type of guidance allows students to be involved with the Web and the information that it offers without becoming overwhelmed. Teachers can also help students with structured information searches by providing them with the appropriate Web tools. Ask Jeeves (http://askjeeves.com) and Alta Vista (www.altavista.com) are search engines that students can use to retrieve valid, reliable, and useful information (Smolin & Lawless, 2003). With planning, teachers can make traveling the Information Highway the most engaging and effective pathway to literacy.

TECHNOLOGY AND WEBSITES

One way to personalize your home page is to include photographs of you, subjects that interest you, or objects you are attempting to explain. There are two ways to include photographs. One method is to take any favorite picture that was taken with your regular camera and scan it onto your home page; the one extra piece of equipment you will need is a scanner.

A second way to include pictures is to use a digital camera, which records the image directly onto computer chips. Instead of film, digital cameras have either a removable memory card or a disk. Besides the digital camera, one needs a connection cable and transfer software, which are usually included with the camera.

Some advantages of the digital camera are that you do not have to pay for film processing and you may use software to edit and touch up pictures. Most digital cameras come with Adobe PhotoDeluxe, which is an image-editing program that is quite easy to use. A good introduction to the use of the digital camera is Julie Adair King's book *Digital Photography for Dummies* (published in 1997 by IDG Books Worldwide, Foster City, CA).

Students can also use digital cameras to create slide show presentations with software programs such as Microsoft PowerPoint. Some other slide show tools that they can use are Kid Pix slide show and Ofoto (www.ofoto.com). Ofoto even allows them to create photo albums and scrapbooks (Smolin & Lawless, 2003).

www.cbcbooks.org

This site contains information about Children's Book Week and links to many children's book publishers.

http://gpn.unl.edu/rainbow

This site describes books featured on the PBS show *Reading Rainbow*, with recommended activities.

www.honors.unr.edu/~fenimore/en297/bohannon/sidewalk.html

Shel Silverstein shares his expertise and ability in drawing his illustrations and writing his poems.

www.reading.org

This is the site of the International Reading Association.

www.harcourtschool.com

This site by Harcourt Inc. has activities designed to be done by individuals or in cooperative groups.

www.eduplace.com/rdg/index.html

This is Houghton Mifflin's educational site for reading and language arts.

www.bookadventure.org

This site allows users to create their own book lists, take quizzes for points and prizes, and offers resources for caregivers and teachers.

www.carolhurst.com/index.html

This site features children's books, ideas for caregivers and teachers, and professional resources.

www.getreadytoread.org

This site offers information and resources on early childhood literacy for caregivers, teachers, health care workers, and advocates. It is sponsored by the National Center for Learning Disabilities.

www.readingrockets.org

This site features authors; voting on favorite books; book lists; forums; and resources for national and state organizations, as well as for caregivers and teachers.

www.spaghettibookclub.com

This site allows teachers to create a reading program utilizing the site as a place where students can write their own book reviews, create activities, and look for resources for the classroom.

www.epals.com

This site brings students from all over the world together via email, forums, and collaborative projects.

http://library.thinkquest.org/2626

This site allows students to collaboratively write stories either by creating new ones, adding to existing stories, or working to illustrate the stories. The students can then submit their work where it can be seen by a large audience.

www.kn.pacbell.com/wired/fil

This site allows teachers and caregivers to enter a subject and locate sources on the Web. These sources can then be used to create learning activities, as well as Web-based instruction, through templates.

www.itools.com

This is a search engine for students. It offers several methods for researching a topic and also provides dictionaries, thesauruses, language translators, and other writing and research tools.

www.educationplanet.com

This is a well-organized search engine geared specifically for educators and students. The user types in a search term and then the engine searches through many educational sites for lesson plans, activities, and information.

www.school.discovery.com/schrockguide

This is Kathy Schrock's Guide for Educators, a categorized list of curriculum resources. It is frequently updated to include the sites for teaching and learning.

Summary

In today's society, reading and writing are not only essential aspects of literacy; they are also crucial for adequate daily functioning. Because reading is now viewed as an interaction between the mind of the reader and the print in the text, it is more important than ever for teachers to help children become independent readers, adept at constructing meaning from print for themselves. Your role as a teacher is to help your students by making use of the results of reading research on readers, text, and necessary instructional strategies. You should help students to take advantage of their prior knowledge, to link the known with the unknown, and to develop reading competencies as needed. Your goal is to create effective and efficient readers who have a repertoire of strategies at their command.

No matter which major approach you use for reading instruction, you will want to expose your students to actual books representing all types of meaningful text. You will want them to be able to monitor their own reading through prediction, summarization, thoughtful reflection, and self-questioning. They can respond to their reading through journals, logs, letters, and various other writing activities.

Throughout your career as a teacher, it will be important for you to reflect carefully on what you are doing and what types of reading materials and strategies you are using. You will need to remain knowledgeable about continuing developments in the field so that you can make decisions about which ideas to implement in your classroom. Most of all, you will want to be sure that what you do mirrors your philosophy and knowledge about reading. Only by practicing a method that you truly believe in will you ever be able to help someone else to learn to read.

ACTIVITIES *with children*

Become a Character

Sometimes children develop a strong feeling for certain characters in a story they have read. You can expand and broaden this sensitivity by having the students compose a short sequel to the story—one in which they actually become the characters in question and behave in ways they deem appropriate. Younger children may want to dictate their ideas to the teacher or onto an audiocassette.

Book Sharing

Children really enjoy sharing books they have read. Also, many children can improve their oral fluency by preparing and reading stories aloud to others, especially to younger children. The older child gets the needed practice, and the younger child acquires a good reading role model.

Book Ads

Children can practice writing and reading summaries by composing ads for stories they wish to "sell" to their classmates. Each ad should include a two- to three-sentence summary highlighting the major points of the story. Both sellers and buyers learn the finer points of summarization.

Context Cloze

Prepare several short reading selections in which you have systematically deleted words not readily recognized by your students. As the children try to understand the text, they will use selected cues from the words surrounding the deletions to help themselves. The purpose of the activity is to highlight the importance of using context to construct meaning. To provide feedback for the students, you may want to include the deleted words on the back of the selections. (See Chapters 9 and 10 for more information on cloze.)

Real Print

Have the students bring boxes, bags, labels, and ads from home. They can then work in pairs and small groups to identify words and common names that they readily recognize. The correctly identified words can be written on cards and added to each child's individual sight-word bank. Children can later group known words in their banks according to sounds (beginning, middle, ending) or match up the word cards with the original words in the advertising.

RELATED READINGS

Atkinson, T. S., Wilhite, K. L., Frey, L. M., & Williams, S. C. (2002). Reading instruction for the struggling reader: Implications for teachers of students with learning disabilities or emotional/behavioral disorders. *Preventing School Failure, 46*(4), 158–162.

Baenen, N., Bernholc, A., Dulaney, C., & Banks, K. (1997). Reading Recovery: Long-term progress after three cohorts. *Journal of Education for Students Placed at Risk, 2*(2), 161–181.

Cabrera, M., & Martinez, P. (2001). The effects of repetition, comprehension checks, and gestures on primary school children in an EFL situation. *ELT Journal, 55*(3), 281–288.

Conteh-Morgan, M. E. (2001). Empowering ESL students: A new model for information literacy instruction. *Research Strategies, 18*(1), 29–38.

Cuddeback, M. J., & Ceprano, M. A. (2002). The use of Accelerated Readers with emergent readers. *Reading Improvement, 39*(2), 89–96.

Cunningham, P., Hall, D., & Defee, M. (1998). Non-ability-grouped, multilevel instruction: Eight years later. *The Reading Teacher, 52*(8), 652–664.

Dudley-Marling, C., & Murphy, S. (1997). A political critique of remedial reading programs: The example of Reading Recovery. *The Reading Teacher, 50*(6), 460–468.

Fashola, O., & Slavin, R. (1997). Promising programs for elementary and middle schools: Evidence of effectiveness and replicability. *Journal of Education for Students Placed at Risk, 2*(3), 251–307.

MacKenzie, K. K. (2001). Using literacy boosters to maintain and extend Reading Recovery success in the primary grades. *The Reading Teacher, 55*(3), 222–234.

Mokhtari, K., & Sheorey, R. (2002). Measuring ESL students' awareness of reading strategies. *Journal of Developmental Education, 25*(3), 2–10.

Ross, S. M., Smith, L. J., & Casey, J. P. (1997). Preventing early school failure: Impacts of Success for All on standardized test outcomes, minority group performance, and school effectiveness. *Journal of Education for Students Placed at Risk, 2*(1), 29–53.

Yadegari, S. A., & Ryan, D. A. (2002). Intensive reading and writing for struggling readers. *The Education Digest, 67*(7), 31–34.

7

Children's Literature: The Cornerstone of a Language Arts Program

I n this chapter you will explore the role that children's literature plays in an integrated language arts program. In addition to finding sources of information about books for children, you will examine techniques for sharing books with children and for facilitating students' varied responses to literature.

CHAPTER OBJECTIVES

After reading this chapter, you should be able to accomplish the following objectives:

1. Define the term *children's literature*.

2. Explain the various categories of children's books.

3. Identify five resources for getting information about books.

4. Describe the guidelines for judging children's books.

5. Describe five books that are sensitive to diversity in the classroom.

6. Explain how a teacher can involve children with books.

7. Describe a literature circle/response group.

8. Describe how to do a story map.

9. Explain the role of storytelling in children's literature.

10. Explain how to do a character perspective chart with a specific children's book.

CHECK YOUR BACKGROUND KNOWLEDGE. Before reading the chapter, complete the K-T-W-L chart based on the chapter overview and objectives provided at left. In column "K," write what you know about the topics in the objectives. In column "T," write what you think you know. In column "W," write what you want to learn. Finally, after you have read the chapter, write what you have learned in column "L."

Know	Think you know	Want to learn	Learned

Children's Literature: The Cornerstone

Well-written children's literature exemplifies the very best of a language and culture. Through meaningful stories, children's books enable children to internalize various aspects of the culture that they are struggling to understand. Books allow children to journey to the past, explore the present, fantasize about what might be, and enjoy the legacy of folktales and fairy tales that illustrate the human condition. Child psychologist Bruno Bettelheim (1976) has claimed that literature is the best way for children to understand their cultural heritage and to develop views and values that give meaning to life. Good literature offers children a whole new world of experiences and feelings—ways of growing and becoming to last a lifetime.

Children's literature not only provides children with perspectives on life but also motivates children to become truly involved with language. When kindergartners hear Bill Martin's *Brown Bear, Brown Bear, What Do You See?* they often begin chiming in when the teacher starts each question-and-answer segment. They pick up the pattern of the refrain, play with it, and make it their own. Children do this because the language and the book are important to them. They realize that the book demands their response. Older students also have ways of responding to good literature.

CHILDREN'S LITERATURE DEFINED

Exactly what is children's literature? It is basically any material written primarily for children that children continue to read and enjoy (Huck, Hepler, Hickman, & Kiefer, 2001). Today the range of children's literature extends from books, magazines, and comics through the media of records, films, videos, and computer adaptations of popular stories. Authors and artists involved in producing children's literature use language and images appropriate for children to convey important ideas and themes. In describing writing children's books, Peggy Parish, author of *Amelia Bedelia* (Thompson, 1984), has stated, "First you have to know what is of interest to children. . . . You have to make every word count. Also, in order to capture and hold a child's attention, there has to be a certain rhythm and flow in a story which complements its essential simplicity" (p. 25). Writing for children, a specialized form of communication, is no easy task.

Among the types of children's books currently available are picture books, poetry books, folktales and fairy tales, realistic fiction, historical fiction, fantasy, biography, and increasingly important information books. Concern with the merits of these books, and the search for proper methods of evaluating them, has led to the establishment of children's literature as a serious, respectable discipline that explores factors distinguishing high-quality children's books from those more commonly and derisively termed *kiddie lit*. Although not every book written for children is a classic, many books that fall short of this goal are entertaining, reasonably good, and very popular with children. The International Reading Association's *Children's Choices*, an annual catalog of books that children choose as their favorites, is testimony to the fact that children have some very definite ideas—and not always the same ideas that scholars have—about the books that they read.

Books abound in today's society. Some are great; some are not so great. As a teacher, you can help students acquire the ability to decide for themselves whether a book is great, reasonably good, or better left alone. The following Classroom Vignette shows how one teacher uses children's literature in her classroom.

VIGNETTE *in the classroom*

One year Ms. Carton decides to use the book *Sarah, Plain and Tall* by Patricia MacLachlan to introduce her fifth-graders to aspects of pioneer life on the prairie. She feels that this is a good way to make the period come alive for the children, to make them see that history is not just facts and events; it is populated with real people who laughed and cried as they lived their everyday lives. When the students finish their first reading of the book, many of them offer initial personal opinions.

John: I really like this book because it has a happy ending, and I love happy endings.

Marie: For me the saddest part of the book was the beginning, when the mother dies. I'm glad Sarah came to help them.

LaToya: I really got to know the people in this story. Now I understand a little of what it was like to live then.

Nilda: I liked the father. It was good for him to get another mother for the children.

Ms. Carton continues this line of thought with the following questions:

- Why is it important for Sarah to like Caleb and Anna and Papa?
- How does Sarah improve everyone's life? How does the family improve Sarah's life?
- How did you feel when Sarah finally decides to stay with the family?
- Which person is most like you—Sarah, Anna, Caleb, or Papa?
- What other books have you read about life on the prairie? How do they compare to *Sarah, Plain and Tall*?
- Have you read any other books by Patricia MacLachlan? What did you think about them?

As a conclusion to the project, Ms. Carton asks each student to explore and write about the message of the story in a daily writing journal. In this way, each child is able to give a unique interpretation to the story. Such activities help children to see the value of a piece of literature—its language, sense of story, moral, characters, and particular style.

CHILDREN'S BOOK CATEGORIES

As you begin to think about children's literature in the classroom, you should explore some of the various types of books available. This section provides brief descriptions of the major children's book genres along with several of the better examples of each type of book. Later, when you use these books with students, you can help them understand what is important about each book and how each story develops. You will thus contribute to their improved comprehension of the stories and increased knowledge of story structure.

Picture Books

Picture books allow children to comprehend a story through pictures alone or through pictures combined with text. Although picture books are generally considered appropriate for preschoolers or primary-age children, there are pictures in every type of book, even those intended for adults. These illustrations may be black-and-white or color drawings, woodcuts or other types of prints, watercolors, paintings, collages, or photographs, among others.

Beyond the classroom

Survey one or two of the teachers in your field experience school. Find out their definitions of the term *children's literature* and how they use it in the classroom. Ask them what techniques they use to help children recognize good books; record responses in your notebook. As you read through this chapter, give some thought to your own plans for using children's literature in the classroom.

In a successful picture book, the illustrations complement the text, add to it, and make it more expressive of the ideas the author is trying to communicate. Some examples of particularly successful picture books are the following:

- Carle, E. (1972). *The Very Hungry Caterpillar.* New York: Philomel Books. Much of the international popularity of this book lies in the colorful, bright collages that portray the eating adventures of the caterpillar.
- Cendrars, B. (1982). *Shadow* (M. Brown, trans. and illus.). New York: Charles Scribner's Sons. This book combines collages, woodblock prints, and paintings to give a true and vibrant description of the energy that is part of the African culture in the book.
- Del Negro, J. (1998). *Lucy Dove* (L. Gore, illus.). New York: DK Publishing. Dark values and colors in this book lend an air of menace as Lucy seeks to defeat a monster in a graveyard.
- Hodges, M. (1984). *Saint George and the Dragon* (T. S. Hyman, illus.). Boston: Little, Brown and Company. Richly detailed and romantic paintings convey the subtleties of this ancient British tale. Even the borders in the book are filled with flowers indigenous to the area.
- Polacco, P. (1994). *Pink and Say.* New York: Philomel Books. This picture book embraces the meeting of two young boys during the Civil War through the burst of color and energetic movement in the illustrations.
- Yolen, J. (1987). *Owl Moon* (J. Schoenherr, illus.). New York: Philomel Books. Schoenherr's soft but precise and clear watercolors convey the pristine winter environment needed for owling. Figure 7.1 is an illustration from this work.

Some subcategories of picture books that have evolved include wordless books and predictable pattern books. Each of these categories provides the

FIGURE 7.1

Illustration from Owl Moon.

For one minute,
three minutes,
maybe even a hundred minutes,
we stared at one another.

Source: From *Owl Moon* by Jane Yolen, illustrated by John Schoenherr, text copyright © 1987 by Jane Yolen, illustration copyright © 1987 by John Schoenherr. Used by permission of Philomel Books, a division of Penguin Young Readers Group, a Member of Penguin Group (USA) Inc.

teacher with special opportunities to meet the language needs of emerging readers and to encourage these young readers to make reading a lifelong habit.

In **wordless books,** pictures alone tell the story. Even young nonreaders can create a story from the illustrations. Such books give children the opportunity to use knowledge about story structure gained from listening to stories to create a story of their own. These books help children to develop inference skills since the entire story develops from whatever the child can "read" in the pictures. Some of the best examples of wordless books are John Goodall's series about a naughty pig, beginning with *The Adventures of Paddy Pork*; Martha Alexander's *Bobo's Dream*, a story about a plucky dachshund; Eric Carle's *Do You Want to Be My Friend?*; and any of Mercer Mayer's works, especially *A Boy, a Dog, and a Frog*. For a more detailed list of wordless picture books, see the bibliography in Jim Trelease's (2001) *The New Read-Aloud Handbook*.

Predictable **pattern books** are picture books that contain repetitive language and enable the young reader to predict which words are coming next. Even if children cannot read the words, they can often join in and follow the pattern. These books are another way of involving children with language learning. *Brown Bear, Brown Bear, What Do You See?* and other works by Bill Martin, Jr., are some of the best examples of this genre. Many other books, such as *The Teeny Tiny Woman* by Margot Zemach, *Chicken Soup with Rice* by Maurice Sendak, and *I Can't Said the Ant* by Polly Cameron, are also available. A selected bibliography of predictable pattern books can be found in *Readers and Writers with a Difference* by Rhodes and Dudley-Marling (1996).

Folklore

Folklore, or traditional literature, has its origins in the oral storytelling of primitive peoples; these tales were used for purposes of instruction and entertainment and were passed down from generation to generation. Often there are similar stories in different cultures: A Chinese version of "Little Red Riding Hood," *Lon Po Po*, won the Caldecott Medal in 1990. Among the different types of folklore are folktales and fairy tales, legends, myths, epics, and fables.

Folktales and **fairy tales** (tales with fairies and other supernatural beings) are among the most important types of children's literature available; one vital characteristic of such stories is the central character's struggle and ultimate victory over hardships. Bettelheim (1976) claimed that this story element teaches children that while life is not without unhappy situations, perseverance can lead to triumph. Other noteworthy story elements of folktales and fairy tales are characters that symbolize either only good or only evil; a long-ago, faraway setting; and a strong plot with much action culminating in the resolution of the original problem or conflict. Some of the tales that have been collected, recorded, and handed down to the present generation are "The Story of the Three Bears," "Cinderella," "Hansel and Gretel," "Rumpelstiltskin," "Beauty and the Beast," "Snow White," and "The Frog Prince."

A **legend** is a tale believed to have some historical basis, although it may not be possible to verify the truth of the story. Many legends originated in the United States—some based on true events, others on tall tales (the stories needed to illustrate the greatness of the new country). Examples of legendary characters still popular with children are Paul Bunyan and Pecos Bill. Some real individuals who have assumed legendary status are Davy Crockett, Johnny Appleseed, and even George Washington.

Myths are folktales that use the supernatural and the spiritual aspects of gods and goddesses to explain the unknown to people. They are a civilization's way of trying to make sense of what is happening around and within it. Generally, a myth attempts to explain the origin of a natural phenomenon, a custom, or a particular type of behavior. A wonderful example of a collection of myths is *In the Beginning* (1988), compiled by Virginia Hamilton and illustrated by Barry Moser. This book catalogs creation myths from around the world and, like most myths, is suitable for older readers.

Epics are tales of heroism describing the adventures of exemplary individuals. The oldest examples of this form are *The Illiad* and *The Odyssey*, which were written by the Greek poet Homer to celebrate the adventures of Odysseus as he battled through the Trojan War and spent years making his way home. Some of the more familiar epics describe the exploits of Robin Hood, King Arthur, Beowulf, Roland, Gilgamesh, and Finn McCool.

The **fable** is a brief story with a strong moral; it often involves animal characters that exemplify a single trait, such as industriousness or flattery. Fables offer many pithy sayings and simple lessons. Who does not remember the fox and the lesson of "sour grapes" or the race of the tortoise and the hare in which slow perseverance wins out over flashy speed? Although Aesop's collection is the best known, fables have also been handed down from India, Arabia, and France.

Modern Fantasy

Fantasy is that which could not be or happen in the world as we know it. Well-written fantasy can ignite children's imagination and provide them with a significant avenue for enjoying literature. An author who writes fantasy can be considered the modern equivalent of the traditional storyteller.

Fantasy ranges from the enchanting tales of Hans Christian Andersen to the magical animal tales of E. B. White and the science fiction of Madeleine L'Engle. Some well-loved examples of the fantasy genre are Michael Bond's *A Bear Called Paddington*, Margery Williams's *The Velveteen Rabbit*, the tales of Beatrix Potter, Rudyard Kipling's *Just So Stories*, and Maurice Sendak's classic *Where the Wild Things Are*. Some tales of enchantment for older readers are Natalie Babbitt's *Tuck Everlasting*, Lloyd Alexander's *Prydain Chronicles*, J. R. R. Tolkien's *The Hobbit*, and the *Harry Potter* series by J. K. Rowland.

Realistic Fiction

Realistic fiction portrays life as it is. It is that which could happen or be in the world as we know it. One of the goals of such fiction is to help children better understand the sometimes-harsh facts of life. Sutherland and Livingston (1984) have claimed that "when books portray characters who have fears or problems similar to those of the reader, they can help point the way to adjustment or solution, and they can ease the child reader's mind by showing that he or she is not alone in being afraid or resentful or discriminated against" (p. 547). "Realistic fiction can also illuminate experiences that children have not had" and "may become one way of experiencing a world we do not know" (Huck et al., 2001, p. 403). Therefore, today's realistic fiction addresses not only the positive aspects of life but also its myriad problems and hardships. Authors such as Judy Blume, Cynthia Voigt, Betsy Byars, Paula Fox, Richard Peck, and Katherine Paterson are articulate spokespeople in outlining some of the very real situations young people face today.

In addition to problematic situations, adventures, animals, and mysteries form the basis of many realistic fiction stories. Typical adventure tales include *Julie of the Wolves* by Jean George, *Island of the Blue Dolphins* by Scott O'Dell, *A Rumor of Otters* by Deborah Savage, and *The Cay* by Theodore Taylor. Stories involving animals continue to be favorites; some of the best are *The Black Stallion* by Walter Farley, *Where the Red Fern Grows* by Wilson Rawls, and *A Time to Fly Free* by Stephanie Tolan. Mysteries arouse the sleuth in children and sharpen their investigative abilities. *The House of Dies Drear* by Virginia Hamilton and *The Callender Papers* by Cynthia Voigt are challenging tales for advanced readers. For younger readers, the mystery cases of Encyclopedia Brown and Einstein Anderson remain favorites.

Historical Fiction

Through **historical fiction,** students can get a realistic view of the past; based on careful research, these stories provide authentic settings, descriptions of events, and examples of people's behavior in a given time period. Such books make the past come alive for children and help them realize that there are real flesh-and-blood people behind historical facts. Nearly every period of history is represented in historical fiction. Young readers can learn about colonial times from Arnold Lobel's *On the Day Peter Stuyvesant Sailed into Town;* Turkle's *Thy Friend, Obadiah;* and Doreen Rappaport's *The Boston Coffee Party,* while their older counterparts can experience this period through Gary Paulsen's *Mr. Tucket.*

James and Christopher Collier's *My Brother Sam Is Dead* gives students some perspectives on the Revolutionary War; Paula Fox's *The Slave Dancer* provides insights about slavery; and Irene Hunt's *Across Five Aprils* depicts some of the conflicts of the Civil War. Pioneer life is accurately recorded in MacLachlan's *Sarah, Plain and Tall;* even the cover, shown in Figure 7.2, faithfully depicts the period. More recent history is represented by Marietta Moskin's *I Am Rosemarie,* which describes life during the Holocaust. Other available historical fiction books include Maxine Schur's *Circlemaker;* Karen Cushman's *Midwife's Apprentice;* Ellen White's *Road Home;* and Paul Curtis's *Bud, Not Buddy.*

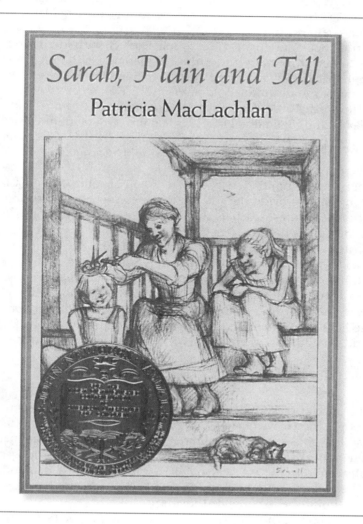

FIGURE **7.2**

Cover illustration from Sarah, Plain and Tall.

Source: Jacket art copyright © 1985 by Marcia Sewall. Jacket copyright © 1985 by HarperCollins Publishers, Inc. Used by permission of HarperCollins Publishers.

Biographies

Biographies (and **autobiographies**) depict the lives of noteworthy men and women from all races and walks of life. As such, biographies provide children with role models as well as information about real places and times. Like historical fiction, biographies can make facts come alive for children; the best examples of this genre are carefully researched and objective in their portrayal of their subjects.

Younger readers enjoy Cynthia Rylant's *When I Was Young in the Mountains* as well as Clyde Bulla's *Lincoln's Birthday.* More advanced readers are drawn to the entertaining works of Jean Fritz, such as *Where Do You Think You're Going, Christopher Columbus?* They also enjoy reading *The First Woman Doctor* by Rachel Baker (the story of Elizabeth Blackwell), *Freedom Train: The Story of Harriet Tubman* by Dorothy Sterling, the Newbery Medal–winning *Lincoln: A Photobiography* by Russell Freedman, and *We Flew Over the Bridge: The Memoirs of Faith Ringgold* by Faith Ringgold.

Nonfiction Books

Nonfiction books provide students with information and explain a variety of concepts. The topics of such books range from recipes to computers. In this Information Age, nonfiction books are assuming a particular importance for readers of all ages and levels.

Nonfiction books often provide young readers with their first experiences with expository text. Usually the earliest books that children come in contact with are alphabet books and counting books. Some of the perennial favorites in the former category are *Brian Wildsmith's ABC*, *Ed Emberly's ABC*, and Maurice Sendak's *Alligators All Around.* Favorite books about numbers include *Anno's Counting Book* and Sendak's *One Was Johnny.* Other nonfiction books that appeal to young readers are Peter Spier's *People*, as well as *The Cloud Book, The Kids' Cat Book, The Popcorn Book*, and *The Quicksand Book*, all by noted author/illustrator Tomie dePaola.

For older readers, nonfiction books are essential sources of data in many content areas; they also provide the information necessary for nurturing each child's unique personal interests. Teachers should pay special attention to selecting books whose information is both current and accurate. Some content area books meeting these criteria are *The Sea World Book of Whales* by Eve Bunting, *The Flight of the Pterosaurs* by Keith Moseley, *The Story of the Statue of Liberty* by Ib Penick, *Black Holes* by Heather Couper and Nigel Henbest, *A Lift-the-Flap Book: Inside the Body* by Giuliano Fornari, and *Crocodiles & Alligators* by Seymour Simon. Books that have personal value for readers include Sheila Cole's *Working Kids on Working* and Helen Benedict's *Safe, Strong, and Streetwise*, a needed book about keeping safe in today's world. In addition, there are many how-to books that students enjoy.

Poetry

Poetry has a special place in the classroom for the sheer enjoyment that it provides. Through poetry, writers express their innermost ideas and feelings about every possible subject; poets use concise and rhythmical language to create images that appeal to both the hearts and the heads of youngsters. Because poetry really exploits the musical qualities of language, it demands to be read aloud. In the elementary school, there should be little emphasis on the analysis of poetry; it should be experienced for itself.

One of the best authors to use when introducing poetry to students is Shel Silverstein. His *Where the Sidewalk Ends* and *A Light in the Attic* are favorites with students of all ages for the humorous images they provide. Other humorous poetry books are *If I Were in Charge of the World and Other Worries* by Judith Viorst and *You Be Good and I'll Be Night: Jump-on-the-Bed Poems* by Eve Merriam. Older children enjoy two Newbery Medal–winning books: Nancy Willard's *A Visit to William Blake's Inn* and Paul Fleischman's *Joyful Noise: Poems for Two Voices*. Other poets whose work children love are Mary O'Neill, Jack Prelutsky, Myra Cohn Livingston, and Lee Bennett Hopkins.

When looking for individual poems to share with your class, check the following anthologies:

- Brown, M. (1993). *Under the Sun and the Moon and Other Poems*. New York: Hyperion Books for Children.
- Crump, F. (1990). *Mother Goose Nursery Rhymes*. Nashville: Winston-Derek Publishers.
- Dyer, J. (1996). *Animal Crackers: Collection of Pictures, Poems, and Lullabies for the Very Young*. Boston: Little, Brown and Company.
- Phillips, L. (1995). *Random House Treasury of Best Loved Poems*. New York: Random House.
- Prelutsky, J. (1996). *Monday's Troll*. New York: Greenwillow Books.
- Schertle, A. (1995). *Advice for Frogs and Other Poems*. New York: Lothrop, Lee, and Shepard Books.
- Sword, E. (1995). *A Child's Anthology of Poetry*. Hopewell, NJ: Ecco Press.

What is important—what lasts—in another language is not what is said but what is written. For the essence of an age, we look to its poetry and its prose, not its talk shows.

PETER BRODIE

Series Books

While series books do not have a reputation as fine children's literature, they are included here because of young readers' fascination with them. Series books, being highly patterned, may provide a clear insight into the rules of reading for many new and transitional readers. Series detective stories allow immature readers to use strategies and make sense of what they are reading. The clues in the series detective stories help develop strategies for reading by providing a prime opportunity for the reader to notice details and then make appropriate choices and predictions. The reader can be caught and entranced by "the excitement of the detective when the clues are discovered" (Ross, 1995, p. 230). As a result, the established formula detective series by the Stratemeyer Syndicate (*Nancy Drew*, *The Hardy Boys*, and *The Bobbsey Twins*) are doing well. Publishers not only are bringing out updated versions of these series but also are publishing a variety of other successful books, including R. L. Stine's *Goosebumps* series and J. K. Rowling's *Harry Potter* books.

However, what is the attraction of series books for older children and young adolescents? According to Moran and Steinfirst (1985), their appeal is based on several characteristics. First of all, they demand little analysis and are easy to read, something for which the less capable, older reader is grateful. Because the plots are predictable (the good and righteous always win in the end), these books really promote comprehension: The reader always has an idea of what is coming. They also provide a respite from more intense realistic fiction while supplying young readers with competent heroes and heroines. However, when closely questioned, middle school readers appear to like more difficult, recommended literature as well as the easier series books (Greenlee, Monson, & Taylor, 1996).

So this is not a recommendation to use series books in place of fine literature, but you might consider them as a starting place for reluctant older readers or even nonreaders. When you convince such students to try series books, you

Beyond the classroom

Begin to be your own judge of children's literature by reading some of the books mentioned in this section. Keep notes about each book in your database. List the book's title, author, publisher, and date of publication. You will probably also want to include a story summary, an estimate of the appropriate reading level, and possible classroom uses. After conferring with your field experience teacher, you might want to try reading one of the books to your class.

open the door to helping them improve both as readers and as judges of good literature; such improvement is impossible if they do not read at all.

Choosing Materials for the Classroom

Because literature plays such an important role in a successful language arts program, teachers need to be knowledgeable about obtaining appropriate materials that their students actually want to read. This section provides a brief overview of resources and guidelines to aid you as you begin selecting books for your classroom. It is particularly important for you to listen to your students and allow their ideas and interests to guide you in choosing classroom materials. You should also consider obtaining books to meet a variety of special needs, ranging from combating racism and sexism to helping students become more sensitive to the elderly and the disabled.

RESOURCES

After reading the preceding section, the first two questions that probably come to mind are, Where do I find all these wonderful books? and How do I know if they are appropriate for my students and our class goals? Fortunately, a number of resources are available to help you find quality books and magazines and to give you some guidance about appropriate classroom uses for them.

Before looking too far, you should first consult the librarians at your school and at your branch of the public library. They have a wealth of information about many different types of books and magazines that you can use in your classroom. You may want to consult anthologies of literature, directories of special books, publishers' catalogs, and biographical dictionaries listing authors and illustrators of children's books. One excellent example of a biographical dictionary is Barbara Rollock's (1988) *Black Authors and Illustrators of Children's Books*. In addition to these general references, other sources are available to professional educators. Appendix A contains a list entitled "Resources for Finding Magazines and Books for Classroom Use."

GUIDELINES FOR EVALUATING BOOKS

Using resources to locate recommended books is only the first step in acquiring appropriate materials for the classroom. You also want to be sure that the books you choose and help children choose for themselves combine high quality with the ability to meet particular needs within the classroom. Books that have won the Caldecott Medal (for illustration), the Newbery Medal (for literature), or other awards are certainly high-quality books (see Appendix A for listings of these books). However, to be sure that a book meets your own criteria for excellence in the classroom, you need to examine it yourself. You likewise need to encourage your students to examine books and to make their own decisions about the merits and qualities of each book.

When evaluating a book, you may find it helpful to think about the guidelines listed in Figure 7.3. You should also model the evaluation process for your students so that they have a framework of specific criteria to use in judging books on their own.

If you or your students are trying to evaluate a nonfiction book rather than a narrative, be sure that it meets the following two criteria:

1. Facts and information in the text should be both current and accurate.
2. Clear, objective writing should reflect the logical organization of the text.

1. **Prereading Information**

   What kind of book is this?

   What can my students predict about this story from the cover and title? From the illustrations? From the chapter titles? From the print size?

   How can I use this book in class?

2. **Story Line**

   Does the book tell an interesting story?

   What happens and how does it end?

3. **Setting**

   Where and when does the story take place?

   In view of the story line, does the setting make sense?

4. **Theme**

   What is the underlying idea of the story?

   Is this theme something my students can understand?

5. **Characters**

   Who are the characters?

   Are the characters appealing, consistent in their behavior, and free of stereotypes?

6. **Style and Format**

   What is special about the way the author writes?

   Is it easy to understand what the author is trying to say?

   Do the pictures, colors, and cover fit the story?

   Does the cover reflect what is within?

7. **Reactions**

   How does this story make me feel?

   What does the author do in parts of the story to cause these feelings?

   Is this book as good as other books written by the same author? As good as other books on the same topic?

8. **Evaluation**

   Why did I like or dislike this book?

   What did this book help me to understand?

   Would I recommend this book to my students? Why?

FIGURE 7.3

Guidelines for evaluating literature.

CUES FROM CHILDREN

Resources and guidelines are helpful in choosing books for the classroom; however, the most important information comes from children themselves. The students' interests and abilities help to determine what materials are appropriate for them.

Children have definite ideas about what they do and do not like to read, and their ideas about what constitutes a good book are not always in agreement with those of adults. One of the reasons that the International Reading Association publishes "Children's Choices" is to make sure that children's voices are heard and that teachers heed what children have to say.

Research by Abrahamson (1980) analyzing the types of books children choose to read has shown that younger readers really enjoy fantasy, folktales, and realistic fiction. They want a story with a strong, sequential plot in which

Beyond the classroom

Choose a literature book recommended either in this chapter or by another teacher, and use the guidelines in Figure 7.3 to evaluate it for yourself. Then evaluate a nonfiction book according to the criteria presented in the text. Comment in your notebook about the benefits for both teachers and students of evaluating books.

the main character faces and solves a problem. Humorous stories are popular, as are stories about children, animals, and families. Young children want the illustrations to complement the story.

Older readers like a variety of books (Sebesta, Calder, & Cleland, 1981). Their interests range from realistic fiction to nonfiction books. They enjoy books with action, mystery, and suspense. They also want to read books that realistically depict the issues or problems they are currently facing (International Reading Association, 1996); this allows them to escape problems through fantasy and science fiction. Sports stories also are of interest to both boys and girls (Feeley, 1982).

When trying to figure out which books appeal to your students, you need to get information about their special interests. Questioning them about the following areas should prove helpful:

- *General interests.* Leisure-time activities; favorite TV shows; hobbies; interests in games or sports; membership in clubs or groups; pets; favorite movies or videos
- *Literary interests.* Current books children are reading; favorite topics; books they own; books they would like to own; involvement with the library; comic books preferred; magazines; next book on their agenda

Beyond the classroom

For more information about magazines, read "Magazines in the Classroom: Beyond Recreational Reading" by Olson, Gee, and Forester in the May 1989 issue of *The Journal of Reading,* or consult *Magazines for Kids and Teens* by Donald Stoll (1997). Note the variety of magazines available for children and see which ones are used in your field experience school.

Once a reading range is established within a class, the teacher needs to make sure that a wide variety of interesting books within that range is available. The teacher needs to guide students to materials that will provide successful experiences for both the gifted and the less capable readers. Although many children can choose books for themselves, individual conferences may be helpful for others.

Another way in which teachers can help to accommodate the varying interests and reading ability levels within a class is to use some of the excellent children's magazines that are available. The magazines are professionally packaged and include a variety of literary genres, writing styles, and reading levels. In your own class, you may want to include some of the magazines listed here:

- *Children's Literature.* 7513 Shadywood Road, Bethesda, MD 20817-2065. Literary magazine that features well-known authors and illustrators.
- *Cobblestone.* Cobblestone Publishing Company, 30 Grove Street, Suite C, Peterborough, NH 03458. Social studies.
- *Cricket.* Open Court Publishing Company, 315 Fifth Street, P.O. Box 300, Peru, IL 61354. Features interesting stories for children.
- *Go Wild!* c/o National Wildlife Federation, 11100 Wildlife Center Drive, Reston, VA 20190-5362. Grades 1–7. Wildlife.
- *Highlights for Children.* 2300 Hidden Picture Drive, P.O. Box 182112, Columbus, OH 43218-2112. Preschool–grade 7. General information.
- *National Geographic World.* 1145 17th Street NW, Washington, DC 20036 (1-800-422-6202). Grades 3–8. Social studies and general interest.
- *Odyssey.* Cobblestone Publishing Company, 30 Grove Street, Suite C, Peterborough, NH 03458. Astronomy and space science.
- *Spider.* Cobblestone Publishing Company, 30 Grove Street, Suite C, Peterborough, NH 03458. Illustrated monthly publication for six- to nine-year-olds.

BOOKS TO MEET SPECIAL NEEDS

Choosing books to meet particular needs is an important part of any classroom literature program. Because today's society is complex and culturally diverse, it presents many situations that can cause confusion and misunderstandings in children. In addition, many students' personal lives involve problems and needs that can cause tension and frustration. Teachers can use books to help students understand themselves and others by sensitizing them to the variety of social issues in today's culture. While teachers may be hesitant about engaging in direct bibliotherapy and using books to promote mental health (Overstad, 1981), they can recommend books to promote social awareness and even *socioemotional growth* (Jalongo, 1983). Literature can become a way of meeting some of the special social needs of students living in a diverse culture.

At present, there is no doubt that the school population is multicultural, and respect for all ethnic groups is essential. Books that portray members of different cultural groups in a positive manner need to be part of every classroom.

To ensure that the books in your classroom adequately reflect today's social reality, you may want to consult several resources. Appendix A contains a list of resources to help you locate books that will help both you and your students to meet the needs of living in a diverse culture and to develop positive views of the elderly, women, and the disabled.

Finally, teachers need to remember that children also face personal problems and stressful situations. Making appropriate books available to them can help them to see how others handle similar problems and to develop their own coping strategies. For example, children who have had an experience with death might appreciate reading Judith Viorst's *The Tenth Good Thing About Barney*, which tells of a boy whose cat has died, or Carol Carrick's *The Accident*, in which a dog is lost. A child involved in a divorce could identify with *The Kids' Book of Divorce* by Eric Rofes and be relieved to know that he or she is not alone in this situation. Other problem situations depicted in books range from sibling rivalry to sexual abuse. Although individual bibliotherapy is not within your realm as a teacher, having books available that address these issues can make a child's adjustment easier.

> *Books are the windows through which the soul looks out.*
>
> **HENRY WARD BEECHER**

Beyond the classroom

Read four books that have been recommended to meet special needs. Add the entries to the literature list that you started at the beginning of this chapter.

Children's Literature and Language Learning

The major focus of any integrated language program is to involve children with real language, to provide classroom experiences in which the language used really means something to the children (Goodman, 1986). With the exception of their own oral language, there is no language more meaningful to children than the language of books. A good book tells a story, a story definitely worth reading. And in telling these stories, such books provide both oral and written language models that shape the children's own use of language.

LANGUAGE MODELS

The language of books makes children aware of the many different ways in which they can use words to express their ideas. Children who have heard fairy tales use the traditional beginning "Once upon a time" in their own made-up tales. These words help children convey the idea of something that happened a long time ago. Without the model of the fairy tale, children might never learn how to convey this idea.

From books, children also learn that words express ideas. Books help children to expand their vocabularies as they develop a variety of concepts. For example, a book such as Tana Hoban's *Push-Pull, Empty-Full* helps youngsters learn about word opposites in a meaningful way. Eric Carle's books *The Very Hungry Caterpillar, The Grouchy Ladybug,* and *The Very Busy Spider* help children acquire proper scientific vocabulary in their ongoing study of scientific concepts.

Books also help children understand the intricacies of language. A book such as Mary Ann Hoberman's *A House Is a House for Me* introduces very young children to the figurative language of metaphors. Students learn that a rose is a house for a smell, a carton is a house for crackers, and a shell is a house for a snail. Other books handle figurative language humorously, such as Peggy Parish's *Amelia Bedelia* books and Fred Gwynne's *The King Who Rained* and *A Chocolate Moose for Dinner.* Still other books, including those of Dr. Seuss and Shel Silverstein, encourage children to actively play with language and zany ideas.

TEXT STRUCTURE

Another major advantage of using books is that they allow children to understand the structure of both *narrative* (stories) and *expository* (informational) text. Every story or narrative has a somewhat similar structure (Stein & Glenn, 1979). Figure 7.4 shows Cunningham and Foster's (1978) story grammar model, which succinctly describes the structure of stories.

FIGURE 7.4

Story grammar.

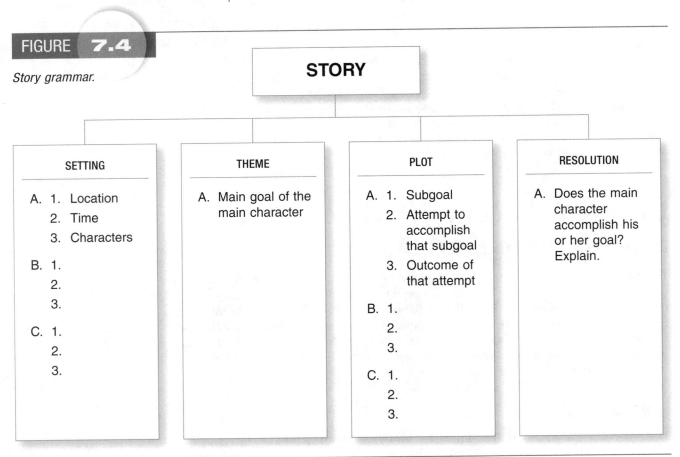

STORY

SETTING

A. 1. Location
   2. Time
   3. Characters

B. 1.
   2.
   3.

C. 1.
   2.
   3.

THEME

A. Main goal of the main character

PLOT

A. 1. Subgoal
   2. Attempt to accomplish that subgoal
   3. Outcome of that attempt

B. 1.
   2.
   3.

C. 1.
   2.
   3.

RESOLUTION

A. Does the main character accomplish his or her goal? Explain.

Source: From Cunningham, James W. (1978, January). The ivory tower connection: A case study. *The Reading Teacher, 31*(4), 365–369. Reprinted with permission of James W. Cunningham and the International Reading Association.

Children can only develop a sense of this story structure schema by listening to stories or by reading stories themselves. After many book experiences, children begin to understand that stories have characters, a plot, a setting, and a theme. This understanding is particularly important because research (Marshall, 1983; Moore, 1995; Whaley, 1981) has shown that there is a relationship between children's awareness of these components and their ability to comprehend the story.

Informational or expository books do not necessarily share a single structure in the same way that narratives do. Actually, several studies (McGee & Richgels, 1985; Meyer & Freedle, 1979; Piccolo, 1987) have outlined five different patterns or text structures for such books: description, sequence, comparison/contrast, cause/effect, and problem/solution. Very often writers combine the text structures in their writing. The following excerpt from *Lincoln: A Photobiography* by Russell Freedman (1987) is an example of description:

> Lincoln was visibly nervous. He was wearing a new black suit and sporting a neatly clipped beard. He held a silk stovepipe hat in one hand, a gold-headed cane in the other. He put the cane in a corner, then looked around, trying to find a place for the hat. Stephen Douglas smiled and took the hat from him. (p. 68)

As is the case with narrative text, a student's knowledge of the structure or pattern of expository writing can affect comprehension (McGee & Richgels, 1985; Sinatra, 1991). With the variety of patterns utilized, it is not surprising that this type of writing provides more of a challenge for young readers than narrative stories. But by repeatedly exposing your students to informational non-fiction books and other expository writing, you can help them to be more sensitive to the language and text structures used in such books. Select nonfiction books for read-aloud sessions and include them in your science and social studies units. For example, a unit on Native Americans for students in the middle grades could be enhanced by some of the following informational books:

Beyond the classroom

Reflect on some of the statements that have been made about the benefits of using literature with children, and make notations in your notebook about your reactions to these ideas. You may also want to note your reaction to any particularly beneficial literature activities that you see used in your field experience classroom.

- Anderson, M. (1994). *The Nez Perce.* New York: Franklin Watts.
- Bruchac, J. (1999). *Lasting Echoes: An Oral History of Native American People.* New York: Silver Whistle.
- D'Apice, R., & D'Apice, M. (1990). *The Algonquian.* Vero Beach, FL: Rourke Publications.
- Hayden, K. (2002). *Plains Indians: Come and Discover My World.* Bt Bound.
- Kamma, A., & Gardner, L. (1999). *If You Lived with the Hopi.* New York: Scholastic.
- Landaue, E. (1994). *The Hopi.* New York: Franklin Watts.
- Phillip, N. (2001). *The Great Mystery: Myths of Native America.* New York: Clarion Books.

Involving Children with Books

In a school program promoting the development of language and reading abilities, one important goal is to make children want to read (Cullinan, 1987). Locating good stories worth telling and using them in the classroom definitely make students want to be involved with books. Good stories draw the reader in and ignite a special, personal response from each child (Kilpatrick, 1993). A great story, such as Sendak's *Where the Wild Things Are*, ignites as many reactions as there are children in the class. Some students identify with the main character Max's defiance and punishment; others are thrilled and horrified by the "wild things." Still others focus on their relief when Max finally returns to his own room and the hot supper waiting for him.

ENVIRONMENT

Teachers need to do more than merely locate good books and make them available for reading. They need to create an environment that draws children and books together and enables the students to grow and develop as readers. Setting aside special areas for quiet reading, establishing an accessible and well-stocked classroom library, and designing stimulating book displays and bulletin boards are all ways to promote successful book involvement. While there is no one set way to arrange a classroom, the floor plan in Figure 7.5 presents an arrangement that one teacher used successfully to establish a literature-oriented environment.

FIGURE 7.5

A reading-friendly room arrangement.

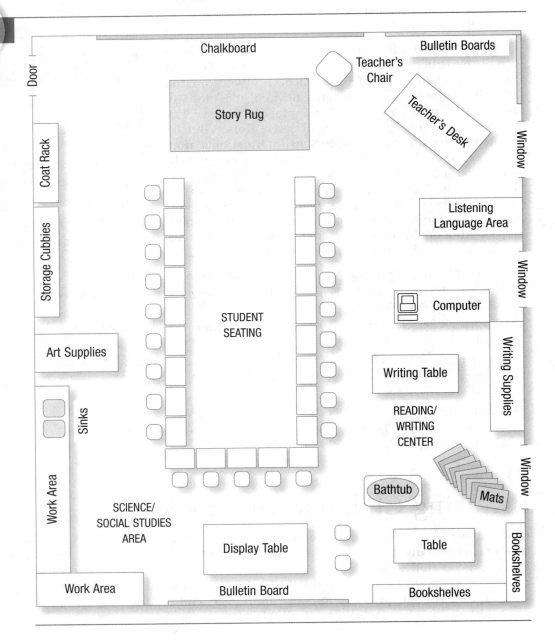

Book displays in the form of bulletin boards, dioramas, or easels are especially effective in featuring books associated with particular units of study in literature, science, social studies, and the other content areas. Successful displays can include book jackets or illustrations, book ads created by children, models of scenes from books, children's letters to the main character or author of a book, "wanted posters" for book characters, and journal entries from students who have particularly enjoyed a book. Book promotion initiates book involvement.

Other methods of book promotion are teacher modeling, book talks, reading aloud, the shared book experience, sustained silent reading, and storytelling.

MODELING

Successful literature-oriented teachers enjoy books and let their classes know it. They set aside time each day for reading aloud as well as for silent reading. They encourage their students to own and borrow books and make sure that classes have regular trips to the school library and media center. Such teachers can also guide students' thinking about books by providing a model of how to approach a book, proceed through it, and finally evaluate it.

BOOK TALKS

In a classroom, teachers are not the only ones who like to talk about books and share them with others. Among children, talking is a primary means of letting others know about special books and making recommendations for further reading. Book talks can take place any time during the school day. They can occur in informal small groups during free time or as more formalized talks to an entire class. O'Halloran (1988) has noted that relatively informal book talks not only help children to get involved with books but also allow them to respond to books spontaneously in lieu of an assigned postreading activity.

Books are friends that never fail.

THOMAS CARLYLE

READING ALOUD

Everyone loves hearing a story, especially when the reader is excited and enthusiastic about it. Teachers who advocate and model reading aloud in their classrooms have found that this technique works with groups as diverse as preschoolers and university graduate students. There is just something about a good story that captures everybody's attention.

One of the most important aspects of reading aloud in the classroom is that it allows a teacher to promote books to students. It tells children that reading books is not just something to supplement the curriculum; it *is* the curriculum (Trelease, 2001). Students begin to realize that books are important, that they are the core of what goes on in the classroom and a primary means of getting information. They begin to see themselves following the lead of their teacher and reading books on their own.

When you start to use reading aloud in your classroom, you may want to keep in mind the following general procedures, adapted from the recommendations of Jim Trelease (2001):

- Examine and read a variety of children's books. In class, however, only share those books that you yourself enjoy—books that generate a great deal of enthusiasm.

- Practice reading a book outside of class and decide if you want to add to, shorten, or delete any particular parts.

- Set aside a specific period each day for reading aloud. Children like routine and knowing that they can count on this activity each day.

- Make sure that you provide variety in the materials you read. Intersperse informational books with stories. Sometimes use a filmstrip and an audio-cassette of a book for the read-aloud session.
- When reading a book to the class, make sure that everyone can see you and the book.
- When you begin reading, help the students to get settled by asking them what they know or remember about a story. This helps them tune in to the session.
- Be sure to read slowly and clearly and to use expression in your voice. Make sure that the way you read reflects what is being said in the story.
- When possible, use props to add to the story and make it more visually appealing to the children. For example, if you were reading *Cranberry Thanksgiving*, you might want to bring in some cranberries to show the students.
- Allow time for children's questions and comments. Talking about the book helps students understand it and make it their own.
- Do not panic if things do not go smoothly the first time. Good read-aloud habits take practice.

SHARED BOOK EXPERIENCES

The shared reading of books is a literature approach to language learning suited for beginning readers. Based on the work of Holdaway (1991), this method is a classroom adaptation of the natural reading experiences that occur when a care-giver shares a book with a young child.

In the classroom, the teacher reads to groups of children and therefore uses oversized **Big Books** that allow everyone to see the pictures and text clearly. Before actually reading the Big Book, the teacher shows the title and illustrations and asks the students to predict what might happen in the story. Then she or he reads aloud while pointing to the words in the text. After the first reading, the whole group joins in reading the words in unison. This process continues until the children are familiar enough with the book to read it on their own. Cullinan (1987) has recommended that regular-size copies of the books also be available for individual reading.

Because children pick up rhymes and repetitive chants easily, predictable books are highly recommended for this activity. When a teacher is reading Paul Galdone's *The Three Billy Goats Gruff*, it is natural for the children to chime in with the "Trip-Trap, Trip-Trap" of the goats crossing the bridge. The same thing occurs with the refrain of "Not I" that is repeated by the cat, the dog, the mouse, and the other animals in response to the hen's query in *The Little Red Hen* by Galdone. For teachers interested in using predictable books, Saccardi (1996) has recommended using three different types of texts: those with repeated cumulative events, those that invite drama, and those that lead to writing.

Obtaining the Big Books necessary for the shared book experience has sometimes been a problem. Some books are now available in this format from Scholastic (Mary Hoberman's *A House Is a House for Me*; Maurice Sendak's *Chicken Soup with Rice*; Margaret Wise Brown's *Goodnight, Moon*; and many others) and the Wright Group (Wright Story Box Program). But many young readers enjoy helping teachers make their own Big Books and thus using a hands-on approach to literature.

SUSTAINED SILENT READING

Sustained silent reading (SSR)—sometimes known as uninterrupted sustained silent reading (USSR), drop everything and read (DEAR), or go read a book (GRAB)—should be an important aspect of any literature-oriented program. SSR involves setting aside classroom time for the students and the teacher to read books. It gives students the opportunity to practice their reading competencies with literature of their own choice.

Over the years, many researchers (Berglund & Johns, 1983; Hunt, 1970; McCracken, 1971) have suggested guidelines for implementing SSR. A key issue in the success of the strategy is modeling, for the teacher's own reading shows students that reading is important. In addition, the following five class rules are helpful in promoting successful SSR sessions (Blake, 1979):

1. Everyone reads.
2. Everyone makes his or her own reading choice. It can be anything within reason—a comic book, a cereal box, a magazine, or *War and Peace.*
3. No one can interrupt once SSR begins. If someone does, everyone stops.
4. Students do not have to report on what they are reading, but if they want to, that is okay.
5. The SSR period is held at the same time every day.

SSR is really an excellent opportunity to let children practice their reading and become better readers. It can also be a major factor in awakening students to the joys of independent reading.

STORYTELLING

Storytelling was described in Chapter 5 as one method of stimulating children's vocabulary development and helping them master the sentence patterns of oral language. However, as a means of promoting interaction between the teller and the listener, storytelling also provides a way of sharing books with children and exposing them to the rich language models of literature (Strickland & Morrow, 1990). Imagine the delight of the child who hears, imitates, and even dramatizes the giant's refrain in "Jack and the Beanstalk": "Fee. Fie. Foe. Fum. I smell the blood of an Englishman." Equally important is the comfort found by the second-grader who is able to ease the pain over the loss of a poodle by recalling that the dog was frisky and smart and funny and clean; it was also snuggly and beautiful, and only once did it bite the cat's tail. In all, the child can list 10 good things about the little dog—a pattern internalized after listening repeatedly to the story *The Tenth Good Thing About Barney,* in which a boy fondly remembers his dead cat. How wonderful and satisfying it is for such a child to be able to reach into his or her storehouse of literature and find just the right words to express ideas and feelings.

Storytelling promotes the reading of literature. When a teacher tells a particular tale to children, he or she is issuing an invitation for them to read the book, to become better acquainted with the characters, and to establish their own personal understanding of the events. Through such storytelling efforts, the teacher gives the children a clear message: I think this is such a great story that I went to the trouble of learning it and preparing it so that you could know about it and enjoy it the way I do.

In and beyond the classroom

Select a story that you really like. After reading it aloud to students, jot down your ideas about the pluses and minuses of reading stories to children. Then prepare and *tell* the same story to a class. In your notebook, write a comparison of the advantages and disadvantages of both approaches to sharing stories, and use this exercise to help you with future decisions about the use of the techniques in your classroom.

Storytelling does have some important benefits that are absent in reading aloud. In storytelling, there is greater interaction and eye contact between the teller and the audience because the book is no longer a barrier between them. The teller can also improvise with the story and make it a richer experience for the audience. Finally, the variety of props that can be used in telling a story motivates children to use a similar collection of items in their own telling and retelling of the tale.

As a beginning storyteller, you may find it valuable to read about a storytelling experience of one of the authors in the Classroom Vignette that follows.

VIGNETTE *in the classroom*

When I was trying to convey the importance of storytelling to my undergraduates, I decided that the only thing that would work would be an actual demonstration with a small group of children. I arranged for my students to observe me telling a story to a small group of five-year-olds in the kindergarten class associated with the college.

Because I wanted to ensure a measure of success, I chose to use a story from a book that I had previously read aloud to numerous kindergartners, first-graders, and second-graders. However, there were several other reasons that influenced my selection of *Pretzel* by Margaret Rey. First of all, the story is about two dachshunds—my favorite breed of dog. I also like the overall theme of the story, which is the importance of valuing each individual's unique traits. In addition, the story has a limited number of characters (two main characters) and a series of well-defined events.

Some professional storytellers feel that stories are not enhanced by props and should be told without them. I, an amateur storyteller, do not subscribe to that philosophy. I believe that the right prop can really enhance a story and help to focus the storyteller. Therefore, I began to explore which type of prop I might want to use.

Because I wanted to show the contrast between Pretzel's unusual length and the size of other dachshunds, and because the story has a limited number of characters and objects, I decided to use a flannel board. I made that choice based on data from *Storyteller,* in which Ross (1996) recommends using flannel boards to illustrate stories involving a comparison of sizes, folktales, scientific tales explaining phenomena, and accumulative tales such as *I Know an Old Lady Who Swallowed a Fly.*

I made my flannel board by covering a portable cork bulletin board with a large piece of tan felt. For the figures in the story, I chose brightly colored pieces of felt and enhanced facial features and decorations with magic markers.

Once the props were completed, I began preparing *Pretzel* for the kindergartners. As recommended by many authorities (Ross, 1996), I did not memorize the story. Instead I read it over many times to get a sequence of the events, and I developed a general time line in my mind of what happened first, what happened second, and so on. I also tried to develop the personality and voice for Pretzel—who was proud, dignified, and helpful—and the traits of Greta, the other dachshund in the story—who was selfish, stuck-up, and spoiled. Once I began telling the story to myself, I began to use particular story phrases such as the following:

One morning in May five little dachshunds were born.

Pretzel suddenly started growing—and growing—and growing.

"I don't care for long dogs," said Greta.

Other than developing the haughty sniff associated with Greta, I didn't add any gestures to the story. However, I did decide to start the story by telling the children a little about my dachshund and allowing them to share some information about their pets. I also decided to let the close of the story be informal by giving the children some time to express their feelings about the story or to handle the felt props. Most of all, I practiced the story on tape, in the mirror, and in front of friends until they knew it almost as well as I did.

The actual telling went smoothly. With some help from the class's regular teacher, I set the board on a chair and gathered the small group of children around it. As planned, we spent a few minutes talking about my dachshund and the children's experiences with dogs and other pets. Then I launched into my rendition of *Pretzel.* I found that the practice really helped, and I was able to portray Pretzel and Greta in exactly the right light. The children really loved the characters and the story, and we spent several minutes at the end of the story handling the props and telling what we liked best about the tale.

The best part of the experience came after the actual storytelling. Because the children enjoyed handling the props so much, the teacher asked me to leave them in the classroom—a request I was glad to honor. She later told me that the children used the flannel figures frequently in attempts to retell the story and that she was reading the book to them to assist their comprehension of the story.

Also, the experience convinced my students that storytelling is not just a frill—something extra to do on a dreary afternoon. They began to understand that books and storytelling form a core component of a language development program.

Although flannel boards and puppetry are two of the more popular methods for enhancing storytelling, other methods are also effective. Transparencies, slides, filmstrips, films, and videos are sometimes used by teachers to tell stories and by students to retell them to each other. The medium used often depends on the size of the group to whom the story is being told, the aspect of the story that is being emphasized, and the overall language competencies that the students are trying to master.

Children's Responses to Literature

Through experiences with good literature, children develop a greater comprehension of story structure, gain more control over language, increase their oral fluency, develop the habit of reading daily, and experience emotional reactions. They become mature and sophisticated readers. This section explores activities to facilitate those responses: discussions, literature circles, strategies for retelling, book publishing, creative drama and choral speaking activities, and oral and written methods for sharing books. All the activities help children to see how vitally important books are in every aspect of life. For a more detailed discussion of children's responses to literature, see Huck, Hepler, Hickman, and Kiefers (2001) *Children's Literature in the Elementary School.*

DISCUSSIONS

Talk is a vital force for learning in the classroom. Modeling and book talks have already been discussed as ways in which to interest and involve children in literature. *Discussions* allow children to express personal responses informally, without preparation. Even if a child really dislikes a book, she or he should have a right to say so and to hear others' reactions to his or her feelings.

Discussions can be large-group or small-group activities, either guided by a teacher or controlled by the students. In one study (Strickland, Dillon, Funkhouser, Glick, & Rogers, 1990), several teachers/researchers studied literature response groups in which the children took control of the questioning and discussion. In such groups, talk proved to be an empowering force in learning.

Very often discussions can follow retellings or book talks and begin with personal responses. Students can then explore questions about the literary elements of characterization, setting, plot, and theme. They can also make predictions about books and compare books that they have read individually. The Classroom Vignette at the beginning of this chapter, discussing the use of *Sarah, Plain and Tall,* provides one example of a focused book discussion.

LITERATURE CIRCLES

Literature circles are specialized discussion groups in which children engage in student-led sessions about books that they themselves have chosen to read (Tierney & Readence, 2000). These circles meet regularly with each member assuming a particular role and preparing to meet the responsibilities of that role at each meeting. Necessary roles include a director, who keeps the discussion going; a literary luminary, who decides which sections of the passage would be appealing or exciting to the group (may read them aloud); a connector, who connects the story to the experiences of the group; and an illustrator, who draws for the group. Optional roles range from the summarizer to the vocabulary enricher (Daniels, 1994). Guidance and support by the teacher are essential in making this process work. Teachers need to monitor students during the process and gather artifacts from each student's role to determine progress. This approach takes time, patience, and lots of modeling.

RETELLING ACTIVITIES

Retelling the story line of a book is a way for a child to reconstruct the story's meaning. The child is able to respond to literature by creating his or her similar version of the tale. According to Morrow (1985), retelling stories is a strategy that can improve oral language fluency, sense of story, and overall comprehension. Retelling strategies can include storytelling; the use of story structures, guides, and maps; the creation of books; and various forms of creative drama (described in detail in Chapter 5).

Storytelling

Storytelling comes naturally to children (Hamilton & Weiss, 1993). They are continually telling their teachers and peers the daily stories of their personal lives. From these stories, it is an easy progression to creating and telling the story lines of wordless picture books, such as *Bobo's Dream*.

Children can make effective use of all the props available to teachers: puppets, flannel boards, chalk stories, transparencies, slides, and self-created filmstrips. One type of story that works particularly well for children is the object story, in which the student uses an object or objects from the story to aid the retelling. At Christmastime one year, a sixth-grader decided to tell a modified version of Chris Van Allsburg's *The Polar Express* to a group of primary children. Her props were a small train model and a reindeer sleigh bell, which helped to prompt her memory of the events in the story. The whole project turned out to be a successful activity that not only delighted the young children (who were able to jingle the bell) but also enhanced the sixth-grader's self-esteem and self-confidence as a speaker.

Story Grammars, Charts, and Maps

Helping children understand story structure and develop a story schema increases recall, comprehension, and ability to make predictions based on text (Mandler & Johnson, 1977). Research by Morrow (1985) has shown that this is especially true for young children. After children have experienced an emotional response to a book, it is important for the teacher to go back and help them understand why they enjoyed it by looking at the elements that are part of the story structure.

A **story grammar** (Cunningham & Foster, 1978; Mandler & Johnson, 1977) builds an outline of the major elements of a story and unites those elements into a readily comprehensible and usually typical structure (Smith & Bean, 1983). Figure 7.6 shows a sample story grammar of "Goldilocks and the Three Bears." This sample highlights a story with a sequential pattern. (A circular story is represented in Figure 7.8 with the story *Hey, Al.*) Stories also can have predictable patterns such as *Brown Bear, Brown Bear, What Do You See?*

Character perspective charts (Shanahan & Shanahan, 1997) are another way of helping children respond to literature; based on the cited research related to story grammars, a **character perspective chart (CPC)** appears to help children develop a more complete and well-rounded appreciation for stories and the viewpoints of all the characters therein. Such charts are especially good for stories

Sample story grammar: "Goldilocks and the Three Bears." FIGURE **7.6**

CLIMAX
The three bears return. They realize that someone has been in the house and confront Goldilocks in the baby bear's bed.

EVENT
Goldilocks wants to take a nap. After trying all the beds, she falls asleep on the small bear's bed.

EVENT
Goldilocks tries all three chairs. She decides on the small bear's chair and breaks it.

EVENT
Goldilocks tries all three bowls of porridge and eats the small bear's portion.

PROBLEM
While the bears are away, a little girl named Goldilocks comes by and decides to explore what is not hers.

SETTING
The three bears live in a house in the woods.

RESOLUTION
Goldilocks jumps from the bed and out the nearest window. The bears never see her again. They do not miss her.

Source: Adapted from L. Galda (1987), "Teaching Higher Order Reading Skills with Literature."

where specific characters may be in conflict, such as Nyasha and Manyara of *Mufaro's Beautiful Daughters.* One fourth-grade teacher initiated a class discussion of that book by using the CPC illustrated in Figure 7.7. Such a chart is most helpful in organizing an in-depth analysis of different points of view in a story.

Story maps also build upon story structure and can be used along with questions to guide youngsters through a re-creation of a story. Some story maps follow a sequential story line (Beck & McKeown, 1981), whereas others depict circular tales (Jett-Simpson, 1981).

To teach the use of story maps, begin with a very simple story, which in turn has a simple map drawing. After hearing a number of these stories, the children begin to internalize the structure of stories; this means they have created a mental schema they can apply to later stories heard or read. This mental schema allows youngsters to predict events and outcomes in new stories based on stories they have heard or read. To further aid the creation of the mental schema, story maps show the children what the story pattern looks like. Eventually the children can create their own story maps to help them remember and predict details in a story heard or read. The Classroom Vignette on page 265 illustrates the use of narrative story maps to aid listening and reading comprehension.

FIGURE **7.7**

CHARACTER PERSPECTIVE CHART: *MUFARO'S BEAUTIFUL DAUGHTERS*

Sample character perspective chart.

Main character: Who is the main character?

Nyasha

Setting: Where and when does the story take place?

A village and city in Africa.

Problem: What is the main character's problem?

Dealing with her sister's (Manyara) bad temper.

Goal: What is the main character's goal? What does the character want?

To be good and kind and do the right thing.

Attempt: What does the main character do to solve the problem or get the goal?

Continues to be considerate and kind to every living creature.

Outcome: What happened as a result of the attempt?

The king recognizes her goodness; she becomes queen.

Reaction: How does the main character feel about the outcome?

Happy.

Theme: What point did the author want to make?

Kindness and goodness are rewarded.

Main character: Who is the main character?

Manyara

Setting: Where and when does the story take place?

A village and city in Africa.

Problem: What is the main character's problem?

Showing her sister's (Nyasha) kindness to be a weakness/ concealing her bad temper.

Goal: What is the main character's goal? What does the character want?

To marry the king and be queen.

Attempt: What does the main character do to solve the problem or get the goal?

Secretly leaves early for the city to be the first to meet the king.

Outcome: What happened as a result of the attempt?

The king recognizes her faults; she becomes a servant in the king's household.

Reaction: How does the main character feel about the outcome?

Appears to be upset.

Theme: What point did the author want to make?

Selfishness is its own undoing.

Source: Adapted from Shanahan & Shanahan (1997), "Character Perspective Charting: Helping Children to Develop a More Complete Conception of Story." *The Reading Teacher, 50*(8), 668–677. Copyright © 1997 by the International Reading Association.

Constructing a **story map** is simply a matter of helping your children sequence in an illustration the events in a story. For example, suppose you have just finished Arthur Yorinks's *Hey, Al* with your students and you say to them, "Tell me what happened in this story." However, instead of just listing all the events on the chalkboard, you draw a circle and tell the students that they have to put the story events in the correct order around the circle. The completed diagram would look something like the one in Figure 7.8.

BOOK PUBLISHING

Children can use story knowledge to write and illustrate their own books. These stories may take the form of Big Books for younger children or individual books for older ones. (The mechanical aspects of book publishing are discussed in Chapter 8.)

VIGNETTE *in the classroom*

Mr. Funk's fourth-grade class has been listening to and reading various types of stories, including folktales. Today he is going to teach the students about the use of story maps to remember the structure of a folktale.

"I've brought another story today that I think you are going to enjoy," he says. "I want you to listen carefully as I read just the title and opening paragraph of the story. Then I want you to help me draw a kind of map of the story, or of what parts you think the story might contain." He begins reading the story "Clever Gretchen."

"Once upon a time there lived a lord who had a daughter named Gretchen, who was as clever as she was good, and pretty besides. Rich merchants and noblemen came from all over the country to ask her hand in marriage, but her father would have none of them. 'The man who marries my daughter,' said he, 'must be the best huntsman in the world.'" Mr. Funk stops reading at this point.

"What kind of a story do you call this?" he asks.

"A folktale," says Ramon.

"How do you know?" asks Mr. Funk.

"Because it begins with 'Once upon a time.'"

"Good for you," says Mr. Funk. "You remembered other stories we've heard that began the same way."

Okay, using your previous knowledge of folktales, let's draw a map using some boxes and arrows to show the structure of this story, or at least what we think the structure will be. Afterward we'll read the rest of the story to check our ideas."

On the chalkboard Mr. Funk has pasted a large piece of butcher paper that he can write on with a magic marker. "What are the elements you might expect to encounter in this story just from having heard the first paragraph?" he asks.

"Well, there's a setting and some characters," says Bobby. "We already know there's Gretchen and the rich lord."

"There's also a problem," says Lindsay. "They've got to find the best huntsman in the world if Gretchen wants to get married. Otherwise she'll be an old spinster."

Mr. Funk writes the ideas on the paper in a list and then leads the students to create a story map outline.

As the discussion continues, they begin to fill in the map, guessing at the other aspects of the story. Then they listen to the rest of the story. Some of their guesses are correct; others are not and need to be revised. Figure 7.9 shows the revised narrative story map the class produced.

In a preschool class, a teacher had done repeated readings of John Langstaff's *Over in the Meadow*. After the children were completely familiar with the rhyme and the rhythm, they wanted to compose their own additions to the tale. However, the students decided they wanted to use pets in a backyard instead of wild animals in a meadow for their version, and they broke into small groups to compose separate verses, such as the following:

Over in our backyard in the grass and the sun
Lived an old mother cat and her little kitty one.
"Purr," said the mother;
"I purr," said the one;
So she purred and was glad in the grass and the sun.

Over in the backyard where a big bush grew
Lived an old mother hound dog and her little puppies two.
"Bark," said the mother;
"We bark," said the two;
So they barked and were glad where the big bush grew.

FIGURE   7.8

Sample story map: Hey, Al.

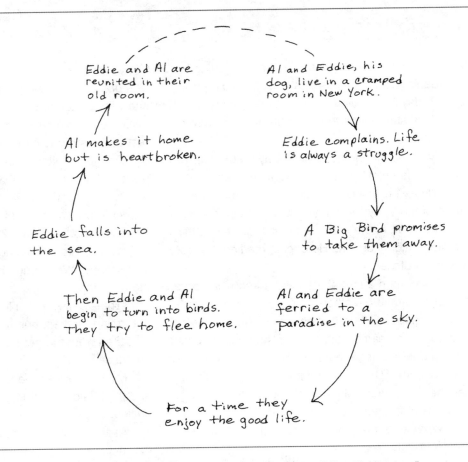

Source: Adapted from L. Galda (1987), "Teaching Higher Order Reading Skills with Literature."

Book publishing not only allows youngsters to respond to literature; it also ignites their continuing interest in reading new books, books that have inspired writing by their peers.

CREATIVE DRAMA

Another way in which students can respond to literature is through the various activities of creative drama, such as pantomime, improvisation, or readers theatre, all of which were discussed in Chapter 5. One additional aspect of creative drama is choral speaking. *Choral speaking* involves the oral reading of poetry or prose. It allows students to become active participants in interpreting and expressing the meaning of a familiar poem or story; it enables them to increase their oral reading proficiency within the security of a whole-group situation. Through choral speaking, children learn how to play with the language of literature and its grammatical structures and how to make it come alive through the clarity and quality of their voices.

You may want to start choral speaking by just repeating some favorite poems to the children and having them join in with you. With longer poems, you may want the students to have copies of the text for reference. One pitfall you need to guard against is allowing this activity to become merely a test of oral fluency. The true goal is to help children understand the meaning of poems and to interpret that meaning through oral expression. For more information about using poems and stories for choral speaking and choral reading, check Virginia

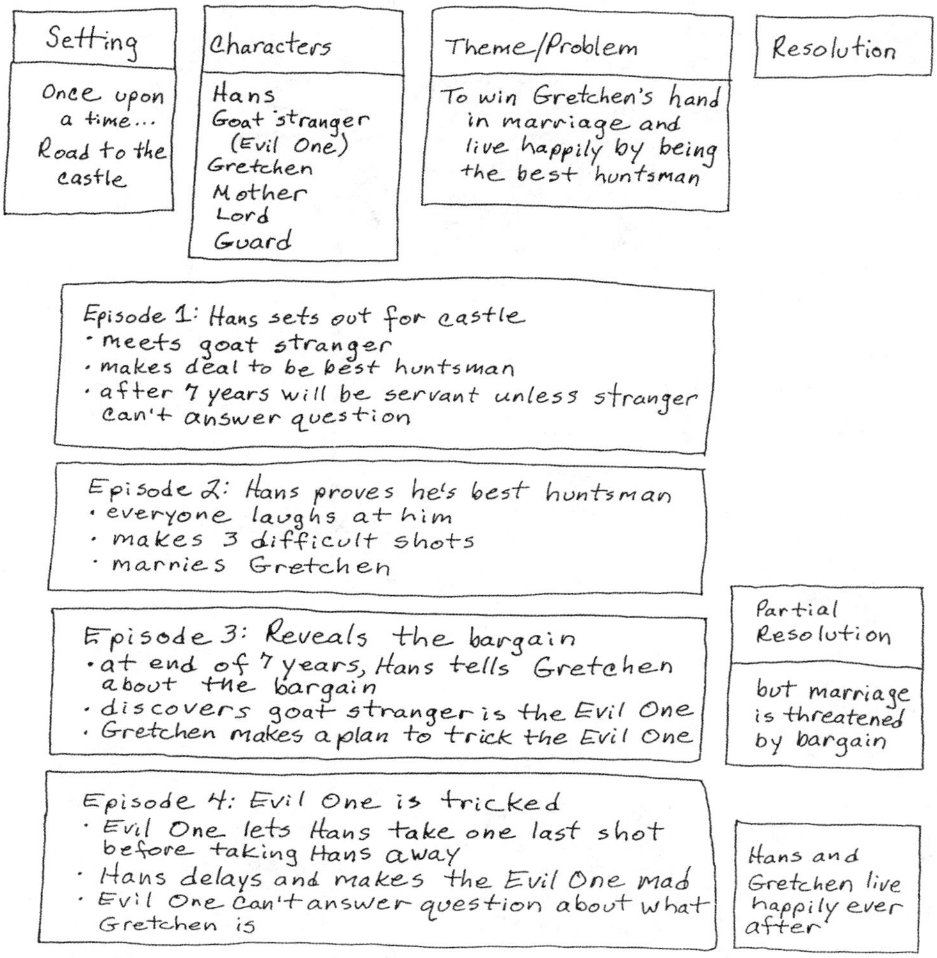

FIGURE **7.9**

Sample story map:
"Clever Gretchen."

Setting	Characters	Theme/Problem	Resolution
Once upon a time... Road to the castle	Hans Goat stranger (Evil One) Gretchen Mother Lord Guard	To win Gretchen's hand in marriage and live happily by being the best huntsman	

Episode 1: Hans sets out for castle
- meets goat stranger
- makes deal to be best huntsman
- after 7 years will be servant unless stranger can't answer question

Episode 2: Hans proves he's best huntsman
- everyone laughs at him
- makes 3 difficult shots
- marries Gretchen

Episode 3: Reveals the bargain
- at end of 7 years, Hans tells Gretchen about the bargain
- discovers goat stranger is the Evil One
- Gretchen makes a plan to trick the Evil One

Partial Resolution

but marriage is threatened by bargain

Episode 4: Evil One is tricked
- Evil One lets Hans take one last shot before taking Hans away
- Hans delays and makes the Evil One mad
- Evil One can't answer question about what Gretchen is

Hans and Gretchen live happily ever after

Tashjian's (1974) *With a Deep Sea Smile* and Virginia Pennock's (1984) "Choral Reading of Poetry Improves Reading Fluency."

SHARING BOOKS

Book talks and bulletin boards have been mentioned previously as motivators for reading. While these activities definitely do interest children in reading books, they are primarily ways for readers to respond to literature. Just as a picture on a bulletin board shows the world what a child thinks about a book, a book talk enables a child to give his or her personal reaction to a story and to retell it in a very personal way. Some teachers extend this activity by encouraging students to write letters to a classmate who has completed a book talk. Figure 7.10 shows the letters that one teacher and two students wrote in response to a book talk.

Some other ways to encourage students to share stories with you and with each other are discussed next.

Journals

Journals can be as simple as having the students keep a brief record of what they are reading and how they feel about it. This type of activity gives clues as to what

FIGURE **7.10**

Sample letters in response
to a book talk.

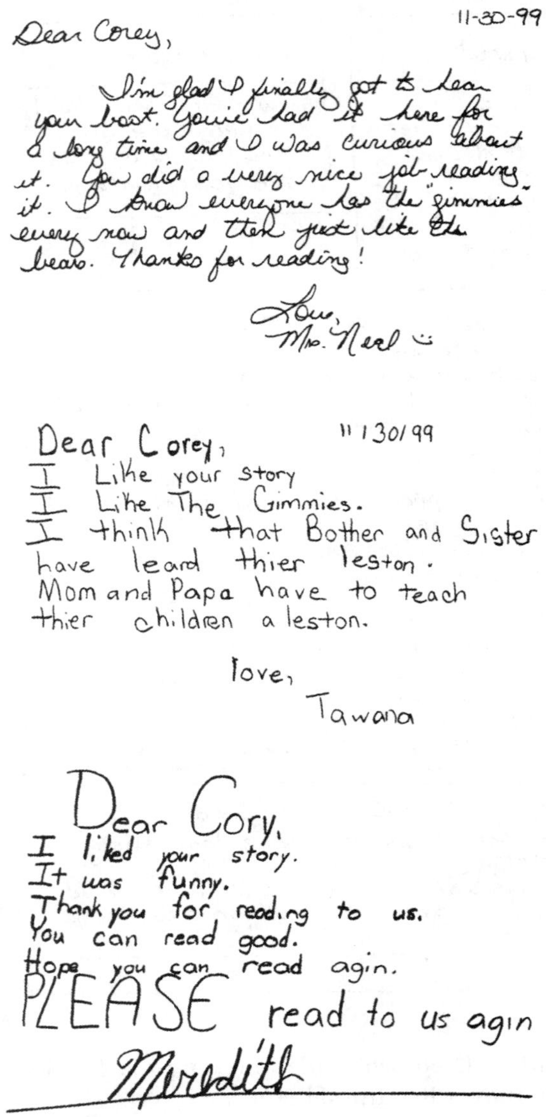

11-30-99

Dear Corey,

I'm glad I finally got to hear your book. You've had it here for a long time and I was curious about it. You did a very nice job reading it. I know everyone has the "gimmies" every now and then just like the bears. Thanks for reading!

Love,
Mrs. Neal

11/30/99

Dear Corey,
I Like your story
I Like The Gimmies.
I think that Bother and Sister have leard thier leston.
Mom and Papa have to teach thier children a leston.

love,
Tawana

Dear Cory,
I liked your story.
It was funny.
Thank you for reading to us.
You can read good.
Hope you can read agin.
PLEASE read to us agin

Meredith

and how much children are reading. You may wish to introduce journal writing to your class by using books in which this type of writing plays a role. Two books to consider are *But I'll Be Back Again: An Album* by Cynthia Rylant and *Diary of an Early American Boy, Noah Blake, 1805* by Eric Sloane. (Also see Chapter 8.)

Letters

Writing letters provides students with an audience and gives them a real purpose or reason for expressing their feelings in response to a book. Some children may want to write to their teachers; others may want to write to the author of the book. One sixth-grade class wrote to Ursula LeGuin, the author of the Earthsea books (Rollin, 1985). Still others may want to write to the characters in the book and tell them just what they think of them. One book that many teachers like to use to encourage letter writing is Beverly Cleary's *Dear Mr. Henshaw*, which chronicles the correspondence between an author and a young fan.

Bumper Stickers

Creating bumper stickers is one interesting way for children to summarize and express their thoughts. You can obtain blank bumper stickers from many local printing companies. Have the students print their sayings on the stickers with indelible markers, as in Figure 7.11.

Wanted Posters

Students can demonstrate their understanding of a character in a story by designing a wanted poster describing the character's outstanding traits. A sample poster is pictured in Figure 7.12.

Book Ads

Children can describe the outstanding attributes of a book by composing a newspaper ad in which they try to sell the book to their classmates. The ads can then be placed on a bulletin board along with student-created book jackets and removed as each new "buyer" decides to read a particular book. The success of an ad depends on whether or not another student chooses to read a book because of it.

FIGURE **7.11**

Sample bumper sticker.

FIGURE **7.12**

Sample wanted poster.

Mobiles, Collages, and Models

Making physical models of a story can help art-oriented students express themselves. For example, a child might make a mobile of all the characters and important artifacts in "Hansel and Gretel." The completed project would include the forest, the bread crumbs, the gingerbread house, Hansel's cage, and the oven, as well as the characters of the mother, the father, the children, and the witch. A collage might include an unusual arrangement of drawings from the story as well as some pieces of important objects mentioned in it. A child who chooses to do a model of a scene from "Hansel and Gretel" might show a miniature version of the interior of the cottage or the witch's gingerbread house.

Beyond the classroom

Think of five other ways in which children can share books. Include them in your notebook with brief descriptions and predictions of how you think they might work in your classroom.

TECHNOLOGY AND WEBSITES

The Internet and CD-ROMs are sources of great information about authors and stories, and many great videos are also available about authors. For example, one Trumpet Club series of videos takes the viewer into the authors' writing studios. While the children "visit" the studios, the authors give some background information about their childhood, explain how they became interested in writing and illustrating, and often tell where they get inspiration for books and illustrations. If a school cannot afford to have an author visit the school, the videos are wonderful, inexpensive ways for the students to meet the authors. Two delightful videos available from Trumpet Club are *Marc Brown: Creator of Arthur*, and *Mem Fox*.

Today many companies make videos based on children's literature. Raymond Briggs's *The Snowman*, released by SVS, Inc., is beautifully done as a wordless video. The music is relaxing, and the scenes spark the imagination as the viewer watches the adventure of the snowman and the little boy.

www.kn.pacbell.com/wired/bluewebn

If you enter SUBJECT and ENGLISH then READING, you will be connected to many authors of children's literature. All authors give details about their books; many include their email address.

www.pbs.org/rogers

This site includes activities for children and a book list of stories that correlate with the Mr. Rogers' TV program's themes. Lyrics for the songs from the show are also included.

www.acm.org/crossroads

This site, written by and for students, includes book reviews and is available in Spanish.

http://scils.Rutgers.edu/~kvander

This site includes great lists of multicultural books by the many different groups represented in the United States. It also lists materials for connecting literature to learning across the curriculum.

www.carolhurst.com

This site gives book reviews, has activities to use with the books, and also lists the books according to themes.

www.ipl.org/div/kidspace/askauthor

This site gives biographical information about authors and has interviews with well-known authors and illustrators.

http://gpn.unl.edu/rainbow

This site gives book lists and describes the books that are on the *Reading Rainbow* show.

www.publishersweekly.com/bsl/currentChildrens.asp

This site has the *Publishers Weekly* children's best-seller lists.

www.janbrett.com

This is Jan Brett's home page, which contains interactive activities for kids to read and draw.

www.acs.ucalgary.ca/~dkbrown/authors.html

This is considered the children's literature Web guide, with numerous authors. Many email addresses are included.

www.isomedia.com/homes/jmele/joe.html

This site has multicultural book reviews.

www.ipl.org/reading/books/index.html

More than 7,000 books are accessible online here.

www.ala.org

This is the American Library Association's home page.

www.ala.org/alsc/caldecott.html

This site lists the Caldecott Medal and honor books, with information about each.

www.ala.org/alsc/newbery.html

This site lists the Newbery Medal and honor books, with information about each.

http://lcweb2.loc.gov/learn

This site is a collection of resource materials for teachers. The site links to the American Memory collection, which highlights items important in America's heritage, history, and culture. It offers lesson plans and related activities.

www.loc.gov/wiseguide

This site is part of the Library of Congress, offering several resources for teaching about American history, as well as contemporary figures in American culture. The "Wise Guide" changes monthly and offers links to the best of the Library's online materials.

www.cyberpg.com/Teachers/folk.html

This site provides an extensive list of resources for teachers K–12 interested in using folktales to enhance lessons. It also provides links to multiple folktale websites.

www.cbcbooks.org

This is the site for the Children's Book Council.

www.ncte.org

This is the site for the National Council of Teachers of English.

www.cultureforkids.com

This site provides information and resources on multicultural activities for the classroom.

Summary

Literature is the central component of language learning. Good books give children reasons to read and provide them with strong language models, which in turn help children to formulate and express their reactions. Your knowledge of the different types of books and magazines available for classroom use will help you in selecting appropriate materials for your class. However, the best method of choosing books is to listen to the needs and wants of your own students. They and their peers are more than willing to give you plenty of ideas about which books to stock in the reading center.

As a teacher, you play a crucial role in involving students with literature. Children imitate adults, so by letting your students see that you read on a daily basis and that you truly enjoy books, you are encouraging them to see reading literature as a desirable, "adult" activity. When you couple your modeling with storytelling, reading aloud, and SSR, you have the basic ingredients to initiate a successful literature-based language program.

Encourage your students to be creative and to respond to literature in a variety of ways. Although discussion and literature circles are commonly used techniques in classrooms, help your students to see that journal writing, retelling stories, using story maps, developing book talks, writing ads for books, and creating murals are equally valid ways of responding to books. Most of all, help children to see how reading literature can be an enjoyable daily habit.

ACTIVITIES with children

Author Experts

Encourage your students to read several books by the same author and to make notes about similarities in the books. Then help them gather some factual information about the author's life and work. When the research is completed, the students can construct a bulletin board display highlighting particular books and important facts about the author's life. The "expert" students can also host a discussion in which they answer other students' questions about the author.

Book Murals

Students can respond to books with particularly intriguing illustrations by creating a class mural (painting on a wall or bulletin board) of a favorite scene. This technique also works very well with nonfiction books, especially those about nature. One first-grade class did a terrific job with a prehistoric mural about dinosaurs.

Book Worms

Help keep track of how many books your students are reading by creating a "book worm." Decorate a face for your worm and attach it to a high spot on a wall. Then cut out the first round segment of the worm and write down the title, author, and location of a book that you have just read. Write your own name at the bottom of the segment and attach it next to the face. Tell your students to do the same every time they complete a book. Before you know it, your book worm will stretch around the room.

Character Parade

Set aside a time for students to dress up as a favorite character in a book. After each student has given three hints about the identity of her or his character, classmates have to guess. The student who successfully guesses the identity of the character becomes the next one to present.

Cigar-Box Stories

Have each child in the class glue a small piece of felt to the inside of a cigar box. Then instruct children to use different colors of felt to make characters and objects from favorite stories they have read. Students can store figures from the different stories in manila envelopes. Whenever a child wants to retell or review a story, the cigar box can be used as a personal flannel board.

Class Book File

Encourage your students to create a file box of children's books for class use. Each time a student finishes a book, ask the student to complete an index card listing the title, author, and location of the book. Also ask the student to include a brief opinion of the book and a signature. When other children are looking for something to read, they can consult the cards in the file for suggestions.

Personal Chronicles

You can help children understand how simple storytelling is by encouraging them to share the stories of their daily lives. You may want to set aside a brief period every day for a few students to share stories of something that happened at home, on the way to school, or at the playground. Some children may even want to record their stories.

RELATED READINGS

Barry, A. (1998). Hispanic representation in literature for children and young adults. *Journal of Adolescent and Adult Literacy, 41*(8), 630–637.

Beck, I., McKeown, M., Hamilton, R., & Kucan, L. (1997). *Questioning the author: An approach for enhancing student engagement with text.* Newark, DE: International Reading Association.

Frank, C. R., Dixon, C. N., & Brandts, L. R. (2001). Bears, trolls, and pagemasters: Learning about learners in book clubs. *The Reading Teacher, 54*(5), 448–462.

Galda, L., & Cullinan, B. E. (2002). *Literature and the child* (5th ed.). Belmont, CA: Wadsworth/Thompson Learning.

Harvey, S. (May/June 2001). Questioning the text. *Scholastic Instructor,* 16–18.

Hendershot, J., & Peck, J. (1998). The view from Saturday: A conversation with E. L. Konigsburg, winner of the 1997 Newbery Medal. *The Reading Teacher, 51*(8), 676–680.

8

The Process of Writing

This chapter introduces you to the notion of writing as a process and the process approach as a way of teaching writing to children. Although there are many models to describe a process approach, we have used a simple three-stage description: prewriting, writing, and postwriting. Within each of these stages you will learn about activities, teaching strategies, and many different types of writing that will help your students become better writers. As you reflect on the ideas in this chapter, think about how the act of writing reinforces the specific skills of writing, which will be discussed in detail in Chapter 9.

CHAPTER OBJECTIVES

After reading this chapter, you should be able to accomplish the following objectives:

1. Explain some different approaches to teaching writing.
2. Describe the stages in a process-writing approach.
3. Explain what is meant by a writer's workshop.
4. Describe the steps in teaching bookbinding to children.
5. Explain what is meant by a Young Authors' Fair.
6. Describe some different types of journal writing.
7. Describe some different types of poetry you will teach and how you will do this.
8. Describe some writing mini-lessons.
9. Describe some ways of assessing writing.

CHECK YOUR BACKGROUND KNOWLEDGE. Before reading the chapter, complete the K-T-W-L chart based on the chapter overview and objectives provided at left. In column "K," write what you know about the topics in the objectives. In column "T," write what you think you know. In column "W," write what you want to learn. Finally, after you have read the chapter, write what you have learned in column "L."

Know	**T**hink you know	**W**ant to learn	**L**earned

Brief History of Writing Instruction

Prior to the beginning of the twentieth century, the teaching of writing was either ignored, minimized, or focused entirely on skill drills. Classroom teachers were most concerned that their students master the mechanics of writing such as handwriting, spelling, punctuation, and capitalization. Consequently, instruction focused on having children copy passages from the board, take dictation, and memorize rules. There was very little actual creative writing done in class.

Up until 1960, the English language arts curriculum emphasized reading instruction at the expense of writing activities. What writing was done was characterized by a rigid reliance on teacher-assigned topics, grammar drills, and rule memorization.

Beginning in the 1960s, a new view began to emerge that linked thought to language to writing. Essentially this view argued that mental processes were enhanced through the use of language, both spoken and written. Vygotsky proclaimed that "thought is born through words." Just as a child's speech is an extension of the child's actions, so too a child's writing is an extension of thought (Vygotsky, 1962, 1978a). The American linguist James Moffett took a similar view. Moffett's theory of language, described in *Teaching the Universe of Discourse* (1968), focused on "the inner workings behind the talking, reading and writing." Mental thoughts, he argued, move through oral and visual representations. The work of Vygotsky, Moffett, and others caused teachers in the 1960s to consider the relationship among thought, speech, and writing.

In the 1970s, James Britton (1973, 1978, 1986) built on the work of Vygotsky and Moffett. His research, done with secondary students in England, led him to conclude that knowledge is a process, not a storehouse of facts. He urged teachers to focus on the process of students' thinking as it related to writing instruction instead of stressing isolated skills. Writing authority Donald Murray, of the University of New Hampshire, similarly urged his students to view writing as an act of discovery, a way of finding what they have to say (Murray, 1978).

Researchers in the 1970s were also changing the way they approached writing. Previously writing research had focused on gathering large samples of writing, counting errors, and then categorizing those errors; such research influenced teachers' instructional focus on error remediation. The newer approach studied smaller groups of students in the actual act of writing. Janet Emig (1971) observed a group of twelfth-graders while they wrote; later she interviewed them about their writing. She found that writing is unique to the individual and does not follow a fixed formula; nor do students rely on memorized rules. This was contrary to the popularly held belief that rule memorization, particularly in grammar instruction, leads to improved writing. Donald Graves (1973) took a similar case study approach to describe the writing processes used by seven-year-olds. He too noted the uniqueness of the writing act and the importance of the classroom environment for encouraging writing. Skills and drills alone, he concluded, do not make a writer.

Other research studies of students' writing were critical of the writing performance of students and the instructional practices of teachers. James Britton and a team of researchers analyzed thousands of essays by British high school students and found that school writing assignments focused almost exclusively on communicating factual information rather than on exploring personal feelings and thoughts or solving problems (Britton, 1973, 1978, 1986).

In the United States, Arthur Applebee conducted a similar large-scale analysis of students' writing. He found that the predominant mode of writing in American secondary schools involved fill-in-the-blank or short-answer exercises. He called this *mechanical writing* (Applebee, 1981). Next he studied the writing samples of 55,000 students in grades 4, 8, and 11 and found that most students in all grades—regardless of economic status—were "unable to write adequately except in response to the simplest of tasks" (1986). Something was still drastically wrong with writing instruction in the schools.

Approaches to Teaching Writing

ASSIGNED TOPICS

For some teachers, creative writing consists primarily of assigning topics to students: "What I did for my summer holiday"; "If I had a dog"; "My scariest Halloween"; "The products of Brazil." Creative writing books still contain these story topics or starter sentences. There is nothing intrinsically wrong with such topics except that students might not want to write about summer vacation, dogs, Halloween, or Brazil. This is particularly true if the teacher assigns a single topic to an entire class of 25 or more students. There is no way that a teacher could expect every one of those students to be excited about the same topic. In other words, assigning topics ignores the principle of motivation. Furthermore, where is the actual teaching in such an approach? Assigning is not teaching.

ONE-SHOT APPROACH

Related to teacher-assigned topics is the one-shot approach to writing: A teacher assigns a topic in class and the students write on that topic in a single sitting (perhaps they are allowed to finish it at home). Each student then turns in the composition, report, or story; the teacher grades and returns it. However, this is clearly not teaching; this is testing. Giving a student one chance to produce a creative, original work in a limited amount of time is a test. It does not teach children anything about where writers get their ideas, how they begin stories and poems, how they organize and develop characters, how they revise and edit. The one-shot approach at its best gives students practice in producing something from scratch. At its worst, it is a painful, often humiliating experience, particularly for the student who fears writing and cannot produce the required piece in the given amount of time.

SKILLS AS WRITING

The third most common approach is to define writing in terms of the skills involved in writing. There are skill worksheets, skill workbooks, skill software packages, and so on. Basically all skill activities are alike in that they dissect the writing act into little pieces: nouns, verbs, adjectives; rules for spelling, rules for capitalizing, rules for punctuating. This dissection often results in the separation of instruction into 10 minutes of spelling, then 15 minutes of handwriting, 15 minutes of grammar, and so on. Donald Graves (1990) called this approach the "cha-cha-cha curriculum."

Defining writing in terms of skills is misleading for another reason: In writing, the sum of the parts does not equal the whole. That is, mastery of all the skills of writing (usually determined by some sort of standardized test) does not make one a writer. You may be a good speller but not be able to write an interesting, coherent sentence. You may know how to identify the adverbs in a sentence but not be able to string sentences together into a logical paragraph. You may be able to list the uses of periods, commas, and quotation marks but still not be able to write realistic dialogue within a story. In short, these skills are the tools used in writing, but they do not *equal* good writing.

WRITING WORKSHOP

In 1974 the federal government funded a grant to support the Bay Area Writing Project at the University of California at Berkeley. Founded by James Gray, the Bay Area Writing Project introduced elementary and secondary schoolteachers to the **workshop approach** to teaching writing. Teachers using this workshop method go through a series of stages in writing, such as drafting, revising, and editing; this came to be known as the process approach.

Teachers who completed the Bay Area summer writing workshops went back to their school districts across the United States and taught this process approach to their colleagues in staff development meetings; another unique aspect of the Bay Area Writing Project was its focus on teachers teaching teachers. The program was so successful that it eventually became the National Writing Project, which now funds workshops for teachers in every state of the union, who in turn disseminate the ideas of process writing (Goldberg, 1989).

The success of the process approach to writing can be seen in the results of the 1992 National Assessment of Educational Progress (NAEP). More than 30,000 students in grades 4, 8, and 12 were asked to respond to various writing tasks. Preceding the task, students were given a blank sheet of paper and encouraged to do prewriting. Data were also gathered on students, teachers, and administrators regarding instructional practices in their schools. The overall results showed that "students whose teachers encouraged certain aspects of process writing averaged higher performance on the NAEP writing assessment" (NAEP, 1996, p. 1).

> *Write without the paraphernalia of scholarship designed to mystify the lay reader and confound one's colleagues.*
>
> MARGARET MEAD

A Process Approach Model

A **process approach** to writing based on the writing workshop involves a series of stages that leads a writer from the discovery of an idea through a number of revisions, culminating in the production of an original work. In the course of the process, writers may spend many hours thinking about writing; talking to other writers; listening to other writers; reading books, magazines, and newspapers; making doodles, notes, and outlines; writing, revising, stopping in disgust or frustration, and then starting again. All this is part of the process; this is how writers write. There is no magic formula to be memorized. There is, however, a general process that can be taught to students as a series of stages that will help them on their way to becoming writers.

James Britton (1978), Janet Emig (1971), L. Flower and J. R. Hayes (1994), Donald Graves (1994), Nancie Atwell (1998), Lucy Calkins (2001), and others have described models of process writing consisting of three main stages: prewriting, writing, and postwriting, all of which act and react with each other in a recursive manner. It should be mentioned at this point that although the leading authorities in literacy education advocate a process approach to the teaching of writing, there are different process-writing models in the literature that use slightly different terminology. For example, in some states a five-step process model is described using the terms *prewriting, drafts, revision, editing, assessment,* and *publishing*. We have chosen to go with a three-stage model that incorporates all of these. Figure 8.1 shows the three stages, their related steps, and the interactive nature of the process.

STAGE ONE: PREWRITING

The process approach does not begin with writing. It begins with thinking about writing: What do I want to write about? What are the things that interest me? What do I care about? These are the thoughts that preoccupy writers,

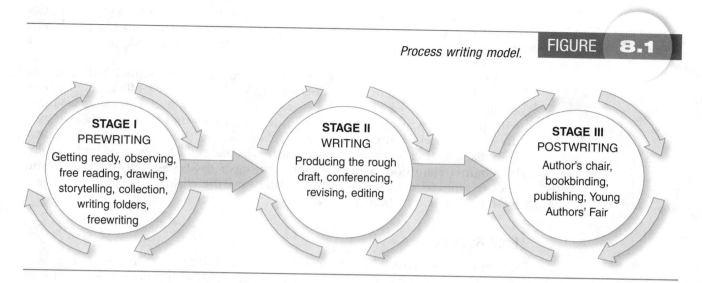

Process writing model. FIGURE 8.1

child and adult alike. Donald Graves has called this the *rehearsal stage* of writing (1994). This is the time when writers plan and organize their thoughts. It is the first essential stage in the writing process. In fact, Donald Murray (1985) has contended that it is the most important stage. It is also the most ignored stage.

The *prewriting stage* consists of a number of steps that teachers may use to support and motivate students during this portion of the writing process.

Getting Ready

Getting students ready to write involves providing them with three things: time to write, space to write, and the materials for writing. A set time should be designated each day as writing time. It can be the first thing in the morning, a period before lunch, or the last period of the day. Teacher and students should decide together when the best time for writing is, based on the school schedule.

Finding just the right place to write is next. For some children, it is a favorite corner of the room or a specially designated writing table; others prefer to write at their own desks. Some students like to crawl under the teacher's large desk and work. In some schools, students can even take their chairs out into the hallway or work in a special section of the library.

The materials for writing include paper (lined and unlined), pencils, pens, felt-tip markers, writing folders, notebooks, crayons, scissors, scotch tape, and paste. For most writers, getting ready to write means going through a mini-ritual of arranging pencils, pens, papers, and so on. Additional materials might include a classroom library for doing research work, reference books such as dictionaries and encyclopedias, computer/word-processing access, and picture files for stimulating the imagination.

Observing

"I can't think of anything to write about, Teacher." This is a complaint heard all too frequently in the elementary grades. Students think that ideas should come to them automatically; they do not realize that sometimes writers need to seek out fresh ideas when their creative wells are dry. One way to do this is through observation.

Observation for the purpose of stimulating writing can be very simple or involve considerable time and planning. For example, one day you might take children on a brief field trip around the school grounds. Have them carefully observe the trees, flowers, plants, and playground equipment. Do they notice something interesting? Something they just took for granted in the past? Why is that chattering squirrel burying nuts beside the large oak tree? There's a story idea!

On another day, take them on a field trip inside the school building. Are there places the students have not been before? The nurse's office, the cafeteria kitchen, and the area behind the curtains of the school auditorium are all filled with potential writing subjects for students. One teacher took her class to visit the boiler room in their elementary school. There they spoke with the custodian. Back in their classroom, their teacher read aloud *The Planet of Junior Brown* by Virginia Hamilton, a story about a young boy who actually hides out and lives in the basement of his school. Afterward the children decided to write a mystery story set in their own school.

Free Reading

Charlotte Huck (1987), an authority on children's literature, has said that reading a variety of books leads children to experiment with different literary forms in their own writing. For example, second-graders who read Judith Viorst's *Alexander and the Terrible, Horrible, No Good, Very Bad Day* wanted to write about their own terrible days. Reading Jean George's *My Side of the Mountain* inspired one fourth-grade boy to keep a journal on his next camping trip. Marguerite de Angeli's Newbery Medal–winner, *The Door in the Wall*, sent a group of girls to the library to research more about fourteenth-century England in order to write their own adventure novel. Scott O'Dell's *Sing Down the Moon* caused a group of Native American students in Oklahoma to write to Navaho students in Arizona. And reading Shel Silverstein's humorous verse has encouraged many a child to try writing poetry.

Thus, a writing program should also include free time each day for students to read and to talk about books (Atwell, 1998). The two cannot be separated nor taught as distinct entities. Rather than talking about the reading program or writing time, Jerry Harste (1990) has argued for a *literacy curriculum*, in which students are invited to read and write throughout the day as a natural part of the learning process—as natural as listening and speaking.

Drawing

For many children, drawing is the best way to get ready to write. Children often have a vague idea of what they want to say but do not know where to begin. So they draw doodles, scribbles, cartoons, or illustrations from stories they have read. As children draw, they are discovering the stories in their head. Drawing for many students is a form of rehearsing; this is even true of older youngsters.

Atwell has written about one student named Jeff. Jeff was older than the rest of the class—already 16—but barely reading at the primary level. He had been retained in earlier grades and was thought to be learning disabled. While the other students in Atwell's class did various prewriting activities, Jeff sat alone, mumbling to himself and drawing. Each day in class while the others wrote, Jeff drew. One day, as Atwell prodded him to get busy and write in class, Jeff explained, "This is the way I do it, the way I write" (p. 8). For Jeff and many other students, drawing is the way to rehearse ideas before putting them into words.

Storytelling

Research has shown a natural link between hearing and telling stories and students' desire to write stories (King, 1989; Short, Harste, & Burke, 1996). From hearing, telling, and reading stories, children intuitively acquire the basic concepts of stories: Aspects of plot, setting, and character and a sense of sequential ordering of events are first tested at the oral level through storytelling. Later, these same storytellers want to write their stories to share with even more people. Like drawing, oral storytelling serves a rehearsal function prior to writing.

Collection

Two things make writing difficult for many youngsters: They feel they have nothing to say, and they do not know how to spell all the words they want to include in their stories. Both issues are real for children and must be addressed by teachers. Too often a potentially good writing lesson degenerates into a sea of waving hands and shouting voices: "Teacher, how do you spell . . . ?" One way to help students overcome these twin feelings of inadequacy is through collection. **Collection** is a type of brainstorming that helps children acquire the ideas, words, and information they will later use in their writing (Murray, 1990).

In this strategy, the teacher introduces a topic to the whole class. Better still, children volunteer topics they would like to write about, such as the NASA space shuttle, the upcoming World Series, or a mystery story set in Tahiti. The class selects one of the topics on which to do a collective brainstorming. Ideas and terms are called out. The teacher writes them on the board. This is done quickly, and everyone's suggestions are accepted. When finished, the class has a graphic representation of the ideas and also an accurate spelling of some of the words they may want to use in their writing. The next step is to transfer this list to a poster, file folder, or word wall that can serve as a source of ideas and correct spellings in the days of writing to come. Once the collection strategy has been demonstrated, youngsters can do their own brainstorming in small groups or individually without the teacher's help.

Collection can also be done in ways other than mere listing. For example, brainstorming can take the form of an outline, a web diagram, or a cluster. *Outlining* begins with mental brainstorming but results in a written outline to help a writer sequence a series of events or points more clearly. It can be used with all types of writing but lends itself particularly well to report writing or persuasive essays. In using outlining, students learn to set up their ideas in a form like the one in Figure 8.2.

Webbing is a technique that extends mental brainstorming by placing the terms generated into a diagram that resembles a spider's web. Each term is connected to another by a strand of the web; the lines in a web diagram indicate the relationships among the various terms generated. Like outlining, webbing

---

GENERIC	EXAMPLE: TEXAS INDEPENDENCE
I. Main Idea	I. Political Issues
1. Supporting detail	1. Expansion of slavery
2. Supporting detail	2. Independence from Mexico
II. Main Idea	II. Economic Issues
1. Supporting detail	1. Trade with United States
2. Supporting detail	2. Expansion of cotton into Texas
III. Main Idea	III. Two Major Battles
1. Supporting detail	1. The Alamo
2. Supporting detail	2. San Jacinto

FIGURE 8.2

Outline format.

Beyond the classroom

Many students start writing or try to start before they are really ready to write. They have not done any preliminary activities such as the ones described here. Visit an elementary classroom and work with a small group of writers in search of topics. Teach them how to outline, web, or cluster. Then observe how the children use these techniques to organize their writing. What positive aspects do you note? What difficulties do the students encounter? Make an outline, web, or cluster to represent your own experience teaching these students.

allows the student to see the entire picture along with the separate parts of the work to be created. Webbing is also referred to as *semantic mapping* (Johnson, Pittelman, & Heinlich, 1986). It is a valuable guide that can keep students on track, show them where they need to go, and maintain a coherent flow in their writing. Figure 8.3 shows a web created by a second-grade class.

A cluster diagram is another variation of the outline; it is similar to the web diagram. To create a **cluster diagram,** students begin with a single word (the theme, subject, or key concept), write it in the center of the page, and circle it; as students think of related terms, they circle them and connect them with lines to the central term. The result is a diagram of lines and circles indicating a type of schema or outline the writer may follow. Tompkins (2003) has recommended clustering as a way to help elementary students recognize how one idea is associated with another and how all ideas in a written work relate to a main theme. Figure 8.4 shows a cluster diagram.

Writing Folders

The writing folder is highly personal; no two look exactly alike. A writing folder can be an ordinary file folder. Students write their names on their folders and decorate them. Each folder contains blank paper for drawing as well as lined paper for writing. Students use these folders daily for drawing, doodling, and making lists of things to write about later. A student's folder may also contain outlines for stories, research notes for reports, character sketches, quotes, or snatches of dialogue. When kept on a regular basis, the folder becomes the

FIGURE 8.3

Sample second-grade web: Animals.

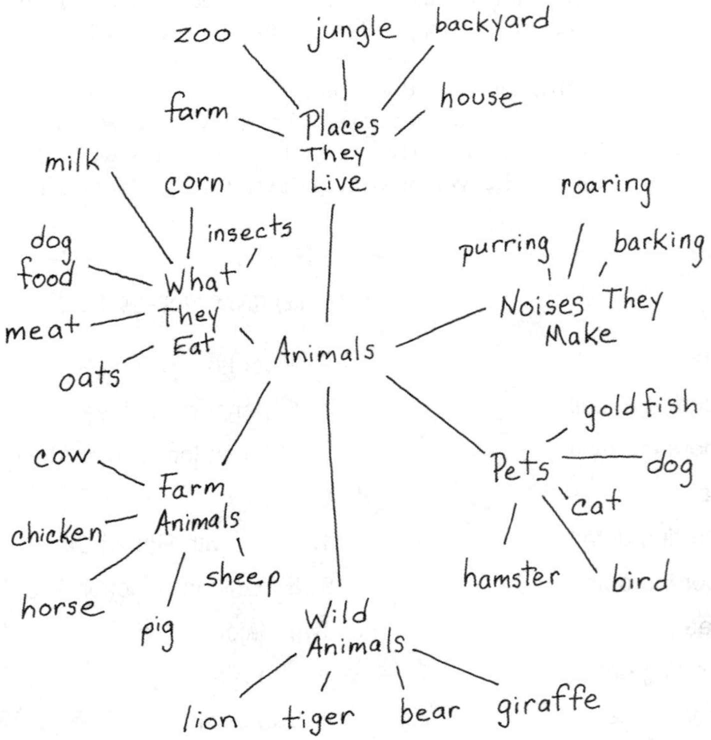

FIGURE **8.4**

Sample cluster diagram:
Monsters

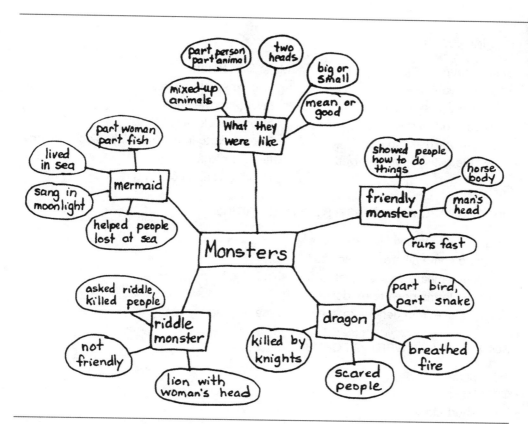

source of ideas for later written works. The key is to use the folder regularly so that writing becomes a daily habit. (Writing folders, or portfolios, are discussed in more detail later in this chapter.)

Nancie Atwell (1998) structures how her eighth-graders use their folders by stapling forms inside the folders. For example, one form is a list of ideas for writing that a student can refer to when the creative well runs dry. Another form lists the titles and dates of work that the student has finished and serves as a chronological record for the school year. Personal skill lists are kept on a form called "Things I can do." Figure 8.5 is an example of some different lists that can be included in folders to help students get ready to write.

Freewriting

A writing program should include time each day not only for free reading but also—obviously—for writing. The term *freewriting* was popularized by Peter Elbow (1973, 1981). Elbow was searching for an activity that would help his freshman English composition students overcome their fear of writing. Freewriting as one of the prewriting activities in a process approach is now also widely used with elementary-grade students who fear the blank page (Frager et al., 1987). For anyone who has experienced "writer's block," **freewriting** is most useful and includes the following three steps:

1. Try to relax and clear your mind for a moment.
2. When the teacher gives the signal, start writing on anything you can think of but do not stop or pause.
3. Continue writing until the teacher gives the signal to stop (usually after about five minutes).

The only way to teach them to write correctly is to have them write.

FANNY JACKSON COPPIN

FIGURE	8.5

Ideas for folder lists.

FINDING IDEAS

Think about:

   people you know

   people you see in the street

   places you've been

   places you'd like to visit

   favorite gifts you've received

Make lists about:

   favorite sports figures

   favorite movie stars

   favorite book titles

   favorite cartoon and comic book characters

   favorite colors

   favorite types of clothing

QUESTIONS TO ASK YOURSELF BEFORE WRITING

What is your main subject?

What are some different subtopics?

Can you compare your subject to something else?

What key terms need to be defined?

Do you move from general to specific, or the reverse?

SOME POSSIBLE WRITING FORMS

Try a poem

Try a letter

Try a short story

Try a chapter in a novel

Try an essay

Try an autobiography

Try a book review

Try a folktale

Try a collaborative (group) writing with friends

Try a mystery story

Try a report

That's it: continuous writing for five minutes without pausing and without worrying about spelling or punctuation or sentence structure. Just let your thoughts flow onto the paper. At first this activity may seem strange to your students, especially if they have been raised on the notion that writing should look neat and mechanically correct on the first effort. Stress that this is an exercise to get them started in writing and that they should relax and enjoy it.

Elbow also described a variety of follow-up activities that can be used with the freewriting exercise. Students can reread their own freewriting material and search for words, phrases, sentences, or ideas they might later want to develop into a story, poem, or essay. Or they can read their freewriting to a friend, perhaps even to the whole class. Elbow suggested focusing freewriting from time to time on specific topics such as, How much allowance should a fourth-grader get and why? The rules are the same except that all the students now write on a single topic for 5 or 10 minutes. Remember that the idea is still to explore a topic rapidly without concern for the mechanics of writing.

The Classroom Vignette that follows depicts one teacher leading her students into writing.

VIGNETTE *in the classroom*

Mrs. Guen is settled into a big, overstuffed chair in one corner of the room. Around her on the floor sit 18 first-graders, listening and watching as she reads to them from Eric Carle's *The Very Hungry Caterpillar.* As she reads aloud, she shows the students the pictures of the caterpillar moving from page to page, gobbling everything up in sight and gradually changing into a butterfly. When she is finished reading, she asks, "What did this story make you think of?" Hands shoot up. She calls on Teri.

"Last week we found that caterpillar and put him in a jar."

"Yeah, and we also found a spider and some ants," chimes in Ramon.

"That's right, boys and girls. We went on a field trip and found all sorts of interesting insects right around our own school. Janey, what was your favorite insect?"

"The caterpillar, I guess," says Janey, looking around shyly.

"Mine was the icky worm we stepped on," says Jonathan, making the rest of the group laugh.

"Okay now. Each one of you imagine your favorite insect, and let's pretend to move around the room like a butterfly, a caterpillar, a spider, or whatever you want."

Soon all the students are crawling, slithering, walking on all fours, flapping their arms. They giggle, laugh, bump into each other, and then collapse in a heap. Then their teacher gathers them together again; they brainstorm all the words they can think of about their insects. The teacher writes the list on a large pad attached to an easel.

"Now, boys and girls, take out your writing folders. There's extra paper and pencils at the writing center if you need them. You may want to draw a picture of what we've been talking about or start a story or perhaps write a poem about an insect."

Most children take a crayon or pencil and go off with best friends to draw. Some of the children go to their desks, hunch over their paper, and begin to write. A few clamor around the teacher, asking for more help to get started on a drawing or story.

STAGE TWO: WRITING

Writing is the second major stage in a process approach; there are four main steps in this stage: producing the rough draft, conferencing about the draft, revising the content and structure of the work, and finally editing to correct the mechanics of writing.

Producing the Rough Draft

All writers write from a *rough draft.* Children need to be taught this beginning in the first grade. Primary-grade teachers sometimes use the term *sloppy copy,* which the children can more easily understand. The children know this is their time to get their ideas down on paper, to begin to shape their stories, poems, pen pal letters, and so on. Intermediate teachers continue to reinforce the idea of the rough draft with their students. By middle school, it should be second nature to the student to work from rough drafts.

Teaching the concept of rough drafts is one way to help young writers achieve that final, polished product that looks like a real story or poem they might read in a book. Generally speaking, the more drafts a child writes, the better the final copy. Each successive draft, like chisel strokes on a piece of marble, refines the work just a little more. This is what Donald Murray meant when he described writing as a craft.

Youngsters who are not used to writing rough drafts need the teacher's assistance to keep them going. Explain to them that in a rough draft the writer's

Good stories are not written, they are rewritten.

PHYLLIS WHITNEY

goal is to get ideas down on paper and complete the work, be it a poem, story, essay, newspaper article, or science report. Get them to focus on the content, not the mechanics; it is the latter that trips up most young writers (Sommers, 1994). Children get frustrated easily when they cannot spell a word, forget how to use capital letters, or make even the slightest error. Primary-grade students scrunch over their papers, biting their lips as they try to draw a *q* or *z*. The first error or smudge, wham! They ball up their papers, throw them away, and start again. It is no wonder that after 20 minutes of so-called writing time these students barely complete one sentence.

In **mini-lesson lectures,** provide students with the following tips for writing rough drafts:

- Write on only one side of the page; use the back for taking notes.
- Skip lines and leave wide margins for adding material later.
- Cross out rather than erase; you may want to reuse something later.
- Date and number your various drafts; keep a record of your progress.

Conferencing

At some point during the writing stage, children discover that they are writing for someone—a reader; this is the concept of **audience.** Awareness of audience is something that teachers work to develop in their student writers, but it takes time and practice. One way to help young writers achieve this sense of audience awareness is through conferencing. Graves (1994), Calkins (1994), Atwell (1998), and Finders and Hynds (2003) have all stressed the importance of conferencing. Before studying the different types of conferences, keep in mind that the three main purposes of **conferencing** are to provide positive feedback and encouragement to the student, to answer any questions the student may have, and to discover any problem areas that may need to be retaught. It is primarily through conferencing—not through the awarding of grades—that students grow as writers.

Teacher–pupil conferences. Once a student has produced a rough draft, she or he is ready for a teacher–pupil conference. Most teacher–pupil conferences are brief and informal. Nancie Atwell (1998) likes to carry a small chair with her and sit next to her students while they read their rough drafts to her. As with all conferences, the first focus should be on the content of the piece, what the writer is trying to say. Later the teacher and pupil may talk about specific trouble spots in a work, such as how to punctuate dialogue in a story. The teacher should move about the room continually, meeting with students for brief chats and listening to them read aloud passages they are proud of or need help with.

Some teachers prefer to set up more formal conferences with their students. The teacher may call a child to his or her desk and ask the child to read the story aloud. Then the teacher and pupil can discuss the written work. If formal conferences are used, the children should know about them in advance. Set up a schedule and post it in the room. This gives students a chance to prepare for the conference and perhaps redo their rough drafts one more time. Donald Graves stressed in *A Fresh Look at Writing* (1994) that teachers should ask questions during the conference rather than make suggestions or give advice: Does your opening paragraph introduce the main character or describe the setting for your story? Have you repeated something that can be omitted? How can you make your dialogue sound more realistic? If your ending comes too soon, how can you keep the reader in suspense a bit longer? A teacher can always tell children how to improve their work; the skill in conferencing is to "nudge" writers toward discovering this for themselves.

In *The Art of Teaching Writing* (1994), Lucy Calkins suggests still another view on conferencing. She argues that the teacher's job in the writing conference is to first understand the student as writer; in effect the teacher is researching the student to better understand the processes he or she is going through. Thus, the questions a teacher would ask focus more on the process of writing than the actual subject matter being written about. Questions such as "How's your writing going?" "What problems are you having in this piece?" or "If you were to do more with this piece what would you do?" focus more on the creative act of writing, rather than on the content being written about.

Peer-to-peer conferences. Paralleling the teacher–pupil conference is the peer conference between two or more children. Peer conferences are important for a number of reasons. First, they relieve some of the pressure on teachers to meet with every student every day. With class sizes averaging 25 or more, it is physically impossible for the teacher to conference with every child each day. Second, feedback from other students is a powerful motivator. It is not necessary for peers to comment and critique every item in one another's papers, just to respond to them. Finally, peer-to-peer conferences reinforce the notion that the teacher is not the only audience willing and able to read what children have written (Calkins, 1991, 1994).

To help students develop some basic conferencing skills, you need to set some guidelines. Discuss with your class and demonstrate some of the kinds of questions the students might ask one another during a conference: questions about the beginning, middle, or end of the work; questions about the characters, setting, or plot. They should focus on the content of the work. Is it clear what the writer is trying to say? If not, where is the problem? Avoid nit-picking about mechanical errors such as spelling, capitalization, and punctuation. Figure 8.6 lists some suggestions for peer conferences.

To reinforce what conferencing should and should not be like, try using the **fishbowl technique.** The teacher asks for a student volunteer to help act out a conference. Teacher and pupil sit facing each other with the rest of the class seated around them observing—like watching two fish in a fishbowl. The teacher and student then role-play two different conferences, a poor one and a good one. A poor conference has the teacher and pupil pointing out each other's errors: "You misspelled *hippopotamus* again, dummy." "Don't you know *Virginia* begins with a capital?" "You forgot to indent your paragraph." Finding errors is easy, but it is certainly not helpful to a writer to hear about them continually. A good conference is one that centers on the content of the piece being read. The reader shows a genuine interest in the work; "Hey, this is really neat about Dracula dying in the end. I'm not exactly sure how it happened. Can you tell me more?" After the children have observed the teacher and student in the fishbowl, the teacher asks for student volunteers to continue the role-playing until satisfied that the entire class has at least some idea as to what should take place during a peer-to-peer conference.

The success of a conference is best measured by the quality of the discussion between the writer and reader. When both parties interact with each other

When I began to write, I found this was the best way to make sense out of my life.

JOHN CHEEVER

1. Bring question list and refer to it.

2. Read draft orally to partner.

3. Do not proofread mechanical errors at these sessions.

4. Rotate conferencing partners.

5. Ask questions rather than give suggestions.

6. Have option of conferencing only with teacher.

FIGURE 8.6

Suggestions for peer-to-peer conferences.

in a positive and constructive manner, both benefit. The author gains a new perspective from the knowledge and insights of another person. Reading and discussing the writer's work allow the reader to see how the other person handled a topic that she or he might be writing on someday.

Revising and Editing

Revising and editing are the two final steps that a writer does during the writing stage. Writers actually revise and edit throughout the entire writing process, beginning with the prewriting stage (writers revise and edit in their heads) and continuing through the rough draft. But it is not until the end of the writing process, when a writer has a completed work in front of him or her, that the focus should be on revising and editing.

The two terms *revising* and *editing* are often confused or used interchangeably. In one sense, revising and editing are the same: They both involve making changes to a rough draft as part of the process of crafting a piece of written work into final form. On the other hand, they are different in perspective: *Revising* involves looking at the entire work, whereas *editing* focuses on changes at the word and sentence level.

The term *revision* means "to resee" a work: to look at a piece of writing with new eyes (Murray, 1990). It also means to rethink and reflect on what you are trying to say (Fulwiler, 1987b). Is your writing clear? If not, perhaps you need to **add** something, possibly an example or additional details to support your argument. Does your writing flow smoothly from one idea or scene to another? If not, you may need to **reorder** your paragraphs, restructure a sentence or two, strengthen your opening, or beef up the middle. Have you chosen just the right words to make your point strong enough? Perhaps another word would do, one that is clearer, more specific, or more colorful. **Changing, omitting, altering, and rearranging** are what revision is about. Revision is the big picture. Figure 8.7 summarizes some issues concerning revision.

The capacity to revise successfully is the mark of a mature writer. Young children therefore find revision difficult. Consequently, they focus on editorial changes, such as correcting spelling mistakes, rather than on redoing an entire sentence or discovering where a paragraph might be omitted. A first-grader may be satisfied with her or his rough draft and merely want to recopy it in neater handwriting. This is not true revision, but at least it establishes a pattern for

---

FIGURE 8.7

Steps in revision.

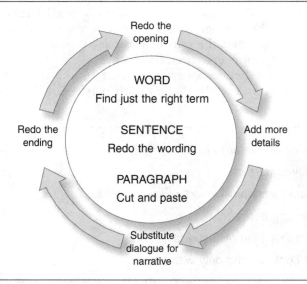

building on later. Second- and third-graders learn to cut and paste, move sentences around, and change words. Still older students may go through three or four revisions, while also discussing their papers with a number of friends, before they feel satisfied that they have said exactly what they intended to say. Professional writers often rewrite an opening sentence in a short story, a line in a poem, or the final paragraph of a novel dozens of times over many months.

There is no one correct way to revise. Some writers rework each sentence before moving on to the next. Others work rapidly, getting down the entire piece as quickly as possible and then going back to smooth and polish the work. Donald Murray (1990) has recommended "listening to the text" while reading it aloud. The key is in recognizing that interesting, clear, effective writing does not happen by accident; it is the result of much rewriting.

If revision means seeing the big picture, then **editing** requires using the fine lens. Both steps are necessary for clear, concise, effective writing; in this sense, editing can be taught as a part of the revision process. However, editing should really be taught as a separate skill that comes after revising.

There are two substeps involved in editing: proofreading and correcting. **Proofreading** is a slow, word-by-word reading to identify errors. Reading slowly in search of misspelled words, incorrectly used punctuation marks, capital letter omissions, tense shifts, run-on sentences, sentence fragments, and so on is difficult for young children. **Correcting** the errors once they are found may be even more difficult. But editing can be made less painful if you use one or more of the following techniques:

- Teach students to read their own work after they are finished.
- Pair off students to read each other's papers.
- Create **editing circles** in which groups of children are taught to skim or read one another's papers but only for a single type of error. For example, one child might read to identify possible spelling errors, another student would look for capitalization errors, a third child for punctuation errors, and so on.
- Remember that you are the final editor, indicating possible changes by a pencil check mark and then returning the paper for the child to make the corrections. Take care not to give the student too many things to correct at once. Figure 8.8 shows examples of some common proofreading marks with which children should become familiar.

When editing skills are taught properly, students see them as part of the refining process. Editing is a final chance to clean up the rough spots in a work in order to communicate more clearly with a reader (Oglan, 2003). Writers understand that misspelled words, incorrectly used punctuation, sentence fragments, and so on throw a reader off track. Too many errors may even cause the reader to begin focusing on the errors rather than the story. This is why editing is so important.

Figure 8.9 shows a student's rough draft with some editing marks. Study it to see what changes the student should make next.

> *There is no good writing, only rewriting.*
>
> **JAMES THURBER**

Beyond the classroom

Select a piece you or someone else has written. Reread it with an eye to revising and editing to make the piece clearer and more concise. Use the proofreading and editing marks as shown in Figures 8.8 and 8.9.

STAGE THREE: POSTWRITING

The final stage in a process approach is *postwriting*, bringing the work to completion in a form suitable for sharing with others. This may mean using a word-processing program to create a professional-looking manuscript either to place on the class bulletin board or to submit to the school newspaper for possible publication. It can also mean reading the work aloud to the entire class or

FIGURE 8.8

Some proofreading marks.

Mark	Use	Example
 ∧	to insert (add) a letter, word, or sentence	The boys ∧ hungry.
 ¶	to begin or indent a paragraph	¶ Four horses left the corral. They headed across the fields and toward the mountains. Soon they were gone from sight.
 ℓ	to delete (take out) a letter, word, or sentence	We had to the leave the party at 8:00 P.M.
 /	to change a capital letter to a lowercase letter	My Friend John left his bike in the street.
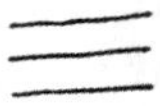 ≡	to change a lowercase letter to a capital letter	They flew to charleston, South Carolina.
 ⬭ SP	to check the spelling of a word	He rode his bicicle to school. SP

FIGURE 8.9

Sample rough draft with editing marks.

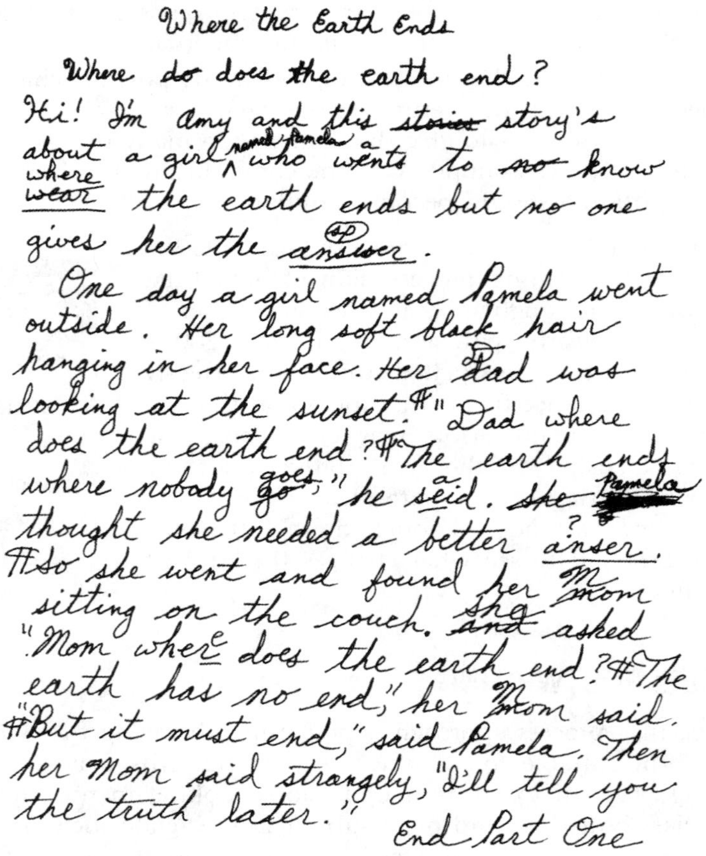

Where the Earth Ends

Where do does the earth end?

Hi! I'm Amy and this stories story's about a girl named Pamela who wents to no know where the earth ends but no one gives her the answer.

One day a girl named Pamela went outside. Her long soft black hair hanging in her face. Her Dad was looking at the sunset. ¶ "Dad where does the earth end? ¶ The earth ends where nobody goes," he said. She Pamela thought she needed a better a inser. ¶ So she went and found her Mom sitting on the couch. She and asked "Mom where does the earth end? ¶ The earth has no end," her Mom said. ¶ "But it must end," said Pamela. Then her Mom said strangely, "I'll tell you the truth later."

End Part One

having still another conference with the teacher. And occasionally postwriting includes getting a written piece ready to submit for a grade.

In the traditional approach to teaching writing, a student always submitted a paper to the teacher to be graded. The teacher thus became the only audience for the child and the grade the sole reason for writing. It is no wonder that so many students hate writing and associate it with red marks and letter grades.

Sharing is a positive alternative to grades. The child who finishes a story, poem, or play wants to share it with as many others as possible. Popular ways of sharing written work include

- displaying the written piece on an author's bulletin board.
- performing the piece as readers theatre with some friends.
- mailing letters to pen pals, businesses, or relatives.
- placing reports in the library for others to use.
- performing an original story or play with puppets.

Following are some additional ways for sharing students' writings that teachers have found to be successful postwriting motivational activities.

Author's Chair

Many primary-grade teachers like to encourage children to be comfortable reading aloud from their own writing to the rest of the class. One way of doing this is by establishing a time for *author's chair* as a part of the regular writing program (Graves & Hansen, 1983).

Renee Rogers, a teacher in Red Rock, OK, uses author's chair with her first-graders as follows: A chair is placed prominently at the front of the room. At a certain time of day, Mrs. Rogers calls the entire class together. Teacher and children alike sit comfortably on the carpet. She then asks for volunteers to read their work. Sometimes these are works in progress, but most often they are finished pieces. While the child is reading, the rest of the group listens politely. When the child is finished reading, Mrs. Rogers asks for comments from the group. The students know they are expected to say something positive about the work. Positive comments—not negative corrections—build self-confidence in young writers. The children can also ask questions of the author if they would like to know more about something. When the students' questions falter, Mrs. Rogers steps in. Not all children volunteer for author's chair immediately, but as the school year progresses, even the shyest child in Mrs. Rogers's class eventually wants to share something he or she has written.

Bookbinding

Bookbinding is an integral and popular part of the process approach to writing. It is also one of the most motivating ways to get students to read. Following are some of the many ways to help children bind their written stories into books that can be read by others for years to come (Rhoten & Yellin, 1993).

Staple bookbinding. Staple pages together with a cover. Use colored mystic tape to cover the staples and reinforce the book spine. Any type of cover may be used, but this technique does not work well with oversized books. A bookbinding learning center can also facilitate this process.

Ring bookbinding. Use a hole punch to make at least two holes along the edge of the pages and the book cover. Insert the rings to form the binding for the book. Shower curtain rings, key rings, even chicken rings (for banding poultry) are excellent for ring bookbinding.

Stitched bookbinding. Using a hole punch, make holes along the left side of the book cover and pages. Using a blunt-end needle or special plastic needle, sew the pages together. Yarn, quilting thread, even dental floss or fishing line all work well.

Library bookbinding. This is the ultimate in bookbinding, and the result is something children will treasure for years. You will need Con-Tact paper, stiff cardboard, needle, thread, and glue or book tape. Since this process is a bit complicated for young children, it is an excellent opportunity to involve caregiver volunteers in your classroom. The steps are as follows:

1. Decide on the size of your book and cut your contact paper larger than the book size.
2. Place two pieces of cardboard for the front and back covers on the contact paper, leaving a half-inch space between the covers and at least a one-inch border around the top, bottom, and sides.
3. Fold back the contact paper to cover the edges of the cardboard, taking care to miter the corners.
4. Cut paper for the book pages that is twice the width (you will be folding it in half) but the same height as the book size you want. Allow an extra sheet for title and end pages.
5. Using your needle and thread, sew the pages together down the middle. This is where the spine of the book will lie.
6. Place the sewn pages on top of the covers, aligning the sewn portion down the spine of the book.
7. Attach the end pages to the book covers using glue or book tape. Glue may also be used to reinforce the spine.

Publishing

For students conditioned to think of writing in terms of red marks and teacher grades, the notion of actually publishing their own writing for others to read may seem strange. Yet all across the country, student-published works are becoming more and more common. Eliot Wigginton's high school students produced original pieces, revised and edited them, and then published the best in a school magazine that was sold throughout the community. For these students, publication was a natural final step in the writing process (Wigginton, 1986).

In Boothbay Harbor, ME, Nancie Atwell's eighth-graders similarly look forward to publishing their stories, articles, and poems in professional journals throughout the country. She calls this "going public" with students' work. It was Atwell, in her book *In the Middle* (1987), who really popularized the notion of publishing the works of student writers as a way of teaching them about various audiences. As Atwell has said, "A sense of audience—the knowledge that someone will read what they have written—is crucial to young writers" (p. 265).

Another opportunity for publishing children's writing is a nationwide contest sponsored by Landmark Editions (1420 Kansas Avenue, P.O. Box 4469, Kansas City, MO 64127), called the Written and Illustrated series. The contest is divided into age groups and students submit their original manuscript stories and illustrations. Every national winner in each age category is then invited to Kansas City, where they work with professional editors and artists to produce a hardcover professional-looking book of their work. Some of the book title winners and their child authors include Stacy Chobsky, *Who Owns the*

In and beyond the classroom

Select one of the suggestions for postwriting activities, such as bookbinding. Then find an elementary classroom whose teacher will allow you to work with a small group of children. Teach the students this activity and record the experience in your journal.

Sun (1988); Lisa Gross, *The Half & Half Dog* (1988); and Elizabeth Haidle, *Elmer the Grump* (1989).

Kids Magazine and *Cricket* are two professional journals that publish children's writing. Bringing these to class and reading a sample article, story, or poem written by children will excite your students to want to submit their own work for publication. You will, of course, need to explain to them that national magazines such as these receive hundreds of submissions every month from children all over the country; therefore, getting a piece accepted for publication is quite difficult. If you do decide to submit students' writing to professional publications, make sure that you read the journal first to acquaint your students with the type of material it publishes, the style it prefers, and any other special requirements. All this information is usually contained in the front of the journal in a section labeled "Information for submitting manuscripts." Figure 8.10 lists some journals that publish student writing, which you may wish to explore with your students. Figure 8.11 lists some websites where students can post original writings.

Young Authors' Fair

One of the most exciting postwriting events a school can conduct for students is a Young Authors' Fair (Hahn, 1983; Oglan, 2003). Such a fair is a celebration of writing, during which students of all ages and all grade levels submit their

---

Boy's Life
1325 Walnut Hill Lane
Irving, TX 75602

Child Life
P.O. Box 567
Indianapolis, IN 46206

Ebony, Jr.
820 S. Michigan Avenue
Chicago, IL 60605

Jack and Jill
P.O. Box 567
Indianapolis, IN 46206

Scholastic Scope
50 W. 44th Street
New York, NY 10036

Cricket
1058 8th Street
La Salle, IL 61301

Highlights for Children
803 Church Street
Honesdale, PA 18431

Kids Magazine
P.O. Box 3041
Grand Central Station
New York, NY 10017

Stone Soup
P.O. Box 83
Santa Cruz, CA 95063

Anthology of Poetry by Young Americans
Anthology of Poetry, Inc.
P.O. Box 698
Asheboro, NC 27204-0698

FIGURE 8.10

Professional publications for students' writing.

---

www.realkids.com
Features true adventure stories written by children ages 8–14.

www.kidpub.com
Publishes any type of children's writing.

FIGURE 8.11

Websites with students' writings.

Young Authors' Fair certificate.

Young Authors' Fair
CERTIFICATE OF PARTICIPATION

This is to certify that

_____

has submitted an original piece of creative writing
to be displayed at the Young Authors' Fair held at
the Stillwater Middle School.

best writing in a bound-book format. The books are displayed on tables in a large area such as the school cafeteria. Caregivers and special guests are invited to attend and browse around the book displays. Students have a chance to visit the fair during the school day to see their own books on display and read books by their friends in other classes.

Organizing a Young Authors' Fair requires schoolwide cooperation. A parent–teacher organization can take a lead role in this project. Classroom teachers need to be reminded of the final date for submitting entries. Students select their best or favorite work to be displayed. Since the purpose of the fair is to provide an opportunity to recognize and praise young writers, no competitive awards are given; every child who contributes an original work in bound-book form receives a certificate of participation. Figure 8.12 is an example of such a certificate.

Teaching with a Process Approach: The Writing Workshop

Today many experienced teachers have altered their lesson plans and rearranged their classrooms to utilize a process writing model within a workshop approach. Writing authorities such as Nancie Atwell (1998), Lucy Calkins (1991, 1994, 2001), Donald Graves (1994), Shelly Harwayne (1992), Linda Rief (1999), and

Gail Tompkins (2003) have long advocated this approach to teaching writing. Many have also described the workshop approach for teaching reading (Reutzel & Cooter, 1991). Some educators simply call it the language arts workshop (Kaufman, 2001). For the purpose of this section, we refer to the method as the writing workshop, but the major principles apply equally well to the teaching of reading and can be used in content-area writing also.

A writing workshop approach differs from the traditional classroom in several important ways. For new teachers who wish to create a writer's workshop within your classroom, keep the following questions in mind as you read further: How is classroom time used in a writing workshop? How is the workshop organized? What is the role of the teacher? What is the role of the student? How is movement managed? How is the workshop evaluated?

First, an entire class period must be structured around the writing workshop, because such an approach requires a *large block of time*. A workshop approach cannot be an add-on to the existing classroom; it must emerge from a conscious rethinking of how teachers and students use their time. The stages involved in process writing (prewriting, writing, postwriting or sharing) cannot be completed with 5 minutes of work here, 10 minutes of work there; interruptions from students who cannot find their proper materials; and so forth. Writing requires big chunks of uninterrupted time.

Second, the teacher, at the beginning of the school year, needs to explain the main elements of the workshop, its organizational structure and important procedural matters (Kaufman, 2001; Rief, 1999). Children must fully understand this new way of learning and behaving before they engage in a writer's workshop. Finally, the teacher should also write along with his or her students. Following is a description of those elements, structures, and procedures.

CHOICE

Students are expected to choose their own topics, reading and writing genres, materials, as well as make choices concerning their first draft, later revisions, and final editing. Making choices is a big responsibility for young children and must be carefully guided, when needed, by the teacher.

RESPONSE

Teachers need to listen to children and conference with them on a regular basis. Teacher conferences may last only a minute when a specific tip or piece of advice is provided a child, or they may last as long as 15 minutes for the child who is struggling or needs extensive feedback from an adult. Peer conferences are another type of response that are very beneficial; students can help one another by reading each other's papers, asking questions, making suggestions. Some students will be further along in the process than others and can therefore help their friends as they move to the next stage of the writing process.

COMMUNITY

To be successful a writing workshop or any workshop approach depends on students sharing their skills and knowledge willingly with their classmates. Students are not competing with one another or trying to see who can finish a piece first. Instead, the teacher encourages children to help one another, to support the child who needs help with spelling a word or finding information. Collaborative writing projects, buddy editing sessions, and group research teams help to create a sense of community within the classroom.

STRUCTURE

A writing workshop should follow a definite routine. Children must first be taught the routine before they can work responsibly and independently in a workshop setting. Here are some examples of the organizational structures that must be taught first to the children:

Status of the class. At the beginning of the workshop period the teacher gathers the entire class around him or her, on the floor or with chairs pulled together in a circle. Then each student briefly informs the teacher about what he or she will be working on that day. The teacher might make a comment or two, but it is important that this not take away too much valuable time from later reading, writing, and research.

Mini-lesson. Next, the teacher presents a brief lecture, demonstration, writing tip, or procedural suggestion. For example, "In your rough drafts, skip a line and leave wide margins on your paper so you will have enough room to make changes later. Here is an example of a student paper with wide margins containing changes the student has made. Are there any questions? Okay, find a comfortable spot in the room and get to work." In addition, some teachers read and write along with their students to model for them the kinds of behaviors they are seeking.

Writing. The bulk of the workshop is spent writing. The children find a place to work on their drafts, revising or editing as appropriate. Some children prefer to work at their desks, others at tables, and some stretched out on the floor. This is quiet time for reading, writing, and thinking. If a child does have to speak to a neighbor, the child does so softly so as not to disturb others who are immersed in serious writing.

Conferencing. A formal conference schedule is established that allows each child to meet one-on-one with the teacher. This is posted on a bulletin board so each child can know in advance when he or she will meet with the teacher. In addition, the teacher moves around the room conferencing with individual children as needed. Finally, children also meet together in peer conferences to discuss their drafts, problems they are having in revising, or questions they may have about editing.

Group sharing. At the end of the period the teacher calls the children back together. Writing problems are discussed. Suggestions for improving the workshop are made. A few students volunteer to share their works in progress in author's chair.

Movement procedures. Because the bulk of time in a writing workshop is independent time, children often have to get out of their seats to go to the class library, to look words up in the dictionary, to approach the teacher with questions. This means that the teacher has to establish careful ground rules for moving about the classroom without disturbing others; freedom of movement within a workshop entails responsibility. For young children, this may mean posting rules of behavior around the classroom or reminding students during procedural mini-lessons of the importance of respecting others who are engrossed in work and do not want to be disturbed.

One result of the writing workshop method is that it helps children to acquire what Lucy Calkins (1994) calls "living the writerly life." This means becoming aware of the everyday world around them and seeing ordinary events

VIGNETTE
in the classroom

One day Ms. Giacobbe is conferencing with Tommy, a first-grader, when she notices he has changed something in his writing. She asks him about it and he replies, "Easy. When I read it, it wasn't right. I left words out."

As Ms. Giacobbe observes Tommy at work over the school year, she notices him rereading what he has written more and more and then revising his work. For example, Tommy draws an arrow to show that a word is missing and needs to be inserted. When asked why he used the arrow, Tommy says he saw his teacher use it at the chalkboard one day. This 7-year-old is discovering for himself how reading and writing work together.

During other conferences with his teacher, Tommy makes still more revisions in his writing. When asked to share his stories with other chil-dren during author's chair, the questions they raise cause him to make still more revisions. Ms. Giacobbe notices that other changes are occurring in Tommy's writing. After doing author's chair a few times, Tommy begins adding more details and trying to explain things more clearly. Obviously Tommy is anticipating the questions the other students might ask him the next time he does author's chair. Tommy has discovered the importance of audience.

For Tommy, writing and reading go hand in hand. The more he writes, the more he reads; the more he reads, the more he writes. As others (teachers and peers) comment on his writing, he is stimulated to write still more and with a greater awareness of his readers.

and objects in a new way. Noticing specific and unusual details that others might miss is what adds spice to one's writing.

Teaching with a process approach and using the writing workshop method demands careful planning on the teacher's part. It means providing freedom and responsibility for students, because such an approach requires students to work on their own or with a buddy or in small groups. To help students, some teachers like to create display posters that remind them what their responsibilities are in a writing workshop, how to conduct peer conferences, what to do if they encounter a problem in their writing, and reinforce the importance of editing (see Figure 8.13). Read the Classroom Vignette above to see how the process approach affects one student's writing process.

Did I . . .	Check if yes
use complete sentences?	☐
capitalize the first word in each sentence?	☐
end statements with periods?	☐
end question sentences with question marks?	☐
indent paragraphs?	☐
check for spelling errors?	☐
capitalize all proper nouns?	☐
use quotation marks to indicate dialogue?	☐

FIGURE 8.13

Editing checklist.

Types of Writing

All the recent research on writing has demonstrated that in order to improve as writers, students must write on a daily basis and—ideally—choose what they write about. Although choice is most important, teachers of writing also introduce children to different types of writing. This is not the same as assigning topics. Within each type of writing, students are still free to write on topics that interest them the most. However, exposing young writers to different types and styles of writing is one of the responsibilities of the teacher.

Many different authors have categorized different types of writing according to the purpose of the writer (Norton, in press; Roe, Stoodt-Hill, & Burns, in press). For example, **descriptive writing** includes stories, poems, and essays whose main purpose is to describe something. **Expressive writing** includes diaries, journals, learning logs, and personal letters; its form is closest to normal speech. **Narrative writing's** main task is to entertain and can also include stories, poems, and plays. **Expository writing** (often emphasized in but not confined to the upper grades) includes research reports and explanations of technical procedures. **Persuasive writing** utilizes the essay format to argue a position or persuade the reader to believe or do something. The actual names of the categories are not as important as the exposure of children at all grade levels to a variety of types of writing. For a more detailed description of some of these categories, visit http://ccweb.norshore.wednet.edu/writingcorner.

Following is a summary of some of the different types of writing activities young people enjoy.

JOURNALS

Clutter is the disease of American writing. We are a society strangling in unnecessary words, circular constructions, pompous frills, and meaningless jargon.

WILLIAM ZINSSER

Writers keep journals; journals are the lifeblood of writing. Through journals, writers explore their thoughts, discover their topics, and try out new techniques. Encouraging primary-grade children to keep journals leads to more reading, increased vocabulary usage, and fluent writing. Thus, introducing students to journal writing is one of the first things a teacher should do (Fulwiler, 1987a; Short, Harste, & Burke, 1996; Tway, 1984).

Spiral-bound notebooks or small looseleaf-binder books make the best journals. Journals can also be made by stapling lined paper into an ordinary folder. The key is not what the journals look like but how they are used. Journals help to establish the writing habit. Toby Fulwiler put it this way: "I no longer trust to chance. . . . Journals work because I use them actively every day to write in, read from, and talk about" (1987b, p. 15). Following are some different types of journals to consider using with your students.

Personal Journals (Diaries)

Many children are already familiar with personal journals. A **diary** is a record of children's personal thoughts or a recounting of the daily events in their lives. Often it deals with the ordinary and the mundane, but it provides a nice record of events of the previous weeks, months, and years. Even very young children can be taught to keep personal journals on a regular basis. Hipple (1985) has described how kindergarten children benefit from journal writing that is a mixture of drawings, scribbles, and random letters. Manning, Manning, and Hughes (1987) found that first-graders became confident writers when they drew and wrote about things that were most personal to them.

One way in which teachers can lead their students into personal journal writing is by reading to them from children's books in which one or more characters keep a journal. Follow-up discussions on why people keep journals helps to motivate youngsters to keep journals themselves. Appendix A lists some popular children's books in which diaries play an important role and the grade levels for which each book is appropriate.

Dialogue Journals

A **dialogue journal** is a written conversation between two people, usually the teacher and a student (Gambrell, 1985; Shuy, 1987). It can be used in a variety of ways for a variety of purposes. For example, sometimes a child wishes to share something with the teacher, but there just is not enough time in class or the child is too shy to speak up in front of others. So the child writes a brief note to the teacher about any topic of his or her choosing. The teacher reads it and then writes back to the child. Sometimes the dialogue journal may be passed back and forth in this manner over many weeks.

Other times a dialogue journal is used by a student to ask questions related to the content in a subject area. "Mrs. Jones, I didn't understand what you meant by a *peninsula* today. I know it's some kind of geography shape, I think. Could you explain it again?" The teacher then writes a response to the child.

An alternative form of dialogue journal that ties into the books children are reading works as follows. A student is reading the book *Dogsong* by Gary Paulsen and finds a quote that interests him or her:

> He heard his father get up and hack and cough and spit into the stove. His father smoked cigarettes all day, rolled them with Prince Albert tobacco, and had one hanging on his lip late into the night. In the mornings he had to cough cigarettes up. The sound tore at Russel more than at his father. It meant something that did not belong on the coast of the sea in a small Eskimo village. The coughing came from Outside, came from the tobacco, which came from Outside and Russel hated it. (pp. 3–4)

After copying the quote into his or her dialogue journal the student would write his or her reaction to it. Later the teacher might reply to the journal entry.

Teachers can also initiate a dialogue journal with their students about nonacademic matters. Staton (1980) found that dialogue journals are excellent for counseling children about personal problems. Often teachers do not have the time to talk with individual children about school or home difficulties that may be interfering with their academic work. So they write about it. Figure 8.14 is an example of the dialogue journal format.

Literary Response Journals

Many young people dislike literature because of the way it is taught: The teacher questions the class as a whole about facts in a book (who did what to whom and why). Teacher questions mean teacher control. Teacher questions also imply that there are specific correct answers that must be guessed or memorized. For many students, this kills the appeal of reading books.

But literature is meant to be enjoyed, to be experienced, to be savored in a highly personal manner. A literary response journal can help students to realize this. The **literary response journal** encourages youngsters to write their feelings and reactions to the books they have read (Barone & Lovell, 1990). Primary through secondary students can use literary response journals to enhance their pleasure and comprehension of books.

One way to introduce literary journals in the classroom is to organize students into small groups based on the book they have chosen to read. Each day in class, the group has time to read and talk about the book. Students may also use some of this time to write about the book. Or they may choose to do their jour-

FIGURE **8.14**

Sample dialogue journal entries.

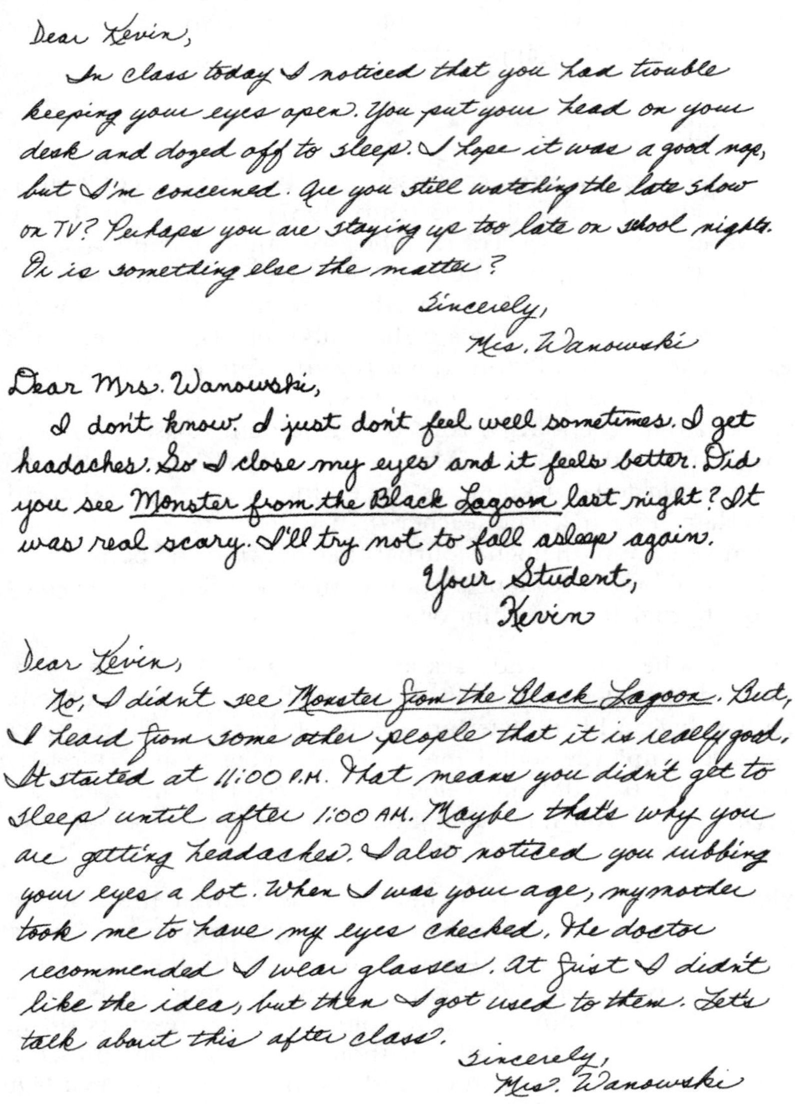

Dear Kevin,

In class today I noticed that you had trouble keeping your eyes open. You put your head on your desk and dozed off to sleep. I hope it was a good nap, but I'm concerned. Are you still watching the late show on TV? Perhaps you are staying up too late on school nights. Or is something else the matter?

Sincerely,
Mrs. Wanowski

Dear Mrs. Wanowski,

I don't know. I just don't feel well sometimes. I get headaches. So I close my eyes and it feels better. Did you see Monster from the Black Lagoon last night? It was real scary. I'll try not to fall asleep again.

Your Student,
Kevin

Dear Kevin,

No, I didn't see Monster from the Black Lagoon. But, I heard from some other people that it is really good. It started at 11:00 P.M. That means you didn't get to sleep until after 1:00 AM. Maybe that's why you are getting headaches. I also noticed you rubbing your eyes a lot. When I was your age, my mother took me to have my eyes checked. The doctor recommended I wear glasses. At first I didn't like the idea, but then I got used to them. Let's talk about this after class.

Sincerely,
Mrs. Wanowski

---

nal writing at home. The key to writing a literary response journal is to focus on personal reactions to the book. James Britton (1973, 1978) has called this **expressive writing,** in which the primary audience is the person writing. Louise Rosenblatt (1989) has referred to this as reading literature *aesthetically*, in which the experience the reader has with the work is the most important factor.

J. D. Salinger's book *Catcher in the Rye* is about the experiences of an angry adolescent named Holden Caulfield. Holden attends a private boarding school, and he has few friends. He curses constantly and is generally portrayed in a negative manner. However, as the book progresses, Salinger leads the reader to experience some of the pain that Holden is experiencing. Following is an excerpt from the literary response journal of one girl who read this book in the class of Marion MacLean (1985). Notice how the writer personalizes her reaction to the main character:

> Holden seems to feel that his parents don't want him because he is always shipped from one boys school to another. And neither of the other children went to boarding school.

He seems to be devistated by his brother's death. Not just devistated, but puzzled and angry at himself, the world, and life. Life most of all. And everyone in it. I think that's why he hates everyone he comes in contact with. It's just a way of letting that deep sadnes and anger out.

Holden at the beginning of this book was a repulsive person who cussed about everything, but by the end of this book I cryed because I felt his pain so much! I wanted to reach out and help him.

Teachers such as Marion MacLean use literary response journals as an integral part of their literature lessons. They find that journal writing about literature encourages students to read aesthetically and to create their own meaning based on personal experiences. Students who keep literary response journals about the books they are reading not only gain an enhanced appreciation for literature but also find that writing stimulates discussions with other students who have read the same book and have had different reactions to it.

Reading Logs

Younger children not accustomed to keeping a literary journal can begin with a reading log. A **reading log** is a list of books a child has read during the school year plus comments about each book. Often this is done on a chapter-by-chapter basis. To guide children in writing in their logs, some teachers provide them with "thought questions." As with the literary response journal for older students, the thought questions are intended to get the young reader to respond to the book at an intellectual or emotional level rather than merely summarizing each chapter. Examples of thought questions include the following:

- Which character in the book might you select as a friend? Why?
- Which character do you dislike? Why?
- Have you ever had a problem similar to the one in this book?
- What in this story is familiar to you? A place? An object? An event?
- What puzzles or bothers you most about this story?
- Would you recommend this book to a friend? Why?
- Can you draw a picture that represents the main thing you remember about your book?

To help young children get started in keeping reading logs, provide them with a sample of the format, in addition to the thought questions. Figure 8.15 is an example of such a format.

FIGURE **8.15**

Reading log format.

		Child's Name: _____		
Title of Book	Author	Date Begun	Date Finished	Comments
The Class Trip (Sweet Valley Twins)	Francine Tripp	Feb. 18, 2004	March 23, 2004	I liked where they went on a trip and Jessica got lost.

Writer's Journals

A **writer's journal** can be a separate journal or it can be incorporated with other types of journal entries such as freewriting exercises, personal diary entries, even reading logs. The difference is that the writer's journal contains reflections on another piece of writing by the author of the journal: how it is going, where the problems lie, what changes need to be made, how much extra research needs to be done. Following is an example of a young girl writing in her journal about a poem she is trying to write. The poem is about saying good-bye to her best friend, who moved to a new home.

> January 14—I'm trying to write a poem about Janey. She was my best friend and I still miss her. I remember how we used to roller skate everyday after school, round and round in our driveway, while we listened to the Beatles. I don't know if I should try and make every other line rhyme or what.
>
> January 20—I've finished my poem, I think. It's longer than I imagined. I think I need to go back and take out some stuff. It sounds corny. But the part about skating to the Beatles is good. I can picture it like it was yesterday.

Learning Logs

Journal writing is a process of reflection, a form of thinking. Toby Fulwiler (1987a) noted that having students record what they have learned in particular subject areas is one way to help them understand difficult subject matter. Lucy Calkins (1994) has referred to these content journals as **learning logs.**

Too often, particularly in the upper grades, teachers pigeonhole writing as something done only in English class. However, many teachers of content areas such as math, science, social studies, art, and music are discovering the benefits of journal writing in their classrooms. They report that students actually learn and retain more information when they are asked to write about what they have learned. This is as true for describing a science experiment as it is for explaining the solution to a mathematics problem or relating how a particular piece of music makes the writer feel.

Fulwiler (1987b) has contended that learning logs can be used at different times and for different reasons. A biology teacher may ask his students to bring their learning logs along on a science field trip to record data. A history teacher might begin a lecture on the Civil War by asking his students to write down what they already know about Abraham Lincoln. A geometry teacher may stop the lesson with 10 minutes remaining and have her students write a summary of what they have learned during the period. Primary-grade teachers could ask their students at the end of the day to complete the sentence, "Today I learned . . ."

Simulated Journals

In the **simulated journal,** according to Tompkins, "students assume the role of another person and write from that person's viewpoint" (1990, p. 44). For example, a fifth-grade social studies class is studying about the early discoverers and explorers. From their textbook and additional biographies found at the library, the children have read about the lives of Columbus, Pizarro, Cortez, da Gama, Balboa, Magellan, Cabot, and Cabral. Their teacher asks them to select their favorite explorer and write a journal as if they were that person. These first-person simulations give students a chance to use their imaginations and at the same time incorporate what they have learned about historical figures. The same learning activity can be used to enhance other subject areas: Students can pretend they are Vincent van Gogh, Marie Curie, or Wolfgang Amadeus Mozart.

Journal-Writing Tips

Whatever kind of journal writing you employ in your classroom, follow these tips:

- Remember that you can collect and read students' journals, but do not grade them. Grading causes children to focus on mechanics rather than on their real thoughts about a subject.

- Remember that journals are rarely rewritten; they are done as first drafts, so allow for misspellings and grammatical errors. Focus on the ideas and the feelings in the writing.

- Have students keep journals on a daily basis. Five or 10 minutes each day is usually all it takes to maintain a journal.

- Encourage children to reread their journal entries and use them as sources of ideas for later writing activities.

- Keep a journal yourself and write with the students in class. Practice what you preach.

STORIES

Children love to create stories. First they create them in their heads; then they want to tell these stories to their friends and family. Eventually they want to write them down. This natural desire to tell stories is what the teacher of fiction writing taps in young children.

All children have a story—indeed many stories—to tell: about the bully who picks on kids after school; about the boy who found a wallet on the school bus; about the day she broke her arm and had to go to the hospital; about the time his dog had six puppies out in the garage; about the strange old woman who lives down the block and chases kids from her yard with a broom; about leaving the old neighborhood to move to another state when Dad got transferred. This is the basis for fiction writing: Experiences, feelings, and beliefs are the source of all writing (Graves, 1989a). Unfortunately, many youngsters do not consider their own lives interesting enough to tell others about. Thus, one of the teacher's first tasks is to convince students that others are interested in what they have to say.

Writing one's own experiences in the form of a story is referred to as **narrative writing.** What makes a story a work of fiction rather than autobiography is that the author alters certain facts—changes the setting, embellishes the characters, or otherwise fictionalizes the events. But at the heart of a good story is an author's own experience. Patricia MacLachlan, a well-known children's author, wrote *Cassie Binegar*, about a girl who liked to hide under the dining-room table and listen to the conversations of others. After she had written this book, MacLachlan's mother told her that she had done the same thing as a child (Courtney, 1985).

How do young children acquire the concept of story to apply to their own writing? First, they must hear stories told and be read to frequently (Applebee, 1978). Professional writers have noted that their earliest inspirations stemmed from hearing stories read to them by their parents (Courtney, 1985). Teachers reinforce story knowledge by reading aloud to their students daily. Second, children must begin to think of themselves as authors to acquire the concept of authorship (Lamme, 1989). Lamme has suggested four ways to do this:

1. Discuss with children that books are written by people called authors, not by some mysterious machine.

2. Reinforce this fact by doing author studies: reading several books by the same author; writing follow-up letters to the author.

3. Invite an author to speak at your school. More and more schools are combining a visit by an author with their Young Authors' Fair program.
4. Make the author's chair activity a regular part of the reading/writing workshop so that children can experience firsthand how an author feels reading his or her work to a responsive audience.

The elements of a story can also be taught in a mini-lesson. A direct instructional mini-lesson includes the following four steps:

1. Identify the specific skill/comprehension area to be taught based on your observations and discussions with children.
2. Select a children's book that exemplifies what you want to teach.
3. Discuss the skill within the context of the book. Do this with the entire class in a mini-lesson.
4. Using a modeling strategy, direct students to practice the skill in their writing. Figure 8.16 is an example of a first-grader modeling the plot of "The Little Red Hen."

Mini-Lesson: Beginning, Middle, and End

Basic to the concept of story are the notions of beginning, middle, and end. These are difficult concepts to grasp if a child has not heard many stories read aloud before coming to school. Typically very young children, who are egocentric and lack recognition of outside audience, start thoughts in the middle, assume their readers can read their minds, and end stories when they run out of paper.

To teach the concepts of beginning, middle, and end, select some highly predictable books that include three easily recognized parts. Pause after the beginning and ask the students what they think the story will be about. The beginning of a book usually introduces the main character(s), the problem to be resolved, and the setting. Next, read the middle portion of the book. Discuss with the children that the middle of the book further develops the characters along with the plot (the action in the story). Finally, read the last section of the book, in which the main character solves the problem and the theme (or message) of the story is revealed.

FIGURE 8.16   *Sample story using modeling strategy and invented spelling.*

The Story of the Little Red Hen
Catherine

Onecs up on a time tere lived a hen pig cat and mouse. The mouse werked with the hen why the pig and cat sleeped. One day the mouse and hen wera walking thay wawnd a Grain of weat. how will help me plant this I wILL seid tucker. But the other aninills ceid not I. Sow the hen and mouse planted the Gran of weat. Soon the weat Grow and Befor you Krow it it was time to harvst the wait will you help me havvst

this Sore seid the mose. naw we will tack it to the mill Just one minet why i Get me Chikes OK So off thay whent. tucker helped Back the cack Soon the house was ful of feresh cack. the cut jvmped up the Powl table and Ran into the kithen So did Pig how will help eat this LoveLy cack I will seid cat I will seid Pig no You wont You did not help me mose did he can help eat So her and her chits and tucker eat the cack

the enD

To help young children grasp the concepts of beginning, middle, and end, have them sketch out their stories first as three separate drawings. Drawing is an important aspect of developing a sense of structure and sequence for stories. Older students can draw cluster diagrams to help them structure stories in their minds. *Where the Wild Things Are* by Maurice Sendak and *Alexander and the Terrible, Horrible, No Good, Very Bad Day* by Judith Viorst are two easy-to-follow books for young children that lend themselves to teaching about beginning, middle, and end.

Mini-Lesson: Plot (Conflict, Climax, and Resolution)

For many young children, what makes for a memorable book is what happens in the story, the action (Seuling, 1984); this is called the *plot*. In fiction, the plot begins with a conflict or problem to be solved. For example, in Jean George's *Julie of the Wolves*, the problem is literally one of how to survive in the wilderness; in Paula Fox's *The Slave Dancer*, a 13-year-old boy is kidnapped and taken to West Africa on a slave ship. Eventually the various events in a story build to a high point, or *climax*; then the action turns and the solution begins to unfold. In the end, there is *resolution*, or a solving of the problem.

To help children write better plots, some teachers use an exercise called the *five-minute plot*. First, set a timer for five minutes. Second, instruct students to quickly sketch out a plot for a story containing a character, a problem, and a solution. Finally, have students compare their five-minute plots for the three main elements. This exercise can be practiced once a week until children become adept at outlining stories quickly.

Mini-Lesson: Setting (Place and Time)

The particular place in which a story is set—a large city, a small country town, the deep woods, an exotic tropical island—is not an accident. Authors choose their settings carefully and research them thoroughly. The time period of a story—past, present, future—is also significant. For example, Esther Forbes's story *Johnny Tremain* takes place around the time of the Revolutionary War. Mildred Taylor's *Roll of Thunder, Hear My Cry* is set in Mississippi in the 1930s; the discrimination felt by the African American family in this story is a reflection of the time and place in which they live. Elaine Konigsburg chose the Metropolitan Museum of Art as the setting for *From the Mixed-Up Files of Mrs. Basil E. Frankwiler*. Other classic children's books in which place and time are especially crucial to the story line are *Strawberry Girl* by Lois Lenski and the *Little House* series by Laura Ingalls Wilder.

Mini-Lesson: Character Development

Fiction books are centered around a conflict or problem to be resolved by a main character. Main characters are often introduced within the first paragraph of a book, which is called the *lead*. The lead sets the tone of the story (Graves, 1989a). Often characters are developed through their actions, the way they resolve their problems. Different types of conflicts or problems are possible. One type involves an individual in conflict with the larger society. In *Journey Home*, author Yochiko Uchida explores the issues of discrimination and prejudice faced by Japanese Americans during and after World War II. In this story, a young girl and her family return home to California after being unjustly placed in a concentration camp in Utah, only to find more injustices awaiting them. A different type of character conflict is revealed in books such as *Call It Courage* by Armstrong Sperry. In this book, the main character, Mafatu, must conquer his fear of the sea and prove himself worthy to be the son of a chief. In *Sam, Bangs and Moonshine* by Evaline Ness, a young girl's innocent lies eventually lead to tragedy, which in turn causes her to face the truth about herself. Finally, there are books in which the main character must face the problem of survival in a hostile natural environment. In *Island of the Blue Dolphins* by Scott O'Dell, young Karana survives alone on an island for 18 years. In two of Jean George's popular books, *Julie of the Wolves* and *My Side of the Mountain*, survival in the wild plays a central role in explaining the development of the main characters.

Mini-Lesson: Theme (Message)

Theme is often confused with plot. *Plot* is the action, what is happening in the story. However, the characters' actions usually have greater significance than is first apparent. Perhaps the main character learns a lesson, grows wiser, matures in some way, or struggles with forces of good and evil; these are the common *themes* of children's books. However, themes are rarely stated directly. Instead, theme must be inferred by the reader from the action in the story. In both *The Yearling* by Marjorie K. Rawlings and *A Day No Pigs Would Die* by Richard Peck, two young boys grow toward manhood by confronting death. Identifying the theme or themes of a book in small groups leads to higher-level discussions and more critical thinking than mere identification of what is happening in the story.

Mini-Lesson: Role of the Narrator

A story can be told in the third person, in which a narrator stands back from the action and relates a story, or the same story can be told in the first person, in which the narrator is the main character in the story, describing events as they occur. In the latter case, the *narrative distance* between the character and the reader is very small; the reader feels as though the events are actually happening to him or her. A story can also be told from the point of view of another character in the story. The importance of who is telling the story can be made clear to young children by reading to them Judy Blume's *The Pain and the Great One*, in which different characters recount the same story. In *The True Story of the Three Little Pigs*, a classic fairy tale is recounted from the wolf's point of view.

PLAYS

Chapter 5, covering speaking skills development, stressed the importance of placing children into small groups to tell stories. Often oral language activities, such as storytelling, improvisation, and readers theatre, lead children to want to write their own plays.

One way to begin play or script writing is to have a group of students work cooperatively on a single play; this is known as **collaborative writing.** The elements of a play are the same as in fiction writing: plot, setting, character, and theme. The main noticeable difference in play writing is the emphasis placed on dialogue. Although dialogue can and often does play an important role in story writing, it plays a preeminent part in a play. The story line or plot is literally carried by what the characters say (McCaslin, 1996).

The key element in writing good dialogue is making it true to the character; that is, the words must fit the character's role. This is why authors use slang expressions, colloquial speech, and regional dialects to emphasize a character's traits. Young children may be confused at first by the unusual spellings that result from an author's attempt to approximate a dialect ("We be workin' mighty hard des deays"). Explain that this is an example not of poor spelling but rather of good dialogue, spoken by a real character.

FIGURE **8.17**

Sample play dialogue.

"Hello!" the woman shouted. "Is anyone there?"

"Ruthie?" Laura's voice asked from the darkness. "Is that you?"

"Yeah, it's me. Where are you? I can't see."

"Gimme a match. I'll turn on the light." Laura moved through the tunnel toward the light.

"Come on," the woman called again. "It's getting cold here."

"Hey, you're not Ruthie," Laura said and dropped her voice to a whisper, now afraid to move.

Figure 8.17 shows some excerpts of a play written by a group of fifth-grade students using dialogue to carry the story line. These students had read a number of plays; eventually they wanted to try their own hand at writing one. Then they wanted to act it out for their fellow classmates. This is the way a natural communication cycle works in the classroom: Children read and hear stories and plays read to them; they begin to tell stories to their friends; they get together as a group and write their own play; and finally they act it out for others to see, hear, and appreciate.

When children first attempt to write dialogue, they will use and misuse quotation marks and other punctuation associated with dialogue. This is only natural, as they are beginning writers. As they read and study models of dialogue written by professional authors, they become more familiar with the proper use of punctuation. As they practice writing dialogue, they eventually develop ease at handling the quotation marks, commas, and periods that once gave them so much trouble.

NONFICTION

Nonfiction writing (also known as **expository writing**) covers a broad range of writing genres; generally speaking, it is written to convey information, share discovered facts, recount a personal event meant to inform or entertain, describe a procedure or instructions for doing something (e.g., a recipe), explain a natural process in science, persuade a reader to believe something, or promote a particular point of view (Wray & Lewis, 1997).

For many elementary-grade students, nonfiction writing is difficult because they have had little experience with it. Unlike narrative writing, which sounds similar to our spoken language, informative writing sounds different from the way we normally speak. Compounding this difficulty is the manner in which it is taught. Many teachers merely assign topics ("Do a report on the African Sahara Desert") without really explaining the steps involved in report research and writing. Wray and Lewis (1997) suggest the following four-step model to lead children into writing nonfiction, informative text:

1. *Demonstration.* The teacher models the steps of researching and writing nonfiction material to the entire class.

2. *Joint activity.* A group of students write a single collaborative piece of nonfiction.

3. *Supported writing.* The teacher provides guiding questions or an outline to assist an individual student.

4. *Independent writing.* The student researches and writes on his or her own, following a process approach and with assistance by the teacher as needed.

The following subareas of nonfiction writing are among the most commonly taught in the elementary and middle grades.

Autobiographies

An **autobiography** is the story of a person's life written by that person. Many famous people have written autobiographies intended for younger audiences. For example, the writer/illustrator Tomie de Paola told about his early life in *The Art Lesson*. Dorothy Hamill has shared with children what it is like to be a champion Olympic ice skater. Hundreds of children have been enthralled by Helen Keller's *The Story of My Life*. Reading any one of these stories or any other autobiography helps young writers to understand the nature of autobiographical writing. Even young children can be encouraged to tell about themselves.

Biography and Research Reports

A **biography** is a story written about a person's life by someone other than that person. For example, Barry Denenberg wrote *Stealing Home*, the story of Jackie Robinson, who broke the color barrier in professional baseball. Biographical writing leads youngsters into exploring the world of research. Research at the elementary-grade level is often misunderstood. Youngsters can do many types of research; the most common is library research. In researching to write a biography of George Washington, a student might

- look up "George Washington" in the encyclopedia.
- examine the card catalog for books about George Washington.
- use the *Dictionary of American Biographies* for a brief sketch of Washington.
- do an Internet search on George Washington, using Yahoo!

The main difficulty in using any of these resources is that they are generally written at a level beyond the reading ability of a child. Thus, children simply copy from books and turn in the work as their own because they know no better. Students must be taught how to **paraphrase** and how to cite a reference source. But these are skills that come much later, through extensive research report writing.

There are other ways to introduce students to the world of biographies and research report writing. For example, young children can write biographies about someone they know, such as a parent, grandparent, friend, or other relative. To do this the teacher should lead students through a series of mini-lessons on how to conduct an interview; how to take notes or tape-record interviews; how to organize notes into an outline; and, finally, how to write a report.

A next step in research writing would be the **I-Search Paper** (Zorfass & Copel, 1995). This can be done individually or in small groups. Students first have to identify a topic they are interested in researching. Then they need to formulate a plan for gathering information. For example, three students in one fourth-grade class wanted to know how burning oil-well fires are extinguished. Their research plan included going to the library to read newspaper accounts of the oil-well fires in Kuwait in 1990. Next they went on the Internet, where they found a website for the Williams Fire Protection company in Houston, Texas, which specializes in oil-well fires. Finally, they contacted a local university that has a program in fire protection and safety technology; they arranged to meet with and interview some firemen there who had had actual experiences with oil-well fires. Later they gathered all of their research notes and with the help of the teacher began to organize them into the rough draft of a research report. When the final copy was completed, they presented their paper orally to the class.

Even young children can write simplified research reports based on their own experiences and following the **All About . . .** format. Susan Sowers reported on one first-grade classroom in which the students wrote *All About . . .* books. The teacher put the separate books together into one large class-collaboration book to share and be displayed in the room (Sowers, 1985). *All About . . .* books are not really research reports but, rather, lists of facts that young children have discovered about some subject. The emphasis is on sharing information. They are a first step in teaching young children how to write research reports. Figure 8.18 gives some examples of one first-grade class's *All About . . .* books. (Note that the teacher chose to correct the children's original invented spelling for the final copy, which is sent home to caregivers. This is not necessary, but it is a teacher's choice.)

Upper elementary and middle school students can also be led to research through the **Quest Project.** In its simplest version a Quest Project involves a student actually doing something he or she has never done before. The students first must examine the topics they are interested in or might be interested in. Then they select something that they would like to do but have never done before. Once their projects have been selected, students try to find someone with expertise in that area to seek if they need help. Mrs. Ally Sharp of Stillwater Middle School uses the Quest Project with her sixth- and seventh-grade students. The class helped her decide on the criteria they would use to evaluate the project as follows: a title for the Quest; a list of materials needed; an estimation of the time required; an explanation of what was learned; and, finally, a step-by-step guide to completing the Quest. Examples of student Quests include constructing a homemade guitar, building a model battleship, riding a unicycle, and fixing a complete dinner for their family.

Research report writing can be fun and interesting if teachers first carefully lead their students through the various steps and allow them to choose their own topics using such approaches as the All About . . ., the I-Search Paper, and the Quest Project. Later, teachers can assign topics on more traditional school research papers that focus more on library and Internet research.

LETTERS

Letter writing should be encouraged at all grade levels as one of the ways to develop students' writing skills. Particularly with young children just learning to read, early letter writing reinforces their reading skills (Clay, 1991). Sending meaningful messages to classmates, caregivers, relatives, as well as school and local officials reinforces the notion of **functional writing**—writing that focuses on content and purpose rather than mere correct form.

Judith LeVine (2002) models letter writing for her kindergarten class each morning by describing the activities for that day. For example, one day she wrote, "Dear Friends, Today we will bake bread. Love, Ms. LeVine." As the school year progresses, individual students are assigned as calendar helpers to write messages to the class. Group class letters are written to caregivers who helped with field trips or class parties. Providing children with a frame such as "Dear

Excerpts from All About . . . *books.*   **FIGURE 8.18**

All About My Cat

My cat is white and black.
My cat drinks milk.
My cat plays with a yarn ball.
My cat is named Checkers.
I really love my cat.

All About My Doll

My doll can speak.
She has a button that you push.
She has blond hair.
The hair is real.
I can dress my doll.
She walks and her arms move.

All About Snakes

I have a pet snake.
Snakes eat mice.
Snakes lose their skin.
Snakes feel smooth.
They are not slimy like people think.
Some snakes are poisonous.
Mine is not.

_____" at the top and "Love, _____" at the bottom helps individual students to compose easier. Such letters are taught under the heading of *friendly letters* because they are written to someone the student knows personally (a friend or relative) or would like to know (a pen pal).

Older students can be taught the form and purpose for writing *business letters*. These are more formal in style and can be written to a local store or distant company to lodge a complaint about a product or make a request. They can also be written to local and national politicians as part of social studies lessons.

Figures 8.19, 8.20, and 8.21 offer suggestions for and examples of the different letter forms.

POETRY

Poetry is music. Think of your favorite rock, western, country, or blues song. Listen to the lyrics and think about why you like this particular song, what it says to you. Poetry is fun. Think of a limerick, a knock-knock joke, a funny commercial based on a play on words. Poetry is emotional. Recall a favorite sermon from church, a high school commencement speech that moved people to tears. Poetry is powerful. Listen to the recorded speeches of Martin Luther King Jr. or John F. Kennedy. Poetry is all of these things.

Unfortunately, too many children are taught to dislike poetry—perhaps not intentionally, but they are taught to regard poetry as something so difficult, highbrow, or complex as to be beyond the gifts of ordinary people. Even adults are intimidated by poetry. Perhaps it goes back to that one terrible day in junior high when you were asked to recite in front of the whole class Edgar Allan Poe's "Annabel Lee." Or perhaps it was your freshman year in high school when the

---

FIGURE 8.19

Suggestions for writing letters.

FRIENDLY LETTER

1. Write to a relative in another town whom you have not seen in a while.
2. Write to a friend you have not seen or heard from in a while.
3. Write to your parents or caregivers, inviting them to come to the next special school event.
4. Write to a pen pal in another class, school, or state. Pen pal information can be found in such magazines as *Teacher, Learning,* and *Instructor* as well as by writing to Pen Pal Letter Exchange, 910 Fourth Street SE, Austin, MN 55912.
5. Write a thank-you letter following a field trip or presentation by a guest speaker.
6. Write a thank-you letter for gifts received for Christmas or a birthday.

BUSINESS LETTER

1. Write for information to the Chamber of Commerce of a state you are studying. The local American Automobile Association in your community can provide the address.
2. Write to a company regarding a product you have bought or wish to buy. In the letter, you can lodge a complaint, offer a compliment, or make a request. The address is printed on the box or package (usually in very fine print).
3. Write letters to the editors of newspapers regarding school and educational issues.
4. Write letters to your congressional representative or senator on issues of interest to young people.

FIGURE 8.20 · *Sample pen pal letter.*

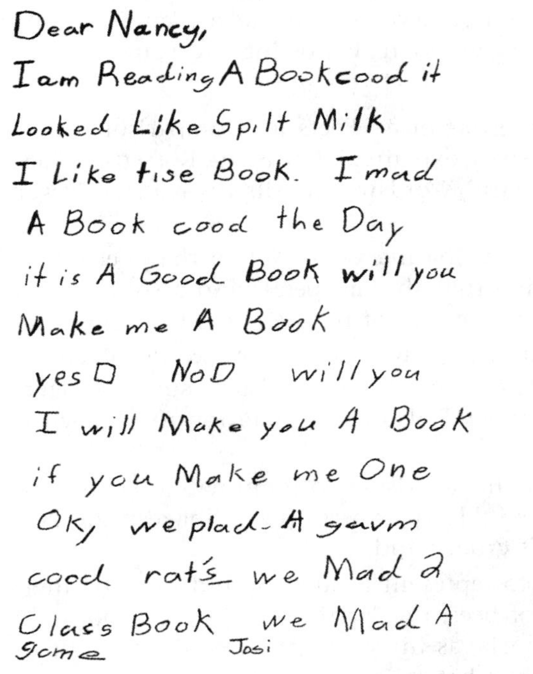

Dear Nancy,
I am Reading A Book cood it
Looked Like Spilt Milk
I Like tise Book. I mad
A Book cood the Day
it is A Good Book will you
Make me A Book
yes ☐   No ☐   will you
I will Make you A Book
if you Make me One
Ok, we plad A gavm
cood rat's we Mad 2
Class Book we Mad A
game   Josi

FIGURE 8.21 · *Sample friendly and business letters.*

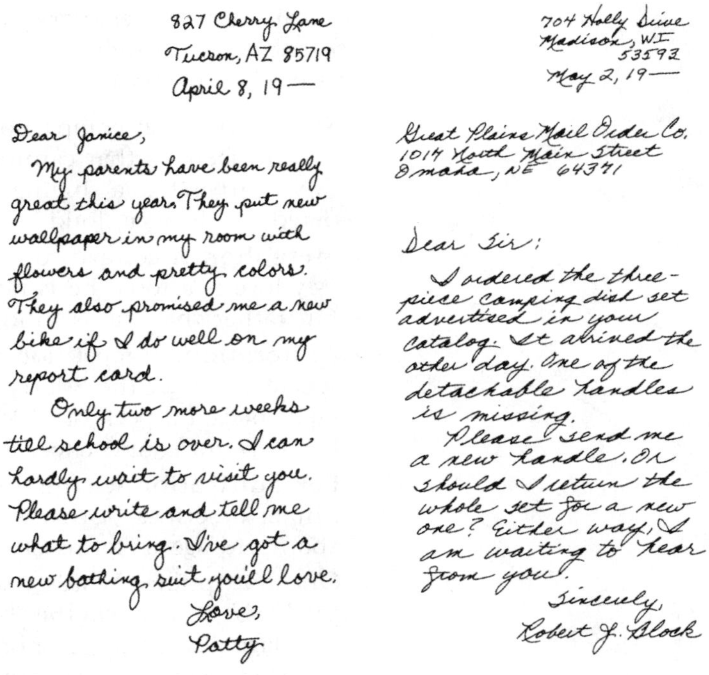

827 Cherry Lane
Tucson, AZ 85719
April 8, 19—

Dear Janice,
My parents have been really
great this year. They put new
wallpaper in my room with
flowers and pretty colors.
They also promised me a new
bike if I do well on my
report card.
Only two more weeks
till school is over. I can
hardly wait to visit you.
Please write and tell me
what to bring. I've got a
new bathing suit you'll love.
Love,
Patty

704 Holly Drive
Madison, WI
53593
May 2, 19—

Great Plains Mail Order Co.
1014 North Main Street
Omaha, NE 64371

Dear Sir:
I ordered the three-
piece camping disd set
advertised in your
catalog. It arrived the
other day. One of the
detachable handles
is missing.
Please send me
a new handle. Or
should I return the
whole set for a new
one? Either way, I
am waiting to hear
from you.
Sincerely,
Robert J. Block

teacher called on you to explain what John Keats was really saying in his poem "Ode on a Grecian Urn." Or perhaps it was that assignment in some long-forgotten class to write a poem using the iambic pentameter form. Talk about pressure. Talk about fear. Talk about frustration.

One result of early negative experiences with poetry is that today teachers either gloss over it quickly in the curriculum or teach it without joy and enthusiasm. The purpose of this section is to correct the bad image that poetry has and to demonstrate that poetry really is fun. Children enjoy reading and writing poetry. It has a genuine place in an integrated language arts curriculum.

What Is Poetry?

> Letting go
> in order to hold on
> I gradually understand
> how poems are made.

Source: How Poems Are Made by Alice Walker.

Poetry involves being sensitive to language, to a particular choice of words, to a specific arrangement of thoughts. A poem can make you laugh or cry. Poems are emotional; they evoke feelings. They are also difficult to fully explain. Sometimes you have to struggle with a poem a bit, to go beyond the surface words to a meaning that lies below.

One of the things that makes poetry difficult for young people is the terminology used in classroom textbooks. Terms such as *iambic pentameter*, *assonance*, and *metonymy* serve only to confuse. Having children analyze poems to search for figurative language or to identify a particular rhyme scheme only results in frustration. Such exercises also consume valuable time that could be better spent helping children enjoy a poem at their own level.

What role, then, does figurative language play? First, the technical terminology of poetry is for the teacher. In order to better understand how poets use language or how certain effects are achieved through words, some knowledge of technical terms is necessary. But it is not necessary to make memorization of these terms the content of your poetry lesson. Following are some common terms used in poetry and prose:

- **Simile.** A direct comparison using *like* or *as*. Poets use comparisons to explain feelings that cannot be easily explained. Christina Rossetti writes, "My heart is like a singing bird." And Wordsworth tells his readers, "I wandered lonely as a cloud."

- **Metaphor.** A comparison without using *like* or *as*. When the poet says, "My love is a rose," he is not saying that she has petals and a spiny stem but rather that she is so lovely that images of nature come to mind.

- **Alliteration.** A repetition of initial sounds in a series of words. Shakespeare writes of the "Merry maids of May." Tongue twisters, such as "Peter Piper picked a peck of pickled peppers," also use alliteration to play with language for sound effect.

- **Personification.** Giving human characteristics to inanimate objects. Joyce Kilmer describes "A tree who lifts its leafy arms to pray." Shakespeare talks about old age in terms of "Time's cruel hand."

- **Onomatopoeia.** Words written to represent a literal sound from nature—the "hiss" of a snake, the "buzz" of bees, the "grrrr" of a tiger. Cartoon language also employs onomatopoeia, as in "snap" (the tree limb in the wind) and "crack" (the sound of the bat as it meets the ball).

- **Hyperbole.** A gross exaggeration to convey strong emotions or evoke humor. An adult writes, "My heart is broken in two." A child writes, "I could eat a horse." Shel Silverstein has poor Cynthia (who would not take the garbage out) creating a trail of garbage across the entire United States.

- **Oxymoron.** A poetic device that creates surprise by placing two opposite or contradictory terms back to back. Here are some examples: slow rapids, jumbo shrimp, silent scream, sweet sorrow, definite maybe, exact estimate, and working vacation.

FIGURE 8.22

Stages in a poetry unit.

1. Exposure
2. Sharing
3. Memorizing
4. Choral speaking
5. Copywriting
6. Illustrating
7. Writing poetry
   A. Free verse
   B. Acrostic
   C. Couplet
   D. Diamante
   E. Haiku
   F. Limerick
   G. Concrete (or visual)

Teaching Poetry: An Alternative Approach

It is the authors' contention that the problem with teaching poetry to young children is the overemphasis on technical terminology and analysis, which can dominate many poetry lessons. Stressing definitions and analysis takes the life and fun out of poetry for young people. It makes poetry so complex as to deny its beauty to the young reader. However, alternative teaching procedures do exist for elementary teachers. These procedures not only teach children something about poetry but, more importantly, allow them to enjoy poetry.

Since poetry is not a usual part of the curriculum in many school districts, each teacher has to create his or her own syllabus. Poetry can be taught throughout the entire school year or incorporated into a unit that might last a few weeks. Figure 8.22 shows the stages in a poetry unit.

Exposure. The simplest way to introduce a poetry unit is by reading poetry aloud with your students—all types of poetry; this is known as **exposure.** As with any oral reading activity, you should first familiarize yourself thoroughly with a poem. Next, practice reading the poem aloud with enthusiasm and feeling. Finally, learn something about the poet to share with your students. In the book *Poetspeak: In Their Work, About Their Work* by Paul Janeczko (1983), various poets have described what it means to write a poem, how poetry is a reflection of their own lives, and how one poem can have many different meanings, depending on the reader.

During this first stage, all the children need do is listen and enjoy. They should not be tested over the poem or asked to do any sort of follow-up activity. The key is for the teacher to select a variety of poetry that holds their interest and appeals to their senses. Appendix A contains a bibliography of poetry sources suitable for the elementary grades.

If you really want to excite students with poetry as performance, bring professional entertainers to your school. Theatrical productions are stimulating as well as entertaining.

Sharing. Once children have heard a variety of poems read aloud by their teacher over the course of a few days, they want to share favorite poems of their own. Most children have a favorite poem they have heard a caregiver recite, read in a book, or learned in a previous class. Not every student will bring a poem to share, but many will. Build on the enthusiasm of a few; the rest of the class will catch the poetry fever.

Sharing can be done as a whole-class activity, with one child reading aloud a favorite poem to the rest of the class. Even better, however, is to break the class into small groups. Arrange their chairs in circles so that everyone is facing one another. Then let each child in the group take a turn sharing a poem she or he has brought. Sharing in small groups develops the affective domain and allows more students the chance to read their favorite poems in a shorter amount of time (Koch, 1970).

Memorizing. It is through memorization that a child really comes to know a poem at a variety of levels. Edmund Farrell (1989) has said that "memorizing poetry is a means of possessing the poem that can be attained in no other way: poetry must move from the head to the heart to the viscera." The key—as with any activity for children—is not to overdo it.

Begin by memorizing a short poem yourself and presenting it to the class. Explain to your students how you prepared for this. Show them the poem on an overhead transparency and go over the lines that you wanted to stress, that you thought were most important. Also share with your students the lines that gave you the most trouble. Let them inside your head. By thinking aloud for students, teachers can take some of the mystery out of basic problem-solving situations.

When the children are ready to try some memorization, let them select their own poems. Do not assign poems to be memorized; again, choice is important. Of course, many children simply look for the shortest poem they can find. This is all right. Children have to begin somewhere, and short poems are certainly less intimidating to memorize than long ones.

Another way to help students with the memorization activity is to pair students and have them work together in memorizing their separate poems. When it comes time for them to present their poems to the rest of the class, they can use the **buddy system:** One child stands before the class reciting a memorized poem while his or her buddy sits directly in front, with the actual poem serving as a prompter if the reciter should forget a line or two. Remember, the emphasis should be on enjoyment.

Choral speaking. In **choral speaking,** all of the children in the class or in a small group take turns reading different parts of the same poem (Stewig, 1981). The emphasis is on the pleasurable sound effect that this creates. Reading poetry aloud to appreciate how it sounds is one of the real pleasures of poetry—a pleasure that is often denied youngsters when the focus is on analyzing the poem for deeper hidden meanings. As with any oral reading, choral speaking requires that the children practice the poem together for optimum effect.

There are a number of different types of choral speaking. The simplest is reading in **unison:** The entire class reads the same poem aloud together. The effect is a strong, clear sound that fills the room. In the **refrain** method, one child serves as lead reader. She or he reads the main part of the poem while the rest of the class joins the leader on the refrain or chorus. **Turn taking** involves dividing the entire class into as many groups as there are lines or stanzas in the poem. The first group reads the first line/stanza, the second group the second line/stanza, and so on. This technique requires careful listening and accurate timing by all readers. Even more complicated but also immense fun is the **round.** In this choral-speaking technique, one group begins by reading a long poem such as *The Charge of the Light Brigade.* When these students reach the second line or stanza, another group begins reading from the beginning of the poem while the first group continues reading. At the next stanza, a third group begins reading while the two previous groups continue their reading. Children enjoy the sound effects of the round and want to try it again.

Copywriting. Copying a favorite poem is a common activity for professional poets (Janeczko, 1983). It is through the act of copying that poets get a feel for rhyme, rhythm, line breaks, imagery, and language used by other poets. Oddly enough, teachers often consider copying a low-level activity. Nothing could be further from the truth. By encouraging students to identify favorite poems and copy them into their notebooks, you are helping them internalize some of the subtler differences between poetry and prose.

Many students want to create their own poetry books of favorite poems. Having them copy different kinds of poems into their notebooks is among the best forms of preparation for writing original poems. Professional poets have done this for years; children can discover it for themselves. Another way to preserve and display favorite poems is to tack them to a bulletin board or hang them from a "poetree" (Hopkins, 1972).

Illustrating. A companion activity to copying poetry is illustrating. On the top half of a page, have students copy a favorite poem. They should leave room on the bottom half to draw an illustration. Many poets, such as Shel Silverstein, illustrate their own poems. At first children may copy these drawings, but eventually they want to select poems without illustrations and create their own. Drawing is a fun exercise and often leads children to want to write their own poems.

Writing poetry. Writing poetry can be a fun and rewarding activity—or it can be frustrating and dull. The key is how the teacher presents it. If you keep the following guidelines in mind, teaching poetry can be one of the most exciting learning experiences your students encounter:

- Remember that not all poetry has to rhyme. In fact, writing rhyming poetry is quite difficult for young children with limited vocabularies.
- Show examples of the different types of poetry forms. Children need to see how poetry looks, how it differs visually from prose.
- Be flexible when teaching a fixed poetic form (such as the haiku); not all children will be able to come up with the exact number of syllables per line as is technically required. Proficiency comes with practice.
- Begin by writing a group poem on the board. The children contribute the lines and you record them. Do not be afraid to change lines. Revision is part of poetry writing, too.

- When the students write, you should write at your desk or at the chalkboard. Let your students see you thinking, composing, revising, and editing.

Types of Poetry

Poetry writing can be taught to any grade. First, show an example of the poetry type (e.g., acrostic) on the chalkboard, a poster, or an overhead. Poetry looks different and needs to be seen before children can write a particular form. Second, read the poem aloud and encourage students to read with you. Enjoy the sound of poetry. In some cases, point out the physical features of the poem, such as the number of lines, the syllables per line, or the rhyme (if any). Third, write a class collaboration of the poem by imitating the poem you have just read. Imitation writing, or patterning, is an important step for children's first attempts at poetry writing. Finally, turn your students loose to write and enjoy whatever poetic form pleases them. Following are some different types to consider.

Free verse is a modern form of poetry invented in the twentieth century; the lines do not rhyme, and it sounds more like prose writing but looks like poetry. Free verse poems can tell a story, paint a picture, or describe a person or a scene. Because the lines do not have to rhyme, free verse is generally easier for young children to write. In Figure 8.23, there is a free verse poem by William Carlos Williams; next to it is an imitated or patterned poem written by a sixth-grade girl from Brooklyn, NY.

Another variation on free verse is *magnet poetry*. A commercial magnet board can be purchased that contains hundreds of individual magnet words. The words can be easily moved around the board to form lines of poetry. Figure 8.24 shows examples of magnet poetry done by second- and third-grade children in Jenks, OK.

The **acrostic** is a simple poetic form in which a single word is written vertically on a page. Then each letter forms the initial letter of a word or line of poetry. Acrostics can have one word per line or be more elaborate. The examples in Figure 8.25 reveal the variety that even a simple form like the acrostic can take. Children may wish to select their own names or a friend's name to begin their first acrostic. Remember to write your acrostic on the chalkboard as the students are writing theirs.

A **couplet** is two lines of poetry. Couplets are the building blocks for longer poems. Figure 8.26 shows Christina Rossetti's poem "Wind," in which the second and fourth lines rhyme, as do the sixth and eighth. Using the patterning technique to introduce poetry writing, first write a class collaboration poem using different first lines. Everyone in the class can contribute lines beginning with the words, "Who has . . ." and "But when . . ." (For example, "Who has touched the sun?" "Who has heard the grass?" "Who has held the rain?")

FIGURE 8.23   *Sample free verse.*

This Is Just to Say
by William Carlos Williams

I have eaten
the plums
that were in
the icebox

and which you were
  probably
saving for breakfast

Forgive me
they were delicious
so sweet
and so cold

Dear Cat
by Lorraine Fedison

Please
for
give
me
for
watching
your
eyes
gleam
in
the
night.

Source: "This Is Just to Say" by William Carlos Williams, from *Collected Poems, 1909–1939, Vol. I.* Copyright © 1938 by New Directions Publishing Corporation. Reprinted by permission of New Directions Publishing Corporation.

FIGURE 8.24   *Sample magnet poems.*

Beautiful butterfly sparkle
with joy
get up and go
stop in wind.
—2nd grade

The color of dreams
sun, cloud, ocean, stars, moon
live in my heart
They are cool
joy and awesome
—3rd grade

FIGURE 8.25

Sample acrostic poems.

Moving	**D**reaming	**S**itting
Around	**A**bout	**A**lways
Running	**V**isions	**M**umbling
Yelling	**E**veryday	

When the snow falls	**A**ubree has an
It makes	**U**mbrella
Nice patterns on	**B**ecause it is
The sidewalk and	**R**aining
Everywhere children are	**E**verywhere
Running and laughing to be free	**E**verywhere

FIGURE 8.26

Sample couplets.

Wind

by Christina Rossetti

Who has seen the wind?
  Neither I nor you:

But when the leaves hang trembling,
  The wind is passing through.

Who has seen the wind?
  Neither you nor I:

But when the leaves bow down their heads,
  The wind is passing by.

The **diamante** is a seven-line poem written in the shape of a diamond (Tiedt, 1970). It follows some strict rules. First, select two subject nouns that are opposites—for example, night and day, boy and girl, child and adult. The first noun goes on the first line; the second goes on the last (seventh) line. On line two, write two adjectives that describe the first subject noun. On line three, write three participles or verbs ending in *-ing* that tell about the first subject noun. On line four, write four nouns—the first two relating to the first subject noun, the last two relating to the second subject noun. (In other words, the focus of the poem shifts in the middle of line four.) On line five, write three participles related to the second subject. On line six, write two adjectives describing the second subject. Figure 8.27 shows some examples of the diamante poetry form.

The **haiku** is a Japanese form of poetry that is very popular both in the United States and in Japan. In fact, all Japanese schoolchildren learn to write haiku (Atwood, 1973). Many Japanese adults have made writing haiku their passion. Even the former emperor of Japan enjoyed spending hours each day composing haiku. But don't be fooled by its appearance: The haiku may look easy, but it is actually a very challenging poetic form because of its restrictions. It has only three lines and a total of 17 syllables. The syllables are arranged as follows: 5 in the first line, 7 in the second, and 5 in the third. Finally, the subject matter of haiku is always nature or the seasons. The best haiku present a single image that conveys a deep emotion. And all this is done in three short lines! Figure 8.28 presents two poems by students modeling famous Japanese haiku.

FIGURE 8.27

Sample diamante poems.

Form	Example
Noun	Elephant
Adjective Adjective	Huge, Leathery
Participle Participle Participle	Lumbering, Charging, Snorting
Noun Noun Noun Noun	Jungle, Beast, House, Rodent
Participle Participle Participle	Scampering, Scratching, Squeaking
Adjective Adjective	Timid, Meek
Noun	Mouse

FIGURE **8.28**   *Sample haiku.*

The first day of spring
walking near the water, now,
one lovely egret.

In the winter snow
a silent mountain waiting
quiet but awake.

FIGURE **8.29**   *Sample limerick.*

There was a young lady of Norway,
Who casually sat in a doorway;
When the door squeezed her flat,
She exclaimed, "What of that?"
This courageous young lady of Norway.

—*Edward Lear*

The **limerick** is a funny five-line verse that follows a specific rhyming pattern: *aabba.* That is, lines one and two rhyme, lines three and four rhyme, and line five rhymes with lines one and two. Edward Lear popularized the limerick in his *Book of Nonsense* published in England in 1846. Figure 8.29 is one of Edward Lear's own limericks.

One of the simplest forms developed by Kenneth Koch is the **"I wish"** poem (Koch, 1970). As a whole class, begin the first line of a poem with the words "I wish . . ." Write this line on the chalkboard. Then ask other children in the class to contribute additional lines to the poem, each one beginning with the words "I wish." This is how a class collaboration poem is constructed. Later, individual students can compose their own "I wish" poems with as many lines as they want. Koch also suggests that for a greater sense of unity, writers should follow two rules:

1. Every line should contain a color, a comic strip character, and a city or country.
2. Every line should begin with the words "I wish."

Another simple form created by Koch is **"I used to . . . But now I . . ."** In this poetic structure, each child in the class contributes a couplet employing the opening words "I used to" on the first line and "But now I" on the second line. By combining many of these couplets through the collaboration process, a longer poem is created. Figure 8.30 shows student collaboration poems based on patterns developed by Koch.

Concrete or **visual poetry** involves writing individual words or entire poems in shapes to represent the meaning of the words or poem. It is a form of word play that children enjoy, just for the fun of it. Sometimes poets incorporate concrete elements into a traditionally written poem for special emphasis or for aesthetic effect. Figure 8.31 gives examples of both ways of using concrete or visual poetry.

FIGURE **8.30**

Sample student collaboration poems.

I wish Superman wore a red cape and lived in Disney Land.
I wish Beetle Bailey didn't wear a frown in Hollywood.
I wish Charlie Brown wore a blue suit to Tulsa and
I wish orange and yellow Garfield lived in Italy eating spaghetti.

I used to be a baby
But now I am a boy.
I used to love arithmetic
But now I play with toys.

FIGURE **8.31**

Sample concrete or visual poetry.

WHAT AM I?
I
am tall
but can be
small. I have limbs,
but cannot walk. I live
for centuries, but can be killed
with powder. I shed, but have no
hair. I cannot think, have no heart, but
I
L
I
V
E

Teachers in the OSU Writing Project like to use the **Where Are You From?** poetry activity. It works like this. First, the teacher brainstorms with his or her class favorite family foods, traditions, TV shows, or games the children enjoy playing. Then the teacher asks the students to write down all of their ideas in their notebook. The next day she asks them to write a poem that answers the question "Where are you from?" But she explains that she does not mean what city they were born in but rather what things make them who they are. Here are some excerpts from two student poems:

> I am from Sunday dinner
> And an afternoon nap.
> I am from the "Little House" books,
> From Ramona Quimby and the Boxcar children.

> I am from swaying wheat fields in the breeze,
>   I am from cattle grazing on the prairie
>   I am from homemade breads and butter,
>   I am from pan-fried chicken dinners.

Poet Gary Snyder spent many years wandering around the United States, particularly the Northwest, which he writes about in his **Things to Do Around** poems. First, ask students to choose a city or town that they know well. Second, ask them to list all of the things they like to do there. Third, have them revise the list, add some things their friends would not think of. Finally, have them write it as a free verse poem. Here is one such poem about David Yellin's home town.

Things to Do Around Stillwater

Take a walk down Main Street and check out the Crazy Day sales.
Share some Cheese Fries with a friend at Eskimo Joe's.
Ride your bike around Boomer Lake but watch out for the joggers.
Read a book at Theta Pond and get chased by the geese.
Go two steppin' at Tumbleweeds.

For more great poetry ideas, investigate the website at www.poetryteachers.com.

Assessing Writing

Assessment of writing through standardized tests is complicated when you consider that what we are trying to evaluate is a creative act. Even experienced teachers disagree on what is an A paper compared to a B paper. Is an 85 percent grade more meaningful than a B minus? In the classroom, teachers have long recognized that red marking a students' written work does more harm than good.

Clearly what is needed for assessing writing are more flexible alternatives to traditional classroom grading practices and standardized high-stakes testing. Fortunately, such alternatives already exist, have been used successfully, and are gaining wider acceptance among teachers, caregivers, and administrators (Tierney, Johnson, Moore, & Valencia, 2000; Yellin, 1991). Following are some alternative methods of evaluating students' writing that stress positive, motivational results rather than punitive, critical assessments.

Great writing evolves more from great encouragement than from great criticism.

JOHN MASEFIELD

TEACHER–PUPIL CONFERENCES

One-on-one conferences between student and teacher about the content of a student's writing are by far the most effective way to evaluate student work. Conferences are supportive, helpful in identifying immediate strengths and weaknesses, and respectful toward the child as an author rather than as an object to be labeled. Conferences can be brief or lengthy, but the focus is always on discussing the content and purpose of the written work. Mechanics are only discussed in terms of how they affect the message that the writer is trying to communicate; a sloppy paper that cannot be deciphered needs to be reworked regardless of how important the content may be.

TEACHER OBSERVATIONS

In an article entitled "Kidwatching: An Alternative to Testing," Yetta Goodman (1978) stressed the importance of teachers watching children in the classroom as a means of assessing their progress and needs. Taking time to watch children is an important but often neglected role of the professional educator. Much can be learned by observing young writers at work: What activities do they engage in during the prewriting stage? Do they outline or diagram prior to writing a rough draft? Do they seek feedback from other students? What kinds of revisions do they make before coming to the teacher for help? Do they make some attempt at proofreading and editing? Without knowledge of a student's behaviors during writing, a teacher is at a loss as to how to help that student improve.

ANECDOTAL RECORDS

Along with observation, teachers need to keep anecdotal records of what students do during the writing process. These can be simple notes jotted in a looseleaf binder, one page per child. Later the notes on a single child can be developed into a brief narrative report to be shared with the child's caregivers. The focus should be on what the student is actually doing—strengths and weaknesses—not merely labeling, grouping, or grading the child.

STUDENT JOURNALS

By reading children's journals about the books they have read and the things they are writing, a teacher (and caregiver) can get an insider's view into what the student is doing and how he or she feels about reading and writing. Student journals are a good record of what actually takes place in the classroom. Unlike a single exam on one day, student journals give a more rounded picture of what a child has done throughout the year.

STUDENT SELF-EVALUATION

Students who keep journals on a regular basis eventually begin to evaluate their own writing. They recognize what they are good at (e.g., writing strong leads that capture the reader's attention) and what they still need to learn (e.g., how to develop a complex plot without giving away the ending too soon). Self-evaluation also applies to the mechanics of writing. Students who think of themselves as writers want to improve their handwriting, spelling, and usage skills, for they know that these can mar an otherwise interesting story. Jane Hansen (1987) has recommended that students keep a three-column chart as follows: "Skills I Learned," "Things I'm Working On," and "Things I Plan to Learn." You will find that students can be very honest in their assessment of their own work and do not need a standardized test score to tell them they need to watch out for run-on sentences.

PORTFOLIOS

The portfolio has become the most popular form of alternative assessment (Farr & Tone, 1998). It is now being used to assess reading achievement and writing development, as well as knowledge and skills learned in content areas (Frazier & Paulson, 1992; Gomez, Grau, & Block, 1991; Valencia, 1990). Portfolios are also one of the great motivating materials to encourage students, particularly low achievers, to take pride in their work.

The writing portfolio is a powerful tool to demonstrate a student's growth and development in literacy. Writing portfolios are used to encourage the student when he or she does not feel like any progress has been made, to integrate writing with thinking, to develop self-assessment, and to act as a springboard for student–teacher discussion when evaluating progress (Farr & Tone, 1998).

Writing portfolios represent students' work. The portfolio folders can be as simple as a file folder that has been decorated by the student. Some teachers prefer the pocket folder so papers do not easily fall out. Some teachers use three portfolios for each student so the writing process remains organized. One portfolio contains the published works that the student does throughout the year. These works are final copies of different genres that were edited and published in the classroom, put in the class or school newspaper, or sent to some individual. This portfolio is called the *Portfolio of Published Works*. The second portfolio for a child contains all the pieces that the student attempted, including all steps of the writing process—brainstorming, first drafts, revisions, and final copy. This portfolio is called the *Portfolio of All My Work*. The third portfolio contains only the composition on which the child is working; it is called the *Working Portfolio*. It is helpful to have each portfolio in a separate storage area that is easily accessible to the student.

In the Portfolio of Published Works, the teacher staples a form that records all published works. Figure 8.32 is an example of a "My Published Works" form. On this form, the student records all the work that he or she has published in some manner. It may be a letter of thanks sent to the principal or a poem written for a school newsletter.

In the Portfolio of All My Work, the teacher can staple a form that records all works with the student's comments. See Figure 8.33 for an example of an "All My Works" form. On this form, students record all the various types of compositions they have attempted. Not all of these works need to be completed; however, students will have a record of everything they tried to write. The comments can be something like "I didn't finish it because I got stuck on it."

My Published Works

FIGURE 8.32

Portfolio form for student's published works.

Name _____

DATE	TITLE	GENRE	AUDIENCE/PLACE OF PUBLICATION
10/14/04	"My Brother's Bike"	Biography/Informational	Fifth-grade class magazine

All My Works

FIGURE 8.33

Portfolio form for student's published works.

Name _____

DATE STARTED	DATE ENDED	TITLE/GENRE	COMMENTS
March 3	March 7	"The Biggest Fish"/ Realistic Fiction	An exaggerated story of a fishing trip I took with my dad.

In the Working Portfolio, the teacher staples a form that records skills the teacher taught the student during the editing stage, a conference, or a mini-lesson. Figure 8.34 is an example of a "Skills I Learned" form. On this form, the students make a record of things they learned during a mini-lesson, during a teacher–student conference, or from a classmate while reading the classmate's work.

In the Working Portfolio, the teacher can also staple a form that records students' ideas for future works. Figure 8.35 is an example of a "Bright Ideas for New Works" form. At times throughout the year, the students may read or hear some-

Skills I Learned

FIGURE 8.34

Portfolio form for skills student learned.

Name _____   Grading Period   1   2   3   4

DATE	SKILLS	EXAMPLE
4/16/04	Two different ways to use the apostraphe	"I can't believe you ate my sister's cake."

FIGURE 8.35

Portfolio form for student's future writing ideas.

Bright Ideas for New Works

Name _____

IDEA	GENRE	WHERE I GOT THE IDEA
A scary story about three boys on a camping trip in the desert who get separated from the rest of the group.	Contemporary realistic fiction/ mystery	A camping trip to the Grand Canyon I took with my family last year.

thing that gives them a great idea for a poem or story; however, they may be in the middle of another story and want to complete it before beginning a new piece.

If the three types of portfolios are used with useful evaluation and comment forms, the portfolios will become a "repository of a student's thought and expression" (Farr & Tone, 1998, p. 10).

In order for the portfolio to be used to integrate writing with thinking, there must be plenty of time for reflection after a student completes a work. Reflection and self-evaluation can be done if the student completes a form for self-assessment such as the one found in Appendix C. During a teacher–student conference, the teacher's quarterly evaluation form (see Appendix C) and portfolio assessment rubric (see Appendix C) can be discussed. At this time, the teacher may receive insight about the student's strengths and writing habits. If they are used properly, the forms can give encouragement to the student. These two forms should be stored by the teacher to be used for evaluation at the end of the grading period.

SIX TRAITS OF WRITING AND OTHER RUBRICS

As high-stakes testing becomes more the norm, various groups and organizations have provided detailed writing assessment guides or rubrics to aid school districts in preparing their children for the writing portion of the standardized test. For example, in Portland, OR, the Northwest Regional Educational Laboratory has produced its Six Traits of Analytic Writing Assessment Guide. Using a scale of 1 to 5 (with 1 being the lowest, for writers who have not achieved the minimum competency in a particular trait of writing), the Six Traits Guide gives teachers and students alike a detailed explanation of the strengths and weaknesses of a student paper. The Six Traits are as follows: (1) development of ideas and content; (2) organizational structure of the paper; (3) voice, or how the writer speaks to the reader; (4) word choice; (5) sentence fluency; and (6) conventions or the mechanics of writing such as spelling, punctuation, capitalization, grammar, usage, and paragraphing. For a more detailed discussion of this writing rubric, visit www.nwrel.org.

Remember that rubrics are scoring guides that assist both the teacher and the student. For teachers, they make grading assignments easier and more objective. For students, they help to clarify how their work will be evaluated and guide them to include specific points, information, and subheadings they might otherwise overlook.

Another website, http://rubistar.4teachers.org, is an excellent source for teachers to help create a myriad of different types of rubrics. In Appendix C, we have included some more complete rubrics for assessing writing.

If you would like to learn more about alternative methods for evaluating students' work, some good sources are *Portfolio Assessment: Getting Started* by Allan De Fina (1992); *Practical Assessments for Literature-Based Reading Classrooms* by Adele Fiderer (1995); *Assessment Is Instruction: Reading, Writing, Spelling, and Phonics for All Learners* by Susan Mandel Glazer (1998); *Classroom-Based Assessment* by Bonnie Campbell Hill, Cynthia Ruptic, and Lisa Norwick (1998); *Alternative Assessment Techniques for Reading & Writing* by Wilma H. Miller (1995); *Creating Writers: Linking Assessment and Writing Instruction* by V. Spandel and R. Stiggins (1990); and *In Teachers' Hands: Investigating the Practice of Classroom Assessment* by R. Stiggins and N. Conklin (1992).

TECHNOLOGY AND WEBSITES

Teachers who use the integrated approach to the language arts want students' writing to have purpose. One excellent way to ensure purpose of writing is to have students use the Internet to correspond with others. There are many ways to incorporate the use of technology with the students' writing. For example, the students can use email to write to their favorite authors. In the websites section, there are a number of sites that have authors who respond to their fans through the use of email. Leu (1997) suggests the following sites for other types of authentic writing:

1. Students can send questions concerning famous scientists, architects, astronauts, and other people to the following:
   - www.askanexpert.com/askanexpert/index.html
   - www.madsci.org

2. If students desire to do collaborative projects with students in other classrooms around the world, they can visit one of the following:
   - www.classroom.net/contact
   or
   - www.gsh.org
   or
   - www.kidlink.org
   (These sites permit teachers either to post a topic that interests their students or to check out the postings and respond to one of the requests.)

3. When students complete an original poem or story, they can share it with the world by posting it on one of the following sites:
   - www.cyberkids.com
   - www.kidpub.com/kidpub

www.sfwa.org
This site discusses careless speech and well-written materials to help writers in understanding the challenge of writing.

www.ncte.org
This is the site for the National Council of Teachers of English. It gives teaching ideas, conversation, public policy, publication information, and much more.

www.Kidpub.com/Kidpub
This is a place for students to publish stories on the Net and to read stories written by other students.

www.Kids-space.org
This site permits students to share their art, music, and writings with others.

www.tea.state.tx.us

This is the site for the Texas Education Agency. It provides information regarding the legislation in Texas dealing with reading and writing requirements for Texas schools as well as standardized tests.

www.nea.org/esea

This is the site for the new Elementary and Secondary Education Act of the federal government.

www.octp.org/octp/readlitpdi.html

The Oklahoma Commission for Teacher Preparation produced this site for teachers interested in the state reading/literacy requirements.

www.nclb.gov

This is the No Child Left Behind site.

www.english.ttu.edu/kairos/nctevis

This is the NCTE resolution on Visual Literacy.

www.wilearns.com/apps

The Wisconsin Literacy Education and Reading Network Source provides a wealth of articles, activities, and teaching ideas for grades K–12.

www.teachers.net/4blocks.column

This is an excellent site for creative ideas within the 4-Blocks Literacy Model.

www.mothergoosetime.com

Many good literacy activities and educational programs for preschool and early elementary grades are found here.

www.bookadventure.org

In Book Adventure, children get to create their book lists and take quizzes on books they have read.

http://rubistar.4teachers.org

This excellent site lets you create your own rubric for just about anything—a great aid for teachers.

Summary

The process approach is one method of teaching writing as part of an integrated approach. In the prewriting phase, teachers try to help their students find ideas to write about by having them keep journals, brainstorm, and tell stories. In the writing phase, students produce rough drafts and then revise and edit those drafts. Teacher–pupil conferences play an important role in revising and editing. Finally, in the postwriting phase, students learn a variety of ways to share their works with others, including author's chair, bookbinding, and publishing.

Along with the process approach to teaching writing, there should be a great deal of writing going on in the classroom every day. There are a number of different types of writing suitable for children, including the writing of journals, letters, stories, reports, plays, and poetry. Whole units can be built around poetry writing.

Finally, alternative ways of assessing writing are becoming increasingly important. In addition to merely giving a grade to written work, teachers now use observations, anecdotal records, and portfolios. These are much more meaningful assessments of what children have actually written and learned about writing.

ACTIVITIES *with children*

Class Bulletin Board

With a group of students, put together a bulletin board of students' writings. Encourage caregivers and administrators to visit your room and examine the bulletin board. This is a first step toward getting away from grading every single paper a child writes.

Young Authors' Fair

Ask each student to select his or her best written piece from the semester and bind it in a hardbound-book form. Then arrange for a large display area, such as the gymnasium or auditorium, to display the children's bound books. Give every student who participates a certificate rather than awarding prizes to the best work.

Class Magazine

With access to a typewriter and a copying machine, you can create your own class magazine. It does not have to be fancy, but it should convey to the students the notion of publication in a real journal. Then invite students to submit their best works (fiction, nonfiction, poetry, and so on). Form a student committee to select works for the magazine. Another committee can help with the proofreading, editing, and layout.

Song Writing

Play some popular rock, country and western, or rap music in class. Discuss the lyrics with your class. Then have children work in small groups to produce their own songs. They should revise and edit them the way they would any other piece of written work.

Teacher Writing

Keep your own journal for a few weeks; then bring it to class to share with your students. Discuss with them why you keep a journal. When students write stories, letters, or poems in class, you should write also. Share your writing with the children. Save your rough drafts and final copies to show development from one stage to another.

Greeting Cards

Ask each student to bring in a commercial greeting card. Discuss the cards as a whole class: the artwork, design, message, poetry, humor, and so on. Then instruct each child to select a special occasion or person and design a greeting card with a message, saying, or original poem.

Writing Recipes

Bring in some food recipes and discuss them with the entire class. Then discuss other areas in which recipes can be used. Here is a child's "recipe for success": "First, take two cups of laughter and mix in a winning smile. Then sprinkle generously with determination. Next, add a cupful of organization. Spread it all over with intelligence. Bake until beautiful." Create other recipes for love, happiness, or good health.

Caregiver Interviews

Have your students find out about their caregivers' childhoods by interviewing them. Were they shy? Popular? Good at sports? Did they have a favorite toy? TV program? Book? Song? What was their most embarrassing moment? Who were their friends? Where did they live? Have students transcribe this oral interview into an article or fictional short story.

Displaced Characters

Take any favorite character from literature. What would that person think, say, or do if she or he lived in the present? For example, take Huck Finn off the Mississippi River and place him in an inner-city classroom made up of children of various ethnic backgrounds. How would he react to the racial tensions today?

RELATED READINGS

Atwell, N. (1998). *In the middle: New understandings about writing, reading, and learning* (2nd ed.). Portsmouth, NH: Boynton/Cook Publishers.

Atwell explains the how and the why of setting up the reading and writing workshop. She uses the workshops with middle school students; therefore, she gives some characteristics of middle school students and examples of their work. She writes as if she is talking to the reader.

Calkins, L. M. (1994). *The art of teaching writing* (2nd ed.). Portsmouth, NH: Heinemann.

Calkins gives background on the characteristics of the different-aged students—from nursery school to adolescents. She clearly explains the structure of the writing workshop and how to encourage students to write in other areas of their lives.

Graves, D. (1994). *A fresh look at writing.* Portsmouth, NH: Heinemann.

The chapters on helping children share their writing with others, helping them evaluate their own writing, and helping them learn conventions of writing are particularly helpful. Graves also explains how to begin using portfolios.

Farr, R., & Tone, F. (1994). *Portfolio and performance assessment: Helping students evaluate their progress as readers and writers* (2nd ed.). Fort Worth, TX: Harcourt Brace College Publishers.

This is a great book for someone who has never used portfolios before. It explains how to set up portfolios so that they become meaningful tools of self-evaluation.

Fiderer, A. (1995). *Practical assessments: For literature-based reading classrooms.* New York: Scholastic Professional Books.

The book has assessment forms that may be copied and used by the classroom teacher. Some are for the teacher to use, and others are for the student to use for self-assessment.

Kohn, A. (2000). *The case against standardized testing: Raising the scores, ruining the schools.* San Francisco: Jossey-Bass.

This is one of the most scholarly arguments against standardized tests and how detrimental they are to children's learning.

Language Arts Journal (November 2001) 79(2).

This issue contains excellent articles on organizing a language arts workshop, writing activities, read alouds, and book clubs.

Smith, J., & Warwick, E. (1997). *How children learn to write.* Katonah, NY: Richard C. Owen Publishers.

This book gives developmental information about children and writing. It explains Graves's process approach, Cambourne's model of literacy, and Flower and Hayes's model of learning.

9

The Tools of Writing

The mechanics or tools of writing are many: legible handwriting, correct spelling, punctuation, capitalization, and a host of grammar skills. All these are necessary tools for the successful writer. In addition, young writers today need computer skills and knowledge of word-processing programs.

In the past, these skills were taught in isolation from real writing. Writing skill instruction emphasized memorization, drill, and repetition. Newer approaches reflecting how children learn argue that children construct their own knowledge about skills by using them in authentic situations. The comprehensive approach incorporates both direct and indirect instruction in the skills of writing.

CHAPTER OBJECTIVES

After reading this chapter, you should be able to accomplish the following objectives:

1. Name the characteristics of legible handwriting.
2. Explain some ways to teach handwriting and spelling.
3. Describe the D'Nealian handwriting method.
4. Explain the stages of developmental spelling.
5. Explain the difference between rhyme and rime in teaching spelling.
6. Explain the difference between grammar and usage.
7. Name four different types of grammar.
8. Explain the differences among sentence combining, expanding, and transforming.
9. Name some rules for capitalizing and punctuating.
10. Explain the use of computers in a writing program.

CHECK YOUR BACKGROUND KNOWLEDGE. Before reading the chapter, complete the K-T-W-L chart based on the chapter overview and objectives provided at left. In column "K," write what you know about the topics in the objectives. In column "T," write what you think you know. In column "W," write what you want to learn. Finally, after you have read the chapter, write what you have learned in column "L."

Know	**T**hink you know	**W**ant to learn	**L**earned

The Beginnings: Reasons for Writing

To understand the importance of the tools of writing, recall the reasons for writing. Chapter 8 stated that all writing depends on experience. Children must have experienced something they want to write about, something they want to express in a more permanent form than speech, something they want to share with others. Experience, permanence, sharing—these are the foundation blocks of writing.

Children also need experience with the world of print. Specifically, they need to see and use the tools of writing. Charles Temple and his associates (Temple, Nathan, Burris, & Temple, 1988) summarized much of the research about how young children go about acquiring the tools of writing in the following sequence:

1. Many children begin writing by drawing.
2. At some point, the child calls his or her drawings writing.
3. Squiggles and scribbles that might be letters appear within the drawing, but only the child can "read" them.
4. By seeing print, children eventually begin to employ the distinctive features of letters and words in their writing, even though they do not yet recognize the relationship between sounds and symbols.

The linguist Noam Chomsky (1974) pointed out that there appears to be an innate capacity in children to use language for communication purposes. Research by Ferriero and Teberosky (1983) has shown that children also have an inborn need to communicate in a variety of ways, including print. Young children, for example, experiment with paints, chalk, clay, paper, and pencil long before they enter school. In this way, they begin to discover and reconstruct for themselves the nature of literacy.

In the preschool years, many children have experiences they wish to share verbally with others. This kind of informal talk should be encouraged by teachers. To make the child's speech record more permanent, a teacher may encourage a child to "write or draw me a picture of what you saw or did." Picture drawings accompanied by scribbled words build on what the child has already experimented with at home. Drawings and early scribbles at home or at school are thus the child's first acquaintance with the tools of written communication.

In school, teachers can build on this natural curiosity about reading and writing by using the child's own language to create stories through the **language experience approach (LEA)** (Stauffer, 1980). Although often considered a beginning approach to reading instruction, LEA is also an excellent way to introduce young children to the tools of writing in the classroom. The steps in LEA are as follows:

1. The child dictates a story.
2. The teacher records the story.
3. The teacher reads the story back to the child.
4. The child reads the story back to the teacher.
5. The child traces or copies the story, with teacher assistance.

It is the last step that makes LEA a viable instructional approach in a writing program. Early in her career of researching the acquisition of literacy, New Zealand's Marie Clay (1975) noted that tracing and copying are strategies commonly used by preschoolers. Clay also noted that children later begin to generate their own writing by employing invented spellings, another strategy in the natural acquisition of writing. Tracing, copying, and inventing symbols provide a young child's first encounters with the tools of writing; thus, they are a part of the LEA, which leads young children into the process of writing. Figure 9.1 gives some teaching suggestions for using LEA as a beginning instructional approach to writing.

Handwriting: An Individualistic Tool

Handwriting is one of the skills or tools taught early and often in the primary and elementary grades. In some schools handwriting is taught as a separate skill from writing; this is known as **direct instruction.** In other schools handwriting is taught in conjunction with the writing process (Christie, Enz, & Vukelich, 2003; Graves, 1994; Norton, 1997); this is known as **indirect instruction.** Although the major focus of this textbook is to teach handwriting and other mechanical skills primarily through the process of writing, we also recommend that at times handwriting needs to be taught explicitly, usually through mini-lessons.

Furthermore, we reject the notion that only through extensive, time-consuming drills can a child improve his or her handwriting. Asking young children to write the letters of the alphabet over and over again creates a negative image of writing. Similarly, having children focus on their body posture, how they position their paper, and how they hold their pencil, and then having them try to re-create perfectly shaped letters is not good teaching practice and is a waste of precious classroom time. Instead, effective teachers help their children to write *legibly* within the context of authentic writing activities (Tompkins, 2003).

LEGIBILITY

Legibility is the single most important point about handwriting to be remembered (Farris, 1991; Hodges, 1991a). **Legibility** means that a child's handwriting can be read by someone other than the writer. It does not have to be perfect; it may not look beautiful. But if the teacher can read the handwriting, it is acceptable. Like so many other aspects of learning, a child's handwriting improves over time as the child sees a need for it to improve. Constant drilling on letter formation or the use of handwriting lessons as

---

- Vary the nature of the experiences used to inspire group charts (class dictates to teacher), key-word vocabulary (individual students' word banks), and individual stories. Use field trips, objects, films, and discussion.

- Try cutting an experience chart story into sentence strips. Later let each child manipulate the strips to reform the story; this is the notion of "composing."

- Type a student's experience story with a primary typeface and make copies for the rest of the class. This is one way to share stories with a wider audience.

- In taking dictation, do not be concerned initially with whether a child's language is grammatically correct. At a later time, when the student is comfortable with the approach, changes in the story form can be made.

- Take dictation from children using a variety of means: chalk, pencil, pen, computer.

- Display experience charts and language-experience stories on bulletin boards around the room and in school hallways for others to read and enjoy.

FIGURE 9.1

Suggestions for using the language experience approach.

punishment only reinforces negative attitudes in children toward handwriting in particular and writing in general. Bing (1988) found that when teachers stressed perfect handwriting, students became so worried about constructing the letters that they lost sight of the purpose of writing, which is to convey thoughts and feelings.

Study Figures 9.2 and 9.3, which show samples from two popular handwriting programs; Zaner-Bloser and D'Nealian. Note the similarities and differences between these two programs, but do not be intimidated by them. Remember that the goal of handwriting instruction is the legibility of students' writing, not some artificial standards of perfection.

The D'Nealian method, is named after its inventor, Donald Neal Thurber (1987). Like other handwriting types (e.g., Zaner-Bloser), the D'Nealian method introduces manuscript and cursive strokes through student workbooks (K–8) that encourage tracing, copying, and much practice of individual strokes and letters. What makes D'Nealian unique is that the manuscript letters are slightly slanted, like cursive letters, and the cursive letters do not contain some of the old-fashioned swirls and flourishes. In theory, this should make the transition from manuscript to cursive writing easier (Graham, 1999). According to classroom teachers who have used D'Nealian, however, this method is no better or no worse than any of the other commercial handwriting materials available. It is what the individual teacher does with the material that makes the difference.

What, then, constitutes legibility? In addition to whether or not handwriting can be read by someone other than the writer, legibility is characterized by four main elements: size, slant, spacing, and distinction.

There are letters of two **sizes** in the English alphabet: lowercase (small) and uppercase (capital) letters. Children need to be taught the difference and encouraged to use each type appropriately. The child who writes with all capital or all small letters eventually discovers that she or he is confusing the reader, particularly in the cases of sentence beginnings and proper nouns. However, even many adults occasionally use small and capital letters inappro-

FIGURE 9.2

Zaner-Bloser handwriting model.

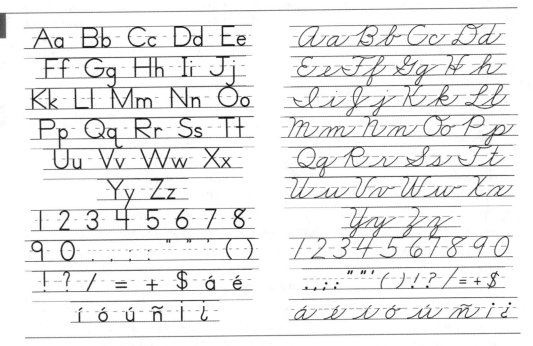

priately, so the teacher should not make a major issue of this with the young child just beginning to write.

In some handwriting programs, a definite rule is also given for the **slant** of letters. For example, a program might advise that all cursive letters slant to the right at a 45-degree angle. This again is an artificial and unrealistic standard to put before children. Some children have no slant in either their manuscript or cursive writing. Other children slant their letters slightly to the right. Left-handed children may slant their letters to the left. As long as the slant is *consistent* it should be acceptable—because it is legible.

There are two types of **spacing** that affect legibility: between letters and between words. A small, consistent amount of space should be left between letters even in cursive writing, in which the letters are joined with a sweep stroke representing the space. A slightly larger, but again consistent, space should be left between words. The key point is *consistency*. If a child uses inconsistent spacing between letters and words, the writing becomes more difficult to read and possibly illegible.

Distinction refers to the fact that certain letters in the English alphabet look alike. For example, in cursive writing, an *i* can be mistaken for an *e* if the writer omits the dot above. Similarly the letters *o*, *a*, and *u*, if not written carefully, can be confused. Clearly, letter distinction is as much an issue of spelling as it is of handwriting, for the two are related. Illegible handwriting looks like sloppy spelling, which only confuses and annoys a reader. Once the teacher identifies for the child which letters need to be written with more care, the student accomplishes the rest through practice in real writing activities. Having students write *aaaaaaooooouuuuu* dozens of times is not the solution.

FIGURE 9.3   *D'Nealian handwriting model.*

Source: D'Nealian® Handwriting Model from *D'Nealian® Handwriting Book 2* by Donald Neal Thurber. Copyright © 1999 by Addison-Wesley Educational Publishers, Inc. Reprinted by permission of Pearson Education, Inc.

Figure 9.4 illustrates the characteristics of legibility. Once you can read a child's handwriting, you can get on with the real teaching of writing: as a process in which students create stories, poems, reports, and so on.

Handwriting is a psychomotor skill, requiring cognitive abilities that are developed over time through practice. The kind of practice a child engages in determines the effectiveness of a handwriting program. This means that handwriting activities should be enjoyable as well as meaningful. They should provide the child with practice in the necessary letter, word, and sentence constructions. All of this means real writing activities such as pen pal letters, short stories, and poems. Thus, handwriting skills are developed not in isolated lessons, but through extensive use of the process approach to writing.

READINESS SKILLS FOR HANDWRITING

Young children need some direct instruction in the formulation of letters. However, not all kindergarten or first-grade children are ready for formal handwriting lessons. According to Lamme (1979), a number of prerequisites

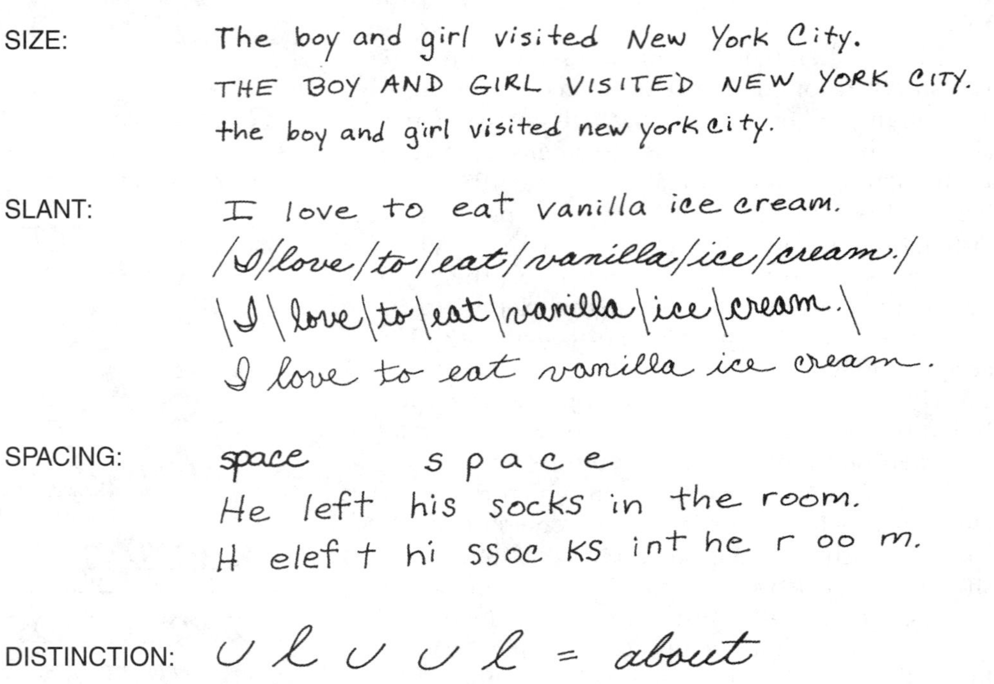

FIGURE 9.4

Characteristics of legibility.

SIZE:
The boy and girl visited New York City.
THE BOY AND GIRL VISITED NEW YORK CITY.
the boy and girl visited new york city.

SLANT:
I love to eat vanilla ice cream.
/I/love/to/eat/vanilla/ice/cream./
\I\love\to\eat\vanilla\ice\cream.\
I love to eat vanilla ice cream.

SPACING:
space   s p a c e
He left his socks in the room.
H elef t hi ssoc ks int he r oo m.

DISTINCTION: ∪ℓ∪∪ℓ = about

should be met before direct instruction begins. These prerequisites are also referred to as the *readiness* skills of handwriting.

Small-Muscle Development

To hold a pencil properly requires development of the small muscles in the hand, fingers, and wrist. Very young children who have difficulty holding their pencils steady may need more practice with manipulative tasks such as assembling jigsaw puzzles and attaching snap beads. Molding with clay and papier-maché also helps develop small-muscle strength. Small-muscle coordination is enhanced by such activities as zipping, buttoning, screwing caps on jars, and tying knots. Art activities such as painting, coloring, and drawing are also good readiness predictors, as is the ability to cut with small scissors.

Eye–Hand Coordination

Writing requires coordination between what the brain thinks, what the eye sees, and what the small muscles of the hand want to do. Manipulative play activities, such as block constructions, typing, sewing, weaving, and hammering nails into wood, all develop the eye–hand coordination necessary for fluency in writing. The ease (or difficulty) with which young children handle paper-and-pencil activities, such as dot-to-dot constructions and mazes, is also a good indicator of readiness for formal handwriting instruction.

Ability to Hold a Writing Tool

Normal-size pencils are difficult for young children to hold and manipulate easily. To prepare students for the writing task, provide them with a variety of utensils, such as bottles, strainers, various-size containers, sticks, toy shovels, and spades, to hold and manipulate. Simple gardening activities and cooking activities also give children practice in holding and manipulating various-size objects. When students wish to write, suggest that they begin with thick magic markers that require less pressure than crayons to produce a clear image on paper. Later, encourage them to use a variety of writing tools, such as felt-tip markers, thick pencils, crayons, and chalk, until they feel comfortable in their ability to hold and manipulate a normal-size pencil.

Letter and Word Perception

In addition to psychomotor skill, handwriting requires visual perception. That is, children need to recognize and note the differences among similar-looking letters and words. In the past, teachers believed that drilling children on the alphabet was the way to achieve this. Today educators recognize that writing readiness parallels reading readiness. By reading aloud to children, allowing them to examine books, and immersing them in a print-rich environment, adults encourage children to naturally acquire a visual knowledge of certain letters and words. These experiences become the building blocks for beginning writing.

DIRECT INSTRUCTION IN HANDWRITING

Although the debate between the relative benefits of direct versus indirect skills instruction continues, in the area of handwriting the experts are in agreement: Some direct instruction in the early grades on letter formation, size, slant, and proper spacing between letters and words is needed (Hodges, 1991a). In addition, children need to be given a specific purpose for why they are writing, help in controlling the pen and pencil to produce legible writing, and of course constant encouragement of their writing efforts.

Finally, a teacher's positive attitude is the key to ensuring positive attitudes toward handwriting in children. Consequently, handwriting exercises should never be used as punishment.

Perhaps the best form of direct instruction that teachers can give their students is modeling of good handwriting practices (Temple et al., 1988). Modeling the strokes of the letters at the chalkboard or on an overhead projector is one way to instruct young children in handwriting. This can be further expanded by using the **VAK** (visual–auditory–kinesthetic) **technique:**

Visual. Let the children see you constructing letters and words on the chalkboard, at an overhead projector, or seated side by side with an individual student. To construct letters and words themselves, children must be able to visualize the strokes involved; to do this, they must see you demonstrating these strokes. To further assist this visual learning, have the letters of the alphabet displayed in the classroom at a child's eye level.

Auditory. Many children are auditory learners. This means that they learn best by hearing the instructions for letter formation. Even predominantly visual learners, however, benefit from auditory reinforcement as part of handwriting instruction. Describe the strokes as you demonstrate them visually. For example, say, "To make the capital B, I first put my pencil at the top of the line and slide it straight down to the bottom line. Next I make two humps. . . ." You can also verbalize about particular features of certain letters; for example, "Notice, children, that the tail of the g goes below the line."

Kinesthetic. The term *kinesthetic* refers to learning that is enhanced through physical movement of the body. Grace Fernald popularized this technique in 1943 as an approach to teaching remedial reading. She believed that

I must write,

I must write at all costs.

For writing is more

than living, it is being

conscious of living.

ANN MORROW
LINDBERGH

children would learn to read words and remember them better if they wrote them. She advocated tracing and copying words as a learning reinforcement. Today kinesthetic activities that reinforce handwriting instruction include writing letters in sand, salt, and shaving cream and shaping letters with clay and yarn.

WHAT SHOULD BE TAUGHT IN HANDWRITING?

Knowing *how* to teach something is only part of the process; your next decision is *what* to teach. This is as true of handwriting instruction as it is of any other content area. Should you introduce one letter at a time until all 26 letters of the alphabet have been studied? And if so, in what order should they be introduced? Or can a few letters be introduced in a single lesson?

One of the primary considerations of any writing program is the element of time: How teachers and pupils use their time in class is crucial. The less time spent on formal, direct instruction in handwriting, the more time is available for real writing activities. Teaching a few letters in a single lesson saves time. One way to do this is to introduce letters based on the similarity of strokes involved in the production of those letters. Figure 9.5 suggests a possible sequence for introducing letters based on the strokes involved.

FIGURE 9.5

Possible groupings of letter strokes.

MANUSCRIPT

Lowercase

Counterclockwise circles: a, c, e, o

Counterclockwise circles, then straight lines: d, g, q

Straight lines: i, j, (k), l, t

Straight lines, then clockwise circles: b, p

Canes or humps: h, m, n, r, (f)

Diagonal lines: (k), v, w, x, y, z

Miscellaneous: (f), k, u, s

Uppercase

Straight lines: E, F, H, I, L, T

Circles: C, G, O, Q

Curved lines: B, D, J, P, R, S, U

Diagonal lines: A, K, M, N, V, W, X, Y, Z

CURSIVE

Lowercase—Beginning Strokes

Undercurve: b, e, f, h, i, j, k, l, p, r, s, t, u, w

Downcurve: a, c, d, g, o, q

Overcurve: m, n, v, x, y, z

Lowercase—Ending Strokes

Undercurve: a, c, d, e, f, h, i, k, l, m, n, p, q, r, s, t, u, x

Overcurve: g, j, y, z

Check-stroke: b, o, v, w

Lowercase—Size or Height

Minimum: a, c, e, g, i, j, m, n, o, q, r, s, u, v, w, x, y, z

Intermediate (or three-quarters): d, p, t

Full upper loop: b, f, h, k, l

Descending: f, g, j, p, q, y, z

Uppercase

Cane-stem: H, K, M, N, Z, U, V, W, X, Y, Z

Backward or direct oval: a, C, D, E, O

Forward or indirect oval: B, P, R

Double loop: G, L

Boats: I, G, O, S, T

Descending: J, Y, Z

Ideally, direct instruction in handwriting should be taught as mini-lessons. In using mini-lessons, the teacher might talk about a few letters, model them on the board, and then allow the students to practice the letter strokes using copying or various kinesthetic activities, but this entire process should only take a short while. Bing (1988) has recommended that no more than 15 minutes per day be spent on handwriting in isolation; the remainder of the period should be spent on real writing activities. For students who need additional practice in making their letters, kinesthetic activities should be set up at learning centers, where students can work at their own pace throughout the day practicing the particular skills they need. Additional practice in handwriting skills can be incorporated into functional activities in the classroom. Figure 9.6 suggests some activities for both primary and intermediate students who need additional practice in handwriting.

SOME ISSUES IN HANDWRITING INSTRUCTION

The major focus of Chapters 8 and 9 is on authentic writing activities done through a series of drafts, revisions, and edits. However, there are some specific issues surrounding the teaching of handwriting that teachers should be aware of. This section addresses some of these issues briefly with the caveat that teachers should not get sidetracked by the controversies.

Tracing vs. Copying

Grace Fernald (1943) popularized the use of tracing over letters in writing to reinforce early reading instruction, a kinesthetic activity still used today. In **tracing** young children write over pre-drawn lines or dots that form letters. This is a widely advocated early activity in most handwriting programs. However, some researchers have argued that **copying,** an activity that has students reproducing letters on a blank page while looking at a letter model in a book or on the blackboard, is a more valuable use of student time (Berninger et al., 1997; Koenke, 1996). Teachers are divided on this issue. Our position is that both trac-

---

FIGURE 9.6

Functional handwriting activities.

PRIMARY GRADES	INTERMEDIATE GRADES
• Label lockers, chairs, tables, closets, centers, and so on.	• Write labels, stories, poems, letters, plays, book reports, reports for social studies, invitations, letters of thanks, announcements, articles for school newspaper, and so on.
• Make nameplates for books.	
• Label paintings and other art projects.	
• Sign dittoed letters sent home to caregivers.	• Keep lists or records, diaries, and journals.
• Sign own milk receipts.	
• Write names to check attendance, lunch count, and so on.	• Take notes in class; make outlines.
• Write stories, poems, and simple plays.	• Keep attendance reports and weather reports.
• Write simple invitations and thank-you cards.	• Make plans for classroom activities.
• Copy and write letters to caregivers about school events.	

ing and copying can be used as part of teacher-led mini-lessons as long as students are then allowed to practice their handwriting in authentic ways such as creating posters and book jackets, and composing stories and poems.

Reversals in Writing and Reading

Many teachers and even more caregivers are overly concerned by the reversals that students make in their writing and in their reading. Reading or writing *was* for *saw* or *b* for *d* is an example of a reversal. The thing to remember is that reversals occur commonly among young children in the beginning stages of reading and writing (Wilde, 1997). Feder and Weber (1986) found that most reversal problems disappear as children grow older and mature. Therefore, reversals should not be seen as a major problem, let alone lead to teachers labeling students as dyslexic!

Instead, you should help children to recognize how these similar letters and words are shaped. Show them the direction of the strokes. Then let the students write without calling attention to the problem. Often by focusing a child's attention on a minor reversal problem, teachers blow the problem totally out of proportion. Soon the fear of making errors keeps the child from putting pencil to paper.

Left-Handed Writers

Left-handed students make up about 10 percent of most classrooms. Some educators suggest that lefties need special handwriting instruction, apart from the rest of the class (Howell, 1978). Others advocate that left-handed students should slant their paper in the opposite direction of right-handed students and crook their hand in a special way (Harrison, 1981). Although these are potentially helpful hints, they also call attention to the left-handed child, singling him or her out, which may actually exacerbate the problem (Bloodsworth, 1993; Graham, 1992).

We suggest a simple solution. Most teachers (and students) are right-handed; therefore, instructional examples are presented from the right-handed point of view. Because the English writing system goes from left to write, right-handed children can rest their hand on the paper and slide it along as they write. Not so for the left-handed child: Because the pencil moves ahead of the hand, the hand is dragged across the paper, thus smearing the writing. With a little personal attention, left-handed children can be taught to raise their wrist slightly so as not to drag their hand across the paper. Using this method, they will soon be able to write as legibly as their right-handed peers.

Cursive Writing

Today most children are taught to write by learning the manuscript stroke first. In kindergarten and first grade, children are introduced to the printed manuscript style. Around grade 3, they are asked to stop using manuscript writing and learn the cursive or continuous joined stroke (Hodges, 1991a). Children are expected to use cursive writing in the remainder of the elementary grades and into middle school. This creates a number of problems, particularly among boys.

A summary of handwriting research studies found that males of all ages dislike handwriting more than females and believe they have very poor handwriting. For some boys, the inability to master cursive writing creates negative attitudes toward school in general and results in poor achievement. Furthermore, research showed that embarrassment over poor handwriting led to low self-esteem and disruptive behavior among boys in the classroom (Graham 1992, 1999).

Sometime around junior high school, formal handwriting instruction drops out of the curriculum entirely, and students are told they can write in either manuscript or cursive, or even type (word process) their papers. The only requirement teachers have is that the students' work be **legible.** One result is that many students—particularly boys—revert back to manuscript writing because it is generally more legible. This raises the question, Why teach cursive writing at all?

Surveys have shown that many students, teachers, and caregivers believe that cursive writing is important because it is faster than manuscript strokes, it is necessary for a legal signature, and it is a more adult or grown-up style of writing (Moore, 1986). The research, however, does not support those beliefs (Peck, Askov, & Fairchild, 1980). First, cursive is no faster than manuscript; if speed were the issue, teachers should be teaching students shorthand. Second, a printed signature is just as legal as a cursive one. Third, many adults use manuscript as their primary writing style; others even mix the two strokes together. Finally, applications and forms usually must be printed or typed. In fact, there is no real reason for teaching cursive writing other than that it allows students to read other people's cursive writing and is a tradition in most schools. Teachers should thus minimize the amount of time spent on cursive writing: Introduce it in grade 3 as a special unit and then drop formal instruction, except for those students who require individual help. Teachers can much better use that valuable time for real reading and real writing in the classroom.

Figure 9.7 shows the handwriting differences in one second-grade class. Some of these students require much teacher assistance, some require a little, and others write nearly as well as many adults.

A number of people have suggested alternatives to spending a large amount of time instructing young children first in manuscript and then in cursive. One

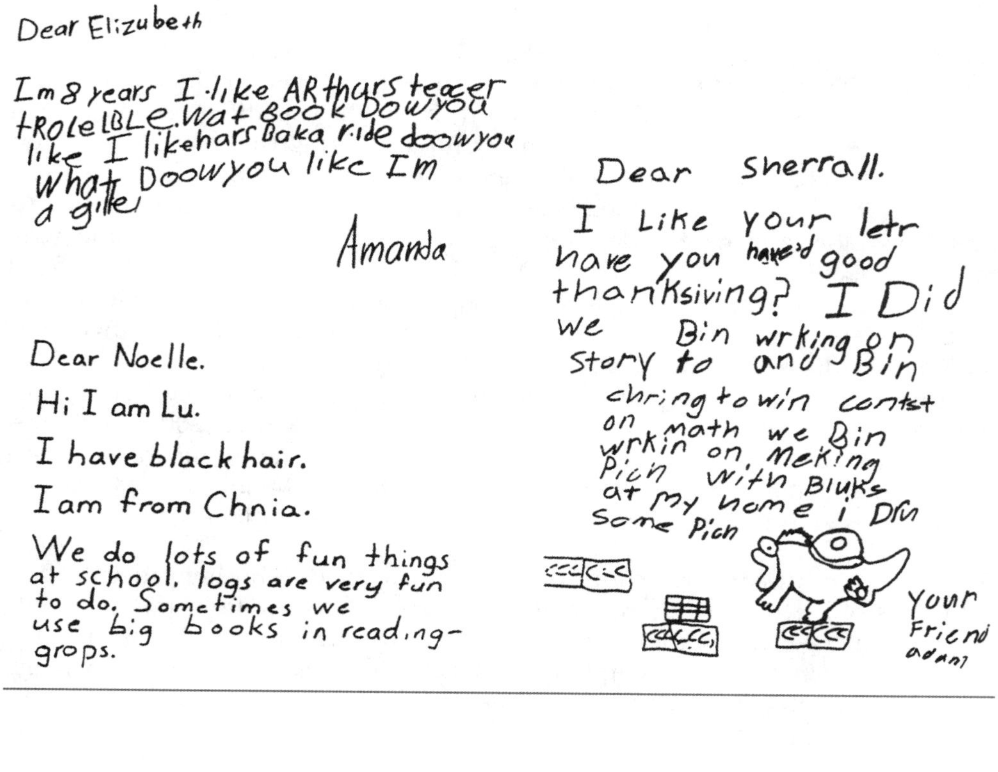

In and beyond the classroom

Visit a preschool or primary-grade classroom. Collect and copy samples of children's handwriting. Identify the four main characteristics in determining legibility in handwriting. Also note how handwriting is taught in the classroom. Is it done in isolation from real writing or integrated into the writing process? At what point does formal handwriting instruction stop in this school? As a follow-up, try teaching a calligraphy lesson to a small group of children.

FIGURE 9.7

Second-grade handwriting samples.

approach combines handwriting instruction and drawing to teach calligraphy (D'Angelo, 1982). **Calligraphy** is the art of beautiful or elegant writing. Children are taught to use a variety of instruments to create a flowery script for decorating and illustrating. In the course of this fun activity, many youngsters find that their normal handwriting improves and becomes more legible. A unit in calligraphy might be just what is needed for students in the upper elementary grades who are frustrated by the rote drill and practice of too much handwriting instruction.

Spelling: Demons and Drills

Children learn to spell in many ways: by taking pretests and retests; doing practice drills such as writing words 10 times each; playing spelling games such as Scrabble; using the dictionary to look up hard-to-remember spellings and meanings; and doing morphology lessons such as synonyms, antonyms, homonyms, and word origins. However, the strongest evidence suggests that young children learn to spell best when they are encouraged to read and write extensively (Buchanan, 1992; Gentry, 1987, 2000; Wilde, 1997). It is primarily through wide reading that children are visually exposed to words that they retrieve from memory and reproduce in their writing activities. The real test of a good speller is how well he or she spells words in essays, compositions, research reports, books reports, and poetry, not how well he or she does on spelling bees or spelling tests (Graham, Harris, & Chorzempa, 2002).

Under certain circumstances, practice exercises or spelling drills can be helpful, such as in learning those hard-to-remember words known as **demons** (e.g., occurrence, committee) or in memorizing the spellings of words borrowed from foreign languages such as *bouquet* from French, *spaghetti* from Italian, or *pretzel* from German. However, spelling drills and rule memorization exercises (e.g., *i* before *e* except after *c*) are often overused to the extent that teachers find there is little time left in the class period for authentic writing activities.

DEVELOPMENTAL STAGES OF SPELLING

Since the 1970s, researchers have learned a great deal about how the spelling of young children develops (Hodges, 1991b). Careful observation of young children engaged in writing has revealed that children learn to spell gradually, in stages, as they try to discover the rules that govern the English spelling system through trial and error (Buchanan, 1982; Chomsky, 1971). During this process of discovery, children construct for themselves **experimental** or **temporary spellings** (Gentry, 1984; Read, 1986), which enable them to proceed with their writing. As they grow older and have wider contact with words through reading and writing, their spelling improves. This process, described widely in the literature, is known as the developmental stages of spelling (Beers & Beers, 1981; Graham et al., 2002; Templeton & Morris, 1999). In recent years, different authors have chosen to use different terms for these developmental stages. For example, Bear, Invernizzi, Templeton, and Johnston (2000) refer to them as emergent, beginning, transitional, intermediate, and advanced, while Leu and Kinzer (2003) prefer precommunicative, semi-phonetic, phonetic, transitional, and standard. We have chosen to use prephonetic, phonetic, orthographic, and morphemic/syntactic because these terms remain familiar and consistent in the literature.

Prephonetic stage. Preschoolers and primary-grade children invent their own ways of spelling words and writing sentences, ranging from random scribbles to actual letters in the *prephonetic stage*. Early invented spellings lack any relationship between sounds and symbols. Later invented spellings approximate consonant sounds but omit vowels entirely.

Phonetic stage. During grades 1 through 3, youngsters become more aware of the sound–symbol relationship of written language in the *phonetic stage.* In their writing, both consonant and vowel sounds are represented by actual letters of the alphabet. Vowels, however, are often still misused or omitted. The concept of words (as represented by larger spaces between groups of letters) develops. Though invented spellings are still used, the child's writing now more closely approximates standard English spelling.

Orthographic stage. The *orthographic stage* overlaps with the phonetic stage, depending on the individual child's development. In this stage, there is a more consistent use of vowels within syllables and an expansion of the correct use of consonants. The child's awareness of spelling patterns grows enormously. Problem areas still persist with double consonants, the *schwa* sound, contractions, and silent letters.

Morphemic/syntactic stage. If children have been exposed to print and encouraged to write using their invented spellings during the primary grades, sometime around the upper elementary grades they should begin to acquire an understanding that the English spelling system is influenced by word meanings and word order as well as pronunciation; this is the *morphemic/syntactic stage.* Word meanings influence knowledge of spelling because similar words are spelled alike. For example, *family, familiar,* and *familiarity* and *manage, manager,* and *managerial* are related morphologically, and this relationship is reflected in their spelling. Similarly, understanding word parts and word order (*syntax*) helps students correctly spell words with prefixes and suffixes (*jumped, running,* and *remaking*). Knowledge of word meanings and grammar, along with phonetic understanding, thus helps the child become a more accurate speller. Figure 9.8 gives examples of writings from each of the developmental stages of spelling.

The Classroom Vignette that follows discusses how a little girl named Brittany progressed through the various stages of spelling.

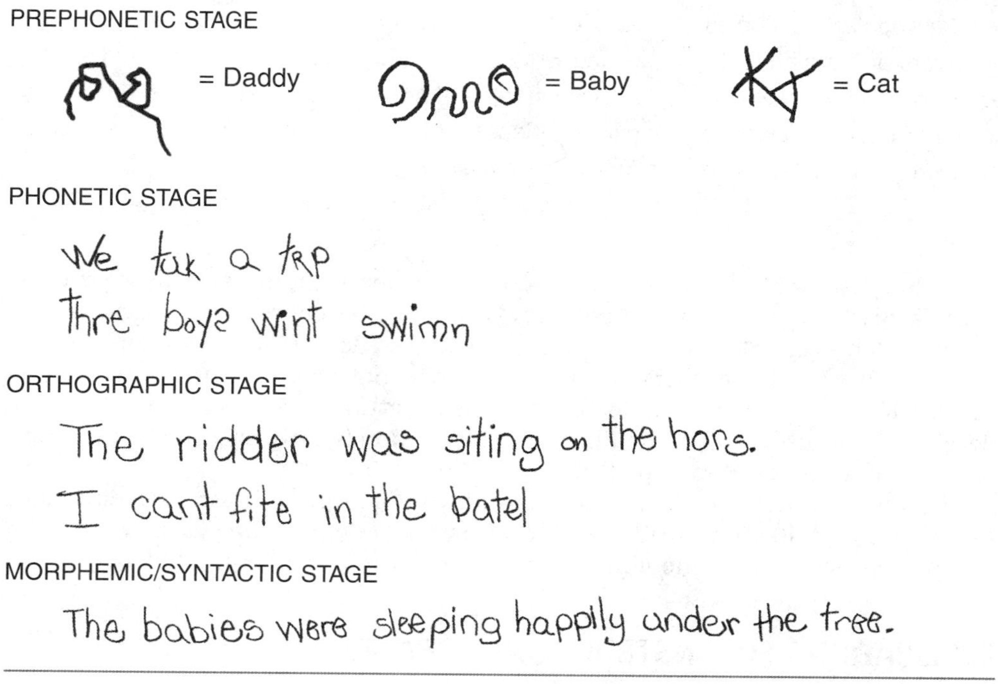

PREPHONETIC STAGE

= Daddy   = Baby   = Cat

FIGURE **9.8**

Examples of the developmental stages of spelling.

PHONETIC STAGE

We tuk a trp
Thre boys wint swimn

ORTHOGRAPHIC STAGE

The ridder was siting on the hors.
I cant fite in the batel

MORPHEMIC/SYNTACTIC STAGE

The babies were sleeping happily under the tree.

Source: Adapted from C. Beers and J. Beers (1981), "Three Assumptions About Learning to Spell"; C. Read (1986), *Children's Creative Spelling;* J. R. Gentry (1987), *Spel . . . Is a Four-Letter Word.*

VIGNETTE *in the classroom*

Brittany has written over 40 books. She is 7 years old. Her mother, a teacher, has been saving all of her drawings, scribbles, and writings since she was an infant. A look at Brittany's progress as a writer exemplifies the developmental stages of spelling. The only difference is that Brittany has moved at a much faster pace than most children, perhaps because she was encouraged by her parents.

Brittany's first interest in print occurred when she was only a few months old. Books were among her favorite playthings, often winning out over toys. Her parents read to her every day. Two of her favorite books were *Animal Sounds* and *My Goodnight Book.* She also enjoyed sitting with books, examining them carefully page by page.

When Brittany was 2 years, 3 months old, her mother purchased some magnetic letters to place on the refrigerator. One day, without being instructed, Brittany took the letters down and began matching them to letters in her picture books. Within a few months, she was playing games with her parents, such as "What does _____ begin with?" Her parents continued reading to her, and her personal library continued to grow.

At age 3 1/2, amid her drawings and scribbles, Brittany began printing the letters of the alphabet. Her parents bought her an assortment of crayons, pens, markers, and paper as her interest in writing grew. During this time, her spoken vocabulary also expanded enormously. By age 4, she was continually asking about the words on signs, billboards, cards, junk mail, and the Sunday comic strips. One month after her fifth birthday, she wrote her first word using experimental spelling: BLREA (ballerina).

Early in her writing, Brittany began labeling her drawings and creating little books she could read to her parents. Figure 9.9 shows Brittany's early experimental spellings and some of her drawings; the typed comments are her mother's.

When Brittany entered kindergarten, the teacher used various learning centers in the room. One of these was a writing center, where the children were encouraged to write using their experimental spellings. Crayons, pens, pencils, and colored paper were available to the children. Brittany often chose to work at the writing center. Figure 9.10 is one of her earliest examples from school using experimental spellings.

One day during Brittany's kindergarten class, an Oklahoma storyteller, Lynn Moroney, told the Native American story of "Baby Rattlesnake." Brittany was so inspired that she sat down the next day and wrote her own story. As with her previous books, Brittany drew the pictures first and then added the text. The story is fragmented; this is common among young writers, who often assume that their audience knows what they know and thus fail to fill in the missing pieces. Figure 9.11 shows Brittany's version of "Baby Rattlesnake."

What can we as teachers and researchers learn from Brittany's writing? Clearly, Brittany is learning to spell and write in the course of her experimenting with language. Her growth is evident. The so-called errors that she makes are part of that growth. Teachers and caregivers will not be concerned by children's invented spelling when they recognize it as a natural part of children's writing development, just as overgeneralizations in children's early speech are a natural part of language development (Weaver, 1996).

If you would like to learn more about young children's early development in writing and spelling, read Lester Laminack's *Learning with Zachary* (1991), a year-by-year account of one child's growth in written language.

IMPLICATIONS FOR INSTRUCTIONAL PRACTICES

The significance of the research surrounding the developmental stages of spelling cannot be overstated. Regardless of the terms used to describe the stages

FIGURE **9.9**

She drew and labeled a whole zoo of animals, each on its own sheet of paper:

HBPADAS (hippopotamus)

ALAFAT (elephant)

KAML (camel)

BALEGOT (billy goat)

LAPRD (leopard)

TAIGR (tiger)

BDRFLAIE (butterfly)

SWAND (swan)

BAR (bear)

ALGADR (alligator)

GRAF (giraffe)

Excerpt from BRITTANYS ANLBOK.

I showed her how the papers could be arranged and stapled together with a front and back cover. A title was added, <u>BRITTANYS ANLBOK</u> (animal book), and so began Brittany's career as an author.

Source: Reprinted with permission of Diane and Brittany Moser.

FIGURE **9.10**

HADDDLKAT	hey diddle diddle cat	TSESSHTAN	to see such fun
ATHAFATL	and the fiddle	THDASHRAN	the dish ran
KOGAMTOVR	cow jumped over	AWAWAAIS	away with a sp
THEMON	the moon	ON	oon
THADOGLAF	the dog laughed		

Brittany's experimental spellings.

of spelling, the constructivist principle remains the same: As children mature over time and engage in experiences with print, their spelling becomes less invented and more conventional. Consequently, teachers use classroom strategies and activities to encourage this development. The following sections describe some of those activities.

Word box. Divide sheets of paper into the number of letters that are in a word. For example in the word *hot*, there are three letters so the sheets of paper would be divided into three boxes. Provide children with counters (small, colored plastic discs) to represent the sounds of the letters. When the children recognize the /h/ sound, they place a counter in the first box. When they recognize the /o/ sound, they place a counter in the middle box. Finally, when they recognize the /t/ sound, they place a counter in the third box. Later actual cut-out or magnetic letters can be used to replace the counter in order for the children to see the exact spelling of the word (Joseph 1998/1999). See Figure 9.12 for an example of a word box.

Labeling. First encourage children to write their names on strips of paper and then attach the strips to their desks. Next, label other places and objects in the classroom such as the "closet," "water fountain," "supply cabinet," "reading center," "pencil jar," and "finger paint area."

Brittany's THE STORE ABAT
BABY RATLSNAK.

Baby rattlesnakes went outside and found a present. What was in it?

He went back in the rocks where his mother was.

Then he went to find the chief's daughter.

She was very beautiful.

Then he went in the rocks and hid.

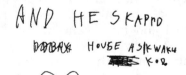

And scampered out to go ch-ch-ch-ch.

Then she stepped on his tail.

And he scampered home as quickly [as he] could.

Source: Reprinted with permission of Diane and Brittany Moser.

Language experience charts. Let groups of children compose language experience charts using their own invented spelling. Then using the LEA method have them dictate the story again to you, the teacher, and write their story in standard spelling. Encourage the children to study and compare the two versions.

Pocket charts. Provide children with word cards and have them arrange the cards into phrases and sentences in a pocket chart. Later, encourage children to

FIGURE **9.12**

Word box.

H	O	T

write words on blank cards and form their own sentences and then place them in the pocket chart for other students to read.

Word wall phonics. Let children write their favorite words on the word wall, sounding them out as best they can. Later, in discussing the children's words, show them the standard spelling for the word without discouraging their creative attempts.

Sustained silent reading and sustained silent writing. Devote some time each day to sustained silent reading and sustained silent writing. This is a time when children explore and discover about literacy without corrections or instructions by the teacher. Later, phonics, spelling, and reading comprehension lessons can build on these early explorations.

Personal dictionaries. As children read and write they encounter and want to use new words. Have each child keep a notebook called "My Personal Dictionary." In it are words that the child wants to learn. The teacher or a caregiver can help the child with the spelling of the word initially; afterward, the child uses the book like a real dictionary to help with his or her spelling.

Strategy charts. Along with the class create a chart of simple suggestions to help children in their writing when they get stuck on a word. Here are some possible suggestions: (1) sound it out as best you can, (2) think of another word you know that sounds like the new word, (3) write the first sound and leave dashes for the rest of the word, (4) ask a friend for help if the teacher is busy.

Acronym charts. An acronym is a word made from the first letters of a series of words. For example, in reading, DEAR time stands for Drop Everything and Read; the popular TV show M.A.S.H. stands for Mobile Army Surgical Hospital. Ask your students to collect acronyms they find in newspapers and magazines and place them on a chart for others to read and use.

Compound word charts. A compound word is one word formed from two or more smaller words, such as *baseball, classroom, birthday.* Encourage students to look through favorite newspapers, magazines, or books for compound words to bring to class and write on the chart to share with others.

Crossword puzzles. Teach children how to create simple crossword puzzles. Then using the spelling words for that week, have children design their own crossword puzzles for their friends to solve. Upper grades can include additional words not on the weekly spelling list to make the puzzles more challenging.

TEACHING SPELLING THROUGH ANALOGIES

In Chapter 6 you learned that young children must first develop phonemic awareness (the ability to hear the separate sounds within words) before they can be taught phonics (the ability to match letters to sounds). Phonemic awareness and phonics abilities also apply to children's spelling. One way teachers can help their students acquire this ability is to teach them about onset rimes and analogies (Smith, 2002).

Onset-rime theory (not to be confused with rhyme) breaks the English syllable down into an **onset** (any consonant that comes before a vowel) and the **rime,** the vowel plus any consonants after it (McKay, 1972). For example, in the word *best*, the /b/ is the onset and /est/ is the rime. Rimes are also referred to as phonograms or word families. The rime /est/ can be further broken down into its three separate phonemes /e/ /s/ /t/. Teachers often stress the importance of recognizing phonemes for reading and writing; however, awareness of phonemes in young children develops slowly. Research has found that children can actually analyze onsets and rimes (syllables) more easily than phonemes (Goswami & Bryant, 1990). This suggests an alternative instructional procedure for teaching children to read and spell: Teach children to use onsets and rimes as a way of learning letter–sound correspondences (Moustafa, 1997).

Using onset-rime theory along with rhymes and analogies, Smith (2002) has developed a unique approach for teaching young children to read (a receptive skill) that can also be applied to teaching them to spell (the productive corollary of reading). Here are the teaching steps:

1. Teach children about words that rhyme (e.g., hat, cat, bat).
2. Read a book aloud to the class with a rhyming pattern (e.g., *Sheep in a Jeep* by Nancy Shaw [1986]; see Appendix A for more books).
3. Teach some target words and their spelling patterns (rimes) as a way to learn new words by analogy (e.g., target word = jeep; rime = eep; analogies = keep, sheep, steep, weep).
4. Together with the children rewrite a predictable book using a structured frame as follows (adapted from Walker, 2000):
    * Frame (taken from the *Beast Feast* by Douglas Florian [1994]):

      The bat is batty as can be

      It sleeps all day in cave or tree,

      And when the sun sets in the sky

      It rises from its rest to fly.
    * Teacher/student-made frame:

      The _____ is _____ as can be.

      It _____ all day in _____ or _____.

      And when the sun sets in the sky,

      It rises from its rest to fly.

INDUCTIVE APPROACH

In the **middle and upper elementary grades** spelling typically becomes a more formalized part of the curriculum. Practice exercises are completed, tests are given on spelling lists from workbooks, and grades are awarded. An additional exercise for upper elementary children is to present spelling patterns **inductively,** as a problem-solving task. Children are presented with groups of related words and told to study them. In small cooperative groups, the students discuss the similarities and differences among the words. The groups also hypothesize about the possible spelling principles exemplified by each word. To test their hypotheses, they need to come up with other example words. In the Classroom Vignette that follows, the teacher is using the inductive approach to teach a mini-lesson on spelling.

Figure 9.13 lists a number of high-utility spelling rules. These are traditional spelling rules taken from commercial texts. They may be taught as mini-lessons using the inductive approach rather than merely memorized by students. Remember, however, that too much time spent on any form of rule learning is time taken away from writing activities, in which the real learning takes place.

Figure 9.14 has some general information concerning letter sounds that may be helpful to you as a teacher. They may also be taught as mini-lessons to your students.

Figure 9.15 has some generalizations relating to syllabication. Again, these are given to you, the teacher, in order for you to help your students.

DIRECTED SPELLING–THINKING ACTIVITY

Zutell (1996) explains the directed spelling–thinking activity (DS-TA), which is patterned after the directed reading–thinking activity. The DS-TA is based on the belief that students need to be actively engaged when attempting to solve spelling problems. The DS-TA, which is done as a class activity, uses the following eight steps:

1. The teacher gives a brief spelling test on words that have a related pattern (e.g., trade, brave, came, bake, which follow the VCe pattern).
2. Students offer predictions of the spelling of the new word.
3. Students give reasons for their spelling.

VIGNETTE *in the classroom*

In the past, Mrs. Jones has taught spelling to her fourth-grade students by presenting a list of words to them on Monday, having them do drill exercises during the rest of the week, and taking a retest on Friday for a spelling grade. This was mostly a copying routine with little thought or discussion. Now she uses a mini-lesson to encourage students to think and talk about their spelling words.

She begins by saying, "I've written two groups of words on the board. Study them carefully. What do you notice about them that makes them alike? In your cooperative groups, talk about these similarities. Can you discover any rules about the sound of /f/ that will help you as spellers?" The teacher reveals the following two groups of words for the children to examine:

1. fun   foolish   free
   stiff   bluff   puff

2. rough   cough   tough
   photo   graph   telephone

The children study the words for a few minutes, then get into their groups. They talk and write and point to the words. Mrs. Jones walks about the room encouraging the discussion. Eventually some of the groups come up with the following rules:

RULE 1: The sound of /f/ at the beginning of words is often spelled *f,* while at the end of words it is spelled *ff.*

RULE 2: The sound of /f/ can also be represented by *gh* in the final position of words and *ph* in any position within a word.

"That's great," says Mrs. Jones. "Now let's test our rules by finding other words with the sound of /f/."

FIGURE 9.13

High-utility spelling rules.

RULE 1
When two vowels appear together in the same syllable, a single long vowel sound is often heard.
> *Examples:* seizure, siege, loathsome, feasible, drainage, sleazy, leasable

RULE 2
The long vowel sound /e/ at the end of a word is often spelled -*y.*
> *Examples:* dropsy, gypsy, stability, hegemony

RULE 3
In spelling the vowel digraphs *ie* and *ei,* the *i* usually comes before the *e* and you hear the long /e/ sound. However, after the letter *c* or when the digraph sounds like long /a/, then the *e* comes before the *i.*
> *Examples:* believe, receive, neighbor, viewpoint, conceive, reign

Exceptions: weird, seize, science

RULE 4
When adding a suffix that begins with a vowel (-*ing*) to words ending in silent *e* (*bake, dance*), remember to drop the silent *e.* When adding a suffix beginning with a consonant, keep the *e.*
> *Examples:* dance/dancing, value/valuable, fame/famous, elope/elopement, imagine/imaginary

RULE 5
Monosyllabic words ending in a single consonant preceded by a single vowel double the consonant when adding a suffix that begins with a vowel.
> *Examples:* drum/drumming, stop/stopping, big/biggest, snub/snubbed, skim/skimmed

RULE 6
Words ending in -*y* and preceded by a consonant change the *y* to *i* before adding the suffix unless the suffix begins with *i.*
> *Examples:* carry/carrier, carrying; study/studious, studying; fly/flies, flying; luxury/luxurious

RULE 7
Add the suffix -*able* to root words that end in silent *e* or to root words that take the prefix *un*- (*available, advisable*). Keep the *e* with soft *c* and *g* words (*manageable, serviceable*). Add the suffix -*ible* to root words that combine with -*ion* (*suggest/suggestion/suggestible*) and to words that without the suffix ending are not meaningful (*incredible, visible*).
> *Examples:* admirable, confirmable, indescribable, immiscrible, accessible, perfectible

Source: Reprinted with permission of David Yellin and the *Daily Oklahoman.*

FIGURE 9.14

Generalizations about letter sounds.

1. The *k* is silent when followed by *n* (know, knob).
2. When *gh* follows the vowel *i,* the *gh* is silent (might).
3. At the beginning of a word, the *w* is silent when followed by *r* (write).
4. At the end of words, the *b* is silent when it follows *m* (comb).
5. *C* sounds like /k/ when followed by *a, o,* or *u* (cat, cot, cut).
6. *C* sounds like /s/ when followed by *i, e,* or *y* (city, center, Cinderella).
7. *G* sound like /g/ when followed by *o, a,* and *u* (gone, game, gun).
8. *Ph* is /f/ (telephone, photograph).
9. *Q* is always followed by *u* and sounds like /kw/ (quick).

Source: Adapted from *Phonics in Proper Perspective* (8th ed.) by Arthur W. Heilman, © 1989. Reprinted by permission of Prentice Hall, Inc., Upper Saddle River, NJ.

1. Syllables are determined by vowel sounds (road = 2 vowels, but only 1 vowel sound; com-plete = 3 vowels, but only 2 vowel sounds; si-tu-a-tion = 5 vowels, but 4 vowel sounds).

2. When there are double consonants in the middle of words, the word is syllabicated between the two consonants (hid-den, gen-tle).

3. When there is one consonant in the middle of a word, the consonant goes with the second syllable if the preceding vowel is long (stu-dent, be-gan). If the preceding vowel is short, the consonant goes with the first syllable (mod-el, pan-el).

4. Digraphs and consonant blends remain together (teach-er, fa-ther).

5. The affixes form separate syllables (re-peat-ing, grate-ful).

FIGURE 9.15

Generalizations relating to syllabication.

Source: Adapted from *Phonics in Proper Perspective* (8th ed.) by Arthur W. Heilman, © 1989. Reprinted by permission of Prentice Hall, Inc., Upper Saddle River, NJ.

4. Students formulate evidence of the pattern.
5. Students brainstorm for other words that follow that pattern and add them to the list.
6. Students continue to add words that they find to the list.
7. The teacher reminds them of the pattern when they are struggling with a word that follows the pattern.
8. Students keep a personalized list of words they know, sorting them according to the patterns.

With the DS-TA, students are discovering the pattern while working with the words instead of the teacher giving the spelling pattern and then the list of words for the students to memorize.

ADDING CREATIVITY TO THE SPELLING PROGRAM

Another helpful resource for teachers wishing to add more creativity to their spelling program is Diane Snowball and Faye Bolton's book, *Spelling K–8: Planning and Teaching* (1999). Snowball and Bolton correctly tie spelling instruction to general reading and writing instruction and to lessons in content-area subjects such as science and social studies; that is, spelling should be taught as part of all subject areas that involve writing. For example, the social studies teacher might begin a lesson on the American Colonial and Revolutionary period by writing on the board and reviewing the spelling and meaning of such words as *revolutionary, colonist, Battles of Lexington and Concord, Puritan settlers,* and *founding fathers.* Snowball and Bolton also suggest using high-frequency spelling word lists such as those by Edward Dolch and Edward Fry. Another excellent source of words on all sorts of topics is *The Reading Teacher's Book of Lists* (1993) by Fry, Kress, and Fountoukidis. Finally, they recommend having students investigate specific spelling patterns based on their own writing needs such as long vowel words, words ending in a suffix, contractions, and words with an apostrophe to show plurality and possession.

SPELLING AND THE PROOFREADING PROCESS

There is also developmental research to support the direct instruction in proofreading skills for elementary and especially middle school, junior high, and high school writers (Riefer, 1987). **Proofreading** is the ability to read a text to discover errors that need to be corrected. In spelling, this means carefully reading what you have written to recognize words that just do not look or sound right. According to Wilde (1996), proofreading for spelling errors is best taught in conjunction with the editing stage of a process approach to writing. For young children, however, proofreading is a difficult skill that will take years to develop, but it is important enough for teachers to introduce it early. The simplest instructional approach is to ask children to reread what they have written, looking for any possible spelling errors (Riefer, 1987). Working with a friend could make this a fun activity, but it is the individual habit of proofreading that the teacher is really trying to develop.

USING THE DICTIONARY

Elementary-grade students need to be taught to use the dictionary. Adults know that when they do not know how to spell a word, they can either ask a friend or look it up in the dictionary. Even young children can use simple speller dictionaries. Elementary-grade students can be taught to use junior dictionaries or an electronic dictionary, which has made dictionary use fun for students. Large, unabridged dictionaries should be avoided because they contain too much extraneous material and too many abbreviations for children to use easily. And ease of use is the key to dictionary lessons. If a child cannot be taught how to find a word in the dictionary quickly, he or she will grow up with a distaste for using dictionaries.

Dictionary lessons should begin by reviewing the alphabet. When children know the position of each letter within the alphabet, they can turn to that portion of the dictionary on the first try. Start by dividing the dictionary into three parts: beginning (*a* through *h*), middle (*i* through *p*), and end (*q* through *z*). Ask students, "Which part of the dictionary would you turn to first to find the word *clarion*?" Next, teach children about the guide words found at the upper corners of the page. All the words on the page fall between these two guide words. This activity takes considerable practice, but it is well worth it if it helps students to feel comfortable using the dictionary as a tool in writing.

As students become comfortable using the dictionary as a learning resource on a regular basis, they note that spelling and vocabulary knowledge go hand in hand. Knowing how to spell a word without knowing what it means makes no sense. Such words will never be used in a child's writing.

Regular use of the dictionary as part of a writing program leads children to learn about prefixes, suffixes, and root words. Dictionaries also contain synonyms and antonyms of words. This knowledge, in turn, helps children to enlarge their vocabularies and improve their spelling. Further use of the dictionary leads older students into lessons about the origins of words. For example, most students are surprised to learn that many common English words were actually derived from foreign place-names: *baloney* comes from the Italian city of *Bologna*; *frankfurter* comes from *Frankfurt*, Germany; the *sardine* gets its name from the island of *Sardinia*; *tangerine* refers to the port city of *Tangiers*, Morocco; and even the common word *turkey* refers to the African guinea fowl that was imported to Europe from *Turkish* ports.

SPELLING LOGS

A companion to using the dictionary is teaching children to keep their own spelling logs (Zutell, 1996). **Spelling logs** are records of an individual child's misspellings on tests and from written work; next to the misspelling is the correct spelling. Students who study the spelling words they want to use in their writing are more likely to learn these words. Spelling tests can even be generated from the words that children want to learn rather than from artificial lists in spelling books. By individualizing spelling in this manner, teachers can help each student to grow as a speller and a writer without comparison to other children and without overemphasizing spelling list memorization.

WORD STUDY GROUPS

Bear et al. (2000) suggest using word study groups within a class. First the teacher must do a spelling assessment of each child in the class. Once the assessment is complete, the teacher can then group the children homogeneously based on their spelling level and needs. For example, children who can spell one-syllable words correctly and are now ready to tackle two-syllable words form one group. Children who confuse long and short vowel sounds in words become a second group. A third group could focus on double consonants and silent letters in words. Once the groups are formed, the teacher provides each group with an appropriate list of words to study and discuss. Through discussion and inductive reasoning, the groups should construct their own strategies for remembering the spellings of certain kinds of words.

SORTING ACTIVITIES

Sorting activities refer to gamelike experiences that require children, working in small groups and later individually, to arrange or categorize objects, pictures, and words based on their common elements or patterns. For example, children can be given pictures of fruits, animals, and houses and asked to group them in three piles and explain why they grouped as they did. Later, children are given a letter sound (e.g., /m/) and a group of pictures, some of which begin with the /m/ sound (e.g., milk, money, mop). Next children are given word cards to sort by various categories (e.g., similar initial consonants, long vowel *a*, short vowel *e*, words with prefixes, words with suffixes). In all cases, the purpose is to get children talking about the words and categories and to recognize common patterns in words. In this way they become conscious of the various elements in words and can generalize about their spelling knowledge to new words.

GENERIC GAME BOARDS

Teachers can construct generic game boards that can be used for a variety of reading and writing activities. Get a large piece of oak tag. Draw boxes or circles in a winding, twisting pattern. At the bottom label the first box/circle "Start" and the last box/circle "Finish." Next create cards with words or rimes or rhymes. Different cards can be created for different purposes using the same generic game board. You can also create cards such as "Free Ride: Advance two spaces," or "Sorry, go back one space." Finally, write some simple directions for playing the game such as: "Choose a card and read the word. Now think of another word with the same onset or rime and write it down on a piece of paper. If you get it correctly advance your token one space." A variation could involve having each player roll a die and if the player reads and writes correctly he or she gets to advance the number of spaces indicated by the die.

For additional games and activities for reading, writing, spelling, and vocabulary development see the following sources: *Words Their Way: Word Study for Phonics, Vocabulary, and Spelling Instruction* (2000) by Bear et al.; *Ways of Writing with Young Kids* (2003) by Edwards, Maloy, and Verock-O'Loughlin; *Voices on Word Matters: Learning About Phonics and Spelling in the Literacy Classroom* (1999) edited by Fountas and Pinnell.

THREE PLANS FOR TEACHING SPELLING ON A WEEKLY BASIS

Again, it is the contention of the authors that spelling improves best when done through real writing activities as part of a process writing approach. However, many schools require their teachers to teach spelling in a systematic fashion on a weekly basis (Chandler & the Mapleton Teachers research group, 2000). Such schools also require that teachers test spelling weekly. For that reason, this chapter includes three fairly traditional plans for teaching and testing spelling on a weekly basis. Spelling authority Edmund Henderson (1985) has noted that formal weekly spelling plans are often tied to basal reader programs. The plans presented here are suitable for third grade and above, provided the students are well into the orthographic stage of spelling proficiency. You will want to modify them to suit your needs. Note that the key to preparing students for weekly tests in each plan is the variety of practice activities.

Plan 1: Pretest/Study/Retest

This first plan is a widely used approach to teaching spelling in the elementary grades (DiStefano & Haggerty, 1985). A *pretest* is given at the beginning of the week, usually on Monday. The teacher says each word, uses it in a sentence, and then repeats it. Students copy the words in their notebooks. Students may exchange papers or grade their own papers as the teacher calls off or writes the correct spellings on the board. Sometimes the teacher discusses specific features of words—silent letters, unusual endings—that might confuse children.

The *study* portion of this plan occurs during the middle days of the week. Each day, for about 15 minutes, students do various practice activities: writing the words five times each, writing the words in sentences, alphabetizing the words, looking up the words in the dictionary, completing a spelling crossword puzzle, and using the words in a short story or poem. The best activities, of course, are those that relate spelling and meaning in some purposeful content.

At the end of the week, a *retest* is given. Every elementary school child knows that this is the test that counts: It is for a grade that goes in the teacher's gradebook. Usually the teacher collects these papers, grades the tests, and returns them on Monday. Some teachers have experimented with allowing students to grade their own papers immediately after each test. Other teachers have formed student committees to help grade the tests. This practice is appropriate if you want your students to assume some of the responsibility for learning.

There are a number of major drawbacks to this first plan, despite its widespread popularity. First, too much time is often spent testing. Second, teachers assume that the students copy the words correctly at the beginning of the week and study this corrected list for the test on Friday. Don't assume! Teachers should move about the room and check that the children have indeed corrected their spelling errors accurately. Finally, many teachers tend to rely on a single practice activity, usually, "Write your words 10 times each." By varying the practice activities, teachers provide more quality study time for their students (Bear et al., 2000; Brown & Ellis, 1994; Moats, 1995).

Plan 2: Study/Test/Study

Plan 2 differs from plan 1 in organization. On Monday and Tuesday, children *study* their spelling words, which have been introduced with a ditto handout or on the chalkboard. Practice activities again should be varied and interesting: Have students use a spelling game such as *hangman* or *concentration* as well as student-created *word-search puzzles*. Have each student pair off with a buddy and devise study activities. Again, these activities should not exceed 15 minutes per day for optimum effect.

During the middle of the week—on Wednesday or Thursday—the *test* is given. This is a single test given for a grade. The teacher may grade the papers, or again students may be involved in their own grading. A criterion is set before the test, say, 90 percent. Any child who meets the criterion is excused from further study activities later in the week. This is the incentive to do well on the midweek test.

During the final day or two of the week, only those students who failed to meet the criterion *study* the spelling words. Again, it is important that the study activities be interesting ones (e.g., generic board games) that the students do not resent. If the group of children engaged in this study period is small, this is also an opportunity for the teacher to work with individual students who may need more help.

This plan has a few obvious advantages. Since there is only one test during the week, there is more time to study and more time to do practice exercises relevant to writing. The students who do well on the test can use the additional time at the end of the week for free reading and creative writing activities of their own choosing. A potential disadvantage is the negative attitudes of those students who do not do well on the midweek test and must do additional practice. But a teacher's positive attitude and rapport with students can offset this. If students perceive the additional practice exercises as punishment, something is wrong and needs to be changed (Bear et al., 2000; Brown & Ellis, 1994; Moats, 1995).

> ### *Beyond the classroom*
>
> Examine a spelling book used in the elementary grades. Evaluate it critically in terms of the practice exercises and time spent testing versus time spent studying the words. Also note the similarity between spelling book exercises and phonics lessons. Spelling and phonics are closely related. What opportunities are there for creative writing activities and varied testing approaches?

Plan 3: Self-Study

In the third approach, a test is given at the beginning of the week in the traditional manner (say the word, use it in a sentence, repeat the word). Immediately following the test, the children *self-correct* their papers. The teacher calls off the correct spelling *letter by letter* and displays the words visually on an overhead projector. This is to ensure that the students copy the correct spellings of the words they must study. As with the first plan, the teacher should still walk about the room double-checking that some students have not made careless errors in their correcting. Such errors are more common than most teachers realize.

The remainder of the week is spent doing a variety of practice exercises. Students can complete cloze exercises using their spelling words, break into teams for spelling games, engage in classwide spelling bees, play spelling tic-tac-toe with a partner, and so on. Using spelling words in their written stories, reports, letters, and poems is still, of course, the best practice children can get.

Retesting for a grade does not take place at the end of the week. Instead, the following week, a new list of words is given and the practice exercises continue. About once every three or four weeks, there is one fairly long spelling test that all students must take. Such an approach has the advantage of minimizing the amount of time spent testing for grades and maximizing the study time. However, the one monthly test is a real challenge to most students' ability to study a large number of words. For this reason, this plan is recommended only for older students who are well into the morphemic/syntactic stage of spelling.

School systems that use weekly approaches to spelling instruction generally utilize spelling books or spelling lists to determine the words to be tested. Selecting children's spelling words from prescribed lists leaves much to be desired. If you must teach, test, and grade spelling on a weekly basis, some of the words should come from the children. Examining their writing will clue you in to the kinds of words that each student misspells most frequently; often children in the same grade have similar spelling-word difficulties. Another source of spelling words should be the other content-area subjects that the children are studying. Words taken from social studies, science, math, art, music, and so on help to reinforce learning in those content areas as well as to give students practice in spelling. Such functional spelling lists are superior to textbook lists, which often have little relevance to the spelling needs of a particular class and even less relevance to the individual student.

In summary, spelling is currently taught in most classrooms on a weekly basis. Formal spelling lists are still used in most schools, but teachers supplement these commercial lists with functional lists that students generate from their own writing or from other content areas such as science, social studies, and math. See Figure 9.16 for some spelling tips to use when teaching spelling. Teachers of young children must continually remind themselves of the developmental nature of spelling and be more accepting of children's invented spelling efforts. At all grade levels, spelling is best taught within the stages of the writing process where learning to spell and edit is a natural part of learning to write (Gentry, 1987; Hodges, 1991a; Wilde, 1996).

FIGURE 9.16

Spelling tips.

1. *Use daily free reading.* By encouraging regular reading, students are exposed to thousands of new words. Over time and with use in writing, these words become part of a student's spelling vocabulary.

2. *Use daily free writing.* Spelling develops through practice: the more practice, the better. Incorporating some free writing time each day reinforces weekly spelling skills lessons.

3. *Keep a personal speller dictionary.* From both their reading and writing, students are encouraged to write down the words they wish to learn in their own speller dictionary. The correct spelling of the word, along with a simple definition, is all that is needed.

4. *Use the dictionary.* Students need to be introduced to the dictionary as a resource tool early in their school years. Begin with simple primary-grade dictionaries and work up to the large unabridged dictionaries. Finding the spelling of an unfamiliar word requires predicting the spelling of the word and then using a trial-and-error approach. Dictionary usage is a habit that takes time to develop.

5. *Maintain a class word wall.* Many teachers cover one section of a class wall with butcher-block paper. Children are encouraged to write their favorite words or new and unusual words they have encountered in their reading on the wall. Throughout the year, the word wall list grows and remains for an easy reference.

6. *Use spelling games.* Practicing spelling is drudgery for some students. Effective teachers try to make this practice more fun by incorporating various spelling games such as word searches, crossword puzzles, spelling jumbles, spelling relay, or big words (see the activities at the end of the chapter).

Grammar: Meaning, Not Memorizing

In 1963, Braddock, Lloyd-Jones, and Schoer completed a report titled *Research in Written Composition.* After reviewing the research studies dealing with all aspects of written composition, they concluded that "the teaching of formal grammar has a negligible or, because it usually displaces some instruction and practice in actual composition, even a harmful effect on the improvement of writing" (pp. 37–38). In 1986, George Hillocks of the University of Chicago edited a similar review of the research on written composition and concluded—as had Braddock, Lloyd-Jones, and Schoer—that grammar instruction, particularly in the elementary grades, does more harm than good to the development of children's writing: "None of the studies reviewed for the present report provides any support for teaching grammar as a means of improving composition skills. If schools insist upon teaching the identification of parts of speech, the parsing or diagramming of sentences, or other concepts of traditional grammar (as many still do) they cannot defend it as a means of improving the quality of writing" (p. 138). Research done by Constance Weaver (1996) reaffirms the case against teaching formal grammar lessons in the elementary and middle school grades. Instead, she finds that the best way for students to apply and learn grammatical concepts is through revising and editing their own writing. Other well-known English educators have recommended that at the very least formal grammar instruction be postponed until the high school years (Haley-James, 1981; Moffett & Wagner, 1983; Noguchi, 1991).

Despite this research evidence against teaching grammar in the elementary and middle grades, the practice continues. Like cursive writing, it is a tradition that persists in the face of research to the contrary. For this reason, the following section addresses the whys, whats, and hows of grammar. But as long as grammar instruction is part of the elementary curriculum, teachers need to understand and teach it in proper perspective to the rest of the language arts curriculum.

Most of us speak or write conventionally without being able to specify the rules.

FRANK SMITH

GRAMMAR AND USAGE

Some textbooks use the terms *grammar* and *usage* interchangeably. This is more confusing than helpful, since there are distinctions between the two. **Grammar** provides the terminology and rules to describe the structure of a language, including words and sentences. How words are structured is known as **morphology,** while the way in which those words are arranged in sentences is called **syntax.** Grammar study includes both the word and sentence levels of language. Although people can be said to speak with proper grammar, more often *grammar* refers to written forms of language that do or do not conform to certain rules (Weaver, 1996).

Usage, on the other hand, is more concerned with the particular choice of words or language structures (phrases and sentences) used by an individual, generally at the oral level. Whereas grammar is structured by written rules, usage is influenced more by regional and situational factors. Some people talk about usage in terms of acceptable and unacceptable language, depending on the social situation. For example, the use of slang expressions (ain't) and double negatives (they don't know nothing) may be appropriate among teenagers on the basketball court but inappropriate during a job interview. Some grammarians even equate usage with language etiquette (Newkirk, 1978). Earlier chapters described the issues surrounding standard and nonstandard speech; these are usage issues.

Clearly, then, part of the confusion for teachers and students alike is that most people have different conceptions of what grammar really is or is not (Weaver, 1996). Some would say that grammar equals the parts of speech, the

The difference between the right word and the almost right word is the difference between lightning and the lightning bug.

MARK TWAIN

major word elements of language. Others would argue that grammar is the larger units, the syntactic structures of our language, such as phrases, clauses, and different types of sentences. Your grandparents probably think of grammar in terms of correctness: using correct subject–verb agreement or avoiding double negatives. Your English composition professor probably discussed grammar under sentence style and effective syntactic options. Finally, there still persists among some the belief that studying formal grammar enhances mental discipline and social graces (Woods, 1986).

WHICH GRAMMAR SHOULD BE TAUGHT?

Added to the controversy over whether or not to even teach grammar in the elementary grades is the issue of which grammar to teach because there are many grammars. This section discusses four of those grammars (traditional, structural, transformational-generative, and Shurley English) and identifies the strengths and weaknesses of each.

Traditional Grammar

Traditional grammar is the oldest of the grammars and also the one most frequently taught in schools in the United States. It is sometimes referred to as *prescriptive* grammar because it prescribes or lists the rules that govern language. Based on a model from Latin, which at one time was considered the perfect language, **traditional grammar** focuses on rules and definitions. The most well known of these rules and definitions concern the eight parts of speech. Indeed, the parts of speech are taught throughout the elementary grades and well into high school. This fact alone should give you some idea of the complexity associated with traditional grammar and why many educators believe it is inappropriate to teach traditional grammar at the elementary level. The following summary (Pixton, 1978) only scratches the surface of the information related to the parts of speech:

1. *Nouns.* Names of persons, places, and things. Nouns also serve as subjects and as direct and indirect objects. They may be common (*university*) or proper (*Oklahoma State University*) and show possession (*the boy's coat*). Nouns are also either singular (*fox*) or plural (*foxes*).

2. *Pronouns.* A subclass of nouns that take the place of nouns. There are personal pronouns (*I, you, he, she, it, we, they*) and relative pronouns (*who, whose, whom, which, that*).

3. *Verbs.* Words that express action or state of being. Verbs can change form to indicate time, which is called *tense*: present (*takes*), past (*took*), future (*will take*). Linking verbs are forms of the verb *to be* (*is, are, was, were*).

4. *Adjectives.* Words that modify or describe nouns (the *large, green* tree). Adjectives can indicate comparisons, such as *pretty/prettier/prettiest*. The articles *a, an,* and *the* are sometimes considered a special group of adjectives that mark the presence of a noun.

5. *Adverbs.* Words that modify or describe verbs (Robin *frequently* jogs to work), adjectives (The horse was *extremely* hungry), or other adverbs (Betty left the room *very* angrily).

6. *Prepositions.* Words that show a relationship between the subject noun of a sentence and another noun or pronoun (called its *object*). Common prepositions are *under, over, on, into, by, for,* and *from.*

7. *Conjunctions.* Words that join or connect words, phrases, or clauses. Coordinating conjunctions, such as *and, but, for,* and *or,* join equal elements in a sentence (Amy *and* Harry are doctors).

8. *Interjections.* Exclamatory words that express strong feeling or emotion without serving any other grammatical function in a sentence (*Oh!*).

Parsing. The main teaching approach to traditional grammar uses textbook and workbook exercises in which children underline and label the parts of speech, illustrated as follows, which is known as *parsing:*

> N.   V.   Prep.   Adj.   N.
> The boy walked near the big house.

Although parsing is now considered an old-fashioned activity, this is the way standardized tests still evaluate knowledge of grammar. Another traditional grammar exercise involves labeling the four kinds of sentences: declarative (statement), interrogative (question), imperative (command), and exclamatory (exclamation). Additional activities include identifying phrases and clauses and classifying sentences as simple, compound, complex, and so on. Such exercises are essentially passive; they give students practice in underlining and labeling but do not require them to create sentences or paragraphs.

Diagramming. Another activity associated with traditional grammar is diagramming sentences. Although also considered old-fashioned, it is still found in many textbooks and required in many upper elementary and middle school curriculums. A *sentence diagram* is a visual picture that identifies the parts of speech in a sentence. Instead of defining the parts of speech verbally, the sentence diagram does it visually. Figure 9.17 shows some sample sentence diagrams. Note that these are among the easiest of sentences to diagram. Diagramming compound and complex sentences is considerably more difficult.

Sentence diagramming is difficult to teach and frustrating for many children to learn. Most teachers resort to direct lecture presentations, and children memorize the sample patterns to pass the test. Above all, these activities take up large amounts of class time that could be much better spent in other ways. At

FIGURE 9.17

Sample sentence diagrams.

1. Horses gallop.

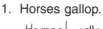

2. Lizards eat flies and earthworms.

3. Lena was named to the team.

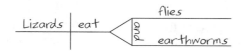

4. The girl plays piano beautifully.

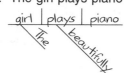

one time, it was believed that diagramming sentences made students better writers; this was the justification for spending so much time on this activity. Research has shown this not to be the case (Braddock et al., 1963; Hillocks, 1986). The best that can be said about sentence diagramming instruction is that it makes children better sentence diagrammers. It does not make them better writers or speakers of the language.

Structural Grammar

A second type of grammar, structural grammar, is also referred to as *descriptive grammar* because it describes language rather than prescribing rules. One of the first linguists to utilize the structural/descriptive approach was Edward Sapir in *Language: An Introduction to Speech* (1921). As the title of his book suggests, **structural grammar** views speech or oral language as being of primary importance. Other important structuralists and their works include Leonard Bloomfield, *Language* (1933), and Charles Fries, *The Structure of Language* (1952).

Although some grammarians view structural grammar as a big improvement over traditional grammar, the two are similar in many ways. Structuralists still talk about the eight basic parts of speech, although they use different terminology. For example, *function* words are those parts of speech that serve only grammatical functions, such as articles and some conjunctions. Prepositions are referred to as *phrase markers.* As with traditional grammar, structural grammar is quite complex and difficult for elementary-grade children to learn beyond superficial memorization of technical terms and examples.

Another aspect of structural grammar that is readily visible in many elementary classrooms is the use of sentence patterns to teach English. According to the structuralists, by learning the common patterns of English, students can find similar patterns in books to enhance their reading and utilize these patterns to improve their writing. Indeed, increasing complexity of language structures is one mark of a maturing writer. Figure 9.18 shows examples of seven common sentence patterns. Each pattern is represented by a pair of sentences: one constructed by a child, the other taken from a children's literature book. Such grammar activities do seem to be an improvement over rule memorization or sentence diagramming.

In one sense, then, the structural approach to grammar—particularly its emphasis on sentence patterns—is an improvement over traditional grammar. It takes the focus away from individual words in isolation and places it on large, meaningful units. By discussing sentence patterns and having children actively create sentences, teachers are giving their students a more realistic taste of what writing is about and how grammar relates to writing.

Beyond the classroom

Examine some children's literature books and select passages from these books that represent the various patterns of the English language. Then use these to teach children to write their own sentences by modeling the pattern. Avoid using technical terminology. Notice how even young children can model various sentence patterns correctly without knowledge of grammatical terms.

Transformational-Generative Grammar

Transformational-generative grammar is the brainchild of the linguist Noam Chomsky; it is described in his seminal work *Syntactic Structures* (1957). **Transformational-generative (TG) grammar** is concerned with analyzing and describing the intuitive rules of language that all native speakers possess. It is this unconscious knowledge that allows children to produce grammatically correct sentences and recognize ungrammatical ones even at a very young age. More recently, Stephen Krashen (1991) showed that the same intuitive principles are at work in the acquisition of a second language.

FIGURE **9.18**

Pattern 1   Noun phrase–Verb

 Examples: The two girls danced.
              The train started.

(Bishop, B. [1979]. *Ralph Rides Away.* New York: Doubleday and Co)

Pattern 2   Noun phrase–Being verb–Prepositional phrase

 Examples: The ladies were at the circus.
              The elephant was on the phone.

(Reinach, J. [1980]. *Wait! Wait! Wait!* New York: Weekly Reader Books/Euphrosyne)

Pattern 3   Noun phrase–Action verb–Prepositional phrase

 Examples: The boy leaped into the pool.
              Everyone stared at the goggles.

(Keats, E. [1969]. *Goggles.* Toronto: Macmillan)

Pattern 4   Noun phrase–Helping verb with action verb–Prepositional phrase

 Examples: The children were reading from their book.
              I am calling on the telephone.

(Hoban, R. [1964]. *A Baby Sister for Francis.* New York: Harper & Row)

Pattern 5   Noun phrase–Verb-Object

 Examples: The boy kissed the girl.
              Paul licked the spoon.

(Brown, M. [1963]. *Ice Cream for Breakfast.* New York: Franklin Watts)

Pattern 6   Compound elements

 Examples: The boy walked to the store and bought some candy.
              She cooked the meals and washed the dishes and made
              the beds.

(Galdone, P. [1973]. *The Little Red Hen.* New York: Seabury Press)

Pattern 7   Complex sentences and compound-complex sentences

 Examples: She walked into the kitchen where she found a large carriage
              with a large doll lying in it.
              The town where he lives is secluded, and I would like to live
              there, too.

(Schlein, M. [1975]. *The Girl That Would Rather Climb Trees.* New York: Harcourt Brace Jovanovich)

Common sentence patterns and their children's literature sources.

There are a number of differences between TG grammar and the other grammars. First, TG grammar focuses on studying the meaning of real sentences rather than on memorizing rules, labeling isolated words, or imitating sentence patterns. Second, TG grammar identifies two distinct levels of language: surface structure and deep structure. *Surface structure* refers to the physical features of language: sounds and symbols. This is what the previous grammars focused on exclusively. TG grammar stresses the second and more important level, *deep structure,* which describes the underlying meaning of a sentence.

A few examples clarify the significant differences between the two levels. In the sentences *Felipe hit the ball* and *The ball was hit by Felipe,* the same deep structure meaning is evident even though the surface structures of the sentences appear different. TG grammarians would say these sentences are basically the same; traditional grammarians would say they are different because the subjects of the sentences are different. Conversely, in the sentences *Juan is easy to please* and *Juan is eager to please*, the surface structures are almost exactly the same, but the deep structure meanings are very different. In reading and writing, underlying meaning—not surface appearance—is most important. By focusing on sentence meaning rather than appearance, TG grammarians anticipated holistic language arts practices that begin with meaningful texts to discover underlying principles.

The next group of sentence examples should clarify these differences even more. Examine the following sentences carefully:

Flying planes can be dangerous.

Visiting professors can be a bore.

If you were told to diagram or label these sentences, you might have difficulty because each of these single sentences contains at least two distinct meanings. Can you identify them? These are called *ambiguous* sentences. To fully understand which meaning was intended by the author, the reader needs to know the context in which they appeared.

Although by focusing on meaningful whole sentences TG grammar leads in the right direction, it is still too complex and esoteric for elementary school children. Chomsky described a grammar to be discussed and debated at the graduate level in college, not taught in the fourth grade. However, other linguists and educators have devised activities based upon the concepts of TG grammar that can be appropriately taught in the upper elementary and middle schools. These include sentence transformations, word substitutions, sentence expansions, and sentence combining, which are discussed later in the chapter.

Shurley English

In some parts of the United States, particularly in the Midwest and Southwest, the Shurley English Method has become popular with school districts. Developed by Brenda Shurley, a schoolteacher from Cabot, AR, this program emphasizes the teaching of the eight parts of speech through labeling pre-designed sentences (Shurley & Wetsell, 1989, 1997). The program is designed for students in grades 1 through 8 and utilizes drill and repetition through group chants, jingles, and question-and-answer flows. Shurley believes that students must first develop an understanding of how the eight parts of speech work together in a sentence before training in actual writing can begin.

The heart of the Shurley English Method* is oral memorization of the eight parts of speech. To do this, children are taught jingles that identify the grammatical function of each word in a sentence. Here, for example, is the jingle for nouns:

This little noun
Floating all around
Names a person, place, or thing.
With a nick, nack, paddy wack
These are English rules.
Isn't language fun and cool.

---

* Jingle and question and answer examples from Shurley, B., & Wetsell, R. K. (1997). *The Shurley Method: English Made Easy.* Cabot, AR: Shurley Instructional Materials. Reprinted by permission of the author.

Another aspect of the Shurley English Method is the question-and-answer flow. This is a series of questions and answers with the entire class reciting as the teacher or a single student writes the appropriate labels on the chalkboard sentence. Here is one sentence example:

1. Entire class reads the sentence aloud: "The five pretty baby kittens jumped playfully today."

2. What jumped playfully today? kittens—subject noun (SN)

3. What is being said about kittens? kittens jumped—verb (V)

4. Jumped how? playfully—adverb (Adv)

5. Jumped when? today—adverb (Adv)

6. What kind of kittens? baby—(Adj)

7. What kind of kittens? pretty—(Adj)

8. How many kittens? five—(Adj)

9. The—article adjective (A)

10. SN V P check (subject noun–verb–pattern–one check)

11. Period—statement—Declarative Sentence (D)

12. Go back to the verb—divide the complete subject from the complete predicate (/).

The final completed sentence on the board would look like this:

$$\underset{\text{P 1}}{\underline{\text{SN V}}} \quad \begin{matrix} \text{A} & \text{Adj} & \text{Adj} & \text{Adj} & \text{SN} & \text{V} & \text{Adv} & \text{Adv} \\ \text{The} & \text{five} & \text{pretty} & \text{baby} & \text{kittens/jumped} & & \text{playfully} & \text{today.} & \text{D} \end{matrix}$$

From our previous discussion of traditional and structural grammars, you should recognize elements of both in Shurley English. For instance, the use of the labeled abbreviations for the various parts of speech is an example of parsing, a traditional grammar approach. In addition, five different sentence patterns are presented, beginning with pattern 1, a subject noun followed by a simple verb pattern, and progressing to a more complex sentence. This is taken from structural grammar. The use of whole-class chanting is also an example of more traditional forms of teaching.

OTHER WAYS TO TEACH GRAMMAR

Cloze technique. An alternative to emphasizing memorizing and diagramming is to teach the parts of speech using the cloze technique. Recall that the **cloze technique** was originally designed to assess reading comprehension by omitting every nth term from a passage and asking the student to provide the exact missing terms. Cloze has also proven to be a successful teaching technique (Marlow & Reese, 1992). For teaching the parts of speech, the teacher photocopies a passage from a basal reader or children's literature book and deletes the parts of speech she or he wishes to emphasize—verbs, for example. Students then have to provide the missing words or ones "close" enough in meaning to be acceptable. Using the cloze technique to teach grammar within the context of real sentences is a preferable activity to labeling and underlining. Figure 9.19 summarizes the steps of this technique. Figure 9.20 is a sample of a cloze test.

Proofreading. As part of the process-writing approach, children are taught to proofread and edit their own writing from rough copy to final copy (Tompkins, 2003). This activity also helps students to distinguish correct grammatical structures from nonsentences. In the process-writing approach, although teachers do not stress grammatical terminology, the students are actually dealing with and learning about the eight basic parts of speech. Correcting written work so that

FIGURE 9.19

FIGURE **9.19**

Steps of the cloze technique for teaching grammar.

Step 1   Present a sentence or paragraph with all the examples of a single part of speech omitted, such as verbs.

Step 2   Ask the students to brainstorm in small groups all the possible words that fit in the blanks.

Step 3   Ask students, "What do all these terms have in common?" Again the groups can discuss and brainstorm to come up with a generalization. This generalization may or may not fit the definition of a verb.

Step 4   Have the students generate their own sentences with verbs omitted and exchange these with friends.

the message comes across clearly to the reader involves a writer's intuitive understanding of and ability to use the rules of language to create meaningful sentences (Smith, 1986). Thus, process writing actually helps children acquire traditional grammar knowledge, albeit at the unconscious level.

Children's literature.   One of the best alternatives to teaching about grammar (parts of speech, figurative language, capitalization, and punctuation) is to let children see and analyze how real writers use the language. Thus, reading and discussing children's literature books is also a way to develop children's awareness of grammatical concepts (Tompkins, 2002). The following steps can be used in teaching grammar with children's books.

1. Identify the part of speech, or specific skill you want to teach.
2. Select a favorite children's book, one with which the children are already familiar.
3. Find a passage in the book that contains the element you want to teach.

FIGURE **9.20**

A sample cloze test.

Directions: Read the two paragraphs. Fill in the missing blanks with verbs to make the sentences correct.

When Wilma Rudolph _____ four years old, she _____ an attack of double pneumonia and scarlet fever. She was _____ crippled, her left leg paralyzed. The doctors _____ that only with special treatment could she _____ to _____ back the use of her leg.

Every week Wilma's mother _____ her on the long round trip between Clarksville, Tennessee, and the clinic in Nashville. The entire family _____ the proper way to _____ Wilma's leg. By the time she _____ eight years old, Wilma _____ able to walk again with the help of a specially built shoe.

Corrected Version

When Wilma Rudolph _was_ four years old, she _had_ an attack of double pneumonia and scarlet fever. She was _left_ crippled, her left leg paralyzed. The doctors _said_ that only with special treatment could she _hope_ to _get_ back the use of her leg.

Every week Wilma's mother _took_ her on the long round trip between Clarksville, Tennessee, and the clinic in Nashville. The entire family _learned_ the proper way to _massage_ Wilma's leg. By the time she _was_ eight years old, Wilma _was_ able to walk again with the help of a specially built shoe.

4. Make a PowerPoint slide or an overhead transparency of that passage and display it for the children to analyze and discuss.

Here are some examples. In Wilson Rawls's *Summer of the Monkeys* (1976), the narrator says that when he was born, "I was as pink as a sunburnt huckleberry, and as lively as a young squirrel in a corn crib" (p. 10). This passage provides a teacher with a great opportunity to discuss the use of similes and descriptive language using adjectives. The children can discuss what they enjoy about the passage and then try their hand at writing similar descriptive paragraphs. In *Holes* (1998), author Louis Sachar writes the following: "The next time the water truck came it was driven by Mr. Pendanski, who also brought sack lunches. Stanley sat with his back against a pile of dirt and ate. He had a baloney sandwich, potato chips, and a large chocolate chip cookie" (p. 35). For this passage ask the class to identify the different ways the author uses capital letters and commas. Then have them write short passages practicing this skill based on the model they have seen. A final example comes from the Newbery Award winner *A Year Down Under* (Peck, 2000). Study the different ways Peck uses verbs and the conjunction: "Grandma filled the door, and people looked up in alarm and surprise. She was famous for keeping herself to herself, but she was everywhere at once, if you asked me. We parted the party like the Red Sea, bearing in our pies" (p. 35).

Ruth Heller has also written concept books that focus on the parts of speech. A teacher can do many activities with one of these books. For example, after reading and discussing Heller's *Many Luscious Lollipops: A Book About Adjectives*, a teacher can write down on the chalkboard all the adjectives that the students remember from the book. Then he or she can have the students use those adjectives to describe items in the classroom. Using the same book, the teacher could go through the book again and write on Post-it notes different adjectives that the students can use to describe the delightful illustrations. For a third activity, the teacher could have the students make their own book of adjectives by drawing pictures and using adjectives to describe their illustrations.

Using another book, the teacher could have the students substitute their own words in sentences selected from the book read. The substituted words would be directed at specific parts of speech, such as adjectives or adverbs.

The books found in Figure 9.21 lend themselves to lively discussions about parts of speech that can later be incorporated into mini-lessons based on students' writing needs.

Approach writing like life, with a passion— be involved.

JANE YOLEN

Sentence transformations. According to TG grammar, the basis for all sentences is the **kernel sentence**: a simple, active, declarative sentence. Kernel sentences, in turn, can be changed or transformed into other surface structures. Native speakers of a language make these transformations unconsciously. However, by understanding how kernel sentences are transformed into more complex sentences, students can utilize this knowledge to improve their own writing. Study the following example of six transformations beginning from one kernel sentence: *The boy sells papers.*

1. *Negative.* The boy does not sell papers.
2. *Passive.* Papers are sold by the boy.
3. *Negative-passive.* Papers are not sold by the boy.
4. *Question.* Does the boy sell papers?
5. *Negative-question.* Doesn't the boy sell papers?
6. *Negative-passive-question.* Aren't the papers sold by the boy?

Try your own kernel sentence and make similar transformations. In working with young children, teach one transformation at a time when you feel the children are ready to handle that new structure.

A mini-lesson on the formation of questions might involve a teacher instructing the class as follows.

> I've noticed in your writing that some of you are beginning to use the question mark. Today I want to talk to you about how question sentences are written. On the chalkboard, I've written a sentence, *Anna plays jump rope after school.* Beneath it, I've changed this sentence into a question sentence, *Does Anna play jump rope after school?* Notice that to make a question I used the word *does*, changed *plays* to *play*, and ended the sentence with a question mark. Here is another way to write a question sentence: *Will Anna play jump rope after school?* Who can come to the board and write still another question sentence?

A few students volunteer and come up to write their questions. "That's good," concludes the teacher. "Now everyone continue working on whatever you were writing. I'll come around if you need help."

Notice how the mini-lesson takes the form of a brief lecture supplemented by a few examples. The teacher could also have assigned a page in a workbook or textbook for additional practice. Instead, he directs the students to spend the rest of their time writing on their own. As he assists children in the course of the week, some of the students experiment with writing questions.

Word substitutions. Even very young children can learn to create new sentences when given an existing sentence. To begin a mini-lesson on this topic, a teacher writes a sentence on the chalkboard with one word underlined: *Maria likes to play.* She then draws a line through the underlined word and above it substitutes another word—*jump, run,* or a similar verb. Then she asks, "Children, does this word still make sense in the sentence? How does it change the sentence?" After a brief discussion, she directs the students to work in small groups and create their own sentences by changing the underlined word. Next she underlines two words in the sentence: *Maria likes to play.* Again the children work in small groups creating new sentences such as *Betty likes to study* and *He likes to swim.*

Notice that in this mini-lesson the teacher uses a cooperative learning discovery approach. The children working in small groups help one another to discover new ways of changing sentences. Substitution exercises such as this one give students practice in revision at the word level; writers often go back to change words in sentences to convey just the right meaning.

Sentence expansions. Young children begin by writing simple sentences and generally work up to writing longer, more involved sentences. The following exercise gives students practice in expanding their sentence repertoire. This is another example of a practice exercise that develops students' ability to revise their writing.

A mini-lesson on sentence expansion might begin with the teacher showing the children some short, simple sentences on the board: *The boy runs. The puppy barked.* Next the teacher explains that one way to develop sentences is by adding adjectives, adverbs, articles, and so on to make them longer and more interesting: *The young boy runs to school. The happy puppy barked excitedly.*

The teacher writes another example on the board: *Trees sway.* This time she asks the students to work in small groups, adding a word (or words) to see how long they can make the sentence. After a few minutes, she asks one of the groups to come forward and write its expanded sentences on the board:

Trees sway.

Tall trees sway.

Tall trees sway lazily and softly.

Tall trees sway lazily and softly in the afternoon breeze.

Sentence combining. Sentence combining has a relatively long history (Christie, 1980; Cooper, 1973; Mellon, 1969; O'Hare, 1973; Strong, 1993). The purpose of sentence combining is to expand students' syntactic fluency in writing by getting them to create structures they might not ordinarily write. The principle behind this technique is similar to sentence expansion but requires a greater facility with written language structures. In doing sentence combining exercises, teachers need to remember that there is more than one correct way to combine sentences. The mini-lesson example uses a discovery-type format.

The teacher might start by writing two sentences on the board. Beneath them, he writes one more sentence that combines the information from the first two. Then he gives the rules for sentence combining as follows: (1) You may move words around and change punctuation, (2) you may also add or delete words, but (3) you must write only one sentence that still retains the meaning of the first two sentences. Following are some examples:

1. a. The wind was strong. The leaves fell to the ground.
   b. The leaves fell to the ground because the wind was strong.
2. a. Philip is my friend. Philip plays basketball. Philip likes to do chemistry experiments.
   b. My friend Philip plays basketball and likes to do chemistry experiments.

The largest body of research on writing and writing instruction concurs: Teaching grammar in isolation from authentic writing does not result in writing improvement (Amiran & Mann, 1982; Elley, Barham, & Wyllie, 1976; Hillocks & Smith, 1991; McQuade, 1980; Neill, 1982; Rosen, 1987; Weaver, 1996). As with any other teaching approach, teachers need to compare the amount of time spent in class to the benefits to students.

The grammar activities described in the previous sections appear to help students in some aspects of writing. However, they are still highly artificial, forcing students to work from someone else's examples. More simply put, letting students write their own sentences, paragraphs, and stories on topics they really care about is a much better reinforcement of the skills you are trying to teach. Letting students discuss their writing at length with fellow students and yourself is the best way to get them to revise and edit their own work. In the course of these genuine writing activities, grammatical growth and understanding take place naturally in an atmosphere that is positive and supportive.

The research arguments against the teaching of formal grammar in isolation from real reading and writing activities are formidable but complex. If you would like to read more about studies done on grammar methods and their effectiveness or lack thereof, we recommend Constance Weaver's book, *Teaching Grammar in Context* (1996), as a recent summary of the research in this area.

Punctuation and Capitalization: Two More Tools of Writing

The issues surrounding punctuation and capitalization are ones that are best dealt with in the middle steps of the process-writing approach under proofreading and editing (Tompkins, 2002). As discussed earlier, the following is a possible five-step approach for teachers to take in this area:

Teaching demands not just desirable personality attributes but specific skills. Skills are not ends in themselves, but they are necessary tools.

JACOB S. KOUNIN

1. In a mini-lesson, model for students how to proofread. Photocopy a student's composition and demonstrate proofreading on an overhead in front of the class. Read the composition aloud, letting your voice indicate pauses, stops, rising, and falling. Do this only for punctuation and capitalization errors. Leave spelling, handwriting, paragraphing, and other editing for later lessons. Trying to teach too much in one lesson is a common fault.

2. Edit (make the changes) on the overhead copy for all the students to see. Use a grammar textbook to check any corrections if you need to; this shows students how reference books were intended to be used.

3. Provide the class with sample paragraphs in which the punctuation and capitalization have been omitted. Allow students to work in pairs or small cooperative groups to correct these paragraphs.

4. Allow the rest of the period for students to write. As individual students complete their rough drafts, encourage them to use their proofreading and editing skills. Then have them get together with fellow students for a second proofreading/editing session.

5. Conduct proofreading/editing conferences with individual students. Although conferences should focus on the content and ideas of the written work, this is also the ideal time for the teacher to assess a student's skill in handling punctuation and capitalization matters. Based on this evaluation, additional mini-lessons on specific areas can be designed for small groups of students or perhaps even the whole class if necessary.

PUNCTUATION

Punctuating sentences properly is difficult for young children, particularly for beginning writers who have not read much. As children move through the grades, if they have been allowed to read and write a great deal, their punctuation skills improve automatically (Atwell, 1998; Calkins, 1994). Why is this so?

There are two views regarding punctuation and how it should be taught. One view holds that punctuation is part of traditional grammar and can be taught by memorizing rules. A second view argues that punctuation is a reflection of spoken language—the pauses, stops, pitch, and stress that people give to language when they speak (Chafe, 1988). Most professional writers subscribe to the latter view, claiming that when they write, they also try to hear how the language sounds. Reading aloud, hearing the sounds of the words, and noting the amount of emphasis they wish to convey in a particular sentence determine how writers punctuate (Welty, 1983). Obviously, however, such writers are also familiar with the rules of punctuation and with what commas, periods, exclamation marks, and other marks tell a reader. Thus, it appears that punctuation is a matter of both recognizing intonation units (by reading aloud or hearing your inner voice) and applying appropriate punctuation. There is also evidence to support the notion that, just as with spelling, young children invent their own punctuation marks and creative use of punctuation (Cordeiro, Giacobbe, & Cazden, 1983). For example, young children will commonly put a period at the end of every line they write, despite instructions from the teacher to put the period at the end of the sentence. For the beginning writer, a line of writing is a sentence. The more children read and write, the more they acquire what Chafe (1988) has called the "mental image of sound" necessary to convey meaning through punctuation.

Figures 9.22 and 9.23 summarize the uses of some of the common punctuation marks. These lists should serve as a reference for you in helping students and as a guide to the kinds of mini-lessons that might be taught; the latter, of course, should be determined by the needs of your students—based on their own writing, not the directives of a textbook.

Period

Use a period . . .

1. at the end of a sentence making a statement

2. after abbreviations of titles when the name of the person follows

3. after abbreviations of days of the week and months of the year

Examples

1. The men drilled for oil.

2. Mrs. Baker, Dr. Jones, Capt. Ahab, Rev. Smith

3. Mon., Wed., Sun., Jan., Aug., Oct.

Comma

Use a comma . . .

1. to separate the day from the year

2. to separate the names of a city and a state

3. after the greeting in a friendly letter

4. after the closing of a letter

5. to separate items in a list

6. between long independent clauses connected with *but, and, or, nor*

7. to set off parenthetical information

8. to separate the speaker from a quotation

Examples

1. Lindsay was born on May 4, 1982.

2. Bethany, OK 73008

3. Dear Pamela,

4. Yours truly,

5. Karen bought milk, bread, and cheese.

6. Aubree thought she would swim all day, but the rain changed her plan.

7. Pat Jones, our coach, led the team.

8. John said, "I'm leaving."

FIGURE 9.22

Rules for using periods and commas.

FIGURE **9.23**

Rules for additional punctuation marks.

Rules	Examples
1. Use a *question mark* after a sentence that asks a question.	1. What is the capital of Virginia?
2. Use an *exclamation point* after a sentence that expresses strong feeling.	2. Help! My desk is on fire!
3. Use an *apostrophe* to . . .	3.
A. indicate a contraction	A. cannot = can't
B. show possession	B. Mary's dress is lovely.
4. Use *quotation marks* . . .	4.
A. to set off a direct quotation	A. Henry said, "Leave here at once!"
B. for titles of articles	B. "The Day I Left Here"
C. for poem titles	C. "Casey at the Bat"
D. for song titles	D. "The Star-Spangled Banner"
5. Use a *colon* . . .	5.
A. to indicate a following explanation or listing	A. They brought the following items to camp: sleeping bag, toothbrushes, and clothes.
B. after the greeting in a business letter	B. To Whom It May Concern:
6. Use a *semicolon* to separate two closely related independent clauses.	6. Harold made the highest grades in school; he expects to win a scholarship.
7. Use a *hyphen* to divide a word at the end of a line (but only at a syllable junction).	7. He did not believe what the pres-ident had said.

A mini-lesson on the period or comma might be conducted like this: After explaining one or more of the rules for using periods or commas, the teacher reads a brief paragraph taken from a children's literature book. When finished, she or he displays that same paragraph on an overhead transparency with the periods and comma omitted. Together, the teacher and students discuss how to punctuate the paragraph. When they are finished, they compare their work with the original paragraph. Next, another unpunctuated paragraph is given to small groups of students to punctuate. Again, the answers can be compared with the original work.

CAPITALIZATION

As with all other aspects of grammar, there are a number of ways to teach children to capitalize properly. Direct instruction lessons that focus on having children memorize a single capitalization rule (see Figure 9.24) and then apply that rule in their own writing is one way; however, having students memorize rules before they are ready for them is not a good teaching practice. Make your decision on what rules to teach based on your analysis of the children's own writing.

FIGURE **9.24**

Rules for capitalization.

Capitalize . . .	Examples
1. the first word in a sentence	1. Our school play is tomorrow.
2. the names of people	2. Margaret and Susan are sisters.
3. the pronoun *I*	3. Do you think I should go to the party?
4. the names of streets, cities, and states	4. We live on Mulberry Road in Sacramento, California.
5. the names of days, months, and holidays	5. On Thursday, December 25, we will celebrate Christmas.
6. the names of rivers, countries, and continents	6. The Amazon River flows through Brazil in South America.
7. the names of languages and nationalities	7. The French, Spanish, and British signed the treaty.
8. the sections of a country	8. They live in the Southwest.

Mini-lessons on specific aspects of capitalization are a good way to teach the concept and still leave time for children to practice it in their writing. Stress to the children that when writers capitalize properly, they are helping their readers to identify proper nouns and to know when a sentence begins. This helps the reader to understand the message that the writer is trying to convey.

Recall that many teachers now use examples from actual children's books to teach concepts such as capitalization. For example, in the informational picture book *So You Want to Be President* (St. George & Small, 2000), the following passage demonstrates different ways of using capital letters: "Not all Presidents danced, but most had a sport. John Quincy Adams was a first-rate swimmer. Once when he was skinny-dipping in the Potomac River, a woman reporter snatched his clothes and sat on them until he gave her an interview" (p. 30). After writing this passage on the chalkboard, the teacher would first ask the children to find all the capital letters in the passage. Then she might ask questions such as, "Why are *Not* and *Once* capitalized?" "Why is *Presidents* capitalized?" "What about *John Quincy Adams* and *Potomac River*?" The children would then discuss the passage and the teacher would encourage them to practice using capital letters in their writing.

In and beyond the classroom

Select a paragraph from a favorite children's literature book. Retype that paragraph, omitting all capital letters and punctuation marks. Then teach a mini-lesson to a small group of students on some of the common rules of capitalization and punctuation. Give them your paragraph to correct and discuss.

DAILY ORAL LANGUAGE PROGRAM

Some classroom teachers have approached the teaching of writing skills using a unique variation on the mini-lesson. Each day the teacher writes two or three sentences on the board. These sentences contain either errors of the type that the students have been making in their writing or difficult skill questions from standardized tests that the teacher has noted from previous classes. The children can volunteer the corrections orally, or they can work on the sentences at their seats. In a brief mini-lesson of 5 to 10 minutes, the teacher reviews with the whole class the corrections to be made.

In 1989, Vail and Papenfuss published a complete series of these sentences, along with mini-lessons, to aid the teacher. Known as the **daily oral language program,** this is another way that teachers can present skills knowledge in writing without taking much time away from the revising, editing, and publishing stages of process writing.

The Computer and Word-Processing Programs: Another Tool for the Writer

More and more computers are appearing in elementary schools. In some cases, they are found in individual classrooms. In other schools, a special room is designated as the computer room; it contains 20 or more machines. Students are sent to the computer room for instruction on a fixed schedule during the week.

Computers have become useful tools for the young writer; however, keyboarding can be an issue when using them. Although there is some disagreement about the exact role of rigorous keyboarding instruction, more schools are realizing the importance of students being proficient in keyboarding and publishers are providing programs to implement it. Among the programs that have been reviewed are the following: Microtype, UltraKey, Kid Desk, The Wonderful World of PAWS, Success with Typing, Superkey, Type of Learn, Typing Tutor III, and Keyboard Success.

Many educators maintain that students do benefit from possessing adequate keyboarding skills and knowledge about the major keys and functions of the word-processing programs. When working with keyboarding, teachers should remember to give students plenty of time to practice their keyboard competencies and to monitor each student's progress by providing appropriate feedback.

In any integrated language arts classroom, word-processing programs should be an important feature. Although other types of information processors do have implications for classroom instruction, word-processing programs have the potential to revolutionize both reading and writing instruction.

Word-processing programs can be used to input, edit, format, and generally arrange text—as well as to do graphics and illustration—on a page. Any word-processing program combined with a printer enables the writer to outline, write, edit, revise, and print out anything he or she might want to express. One aspect of these programs that is especially helpful in the editing stage is the spell checker and grammar checker. These programs can also save paper when the editing is done on the computer.

Fortunately, some word-processing programs are designed for the primary reader/writer. Among these are Bank Street Writer III and Magic Slate II, both of which have picture icons to help children decide which function of the program they want to use. Write for Kids has picture icons plus the capability of reading back the child's story.

There are also many programs that support children's initial writing attempts by including graphics with text. Some examples are The Story Starter, The Story Maker, Story-Book Weaver Deluxe, Storybook Maker, Dazzle Draw, KoalaPad, The Print Shop Deluxe, SuperPrint, and Explore-a-Story. Claris Words is another word-processing program that permits students to use the mouse to illustrate their stories and then to add color.

Beyond the classroom

Select one of the word-processing programs listed here and use it. Then write a critical review of the program in terms of its usefulness with elementary-grade children.

TECHNOLOGY AND WEBSITES

Computer-assisted instruction (CAI) consists of drill-and-practice programs and tutorials that can be used to provide reinforcement and instruction in the individual language arts skills. Although some of these programs have been criticized as expensive "workbooks" that should not be overused or abused, they may have a place in your classroom as you seek to improve or reinforce particular competencies in your students. However, if you do use these programs, make sure they are related to meaningful classroom learning experiences.

If you desire to use CAI in your classroom, what should be some of your concerns? First, there should be a close match between the program and the goals and content of your language arts curriculum. Second, the type and amount of reinforcement the program provides should be adequate and motivational; the program should be self-pacing for the students and easy to use. If these features are missing, the program will probably not meet the needs of your students.

Drill-and-practice programs can provide reinforcement for previously taught areas of language instruction. As such, they may enhance language, reading, and writing competencies in children. In a drill-and-practice program, a student is given a structured sequence of related tasks to be completed. Since practice is a key factor within these programs, the student is often given several chances to complete each task correctly and then given feedback on the correctness of the answers. Students should be rewarded for correct answers and given minimal discouragement for those that are incorrect. *The Sticky Bear Series, Reading Rabbit, Bailey's Book House,* and *Super Solvers Spellbound* are four programs that have worked well and provided acceptable reinforcement with early learners. *Cloze Plus* and *Cloze Test* are two programs that provide reinforcement in using context clues to figure out a word in a passage.

One way of ensuring that a CAI program focuses on the overall language needs of students is to determine whether the software has a teacher utility. Such a feature allows the teacher to customize instruction by using words that are currently part of the students' language, reading, writing, and researching activities. If a class is researching dinosaurs, a teacher might want to reinforce students' new vocabulary about dinosaurs with computer puzzles, word searches, cloze exercises, spelling checkups, or sight-word flashcards. To do this, the teacher might select programs such as *Crossword Magic, Wordsearch, Magic Spells,* and *E-Z Learner.* A teacher can use these programs as word banks for the new vocabulary words the students are acquiring.

www.puzzlemaker.com
This site permits you to create mazes, word searches, crosswords, and more for any lesson.

www.wfu.edu/~cunningh/fourblocks
This is Patricia Cunningham's Four Blocks curriculum model site with many good teaching suggestions and discussion of ideas relevant for classroom teachers.

www.kidsdomain.com
This site is part of the Kaboose network and is designed for kids. It provides all sorts of activities and ideas for the classroom.

www.greenwoodinstitute.org
The Greenwood Institute site provides teachers with information regarding mainstreaming, home schooling, and educational research projects.

www.ciera.org

CIERA is the Center for the Improvement of Early Reading Achievement, and its site has articles and ideas regarding literacy for early childhood and elementary educators.

www.readingrockets.org

Reading Rockets is a national organization to help launch young readers. The site includes many helpful ideas on teaching spelling and handwriting. It is a service of public television station WETA in Washington, DC.

www.eleaston.com/writing.html

This site has specific ideas to help with all types of writing. It provides information on citations, grammar, handwriting, punctuation, spelling, and vocabulary.

www.grammarnow.com

This is a great site where you can email questions about grammar problems, composition issues, proofreading, and editing.

www.ccc.commnet.edu/grammar

Capital Community College maintains this site, which provides helpful ideas for grammar and writing.

www.spellingbee.com

This is the home page for the Scripps Howard National Spelling Bee. Students in your class may wish to investigate it.

http://owl.english.purdue.edu/handouts/grammar

This is an online writing lab that helps older students with writing, grammar, punctuation, and spelling.

www.funbrain.com/funbrain/spell

This is a good site to help improve your spelling. Many fun games for children of all ages and grades are found here. Your students will wish to investigate this site.

www.spelling.hemscott.net

Spelling it Right helps you to gain confidence in your spelling.

http://ipl.si.umich.edu/div/kidspace/askauthor

This site connects you to home pages of young adult authors. You can dialogue with the authors through email.

www.snowcrest.net/kidpower/authors.html

This site lists authors who are willing to visit your school.

www.grammarlady.com

This site includes grammar rules and is a hotline for posting questions about composition.

www.wolinskyweb.com/word.htm

This site features resources of sites that have fun with words.

Summary

To be an effective writer means to communicate clearly with an audience. This requires the effective use of the mechanics or tools of writing. In the past, so-called writing programs overemphasized the teaching of handwriting, spelling, grammar, capitalization, and punctuation to the extent that little actual writing ever took place in the classroom. This is changing with the emphasis on process writing.

Today the tools of writing are seen in a comprehensive perspective and taught as part of the process approach. Handwriting is taught in the early grades and emphasizes the legibility of a child's handwriting. In the area of spelling, invented spelling is recognized as a developmental part of children's writing growth. Punctuation and capitalization are taught through mini-lessons and the discovery approach when appropriate. Rote memorization and drills are minimized. The role of grammar instruction as isolated drill is also being reexamined in favor of more meaningful activities with direct application to real writing and reinforced through extensive reading. Finally, the potential of the computer, with word-processing programs, is being integrated in elementary school writing programs as another tool to aid the writer in the creative process of composing.

A final suggestion would also be in order. Although most classrooms rely on textbooks to teach grammar, punctuation, capitalization, and so on, the textbooks are generally too complex and too confusing for easy understanding. We instead recommend two handbooks, written expressly for young children to answer the questions they have about the mechanics of language. For grades 4 and 5, see *Writers Express: A Handbook for Young Writers, Thinkers, and Learners* (1995) by Kemper, Nathan, and Sebranek (published by Write Source, Burlington, WI). For grades 6–8, see *Write Source 2000: A Guide to Writing, Thinking, and Learning* (3rd ed.) (1995) by Sebranek, Meyer, and Kemper (also published by Write Source, Burlington, WI).

ACTIVITIES *with children*

Big Word Spelling

Write a word on the blackboard in jumbled alphabetical order, for example, aeefgiorrrrt. Ask students, "Using all the letters, what word can you come up with?" If students are unable to come up with the answer, provide it for them: refrigerator. Next ask students to draw three columns on a sheet of paper: column one for two-letter words, column two for three-letter words, and column three for four-letter words. Now ask them to list as many words as they can in each of the columns using the original letters. Finally, have students do this activity with a word of their own choosing and give it to a friend.

Spelling Relay

In small groups, students collaboratively spell words. One student begins by naming the first letter of a word. Each subsequent student adds a letter toward the creation of a real word. As each student adds a letter, the word that the next student is thinking of may change. Students keep going until one student either is stuck or can only add a letter that will complete the word.

Sentence Relay

Play this game in the same way as spelling relay, except have each person in the group add a word. The object is to build long sentences without completing a sentence. The game ends when a word is given that makes a complete sentence.

Chain Spelling

This spelling game is played using the same rules as Geography Train (see the activities section in Chapter 5). A student begins by spelling any word. The next person in the group must think of and spell a word that begins with the last letter of the word spelled by the first person. The game continues until someone cannot think of a word beginning with the last letter of the previously mentioned word.

Handwriting Pictures

Using individual letters or groups of letters from the alphabet, have students create pictures. They can add eyes, legs, and so on to create stick figures or add other features to create houses, trucks, and trains.

Jumbled Sentences

Select headlines or lead sentences from newspaper articles. Cut up the sentences into separate words. Give the separate words to a group of students to unscramble. Depending on which aspect of grammar or punctuation you want to emphasize, the jumbled sentence or headline could contain descriptive adjectives, prepositional phrases, semicolons, and so on.

Crossword Puzzles

Share some crossword puzzle examples with your class. Describe how they are created, with definitions, words running horizontally and vertically, and blank spaces darkened. In small groups, have the students create their own crossword puzzles using the week's spelling words.

Touch Center

Create a learning center around tactile activities for reinforcing handwriting and spelling. Use sand trays, shaving cream, glue and macaroni, strings, and clay. Young children can create the letters of the alphabet, while older students can practice writing difficult spelling words.

Punctuate This!

Ask students to copy one paragraph from the book that is being read but to omit the punctuation marks and capital letters. Have students exchange paragraphs around the group and correct one another's paragraphs. They can use the book model to check their work.

Combining Sentences

Books written for young children use many short sentences. Have your upper elementary and middle school students select a children's book written for primary-grade children. Then ask them to rewrite three or four sentences, combining them into one sentence. Remember, they may add and delete words as well as add new punctuation marks.

Labels, Labels

To help students practice their handwriting skills with a functional purpose, take a class "trip" around your room and identify all the things that need labels. For example, children can label their desks and lockers, various learning centers, supply closets, bulletin boards, and special file cabinets.

Spelling Patterns

Teach children some simple English spelling patterns. Then have them look through their reading books for example words to fit the patterns. How many words of the same patterns can they find? Examples: C–V–C (*cat, hat, bad, sad, pig, dog, wig*); C–V–C+E (*save, game, bike, like, tone, dove, bone*); C–V–V–C (*rain, leaf, coat, need*).

Circus Spelling

Pretend that students are attending a circus. For each ride they want to go on, they have to get a ticket. To get a ticket, they have to spell the three words listed on the ticket. See who can collect the most tickets. Example words: *clown, popcorn, roller coaster*. Some variations on this activity can be County Fair, Sports Events, or Travel Agents.

RELATED READINGS

Buchanan, E. (1992). *Spelling for whole language classrooms.* Winnipeg, Canada: Whole Language Consultants Ltd.

This book gives detailed descriptions of the spelling stages through which most children pass. It also gives strategies to use for each stage; many are in the form of games.

Cunningham, P. M. (1995). *Phonics they use: Words for reading and writing* (2nd ed.). New York: HarperCollins College Publishers.

This book explains the main aspects of the sounds of words and gives a great number of strategies to use to facilitate children's becoming aware of the different sounds within words.

Goodman, K. (1993). *Phonics phacts: A common-sense look at the most controversial issue affecting today's classrooms!* Portsmouth, NH: Heinemann.

Goodman explains why teaching phonics in isolation is not effective. In detail, he explains phonology, orthography, and phonics. He also gives some background on the politics of phonics.

Heilman, A. W. (1998). *Phonics in proper perspective* (8th ed.). Upper Saddle River, NJ: Merrill.

Heilman explains the purpose and the limitations of phonics as well as the controversy over direct instruction of phonics. He does give some generalizations that teachers should know as they help young learners to read and write.

Owen, R., Hester, J., & Teale, W. (2002, April). Where do you want to go today? Inquiry based learning and technology integration. *The Reading Teacher, 55*(7), 616–625.

This is a very readable article on integrating technology within the language arts classroom.

Strickland, D. S. (1998). *Teaching phonics today: A primer for educators.* Newark, DE: International Reading Association.

A well-known educator/researcher gives some good guidelines to finding the balance between intensive phonics and the holistic approach. She gives practical strategies that support beginning readers and writers. She has one chapter on communicating the phonics issue to caregivers and the community.

Weaver, C. (1996). *Teaching grammar in context.* Portsmouth, NH: BoyntonCook division of Heinemann.

This is one of the most readable books on grammar.

Wilde, S. (1997). *What's a schwa sound anyway? A holistic guide to phonetics, phonics, and spelling.* Portsmouth, NH: Heinemann.

This is an excellent resource book that gives some basic insights into linguistics that teachers should know as they work with students. The more teachers know, the more helpful they can become when students struggle with reading and writing.

10

Reading and Writing Across the Curriculum

his chapter introduces you to the directed reading–thinking activity, graphic organizers, semantic feature analysis, and semantic webbing. Special emphasis is placed on utilizing techniques that help students become strategic readers. You will also learn about using thematic units in the classroom.

CHAPTER OBJECTIVES

After reading this chapter, you should be able to accomplish the following objectives:

1. Explain why reading and writing need to be integrated across the curriculum.
2. Define content literacy and a literacy event.
3. Explain the organizational patterns of text.
4. Explain the concept of readability and its role in reading and writing.
5. Describe graphic organizers, semantic maps, and semantic features analysis.
6. Give examples of possible sentences.
7. Indicate the differences between a semantic map and a semantic web.
8. Describe the similarities between the directed reading–thinking activity (DR-TA) and the K-T-W-L chart.
9. Describe the differences between writing for yourself and writing for others.
10. Explain the benefits of using thematic units to integrate the curriculum.

CHECK YOUR BACKGROUND KNOWLEDGE. Before reading the chapter, complete the K-T-W-L chart based on the chapter overview and objectives provided at left. In column "K," write what you know about the topics in the objectives. In column "T," write what you think you know. In column "W," write what you want to learn. Finally, after you have read the chapter, write what you have learned in column "L."

Know	**T**hink you know	**W**ant to learn	**L**earned

Why Reading and Writing Across the Curriculum?

Over the years, there have been many different views about the role of reading and writing within the elementary classroom curriculum. The discrete view sees reading and writing as activities that should be done for their own sake. In this approach, reading and writing are often taught in separate periods of the school day, are seldom related to each other, and are rarely—if ever—integrated with the other content areas.

The whole language and the integrated approaches consider reading and writing as closely related ways of learning new information. Through experiences with reading and writing, children learn how to learn. They become literate and develop into independent self-educators who can acquire all types of content information.

Not only do reading and writing help people to learn, but they are actually motivators for each other. In reading, people are trying to find information, locate ideas, and comprehend what the text really says. To accomplish this task, readers use prior knowledge and often make predictions about what they expect to learn. In writing a summary of material or including it for an entry in a reading/writing log, readers are able to clarify and even analyze the ideas they have gathered. And it is this analysis that may further motivate a person to reread and study the material or to seek out other information to enhance what was learned from the text. In other words, reading promotes writing, which in turn encourages further reading (Vacca, Vacca, Gove, Burkey, Lenhart, & McKeon, 2003). The processes build on each other as ways of obtaining meaning.

In an integrated approach, reading and writing become natural ways of making content come alive for students. Through these processes, students can take charge of their learning by interacting with textual material in a variety of ways. To get a better idea of how this happens, read the following Classroom Vignette, in which content and process learning are integrated.

SUPPORTIVE RESEARCH

A great deal of the rationale for integrating reading and writing across the curriculum comes from research and published reports that have outlined what the United States needs to do to become a "nation of readers." Research has indicated that the most logical place for developing reading, writing, and thinking competencies is in content areas such as social studies and science (Anderson, Hiebert, Scott, & Wilkinson, 1985).

Because reading materials in subject areas are much different from the narrative stories that many young readers are accustomed to reading, they can present a challenge to constructing meaning and achieving complete comprehension (Anderson et al., 1985). Instructional approaches that help prepare students for complex textual concepts and ideas, that show them how to use specific learning processes and strategies, and that outline ways for them to respond to varied textual resources can go a long way toward helping students comprehend needed information. In other words, literacy instruction in the content areas makes a difference (Vacca, 2002a).

Reading and writing are tools for learning that allow students to clarify, refine, and apply their knowledge. Because reading and writing strategies are so vital to students in comprehending new information, researchers have coined the term **content literacy**—the ability to use reading and writing for the acqui-

VIGNETTE in the classroom

Mrs. Castleberry's second-grade class has just embarked on a unit of study involving caterpillars and the ways in which they grow and change. The title for the thematic unit is "Caterpillars and Change—What Really Happens?" The basic information for much of the unit comes from science. However, reading, writing, literature, poetry, health, math, art, and social studies all play major roles in the project.

As a way of arousing the children's interest in the topic, Mrs. Castleberry reads *The Very Hungry Caterpillar* by Eric Carle to them. Not only are the students fascinated by Carle's lively and imaginative pictures, but they are also very interested in the variety of foods that the caterpillar ate. When they learn that the caterpillar got a stomachache from all its eating, several of the children exclaim, "I'd have one too if I ate all that stuff!" In the end, everyone is delighted that the caterpillar turned into a beautiful butterfly, an event that they celebrate by decorating colorful tissue-paper butterflies.

To prepare the students for the information they will be encountering throughout the unit, Mrs. Castleberry also has them begin to fill in the Caterpillar Information Chart (pictured in Figure 10.1). It is an adaptation of an interactive learning chart that is sometimes used in the directed reading–thinking activity (Monahan & Hinson, 1988).

For the next few weeks, the entire class is involved in a series of caterpillar-related activities. In addition to engaging the help of the school librarian in locating simple entries about caterpillars from encyclopedias and dictionaries, students consult a variety of information books, including the following:

Boring, M., & Garrow, L. (1996). *Caterpillars, Bugs, and Butterflies.* Chanhassen, MN: Creative Publishing International.

Ehlert, L. (2001). *Waiting for Wings.* San Diego: Harcourt.

Heiligman, D., & Weisman, B. (1996). *From Caterpillar to Butterfly.* New York: HarperCollins Children's Books.

Hogner, D. (1964). *Moths.* New York: Thomas Y. Crowell Company.

Hunt, J., & Selsam, M. (1987). *A First Look at Caterpillars.* New York: Walker & Co.

Norsgaard, E. J. (1988). *How to Raise Butterflies.* New York: Dodd, Mead & Co.

Ryder, J., & Cherry, L. (1996). *Where Butterflies Grow.* New York: Pearson.

Shapiro, K., & Cassels, J. (2002). *Butterflies.* New York: Scholastic.

Terry, T. (1988). *The Life Cycle of a Butterfly.* New York: The Bookwright Press.

Watts, B. (1986). *Butterfly and Caterpillar.* Morristown, NJ: Silver Burdett.

Watts, B. (1989). *Keeping Minibeasts: Caterpillars.* New York: Franklin Watts.

As a way of summarizing its findings, one group of children writes a book of information about caterpillars entitled *Caterpillars—Everything You Always Wanted to Know and Then Some.*

Many students also do firsthand research by observing a variety of caterpillars, cocoons, and chrysalides with a magnifying glass and recording data about their findings on a features chart (pictured in Figure 10.2). The class is a bit surprised to find such a variety of different caterpillars and to learn that some caterpillars turn into moths rather than butterflies.

Mrs. Castleberry finds that most of the class is very interested in learning what caterpillars eat. She has one group of students research the different food sources of caterpillars and report on them to the class. The group that undertakes this task finds that the diet of the caterpillars is primarily vegetarian, with an emphasis on green, leafy foods. The children feel that this is a very healthy diet and decide to apply this to their own lives by becoming more aware of healthy foods they should be eating. They enjoy this aspect of the unit so much that as a

(continued)

culminating activity for the project the class decides to have a Healthy Caterpillar Snack Party at school. They plan and write a menu and an invitation for the other second-grade class:

Please come to a Healthy Caterpillar Snack Party

Where: Room 213 in Longmeadow School

When: April 12, 10:30 A.M.

Given by: Mrs. Castleberry's class

Menu: Carrot sticks

Celery sticks with peanut butter

Radish curls

Apple slices

Pear halves

Lettuce leaves with pineapple

Apple juice

Door prizes will be 3-D paper caterpillars made by members of the class. R.S.V.P. by April 5.

Needless to say, the students in both second-grade classes have a great time and enjoy some very healthy snacks.

FIGURE 10.1

Caterpillar information chart.

Caterpillar Information Chart			
What We Know About Caterpillars	What We Think About Caterpillars	What We'll Learn About Caterpillars	What We Learned About Caterpillars
Caterpillars turn into butterflies. We like them.	Spring might be the best time to see them. Some live in a chrysalis.	We'll be able to find out if a caterpillar lives in a chrysalis or a cocoon.	We learned that there are many kinds of caterpillars. The ones that turn into butterflies live in a chrysalis. The ones that turn into moths live in a cocoon.

sition of new content (McKenna & Robinson, 1990). Content literacy includes general literacy skills, content-specific literacy skills (such as map reading), and some prior knowledge of content. Once students have acquired content literacy, the process of building new knowledge is greatly facilitated. Typical daily instruction allows such students to engage in the active construction of content knowledge through the use of reading activities (directed reading–thinking activity [DR-TA], graphic organizers) as well as writing strategies (dialogue journals, reading logs).

This approach to learning content gives children the opportunity to find things out and to think for themselves. William Bigelow's (1989) students dis-

FIGURE **10.2**

Caterpillar Data							
Name	Moth/ Butterfly	Hair	Spines	Pattern	Body	Horns	Tail
Wooly Bear	Moth	Fine		Light, middle, and dark end	Curls, round	No	Curls, not forked

Caterpillar data collection chart.

covered this when they learned in their social studies class that textbooks had not told them the whole truth about Columbus's "discovery" of America. They found out that the real reason Columbus came to America had more to do with money and economics than with proving that the world was round. They were also amazed by the cruel way he treated the people who were already living in the Americas. These students found out that they should not necessarily trust authorities for all their information; they realized they needed to become active participants in their learning, to create their own meaning as they progressed (Bigelow, 1989).

A PURPOSE FOR REAL READING AND WRITING

Goodman (1996) has stated that children should read "real language," material that is really worth reading. According to Goodman and many other educators, a child's experiences with text should be *literacy events*, in which the child reads materials that he or she needs and wants to read. These literacy events can involve reading a story, an informational text, or a combination of several different types of texts. The important thing is that the child have a self-imposed purpose for reading and writing—such as finding out about caterpillars and their characteristics, their eating habits, and the variety of ways in which they change. When children have such a purpose for acquiring information, they can then become active information seekers and can begin to develop an integrated knowledge base. This type of knowledge resembles the information obtained in the real world rather than the segmented bits of isolated information that are too often found in classrooms.

Integrating the reading and writing processes across the curriculum thus establishes a clear purpose for learning. The content of the curriculum provides

Beyond the classroom

Interview two or three classroom teachers in your field experience school to find out how they integrate aspects of the language arts across the curriculum. Ask them for specific ideas related to units and activities they have developed. Then take notes on your findings in your journal and refer to them as you gather more information to use in your own classroom.

students with a reason for acquiring information; the actual reading and writing make the learning an active process in which the readers are involved with the material. Teachers also need to help students see the connection between school and real-life situations. For example, students can easily see the relationship between reading directions and knowing how to use the Internet.

Through this content literacy process, children are able not only to acquire content information but also to improve their reading and writing competencies. Children do not learn to read and write in a vacuum; they learn to read and write by reading and writing about something (Tompkins, 1997). When reading and writing become tools for understanding, creating, and communicating information, children have the opportunity to practice, refine, and extend the literacy skills they already possess by engaging in something meaningful.

CONSTRUCTING CONTENT KNOWLEDGE

Active involvement in reading and writing about a topic leads to the construction of new knowledge and adds to each student's base of content information. In turn, this growing base of knowledge helps students to understand any new information they encounter. Actually, there is a cyclical pattern to the relationship between a student's base of content knowledge and the use of reading and writing activities as methods of acquiring further information (Vacca et al., 2003). The more background knowledge a student possesses, the easier it is for that person to implement reading and writing activities to integrate new content, thus increasing the base of knowledge and facilitating the continued use of reading and writing strategies. In effect, the more knowledge one has, the more one is able to acquire.

In such an approach to learning, both content and process goals are important. The *content goals* relate to the significant information in the text, while the *process goals* focus on what the student needs to do to acquire that knowledge. To attain both sets of goals, the emphasis prior to reading should be on activating each student's prior knowledge. During reading, teacher-modeled strategies should be used to actively involve students in learning. And after reading, students should work to organize and synthesize information for transfer to other learning situations (Tompkins, 1997).

Reading and writing across the curriculum helps students to maximize their acquisition of content knowledge. They are able to acquire significant chunks of information rather than fragmented, isolated bits. Learning is holistic and meaningful. Also, by building up a store of knowledge, students enhance their ability to use reading and writing to process information and construct new knowledge. They become able to extend their knowledge and to add to their store of information whenever they wish (Tompkins, 1997). This integrated approach puts students in charge of learning, which is really what education is all about.

> *You can be indifferent to a term paper, a grocery list, but you cannot be indifferent to your writing.*
>
> **JANE YOLEN**

Text Considerations

Because reading and responding to text form a significant part of any content curriculum, one of the first things you must consider when you are integrating the language arts across the curriculum is the impact of the different types of text upon your students. Books in the various content areas tend to be difficult for youngsters to comprehend. Factors that contribute to text difficulty include the organization and structure of the text, the number of concepts the text addresses, the readability of the text, the appropriateness of the text for the students and the purpose of the class, and the accuracy of the information in the text (Vacca et al., 2003). Textbooks in the various content areas also make use of the specialized vocabularies of those subjects, many of which can be confusing and difficult for students to acquire.

ORGANIZATIONAL PATTERNS

As described in earlier chapters, stories (or narrative text) have certain elements that include a setting, characters, a theme, a plot of actions or events (all of which are related to the goals of the characters), and a resolution. Moving into the different content areas involves a transition from structured narrative stories to informational, or expository, text. This type of text generally has not one but many structures, which can be especially confusing for young readers. Typical expository text can be organized according to cause–effect, comparison–contrast, enumeration, sequence, and problem–solution (Vacca & Vacca, 2002).

Cause–effect texts show the causal relationship between one set of ideas and facts and the resulting outcomes. This pattern or relationship points out that one item is unable to exist without the others. The following paragraph is typical of a cause–effect text:

> Hurricane Hugo hit the South Carolina coast with greater force than any storm in current history. As a result, homes, businesses, beaches, wetlands, and forests were completely destroyed. Damages were estimated in the billions of dollars.

The *comparison–contrast* pattern of text organization focuses on the similarities and differences that are evident in the topics of particular passages. For example:

> After the Civil War, many of the farmers who had lived in Vermont decided to move to the new lands of the West. In setting up their new lives and farms, these people continued with many of the familiar chores associated with farm life: clearing the land; setting up barns and fencing pastures; plowing, planting, and harvesting the fields, as well as caring for the livestock. However, there were some major differences between the western land and that of Vermont. The new land had few rocks and fertile soil—two benefits the hearty Vermonters could really appreciate.

In *enumeration*, or listing, the author describes important information about a particular topic. The author may focus on facts or on particular characteristics and features. The following would be a typical listing passage:

> Polar bears live in the very cold Arctic regions of Russia, Canada, Norway, and Greenland. Their black skin, which absorbs the sun, helps to keep them warm even though their fur is white. The polar bears' fur is actually unique. The hairs are hollow, which helps collect the sun's rays and drive the heat right to their black skin. Another part of their body that keeps them from freezing is their four inches of fat. They have fur on every part of their body except their noses. They even have fur on their feet to keep them warm and to keep them from falling on the ice. Their favorite foods are seals, walruses, and fish.

Sequence involves putting ideas and topics into a particular time order. One way to recognize sequence is through its use of dates and time periods to help organize a passage. An example of this pattern might be as follows:

> In 1991, when Magdalena Estrada was six years old, she contracted a serious virus that left her right leg limp and lifeless. After two years of treatment, doctors in her native Guatemala felt that they could do no more for Mag-

dalena. So, in 1994, several children's relief organizations arranged to bring Magdalena to the United States for further treatment and physical therapy. Within six months Magdalena was able to walk with only the help of a cane, and within a year she was able to walk on her own again.

One final organizational pattern of expository text is that of *problem–solution*. Such a pattern shows how a problem develops and then outlines the solutions to the problem. Take a look at the following example:

> The increasing incidence of acquired immunodeficiency syndrome (AIDS) has been a cause of great concern within the American population. To counteract this problem, many groups have lobbied for more government support for research regarding the treatment of AIDS victims. The resulting publicity from these efforts has caused a heightened awareness of the disease and its consequences. People have finally begun to recognize the value of education in stopping the spread of AIDS.

Researchers such as Meyer (1975) have long recognized these patterns but have described them with somewhat different terminology: covariance (cause–effect), adversative (comparison–contrast), attribution (enumeration), time order (sequence), and response (problem–solution). However, no matter which terminology is used, the fact remains that the complex patterns of organization in expository text make it more difficult for students to comprehend and respond to the essential information.

Therefore, it is crucial that expository materials used in the classroom be as clearly written and as well organized as possible. They should also be written at a level within the conceptual reach of the students who will be reading them. As a teacher, you will need to take a role in deciding whether or not the texts you use have these characteristics. One of the ways you can work toward this goal is by checking on the readability of the materials that you want to use with students.

READABILITY

How readily or easily a text can be read is called *readability* (Monahan & Hinson, 1988). Recently, the definition of readability has been expanded to encompass factors within the reader as well as aspects of the written text. The level of difficulty of the textual material quite definitely has an impact upon comprehension. How difficult a text is depends upon the length of the sentences, the complexity of the words and language, the writing style and purpose of the author, the organization of the content, and the layout or appearance of the material. In addition, each reader's prior knowledge of the content, purpose for reading, understanding of the vocabulary, and interests and attitudes have an effect on how well that person is able to understand what she or he is reading (Manzo, Manzo, & Estes, 2000).

One way of helping to determine readability is with conventional **readability formulas,** which generally graph the average length of the sentences and the average number of syllables per word (word complexity) in a text. Among the accepted and used formulas is the Fry readability graph (Fry, 1977). Estimates of textual difficulty can be hand calculated by following directions and then graphing the results, as illustrated in Figure 10.3. Readability can also be computed with specialized computer programs, which greatly ease the burden of this task for the teacher. However, readability formulas are often unreliable.

In the 1990s alternatives to using readability formulas arose. One of these alternatives is the Lexile system, which rates texts through the college level. Although the developers of the Lexile text analysis (Smith, Stenner, Horabin, &

FIGURE **10.3**

Fry readability graph.

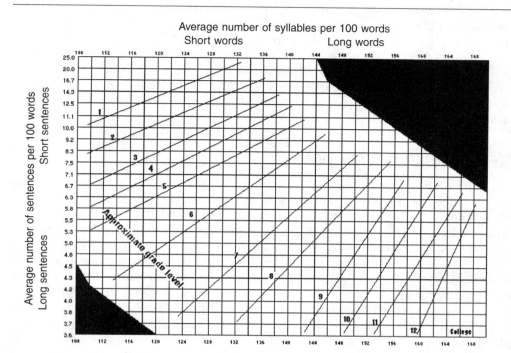

Average number of syllables per 100 words
Short words   Long words

Expanded Directions for Working Readability Graph

1. Randomly select three (3) sample passages and count out exactly 100 words each, beginning with the beginning of a sentence. Do count proper nouns, initializations, and numerals.

2. Count the number of sentences in the hundred words, estimating length of the fraction of the last sentence to the nearest one-tenth.

3. Count the total number of syllables in the 100-word passage. If you don't have a hand counter available, an easy way is to simply put a mark above every syllable over one in each word, then when you get to the end of the passage, count the number of marks and add 100. Small calculators can also be used as counters by pushing numeral 1, then push the + sign for each word or syllable when counting.

4. Enter graph with *average* sentence length and *average* number of syllables; plot dot where the two lines intersect. Area where dot is plotted will give you the approximate grade level.

5. If a great deal of variability is found in syllable count or sentence count, putting more samples into the average is desirable.

6. A word is defined as a group of symbols with a space on either side; thus, *Joe, IRA, 1945,* and *&* are each one word.

7. A syllable is defined as a phonetic syllable. Generally, there are as many syllables as vowel sounds. For example, *stopped* is one syllable and *wanted* is two syllables. When counting syllables for numerals and initializations, count one syllable for each symbol. For example, *1945* is four syllables, *IRA* is three syllables, and *&* is one syllable.

Note: This "extended graph" does not outmode or render the earlier (1968) version inoperative or inaccurate; it is an extension. (Reproduction permitted—no copyright)

Source: "Fry's Readability Graph: Clarifications, Validity, and Extension to Level 17," *Journal of Reading, 21* (December 1977), 249.

Smith, 1989) claim that it is not a readability formula, it does use the same criteria to compute levels: semantic difficulty (high-frequency words on a list) and syntactic difficulty (sentence length) (Hiebert, 2002). Like the readability formulas, Lexiles are not without their problems, such as rating the children's book *Charlotte's Web* on the same level as Grisham's *The Firm* (Hiebert, 2002). To really determine the suitability of texts for students, it is best to heed the recommendations outlined in *Becoming a Nation of Readers* (Anderson et al., 1985), which urges analysis of a variety of other factors related to successful text comprehension.

TEXT/READER INTERACTION

To determine how suitable textual material is for particular children, it is wise to consider the interaction that should occur between the reader and the text. A teacher needs to examine the background knowledge or experience of the reader; the purpose of the material; its relevance, interest, and appropriateness; and the overall predictability of the material for the reader (Manzo et al., 2000).

Some teachers may even wish to make use of an interactive strategy such as cloze (Bormuth, 1968) to help determine how well a child can read and comprehend a particular selection (see the box on the next page). Words are systematically deleted from a passage of text; the student is then required to predict the correct word for each deletion. This technique is effective because it provides some information about the individual's prior knowledge of that material and also indicates how predictable and cohesive the language of the material is for the child. In essence, cloze identifies a child's potential for comprehending selected materials.

Beyond the classroom

For more information about choosing suitable materials for students to read, check out "Making Reading Relevant for Adolescents" by Thomas W. Bean in the November 2002 issue of *Educational Leadership*.

Although the cloze procedure may not be something you want to use with every selection of text, it is one way of assessing children's potential for interaction with text. It can supplement your knowledge about the literary quality, cohesion, and teachability of particular texts.

Helping Children Build Information

Reading and writing across the curriculum helps children to build their store of knowledge—a cognitive stockpile of information that can be used to facilitate comprehension of any future text.

Within an integrated curriculum, teachers basically need to be concerned with helping students to develop the following comprehension and communication competencies:

- understanding and effectively using the specific vocabularies of the various subject areas
- developing strategies to guide and facilitate individual comprehension
- knowing how and when to implement such strategies
- being able to use a variety of resources to reinforce and support comprehension
- developing writing as a learning tool for comprehension and communication

In the following section, these various strategies and techniques are classified into two major groups: those that are most often used for concept understanding and those that guide and assist comprehension.

To use cloze successfully:

1. Select a text passage somewhere between 100 and 500 words. This material should come from a prospective reading assignment that is not familiar to the students.

2. Leave the first and last sentences intact. Then randomly select a word in the second sentence to delete. Continue deleting every 5th word until 50 words have been removed. (Avoid deleting proper names.) For younger children or those who find reading difficult, consider deleting every 10th word.

3. Administer the test passage to the students by first explaining to them that they should do this activity individually, without assistance from any textbook. Students may take as long as they need to complete the passage filling in missing words as they read. (Consider giving students some prior experiences with cloze passages before you use this technique for assessment. That way students will be familiar with the procedure and will not experience initial confusion, which might invalidate the results of the procedure.)

4. When scoring the student passages, only count as correct the exact words deleted from the text. Accepting synonyms usually does not change a score radically and may interfere with the accuracy of the measurement.

5. Determine and record each student's cloze percentage score (number correct × 2). A score of 60 percent or above is an indication that the selection can be read independently by a student. A score between 40 and 60 percent implies that the selection can be used for instruction. However, you will need to supply the students who score in this range with some instruction or guidance. Any score below 40 percent suggests that the passage is too difficult for the student and may be a cause of frustration. It would probably be better to find another selection.

When Wilma Rudolph was four years old, she had an attack of double pneumonia and scarlet fever. She was left crippled, _1_ left leg paralyzed. The _2_ said that only with _3_ treatment could she hope _4_ get back the use _5_ her leg.

Every week Wilma's _6_ took her on the _7_ round trip between Clarksville, Tennessee, _8_ the clinic in Nashville. _9_ entire family learned the _10_ way to massage Wilma's _11_ . By the time she _12_ eight years old, Wilma _13_ able to walk again _14_ the help of a _15_ built shoe.

However, being _16_ to walk wasn't enough _17_ Wilma. She became very _18_ in sports. When she _19_ high school, she decided _20_ try out for the _21_ team. Wilma made the _22_ . By her sophomore year, _23_ had become the outstanding _24_ . The track coach of Tennessee State University _25_ her play. He suggested _26_ she should try out _27_ the track competition. She _28_ and was an unbeatable _29_ star throughout high school.

Wilma _30_ for a track competition _31_ the U.S. and the Soviet Union. _32_ illness struck. It took _33_ for her to regain _34_ health. She had to _35_ harder than ever to _36_ . And qualify she did, _37_ while running she pulled _38_ thigh muscle. Another setback. _39_ , a few months before _40_ was to enter the Olympics, _41_ had to have her _42_ out. Complications arose, and _43_ took weeks for her _44_ recover. All the time _45_ kept thinking hard about _46_ Olympics.

When the doctors _47_ said Wilma was well, _48_ began to make up _49_ lost time. She trained _50_ the other athletes rested, always keeping in mind the Olympic games. After days of hard training, Wilma qualified. And in the Summer Olympics of 1960, Wilma Rudolph ran away with three gold medals.

1. her	10. proper	19. entered	28. did	37. but	46. the
2. doctors	11. leg	20. to	29. track	38. a	47. finally
3. special	12. was	21. basketball	30. prepared	39. Then	48. she
4. to	13. was	22. team	31. between	40. she	49. for
5. of	14. with	23. she	32. Again	41. she	50. while
6. mother	15. specially	24. player	33. months	42. tonsils	
7. long	16. able	25. saw	34. her	43. it	
8. and	17. for	26. that	35. train	44. to	
9. The	18. interested	27. for	36. qualify	45. she	

Source: Text adapted from *Skill by Skill Organizing Information* by Sandra M. Brown and Sharon Levitt. Copyright © 1983, 1976 by Modern Curriculum Press.

CONCEPT UNDERSTANDING

Successfully acquiring content information depends on the ability to understand a wide variety of concepts. And understanding these concepts is, in turn, dependent on being familiar with the specific or technical vocabulary of a particular subject area. Therefore, in order to obtain information from the curriculum, students need to have extensive word knowledge *and* be aware of the strategic links between specialized content vocabularies and their underlying concepts.

Teachers can assist students in their endeavors to obtain information by providing learning experiences that expose children to strategies that help them learn how to develop vocabulary knowledge independently. Then the students can continue to gather information on their own. Some of the strategies that teachers have used successfully to accomplish this are graphic organizers (or word maps), semantic mapping techniques (list–group–label), semantic feature analysis, and possible sentences.

Graphic Organizers

A **graphic organizer** provides a visual structure for new vocabulary and uses charts, timelines, and so forth to organize the vocabulary and concepts of a particular topic (Parks & Black, 1990). A graphic organizer is really a framework for comprehension: It enables students to visualize the relationships among concepts in a text or passage and then to analyze how those concepts work together. Some of the different formats for graphic organizers include outlines, diagrams, timelines, flowcharts, hierarchic organizers, webs or mapping charts, and causal charts. See Figures 10.4 through 10.7 for examples.

It should be noted that graphic organizers have multiple uses. They can be developed by the teacher to introduce new vocabulary and concepts. To do this, a teacher should identify the key words in a lesson, arrange them in a diagram, and present it to the students (Vacca & Vacca, 2002). Organizers can also be

FIGURE 10.4

Timeline organizer.

MAGDALENA ESTRADA

Magdalena was born	She got a virus and her leg went limp	Guatemala doctors could do no more for her	Went to the U.S. for help	She could walk again
1985	1991	1993	1994	1995

FIGURE 10.5

Problem–solution organizer.

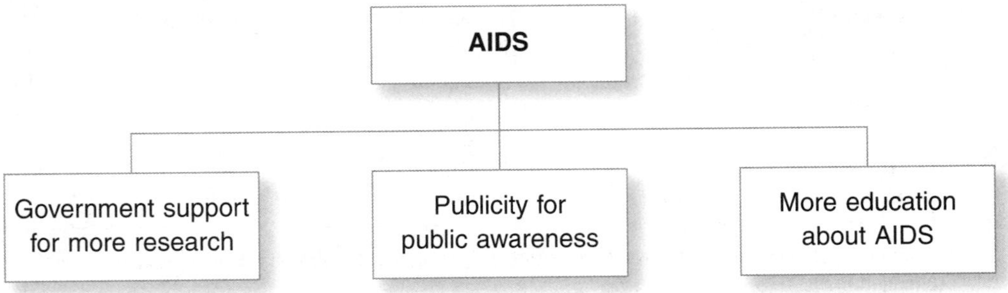

AIDS

- Government support for more research
- Publicity for public awareness
- More education about AIDS

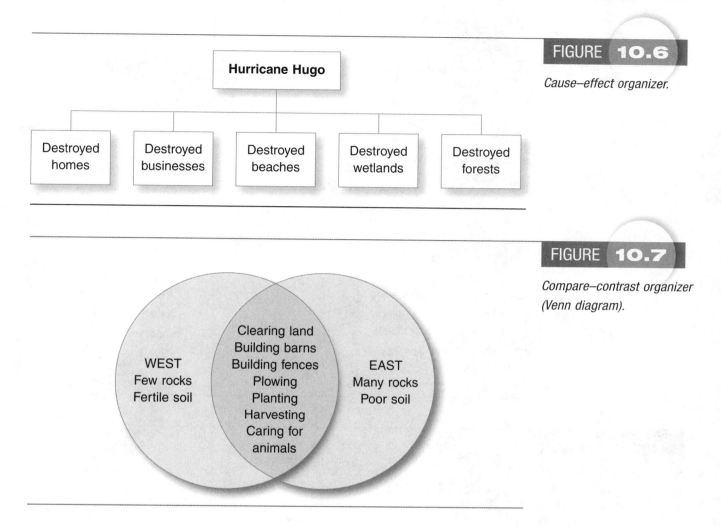

FIGURE 10.6

Cause–effect organizer.

FIGURE 10.7

Compare–contrast organizer (Venn diagram).

used for a comprehension check or review. In this approach, the teacher provides the children with copies of key vocabulary and allows them to work in small groups to construct their own diagrams. Of course, the teacher provides assistance and support (Parks & Black, 1990). In a review lesson, it may also be beneficial to give students a diagram that has been partially completed and then let them finish it on their own. The additional guidance of the diagram serves as a catalyst for the students' recollection of concept organization. Figures 10.8 and 10.9 show two approaches to using graphic organizers to build visual as well as verbal structures for specialized vocabulary.

Semantic Mapping

Semantic mapping is a vocabulary strategy (Johnson & Pearson, 1984) also called *list–group–label* (Taba, 1967; Tierney & Readence, 2000); as a visual technique, it helps students to expand, organize, and remember new concepts. Although the format of a semantic map is similar to the map version of a graphic organizer, the actual development of it is not. Students play an active role in the formation of the map. Their interaction and discussion with the teacher determine the configuration that the map takes. The key to this strategy is the empowerment of students: helping them to use their own knowledge and categorization skills to see new relationships among concepts and vocabulary terms.

FIGURE **10.8**

Mapping chart: Trees.

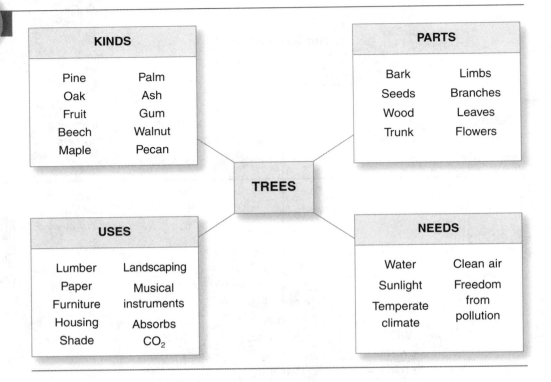

FIGURE **10.9**

Hierarchic organizer:
The newspaper.

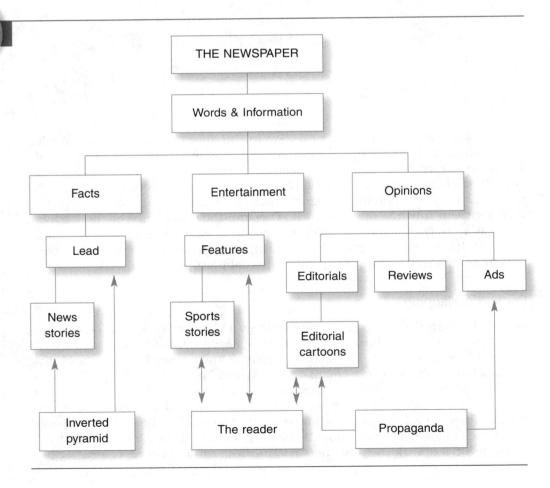

These six steps are helpful in developing a semantic map (Johnson & Pearson, 1984):

1. Choose a central word from a text that the children are using. If you are doing a unit on different wildlife and their habitats, for example, you might choose the word *owls*.
2. List the word on a large piece of paper or on the chalkboard.
3. Encourage the children to list words related to the chosen topic on a separate piece of paper and to categorize them if they can.
4. Have students share their lists of words orally. Put words on the map in agreed-upon categories.
5. Be sure to have students label the categories on the map. It helps them with categorization.
6. Encourage the students to discuss the map with you and with one another. In this way, they begin to see the relationships among the terms.

A semantic map developed about owls might look like the one depicted in Figure 10.10.

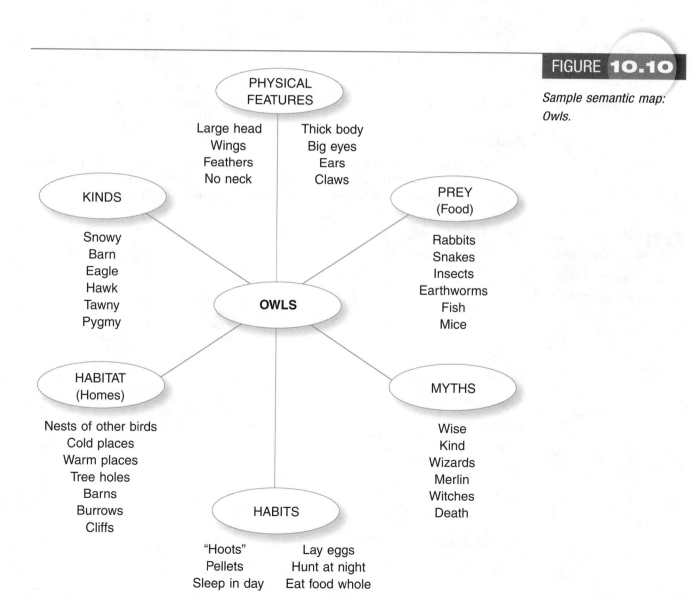

FIGURE 10.10

Sample semantic map: Owls.

PHYSICAL FEATURES

Large head
Wings
Feathers
No neck

Thick body
Big eyes
Ears
Claws

KINDS

Snowy
Barn
Eagle
Hawk
Tawny
Pygmy

PREY (Food)

Rabbits
Snakes
Insects
Earthworms
Fish
Mice

OWLS

HABITAT (Homes)

Nests of other birds
Cold places
Warm places
Tree holes
Barns
Burrows
Cliffs

MYTHS

Wise
Kind
Wizards
Merlin
Witches
Death

HABITS

"Hoots"
Pellets
Sleep in day

Lay eggs
Hunt at night
Eat food whole

Semantic Feature Analysis

A **semantic feature analysis,** also called features analysis (Tierney & Readence, 2000), is a categorization activity that uses a matrix to illustrate the similarities and differences among related terms. It enables all types of students to activate their prior knowledge as a way of facilitating the acquisition of specific content vocabulary and concepts.

When preparing to use this strategy with your students, use these six steps as a guide (Johnson & Pearson, 1984):

1. Decide upon a category or topic, such as *sea habitats.*
2. List some terms in this category (*ocean, salt marsh, coral reef*) in a column on the left side of a page or the chalkboard.
3. Help children to decide on some characteristics or features shared by the words (salt water, cold water, waves, plants, animals). List these across the top of the page or chalkboard.
4. Place a + in the appropriate box to indicate that an item in the category possesses a feature and a − to indicate that the item does not have the feature.
5. Add any new terms or features.
6. Discuss the matrix and help students to note the features shared by the words as well as the uniqueness of each word.

In a science project developed at the elementary school located on Sullivan's Island, SC, some students completed the feature analysis illustrated in Figure 10.11. Because of the school's location on the Atlantic Ocean, studying water habitats has become an essential educational experience.

Possible Sentences

Not all vocabulary techniques have to be visual illustrations. One successful strategy, called **possible sentences** (Moore & Moore, 1986; Tierney & Readence, 2000), relies primarily on verbal predictions to enhance vocabulary and concept

---

FIGURE 10.11

Sample semantic feature analysis: Sea habitats.

	Salt water	Deep water	Shore or shallow water	Rocks	Sandy or muddy bottom	Cold water	Warm water	Brackish water	Waves	Plants	Animals
Ocean	+	+	+	+	+	+	+	−	+	+	+
Rocky intertidal	+	−	+	+	?	+	+	−	+	+	+
Kelp forest	+	−	+	+	?	+	−	−	+	+	+
Estuary	−	−	+	−	+	+	+	+	−	+	+
Salt marsh	−	−	+	−	?	+	+	+	−	+	+
Sandy beach	+	−	+	−	+	+	+	−	+	+	+
Continental shelf	+	+	+	−	+	+	+	−	+	+	+
Coral reef	+	+	?	+	−	−	+	−	+	+	+
Sea grass bed	+	−	+	−	+	+	+	+	+	+	+
Mangrove swamp	+	−	+	?	+	−	+	+	?	+	+

development. Teachers introduce their students to this procedure by presenting new vocabulary in conjunction with familiar words. The students use the words to make up sentences; then they read textual material to verify the correctness of their sentences. Using possible sentences involves the following five steps:

1. List important vocabulary terms. For the passages related to the sea habitat project mentioned previously, a teacher might start by listing and pronouncing the following terms with the children: *ocean, rocky intertidal, salt water, tides, seaweeds, kelp forest, waves, beach, estuary, sea grasses, mud,* and *brackish water.*

2. Formulate sentences. The students in the class are then asked to use two or more of the words from the list in a sentence. This sentence should contain information that students think will actually be in the text. Even if the "possible sentence" is not correct, the teacher records it. This process continues until all the words have been used at least once. Sentences produced from the list in the sea habitat project might include the following:

- A *kelp forest* has lots of *seaweeds* and *salt water.*
- *Tides* and *waves* have an effect on a *rocky intertidal.*
- In an *estuary,* the *mud* and *brackish water* provide a good home for young sea animals.
- *Sea grasses* limit the *ocean's* ability to erode the *beach.*

3. Check sentences. Children read the passages to see if their sentences are correct.

4. Evaluate sentences. After everyone has completed the reading, each sentence is evaluated. Some sentences may need to be omitted; others may need to be restated. For example, students may want to clarify the fourth sentence by stating that sea grasses actually protect the beach from being battered by the ocean's waves.

5. Generate new sentences. The last step is to generate new sentences and to check them for accuracy. Once these are confirmed, children should be encouraged to add them to their reading logs or journals.

This technique is especially good for arousing prior knowledge and encouraging interaction with the text through the use of predictions. It is a good activity for involving an entire class with a text.

Beyond the classroom

For more information on vocabulary development in the content areas, consult Chapter 10 of *Reading Strategies and Practices: A Compendium* by Tierney and Readence (2000). In addition, you may want to record some activities that teachers in your field experience school use and even try your own hand at developing a vocabulary activity for the students in your field experience class.

COMPREHENSION ACROSS THE CURRICULUM

Although understanding the definitions and meanings of vocabulary words is definitely part of comprehension, true understanding comes from being able to interpret extended passages of text. To do this, children must be able to use what they already know as a way of understanding new information. They must be able to access their prior knowledge and connect the unknown with the known. In this way, they are able to process information and construct new knowledge for themselves.

Strategies for Building on Prior Knowledge

It has often been stated that teachers are to build on prior knowledge. Guillaume (1998) offers the following five strategies to use when activating students' prior knowledge:

1. Inspect the pictures of the text to be read and discuss and/or predict what is happening in the pictures.
2. Provide any artifacts, posters, models, and so forth of the topic to be studied and discuss them before beginning the study.
3. Provide music, art, or poems that relate to the topic and discuss them before the study.
4. "Factstorm" by giving students two to three minutes to jot down words or phrases that they think are associated with the topic.
5. Prepare a wall chart of K-W-L (What I *know*, What I *want* to learn, and What I *learned*) and fill it in with the students' information and questions. See Figure 10.12 for an example on polar bears.

Many strategies are available to help teachers facilitate the growth of comprehension in their students. This section presents some of these strategies in two groups: questioning strategies and guidance strategies.

As with all teaching, you must realize that you need to model the strategies, give students the opportunity to practice them, and provide feedback as the students attempt to make them their own. It might be a good idea to use modelling as described in Chapter 6 for helping your students to internalize some of the techniques recommended.

Questioning Strategies

Questioning is probably the most frequently used technique for aiding comprehension. Through the use of questions and *questioning strategies*, teachers can help students achieve the various levels of comprehension and know where to locate specific types of information. Chapter 6 included a discussion on how to use knowledge of the *question–answer relationship* as a way of guiding and simplifying the search for information. By helping students understand exactly where to look for information (on the page, in their own heads, or in both places), teachers enable them to have more control over their own learning.

ReQuest. ReQuest is another way in which teachers can use questioning as a means of empowering students by helping them learn how to ask their own questions. However, in order to do so, teachers need to follow the modeling guidelines set forth by Manzo (1968, 1969). The technique he developed incorporates reciprocal questioning and critical thinking in a one-on-one teaching situation.

A teacher prepares for **ReQuest** by making sure that the material used for developing the questions is appropriate for the student and lends itself to making predictions, selecting several points at which the student can pause and make some predictions, and initiating the session through the following nine steps (Manzo, 1968; Searfoss & Dishner, 1977; Tierney & Readence, 2000):

FIGURE 10.12

Sample wall chart.

TOPIC: POLAR BEARS

WHAT I KNOW	WHAT I WANT TO LEARN	WHAT I LEARNED
They are white. They live in Arctic.	What do they eat? Are they mean?	They have fur on their feet to keep them from slipping on the ice.

1. Each participant receives a copy of the reading selection.

2. Both the teacher and the student read the first sentence(s) silently. Then the teacher closes the book and tells the child to ask the types of questions a teacher would ask and to ask them the way a teacher would ask them. The student asks as many questions as he or she sees fit.

3. The teacher responds to the questions, reinforces appropriate questions, and requests rephrasing of questions that are unclear.

4. The child finishes questioning and closes the book. Then the teacher takes over questioning the student. At this time, the teacher tries to model appropriate questioning behavior and to use a variety of question types.

5. The procedure is repeated with the second sentence. (With older students, a teacher may want to start reading a few sentences at a time rather than just one.)

6. This process continues until enough of the selection has been read (probably the first paragraph or so) for the student to make a prediction about what the rest of the selection is about.

7. The teacher then asks the student to justify the prediction. If the prediction is reasonable, the student continues with silent reading. If not, the exchange of questions continues and the student makes another prediction at a later point.

8. Now the teacher directs the student to read to the end of the selection in order to compare the prediction with what really did happen.

9. The teacher follows up with a discussion about the merits of the prediction and why it might be possible to have several logical and plausible conclusions to the same selection. It is best to avoid the idea of one right answer. The student might even be given the opportunity to write a new ending for the text.

Semantic webbing. Still another comprehension activity based on questioning is semantic webbing (Meinbach, Rothlein, & Fredricks, 1995; Parks & Black, 1990). **Semantic webbing** helps students develop a map of the information by organizing ideas and visually illustrating the relationship among concepts in the reading material. At the center of each web is the *core question.* Attached to the center are several web strands representing the children's answers to the question. The strands, in turn, are supported by the strand supports, which generally consist of important facts and information from the story. The strand ties show the relationship of the strands to each other. Figure 10.13 shows a semantic web based on "The Three Little Pigs."

Such a web organizes the story so that the children can see certain relationships and gain a deeper understanding of what the material is about. How the web develops depends on the core question. If the question had been "What happened?" the web would have taken a different direction: The information would have been organized around the sequence of events in the story. The question and how it is stated assist the students in getting the information.

Beyond the classroom

Try to extend your knowledge about semantic webbing by reading "Using Maps to Teach Note Taking and Outlining for Report Writing" (Pieronek, 1994) in *Social Studies.* This article illustrates how to use semantic webs in the content areas. After reading it, you may want to try developing a semantic web with some of the students in your field experience class.

Guidance Strategies

Guidance strategies empower students to become strategic readers, readers who have developed metacognition and are able to motivate and monitor themselves as they comprehend information. By providing assistance based on the needs of

FIGURE **10.13**

Sample semantic web:
"The Three Little Pigs."

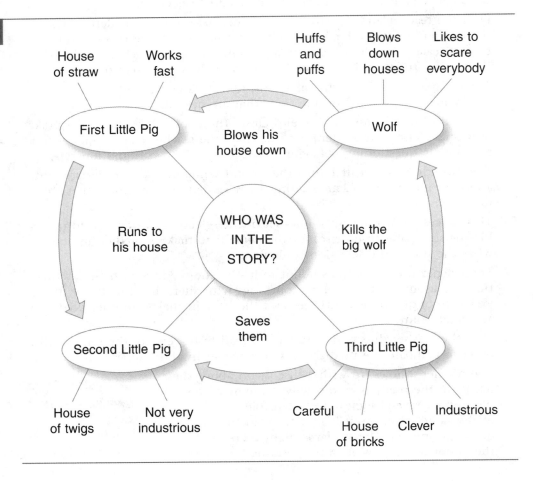

your students, you can help them to become independent, self-confident learners in all areas. (See Chapter 6 for more information on metacognition and strategic readers.)

In general, *guidance strategies* are used during the reading process as a way of arousing interest and focusing attention. They help children to activate prior knowledge, to monitor the comprehension process, and to provide needed follow-up during the postreading period. This section describes three strategies to help guide the reading process from beginning to end: the DR-TA, the guided reading procedure, and reading guides.

Teaching is the art

of assisting discovery.

MARK VAN DOREN

Directed reading–thinking activity (DR-TA). Stauffer (1969) originally conceptualized the DR-TA as a process to help students set purposes for reading. As such, it is particularly suited for selections in the content areas (Tierney & Readence, 2000).

During the **DR-TA,** the teacher helps the reader identify purposes for reading, guides the reader through the reading process, monitors the reader to determine any difficulties, helps the reader develop comprehension, and helps the reader develop particular skills as appropriate. Activities during the prereading, reading, and postreading stages are as follows:

- *Prereading.* Have students activate any prior knowledge by viewing the title, pictures, and headings of the material. Encourage students to make predictions about the selection based on their observations. Write their ideas on the board or a chart.

- *Reading.* Have students read to verify their predictions. Extend their thinking by encouraging them to verify their predictions, summarize what they have read, and predict what might happen next.
- *Postreading.* Discuss what the students have read and the accuracy of their predictions. Encourage the children to point out sections of the material that support or disprove their predictions. Allow the children to discuss the process and summarize what they have learned for themselves.

After the postreading session, you might want to go back and use this particular material for the development of specific student competencies, such as the use of context clues or summarization.

The DR-TA has proved to be a very successful reading strategy—so much so that in recent years much attention has been focused on it. One modification has been the development of the chart in Figure 10.14. This chart serves to activate and record each reader's prior knowledge about a topic as well as her or his predictions and summarization notes about the reading selection.

Guided reading procedure (GRP). The guided reading procedure, as discussed in Chapter 6, is intended to provide practice in certain strategies needed to develop as an independent reader. The **GRP** involves student collaboration, the use of self-questioning and self-correction techniques, and the organization of information. It is most appropriate for materials containing a multitude of facts needed for future reference.

Reading guides. Both the DR-TA and GRP are designed to be used as group strategies. However, at times you may want to employ an activity that individual students can use independently. The **reading guide** consists of having individual students make decisions about a series of statements at the different levels of comprehension; the purpose of the strategy is to guide the student in comprehending a selection by showing him or her the relationship among the ideas. The statements in the guide also serve as initiators for student discussion of the material.

Figure 10.15 presents an example of a guide that a primary teacher used to help the children in her class understand that animals are adapted in special ways in order to survive in their habitats. She wanted them to organize their ideas about this concept by classifying the animals according to where they live.

FIGURE **10.14**

DR-TA adaptation chart.

WHAT DO YOU . . .

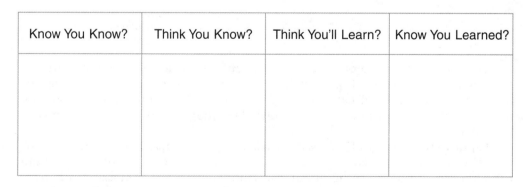

Know You Know?	Think You Know?	Think You'll Learn?	Know You Learned?

FIGURE **10.15**

Sample reading guide.

Topic: Animals are adapted to live in different habitats.

Part I   As you read the text, check the statements that are true.

☐   1. *Adapted* means that an animal fits into its habitat.

☐   2. An animal that is adapted cannot get food and water.

☐   3. Deserts are hot and do not have much rain.

☐   4. The polar areas near the North and South Poles are cold most of the year.

☐   5. Polar bears live near the North Pole.

☐   6. Penguins live near the South Pole.

☐   7. Some of the biggest and fastest animals live in the grasslands.

☐   8. Rain forests are hot and wet.

☐   9. Whales live in the ocean.

☐ 10. Whales breathe through fins.

Part II   Classify the animals listed according to where they live. Write each word under the proper heading.

blue whale	kangaroo rat	cattle	ptarmigan	jackrabbit
boa	rattlesnake	buffalo	shark	ermine
zebra	camel	sheep	tree frog	octopus
rhino	penguin	ocelot	seal	arctic tern
musk ox	polar bear	killer whale	walrus	parrot
arctic hare	giraffe	sea urchin	lizard	monkey

Deserts	Polar Areas	Grasslands	Rain Forests	Water

One specialized type of guide calls students' attention to the dominant textual pattern in the reading materials. By helping students to recognize and then use a major textual pattern to organize their ideas, you can encourage students to develop metacognitive knowledge about relationships in textual information.

Figures 10.16 and 10.17 show two pattern guides that have been successfully with middle school students. Both guides were developed to facilitate the children's understanding about the Hohokam and the Anasazi Indians as part of a unit on Native Americans. One guide was developed to highlight the interaction of causes and effects on various aspects of tribe members' lives; the other compares the two groups on a variety of factors.

THE HOHOKAM AND THE ANASAZI

Match the effects on the right with the causes on the left.

FIGURE 10.16

Sample reading guide (cause–effect).

Causes

_____ 1. The Ice Age ended and the desert formed.

_____ 2. The Hohokam lined the irrigation canals with clay.

_____ 3. The Hohokam built and lived in pit houses.

_____ 4. The Anasazi planted crops near streams with plenty of rain.

_____ 5. The Anasazi took great care in building the pueblos.

_____ 6. The Anasazi could remove the ladders to the pueblos.

_____ 7. A great drought came.

Effects

A. Enemies could not get into the homes.

B. They were even better farmers than the Hohokam.

C. The Anasazi packed up and disappeared.

D. After thousands of years, the people learned to farm to survive.

E. The farmers were protected from the hot daytime sun and the sharp cold at night.

F. Many of the Anasazi pueblos are still standing.

G. The water took longer to soak into the ground.

FIGURE 10.17

Sample reading guide (comparison–contrast).

THE HOHOKAM AND THE ANASAZI

The Hohokam	In relationship to:	The Anasazi
	Geographic Location	
	Farming Techniques	
	Housing	
	Crafts	
	Fate	

Responding to Information: Writing to Learn

Previous chapters have described the writing process and stressed its importance in developing children's communication competencies. Chapters 8 and 9 also outlined specific methods for enhancing classroom writing as well as appropriate approaches to evaluation.

This section focuses on the benefits of using writing as a tool for learning throughout the curriculum. Because writing is part of the total communication process, it should be united as much as possible with the other language arts of reading, listening, speaking, viewing, and visually representing. Through writing, many students can get ready for reading and learning; then they can use writing to respond to what they have read and to link or summarize all the information they have acquired. For students, the curriculum can become a cycle of writing, reading, thinking, and then more writing to reflect upon and extend their thinking (Tompkins, 1997).

Writing is very much an individual process. It lets people clarify their own thoughts and helps them to understand themselves and to make their ideas understood by others. Therefore, classroom writing should not be forced but should come as a natural part of learning (Tompkins, 1997).

It is important to allow students the same opportunities for self-expression and communication with others that they have in real life. With this concept in mind, the following section is organized around two broad ideas: writing for self—which includes freewriting as well as writing journals, diaries, and logs—and writing for others—which includes various types of letters, telecommunications activities, the use of language experience, paragraph frames, and book publishing. Many of these concepts have been introduced in earlier chapters but deserve further consideration in the context of writing across the curriculum.

WRITING FOR SELF

Writing for self encompasses the idea of **freewriting** (also called *quickwrites*) for personal expression (Elbow, 1973), a way of communicating your ideas to yourself, digging within yourself, and just saying what comes to mind about whatever you are involved in. This might mean writing a poem, a personal statement, a daily diary, or just a series of jottings. These ideas were explored in Chapter 8, which chronicles the writing process. However, one type of personal writing particularly suited to the content areas is that of keeping a journal.

Journal writing actually allows writing to become a natural part of the classroom process. Students can use their journals as a way of reflecting on classroom situations or of keeping a record of science experiments, social studies research, or personal reactions to classroom presentations in art or music.

To be successful, journal writing should become part of the daily classroom routine, with a particular block of time (5–20 minutes, depending on your class) devoted to it in the same way that time is set aside for sustained silent reading. In this type of individual activity, children should have the freedom to write whatever they feel and think without having to worry about spelling, grammar, and mechanics.

Following are two journal entries written by two different children in Ms. Terri Neal's third-grade class showing how they responded to a classroom science presentation on snakes:

> Today we had a visitor, her name was Karen she had snakes, there—names were Checkers. Because it's stomach looked like checkers. And the other snakes name was Tasha! I don't know why she named her that! We asked questions too! The class had fun! Some people got scared! I wish the snake would eat the rat! Checkers started to get out of the aquairam!
>
> I like when the snake was chasing the mouse. And Tosha tried to whrap around the mouse and the mouse got away. I am glad that the snake did not get the mouse. If I was little I would not be scared, I got to hold Tosha and checkers.

Another way of referring to this type of journal is as a *learning log* (Vacca & Vacca, 2002). This name gives the student the idea that the entries are supposed to chronicle her or his learning. It is also a way for students to state problems and clarify certain aspects of learning in a risk-free atmosphere.

A specialized form of journal writing begins to cross the bridge between writing for self and writing for others. In a **dialogue journal,** students

FIGURE **10.18**

Sample dialogue journal entries.

Feb. 28, 2004

I loved "James and the Giant Peach". The cariter I liked was the Cenepede. I wish that the anuts were nicer. I am Glad the James found a nice home even if it was a seed. I an glad that James have lots of friends.

Gadeer,

I agree. This story is great. However, I think that my favorite character is James.

Like you, I'm glad that he did find a home and has lots of friends.

If you like this type of fantasy writing, you will probably enjoy some of the other books that Roald Dahl has written. If you'd like, I'll get a list of titles together.

T. Johnson

write their thoughts and messages to the teacher, who then responds to them in a supportive and nonevaluative manner. This type of journal, described in greater depth in Chapter 8, allows children to carry on a "conversation" in writing (Atwell, 1998). It also enables the teacher to provide a writing model for students. Some sample dialogue journal entries appear in Figure 10.18.

As with all personal classroom writing, when engaging in dialogue journals, you as the teacher must be careful to respect the privacy of students in addition to respecting the value of their thoughts.

WRITING FOR OTHERS

Writing for others involves communication and sharing of ideas. One of the easiest, most basic, and most widely used activities in writing for others is letter writing. Letters may be written in response to material being studied in class and may or may not be sent. Letters not intended to be sent (Vacca & Vacca, 2002) can be used to engage students in a role-play situation to expand their thinking about information they have acquired. For example, students who have been studying about the destruction of the rain forests might summarize their findings in an open letter to Brazilian ranchers and developers. In such a letter, the students might point out the need to save the forests for the welfare of the world as well as that of Brazil.

On the other hand, letters to be sent can engage the students in real-life communication with teachers, classmates, caregivers, and even authors of books being used by the class. Strickland (1987) has termed letters that catalog a continuing interaction between students and teachers about a particular topic or book *dialogue letters.*

An extension of sending letters is the use of email. Students can become involved in their school or district or even nationally. They can exchange ideas, letters, jokes, and any other imaginable information by sending email messages. Classes have even become involved in networks that allow them to have pen pals in other parts of the country and all over the world. When students send information to such faraway friends, they invariably take great pains to make sure that it is interesting and accurate in every way.

Another method of using writing to develop and extend knowledge is through *language experience.* The content areas generally provide a wealth of experiences for both primary- and middle-level students. They have experiments in science, problems to solve in math, simulations and role-plays in social studies, projects in art, and performances in music and theatre. Completing a language-experience chart following one of these activities or events allows the children to think about and internalize the learning as well as to communicate it to others. Barrow, Kristo, and Andrew (1984) have recommended using science language experience with individuals and small groups who have investigated or manipulated science-related objects. This process has four steps (Barrow & Andrew, 1981):

1. The teacher provides manipulatives for students to investigate. The teacher may post questions about the manipulatives to stimulate discussion.
2. Students dictate or write about their observations.
3. Children illustrate these stories as an additional interpretation of the experience. The teacher may direct younger students to draw what they see first, as a support for the subsequent writing.
4. Students share their experience stories and illustrations with teachers, peers, or caregivers.

Two examples of science language-experience stories appear in Figure 10.19.

A further extension of using writing to learn in the primary grades involves the use of *paragraph frames* (Cudd & Roberts, 1989). These frames use a cloze procedure of sentence starters to help organize a child's paragraph into one of the common organizational patterns of content-area text. Frames can be organized to sequence, enumerate, react to reading, or compare and contrast. A sample paragraph frame is illustrated in Figure 10.20.

As always, book publishing, either individually or as a group, is another way for children to consolidate and internalize information for themselves as

---

FIGURE 10.19

Sample science language-experience stories.

Meal Worm

He is squshy and squirmy. He is sleppy. He has rough skin. They are slow and thin. They are little. He is scraney Kathryn

The meal worm

This worm lives in a forest. He is very happy. One day a boy got the worm and put him in a jar. The boy said this worm is little, soft and ticklish. The worm was happy from then on. Peter.

FIGURE **10.20**

Sample paragraph frame.

Example 1   (Elena, grade 2)

Before a frog is grown, it goes through many changes. First, the mother frog _____

_____.

Next, _____.

Then, _____.

Finally, _____.

Now they _____

_____

> Before a frog is grown,
> it goes through many stages. First,
> the mother frog lays the eggs. Next,
> the eggs hatch and turn into tadpoles.
> Then slowly the tadpoles legs begin
> to grow. Finally, the tadpole turns
> into a frog. Now and then they
> have to go into the water to keep
> their skin moist.

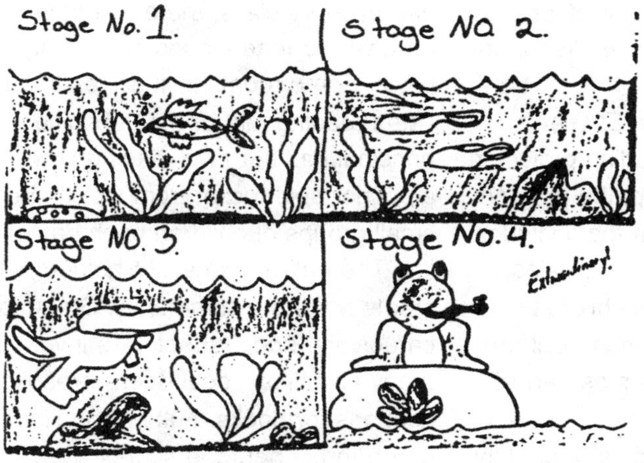

Stage No. 1.   Stage No. 2.

Stage No. 3.   Stage No. 4.   Extraordinary!

---

they communicate it to others. Book publishing can take a variety of forms. Many children create books by retelling stories they have read or that have been read to them. In the content areas, children can vary this approach by publishing books containing factual information. Yet another interesting approach to the mechanics of writing was demonstrated by one sixth-grade class that wrote its own grammar book and kept it as a resource in the classroom. (See Chapter 8 for a discussion on book publishing.) Read the Classroom Vignette that follows to see how some schools use reading and writing across the curriculum.

VIGNETTE
in the classroom

What do Avondale Elementary School (Birmingham, AL), Bertrun E. Glavin Elementary School (Winnipeg, Manitoba), Bel Pre Elementary School (Silver Spring, MD), Dunn Middle School (Danvers, MA), Delmar-Harvard School of Investigative Learning (University City, MO), Capshaw Elementary School (Cookeville, TN), and Sheldon Elementary School (Sheldon, VT) have in common? These are some of the winners of Exemplary Reading Program Awards given by the International Reading Association. Another thing these schools all have in common is their integrated focus on using reading and writing throughout the curriculum.

At the Avondale Elementary School, children in grades 1 through 3 take a writing workshop twice a week. Older students can select a writing club as part of their extracurricular activities. The school also hosts children's book authors as well as professional storytellers and illustrators at a daylong workshop for caregivers and children.

In Winnipeg, Manitoba, the Bertrun E. Glavin Elementary School started a home reading project in 1990. From a home–school partnership, the program has evolved into an integrated program that includes gifted and talented classes, multicultural activities, and conflict management programs. All children in the program check out books from the school library to bring home to read to their caregivers as part of the school curriculum.

The Bel Pre Elementary School hosts a monthly books and breakfast program for caregivers of Title 1 students. Professional educators demonstrate techniques caregivers can use with their children to support reading and writing at home. The program also encourages caregivers to volunteer at the school in various capacities.

In Danvers, MA, the Dunn Middle School launched a reading and study skills training program for all its sixth-grade teachers of math, science, social studies, and English. Teachers even got the school schedule changed to allow for a yearlong course for students titled Reading in the Content Area.

In University City, MO, the students at Delmar-Harvard School of Investigative Learning write, illustrate, and edit books about their families and community. Caregiver volunteers help with the typing and binding of the books.

The students of Capshaw Elementary School do sustained silent reading on a schoolwide basis every day. In every class, there is a specially designated area where read alouds and silent reading take place. Some rooms include reading tents, an elevated reading loft, or bathtubs filled with pillows. The principal has her own reading corner equipped with a comfortable rocker from which she reads aloud to small groups of children each day of the week.

The entire village of Sheldon, VT, is working to create a literate community. Grandparents, parents, caregivers, and students are involved in various literacy activities. Local bookstores issue free coupons for books. Author and illustrator workshops go on throughout the school year. Children and adults alike take the literacy pledge to turn off the television and read.

Thematic Units: The Key to Integration

There are three types of thematic units: the intradisciplinary, the interdisciplinary, and the inquiry-based. Each uses a theme and is based on the philosophy of using authentic viewing, reading, writing, and hands-on activities to learn more about the world in which students live. All three of these types emphasize the interrelatedness of the language arts; however, the planning of each is somewhat different. In the intradisciplinary unit, all the aspects of the language arts (reading, writing, listening, speaking, viewing, and visually representing) are integrated as the students study an author or a particular genre that the teacher selects. In the interdisciplinary unit, the teacher goes beyond literature and authors and selects a theme, such as the rain forest or ocean life, and integrates the theme in all content areas: math, social studies, art, literature, music, science, and so forth. In the inquiry-based unit, the teacher permits the students to select the topic, which might be gum and candy, and integrates that topic in all the content-area subjects. Figure 10.21 shows the similarities and differences among the three types of units. From the diagram, it is easy to see that the common thread of all three types of units is the interrelatedness of the language arts.

INTRADISCIPLINARY UNIT

With the **intradisciplinary unit** approach, the teacher integrates the language arts while studying authors or a particular genre. The students read books of their choice that are appropriate for their reading level, they view different types of material, they listen to classmates' points of view in literature discussion circles, and they visually present their responses to the literature. The teacher selects the author or genre and plans appropriate activities for the unit. Specific skills are taught as the need arises during the actual unit.

For example, a first-grade teacher may choose to study Eric Carle, a favorite author of many first-graders. One week before the unit is to begin, the teacher announces the study and encourages students to browse through the books that she or he has placed on a table in the classroom. The teacher knows that most first-graders cannot read the texts, but they can view the pictures. On the Friday before the unit begins, the teacher takes a poll of the students' favorite Carle books. On Monday, the teacher begins to read to the students the book that received the most votes. While reading, the teacher has the students look at the pictures and predict what will happen. The teacher may decide not to finish the book when reaching the climax and have the students as a class dictate an ending while the teacher writes it on a large chart. Or the teacher may have each student draw his or her ending; then the teacher would write a caption under each student's picture. The teacher encourages students to share their endings at the end of the work time. Afterward, the teacher reads the rest of the book in order for the students to compare their ending with Eric Carle's ending. On Tuesday, the teacher takes another Eric Carle book and does a different activity with it. Throughout the unit, the teacher has the students discuss and compare the unique artwork of the books and then teaches the children how to create collages from tissue paper, the technique that Carle uses. The teacher also gives some biographical information about Eric Carle. Throughout the unit, the language arts are integrated while students spend time viewing, reading, discussing, writing, and visually representing.

When teachers use the intradisciplinary unit approach with older students, the classroom may become a reading/writing workshop. A teacher's goal for the

The teacher's task is not to implant facts but to place the subject to be learned in front of the learner and, through sympathy, emotion, imagination and patience, to awaken in the learner the restless drive for answers and insights which enlarge the personal life and give it meaning.

NATHAN M. PUSEY

	Integration of Language Arts	Integration of Content Areas	Planner
Intradisciplinary	Yes	No	Teacher
Interdisciplinary	Yes	Yes	Teacher
Inquiry-based	Yes	Yes	Students

FIGURE 10.21

Relationship among the three approaches to integrated units.

school year may be to expose the students to the different genres. At the beginning of each new unit, the teacher would introduce the genre, such as historical fiction, by explaining that type of literature, introducing authors who write historical fiction, and providing large stacks of books of varying reading levels from various authors. Students would choose which books to read and choose how to respond to the literature. Some students who choose the same author would form literature circles to discuss the similarities and differences of the various books. If the author is living, students could email the author or browse the author's Web page. During a historical fiction unit, another group of students who all read different books from a particular era, such as the Civil War, could combine the information they learned into a skit and perform it for the class.

As you can see, the language arts are totally integrated in the intradisciplinary unit approach: The students are listening to others, reading books of their choice, writing pieces that are authentic, viewing different types of materials, and visually presenting their responses to the literature. It is difficult to separate these language arts skills because they complement each other. The Class Vignette that follows is an example of the intradisciplinary unit approach in a fifth-grade classroom.

INTERDISCIPLINARY UNIT

The interdisciplinary unit uses a somewhat different type of integrated approach. The **interdisciplinary unit** integrates the entire curriculum by using one unifying theme that includes many content areas, such as math, science, social studies, literature, music, and art. The interdisciplinary unit integrates more than the language arts. Reading, writing, listening, speaking, viewing, and visually representing are the means to gather information and to share infor-

VIGNETTE *in the classroom*

One fifth-grade teacher decided to do an author study on Beverly Cleary. The teacher collected many of Cleary's books and made them available to the students. Four students chose to read the same book, *Dear Mr. Henshaw* (1983). Since the story is told entirely through the letters and diary of a young boy, the students also became interested in letter writing.

One day the teacher joins the group. John wants to share with her a serious passage about divorce, a topic that is painfully real to him. The teacher encourages him to read it aloud so that the group can discuss it. However, Alex, another boy in the group, says that he thinks the book is actually pretty funny. Again, the teacher encourages him to read aloud to support this. After both students have read aloud from their chosen passages, the entire group

wonders how a book can be funny and serious at the same time. Two students decide to write their own letters to the author, asking her some of the questions that are puzzling them. One student decides to write his own book, using letters to tell the story. The last student decides to make a diorama that depicts the book.

The students selected their own book to read. They met in literature discussion groups periodically to talk about the book and to share favorite passages. Choice of reading material, silent reading, discussion, and writing—these are the elements that make up the integrated approach. Note, too, that the book choice and related activities were student initiated. The teacher chose the author and then served as a resource to help students, but she did not dictate exactly what students were to do.

mation that is learned. This approach provides students the opportunity to understand concepts in a holistic fashion as they relate to the world. A broad conceptual theme, chosen by the teacher, is used to promote cognitive growth in the content areas. Large blocks of time are given to students to learn about many aspects within the overall theme.

Central to the success of the interdisciplinary unit is appropriate planning of the unit (Vacca & Vacca, 2002). Because the theme is the core of the unit and provides a structure for organizing activities, it is important for the teacher to spend some time thinking about which themes would be most appropriate for the class, would involve the greatest number of available resources, and would encourage students to be active learners. The themes that are eventually chosen should reflect the curriculum for that grade level and the overall objectives for that group of students. When developing the unit, the teacher must be sure that it contains the following information and guidelines (Seely, 1995):

- The title and theme must reflect the content of the unit that will interest the students as well as fit the required state curriculum.
- The major objectives of the unit and the concepts to be learned must reflect the required skills for that grade level.
- The resources to be used by the students and teacher may be classified as either reading materials or media resources. They can include websites; addresses (both email and postal) of businesses, experts in the field, clubs, authors, and so on; and possible guest speakers.
- The projects and activities can be whole group, small group, or individual. They can also be Internet projects with students from other places.
- The methods for evaluating the unit, such as learning portfolios, anecdotal records, checklists, or informal testing, must be made known to the students before the unit begins.

One example of an interdisciplinary unit may be the history of the state in which the students are living. Some possible areas within this broad theme would be the history of the state, its natural resources, and exciting places to visit as well as great authors, famous people, and great inventors from that state. In order for the interdisciplinary approach to be successful, the areas studied and skills developed during the time the topic is studied must be relevant and authentic; they cannot be "tacked on." Lapp, Flood, and Farnan (1996) believe that "effective curriculum integration occurs when the content from one subject area is used to enhance or enrich the content of another" (p. 418).

Choice is given to the students. They get to choose which questions to answer, which resources to use to gather the information, and how to present their findings to the rest of the class. They may choose to write an informational book, write and perform a skit, make a diorama, draw a mural, create a computer presentation, write a script and videotape a presentation as a documentary, or use any other creative way. In this type of classroom, the necessary material is learned because the students share their findings with other students; however, all the students did not read the same chapter of one text nor did they listen to the teacher lecture on the information.

Figure 10.22 shows an interdisciplinary unit on Oklahoma, a required unit for fourth-graders in Oklahoma. Figure 10.23 is a list of possible integrated projects for the unit. Figure 10.24 has a list of books by Oklahoma authors. This

FIGURE 10.22

Interdisciplinary study of Oklahoma.

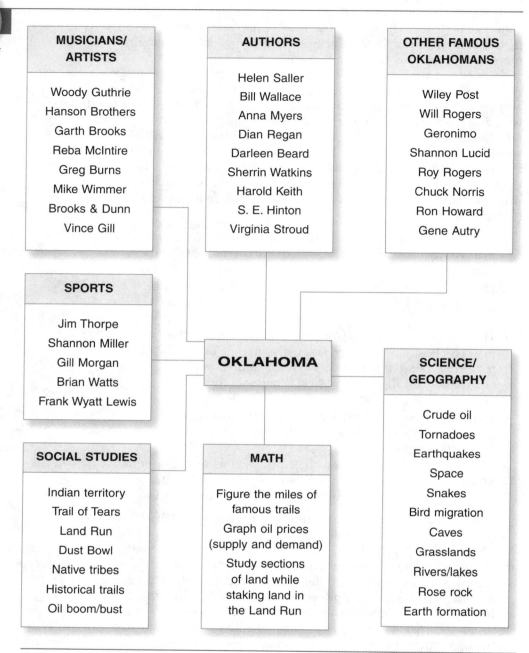

MUSICIANS/ARTISTS

Woody Guthrie
Hanson Brothers
Garth Brooks
Reba McIntire
Greg Burns
Mike Wimmer
Brooks & Dunn
Vince Gill

AUTHORS

Helen Saller
Bill Wallace
Anna Myers
Dian Regan
Darleen Beard
Sherrin Watkins
Harold Keith
S. E. Hinton
Virginia Stroud

OTHER FAMOUS OKLAHOMANS

Wiley Post
Will Rogers
Geronimo
Shannon Lucid
Roy Rogers
Chuck Norris
Ron Howard
Gene Autry

SPORTS

Jim Thorpe
Shannon Miller
Gill Morgan
Brian Watts
Frank Wyatt Lewis

OKLAHOMA

SCIENCE/GEOGRAPHY

Crude oil
Tornadoes
Earthquakes
Space
Snakes
Bird migration
Caves
Grasslands
Rivers/lakes
Rose rock
Earth formation

SOCIAL STUDIES

Indian territory
Trail of Tears
Land Run
Dust Bowl
Native tribes
Historical trails
Oil boom/bust

MATH

Figure the miles of famous trails
Graph oil prices (supply and demand)
Study sections of land while staking land in the Land Run

unit can be modified to fit any state by changing authors, famous people, natural resources, and so forth.

Another example of a curriculum web developed around the interdisciplinary unit of beasts and monsters is found in Figure 10.25. The starting point for the unit was the book *The Beast of Monsieur Racine* by Tomi Ungerer.

A third example of an interdisciplinary unit title, "Fish—Our Friendly Neighbors," was developed by some elementary-school teachers in South Carolina. The concepts that they wanted their students to understand were the following:

1. A wide variety of fish are available in local South Carolina waters.
2. All the fish have distinctive characteristics that are adapted to their needs and specific habitats.

1. Using an Oklahoma state map, have students find the shortest distance between various towns, cities, and vacation spots.

2. Using an Oklahoma state map, trace Route 66 and have students find how many miles long the route is in Oklahoma. Have them research Route 66 to find out why and when it was an important route through Oklahoma.

3. Using an Oklahoma state map, have students trace the Chisholm Trail and find out how many miles long it was. Have them research the trail to find out when and why it was so important.

4. Have students research the significance of the Trail of Tears; have them write and perform a play based on their findings.

5. Interview an oil-field worker to find out how oil rigs are set up and how much oil they pump. Have students build a model of a rig that will pump oil (cooking oil).

6. Have students find out the price of oil per barrel for the last 40 years and use a bar graph to show their findings.

7. Research the Land Run and reenact it with the other fourth-graders, wearing costumes that fit the era. Have students build covered wagons.

8. Have groups of children find out why one of the people listed under "Other Famous Oklahomans" (see Figure 10.22) was famous. Have them make a class book of famous Oklahomans.

9. Have groups of students research living recording artists (Hanson Brothers, Garth Brooks, etc.) to determine how they became popular and what it takes to record a CD; have them trace one of the recording artist's world or national tours. Have groups of children compose a song and record it on tape to play to the class and/or caregivers.

10. Read some books written by Oklahoma authors (see Figure 10.22) and have the children invite one of them to their school to talk about their work.

11. Invite an Oklahoma artist (e.g., Greg Burns or Mike Wimmer) to your school to tell about his or her artwork. Have students draw or paint, using techniques similar to those the artist used.

12. Give small groups of students a Native American tribe to research. Using a video camera, have the students produce a TV special about their findings. Have them invite some members of various tribes to talk to the class about their customs and use the presentation as part of the video.

13. Read *Children of the Dust Bowl* by Jerry Stanley; then have some children write and perform a skit or play based on this book and other sources.

14. Research Shannon Lucid's life to determine how she became an astronaut who was chosen for the spaceflight with the Space Station Mir.

15. Invite Shannon Miller to your class to talk about gymnastics and the Olympics.

16. Invite a TV weatherperson to come and explain tornadoes and how people can protect themselves during a tornado.

17. Have a small group research the types of snakes in Oklahoma and create an information brochure on these snakes.

18. Have students map bird migration to and from Oklahoma on a U. S. map.

19. Have a small group of students study the terrain of Oklahoma and create a model of it.

20. Have a small group of students research the rock formation in which crude oil is found; have them create a model.

21. If your school is named after a famous Oklahoman (e.g., Wiley Post, Jim Thorpe), have the students find out why she or he was famous; then have students write a pamphlet to publish and share with caregivers during an open house.

FIGURE 10.23

Some possible projects for an integrated unit on Oklahoma.

FIGURE **10.24**   *Recommended books by Oklahoma authors (with possible extended studies).*

Darleen Bailey Beard

The Babbs Switch Story (2002). New York: Farrar, Straus, & Giroux. (coping with a sister with mental retardation and growing up in the 1920s)

The Pumpkin Man from Piney Creek (1995). New York: Simon & Schuster. (pumpkin farming and honesty)

The Flimflam Man (1998). New York: Farrar, Straus, & Giroux. (origins of town festivals and how people bamboozle one another in business)

Twister (1999). New York: Farrar, Straus, & Giroux. (Oklahoma weather)

Sherrin Watkins

White Bead Ceremony (1994). Tulsa, OK: Council Oak Books. (customs of the Shawnee tribe; pronunciation key of Shawnee words included)

Ceremony of the Green Snake (1995). Tulsa, OK: Council Oak Books. (customs of the Shawnee tribe)

Harold Keith

Rifles for Watie (1957). New York: A Harper Keypoint Book. (Civil War and the Cherokee Indians, with their alphabet)

Chico and Dan (1998). Austin: Eakin Publications. (a young boy's attachment to a wild horse)

Anna Myers

Red-Dirt Jessie (1992). New York: Walker & Co. (death and dying and trust)

Rosie's Tiger (1994). New York: Walker & Co. (Korean War and Koreans attempting a life in the United States)

Graveyard Girl (1995). New York: Walker & Co. (yellow fever and the effects on society)

Spotting the Leopard (1996). New York: Walker & Co. (the Great Depression as well as zoo animals and their natural habitats)

The Keeping Room (1997). New York: Walker & Co. (Quakers)

Captain's Command (2001). New York: Walker & Co. (how a family readjusts as one of its members becomes missing in action during WWII)

Stolen by the Sea (2001). New York: Walker & Co. (how an adolescent girl struggles with her feelings of jealousy, shame, and nobility)

Tulsa Burning (2002). New York: Walker & Co. (race relations and family triumphs)

Dian Curtis Regan

The Curse of the Trouble Dolls (1992). New York: Henry Holt & Co. (different customs)

The Thirteen Hours of Halloween (1993). Morton Grove, IL: Albert Whitman & Co. (origins of the many Halloween costumes)

Princess Nevermore (1995). New York: Scholastic. (royal protocol and the world of magic)

Dear Dr. Sillybear (1997). New York: Henry Holt & Co. (homonyms)

Chance (2003). New York: Philomel Books. (leaving home and discovering what home really is)

Virginia Stroud (author and illustrator)

Doesn't Fall Off His Horse (1994). New York: Dial Books. (how a Cherokee boy becomes a man and other ceremonies of the Cherokee tribe; also the type of art Stroud uses)

A Walk to the Great Mystery (1995). New York: Dial Books. (ways of the Cherokee medicine woman; also the type of art Stroud uses)

Bill Wallace

Beauty (1988). New York: A Minstrel Book. (how to care for horses)

A Dog Called Kitty (1988). New York: A Minstrel Book. (various types of dogs and how to care for them)

Christmas Spurs (1990). New York: A Minstrel Book. (Stetson cowboy hats and the cowboy's life)

The Final Freedom (1997). New York: A Minstrel Book. (Geronimo and Native Americans as well as the World Fairs)

Upchuck and the Rotten Willy (1998). New York: A Minstrel Book. (characteristics of pets)

Coyote Autumn (2002). New York: Holiday House. (adjusting to new environments and experiencing wildlife)

Mike Wimmer (illustrator)

All the Places to Love by Patricia MacLachlan (1994). New York: HarperCollins Publishers. (oil painting)

Home Run by Robert Burleigh (1998). San Diego: Harcourt Brace. (oil painting and the world of Babe Ruth)

Summertime: From Porgy and Bess (1999). New York: Simon & Schuster. (an African American family's life together depicted in oil paintings)

Other Sources

Children of the Dust Bowl by Jerry Stanley (1992). New York: A Trumpet Club Special Edition. (photographs of families and the account of their trek to California during the 1930s)

Oklahoma Adventure Guide, 8005 South I-35, Suite 205, Oklahoma City, OK 73149-2932. (set of three guides featuring highlights from the following three areas of Oklahoma: central, northeast, and northwest)

Oklahoma Today: Official Magazine of the State of Oklahoma. Oklahoma City, OK: Oklahoma Today. (features people, places, and events in Oklahoma; published seven times a year)

Out of the Dust by Karen Hesse (1997). New York: Scholastic. (study of the Dust Bowl in Oklahoma and Newbery Award books)

Sample curriculum web: The Beast of Monsieur Racine. **FIGURE 10.25**

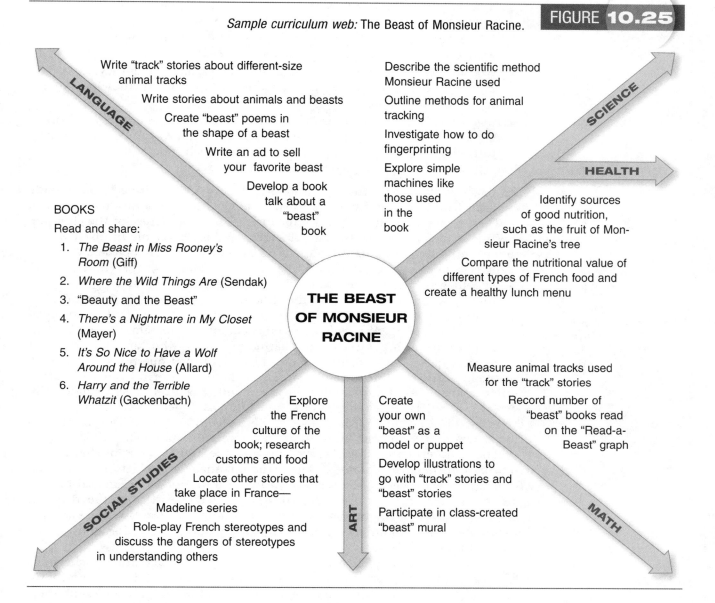

LANGUAGE

Write "track" stories about different-size animal tracks

Write stories about animals and beasts

Create "beast" poems in the shape of a beast

Write an ad to sell your favorite beast

Develop a book talk about a "beast" book

SCIENCE

Describe the scientific method Monsieur Racine used

Outline methods for animal tracking

Investigate how to do fingerprinting

Explore simple machines like those used in the book

HEALTH

Identify sources of good nutrition, such as the fruit of Monsieur Racine's tree

Compare the nutritional value of different types of French food and create a healthy lunch menu

BOOKS

Read and share:

1. *The Beast in Miss Rooney's Room* (Giff)
2. *Where the Wild Things Are* (Sendak)
3. "Beauty and the Beast"
4. *There's a Nightmare in My Closet* (Mayer)
5. *It's So Nice to Have a Wolf Around the House* (Allard)
6. *Harry and the Terrible Whatzit* (Gackenbach)

THE BEAST OF MONSIEUR RACINE

MATH

Measure animal tracks used for the "track" stories

Record number of "beast" books read on the "Read-a-Beast" graph

ART

Create your own "beast" as a model or puppet

Develop illustrations to go with "track" stories and "beast" stories

Participate in class-created "beast" mural

SOCIAL STUDIES

Explore the French culture of the book; research customs and food

Locate other stories that take place in France— Madeline series

Role-play French stereotypes and discuss the dangers of stereotypes in understanding others

3. Local fish are a natural resource that provides us with benefits.

4. Fish have been important in all cultures.

With these ideas in mind, the teachers went about locating many resources available to themselves and their students. They started by contacting the local offices of the South Carolina Wildlife and Marine Resources Department, where they were able to get information on available pamphlets, films, and videos as well as appropriate sites for field trips. They were even able to have several local marine biologists come to the school and serve as research consultants to the children. Library resources were available at the school and through the main branch of the public library. The books were targeted for children in grades K–5. A small sampling of these books follows:

As you teach, emphasize what interests you.

WILLIAM GLASSER, M.D.

- Carle, E. (1987). *A House for Hermit Crab.* Saxonville, MA: Picture Book Studio, Ltd. Tells of a hermit crab that has outgrown its old shell and moves into a new one, which it decorates with various sea creatures. (K–2)

- Cole, J. (1986). *Hungry, Hungry Sharks.* New York: Random House. Contains a simple discussion of the different types of sharks and their behavior. (1–3)
- Cole, J. (1992). *The Magic School Bus on the Ocean Floor.* New York: Scholastic. Describes all types of life in the ocean. (2–5)
- Osborne, M. P. (1993). *Mermaid Tales from Around the World.* New York: Scholastic. Contains a collection of mermaid tales (fish mythology) from various cultures. (3–8)
- Paige, D. (1981). *A Day in the Life of a Marine Biologist.* Mahwah, NJ: Troll Associates. Follows a marine biologist through a day at the oceanographic institute as she gathers samples, charts animal behavior, and works on her own research. Photographs. Reading Rainbow Series. (3–5)

The teachers also referred to the annual listing of "Outstanding Science Trade Books for Children," published in *Science and Children*, for additional books.

Then began the planning and implementation of activities for the children. The initial motivation for the unit in each of the classrooms involved taking students on a walk on a nature trail along the beach and having them compose a language-experience chart about what they saw and felt. The children were also encouraged to speculate about what might be in the ocean.

Through inquiry and research, the children were able to gain a great deal of information. They made use of the school library and its standard resources of dictionaries, encyclopedias, videodiscs, and computer programs. They also had the opportunity to interview several marine biologists, who came to the school during designated blocks of time. The students outlined questions for the biologists addressing the three major concepts of the unit prior to each visit. Other activities for getting information from trade and reference books included DR-TA, GRP, a variety of reading guides, and journals or learning logs. One class even developed a standard data sheet to help record and organize the information they found. Figure 10.26 illustrates a completed data sheet.

The children used language, writing, and the arts as a way of sharing the information they had obtained. Some students made a booklet of "Fish Facts" from their data sheets. Other classes created a mural of an ocean full of fish, posters of fish, and want ads describing the characteristics of the fish. An alternative activity might have been a skit called "A Day in the Life of a Marine Biologist," about the marine biologists who had served as consultants at the school.

When it came time for evaluating the interdisciplinary unit, teachers felt that it was most appropriate to keep work portfolios of the inquiry and writing activities that the students completed. In addition, teachers kept their own journals of the project, in which they included anecdotal records of the students' progress. Teachers also monitored the journals the children kept and made comments that helped to guide each student's work.

Beyond the classroom

You might wish to try brainstorming a curriculum web—the initial step in planning a unit. Pick a topic or theme and use the web illustrated in Figure 10.27 as a guide. It might help to choose a selection of literature as the core for the unit. Then ask your field experience teacher to give you feedback on it; record the web and comments in your journal.

INQUIRY-BASED UNIT

The **inquiry-based unit** is much like the interdisciplinary unit; however, the students as a class brainstorm for broad topics that interest them and then vote as a class on which one to study. After they decide on the broad topic (i.e., space), they brainstorm the many different areas to study that are related to the broad topic, such as planets, Kennedy Space Center, and astronauts. During this brainstorming session, it is important that the students, with guidance from the teacher, decide on

FIGURE 10.26

Completed data sheet: Fish.

SOUTH CAROLINA FISH   Name Jamie G.

Common fish name **fiddlercrab** Scientific name **crustaceans**

In what part of S.C. is it found? Charleston

Size range (How small or big is it?) about 5 cen.

What does it look like? Describe it in words and draw a picture.
(color—patterns—fins—tail)

Drawing	Description
	He has oo like eyes. It has four legs, no nose & one mouth

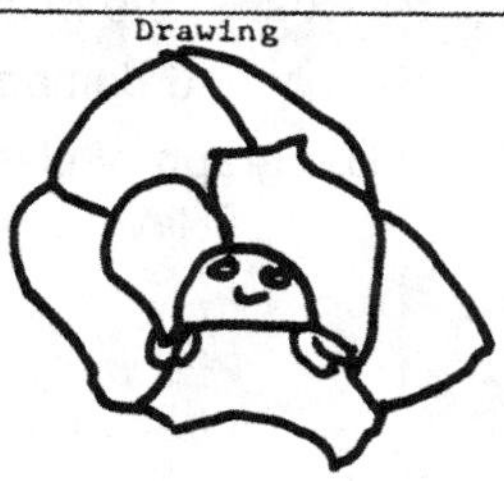

In which aquatic habitats can this fish be found? (Check them)

____ocean   ✓ sandy beach   ____river   ____continental shelf

____estuary   ____lake   ✓ salt marsh   ✓ coral reef

Describe the habitat of this fish. Where is it most likely found? Their habbitat is on a beach. They're most likely found on the beach

During which months of the year can you find this fish? Summer

Is this a good fish to eat? no

Tell an interesting fact about this fish It is so small you could step on it and not even know it

Fisherman interviewed Mr. Harris & Bob Graham.

Name of book used to check information Fiddler Crabs.

questions that the individual students want to answer in order for there to be structure. The teacher needs to carefully guide students in making sure all the content areas are covered and that the study and activities are both well balanced and possible within the set amount of time given for the unit.

The following scenario is an example of the inquiry-based approach. After a discussion among the students of why gum chewing was "outlawed" in their new building, they decided that gum/candy would be a great topic to study. The teacher asked for suggestions on how to incorporate the various subjects, such as math, science, social studies, music, art, literature, and health. The teacher was confident that plenty of reading, writing, viewing, listening, and discussion would emerge from the study. After brainstorming, the students decided on the areas pictured in Figure 10.27.

FIGURE 10.27

Web for inquiry-based unit on candy and gum.

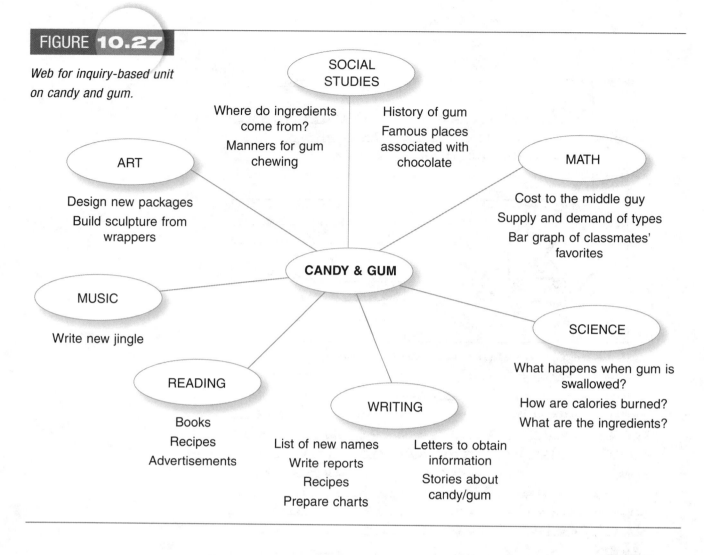

Researchers who promote the inquiry-based approach to language arts "surmise that learners will feel more of an investment in their studies if they peruse meaningful content through student-directed inquiry in small groups or individually" (Guthrie & McCann, 1997, p. 130).

ASSESSING THE INTEGRATED CURRICULUM

In all three integrated approaches using thematic units, the assessment must be different from teacher-made tests and worksheets with single right answers. The assessment must be authentic in nature and "based on what students actually do in a variety of contexts at different points throughout the instructional year" (Seely, 1995, p. 59). The assessment may include checklists, anecdotal records, learning logs, dialogue journals, portfolios, teacher conferences, peer assessment, and self-assessment (Manning, Manning, & Long, 1994; Meinbach, Rothlein, & Fredricks, 1995). Since so much of the time is spent in the process, there must be assessment of how each student spent each day and how well the student worked cooperatively in small groups. See Appendix C for some alternative assessment forms. Appendix C, p. 498 is a rubric for a writing assignment. Different elements of the writing assignment are given points; the points reflect the importance of that particular element as it pertains to the entire writing project. Other authors with assessment forms and ideas for evaluation are Atwell (1998), Fiderer (1998), Rickards and Cheek (1999), Spandel and Stiggins (1990), and Tierney and Readence, (2002).

SAMPLE THEMATIC UNIT—FOLKTALES

Following is a thematic unit on folktales, developed by Jerita Whaley, a fourth-grade teacher at Westwood Elementary School in Stillwater, OK. Each student signed an individual contract (see Figure 10.28) indicating which activities he or she would do to meet the requirements for a specific grade; the teacher also signed each contract. The signatures showed that both pupil and teacher understood the terms of the contract. Also included are lists of the activities from which students could choose and an annotated bibliography.

From the Learning Skills Activities, it is easy to see that the teacher engaged the students in higher-level thinking skills. From the Literature Appreciation Activities, it is evident that there is an integration of literature, geography, history, language, music, drama, visual art, and poetry as the students engage in all areas of the language arts.

FIGURE 10.28

Thematic unit on folktales, including a student contract, a list of possible activities, and an annotated bibliography.

Contract

Student _____ Date _____

Teacher _____

I, _____, agree to read _____ folktales and finish the activities required in order to obtain a particular grade.

The grade I contract for is _____

A	=	Assignments from:	
		Learning Skills	Choice of 3 activities
		Literature Appreciation	Choice of 3 activities
		Art/Music/Drama	Choice of 2 activities
B	=	Assignments from:	
		Learning Skills	Choice of 2 activities
		Literature Appreciation	Choice of 2 activities
		Art/Music/Drama	Choice of 2 activities
C	=	Assignments from:	
		Learning Skills	Choice of 2 activities
		Literature Appreciation	Choice of 1 activity
		Art/Music/Drama	Choice of 1 activity

I, _____, understand my responsibilities and will fulfill them to the best of my ability.

Date contract fulfilled _____

Student's signature _____

Instructor's signature _____

(continued)

FIGURE 10.28 *Continued.*

LEARNING SKILLS ACTIVITIES

1. Choose your favorite folktale and write it as a sensational news story for the school paper. (Application)

2. After reading at least two versions of the same folktale, make a list of ways they are alike and ways they are different. (Compare & contrast/analysis)

3. Make a list of new words as you read each folktale. Choose a friend to help you make a crossword puzzle. (Vocabulary knowledge/synthesis)

4. Read the first two pages of a folktale with a friend. Each of you write a prediction for the next event. Read the folktale, then compare your predictions with what happened next. Which do you like best? Why? (Prediction/evaluation)

5. Make a story web or map of one of the folktales you read. (Comprehension/analysis)

6. Rewrite one event in a folktale so that the ending is different. Rewrite the ending. (Analysis/prediction)

7. Invent a code system and send a message about a character in a folktale to one of your friends. (Synthesis)

8. Choose a folktale character and pretend that you have the power to bring that character to your house for an evening. Without telling your family the details about the character, how do you think they will react to the way your "friend" behaves? Write about your family's response. (Inference/analysis)

9. Memorize a poem from another country and share it with the class. (Knowledge)

10. Imagine a setting for a story. When the picture is clear in your mind, draw a picture of the setting. Write a description. (Synthesis)

11. Select a story to retell from another point of view. You could, for example, be the "bad guy" and justify your actions. (Evaluate)

LITERATURE APPRECIATION ACTIVITIES

1. Interview 20 people to determine their favorite folktales. Graph your findings.

2. Read folktales to five other people in school. You must make arrangements with teachers for the reading. Get signatures from each person you read to.

3. Draw a map of a country and list at least three folktales that have been popular in that country.

4. Write a report about your favorite folktale author, reteller, translator, editor, or illustrator. Share it with the class.

5. Make a list of the "bad guys" in at least 10 different folktales. Write a sentence about each, describing that person's rottenness.

6. Make a list of all the "good guys" mentioned in at least 10 different folktales. Try to think of one or two traits each one possesses that makes that person a "good guy."

7. Write your own folktale or version of a folktale. Get a friend to illustrate it for you.

8. Lead your literature group in a brainstorming activity and make a cluster diagram of the discussion. Possible topics might be giants, enchanted people, talking animals in folktales, ways magic is used, and so on.

9. Make a list of words or phrases used in making comparisons. Find at least 10 similes or metaphors, and identify the folktale you found them in.

10. Write a riddle about one of the characters in a fairy tale of your choice. See if a friend can guess the riddle.

11. Use a haiku to describe the setting from one folktale. Select the words to give a complete picture.

12. An acrostic poem begins each line with a letter from a person's name. Select a character, and write his or her name vertically on a sheet of paper. Each line should tell something about the character of your choice.

13. Write a poem or song expressing your response to events in a folktale.

ART/MUSIC/DRAMA ACTIVITIES

1. Make a tape of at least five folk songs for a class sing-along.

2. Choose an illustrated folk song book to practice, sing, and share with a small group.

3. Make a mobile to illustrate your favorite folktale.

4. Make an attractive book jacket for a folktale.

5. Design and draw a dragon or other monster suitable for a great folktale. Write a detailed description of the monster's unique physical qualities.

6. Find three or four other people who have read the same folktale and perform one or two episodes from the book.

7. Draw your four favorite castles, whether they come from your dreams or something you have seen.

8. Memorize a folktale for a storytelling session with a small group in kindergarten or first grade.

(continued)

9. Illustrate a folktale for a friend, or draw four or more detailed illustrations for a folktale of your choice.

10. Practice calligraphy and write a "Hear Ye, Hear Ye" message that the town crier might proclaim about an important event in a fairy tale you like. Mount it on two dowel rods or pencils.

11. Study heraldry and design a shield to represent your family. Make it in felt for the bulletin board.

ANNOTATED BIBLIOGRAPHY

Ahlberg, J., & Ahlberg, A. (1986). *The jolly postman or other people's letters.* Boston: Little, Brown & Co. The postman makes deliveries, "Once upon a bicycle," to favorite fairy tale characters. This book can be a wonderful inspiration for all kinds of writing activities.

Andersen, H. C. (1986). The Emperor's new clothes. In W. F. Russell (ed.), *More classics to read aloud to your children.* New York: Crown. The Emperor's new clothes are the biggest hit ever until a child in the crowd tells the truth. If an innocent child cannot see the clothes, then the Emperor has none. (Denmark)

Bierhorst, J. (ed.). (1997). *The dancing fox: Arctic folktales* (M. K. Okheena, illus.). New York: William Morrow & Company. Eighteen folktales on the Inuit people provide a glimpse into the humor and daily life of these people. Black-and-white drawings compliment these enchanting tales.

Bower, T. (2000). *The shipwrecked sailor: An Egyptian tale with hieroglyphs.* New York: Atheneum Books for Young Readers. This book uses lively language and authentic illustrations, decorative borders, and helpful notes to pique children's interest in Egyptian symbols and hieroglyphs.

Carrick, C. (1989). *Aladdin and the wonderful lamp* (D. Carrick, illus.). New York: Scholastic. This tale from Arabia is a less detailed version of the lamp than the version by Andrew Lang. (Arabia)

Demi. (1997). *One grain of rice: A mathematical folktale.* New York: Scholastic Press. A young girl teaches the Rajah to appreciate math in this folktale.

Donoghue, E. (1997). *Kissing the witch: Old tales in new skins.* New York: HarperCollins. Several female narrators occupy the places and live the events of a familiar fairy tale, but the story is a little different when these women become friends.

Doucet, S. A. (1997). *Why Lapin's ears are long: And other tales from the Louisiana bayou.* New York: Orchard Books. Follow Compere Rabbit, Br'er Rabbit's Louisiana cousin, in his adventures as he milks a wildcat, snatches an alligator's egg, and steals a grizzly's tooth. He may be small, but he is tricky.

Ehrlich, A. (1981). *Hans Christian Andersen's "The wild swans"* (S. Jeffers, illus.). New York: Dial Books. A courageous princess must face terrible hardships to free her 11 brothers from a wicked curse. Susan Jeffers's enchanting illustrations are vibrant with life and form a perfect backdrop for this incredible story, in which love again is triumphant. (Denmark)

Gregorowski, C. (2000). *Fly eagle, fly! An African tale.* New York: Margaret K. McElderry Books. A farmer finds an eaglet and raises it as a chicken in this book about the human spirit and its need to soar.

Grimm, J., & Grimm, W. Snow White. In N. Lewis (ed.), *The twelve dancing princesses and other tales from Grimm* (L. Postma, illus.). New York: Dial Books. This version is a translation true to the original tale from the Brothers Grimm. The witchy stepmother gets it in the end. (Germany)

Hastings, S. (1985). *Sir Gawain and the loathly lady* (J. Wijngaard, illus.). New York: Lothrop, Lee & Shepard Books. King Arthur's life depends upon his answer to the question, What is it that women most desire? Beautiful illustrations depict how Arthur is saved by the loathly lady who gives him the answer in return for being allowed to marry one of his knights. (England)

Hodges, M. (1984). *Saint George and the dragon* (T. S. Hyman, illus.). Boston: Little, Brown & Co. This golden legend from Edmund Spencer's The Faerie Queen tells of George, the Red Cross Knight, and fair and faithful Una, who encourages him to slay the terrible dragon that has been terrorizing her father's kingdom. The illustrations by Hyman in this English tale are her best yet. (England)

Huck, C. (2001). *The black bull of Norway: A Scottish tale.* New York: Greenwillow Books. Watercolors in deep shades and the Black Bull's lifelike depiction make this folktale unforgettable for all generations. This is an old story of a girl who struggles with spells and seven years of hard labor to find true love.

Kaplan, I. (1967). Little Rosa and Long Leda. In *Fairy tales from Sweden* (C. Calder, illus.). Chicago: Follett. This version of the Cinderella–Snow White tale does not involve a glass slipper, but the stepmother is a real witch. Despite being changed into a goose

(continued)

FIGURE 10.28   *Continued.*

by the stepmother's evil magic, kind Queen Rosa is saved by her husband, the King, and they all live happily ever after. (Sweden)

Lelooska, D. (1997). *Echoes of the elders: The stories and paintings of Chief Lelooska.* New York: DK Ink. This is a collection of five enchanting and sometimes shocking stories from the Kwakiutl people of the Northwest coast. An accompanying CD brings to life Chief Lelooska's own chants and drums.

Louie, A. (1982). *Yeh-Shen* (E. Young, illus.). New York: Philomel Books. This tale dates from the T'ang dynasty (618–907 A.D.); the oldest version of the "Cinderella" tale is Italian, dating from 1634. Since the Yeh-Shen story predates that tale, Cinderella seems to have made her way from Asia to Europe. In this version, a young Chinese girl overcomes the wickedness of her stepsister and stepmother to become the bride of a prince. Instead of a fairy godmother, she has the help of a golden fish. (China)

Macaulay, D. (1977). *Castle.* Boston: Houghton Mifflin. This Caldecott Honor book and ALA notable traces the step-by-step planning and construction of a thirteenth-century castle and town, from the hiring of a skilled master engineer to the testing of the buildings' defenses when hundreds of Welsh soldiers attack. The incredible pen-and-ink illustrations show the castle and town, the tools the workers used in their labors, and the weapons the soldiers used to defend their castle and town.

MacMillan, C. (1967). *The Indian Cinderella.* In V. Haviland (ed.), North American legends. New York: Collins. The younger sister escapes her cruel older sisters when she wins the sometimes-invisible Strong Wind as her husband. (Northeast Woodland Indians)

Martin, R. (ed.). (1996). *Mysterious tales of Japan* (T. Kiuchi, illus.). New York: G. P. Putnam's Sons. Ten haunting tales of Japanese culture coupled with striking illustrations make this book a magic journey over the Pacific.

Mobley, J. (1979). *Star husband* (A. Vojech, illus.). New York: Doubleday & Company. This sensitive story from the legends of the Great Plains Indians is a beautiful adaptation of a story told by the Old Ones. Full-color illustrations depict the stars as people and show a mortal girl who wishes for one beautiful star, which becomes her husband. This is a reassuring affirmation of the natural cycle of life, death, and rebirth. (Great Plains Indians)

Morris, W. (1987). *The magic leaf* (J. Chen, illus.). New York: Atheneum. Through vibrant watercolor illustrations, readers are introduced to a swordsman and scholar named Lee Foo. Because he reads so many books, Lee Foo thinks he is very clever. He solves his problems so foolishly in trying to appear clever that he gets into a great deal of trouble. When he returns home humbler and wiser, he finally realizes that he is no longer interested in clever plans. (China)

Myers, S. (1979). *The enchanted sticks* (D. Diamond, illus.). New York: Coward, McCann & Geoghegan. This Japanese tale is about an old man who conquers a robber chief with the help of enchanted sticks. The enchanted sticks have already kept the old man company, dancing, playing games, and spelling out messages. Later they lead him in rescuing a young maiden from the terrible robbers. The end of the story also offers a good opportunity for a math exploration. (Japan)

Newman, D. L. (1967). *The tar baby.* In V. Haviland (ed.), North American legends. New York: Collins. The lazy rabbit outwits the other animals even after he gets stuck in the tar baby. This is very much like an Uncle Remus tale. (West Virginia)

Norman, H. (1997). *The girl who dreamed only of geese: And other tales of the Far North.* (L. Dillon & D. Dillon, illus.). New York: Harcourt Brace. Inuit stories come to life as Norman adapts these provocative tales for younger readers, including story notes cataloging his sources for those who wish to learn more.

Pevear, R. (1987). *Our king has horns.* (R. Rayevsky, illus.). New York: Macmillan. A young barber is about to lose his life for revealing the king's terrible secret. This version of an old Georgian folktale about the persistent nature of truth is retold with wit and beautiful illustrations. (Russia)

Philip, N. (ed.). (1999). *Stocking of buttermilk: American folktales* (J. Mair, illus.). New York: Clarion Books. Sixteen stories with bright illustrations allow the reader to taste a variety of cultures from all over America.

Poranzinska, J. (1987). *The enchanted book: A tale from Krakow* (B. Smith, trans.; J. Brett, illus.). New York: Harcourt Brace Jovanovich. In this folklore from Poland, the miller's youngest daughter succeeds in outwitting an evil sorcerer. There is a common element of girls becoming enchanted birds with the German tale of Jorinda and Jorjingle. (Poland)

(continued)

Robinson, A. (1979). Kelfala's secret something. In *Three African tales* (C. Byard, illus.). New York: G. P. Putnam's Sons. The jester is an important part of African culture, even today. This story from Kenya is told by the Kikuyu, who provide a view of their culture through this tale about a clown named Kelfala who falls in love with the beautiful Wambuna and tries to win her with his clever trick. (Kenya)

Rogasky, B. (1982). *Rapunzel* (T. S. Hyman, illus.). New York: Holiday House. This is a favorite version of this classic tale from the German Brothers Grimm about a girl raised by a witch in a tall tower. This version's happy ending includes the handsome prince and twins. The illustrations are incredibly beautiful and detailed. (Germany)

Rogasky, B. (1986). *The water of life* (T. S. Hyman, illus.). New York: Holiday House. This Brothers Grimm tale, by this author–illustrator team, is even more beautifully done than Rapunzel. It has all the classic elements of a great story. To cure his dying father, a prince searches for the Water of Life. He finds an enchanted castle, a magic sword, and a beautiful princess. Despite his brothers' treachery, goodness and love triumph. (Germany)

Seeger, P. (1986). *Abiyoyo* (M. Hays, illus.). New York: Macmillan. After a man and his son are ostracized from a town because the people are upset by their singing and magic tricks, they use their talents to make Abiyoyo, the terrible giant, disappear. The people then bring them back into the town and join in the song, Abiyoyo! (Africa)

Sierra, J. (1996). *Nursery tales around the world* (S. Vitale, illus.). Boston: Houghton Mifflin. Oil paintings on wood provide a remarkable backdrop for 18 familiar tales from the oral traditions of many cultures.

Stewig, J. (1988). *The fisherman and his wife* (M. Tomes, illus.). New York: Holiday House. Stewig uses clear descriptive language in his version of this Brothers Grimm tale. He unveils a story of the satisfied fisherman, his demanding wife, and a magic fish. The wife's greediness brings riches, power, and glory to her while depleting the earth's resources. At last she gets what she deserves. This tale could lead children to ask, If we greedily devour the earth's resources, will we get what we deserve? This is a wonderful classic. (Germany)

Van Laan, N. (1997). *Shingebiss: An Ojibwe legend* (B. Bowen, illus.). Boston: Houghton Mifflin. Shingebiss, a little merganser duck, must face the harsh winter of the Great Lakes region. The tale is authenticated by Ojibwe terms and woodcut block prints.

Williams-Ellis, A. (1987). Baba Yaga. In *Tales from the enchanted world* (M. Kemp, illus.). Boston: Little, Brown & Co. A young girl's stepmother sends her to the witch's house on an errand. Her clever consideration and kindness to the witch's animals and servant help her escape from the terrible clutches of Baba Yaga. (Russia)

Wolkstein, D. (ed.). (1996). *White wave: A Chinese tale* (E. Young, illus.). San Diego: Harcourt Brace. A farmer finds a shining shell and then discovers that it contains the Moon Goddess. She brings him fortune and companionship until the day he wants too much.

Yep, L. (1997). *The Khan's daughter: A Mongolian folktale* (J. Tseng & M. Tseng, illus.). New York: Scholastic. Only three tests stand in the way of a poor peasant who wishes to marry the Khan's daughter. To his surprise, she gives him the toughest test of all. This is a traditional love story set in the Mongolian highlands.

For more information on children's folktales, visit http://capitolchoices.communitypoint.org.

TECHNOLOGY AND WEBSITES

Simulations deserve a place in language arts instruction because they provide motivation for reading, researching, and writing. Simulations allow a particular situation or aspect of a content area to come alive for students and also allow children to experience something that would not be possible merely through a test. Because many simulations involve text, they motivate students to read. Further, software programs, such as *Oregon Trail Fifth Edition*, *Road Adventures USA*, and, *Colonization*, require students to make decisions about budgets, relations with other cultures, and time management while playing, thus encouraging higher-level thinking skills.

Computer programs may be categorized in various ways according to their problem-solving capabilities. These programs demand logical reasoning from those who play them. Some software programs that do involve problem solving and decision making are *Liberty's Kids, Star Flyers Royal Jewel Rescue, Where in the USA Is Carmen Sandiego? Carmen Sandiego Word Detective*, and *The Reading Trek*. These text-based programs encourage users to try the predictions and evaluation strategies common to the psycholinguistic theory of reading in order to make decisions and solve problems. In *The Reading Trek*, students complete five lessons in different genres of reading: poetry, fiction, nonfiction, practical reading, and drama. They complete five activities for each genre that encompass prereading; reading; comprehension; reflection; and "on your own," in which users write based on what they have learned in the lesson. The lessons also involve comprehension and quizzes.

Two CD-ROMs offering a wealth of information are *Encyclopedia Britannica 2003 Deluxe* by the Learning Company and *National Geographic 110 Years* by National Geographic Interactive. Both of these include much reading with interaction by the user and cover a variety of topics.

www.Biologylessons.sdsu.edu

This site includes lessons about molecules, cells, and population biology. The lessons have students predict, answer questions, collect data, and reflect.

http://educate.si.edu

This site informs teachers about Smithsonian educational resources and provides approaches to integration of the various subjects.

www.solarview.com

This site is a beautiful introduction to the solar system and includes science and history.

www.fi.edu/weather/nino/nino.html

This site explains El Niño in simple terms.

www.althorp-house.co.uk

This site takes visitors to the late Princess Diana's home.

www.stpauls.co.uk/index.htm

This site takes you to St. Paul's Cathedral, where Princess Diana was married to Prince Charles.

www.ipl.org/div/potus

This site links to POTUS: Presidents of the United States. It includes texts, sound bites, photos, and film clips.

www.ipl.org/div/news/?unresolved=/cgi-bin/reading/news.out.pl

This site contains numerous newspapers from the United States and around the world.

http://sln.fi.edu

This Franklin Institute Science Museum site is great for teachers and students.

www.enc.org

This is the site of the Eisenhower National Clearinghouse for Mathematics and Science Education. It has action ideas and lesson plans for all grades.

www.learner.org/exhibits/garbage/global.html

This site is about garbage and how to shrink landfills.

www.monticello.org

This site, based on Jefferson's home, has information about all his talents.

www.nortonsimon.org

This site has information about Michelangelo and his art in Florence, Italy.

http://kids.msfc.nasa.gov/defaultNoFlash.asp

This site is designed for students to learn about space, astronauts, spacesuits, shuttles, and other planets.

www.kidsfood.com

This site is designed for third- to fifth-graders to teach them about food and nutrition. A teacher's guide, which gives lesson plans and activities, is provided.

www.envirolink.org

This site is an environmental information service that focuses on environmental, cultural, and exploration issues around the world.

http://volcano.und.nodak.edu

This is a site designed for teachers and students who desire to learn more about volcanoes.

www.usgs.gov

This site has U. S. maps and earth science data.

www.ngdc.noaa.gov

This site is a data center for geophysics, climatology, and glaciology.

www.nasa.gov

This is NASA's home page.

www.castles.org

This site has information about specific castles and how they were built.

www.middleweb.com/CurrMiddleAge.html

This site provides links to sites about the Middle Ages and the customs of that time.

www.madison.k12.wi.us/tnl/detectives

This site provides links to different sites dealing with curricular areas.

www.jaguar-sun.com/maya.html

This site provides information on Mayan history and culture, geared toward upper elementary/middle school students.

www.americaslibrary.gov/cgi-bin/page.cgi

Part of the Library of Congress, this site allows students to explore American history, important Americans, and learn about different places in the United States.

www.brainpop.com

This site is geared toward various curricular areas. Visitors can watch movies on grammar usage, science, technology, math, and health. There is also a section for teachers with lesson plans and standards correlation.

www.historychannel.com/classroom.html

This site has information and activities on historic people, places, events, and speeches. There is also a section where teachers can share their ideas on history activities for the classroom.

http://Yosemite.epa.gov/oar/globalwarming.nsf/content

This site provides information on global warming. There is a section devoted to children's activities and games as well as useful links.

www.nineplanets.org

This site offers a multimedia tour of the solar system with information on the history, weather, atmosphere, and mythology of the planets.

www.mojavewater.org.Mwa800.htm

This site has information on water conservancy and the "Kids' Corner" provides easy-to-understand facts as well as games and activities.

www.touregypt.com/kings.htm

This site offers quick and easy-to-find information on the rulers of Ancient Egypt.

www.luminarium.org/lumina.htm

This site provides information on art, culture, and literature on three time periods: Medieval, Renaissance, and the seventeenth century.

Summary

Using reading and writing in the content areas is a natural, almost common-sense way of allowing students to apply and extend what they know about language. Such an approach gives special meaning to reading and writing instruction because it encourages students to use these processes in acquiring real and necessary information.

Using reading and writing in the content areas is also important not only in expanding language competencies but also in developing each student's content literacy—the cyclical ability both to use a store of background knowledge in comprehending new content information and to know what strategies to use to facilitate getting and applying that information. Students may then use the newly acquired knowledge to facilitate further comprehension.

Remember that the purpose of using reading and writing across the curriculum is to aid students in their ability to internalize knowledge—and to give children a real and meaningful reason for using reading and writing. By doing this, teachers can help children not only to appreciate language but to become proficient users of it in their daily lives.

ACTIVITIES *with children*

Class Choice

Have the class vote on a favorite book and build a unit around it. Then brainstorm activities related to the book. Use a diagram with the six branches of reading, writing, listening, speaking, viewing, and visually representing. This diagram should get you started on planning a literature unit.

Community Communication

As part of a social studies unit on community and community service, children can correspond with individuals in local nursing homes or other institutions. The exchange of letters will give the students many opportunities for reading and writing. They may want to share events of their daily lives, important happenings, or original writings.

Make a Map

After students have had a number of experiences reading, drawing, and labeling maps, they may want to create a map depicting the location of a favorite story.

For example, after reading *Owl Moon*, several children might want to draw a map showing the route that the little girl and her father took from the farm to the woods and back again.

Learning Log

Encourage each student to keep a learning log in which he or she summarizes what learning has taken place each day. Periodically, you may want to make comments in their logs.

Class Newsletters

Let students assume the responsibility for writing a weekly or monthly newsletter home to caregivers. In it, they can summarize the progress of learning in the classroom and highlight special events. You may even want to do the newsletter on the computer with the help of software such as *The Newsroom*.

Fact Books

In many areas of the curriculum, students can create their own books of facts. Whenever children study a particular topic, such as animal habitats, they can begin to collect particular facts that interest them. Then they can organize these facts into a book format and publish it for others to enjoy.

RELATED READINGS

Barton, M. L., Heidema, C., & Jordan, D. (2002). Teaching reading in mathematics and science. *Educational Leadership*, 60(3), 24–28.

Beck, I. L., & McKeown, M. G. (2002). Questioning the author: Making sense of social studies. *Educational Leadership*, 60(3), 44–47.

Chancer, J., & Rester-Zodrow, G. (1997). *Writing, art, and inquiry through focused nature study*. Portsmouth, NH: Heinemann.

This book explains how one California class used the moon and its changing position as a topic for their inquiry study for 28 days. The children, with their parents, recorded in their journal the moon's position and any questions they had. Each day, they were given time to share their questions and find answers. The teacher included writing, reading, art, science, and music in the study.

Davenport, M. R., Jaeger, M., & Laurintzen, C. (1995). Negotiating curriculum. *The Reading Teacher*, 49(1), 60–67.

This article gives information on a thematic unit of the culture and geography of the Appalachian region of the United States.

Fennessey, S. (1995). Living history through drama and literature. *The Reading Teacher*, 49(1), 16–19.

This article explains how a thematic unit on Langston Hughes and the entire idea of racial prejudice came alive when the students used drama to interpret parts of history.

Fiderer, A. (1995). *Practical assessments for literature-based reading classrooms*. New York: Scholastic Professional Books.

This book has ready-to-use forms for response evaluations, miscue records, self-evaluation checklists for literature responses, and home-reading records.

Fisher, D., Frey, N., & Williams, D. (2002). Seven literacy strategies that work. *Educational Leadership*, 60(3), 70–73.

Fry, E. (2002). Readability versus learning. *The Reading Teacher*, 56(3), 286–291.

Jacob, V. A. (2002). Reading, writing, and understanding. *Educational Leadership*, 60(3), 58–61.

Topping, D. H., & McManus, R. A. (2002). A culture of literacy in science. *Educational Leadership*, 60(3), 30–33.

CHAPTER 11

Working with a Diverse Population

This chapter emphasizes the importance of teachers embracing all diverse learners. The diverse learners who are highlighted in this chapter are students with cultures that are different from the teacher's, students with different language backgrounds, students with various disabilities, and students with academic giftedness.

CHAPTER OBJECTIVES

After reading this chapter, you should be able to accomplish the following objectives:

1. Name some strategies teachers can use to promote multicultural awareness.

2. Name some strategies teachers can use to promote acceptance of all dialects.

3. Name some strategies teachers can use to aid students whose native language is not English.

4. List some characteristics of ADHD students.

5. Explain compacting.

CHECK YOUR BACKGROUND KNOWLEDGE. Before reading the chapter, complete the K-T-W-L chart based on the chapter overview and objectives provided at left. In column "K," write what you know about the topics in the objectives. In column "T," write what you think you know. In column "W," write what you want to learn. Finally, after you have read the chapter, write what you have learned in column "L."

Know	**T**hink you know	**W**ant to learn	**L**earned

Children with Special Needs

Today's classroom is characterized by diversity of all sorts. Teachers encounter students with varying intellectual, physical, linguistic, emotional, social, and cultural needs in the same classroom. The challenge for teachers is to embrace this diversity and strive to meet the individual needs of all students.

Teachers need to understand that all students, no matter what their race, socioeconomic status, physical abilities, or ethnicity, are "at risk" sometime during their school career because they experience short-term or maybe long-term personal, social, or family difficulties. Reflect on why the following students may be at risk:

Students whose parents are workaholics.

Students who live with two dads or two moms in a community where no one else has the same living condition.

Students whose parents stress the importance of being good-looking, thin, and popular.

Students whose father or mother just lost a job.

Students who live in a blended family.

Students who live with an aunt or a grandparent.

Students whose parents are addicted to drugs or alcohol.

Students who live with aggressive, abusive parents.

All these students may be at risk for a period of time; however, teachers need to be cautious not to categorize these students as if they all have the same needs. For example, some children live with grandparents or in blended families that are harmonious and more stable than their previous living arrangement.

Often teachers and researchers attempt to categorize students according to geographic area, socioeconomic status, race, ethnicity, or exceptionalities. There is a danger in doing this. For example, rural students are often categorized as students who lack cultural experiences. Their cultural experiences may be different from those of suburban students, but these experiences are just as rich. Oftentimes, teachers categorize urban students as those who live in extreme poverty, come from broken homes, live a life of crime, are on drugs, and are underachievers. However, many urban children come from nurturing homes where caregivers work hard to provide a safe home life for their children. Suburban students are often categorized as children who live with both parents in a nurturing home where there are no drugs or physical abuse, but this is not a complete picture of children living in the suburbs. Many students with special needs require additional attention. They are students who do not have sufficient English skills, who lack preschool experiences, who live in extreme poverty, or who have mild learning disabilities. Again, labeling these students is not prudent because teachers then tend to think that all students who fall into one of these categories have identical needs, when in reality, no two students have the same needs.

In many traditional classrooms, children encounter a narrowly defined environment with hard-and-fast expectations for achievement. Such expectations are based on a business-management mentality in which learning is measured primarily by test scores derived from standardized achievement tests. The quality of education is defined by how well children perform in reading, writing, and arithmetic in comparison with children with no disabling conditions who are from predominantly white, middle-class homes. How such a system has emerged in this highly developed society is a matter for sociological debate; the outcome, however, is about a 20 percent yearly school dropout rate (National Center for Education Statistics, 2000). The difference between dropout rates for whites and African Americans narrowed during the 1970s and 1980s; however, since 1990 the gap has remained fairly constant (National Center for Education Statistics, 2000). In 2001, the most recent year for which data are available at the time of this publication, the dropout rate for Asian/Pacific Islanders was 3.8 percent, for Hispanics was 27.8 percent, for African Americans was 13.1 percent, and for whites was 6.9 percent.

Numerous studies have attempted to analyze the reasons why so many children and adolescents leave the school system before graduation. Lists of contributing factors include both student variables and school or organizational variables. Student characteristics include low reading scores, low cognitive scores and low socioeconomic status (Pransky & Bailey, 2002/2003), grade repetition, poor attendance, and disruptive behavior.

Minority students may also find themselves in the at-risk category (Pransky & Bailey, 2002/2003). This is particularly true for many African American, Native American, and Hispanic students who have lower academic achievement scores than their middle-class peers. Low academic achievement and low socioeconomic status are two of the major factors that cause students to drop out before graduation (Rumberger & Larsen, 1998). In the past two decades, the minority populations in U.S. schools have increased enormously. Today, Hispanics are the largest minority group in the United States; thus, they are the fastest-growing student population (U.S. Department of Education, 2001). Yet, they have the highest dropout rate. Interviews with Hispanic students revealed that they felt they were invisible and not a part of the school. Because of their limited English, teachers often had low expectations for them and thus used low-level skills and drills instead of giving them higher-level thinking activities in which they would have the opportunity to express their opinions (Rolon, 2002/2003).

Clearly, some of the responsibility of the high dropout rate belongs to the educational system itself. Obviously, the system has difficulty adapting to students whose needs are not addressed in schools founded on a middle-income, normal learning-abilities model. Larry Bell (2002/2003), a researcher who focuses on best practices for at-risk students, offers some strategies that have worked in schools where there is no achievement gap between at-risk students and students who are not at risk. He found that schools that had no gap do the following:

- *"Emphasize reading skills."* Students support one another's reading in book clubs, and teachers provide motivational books and books about role models with whom students can identify.

- *"Teach higher-order thinking skills to all students."* Teachers use open-ended questions, where students must give reasons for their answers.

- *"Routinely reteach."* Teachers spend four to five minutes reviewing previous lessons, and after tests, they discuss all questions so that students can correct any incorrect answers.

- *"Make at-risk students participate."* Teachers use the "fishbowl" technique, by putting all students' names in a bowl and randomly drawing them.

- *"Require students to speak and write in complete sentences."*

- *"Get students emotionally involved."* Teachers ask students how they feel about controversial topics. They also use events, people, experiences, and perspectives that reflect the students' culture.

- *"Demonstrate patience and caring."* Teachers do not expect overnight success; however, they celebrate small steps of success and continue to build positive relationships with students. Students need to know that teachers care about their success. (pp. 32–34)

The following is a list of books that prospective teachers and veteran teachers alike should read as they prepare themselves for working with diverse

All students can learn.

CHRISTOPHER MORLEY

Beyond the classroom

Ask an administrator in your local school district or the teacher in your field experience class to identify the kinds of exemplary language arts programs being provided. Secure permission to visit one of these programs and note in your journal how the practices promote learning for all children.

populations in the twenty-first century (all published by the National Educational Service in connection with Phi Delta Kappa of Bloomington, IN):

- *Building Cultural Bridges* (1997) by Robinson, Bowing, and Ewing. This book provides teachers with interactive lesson plans aimed at helping adolescents deal with cultural differences and prejudices.

- *From Rage to Hope: Strategies for Reclaiming Black and Hispanic Students* (1997) by Crystal Kuykendall. This book, written by the former executive director of the National Alliance of Black School Educators, focuses on the underachievement and social problems experienced by African American and Hispanic youth. There are strategies for working with discipline problems in the classroom and involving caregivers, among other activities.

- *Achievement for African-American Students: Strategies for the Diverse Classroom* (1997) by Gary Reglin. Providing meaningful classroom instruction with greater sensitivity to the needs and expectations of African American students in grades K–12 is the focus of this book. There are strategies for resolving conflicts in the classroom, involving caregivers, and improving social interactions.

- *Educating Language-Minority Students* (2003) by Michael S. Mills. This book helps teachers and principals understand and apply the legal principles that involve language policies. It includes a guide to federal legislation.

- *Teaching for Diversity* (2003) by Ricardo L. Garcia. This paperback helps teachers understand students from diverse cultures and gives suggestions on how teachers can help diverse students to live in a diverse society.

Meeting Special Needs: Cultural Factors in the Classroom

The societal changes of the last decade are reflected to a great extent in the public schools. Schools have generally been assumed to transmit societal norms and values. While education helped assimilate the immigrants of the late 1800s and early 1900s, societal needs have taken a sharp turn away from the melting-pot mentality of that period.

Sometime in the early 1970s, educators began to realize the importance of ethnicity and the need to teach their students how to understand and accept cultural differences. "One of the main challenges for many 'at-risk' students is bridging the gap between their home cultures and the culture of the public school" (Pransky & Bailey, 2002/2003, p. 373). Take, for example, Ms. Graves, a white, middle-class teacher who has good intentions, but never considers the culture clash between her Cambodian students and herself. Ms. Graves decides to use a teaching strategy that is considered to be one to encourage students to challenge what they hear. But look what occurs instead.

> During a unit review of Egypt, Ms. Graves instructs her students that she is going to state some facts they learned during the unit; some facts are correct, whereas others are incorrect. She instructs the students to listen carefully and correct her when they all hear the incorrect fact. Ms. Graves interprets the Cambodian students' silence to mean that they do not know which facts are incorrectly stated. However, the real reason for the students' silence is respect for the teacher. In their homes, they are taught never to challenge an adult; an adult is always correct.

Pransky and Bailey (2002/2003) understand the importance of teachers understanding the cultures of their students. They remind teachers that in order "to meet your students where they are, first you have to find them" (p. 370).

Pransky and Bailey designed a conceptual framework to aid teachers as they work with students from various cultural backgrounds. Their conceptual framework is based on Vygotsky's (1986) zone of proximal development (ZPD) and Gee's (1990) concept of discourse community. The ZPD refers to the gap between what students can do independently and what they can do with assistance. Thus, there is a need for teachers to identify specific tasks with which students need assistance.

Discourse community is the unspoken, acceptable way a group uses language, acts, believes, and values. Everyone belongs to a variety of discourse communities. One's family, religious group, ethnic group, and local community are all discourse communities. Each community has its own set of rules, and members understand how they are to conduct themselves while in the community. The discourse community of the majority of our public schools is based on a white, middle-class set of rules. Students who come from different discourse communities with different sets of rules may be at risk when they come to school because they do not fully understand the school culture, and their culture may conflict with that culture.

As teachers work with students from many cultures, they need to understand how the school's discourse community differs from the culture found in their classroom. As teachers set learning expectations for a lesson, they must consider the level of language proficiency students need in order to participate in the lesson. Teachers must also consider the kinds of interaction between teacher and student and between student and student that will occur during the lesson, and what background knowledge the students will need to have. Furthermore, teachers must consider the nature of the task for the lesson, and then what skills the students need in order to perform the task. These skills not only include academic skills, but also the students' cognitive, cultural, and language skills. Figure 11.1 depicts Pransky and Bailey's (2002/2003) conceptual framework. The items listed in each box are areas that teachers must consider as they plan and teach the lessons.

I have plowed and planted and gathered into barns . . . and ain't I a woman?

SOJOURNER TRUTH

Zone of proximal development in the teaching/learning process: A conceptual framework.   **FIGURE 11.1**

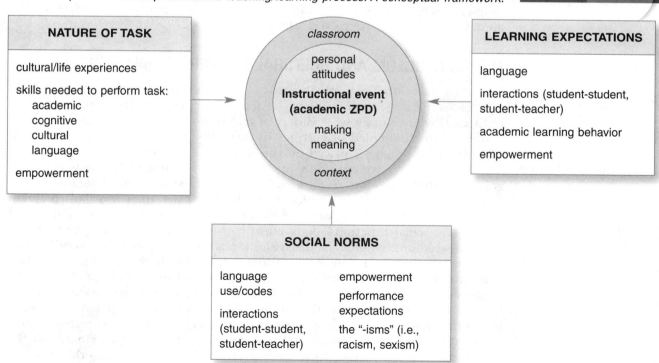

Source: H. Pransky & F. Bailey (2002/2003). To meet your students where they are, first you have to find them. *The Reading Teacher, 56*(4), 370–383. Reprinted with permission of H. Pransky and the International Reading Association.

CLASSROOM CLIMATE AND CULTURE

At the beginning of the twentieth century, the majority of students in American schools were from Western European countries; thus, the Anglo-Americans were the macroculture. As the twenty-first century begins, the Anglo-American population in many schools is now the minority; however, the majority of American teachers are Anglo-Americans. Some cultures have different value systems and different ways of communicating with one another. Listed below are some areas that teachers must consider (DeVries, 2004).

- Some families value cooperation; therefore, the children share answers with someone who does not know the answer.
- Some caregivers instruct children to lower their eyes when they are being reprimanded; they never look into the eyes of teachers when they are being reprimanded.
- Some caregivers would never ask a child a question if the caregiver already knew the answer to the question. These children may not respond to questions if they thought the teacher knew the answer.
- In some families, the child brings disgrace to the family if they do a task incorrectly. These children may not respond or hand in work unless they know the answers are correct.
- In some families, men may not expect a woman to tell them what to do, and they may not accept instruction from a woman.

All teachers must strive to understand and accept the cultures of their students. Students whose culture differs from the teachers' must never be made to feel that their behavior is wrong, strange, or unacceptable. They deserve an environment that respects their individual culture and helps them adapt to the dominant cultural patterns (Pransky & Bailey, 2002/2003).

THE CURRICULUM AND CULTURALLY DIVERSE CHILDREN

Educators have long been challenged to design curriculum models that facilitate self-actualization of students. Focus must be on the student as an individual who brings a wide variety of traditions and knowledge to the subject matter. With the myriad of cultures in our schools, this advice must be taken seriously, with emphasis placed on the student as a person.

One way to engage culturally diverse learners is through the book club program, which focuses on reading, writing, and talking about books (Kong & Fitch, 2002/2003; Raphael, Pardo, Highfield, & McMahon, 1997). This program is based on Vygotsky's (1978b) sociocultural theoretical view that reading and writing are social functions. Book clubs consist of four major elements: small-group discussions, whole-class discussions, reading, and individual writing. The main part is the discussion, when students learn about themselves, each other, and other cultures while reading, discussing, and writing about good literature. In the book club program, first all the students read the same book, which features a culture other than the middle-class white culture. Then they write individual responses to teacher-prepared prompts, which are open-ended questions. Next small groups discuss their responses to the prompts. Finally, all the students in the class discuss their responses to the prompts and other parts of the book that interest them. During discussions, students are encouraged to express their ideas, listen to differing opinions of their classmates, and learn from one another.

Beyond the classroom

Interview several general education teachers. Ask them how they make a new child feel welcome. Then ask them what—if any—differences occur when they are trying to make a student with a disability or a child from a minority culture feel welcome. Reflect upon their answers, and determine what you would do through language arts to achieve a sense of welcome for a student with a disability or from a minority culture.

A child miseducated

is a child lost.

JOHN F.

KENNEDY

The books used for book club must be age appropriate, have the necessary elements of a story so that the teacher can teach literary concepts, and be great for discussion. Appendix A lists books from the various cultures that are appropriate for the book club program.

Language arts programs should be extended to include the experiences of many different ethnic groups. Such groups include Greek-Americans, Italian-Americans, and Anglo-Saxon Protestants, as well as Native Americans, Mid-Eastern Americans, African Americans, and Hispanic-Americans. A comparative approach to cultural diversity through language arts activities allows students to enjoy the challenges, joys, and humanity shared by one people of the world while diminishing ethnocentric bias or stereotyping. (Refer back to the literature bibliographies in Chapter 10 for some ideas on books to use.)

By utilizing language arts materials and activities that represent the cultures of children in the classroom, the teacher demonstrates the value of diversity as well as the value of individuals in the room. Presentation of language arts materials based on ethnic diversity enhances students' beliefs that they are recognized, esteemed, and valued as part of a network of shared communication and commitment by peers and teachers.

> ## In and beyond the classroom
>
> Visit a classroom in which the teacher has a reputation for providing a strong, positive classroom climate. Ask to observe or volunteer to participate in activities. Observe the dynamics of the classroom; try to identify three activities that show the children that they belong to a supportive classroom. An alternative activity is to select a section of interest from *The Whole Language Catalog* (Goodman, Bird, & Goodman, 1992) and identify characteristics of the whole language approach associated with developing a positive classroom climate.

Children with Language Differences

As discussed in Chapter 4, language acquisition is a normal and exciting developmental process in all children. Children are surrounded by language and interact with the language—or languages—of their environment. They naturally gain facility in talking, gesturing, intonation, listening, singing, and all other forms of social communication.

No precise timeline or specific sequence of skills is appropriate for describing language development in all children (Freeman & Freeman, 2001). Children proceed at their own rates through a process that in many ways remains a mystery. However, they do appear to follow a general developmental sequence building from simple to more and more complex use of communication: Sounds, for example, precede words; words precede phrases; and phrases precede sentences. Children of all cultures appear to follow this developmental sequence, beginning with prelinguistic abilities and culminating in mastery of complex language rules.

We must see that every child has equal opportunity, not to become equal, but to become different—to realize the unique potential he or she possesses.

JOHN FISCHER

AFRICAN AMERICAN VERNACULAR ENGLISH (AAVE)

On December 18, 1996, the school board of Oakland, CA, adopted a resolution that concerns the use by a majority of African American children of their home/community language (often referred to as **African American Vernacular English, AAVE**) in the public school classrooms.

The resolution further stated that teachers in the Oakland school district need to acquire knowledge about the nature and history of AAVE in order to help their students become more successful in the classroom. This echoed a famous 1979 case involving a group of African American students from the Martin Luther King Jr. Elementary School in Ann Arbor, MI. Attorneys for the children argued that the Black English vernacular spoken by these youngsters was so different from standard English as to constitute a separate language. Therefore, they contended that the children should be entitled to separate and special instruction. The judge in the case agreed with this argument and ordered the Ann Arbor teachers to attend special training sessions in dialect awareness (Baugh, 2002; Yellin, 1980). Nearly 20 years later, the teachers of Oakland faced a similar situation.

Issues Related to the AAVE Controversy

To fully understand the significance of the Oakland Resolution for the education of African American children, teachers must be aware of the various issues related to this controversy. The following is just a summary of those issues.

Language or dialect?   A **dialect** is defined as "any language variety that is shared by a group of people. Dialects that are socially favored are often referred to as standard, and those that are socially stigmatized are often referred to as nonstandard or nonmainstream, even though all dialects of a language have been shown by linguists to be equally complex and systematic" (Oetting & McDonald, 2002, p. 2 of 19).

Is AAVE (also called Ebonics) a legitimate separate language, or is it a dialect variation of standard English? This question continues to plague the discussion surrounding the use of AAVE in the classroom. As far back as 1972, the linguist William La Bov argued that Black English was a distinct language because it possessed a systematic, rule-governed grammar and vocabulary that distinguished it from standard English. In 1997, the linguist Wayne O'Neil similarly argued for defining AAVE as a language, but for social and political reasons in response to the wishes of the majority of the African American population (O'Neil, 1997)—in spite of the fact that newspapers reporting on the Oakland controversy characterized AAVE as a substandard dialect variation lacking consistent spelling, pronunciation, or rules. Stanford University's John Rickford also takes the position that whether a speech form is described as a separate language or dialect depends more on social and political climate than on linguistic arguments (Rickford, 1997b). For example, Norwegian and Swedish share many vocabulary terms yet are considered different languages. But Mandarin and Cantonese are regarded as different dialects of the same language yet are mutually incomprehensible. Rickford (1997a) concludes that although AAVE is best described as a dialect, "it is the most distinctive dialect in the U. S. and the one that has gotten the attention of linguists more than any other for the last 30 years" (p. 12).

Beyond the classroom

Visit your local children's library. Make a list of books and tapes that describe how children and teachers help each other to feel like they belong to part of a social group. An alternate activity is to identify three biographies or storybooks that reflect various cultural groups and that can be used in conjunction with particular science, math, and social studies topics.

Issues of power and identity.   Underlying the arguments, complexities, and issues surrounding AAVE is the notion of power and identity. For many African American children, life in America is one of powerlessness, a feeling that they have less and are less than their white peers. The acclaimed novelist James Baldwin, writing in 1997 in response to the Ann Arbor case, put it this way: "It goes without saying, then, that language is also a political instrument, means and proof of power. It is the most crucial key to identity: It reveals the private identity, and connects one with or divorces one from the larger public or communal identity" (Baldwin, 1997, p. 16).

Like Baldwin, researcher/writer Lisa Delpit (1997) believes that there is a wealth of information linking children's identity and self-esteem to their local dialect. For example, research among the Pima Indian children of Arizona showed that in grades 1 through 3 the children were approximating the standard English speech of their teachers. One would expect that as they grew older, their standard English proficiency would improve. This was not the case. By grade 4, their language moved more toward the local dialect of the community. That is, these children chose to use their local dialect over the standard form of school talk. By ages 8 and 9, children become aware that they are members of a group; that group identity, in turn, influences their identity of self. Delpit argues that the language form African American children bring to school is an expression of themselves, their family, and their community and must be respected as such by the teachers.

Some Characteristics of African American English Vernacular (AAVE)

Many aspects of AAVE, such as vocabulary terms, verb tenses, inflections, and grammatical constructions, differ from standard English and often cause confusion among teachers and other students who may not be familiar with these differences. Phonologically, for example, *jump* is pronounced /jum/, *desks* is pronounced /desses/, *they* is pronounced /dey/, *tooth* is pronounced /toof/, *sister* is pronounced /sistuh/, *pig* is pronounced /pick/, and *hundred* is pronounced /hundret/ (Fashold & Shuy, 1970).

Syntactically, AAVE also differs from standard English in many ways, most prominently in the verb *to be* (Smith, 1997). Examples of grammatical structures in AAVE include "He be doin' that," "They be tired," or "They tired." Other nonstandard examples commonly used in AAVE speech include, "That teacher she mean," "That girl she smart," "They done came," or the use of double and triple negatives as in "I ain't never had no trouble wit none of them" (Fashold & Shuy, 1970; Hoover, 1997; Smith, 1997).

Smitherman (1997) explains that AAVE is also much more than phonological differences or grammatical changes. AAVE also includes a style of speaking that differs from standard English. For example, **signifyin'** is a "form of ritualized insult in which a speaker puts down, talks about, needles—signifies on—other speakers" (p. 9). One type of signifyin', called "playin' the dozens," involves linguistic insults at a person's mother or other relatives, as in this exchange between two women about a hairstyle. First woman: "Girl, what up with that head?" Second woman: "Ask yo momma" (i.e., It's none of your business). Another example would be this exchange between two males. First male: "Yo momma wear combat boots and concrete drawrs." Second male: "Yo momma so ugly, she scare the white offuh rice." Signifyin', playin' the dozens, and other humorous retorts reveal a person's language skills in the African American community yet are often viewed negatively by the majority white community. See Figure 11.2 for features of AAVE.

> ## *Beyond the classroom*
>
> As classroom teachers, you will need to be well informed regarding the many ramifications of the AAVE controversy. By reading the works of many of the scholars referred to in this section, you will gain a deeper understanding of the complex issues surrounding AAVE. Here is a list of some authors and their works you might wish to read: Geneva Smitherman, *Talkin and Tesifyin: The Language of Black America; Norton Anthology of African American Literature*, edited by Henry Louis Gates, Jr. and Nellie V. McKay; Mary Rhodes Hoover, *Super Literacy*; Lisa Delpit, *Other People's Children: Cultural Conflict in the Classroom*; and Evelyn Dandy, *Black Communications*.

Classroom Implications for Teachers

Classroom teachers cannot ignore the issue of nonstandard speech in their classrooms, nor can they pretend it will take care of itself. To do so only dooms thousands of African American children to years of frustration and failure and ultimately leads to the high dropout rates we currently witness among minority students. Instead, teachers must address the controversies and issues surrounding nonstandard speech with sensitivity and innovative approaches.

FIGURE 11.2

Features of AAVE.

	STANDARD ENGLISH	AAVE
Final consonant sounds	send, sent	sen
	six	sic
	asked	asc
	walked	walk
	five cents	five cent
	running, going	runnin, goin
Consonant sounds /l/ and /r/	school	schoo
	teacher	teachuh
	help me	hep me
"Th" sounds as /d/, /v/, or /f/	this, that, these	dis, dat, des
	with	wid
	brother	brovah
	death	deaf
Articles *a, an*	an apple	a apple
	an egg	a egg
Double negative	I don't have any money.	I ain't got no money.
Tense marker	He is playing over there.	He playing der.
	Pete has four dogs.	Pete have four dog.
	She works every day.	She work every day.
Present tense used for both present and past	he said	he say
	he got	he get
Verb *to be*	She is busy now.	She be busy now.
	They are busy now.	They be busy now.
Helping verbs	John is coming at 6:00 P.M.	John come at 6:00 P.M.
	Mary has gone away.	Mary gone away.
Pronouns	That's mine.	That mines.
	He did it himself.	He did it hisself.
Subject noun and pronoun	John said that.	John, he say dat.
	Miss Jones always says.	Miz Jones, she alway be saying.

Source: Adapted from J. Lindfors (1987), *Children's Language and Learning* (2nd ed.).

Lisa Delpit (1997) has reviewed the research on classroom practices that have been successful with minority students. Here is a summary of some of her suggestions:

- Make the study of language diversity an actual part of the school curriculum. Even young children can discuss the way different television characters or people from different cultures speak.
- Audiotape stories narrated by speakers from different cultures, including stories that contain AAVE speech such as "Flossie & the Fox" by Patricia McKissack.
- Have students become "language detectives," where they interview different people, listen to different speech variations on the radio and television, and identify similarities and differences in talking.

- Help students to create bilingual dictionaries of their own language forms and those of standard English. Teacher and students work together to decide which appropriate translations to include in the dictionaries.
- Use role-playing and other dramatics activities to encourage students to switch back and forth from one language form to another (code switching). Memorizing dramatic parts in another dialect or in standard English is a good way to practice language skills without fear of constant correction.
- Videotape student presentations and then use them in self-critique class lessons to develop awareness of and improvement in standard English.
- Have students use a tape recorder in class during ordinary lessons. Afterward, upon listening to the tape, have students note how often and under what circumstances they switch between AAVE and standard English.
- Have young children create puppet shows or role-plays using cartoon characters to address issues of AAVE or standard English in the classroom. As with other forms of dramatic play, puppetry allows students to use and deal with various language forms without fear of corrections or negative reactions from the teacher.

Beyond the classroom

Discover for yourself some of the richness of the African American experience by reading authors such as Maya Angelou, James Baldwin, Paul Laurence Dunbar, Langston Hughes, Malcolm X, Terry McMillan, Toni Morrison, and Walter Dean Myers.

- Have students present daily news reports to their classmates modeling their favorite newscaster, such as Tom Brokaw or Dan Rather. Television newscasters are often held up as good examples of standard English speakers because regardless of their sex, age, or race they must communicate clearly with a wide and varying audience.
- Use children's literature to develop students' awareness of dialect and cultural differences among characters. For example, in "Flossie & the Fox" by Patricia McKissack, lessons could include translations of Flossie's speech into standard English identifying the wordplay and humor in the book, role-playing scenes from the book, and writing extensions of the story.
- Use children's books to identify specific contrasting language patterns between standard English and AAVE. For example, in *Millions of Cats* by Wanda Gag, children will encounter the pattern "hundreds of cats, thousands of cats, millions and billions and trillions of cats." This pattern is repeated throughout the story, providing children with a model for the use of the standard English plural form *s*, which is often omitted in AAVE. Oral repetitions of the plural *s* pattern can be supplemented with other activities, such as acting out parts of the story, retelling the story into a tape recorder, or retelling the story using puppets (Tompkins & McGee, 1983).

Reising and Perry (2001) found some specific strategies that assisted Black English dialect speakers as they moved toward standardized English. The following strategies were especially helpful:

If you have no confidence in self you are twice defeated in the race of life. With confidence, you have won even before you have started.

MARCUS GARVEY

- Focus on one sound or grammatical item at a time.
- Have students listen carefully to the correct sound or grammatical structure.
- Have students practice saying the correct sound or grammatical structure.
- Help students hear the difference between the Black English dialect and the standardized sound or structure.
- Have students repeat the Black English dialect sound or structure and then the standardized sound or structure to demonstrate that they can discriminate between the two.
- Encourage students to use the standardized sound or structure in their speech in the classroom.

VIGNETTE *in the classroom*

Carrie Secret teaches fifth grade in Prescott Elementary School in Oakland, CA. Prescott was one of the few schools where a majority of the teachers adopted the Standard English Proficiency (SEP) program. This is the statewide initiative that uses systematic instruction in AAVE while having as its goal that children learn standard English.

Mrs. Secret has been at Prescott, a troubled inner school, for 31 years. She has seen teachers come and go, but she herself has elected to remain in this school. As she puts it, "I've never desired to do anything but teach. I have never desired to leave the classroom for any other position. Teaching is my passion."

She is a strong believer in the SEP program, which uses many strategies from second-language learning programs. In SEP, there are three emphases: culture, language, and literacy. "Our program," she states, "is not just a language program that stresses how well you acquire and speak English. We emphasize the learning of reading by incorporating a strong literacy component. Another crucial issue is that we push students to learn the content language of each area of the curriculum."

In explaining her approach to instruction, Mrs. Secret explains, "In fifth grade, I encourage the students to practice English most of the instructional time. I say encourage because *required* is a word that sends a message that if you don't use English, then you are operating below standard."

Some days Carrie Secret announces to her class, "While you are working, I will be listening to how well you use English. In your groups, you must call for translation if a member of your group uses an AAVE structure." Other days she tells her children they are attending Spelman or Morehouse College (historically African American colleges) and that they are expected to use the language the professors use, which is standard English.

Carrie Secret also believes in reading aloud to her students regularly, particularly when she taught in the younger grades. She would read to them first thing in the morning, after recess, and again after lunch. She still reads aloud to her fifth-graders and stresses not only reading for information but also for pleasure. She also shares poetry aloud each day and has the whole class singing songs such as "I Believe I Can Fly" and "Step by Step."

Source: Adapted from "An Interview with Carrie Secret," in *The Real Ebonics Debate*, Theodore, AL: Beacon Press, 1997.

ENGLISH AS A SECOND LANGUAGE (ESL)

"For the rich, learning a second or foreign language has always been valued and expected, whereas for the poor, speaking a language other than English has been seen as a deficit to be remediated, replaced or eradicated" (Nancy Lemberger, 1997).

One of the most interesting and controversial aspects of American education is the proliferation of students who do not speak English or who speak another language in addition to English. Much has been written about this under the headings of Second-Language Acquisition and Bilingual Education. This section is intended to give you an overview of the whole area of bilingual education and make you aware of some of the issues, along with their complexities.

One thing is for certain: The demographics of America since 1990 have changed and are continuing to change, and these changes are readily seen in the classrooms. Since 1991, the number of English-as-a-second-language (ESL) students has increased 95 percent, which resulted in 4,747,763 ESL students in public schools in the 2001–2002 school year (U. S. Department of Education, National Center for Education Statistics, 2001). Six states (Texas, California, Arizona, Illinois, New York, and Florida) each had more than 100,000 limited-English-proficiency students, and another 20 states had between 20,000 and

100,000 ESL students. Since 1991, the population of ESL students in Alaska, Arkansas, Idaho, Kansas, Nebraska, Oklahoma, and Oregon schools has increased greater than 200 percent. The challenge for classroom teachers not only comes from increasing numbers of ESL students, but also from the many different languages of the ESL students. The ESL population represents 327 different languages. The most common languages are Spanish, Vietnamese, Hmong, Haitian Creole, Korean, Arabic, Chinese Cantonese, Russian, Navajo, Portuguese, Chinese Mandarin, Japanese, Serbo-Croatian, Urdu, Khmer, and Tagalog (U.S. Department of Education, National Center for Education Statistics, 2001).

> ## Beyond the classroom
>
> Meet with a linguistics or language arts professor at your college or university. Bring along a copy of a language arts lesson plan that you have designed and discuss how it can be adapted to meet the needs of students who speak nonstandard English.

Throughout the 1970s and 1980s, while various bilingual approaches and programs were being tried all under the umbrella terms of bilingual education, the stream of immigrants from Mexico, Latin America, and Asia to America became a flood. Making the adjustment from their native language to English often took six to seven years of participation in a bilingual education program. During that time, many of these students dropped out of school. Predictably, a conservative, antibilingual reaction emerged. Its most vocal proponent was California's U. S. senator and former professor of linguistics, S. I. Hayakawa. In 1981, Senator Hayakawa went so far as to introduce an amendment to the U. S. Constitution to make English the official language of the United States. During the 1980s, this English-only movement gained great momentum. In 1985, Secretary of Education William Bennett declared bilingual education a "failed path" and called for its dismemberment in favor of English-only curriculums in America's public schools. Bilingual education as we had known it since 1974 was under attack from all sides.

In June 1998, voters in the State of California passed **Proposition 227,** called the English for the Children initiative, which for all practical purposes ended bilingual education in the California public schools (Beck, 1998). It provided that after one year of intensive English instruction, all of California's non-English-speaking students would be mainstreamed into regular English instruction classes. Almost immediately a new storm arose. School districts with a majority of non-English-speaking students served by the current bilingual programs said they would not stop teaching just because of the proposition. Clearly the issue of bilingual education is just as much a political issue as an educational issue.

California's Proposition 227 attacking bilingual education as a whole has been roundly criticized by many professional educators and their representative organizations. For example, in 1998 the National Council of Teachers of English issued its National Research Council (NRC) report in which it came out strongly in favor of bilingual education programs (Kaufman, 1998). Furthermore, the report recommended that children who speak a language other than English and who are in schools where there are appropriate materials and fluent teachers be taught to read in their native language while they are acquiring proficiency in spoken English. This is the position of the NRC and the learned research communities; it refutes the direction in which California and other states are going.

Second Language Acquisition

It is easy to recognize the incredible difficulties that bilingual programs present to the individual elementary classroom teacher who might be expected to provide instruction in math, science, and social studies to her or his students who speak three, four, or as many as half a dozen different languages. In response to this need, the entire field of second-language acquisition research took on a new urgency. Leading the way was the work of Stephen Krashen.

Krashen's (1981, 1982, 1985) model of second-language acquisition provides the theoretical foundation for understanding the many approaches to bilingual education; at the same time, it raises questions about many of the negative practices associated with bilingual education programs in America. First, Krashen distinguishes between language learning and language acquisition. Learning another language is associated with school; it involves memorizing new vocabulary terms, studying grammar rules, and translating passages from one language to another. However, knowing about a language is not the same as knowing a language. The latter is more of a subconscious process that enables one to function in a given environment.

To better understand this notion, let's break Krashen's theory down into its components. First, to know language requires what Krashen calls *comprehensible input*, or the ability to understand the general language patterns of what is heard or read and to attach meaning to form in a language environment. Second is Krashen's notion of the *low affective filter*, which refers to the learner's openness to learning as well as a willingness to take risks and make mistakes. Finally, the *monitor hypothesis* is the way in which learners edit or correct their use of the new language based on their conscious understanding of the rules of that language. In sum, Krashen believes that knowing a language begins with indirect, unconscious experiences and later proceeds to direct instruction.

There are two levels of language proficiency. **Basic interpersonal communication (BIC)** is the ability to orally communicate with native speakers at a comfortable level on most topics. It takes the average second-language learner two years to obtain BIC. The second level is **cognitive academic language proficiency (CALP);** this is the ability to read and write academic materials that native speakers of the same chronological age can do. It takes the average second-language learner five to seven years to obtain CALP (Peregoy & Boyle, 1997). At any given time in any given classroom, a teacher may encounter a number of factors that will influence the teaching environment: multiple languages, various levels of literacy, varying background experiences, and various levels of self-esteem (Chamot & O'Malley, 1994).

Following Krashen's work and that of others in the field of second-language acquisition, a number of different program models emerged in the schools. Three main types that emerged were based on three educational theories—behaviorist, innatist, and interactionist (Peregoy & Boyle, 1997).

Programs based on the Behaviorist Theory are **pull-out programs,** in which students leave their regular classroom and go to another room where a specialist works with them for a certain amount of time each day. These programs emphasize repetition of simplified phrases; designers of these programs believe a controlled, simplified vocabulary is the quickest way for the student to acquire English. In these programs, students study English for part of the day until they are proficient in English and can function in the regular classroom for all subjects. These programs have declined somewhat in popularity both because of cost and because research indicates that students learn English best through social interaction with other English-speaking students, not by simplifying some aspect of the language (Goodman & Freeman, 1993).

Programs based on the Innatist Theory use **total submersion programs,** based on the belief that language is naturally learned when it is heard and used (Freeman & Freeman, 2001). In a total immersion program, students spend the entire day in the regular classroom because proponents believe the quickest way for students to learn English is in a regular classroom, learning alongside other students their age. An example would be in some places in Canada where students learn French and English.

The third type of program, based on the Interactionist Theory, states that language is acquired through **nature and nurture.** These programs, which have various names, emphasize the importance of comprehensible input (Krashen, 1989) and social interaction (Vygotsky, 1962). If only one language other than English is being spoken in the classroom, it is possible to find a bilingual teacher or a bilingual paraprofessional. In such cases, the teacher explains the concept in English, checks for understanding in English, and then repeats the concept in the other language. The English-speaking students also benefit from this type of teaching because they learn another language.

Today's ESL Programs

Today the goals for most bilingual educational programs are to provide ESL students access to the core curriculum and to give them the opportunity to become proficient in English while maintaining a high self-esteem. According to Peregoy and Boyle (1997), the best learning environment (1) permits ESL students to use their first language while learning or expressing themselves when necessary; (2) prepares ESL students to learn content in English; (3) provides ESL students comprehensible but challenging materials tailored to the individual; and (4) provides ESL students with many literacy opportunities.

Code Switching

Code switching is a linguistic expression that often occurs with ESL students. **Code switching** is typically defined as the alternate use of two or more languages in the same word, phrase, clause, sentence, or conversation. The following are examples of code switching between Spanish and English (Valdes-Fallis, 1978):

- La consulta era eight dollars. (The office visit was eight dollars.)
- Well, I keep starting some. Como por un mes todos los dias escribo y ya dejo. Last week empece otra vez. (Well, I keep starting some. For about a month I write every day and then I stop. Last week I started again.)

Code switching occurs in both fluent and emerging bilinguals. It seems to be learned at a very early age, and it can be used to clarify meaning or attract or retain attention. Code switching is grammatically and functionally derived from standard language principles (McClure, 1977). In all respects, code switching is deliberate and linguistically appropriate.

The false notion that code switching is a sign of an alingual or nonlingual speaker must be replaced with accurate information. Negative biases can influence how a teacher responds to a child: If a teacher views code switching as a sign of low intelligence, she or he might treat children who code-switch as unlikely to achieve in school. Negative biases can lower the teacher's expectations of success for such children and result in de facto segregation within the classroom if such students are automatically placed in lower reading groups.

Once a teacher understands that code switching represents a combination of the linguistic rules of both languages, a more accurate assessment of the child's language arts needs can be made. A child who engages in code switching is no longer viewed as an unskilled language learner but as a child learning to handle two disparate linguistic systems—an intellectual challenge that his monolingual teachers have not met. Developmental literature suggests that while a child is acquiring two languages, one of the languages may surge ahead or lag behind the other, or both may develop simultaneously (Garcia, 1983). Instead of being some-

In and beyond the classroom

Many school systems have developed both bilingual and ESL programs. Ask the teachers in these classes to define bilingual and ESL programs for you. Visit each of these programs and observe how language arts instruction is conducted. Reflect on how the techniques you observed could be applied in the general classroom. If it is not possible for you to visit such rooms, read the article "Learning About Language Learning" (Piper, 1986) and compare the information found in this article with the information you have read in this chapter.

how inferior in language skills, the child is teeming with language learning—perhaps to a greater extent than any of his monolingual peers.

Language Arts Instruction for ESL Students

So what kind of language arts instruction should students who are codeswitching receive while they are becoming fluent bilinguals? In general, the instruction should be the same as for fluent bilinguals: language arts concepts, information, and skills taught in the language of greater linguistic comfort. Although many classroom teachers are not bilingual, language arts instruction for emergent bilinguals can easily incorporate the cultural heritage associated with the native language and focus on development of self-esteem.

A comprehensive language arts program includes a melding of both whole language and direct instruction practices. For children who are learning English as a second language, Gersten and Dimino (1990) have said, "The rate at which they learn is directly dependent on how clear our explanations and examples are, how careful our instructions are, how much practice we provide, and the wording of the feedback provided to students" (p. 24).

To provide this approach, classroom teachers use a number of strategies. First, the teacher uses inquiry-based instruction to permit ESL students to study concepts that interest them by viewing videos if they cannot read, and later reading books that are at their reading level. Inquiry-based instruction results in small-group learning or buddy learning, which is less threatening to these students. Second, the teacher modifies the lesson so the ESL students will feel successful. Third, the teacher encourages and permits ESL students to use their native language in speech and writing when they cannot find the appropriate English term. At first, students may only be able to draw their understanding of the concept. Fourth, the teacher respects their culture by learning something about it and sharing the information with the class. Finally, the teacher provides time for cooperative learning groups and socialization (Peregoy & Boyle, 1997; Schirmer, Casbon, & Twiss, 1996).

Peregoy and Boyle (1997) suggest that a teacher, while giving instruction, should remember the 11 following points:

1. Do not shout. ESL students are not deaf; they just do not understand English.
2. Speak at a somewhat slower rate, but keep it natural.
3. Speak clearly.
4. Avoid figures of speech and idioms.
5. Repeat key phrases or vocabulary.
6. Use descriptive language.
7. Use many visuals—pictures, charts, videos, manipulatives.
8. Use gestures, but be conscious of gestures that offend some cultures.
9. Teach phrases or sentences instead of isolated words.
10. Relate a new concept to some concept the students already know.
11. Give models or examples of how to complete the assignment.

There are other factors that accelerate second-language learning: (1) The teacher makes reading, writing, and speaking applicable to daily living (Freeman & Freeman, 2001); (2) the teacher celebrates approximations and progress (Freeman & Freeman, 2001); (3) caregivers become involved in the student's education (Peregoy & Boyle, 1997); (4) the holistic approach is used (Goodman & Freeman, 1993); and (5) portfolios are used to reflect students' progress because it is encouraging for them to see their growth (Garcia, 1994).

In and beyond the classroom

Identify a child with a learning disability, a communication disorder, or a mental disability who is mainstreamed for all or part of the day in a class in your field experience school. Discuss the child's IEP as related to language arts instruction with the special education teacher. Discuss how the language arts objectives are being achieved both in the special setting and in the general education classroom.

Painting is just another way of keeping a diary.

PABLO PICASSO

Here are 15 specific practices that teachers can use for second-language learners:

1. Use the language experience approach (LEA) (an activity in which the student dictates to the teacher and the teacher writes exactly what the student says), which permits students to see the words that they can speak in print; it also helps them become aware of the letter/sound relationships (Chamot & O'Malley, 1994). (See Chapter 9 for further discussion of LEA.)

2. Expose students to print even if they are not proficient speakers (Chamot & O'Malley, 1994; Goodman & Freeman, 1993).

3. Read to students as you point to the text so they can follow along; they also get to hear the new language (Peregoy & Boyle, 1997).

4. Use the process-writing approach when writing because it has manageable parts (Farnan, Flood, & Lapp, 1994; Peregoy & Boyle, 1997).

5. Permit students to keep learning logs in their native language as long as necessary (Peregoy & Boyle, 1997).

6. Use small-group discussions so students can try out the language in a non-threatening setting (Chamot & O'Malley, 1994).

7. Permit students to work with a partner (Peregoy & Boyle, 1997).

8. Use dialogue journals with the teacher (Farnan et al., 1994).

9. Be sure the students are doing academic work and not busy work such as coloring pictures from a coloring book (Peregoy & Boyle, 1997).

10. Emphasize comprehension over pronunciation (Chamot & O'Malley, 1994).

11. Use books with a wide range of reading levels as well as multiple books on one topic (Farnan et al., 1994).

12. Connect prior knowledge to new content (Farnan et al., 1994; Goodman & Freeman, 1993).

13. Use books that are linked to students' culture (Allen, 1994).

14. Use electronic books to introduce students to a wide vocabulary (Higgins & Hess, 1999).

15. Label items in the classroom.

Using literature in combination with systematic instruction and feedback is clearly an important means of unifying reading, writing, speaking, and listen-

VIGNETTE *in the classroom*

The students in Mr. Decker's class are planting seeds and later will write about the experience in their journals. The teacher is having a conversation with Sergio, an emergent bilingual English–Spanish speaker. The teacher is a monolingual English speaker.

Sergio asks, "Teacher, where is my semilla?"

The teacher holds up a seed and says, "Are you asking for your seed?"

"Yes, my seed. I'm going to plantarla."

In order to facilitate Sergio's ability to use words in context, the teacher picks up a seed and a cup, and as he hands them to Sergio, he says, "Sergio, here is your seed. You also need dirt and a cup."

Sergio plants his seed in the cup and then goes back to his teacher and says, "Teacher, I'm done. Where's mi diario?" Mr. Decker responds, "I don't understand. What is a diario?"

Sergio points to another student's journal and says, "This." The teacher replies, "Oh, okay, I see. *Diario* means 'journal.' Thanks for teaching me a new word. Your journal is on the counter."

Sergio collects his journal, returns to his work space, and happily begins to write about planting seeds. His teacher assists other students in the class. Both Sergio and his teacher have enjoyed another positive language learning experience together.

ing. Children's literature books not only enhance children's self-esteem but can also provide excellent models of the English language. Take, for example, the book *The Very Hungry Caterpillar* by Eric Carle. Through this story, children are exposed not only to a beautifully illustrated and interesting account of a caterpillar's metamorphosis but also to number, time, and color concepts. For students learning English as a second language, it provides an excellent example of what the English language looks and sounds like—an example that can aid them in their own reading, writing, and speaking.

Children with Disabilities

Today any teacher at any one time may have students who are learning disabled, low achievers, emotionally disturbed, mentally retarded, hearing impaired, or visually impaired, or have attention deficit hyperactivity disorder, some level of autism, or a speech impairment or any other speech problems. For each special need, the teacher is required by law to have an individualized educational plan (discussed next) if the caregiver consents that his or her child receive special education.

In this chapter, only some of the special needs are addressed. It is important to remember that when these children are in your classroom, you are their teacher, not just their babysitter. It is important that they be given learning experiences that fit their needs and abilities.

LEGISLATION AND INDIVIDUALS WITH DISABILITIES

In 1975, Congress passed the Education of All Handicapped Children Act, also called **PL 94-142,** which required that "a free and appropriate education and related services be provided in the least restrictive environment" and that an **individualized educational plan (IEP)** be written for each qualifying student. Since 1975, the law has been amended several times.

In 1983, the amendments emphasized that schools provide transitional services for secondary students and that schools provide caregivers some training in helping their child. In 1986, amendments were passed to extend appropriate education for ages three to five and to provide early intervention programs for children two years old and younger. In 1990, Congress updated and renamed the act Americans with Disabilities Act and in 1997, Congress amended the act as the Individuals with Disabilities Education Act (IDEA '97) so that schools must demonstrate that students with disabilities meet the learning standards established by the state (Sullivan, 2003). With this amendment, high-stakes tests are often given before a curriculum that is aligned with state standards is in place. This results in lower test scores for students who normally do fairly well on standardized tests and even worse test scores for students with learning disabilities (Erb, 2003). It is important that teachers take action so that students' IEP objectives are integrated with state standards. Implementing the integration may be difficult; however, Sullivan (2003) introduced CONNECT as a tool for teachers to use as they differentiate instruction so that students with learning disabilities and an IEP can obtain the state's standards. CONNECT is a seven-step process that assists teachers as they integrate IEP objectives with state standards and the school's curriculum. The steps are as follows:

In and beyond the classroom

There is much disagreement among researchers, educators, and caregivers whether full inclusion is appropriate for all disabled students and for the nondisabled students. You may wish to take some time and reflect on the pros and cons of full inclusion. We recommend that you visit some classroom teachers who have full inclusion in their rooms and ask if you may observe the classroom. While you are there, focus on the interaction between the children with special needs and the other students. Are all students actively engaged in appropriate activities? Are some students shy around students with special needs? Ask the teacher if you may also see the IEP form that the school uses.

1. Consult the IEP for a student with special needs. The plan lists the student's difficulties and any special considerations the student needs in order to reach the short- and long-term goals set by the IEP committee.

2. Optimize learning by linking IEP objectives to state standards. An IEP objective may be for the student to increase reading rate by reading phrases instead of words, and the state standard may require students to be able to understand limericks. The teacher can have the student work on increasing rate while reading limericks.

3. Note strategies for instruction. The IEP lists accommodations that the student needs in order to reach the objective. The accommodations may include large-print materials. In this case, the teacher can enlarge the limericks.

4. INstruct. During instruction, the teacher must monitor the accommodations and make adjustments when needed.

5. Evaluate. The teacher needs to evaluate the student to determine whether the short- and long-term goals are being met. In the case of fluency, the teacher could evaluate the progress by listening to the student or by having the student record some limericks on tape and self-assess the progress.

6. Check for progress. The teacher must collect all the data, including personal observations, and analyze the data to assess whether the student is reaching the objectives and to make sure that the student is being challenged.

7. Tailor instruction to student needs. If the student's fluency is not improving by reading entire limericks, the teacher needs to change instruction. For this student, the teacher may create a tape in which the teacher reads a limerick-line by line, pausing after each line so the student can "echo" each line.

ATTENTION DEFICIT HYPERACTIVITY DISORDER (ADHD)

Many teachers believe that all students in their class have ADHD because of all the wiggles, movement, and calling out. However, wiggles and the true symptoms of ADHD are quite different. Johnson (1992) compiled the following list of symptoms that the classroom teacher may observe in the child with ADHD. She cautions against two incorrect conclusions—a child does not have to demonstrate all the symptoms in order to have ADHD and a child with two or three of the symptoms does not necessarily have ADHD. Children with **attention deficit hyperactivity disorder (ADHD)** may exhibit these symptoms in the classroom:

- *Disorganization.* They often have messy desks, papers, and backpacks.
- *Impulsive reading.* They often make quick guesses. They do not stop to think whether a letter has a line or a hump, and they often do not read past the first or second letter.
- *Impulsive writing.* Their papers are often messy because of writing over letters to make corrections or because they erase so hard that the paper tears. Often they do not stay on the line and crowd their words when they get to the end of the line.
- *Math difficulty.* They often copy inaccurately and will quickly do the math problem without checking to see if the sign indicates addition, subtraction, multiplication, or division.

Beyond the classroom

Arrange to observe a general education classroom in your field experience school in which a child with a sensory or physical impairment is mainstreamed for all or part of the day. Observe the child and how the environment has been modified to assist that student in learning language arts material. Discuss your observations with the child's special and general education teachers. An alternate activity is to describe a real or hypothetical child with a physical or health impairment receiving language arts instruction in the general education classroom. Using a minimum of three current journals as your knowledge base, describe the kinds of modifications you would make for this student. See Figure 11.3 for a list of special education journals.

• *Undetailed drawings.* Drawings are usually done quickly with stick figures and no details. The coloring is usually messy and outside the lines.

• *Impatience with classroom pace.* The pace of the classroom is usually too slow for them; therefore, they talk out of turn about topics that are not being discussed. They cannot stay on task for a long period of time. They are very restless and constantly move around the room, bothering other children. Waiting in line is a difficult task for them.

• *Touching troubles.* They often touch classmates' hair, clothes, and other belongings. They are quick to accidentally hit others.

• *Frequent outbursts.* Because these children feel out of control, they often are bossy and not liked by their peers. This results in low self-esteem.

There are some practical tips for classroom teachers to use with students who have ADHD. Shima and Gsovski (1996) suggest these four:

1. Whether in small groups or with individual work, use creative hands-on activities.
2. Give directions in small segments and restate them often.
3. Help the students organize and monitor their homework by providing contracts and notebook folders with pockets.
4. Insist on high levels of participation by giving the children small jobs and calling on them often.

Listen rather than lecture. Show the road but expect the child to reach his destination on his own.

HAIM GINOTT

Armstrong (1996) suggests that the teacher engage these children in physical, outdoor exercise and sports with no competition. In this way, they can release some of their energy without fear of failure. He also suggests the use of personal contracts so the child can see accomplishments. Computers help students with ADHD feel successful by eliminating messy handwriting. Johnson (1992) found that quiet classical music has a calming effect on students with ADHD and that tutors are useful because the children receive one-on-one attention, which they crave.

AUTISM

Autism is an umbrella term describing a syndrome or cluster of behaviors exhibited by children whose characteristics and needs are actually heterogeneous. Autistic behaviors have been described along a continuum of severity. Definitions of **autism** and autistic disorders generally include the following six behavioral characteristics:

1. profound failure to relate to or emotionally bond with significant people in the environment
2. impaired language acquisition and comprehension; muteness or echolalia (repeating what is said by the other person)

3. under- or overresponsiveness to sensory stimulation

4. inappropriate or flat affective trait (i.e., speaking without emotions)

5. preoccupation with stereotypical, repetitive, self-stimulatory behaviors, such as body rocking or hand tapping

6. profound resistance to environmental change, including modifications in daily routines

Not all children described as autistic or autistic-like exhibit all these behavioral characteristics, nor do they demonstrate these behaviors to the same degree. Nonetheless, autism is one of the most disruptive and severe childhood disabilities.

Some children described as autistic are educated in the regular classroom for all or part of the school day. Since autistic behaviors are idiosyncratic, educational provisions should focus on individual children and their particular behaviors.

With respect to language arts instruction, techniques and materials should be modified according to the behavior of the particular child. For some students, the need to maintain a strict routine is critical; for others, participation in group activities is likely to aggravate negative social tendencies. Some children can participate in all language arts activities with no major modifications but might become highly agitated by environmental factors, such as the sound of a fire engine siren or the sight of popcorn popping. Certain topics found in storybooks may also set off delusional behaviors, and excessive preoccupation with spelling or handwriting style may be observed. Kluth and Darmody-Lathan (2003) offer strategies that have been successful with some students with autism:

- Recognize all literacies. Too often teachers emphasize only reading and writing. However, often autistic students learn through listening and respond through drawings and sign language.

- Capitalize on student's interests. Because students with autism often stay focused for long periods of time on something that fascinates them, teachers can introduce different sources to find information on that topic. For example, information on zoo animals can be found on websites of different zoos.

- Use a range of visual supports. Graphic organizers and other visual representations help clarify concepts.

- Read aloud. Teachers or others reading aloud to students with autism helps build word recognition, fluency, and comprehension.

- Encourage different types of expression and communication. Often students with autism do not like to talk in front of peers; however, they are often successful communicators if they can talk through a puppet or as another character.

Regardless of the instructional topic, the general educator needs to create a reasonably appropriate educational environment for autistic children. Answers to the questions posed in Figure 11.4 should be helpful in establishing a positive learning environment for students with autistic behaviors.

The answers to the last of these questions are particularly helpful when preparing other students in the classroom to accept their autistic classmate in a positive way. The other children need to be prepared for some atypical behaviors and to know how to depersonalize their occurrence. When gaze aversion happens during a conversation, for example, the inattention or lack of willingness to enter into this social activity should be taken no more personally than an interruption of conversation caused by a sneeze or hiccup. The other students also need to realize that delusional or fantasy behaviors are part of their classmate's problem, not a deliberate attempt to be dishonest with them. Preparing the other children in the classroom is as important as understanding the needs of the child with autism if a successful social and learning climate is to be established.

FIGURE 11.4

Questions for assisting autistic children.

- Which teaching strategies have been successful with this student in the past?
- Which procedures can be applied in the classroom without extensive support?
- What is the expected effect of any medications prescribed for the child?
- To what degree have the following behaviors been observed in an education setting: unresponsiveness to social stimuli, gaze aversion, overselective response, language disorders, and excessive fantasy and delusions? How disruptive were these behaviors?

Academically Gifted Children

Most educators today recognize that students who are academically gifted have special needs and fall under PL 94-142. However, there are differing opinions among educators on how to meet these special needs. Some believe that the "least restrictive environment," which is promised to all children in PL 94-142, is a pull-out program, whereas other educators believe gifted students belong in the inclusive classroom. Both groups have reasons for their stance.

Start a program for gifted children, and every parent demands that his child be enrolled.

THOMAS BAILEY

Advocates for pull-out programs argue that the traditional **scope-and-sequence curriculum** (a curriculum that stresses certain concepts must be mastered in a specific sequence and that emphasizes repetition) is restrictive and does not permit a gifted student to grow cognitively. They believe that the scope-and-sequence curriculum includes unnecessary review with no higher-level thinking activities. Often large class size hinders the regular classroom teacher from giving needed time to the gifted; or teachers feel that these students will succeed without any extra help, and many classroom teachers lack the skills for designing and implementing appropriate curriculum for the gifted. Gallagher, Harradine, and Coleman (1997) found in a study of 871 academically gifted students that these students considered core subjects unchallenging, regular classrooms boring, and cooperative learning groups in regular classrooms unfair because they were held back and had to do all the work. There is also the possibility that gifted students choose not to succeed under the regular curriculum because they desire to "belong." To alleviate this problem, proponents of gifted education believe that gifted students need opportunity to excel with other gifted students with an appropriate curriculum that (1) permits the gifted student to reach his or her potential; (2) gives opportunity for in-depth study of concepts that interest the student; (3) allows for divergent thinking; and (4) permits students to solve real-life problems (Renzulli, 2002).

Educators who favor the inclusive classroom for all students believe that gifted students belong in the regular classroom because it reflects society and there students learn to accept the differences of individuals. They believe that the pull-out programs make it more difficult to promote a positive response to differences by labeling gifted students and making them leave the regular classroom.

Most states have legislation that provides for the funding of gifted programs because they see the special needs for students with a high IQ (Doina, 1997). Across states and within states, these programs vary greatly because there are no national guidelines. Some have two-day pull-out programs for the entire district, whereas other districts may have only one hour per day in individual buildings.

The discussion that follows includes characteristics of the gifted student and some strategies that are effective with the gifted student. Also listed are resources that are useful to the classroom teacher.

CHARACTERISTICS OF GIFTED CHILDREN

The National Association for Gifted Children (2003) classifies gifted students as those who (1) have an IQ of 130 or above, (2) have a score on an intelligence test of two standard deviations above the mean on group or individual measures, (3) have a score of 97th percentile or higher on standard achievement tests, (4) have high levels of leadership ability, or (5) have extraordinary talent in visual or performing arts. Gifted students are divergent thinkers, have advanced vocabulary, are fast thinkers, are unusually sensitive to exceptions, are idealistic, and seek justice. Figure 11.5 is a list of additional characteristics of the gifted student that was compiled by the teachers of the Gifted Education Program in Yukon, OK, schools (2002).

Identifying and working with gifted students who have learning disabilities is difficult because teachers trained to work with gifted students are not trained to work with students with other exceptionalities (Kennedy, Higgins, & Pierce, 2002; Renzulli, 2002). Yet, it is imperative that all students—minority, ESL, and those with exceptionalities—be given the opportunity to maximize their abilities (Uresti, Goertz, & Bernal, 2002). To identify these students who are often called twice exceptional, collaboration among classroom teachers, gifted teachers, special education teachers, and caregivers is needed. These teachers and caregivers must form a team and combine their efforts to provide an appropri-

FIGURE 11.5

Characteristics of giftedness.

1. Asks lots of questions.
2. Possesses lots of information on specific things.
3. Is very curious; wants to know "Why?" or "How?"
4. Has concern and is sensitive about social, political, and global issues.
5. Has own ideas about how something should be done.
6. Enjoys debating.
7. Has a better reason for not doing something than you have for doing it.
8. Becomes impatient with work that is not perfect.
9. Expects others to be perfect.
10. Finds assignments unchallenging.
11. Thinks deeply and differently about things.
12. Enjoys exploratory levels of learning.
13. Loves abstract ideas.
14. Has a sense of humor.
15. Has a passionate interest in a specific area.
16. Has many interests and hobbies.
17. Can make personal application of concepts.
18. Has high level of energy.
19. Sees relationships between ideas.
20. Has a good memory.
21. Does not begin a task if there is a possibility of failure.
22. Easily sees subtle cause-and-effect relationships.
23. Prefers to work alone.

Source: Adapted from the Gifted Education Program in Yukon, Oklahoma.

ate differentiated curriculum for the student. At the beginning of the year, the team must meet to create a student profile. Included in the profile is information from previous teachers; test scores; as well as lists of the student's interests, disability characteristics and needs, and extracurricular activities in which the student participated in the past or would like to do.

Kennedy, Higgins, and Pierce (2002) suggest that the following general modifications be made when a team plans a student's instruction at the beginning of the year:

- Consider the student's strengths, interests, and disabilities when planning each assignment.
- Write a contract with the student as to when and how each assignment will be completed.
- Make sure the assignments are challenging but do not interface with the student's disability.
- Compact (omit the assignment when the student understands concepts). See page 450 for detailed information on compacting.
- Provide the student with a critical but fair assessment of each assignment.

REGULAR CLASSROOM ACTIVITIES FOR GIFTED STUDENTS

It is evident that gifted students need appropriate educational opportunities. Whatever type of special program they receive, the majority of the school time is spent in the regular classroom. Therefore, two types of activities that can be used by the classroom teacher in the regular classroom are the enrichment triad model and curriculum compacting. Both of these programs provide the following goals, which professionals agree would be at the heart of all activities that academically talented students encounter (Doina, 1997):

- flexible rate at which to work
- student choice of topic
- studies based on broad themes with in-depth study on one aspect of theme
- open-ended tasks
- alternative assessment

Enrichment Triad Model

Renzulli and Reis (1985), two nationally recognized researchers and leaders in gifted education, designed the **enrichment triad model,** which has three types of enrichment activities. This model, originally designed for gifted programs, is now used for schoolwide enrichment programs (Renzulli, 1994).

Type I enrichment activities are designed to expose students to new topics that they may wish to investigate later in greater detail. Type I activities include listening to outside speakers, watching videos, holding assemblies, going on field trips, visiting interest centers, and completing Bloom's taxonomy tasks (see Figure 11.6 for the levels of Bloom's taxonomy). Bloom's taxonomy task cards can be on any topic or book. The student begins with the first task and continues to the last one. A Bloom's taxonomy task card example on Ruth Heller's *Color* is found in Figure 11.7. After reading *Color*, a concept book about how printers apply color to the

Beyond the classroom

Take some time to reflect on your stance. Permit yourself to list the advantages and disadvantages of pull-out programs. Maybe you were in such a program and can give some insight on how you felt about the program while you were in it. If you were not in a gifted program, you may wish to research the subject in order to validate your stance. Telephone some districts around your university and ask how they meet the needs of gifted students. If they have a pull-out program, ask for permission to visit it.

The national educational movement is toward inclusion (Sapon-Shevin, 1994/1995) and extending the pedagogy of gifted education to all students (Reis, Gentry, & Park, 1996). Therefore, classroom teachers are given more of the responsibility to meet the needs of gifted students.

Knowledge:	Simple recall of learned facts.	
	Student will bring to mind what was read, seen, or heard.	
Comprehension:	Translating or interpreting material from one form to another.	
	Student explains or predicts what did or will happen.	
Application:	Ability to use learned material in personal life.	
	Student applies rules, concepts, or theories to daily life.	
Analysis:	Ability to break down material into its components.	
	Student will identify the parts, be able to see the relationships among parts, and recognize the organization of all parts.	
Synthesis:	Ability to put parts together to form a new whole.	
	Student will research various materials, recognize similarities and differences, and be able to give an oral or written presentation.	
Evaluation:	Ability to judge the value of the material studied.	
	After studying the material, student will give a value statement with clearly defined criteria.	

FIGURE 11.6

Bloom's taxonomy: Type I activity.

Source: Adapted from Bloom, *Taxonomy of Educational Objectives, Handbook I: Cognitive Domain* (1956).

1. Explain the four stages used by a printer when applying color to a page in a book.
2. Explain the magic of creating secondary colors.
3. Using the supplies on the table, mix colors to create your own color wheel.
4. Explain which primary or secondary colors create black.
5. Using four transparencies, draw a picture by using each of the transparencies as part of the entire picture; then place the transparencies over each other to show your complete picture.
6. Survey your classmates to find out which color is their favorite and create a bar graph to show the results of the survey.

FIGURE 11.7

Type I activity: Bloom's taxonomy task on Color *by Ruth Heller.*

pages of a book, the students would individually complete the task folder. All Type I activities are enrichment activities and are not part of the ordinary curriculum.

Type II enrichment activities focus on the development of higher-level thinking skills. These activities include research projects that develop library skills, problem-solving puzzles, mind-benders, and community projects that focus on helping and serving others or promoting pride within one's community.

Type III enrichment activities involve real-life problems. The activities are indepth independent or small-group projects in which a real-life problem is addressed. The goal is to find possible solutions to a real-life problem. Projects may include presenting city officials with a possible solution to a traffic problem around the school, inventing a new product, or writing and illustrating a new storybook or concept book about a favorite topic.

The enrichment triad model can be implemented in the regular classroom. All three types of activities are used, beginning, of course, with Type I. Teachers who use the enrichment triad model set aside special time each week for the activities. When working with Type II and Type III activities, students with similar interests are permitted to work together. A Type III activity may be a group or an individual project.

Compacting for the Gifted

Many teachers are challenged by gifted students. These students are easily bored and can present behavioral problems if they are not challenged. One way to accommodate these students is through **curriculum compacting:** "Curriculum compacting is a flexible, research-supported instructional technique that enables high-ability students to skip work they already know and substitute more challenging content" (Reis & Renzulli, 1992, p. 51).

The most frequently compacted areas are math, reading, language arts, science, and social studies. Compacting is done for individual subjects and for individual students. It is an individualized educational program for the gifted student. A student may be strong in one subject area and be able to compact most of that subject; however, in another content area that same student may not be able to do any compacting. Usually compacting is done by chapter or units and is done for the entire school year.

There are three steps to curriculum compacting. In the first step, the teacher articulates the goals and outcomes for the chapter or unit. While doing this, the teacher makes note of whether the material is review material or new content. In the second step, the teacher identifies all students who have already mastered the objects or goals. One way to do this is to check the students' scores on standardized tests. Then the teacher gives the targeted students the posttest for that chapter or unit that is going to be studied. From the test, the teacher analyzes exactly which skills the students can perform and which concepts they know. Next the teacher lists the skills and concepts that the students have not mastered. If the students are weak in a skill or concept, the teacher will write down the specific parts of the chapter that the students must complete and will determine how they will demonstrate mastery of the skill or concept.

In the third step, the teacher states the project, research, or self-directed activities that the students will accomplish while the class is working on the curriculum. The decision is agreed upon by each gifted student and teacher and is often written as a contract. The student and teacher list specific materials to be read, documents to write, videos to view, or projects to complete. Most schools use the compactor form that Renzulli and Smith (1978) designed (see Figure 11.8).

Besides the gifted students, there may be other students in the classroom who could benefit from curriculum compacting. Starko (1986) listed some behaviors of students for whom compacting may be of benefit: (1) finish tasks quickly, (2)

FIGURE 11.8	**The Compactor**

Sample compactor form.

Student's name _____   Age _____   Teachers _____

Conference date _____   Grade _____   Caregivers _____

Topics to be covered; tests used to prove competency	Parts of chapter to be completed to ensure competency	Enrichment tasks to be completed

Source: Adapted from J. Renzulli and L. H. Smith (1978), *A Guidebook for Developing Individualized Educational Programs for Gifted and Talented Students.* Copyright © Creative Learning Press, Mansfield Center, CT.

appear bored, (3) have test scores that are consistently high despite average class work, (4) have advanced vocabulary, and (5) ask higher-level thinking questions.

The regular classroom teacher who uses both the enrichment triad model and curriculum compacting will be catering to at least some of the needs of gifted students. A list of resource materials that can be used with gifted students is found in Figure 11.9.

FIGURE 11.9

Resources for gifted and enrichment programs.

Challenge Magazine: Reaching and Teaching the Gifted
Good Apple
Box 299
Carthage, IL 62321
(217) 357-3981
www.school-tools.com/Good-Apple.htm
(ready-to-photocopy enrichment activities)

Creative Learning Press
P.O. Box 320
Mansfield Center, CT 06250
(203) 281-4036
www.creativelearning.com
(publisher of Renzulli's materials)

Creative Publications
5040 W. 111 Street
Oaklawn, IL 60453
1-800-624-0822
www.creativepublications.com
(excellent source for logical thinking, brainteaser books)

Critical Thinking Press & Software
P.O. Box 448
Pacific Grove, CA 93950-0448
1-800-458-4849
www.criticalthinking.com
(excellent source for a wide variety of critical-thinking materials)

Free Spirit Publishing Ind.
400 First Avenue, North, Suite 616
Minneapolis, MN 55401
1-800-737-7323
www.freespirit.com
(life skills material; special emphasis on gifted)

Interact
P.O. Box 997-H91
Lakeside, CA 92040
1-800-359-0961
www.interact-simulations.com
(wide variety of simulations on many topics)

TECHNOLOGY AND WEBSITES

There are a number of reasons for you and your students to create a Web page. First, it is an easy, informal way to share information about your class with the entire world. What your students consider commonplace in your area of the country (e.g., trout farms, marine life, peanut farms, or the Grand Canyon) may be new, interesting information to other children. Second, the Web page is a fun way to share students' written work, such as stories, riddles, book reviews, projects, puzzles, and mind-benders, with caregivers, the community, and the world. Third, it is a means for students to display their creative work, such as artwork, cartoons, and graphic designs. Fourth, if the class includes an opportunity for others to email comments back to them, the Web page is a means for building friendships or for creating partnerships in projects. Finally, a Web page can be a means of communicating a newsletter to caregivers and the community about upcoming events or posting a list of materials the class needs for a science project.

It is not difficult to create a Web page. The following three websites provide step-by-step instructions as well as other features:

- www.teachers.net/sampler permits teachers to create a class Web page.
- www.think.com supplies a space and tool for teachers to create Web pages; it also has free email for students and a space and tool to create online discussions.
- www.thegateway.org is sponsored by the U. S. Department of Education. It helps teachers set up Web pages and is the key to one-stop access to educational materials on the Internet.

Once you create your Web page, you need to (1) edit the Web page, and (2) test your links so they are "live" and do not link to inappropriate material. When you publish a Web page, there are some points to consider:

1. Create a Web page that loads quickly. To load quickly, consider the following:
   a. If you include photographs (digital cameras are discussed later) or graphics, do not make them too large.
   b. Use the same background for all the pages because once it is loaded, it does not need to reload for each page.
   c. Use "thumbnails," which permit pictures to be enlarged when the audience is viewing your page.
2. Design your page carefully so it is appealing; a good font is Times New Roman.
3. Map your site carefully and thoroughly by doing the following:
   a. Be sure navigational tools are consistent (where to return to main menu, submenu, etc.).
   b. Be sure menus and submenus are comprehensive and understandable.
   c. Be consistent (e.g., frame all pictures in the same manner).
   d. When linking to other sites, include only the information you want to include.
4. Check copyright laws; one good way is to view the Stanford copyright site.
5. Be sure the home page is visible without having to scroll through it.

One way to personalize your home page is to include photographs of you, subjects that interest you, or objects you are attempting to explain. There are two ways to include photographs. One is to scan onto your Web page any favorite picture that was taken with your regular camera; of course, you will need a scanner to do this.

The second way to include pictures is to use a digital camera, which records the image directly onto computer chips. Instead of film, digital cameras have either a removable memory card or a regular disk. The first digital cameras on the market required a connection cable and transfer software, which were included with the camera. However, with the newer digital cameras, you simply transfer the disk from the camera into the computer without the need for any extra cables and software.

Two advantages of the digital camera are that it does not require film processing and that the software can be edited in order to touch up pictures. Most digital cameras come with Adobe PhotoDeluxe, which is an image-editing program that is quite easy to use. Two disadvantages of the digital camera are that it is expensive (however, the price is lowering as more companies are making them) and that it requires a lot of computer memory (usually 100 MB is recommended) in order to load the pictures.

ENGLISH AS A SECOND LANGUAGE

www.eslcafe.com

This site offers discussion forums, idioms, quotes, and writing ideas for teachers.

http://iteslj.org

This is the home page for the Internet TESL Journal.

www.aitech.ac.jp/~iteslj/cw

This site has fun puzzles for ESL students in a number of categories on various levels of difficulty.

www.csun.edu/~hcedu013/eslplans.html

This site offers lesson plans for teachers who work with ESL students.

www.tesol.org

This site gives information on teaching English as a second language.

www.ncela.gwu.edu.states/stateposter.pdf

This site gives the national statistics for minority students in public school.

LEARNING DISABILITIES

www.ldonline.org

This site offers information about all types of learning disabilities.

www.nichcy.org

This site is the National Information Center for Children and Youth with Disabilities.

www.ku-crl.org/htmlfiles/core.html

This is the University of Kansas Center for Research on Learning, which offers instructional strategies to use with children who have learning disabilities.

www.ncld.org/research/osep%5fswanson.cfm

This site has a meta-analysis of intervention research for students with learning disabilities.

DISABILITIES AND GIFTED EDUCATION

http://ericec.org

The ERIC Clearinghouse site provides information on learning disabilities and gifted education.

www.nagc.org

This is the site for the National Association for Gifted Children.

www.dana.org

This site provides the findings of brain research on diseases and disorders. It also links to other great sites about brain research.

www.newhorizons.org/blab.html

This is an online discussion site on brain research. It includes links to other sites about brain research.

www.necl.org

This site has information regarding at-risk students.

www.quasar.ualberta.ca/ddc/incl/intro.htm

This site includes more than 100 interviews with teachers about inclusion.

www.ascd.org

This site has relevant information about the differentiated classroom.

www.nagc.org/home.htm

This site offers tips for caregivers who have a gifted child.

AAVE

www.cal.org/ebonics
This site disseminates information about Ebonics.

www.yahoo.com/Arts/Humanities/History/Genealogy
This site gives information about the histories of many cultures.

Summary

Many students in elementary schools are at risk of failing in a school system geared toward white, middle-class students who possess "normal" learning abilities. The diverse needs of certain children derive from language and cultural differences, physically based linguistic discrepancies, social and behavioral disorders, and various academic activities.

Effective teachers are concerned about meeting the diverse needs of each student in their ever-changing classroom. Because many classrooms have students from various cultures, teachers must understand and embrace all students' cultures. Teachers must understand and accept individual students whose native language is not English nor do they speak it in their homes. Since teachers cannot be expected to speak all the languages that are represented in their classroom, they need effective strategies to work with students as they become proficient in English.

Students who are academically talented also need special attention as they reach their potential. Using the enrichment triad model and the curriculum compacting strategy permits these students to work at their level and rate within the regular classroom.

Schools provide students with a context and climate for developing self-concepts. The teacher as the classroom leader sets the tone for acceptance or rejection of class members. Effective teachers minimize labels and look beyond categories to the students they are teaching. They celebrate their students *con carino y amor* (with affection and love), for they may not pass their way again.

ACTIVITIES *with children*

Living Languages

Children often learn the meanings of new words through contextual language cues. One way to heighten children's awareness and appreciation of languages is to give students five or six sentences written in English with a non-English word embedded. This word can be printed in any type of script appropriate to the language (Korean symbols for Korean terms). Allow the children to work in small groups and list meanings and how they arrived at these meanings. The students can illustrate their new words or begin a class dictionary.

Money, Money, Money!!!

The day before this activity, ask the children to bring money of any type from home to share with the class. You also bring money from at least three countries to class. Locate the lands represented by the money on the map. Have the students compare sizes, shapes, and value relative to currency from the United States. Next, have the children plan a shopping trip to the land of their choice, real or imagined. Have them describe what they will buy and how much purchases will cost in the currency of the United States and the country of their choice. If a student chooses an imaginary country, then currency will need to be invented.

Walk in Another's Shoes

This writing activity engages children's imagination, prior knowledge, and creativity while building on cultural awareness. Write the sentence *Never judge a person until you have walked two days in his or her moccasins* on the board. Have the students discuss possible meanings of this sentence. Next have the children form small groups; give each group a picture of a kind of "moccasin": for example, a wooden shoe from Holland, a sandal from Guatemala. Ask them to imagine that they are the person who owns the "moccasin" and to write a story about experiences they have had with their "moccasins." Students can share their stories by acting them out, reading them aloud, or placing them in a notebook in the learning center.

RELATED READINGS

Educational Leadership (December 2002/January 2003) 60(4).

This issue's theme is "Equity and Opportunity." Each article gives thought-provoking insights on teaching at-risk students.

Freeman, D., & Freeman, Y. (2001). *Between worlds: Access to second language acquisition.* Portsmouth, NH: Heinemann.

This book helps teachers as they work with ESL students. Chapter 5, "What Are the Principal Theories of Second Language Acquisition," is helpful to teachers who do not have much experience with ESL.

Gonzalez, V., Brusca-Vega, R., & Yawkey, T. (1997). *Assessment and instruction of culturally and linguistically diverse students with or at-risk of learning problems: From research to practice.* Needham Heights, MA: Allyn & Bacon.

This book focuses on the assessment of the various disabilities and how to provide the appropriate classroom for each type of disability. It also gives great information on how the school can work with caregivers.

Johnson, D. A. (1992). *I can't sit still: Education and affirming inattentive and hyperactive children.* Santa Cruz, CA: ETR Associates.

This book offers practical suggestions for parents, teachers, and other care providers of children up to age 10 who have ADHD.

Lessow-Hurley, J. (2003). *Meeting the needs of second language learners: An educator's guide.* Alexandria, VA: Association for Supervision and Curriculum Development.

This book explores the challenges of helping second language learners to keep up in the regular classroom.

Renzulli, J. H., & Renzulli, J. S. (1998). *Total talent portfolio: A systematic plan to identify and nurture gifts and talents.* Mansfield Center, CT: Creative Learning Press.

This book aids teachers as they attempt to identify all gifted students. It also gives ideas for classroom activities to challenge gifted students.

Risko, V., & Bromley, K. (eds.). (2001). *Collaboration for diverse learners.* Newark, DE: International Reading Association.

This book gives classroom teachers practical ideas to use in the classroom. It explains how to involve caregivers, specialists, administrators, and classroom teachers in collaborative decision making.

Tomlinson, C. A. (2001). *How to differentiate instruction in mixed-ability classrooms* (2nd ed.). Alexandria, VA: Association for Supervision and Curriculum Development.

This book gives teachers practical ideas of ways to differentiate lessons for all types of learners.

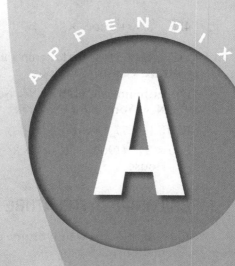

Classroom Resources

Predictable Rhyming Books

Children's Literature Author Websites

Listening Tapes from Scholastic

Resources for Finding Magazines and Books for Classroom Use

Books to Meet Special Needs

Awards Chosen by Adults for Children's Books

Children's Books and Journal Writing

Sources for Poetry

Children's Literature That Reflects a Variety of Cultures

Females in Children's Literature

PREDICTABLE RHYMING BOOKS

Alda, A. (1992). *Sheep, Sheep, Sheep Help Me Fall Asleep.* New York: Bantam Doubleday Dell Books for Young Readers.

Cameron, P. (1961). *"I Can't," Said the Ant.* New York: Coward-McCann.

Cole, J. (1989). *Anna Banana: 101 Jump Rope rhymes.* New York: Morrow Junior Books.

Fleming, D. (1994). *Barnyard Banter.* New York: Holt, Rinehart & Winston.

Florian, D. (1994). *The Beast Feast.* New York: Scholastic.

Fox, M. (1993). *Time for Bed.* San Diego: Harcourt Brace Jovanovich.

Guarino, D. (1989). *Is Your Mamma Llama?* New York: Scholastic.

Hague, M. (1993). *Teddy Bear, Teddy Bear: A classic action rhyme.* New York: Morrow Junior Books.

Hawkins, C., & Hawkins, J. (1983). *Pat the Cat.* New York: G. P. Putnam's Sons.

Hawkins, C., & Hawkins, J. (1984). *Mig the Pig.* New York: G. P. Putnam's Sons.

Hawkins, C., & Hawkins, J. (1985). *Jen the Hen.* New York: G. P. Putnam's Sons.

Hawkins, C., & Hawkins, J. (1986). *Tog the Dog.* New York: G. P. Putnam's Sons.

Krauss, R. (1985). *I Can Fly.* New York: Golden Press.

Lewison, W. (1992). *Buzz Said the Bee.* New York: Scholastic.

Martin, B., & Archambault, J. (1988). *Up and Down the Merry-Go-Round.* New York: Henry Holt & Co.

Martin, B., & Archambault, J. (1989). *Chicka Chicka Boom Boom.* New York: Simon & Schuster.

Martin, B., & Carle, E. (1991). *Polar Bear, Polar Bear, What Do You Hear?* New York: Simon & Schuster Books for Young Readers.

Ochs, C. P. (1991). *Moose on the Loose.* Minneapolis, MN: Carolrhoda Books.

Oppenheimer, J. (1989). *Not Now! Said the Cow.* New York: Bantam Books.

Raffi. (1987). *Down by the Bay.* New York: Crown.

Seuss, Dr. (1965). *Fox in Socks.* New York: Random House.

Shaw, N. (1986). *Sheep in a Jeep.* Boston: Houghton Mifflin.

Shaw, N. (1989). *Sheep on a Ship.* Boston: Houghton Mifflin.

Wood, A. (1992). *Silly Sally.* San Diego: Harcourt Brace Jovanovich.

Avi. www.avi-writer.com

CHILDREN'S LITERATURE AUTHOR WEBSITES

Judy Blume. www.judyblume.com/menu-main.html

Jan Brett. www.janbrett.com

Betsy Byars. www.betsybyars.com

Eric Carle. www.eric-carle.com

Tomie dePaola. www.tomie.com

Mem Fox. www.memfox.net

Jean Craighead George. www.jeancraigheadgeorge.com

Gail Gibbons. www.gailgibbons.com

Dan Gutman. www.dangutman.com

Virginia Hamilton. www.virginiahamilton.com

Phyllis Reynolds Naylor. www.simonsays.com/alice

Katherine Paterson. www.terabithia.com

Gary Paulsen. www.garypaulsen.com

Patricia Polacco. www.patriciapolacco.com

J. K. Rowling. www.scholastic.com/harrypotter/index.htm

Louis Sachar. www.cbcbooks.org/html/louis-sachar.html

Jon Scieszka and Lane Smith. www.kidsread.com/series/series-warp.asp.

Jerry Spinelli. www.carr.lib.md.us/authco/spinelli-j.htm

Audrey Wood. www.audreywood.com

LISTENING TAPES FROM SCHOLASTIC

Primary Grades

The Biggest Pumpkin Ever by S. Kroll

Clifford's First Christmas by N. Bridwell

The Little Old Lady Who Was Not Afraid of Anything by L. Williams

The Popcorn Shop by A. Low

Franklin Is Messy by P. Bourgeois

The Very Hungry Caterpillar by E. Carle

A Busy Year by L. Lionni

The Mitten by J. Brett

Hopper by M. Pfister

If You Give a Mouse a Cookie by L. Numeroff

Intermediate Grades

Pigs Aplenty, Pigs Galore by D. McPhall

Borreguita and the Coyote by V. Aardema

It's Thanksgiving by J. Prelutsky

A Book About Your Skeleton by R. Gross

Harlem by W. D. Myers

Clever Tom and the Leprechaun by L. Shute

Tom by T. dePaola

Days of the Blackbird by T. dePaola

Peppe the Lamplighter by E. Bartone

Turkey's Gift to the People by A. Rucki

RESOURCES FOR FINDING MAGAZINES AND BOOKS FOR CLASSROOM USE

Professional Organizations

- American Library Association (ALA), 50 East Huron Street, Chicago, IL 60611
- The Children's Book Council (CBC), 12 W. 37th Street, 2nd Floor, New York, NY 10018-7480
- International Reading Association (IRA), 800 Barksdale Road, P.O. Box 8139, Newark, DE 19714-8139
- National Council of Teachers of English (NCTE), 1111 Kenyon Road, Urbana, IL 61801

Professional Publications

- *Bulletin of the Center for Children's Books,* published by the University of Chicago Graduate Library School, The University of Illinois Press, 501 E. Daniel Street, ML-493, Chicago, IL 61820
- *The Horn Book,* published by Horn Book, 56 Roland Street, Suite 200, Boston, MA 02129
- *The Lion and the Unicorn,* published by Johns Hopkins Press, 2715 N. Charles Street, Baltimore, MD 21218.
- *The New Advocate,* published by Christopher Gordon Publishers, 480 Washington Street, Norwood, MA 02062

Current Bibliographies

- Allen, M. (1996). *100 Years of Children's Books in America: Decade by Decade.* New York: Facts on File.
- *Children's Books in Print* (annual). New York: Bowker.
- Khorana, M. (1994). *Africa in Literature for Children and Young Adults: An Annotated Bibliography of English Language Books.* Westport, CT: Greenwood Press.
- Lima, C. (2001). *A to Zoo: Subject Access to Children's Picture Books* (6th ed.). New York: Bowker.
- Marantz, S. (1995). *The Art of Children's Picture Books: A Selective Reference Guide.* New York: Garland Publishing.
- Odean, K. (2002). *Great Books for Girls.* New York: Ballantine.

Annual Booklists

- "Children's Choices" published in *The Reading Teacher* by the IRA.
- "Notable Books in the Language Arts" compiled by the National Council of Teachers of English.
- "Notable Children's Trade Books in the Field of Social Studies" compiled by the National Council for the Social Studies and the CBC.
- "Orbis Pictus Award Books" compiled by the National Council of Teachers of English.
- "Outstanding Science Trade Books for Children" compiled by the National Science Teachers Association and the CBC.
- "Teacher's Choices" published in *The Reading Teacher* by the IRA.
- "Young Adult Choices" published in *The Journal of Adolescent and Adult Literacy* by the IRA.

Parent Resources

- Kaywell, J. (1993). *Adolescents at Risk: A Guide to Fiction for Young Adults, Parents, and Professionals.* Westport, CT: Greenwood Press.
- Lindskoog, J. (1999). *How to Grow a Young Reader: A Parent's Guide to Books for Kids* (rev. ed.). Wheaton, IL: Harold Shaw Publishers.
- Lipson, E. (2000). *The New York Times Parent's Guide to the Best Books for Children.* New York: Random House.
- Trelease, J. (2001). *The Read-Aloud Handbook* (5th ed.). New York: Penguin Books.

BOOKS TO MEET SPECIAL NEEDS

Teacher Resources

- Castro, R. (1997). *What Do I Read Next?: Multicultural Literature.* Detroit: Gale Research.
- DeMelendez, W., Ostertag, V., & Peck, J. (1997). *Teaching Young Children in Multicultural Classrooms: Issues, Concepts, and Strategies.* Albany, NY: Delmar Publishers.
- Hahn, J. (1996). "Literary Bridges: Linking Language Arts and Bilingual Education." *Primary Voices K–6,* 6(4), 31–34.
- Helbig, A., & Perkins, A. (1994). *This Land Is Our Land: A Guide to Multicultural Literature for Children and Young Adults.* Westport, CT: Greenwood Press.
- Lind, B. (1996). *Multicultural Children's Literature: An Annotated Bibliography, Grades K–8.* Jefferson, NC: McFarland & Co.

- Rogers, T. (1997). *Reading Across Cultures: Teaching Literature in a Diverse Society.* New York: Teacher's College Press.
- Slapin, D. (1992). *Through Indian Eyes.* Philadelphia: New Society Publishers.

Multicultural Awareness

- Alexander, L. (1992). *The Fortune-Tellers.* New York: Dutton. (African)
- Ancona, P. (1993). *Pablo Remembers.* New York: Lothrop, Lee & Shepard Books. (Latino–Hispanic)
- Clifton, L. (1992). *Everett Anderson's Goodbye.* New York: Holt, Rinehart & Winston. (African American)

- Climo, S. (1993). *The Korean Cinderella.* New York: HarperCollins. (Asian American)
- Cofer, J. (1995). *An Island Like You: Stories of the Barrio.* New York: Orchard Books. (Latino–Hispanic)
- Davis, D. (1992). *Behind Barbed Wire: The Imprisonment of Japanese Americans During World War Two.* New York: Dutton. (Asian American)
- Demi. (1990). *The Empty Pot.* New York: H. Holt. (Asian American)
- Garland, S. (1993). *Why Ducks Sleep on One Leg.* New York: Scholastic. (Asian American)
- Goldin, B. (1994). *Red Means Good Fortune: A Story of San Francisco's Chinatown.* New York: Viking Press. (Asian American)
- Gonzalez, L. (1994). *The Bossy Gallito: A Traditional Cuban Folktale.* New York: Scholastic. (Latino–Hispanic)
- Grimes, N. (1994). *Meet Danitra Brown.* New York: Lothrop, Lee & Shepard Books. (African American)
- Soto, G. (1990). *Baseball in April and Other Stories.* San Diego: Harcourt Brace Jovanovich. (Latino–Hispanic)
- Soto, G. (1995). *Chato's Kitchen.* New York: Putnam's. (Latino–Hispanic)
- Tompert, A. (1990). *Grandfather Tang's Story.* New York: Crown Publishers. (Asian American)

The Elderly

- Ackerman, K. (1988). *Song and Dance Man.* Illustrated by Stephen Gammell. New York: Knopf.
- Aliki. (1979). *The Two of Them.* New York: Greenwillow Books.
- Bauer, M. (1995). *When I Go Camping with Grandma.* Mahwah, NJ: Bridgewater Books.
- Crews, D. (1991). *Bigmama's.* New York: Greenwillow Books.
- dePaola, T. (1973). *Nana Upstairs and Nana Downstairs.* New York: Penguin.
- dePaola, T. (1981). *Now One Foot, Now the Other.* New York: Penguin.
- Drucker, M. (1992). *Grandma's Latkes.* San Diego: Harcourt Brace Jovanovich.
- Rylant, C. (1982). *When I Was Young in the Mountains.* New York: Dutton.
- Williams, D. (1992). *Grandma Essie's Covered Wagon.* New York: Knopf.

Women's Roles

- Avi. (1990). *The True Confessions of Charlotte Doyle.* New York: Orchard Books.
- Beatty, P. (1984). *Turn Homeward, Hannalee.* New York: W. Morrow.
- Creech, S. (1994). *Walk Two Moons.* New York: HarperCollins.
- Cushman, K. (1994). *Catherine, Called Birdy.* New York: Clarion Books.
- Cushman, K. (1995). *The Midwife's Apprentice.* New York: Clarion Books.
- Lindgren, A. (1983). *Ronia, the Robber's Daughter.* New York: Viking Press.
- McCaffrey, A. (1976). *Dragonsong.* New York: Atheneum.
- McCaffrey, A. (1977). *Dragonsinger.* New York: Atheneum.
- Voigt, C. (1982). *Dicey's Song.* New York: Atheneum.

Individuals with Disabilities

- Behrman, C. (1992). *Fiddler to the World: The Inspiring Life of Itzhak Perlman.* White Hall, VA: Shoe Tree Press. (physical disabilities)
- Betancourt, J. (1993). *My Name Is Brain-Brian.* New York: Scholastic. (learning disabilities)
- Butler, B. (1994). *Witch's Fire.* New York: Cobblehill Books. (physical disabilities)
- Duffy, J. (1992). *Uncle Shamus.* New York: Scribner Young Readers. (blindness)
- Gordon, M. (1991). *Jumpin' Johnny Get Back to Work! A Child's Guide to ADHD/Hyperactivity.* DeWitt, NY: GSI. (attention deficit disorder)
- Gould, M. (1991). *Golden Daffodils.* Newport Beach, CA: Allied Crafts. (cerebral palsy)
- Krementz, J. (1992). *How It Feels to Live with a Physical Disability.* New York: Simon & Schuster. (physical disabilities)
- Krisher, T. (1990). *Kathy's Hats: A Story of Hope.* Morton Grove, IL: Albert Whitman. (serious or life-threatening conditions)
- Metzger, L. (1993). *Barry's Sister.* New York: Puffin. (cerebral palsy)
- Osofsky, A. (1992). *My Buddy.* New York: Henry Holt & Company. (physical disabilities)
- Philbrick, W. (1993). *Freak the Mighty.* New York: Scholastic. (learning disabilities)
- St. George, J. (1992). *Dear Dr. Bell—Your Friend, Helen Keller.* New York: Putnam. (deafness)
- Wood, J. (1992). *The Man Who Loved Clowns.* New York: Putnam. (Down Syndrome)

AWARDS CHOSEN BY ADULTS FOR CHILDREN'S BOOKS

Newbery Medal

Each year the Newbery Medal is awarded to the most distinguished literature book for children.

2003 *Crispin the Cross of Lead*, Avi (Hyperion Books for Children)

2002 *A Single Shard*, Linda Sue Park (Clarion Books/Houghton Mifflin)

2001 *A Year Down Yonder*, Richard Peck (Dial)

2000 *Bud, Not Buddy*, Christopher Paul Curtis (Delacorte)

1999 *Holes*, Louis Sachar (Frances Foster/Farrar, Straus & Giroux)

1998 *Out of the Dust*, Karen Hesse (Scholastic)

1997 *The View from Saturday*, E. L. Konigsburg (Atheneum Books for Young Readers)

1996 *The Midwife's Apprentice*, Karen Cushman (Clarion Books)

1995 *Walk Two Moons*, Sharon Creech (Harper-Collins)

1994 *The Giver*, Lois Lowry (Houghton Mifflin)

1993 *Missing May*, Cynthia Rylant (Orchard Books)

1992 *Shiloh*, Phyllis Naylor (Atheneum)

1991 *Maniac McGee*, Jerry Spinelli (Little, Brown & Company)

1990 *Number the Stars*, Lois Lowry (Houghton Mifflin)

1989 *Joyful Noise: Poems for Two Voices*, Paul Fleischman (Harper & Row)

1988 *Lincoln: A Photobiography*, Russell Freedman (Clarion Books)

1987 *The Whipping Boy*, Sid Fleischman (Greenwillow)

1986 *Sarah, Plain and Tall*, Patricia MacLachlan (Harper & Row)

1985 *The Hero and the Crown*, Robin McKinley (Greenwillow)

1984 *Dear Mr. Henshaw*, Beverly Cleary (William Morrow)

1983 *Dicey's Song*, Cynthia Voigt (Atheneum)

1982 *A Visit to William Blake's Inn: Poems for Innocent and Experienced Travelers*, Nancy Willard (Harcourt)

1981 *Jacob Have I Loved*, Katherine Paterson (Crowell)

1980 *A Gathering of Days: A New England Girls' Journal, 1830–1832*, Joan W. Blos (Scribner)

1979 *The Westing Game*, Ellen Raskin (Dutton)

1978 *Bridge to Terabithia*, Katherine Paterson (Crowell)

1977 *Roll of Thunder, Hear My Cry*, Mildred D. Taylor (Dial)

1976 *The Grey King*, Susan Cooper (McElderry/Atheneum)

1975 *M. C. Higgins, the Great*, Virginia Hamilton (Macmillan)

1974 *The Slave Dancer*, Paula Fox (Bradbury)

1973 *Julie of the Wolves*, Jean Craighead George (Harper)

1972 *Mrs. Frisby and the Rats of NIMH*, Robert C. O'Brien (Atheneum)

1971 *Summer of the Swans*, Betsy Byars (Viking Press)

1970 *Sounder*, William H. Armstrong (Harper & Row)

1969 *The High King*, Lloyd Alexander (Holt, Rinehart & Winston)

1968 *From the Mixed-Up Files of Mrs. Basil E. Frankweiler*, E. L. Konigsburg (Atheneum)

1967 *Up a Road Slowly*, Irene Hunt (Follett)

1966 *I, Juan de Pareja*, Elizabeth Borton de Trevino (Farrar, Straus & Giroux)

1965 *Shadow of a Bull*, Maia Wojciechowska (Atheneum)

1964 *It's Like This, Cat*, Emily Neville (Harper & Row)

1963 *A Wrinkle in Time*, Madeleine L'Engle (Farrar, Straus & Giroux)

1962 *The Bronze Bow*, Elizabeth George Speare (Houghton Mifflin)

1961 *Island of the Blue Dolphins*, Scott O'Dell (Houghton Mifflin)

1960 *Onion John*, Joseph Krumgold (Crowell)

1959 *The Witch of Blackbird Pond*, Elizabeth George Speare (Houghton Mifflin)

1958 *Rifles for Watie*, Harold Keith (Crowell)

1957 *Miracles on Maple Hill*, Virginia Sorensen (Harcourt Brace Jovanovich)

1956 *Carry on, Mr. Bowditch*, Jean Lee Latham (Houghton Mifflin)

1955 *The Wheel on the School*, Meindert Dejong (Harper & Row)

1954 *. . . And Now Miguel*, Joseph Krumgold (Crowell)

1953 *Secret of the Andes*, Ann Nolan Clark (Viking Press)

1952 *Ginger Pye*, Eleanor Estes (Harcourt Brace Jovanovich)

1951 *Amos Fortune, Free Man*, Elizabeth Yates (Dutton)

1950 *The Door in the Wall*, Marguerite de Angeli (Doubleday)

1949 *King of the Wind*, Marguerite Henry (Rand McNally)

1948 *The Twenty-One Balloons*, William Pene du Bois (Viking Press)

1947 *Miss Hickory*, Carolyn Bailey (Viking Press)

1946 *Strawberry Girl*, Lois Lenski (Lippincott)

1945 *Rabbit Hill*, Robert Lawson (Viking Press)

1944 *Johnny Tremain*, Esther Forbes (Houghton Mifflin)

1943 *Adam of the Road*, Elizabeth Gray (Viking Press)

1942 *The Matchlock Gun*, Walter Edmonds (Dodd)

1941 *Call It Courage*, Armstrong Sperry (Macmillan)

1940 *Daniel Boone*, James Daugherty (Viking Press)

1939 *Thimble Summer*, Elizabeth Enright (Rinehart)

1938 *The White Stag*, Kate Seredy (Viking Press)

1937 *Roller Skates*, Ruth Sawyer (Viking Press)

1936 *Caddie Woodlawn*, Carol Brink (Macmillan)

1935 *Dobry*, Monica Shannon (Viking Press)

1934 *Invincible Louisa*, Cornelia Meigs (Little Brown)

1933 *Young Fu of the Upper Yangtze*, Elizabeth Lewis (Winston)

1932 *Waterless Mountain*, Laura Armer (Longmans)

1931 *The Cat Who Went to Heaven*, Elizabeth Coatsworth (Macmillan)

1930 *Hitty, Her First Hundred Years*, Rachel Field (Macmillan)

1929 *The Trumpeter of Krakow*, Eric P. Kelly (Macmillan)

1928 *Gay Neck: The Story of a Pigeon*, Dhan Mukerji (Dutton)

1927 *Smoky, the Cowhorse*, Will James (Scribner)

1926 *Shen of the Sea*, Arthur Chrisman (Dutton)

1925 *Tales from Silver Lands*, Charles Finger (Doubleday)

1924 *The Dark Frigate*, Charles Hawes (Atlantic/Little Brown)

1923 *The Voyages of Doctor Doolittle*, Hugh Lofting (Lippincott)

1922 *The Story of Mankind*, Hendrik Van Loon (Liveright)

Caldecott Medal

Each year the Caldecott Medal is awarded to the most distinguished children's picture book.

2003 *My Friend Rabbit*, Eric Rohmann (Roaring Book Press/Millbrook Press)

2002 *The Three Pigs*, David Wiesner (Clarion/Houghton Mifflin)

2001 *So You Want to Be President?* Illustrated by David Small (Philomel Books)

2000 *Joseph Had a Little Overcoat*, Simms Taback (Viking)

1999 *Snowflake Bentley*, Mary Azarian (Houghton Mifflin)

1998 *Rapunzel*, Paul O. Zelinsky (Dutton's Children's Books)

1997 *Golem*, David Wisniewski (Clarion Books)

1996 *Officer Buckle and Gloria*, Peggy Rathmann (G. P. Putnam)

1995 *Smokey Night*, David Diaz (Harcourt Brace)

1994 *Grandfather's Journey*, Allen Say (Houghton Mifflin Company)

1993 *Mirette on the High Wire*, Emily Arnold McCully (G. P. Putnam)

1992 *Tuesday*, David Wiesner (Clarion)

1991 *Black and White*, David Macaulay (Houghton Mifflin)

1990 *Lon Po Po*, adapted and illustrated by Ed Young (Philomel Books)

1989 *Song and Dance Man*, Karen Ackerman, illustrated by Stephen Gammel (Knopf)

1988 *Owl Moon*, Jane Yolen, illustrated by John Schoenherr (Philomel Books)

1987 *Hey, Al*, Arthur Yorinks, illustrated by Richard Egielski (Farrar, Straus & Giroux)

1986 *The Polar Express*, Chris Van Allsburg (Houghton Mifflin)

1985 *Saint George and the Dragon*, retold by Margaret Hodges, illustrated by Trina Schart Hyman (Little, Brown)

1984 *The Glorious Flight: Across the Channel with Louis Bleriot*, Alice and Martin Povensen (Viking Press)

1983 *Shadow*, Blaise Cendrars, translated and illustrated by Marcia Brown (Scribner's)

1982 *Jumanji*, Chris Van Allsburg (Houghton Mifflin)

1981 *Fables*, Arnold Lobel (Harper & Row)

1980 *Ox-Cart Man*, Donald Hall, illustrated by Barbara Cooney (Viking Press)

1979 *The Girl Who Loved Wild Horses*, Paul Goble (Bradbury)

1978 *Noah's Ark*, Peter Spier (Doubleday)

1977 *Ashanti to Zulu*, Margaret Musgrove, illustrated by Leo and Diane Dillon (Dial Press)

1976 *Why Mosquitoes Buzz in People's Ears*, retold by Verna Aardema, illustrated by Leo and Diane Dillon (Dial Press)

1975 *Arrow to the Sun*, adapted and illustrated by Gerald McDermott (Viking Press)

1974 *Duffy and the Devil*, retold by Harve Zemach, illustrated by Margot Zemach (Farrar, Straus & Giroux)

1973 *The Funny Little Woman*, Lafcadio Hearn, retold by Arlene Mosel, illustrated by Blair Lent (Dutton)

1972 *One Fine Day*, Nonny Hogrogian (Macmillan)

1971 *A Story, a Story*, Gail E. Haley (Atheneum)

1970 *Sylvester and the Magic Pebble*, William Steig (Windmill Books)

1969 *The Fool of the World and the Flying Ship*, retold by Arthur Ransome, illustrated by Uri Shulevitz (Farrar, Straus & Giroux)

1968 *Drummer Hoff*, adapted by Barbara Emberley, illustrated by Ed Emberley (Prentice Hall)

1967 *Sam, Bangs and Moonshine*, Evaline Ness (Holt, Rinehart & Winston)

1966 *Always Room for One More*, Sorche Nic Leodhas, illustrated by Nonny Hogrogian (Holt, Rinehart & Winston)

1965 *May I Bring a Friend?* Beatrice Schenk de Regniers, illustrated by Beni Montresor (Atheneum)

1964 *Where the Wild Things Are*, Maurice Sendak (Harper & Row)

1963 *The Snowy Day*, Ezra Jack Keats (Viking Press)

1962 *Once a Mouse*, Marcia Brown (Scribner's)

1961 *Baboushka and the Three Kings*, Ruth Robbins, illustrated by Nicholas Sidjakov (Parnassus)

1960 *Nine Days to Christmas*, Marie Hall Ets and Aurora Labastida (Viking Press)

1959 *Chanticleer and the Fox*, adapted and illustrated by Barbara Cooney (Crowell)

1958 *Time of Wonder*, Robert McCloskey (Viking Press)

1957 *A Tree Is Nice*, Janice Udry, illustrated by Marc Simont (Harper & Row)

1956 *Frog Went A-Courtin'*, retold by John Langstaff, illustrated by Feodor Rojankovsky (Harcourt Brace Jovanovich)

1955 *Cinderella*, illustrated and retold by Marcia Brown (Scribner's)

1954 *Madeline's Rescue*, Ludwig Bemelmans (Viking Press)

1953 *The Biggest Bear*, Lynd Ward (Houghton Mifflin)

1952 *Finders Keepers*, Will Lipkind, illustrated by Nicolas Mordvinoff (Harcourt Brace Jovanovich)

1951 *The Egg Tree*, Katherine Milhous (Scribner's)

1950 *Song of the Swallows*, Leo Politi (Scribner's)

1949 *The Big Snow*, Berta and Elmer Hader (Macmillan)

1948 *White Snow, Bright Snow*, Alvin Tresselt, illustrated by Roger Duvoisin (Lothrop)

1947 *The Little Island*, Golden MacDonald, illustrated by Leonard Weisgard (Doubleday)

1946 *The Rooster Crows*, Maude and Miska Petersham (Macmillan)

1945 *Prayer for a Child*, Rachel Field, illustrated by Elizabeth Orton Jones (Macmillan)

1944 *Many Moons*, James Thurber, illustrated by Louis Slobodkin (Harcourt Brace Jovanovich)

1943 *The Little House*, Virginia Lee Burton (Houghton Mifflin)

1942 *Make Way for Ducklings*, Robert McCloskey (Viking Press)

1941 *They Were Strong and Good*, Robert Lawson (Viking Press)

1940 *Abraham Lincoln*, Ingri and Edgar Parin d'Aulaire (Doubleday)

1939 *Mei Li*, Thomas Handforth (Doubleday)

1938 *Animals of the Bible*, Helen Dean Fish, illustrated by Dorothy P. Lathrop (Lippincott)

Coretta Scott King Award

This award is presented annually at the American Library Association Convention to honor children's books by, for, and/or about African Americans. It was established in memory of Dr. Martin Luther King, Jr., and in honor of Coretta Scott King, his wife. The text award began in 1970, and the illustration award was added in 1979.

2003 Text: *Bronx Masquerade*, Nikki Grimes (Dial Books)

Illustration: *Talkin' About Bessie: The Story of Elizabeth Coleman*, N. Grimes, illustrated by E. B. Lewis (Orchard Books/Scholastic)

2002 Text: *The Land*, Mildred D. Taylor (Phyllis Fogleman Books)

Illustration: *Goin' Someplace Special*, P. McKissack, illustrated by J. Pinkney (Anne Schwarz Books/Atheneum Books)

2001 Text: *Miracle's Boys*, Jacqueline Woodson (G. P. Putnam's Sons)

Illustration: *Uptown*, Bryan Collier (Henry Holt & Co.)

2000 Text: *Bud, Not Buddy*, Christopher Paul Curtis (Delacorte Press Books for Young Readers)

Illustration: *In the Time of the Drums*, K. L. Siegelson, illustrated by Brian Pinkney (Hyperion)

1999 Text: *Heaven*, Angela Johnson (Simon & Schuster)

Illustration: *I See the Rhythm*, T. Igus, illustrated by M. Wood (Children's Book Press)

1998 Text: *Forged by Fire*, Sharon M. Draper (Atheneum)

Illustration: *In Daddy's Arms I Am Tall: African Americans Celebrating Fathers*, Javaka Steptoe (Lee & Low)

1997 Text: *Slam!* Walter Dean Myers (Scholastic Press)

Illustration: *Minty: A Story of Young Harriet Tubman*, Jerry Pinkney (Dial Books for Young Readers)

1996 Text: *Her Stories*, Virginia Hamilton (Blue Sky Press)

Illustration: *The Middle Passage: White Ships Black Cargo*, Tom Feelings (Dial Books)

1995 Text: *Christmas in the Big House, Christmas in the Quarters*, Patricia and Frederick McKissack (Scholastic)

Illustration: *The Creation*, James Ransome (Holiday House)

1993 Text: *Dark Thirty: Southern Tales of the Supernatural*, Patricia A. McKissack (Knopf)

Illustration: *The Origin of Life on Earth: An African Creation Myth*, illustrated by Kathleen Atkins Wilson; retold by David A. Anderson/SANKOFA (Sights)

1994 Text: *Toning the Sweep*, Angela Johnson (Orchard Books)

Illustration: *Soul Looks Back in Wonder*, Tom Feelings (Dial)

1992 Text: *Now Is Your Time! The African-American Struggle for Freedom*, Walter Dean Myers (HarperCollins); *Night on Neighborhood Street*, Eloise Greenfield, illustrated by Jan Spivey Gilchrist (Dial)

Illustration: *Tar Beach*, illustrated by Faith Ringgold (Crown); *Night on Neighborhood Street*, Eloise Greenfield, illustrated by Jan Spivey Gilchrist (Dial); *All Night, All Day: A Child's First Book of African-American Spirituals*, selected and illustrated by Ashley Bryan (Atheneum)

1991 Text: *Road to Memphis*, Mildred D. Taylor (Dial); *Black Dance in America*, James Haskins (Crowell)

Illustration: *Aida*, as told by Leontyne Price, illustrated by Diane and Leo Dillon (Harcourt)

1990 Text: *A Long Hard Journey*, Patricia and Frederick McKissack (Walker and Co.)

Illustration: *Nathaniel Talking*, Eloise Greenfield, illustrated by Jan Spivey Gilchrist (Writers and Readers Publishing)

1989 Text: *Fallen Angels*, Walter Dean Myers (Scholastic)

Illustration: *Mirandy and Brother Wind*, Patricia McKissack, illustrated by Jerry Pinkney (Knopf)

1988 Text: *The Friendship*, Mildred D. Taylor, illustrated by Max Ginsburg (Dial)

Illustration: *Mufaro's Beautiful Daughters*, John Steptoe (Lothrop)

1987 Text: *Justin and the Best Biscuits in the World*, Mildred Pitts Walter (Lothrop)

Illustration: *Half a Moon and One Whole Star*, Crescent Dragon Wagon, illustrated by Jerry Pinkney (Macmillan)

1986 Text: *The People Could Fly: American Black Folktales*, Virginia Hamilton, illustrated by Leo and Diane Dillon (Knopf)

Illustration: *The Patchwork Quilt*, Valerie Flournoy, illustrated by Jerry Pinkney (Dial)

1985 Text: *Motown and Didi*, Walter Dean Myers (Viking)

Illustration: No award given

1984 Text: *Everett Anderson's Goodbye*, Lucille Clifton, illustrated by Ann Grifalconi (Holt)

Illustration: *My Mama Needs Me*, Mildred Pitts Walter, illustrated by Pat Cummings (Lothrop, Lee & Shepard)

1983 Text: *Sweet Whispers, Brother Rush*, Virginia Hamilton (Philomel)

Illustration: *Black Child*, Peter Mugabane (Knopf)

1982 Text: *Let the Circle Be Unbroken*, Mildred D. Taylor (Dial)

Illustration: *Mother Crocodile = Maman-Caiman*, Birago Diop, translated and adapted by Rosa Guy, illustrated by John Steptoe (Delacorte)

1981 Text: *This Life*, Sidney Poitier (Knopf)

Illustration: *Beat the Story-Drum, Pum-Pum*, Ashley Bryan (Atheneum)

1980 Text: *The Young Landlords*, Walter Dean Myers (Viking)

Illustration: *Corn Rows*, Camile Yarbrough, illustrated by Carole Byard (Coward)

1979 Text: *Escape to Freedom: A Play About Young Frederick Douglass*, Ossie Davis (Viking)

Illustration: *Something on My Mind*, Nikki Grimes, illustrated by Tom Feelings (Dial)

1978 *African Dream*, Eloise Greenfield, illustrated by Carole Byard (Day)

1977 *The Story of Stevie Wonder*, James Haskins, illustrated with photos (Lothrop)

1976 *Duey's Tale*, Pearl Bailey, photos by Arnold Skolnick and Gary Azon (Harcourt)

1975 *The Legend of Africania*, Dorothy Robinson, illustrated by Herbert Temple (Johnson)

1974 *Ray Charles*, Sharon Bell Mathis, illustrated by George Ford (Crowell)

1973 *I Never Had It Made*, Jackie Robinson as told to Alfred Duckett, illustrated with photos (Putnam)

1972 *Seventeen Black Artists*, Elton Clay Fax, illustrated with photos (Dods)

1971 *Black Troubadour: Langston Hughes*, Charlemae Rollins, illustrated with photos (Rand)

1970 *Martin Luther King, Jr.: Man of Peace*, Lillie Patterson, illustrated by Victory Mays (Garrard)

CHILDREN'S BOOKS AND JOURNAL WRITING

Ada, A. F. (1994). *Dear Peter Rabbit.* New York: Atheneum Books for Young Readers. (1–3)

Ada, A. F. (1998). *Yours Truly, Goldilocks.* New York: Atheneum Books for Young Readers. (1–3)

Adlier, D. A. (1985). *Eaton Stanley and the Mind Control Experiment.* New York: Dutton. (3–6)

Blos, J. (1979). *A Gathering of Days.* New York: Scribner. (4–6) (Newbery Medal)

Cleary, B. (1983). *Dear Mr. Henshaw.* New York: William Morrow. (3–6)

Cleary, B. (1984). *The Ramona Quimby Diary.* New York: William Morrow. (2–6)

Conrad, P. (1992). *Pedro's Journal: A Voyage with Christopher Columbus.* WA: Turtleback Publishers. (5+)

Denenberg, B. (1997). *So Far from Home: The Diary of Mary Driscoll, an Irish Mill Girl.* New York: Scholastic. (5+)

Denenberg, B. (1998). *The Journal of William Thomas Emerson: A Revolutionary War Patriot.* New York: Scholastic. (5+)

Fitzhugh, L. (1964). *Harriet the Spy.* New York: Harper & Row. (3–6)

Frank, A. (1952). *Anne Frank: The Diary of a Young Girl.* New York: Doubleday. (6+)

Garland, S. (1998). *A Line in the Sand: The Alamo Diary of Lucinda Lawrence.* New York: Scholastic. (5+)

Goffstein, M. B. A. (1984). *A Writer.* New York: Harper & Row. (4–6)

Hahn, M. D. (1983). *Daphne's Book.* New York: Clarion Books. (4–6)

Hesse, K. (1997). *Out of the Dust.* New York: Scholastic Press. (4–6) (Newbery Medal)

Hest, A. (1994). *The Private Notebook of Katie Roberts, Age 11.* Cambridge, MA: Candlewick Press. (5+)

Hoban, L. (1976). *Arthur's Pen Pal.* New York: Harper & Row. (K–3)

Keats, E. J. (1968). *A Letter to Amy.* New York: Harper & Row. (K–3)

Lorbiecki, M. (1997). *My Palace of Leaves in Sarajevo.* New York: Dial Books. (6+)

Lowry, L. (1984). *Anastasia, Ask Your Analyst.* Boston: Houghton Mifflin. (3–6)

Mills, C. (1986). *The One and Only Cynthia Jane Thornton.* New York: Macmillan. (3–6)

Murphy, J. (1998). *West to the Land of Plenty: The Diary of Teresa Angelino Viscardi.* New York: Scholastic. (5+)

Reig, J. (1978). *Diary of the Boy King Tut-Amen.* New York: Scribner. (6+)

Sharmat, M. W. (1982). *Mysteriously Yours, Maggie Marmestein.* New York: Harper & Row. (3–6)

Taylor, E. J. (1986). *Rag Doll Press.* New York: Alfred Knopf. (K–3)

Taylor, J. (1992). *Letters to Children from Beatrix Potter.* New York: Frederick. (5+)

Woodruff, E. (1994). *Dear Levi: Letters from the Overland Trail.* New York: Alfred A. Knopf. (5+)

ANTHOLOGIES OF POETRY

Adoff, A. (1995). *Street Music: City Poems.* New York: HarperCollins.

Baylor, B. (1986). *I'm in Charge of Celebration.* New York: Charles Scribner.

Broderbund, P.O. Box 6144, Novato, CA 94948-9861. J. Prelutsky, *New Kid on the Block* (CD-ROM).

Bruchae, J. (1995). *The Earth Under Sky Bear's Feet.* New York: Philomel Books.

Bruchae, J. (1996). *Between Earth and Sky.* San Diego: Harcourt Brace.

Bruchae, J. (1996). *The Circle of Thanks.* Mahwah, NJ: Bridgewater Books.

dePaola, T. (comp.). (1988). *Tomie dePaola's Book of Poems.* New York: G. P. Putnam's Sons.

Fleischman, P. (1985). *Joyful Noise: Poems for Two Voices.* New York: Harper & Row.

Glaser, I. J. (1995). *Dreams of Glory: Poems Starring Girls.* New York: Atheneum.

Hall, D. (ed.). (1985). *The Oxford Book of Children's Verse in America.* New York: Oxford.

Hopkins, L. (comp.). (1988). *Side by Side: Poems to Read Together.* New York: Trumpet Club.

Hughes, L. (1986). *The Dream Keeper and Other Poems.* New York: Alfred A. Knopf/Borzio Books.

Janeczko, P. B. (comp.). (1985). *Pocket Poems: Selected for a Journey.* New York: Bradbury.

Jones, H. (ed.). (1993). *The Trees Stand Shining: Poetry of the North American Indians.* New York: Dial Books.

Kennedy, X. J., & Kennedy, D. M. (eds.). (1982). *Knock at a Star: A Children's Introduction to Poetry.* Boston: Little, Brown.

Livingston, M. C. (sel.). (1991). *Lots of Limericks.* New York: McElderry Books.

Lobel, A. (1983). *The Book of Pigericks.* New York: Harper & Row.

Morrison, L. (comp.). (1992). *At the Crack of the Bat.* New York: Hyperion Paperbacks for Children.

Opie, I. (ed.). (1996). *My Very First Mother Goose.* Cambridge, MA: Candlewick Press.

Prelutsky, J. (ed.). (1983). *The Random House Book of Poetry for Children.* New York: Random House.

Prelutsky, J. (1990). *Something Big Has Been Here.* New York: Greenwillow Books.

Prelutsky, J. (1993). *A Nonny Mouse Writes Again!* New York: Knopf.

Schenk de Regniers, B., Moore, E., White, M., & Carr, J. (comps.). (1988). *Sing a Song of Popcorn.* New York: Scholastic.

Seattle, C. (1991). *Brother Eagle, Sister Sky.* New York: Dial Books.

Silverstein, S. (1981). *Falling Up.* New York: Harper & Row.

CHILDREN'S LITERATURE THAT REFLECTS A VARIETY OF CULTURES

African American

Adedjouma, D. (ed.). (1996). *The Palm of My Heart: Poetry by African American Children.* Illustrated by G. Christie. New York: Lee & Low Books.

Angelou, M. (1996). *Kofi and His Magic.* Photos by M. Courtney-Clark. New York: Crown.

Belton, S. (1994). *May'naise Sandwiches and Sunshine Tea.* Illustrated by G. G. Carter. New York: Four Winds.

Bloom, V. (1997). *Fruits: A Caribbean Counting Poem.* Illustrated by D. Axtell. New York: Holt.

Burrowes, A. J. (2000). *Grandma's Purple Flowers.* New York: Lee & Low Books.

Clements, A. (2002). *The Jacket.* New York: Simon & Schuster.

Cooper, F. (1994). *Coming Home: From the Life of Langston Hughes.* New York: Philomel.

Curtis, C. P. (1995). *The Watsons Go to Birmingham—1963.* New York: Delacorte Press.

Curtis, C. P. (1999). *Bud, Not Buddy.* New York: Delacorte Press.

Fenner, C. (1995). *Yolonda's Genius.* New York: Simon & Schuster.

Gutman, D. (2003). *Shoeless Joe and Me.* New York: Harper Trophy.

Hoffman, M. (2000). *Boundless Grace.* New York: Puffin.

McKissack, P., & McKissack, F. (1992). *Sojourner Truth: Ain't I a Woman?* New York: Scholastic.

McKissack, P., & McKissack, R. (2003). *Days of Jubilee.* New York: Scholastic.

Mitchell, R. (1997). *The Talking Cloth.* New York: Orchard Books.

Monk, I. (1999). *Hope.* Minneapolis: Lerner.

Moodie, F. (1997). *Nabulela: A South African Folk Tale.* New York: Farrar, Straus & Giroux.

Myers, W. D. (1997). *Harlem.* Illustrated by C. Myers. New York: Scholastic.

Paulsen, G. (1993). *Nightjohn*. New York: Laurel-Leaf.

Polacco, P. (1994). *Pink and Say*. New York: Philomel.

Rappaport, D. (2002). *No More! Stories and Songs of Salve Resistance*. Cambridge, MA: Candlewick Press.

Schroeder, A. (1996). *Minty: A Story of Harriet Tubman*. Illustrated by J. Pinkney. New York: Doubleday.

Tarpley, N. A. (2002). *Bippity Bop Barbershop*. New York: Little Brown Children's Books.

Taylor, M. (1990). *Mississippi Bridge*. New York: Dial.

Wiles, D. (2001). *Freedom Summer*. New York: Atheneum.

Wyeth, S. D. (2003). *Message in the Sky: Corey's Underground Railroad Diary*. New York: Scholastic.

Asian American

Brown, T. (1995). *Konnichiwa! I Am a Japanese-American Girl*. New York: Holt.

Chin-Lee, C. (1997). *A Is for Asia*. Illustrated by Y. Heo. New York: Orchard.

Demi. (1997). *One Grain of Rice: A Mathematical Folktale*. New York: Scholastic.

Garland, S. (1992). *Song of the Buffalo Boy*. New York: Harcourt Brace.

Hamanaka, S. (1995). *Bebop-a-Do-Walk!* New York: Simon & Schuster.

Ho, M. (1996). *Hush! A Thai Lullaby*. Illustrated by H. Meade. New York: Orchard.

Ho, M. (2003). *Gathering the Dew*. New York: Scholastic.

Jiang, J. L. (1997). *Red Scarf Girl: A Memoir of the Cultural Revolution*. New York: HarperCollins.

Kalman, B. (2000). *Japan: The Land*. New York: Crabtree.

Kalman, B. (2000). *Japan: The People*. New York: Crabtree.

Lee, H. V. (2000). *In the Snow*. New York: Henry Holt.

Lee, M. (1997). *Nim and the War Effort*. Illustrated by Yangsook Choi. New York: Frances Foster Books/Farrar, Straus & Giroux.

Levine, E. (1995). *I Hate English!* New York: Scholastic Trade.

Mak, K. (2001). *My Chinatown: One Year in Poems*. New York: HarperCollins.

Muth, J. (2002). *The Three Questions*. New York: Scholastic.

Namioka, L. (2000). *Yang the Second and Her Secret Admirers*. New York: Yearling Books.

Peacock, C. A. (2000). *Mommy Far, Mommy Near: An Adoption Story*. Morton Grove, IL: Albert Whitman.

Rattigan, J. K. (1996). *The Woman in the Moon: A Story from Hawaii*. Illustrated by C. Golembe. Boston: Little Brown.

Salisbury, G. (1994). *Under the Blood-Red Sun*. New York: Delacorte.

Uchida, Y. (1996). *Jar of Dreams*. Boston: Houghton Mifflin.

Wells, R. (1996). *The Farmer and the Poor God*. Illustrated by Yoshi. New York: Simon & Schuster.

Yep, L. (1997). *The Case of the Goblin Pearls*. New York: HarperCollins.

Yep, L. (1997). *The Khan's Daughter: A Mongolian Folktale*. Illustrated by J. Tseng and M. Tseng. New York: HarperCollins.

Yep, L. (1997). *Thief of Hearts*. New York: HarperTrophy.

Hispanic American

Ada, A. (1997). *Gathering the Sun: An Alphabet in Spanish and English*. Illustrated by S. Silva. New York: Lothrop, Lee & Shepherd.

Bunting, E. (1996). *Going Home*. Illustrated by D. David. New York: HarperCollins.

Dominguez, K. K. (2002). *The Perfect Pinata/ La Pinata Perfecta*. Morton Grove, IL: Albert Whitman.

Dorros, A. (1995). *Isle*. Illustrated by E. Klevev. New York: Dutton.

Elya, S. M. (2002). *Home at Last*. New York: Lee & Low Books.

Eversole, R. (1995). *The Flute Player/La Flautisa*. Illustrated by G. B. Karas. New York: Orchard.

Fine, E. H. (2002). *Under the Lemon Moon*. New York: Lee & Low Books.

Gershator, D., & Gershator, P. (1995). *Bread Is for Eating*. Illustrated by E. Shaw-Smith. Austin, TX: Holt.

Herrera, J. F. (1995). *Calling the Doves/El canto de los Palomas*. Illustrated by E. Simmons. New York: Children's Book Press.

Jimenez, F. (2000). *La Mariposa*. New York: Houghton Mifflin.

Johnston, T. (2001). *Any Small Goodness*. New York: Scholastic.

Kleven, E. (1996). *Hooray, a Pinata!* New York: Dutton.

Leiner, K. (2001). *Mama Does the Mambo.* New York: Hyperion.

Lopez, L. (1997). *The Birthday Swap.* New York: Lee & Low Books.

Presilla, M. E., & Soto, G. (1996). *Life Around the Lake: Embroideries by the Women of Lake Patzcuaro.* New York: Henry Holt.

Reiser, L. (1998). *Tortillas and Lullabies.* Illustrated by C. Valientes. New York: Greenwillow.

Ryan, P. M. (2000). *Esperanza Rising.* New York: Scholastic.

Soto, G. (1997). *Snapshots from the Wedding.* Illustrated by S. Garcia. New York: Putnam.

Soto, G. (2002). *If the Shoe Fits.* New York: Putnam.

Van Laan, N. (1996). *La Boda: A Mexican Wedding Celebration.* Illustrated by A. Arroyo. Boston: Little, Brown & Company.

Velasquez, E. (2001). *Grandma's Records.* New York: Walker & Company.

Native American

Ancona, G. (1995). *Earth Daughter: Alicia of Acoma Pueblo.* New York: Simon & Schuster.

Bruchac, J. (1993). *The First Strawberries: A Cherokee Story.* Illustrated by A. Vojtech. New York: Dial.

Bruchac, J. (1999). *Eagle Song.* New York: Puffin.

Bunting, E. (1995). *Cheyenne Again.* Illustrated by I. Toddy. New York: Clarion.

Creech, S. (1996). *Walk Two Moons.* New York: HarperCollins.

Duncan, L. (1996). *The Magic of Spider Woman.* Illustrated by S. Begay. New York: Scholastic.

Heinz, B. (1996). *Kayuktuk: An Arctic Quest.* Illustrated by J. Van Zyle. San Francisco: Chronicle Books.

Hulpach, V. (1996). *Ahaiyute and Cloud Eater.* Illustrated by M. Zawadzki. Translated by P. Hejl. San Diego: Harcourt Brace.

Keams, G. (1995). *Grandmother Spider Brings the Sun: A Cherokee Story.* Illustrated by J. Barnardin. Flagstaff, AZ: Northland.

Lacapa, K. (1999). *Less Than Half, More Than Whole.* Flagstaff, AZ: Northland.

McCain, B. R. (2001). *Grandmother's Dreamcatcher.* Morton Grove, IL: Albert Whitman.

Nex, R. T. (1995). *Forbidden Talent.* Flagstaff, AZ: Northland.

Roessel, M. (1995). *Songs from the Loom: A Navajo Girl Learns to Weave.* Minneapolis: Lerner.

Smith, C. L. (2000). *Jingle Dancer.* New York: Morrow Junior.

Smith, C. L. (2002). *Indian Shoes.* New York: HarperCollins.

Watkins, S. (1997). *White Bead Ceremony: Mary Greyfeather Gets Her Native American Name.* Tulsa, OK: Council Oak Books.

FEMALES IN CHILDREN'S LITERATURE

Adler, David A. *America's Champion Swimmer: Gertrude Ederle.* The life and accomplishments of Gertrude Ederle, the first woman to swim the English Channel and a figure in the early women's rights movement, are described.

Cushman, Karen. *Catherine Called Birdy.* The 13-year-old daughter of an English country knight keeps a journal in which she records the events of her life, particularly her longing for adventures beyond the usual role of women and her efforts to avoid being married off.

Fritz, Jean. *You Want Women to Vote, Lizzy Stanton?* The life of Elizabeth Stanton and the struggle to get women the right to vote is recounted.

Hearne, Betsy. *Seven Brave Women.* A young girl recounts the brave exploits of her female ancestors, including her great-great-great-grandmother who came to America in a wooden boat.

Hoffman, Mary. *Amazing Grace.* Although a classmate says Grace cannot play Peter Pan in the school play because she is a girl and she is African American, Grace discovers that she can do anything she sets her mind to.

Ryan, Pam Munoz. *Amelia and Eleanor Go for a Ride.* This is a fictionalized account of the night Amelia Earhart flew Eleanor Roosevelt over Washington, D.C., in an airplane.

Spinelli, Jerry. *There's a Girl in My Hammerlock.* Thirteen-year-old Maisie joins her school's formerly all-male wrestling team and tries to last through the season, despite opposition from other students, her best friend, and her own teammates.

Willey, Margaret. *Clever Beatrice.* A small, but clever young girl outwits a rich giant and wins all his gold.

Self-Diagnostic Instrument

This short (38-item) test is designed to help you determine the basic skill areas in the language arts in which you are weak. Any errors that you make here should be seen as areas that require your review.

Write your responses on the indicated lines. When you have finished, check your answers against the correct choices listed at the end of this appendix.

Structural Analysis and Phonetics

1. A morpheme placed at the beginning of a word to alter the meaning of that word is called a _____.
2. A _____ comes at the end of a word and alters its meaning.
3. The root word in *redevelopment* is _____.
4. The underlined portion of the word <u>pray</u>ing is called a _____.
5. The common phonetic element in *chop, ship, moth,* and *when* is called a _____.
6. The common phonetic element in *hoist, round, gown,* and *boy* is called a _____.
7. The correct syllabication and accent for *coconut* and *cogitate* are _____.
8. Which of the following words contains a prefix?
   a. record
   b. realize
   c. recruit
   d. recover

1. _____   5. _____
2. _____   6. _____
3. _____   7. _____
4. _____   8. _____

Spelling and Vocabulary

Select the *synonym* of the underlined word in each sentence.

9. Jake is the most <u>ingenious</u> person in our family.
   - a. sincere
   - b. modest
   - c. sociable
   - d. clever

10. Examination determined that the tumor was <u>benign.</u>
    - a. noncancerous
    - b. kind
    - c. malignant
    - d. bestial

11. She reportedly suffered from <u>chronic</u> head colds.
    - a. constant
    - b. bellicose
    - c. painful
    - d. perceptible

12. The <u>mendicant</u> approached them on the street.
    - a. merchant
    - b. police officer
    - c. beggar
    - d. salesperson

Select the *antonym* of the underlined word in each sentence.

13. His <u>nefarious</u> character was well known to all.
    - a. clever
    - b. kindly
    - c. wicked
    - d. generous

14. He made a <u>lucrative</u> investment last year.
    - a. fortunate
    - b. rewarding
    - c. unprofitable
    - d. fraudulent

15. The boy was called a <u>dolt</u> by his teachers.
    - a. clever fellow
    - b. delinquent
    - c. prankster
    - d. doll

9. _____   13. _____

10. _____   14. _____

11. _____   15. _____

12. _____

Choose the word in each pair spelled correctly and write it on the line below.

16. Sarah (recieved, received) a sweater for her birthday.

17. The boys found (their, there) books where they had left them.

18. Today the natural (environment, enviroment) is threatened by industrial pollution.

19. Try to use correct (grammar, grammer) in your composition.

20. The stars were (shining, shinning) brightly in the sky.

21. We will (definately, definitely) meet you at eight o'clock.

22. The city was (fourty, forty) miles from the airport.

16. _____   20. _____

17. _____   21. _____

18. _____   22. _____

19. _____

Proofreading

One word in each line is spelled or used incorrectly. Write the correct word on the line below.

23. There are too main points to
24. be considired. First, the cost
25. of the entire operation must be less then
26. the transpertation of the various materials.
27. Second, the sight of the building
28. should depend on the advise of an expert.

23. _____   26. _____

24. _____   27. _____

25. _____   28. _____

Punctuation, Capitalization, and Parts of Speech

29. Which of the following sentences is punctuated correctly?
    a. The lake which is calm, is not deep
    b. She ran down the steps, and across the street.
    c. The road stretched forever, we drove on until midnight.
    d. "I'll never see you again," she said.

29. _____

Indicate on the line below which word (or words) in each line should be capitalized.

30. They lived on hester street for
31. ten years before moving to michigan,
32. where her husband taught english at the college.

30. _____   32. _____

31. _____

Write the name of the part of speech for the underlined word in each line.

33. There were seventy <u>large</u> elephants
34. in the parade. They walked, <u>slowly</u>
35. swinging their heavy <u>trunks.</u>
36. <u>Around</u> the square they trudged
37. for hours. <u>However,</u> their pace never changed.
38. Which of the following sentences is punctuated correctly?
    a. They gathered up their coats, hats scarves and left.
    b. Where have all the flowers gone!
    c. Today, unlike previous days, the weather is clear.

d. I will leave now: but tomorrow I shall return.

33. _____   36. _____
34. _____   37. _____
35. _____   38. _____

Answers

1. prefix
2. suffix
3. develop
4. blend
5. digraph
6. diphthong
7. có co nut, cóg i tate
8. d (recover)
9. d (clever)
10. a (noncancerous)
11. a (constant)
12. c (beggar)
13. b (kindly)
14. c (unprofitable)
15. a (clever fellow)
16. received
17. their
18. environment
19. grammar
20. shining
21. definitely
22. forty
23. two, *not* too
24. considered, *not* considired
25. than, *not* then
26. transportation, *not* transpertation
27. site, *not* sight
28. advice, *not* advise
29. d
30. Hester Street
31. Michigan
32. English
33. adjective
34. adverb
35. noun
36. preposition
37. conjunction
38. c

Assessment Devices

Sample Interest Inventory

Name _____ Date _____

School _____ Age _____

1. How much do you like to read? (Check one answer.)

   ☐ A little   ☐ A lot   ☐ Not at all

2. What newspapers do you read?

   _____

3. What are your favorite comic strips in the newspaper?

   _____

4. What magazines do you read?

   _____

5. What three living women do you admire most?

   A. _____ B. _____ C. _____

6. What three living men do you admire most?

   A. _____ B. _____ C. _____

7. Who are your heroes (men or women)?

   _____

8. What hobbies do you have?

   _____

9. What are your favorite television programs?

   _____

10. How many television programs do you watch each day?

    _____

11. How many hours each day do you usually spend watching television?

    _____

12. How many hours a day do you spend on the computer?
    Do you use the computer to play games or to search websites?

    _____

13. What are your favorite movies?

    _____

14. Who are your favorite movie, television, and music stars?

   _____

15. What are the three best fiction books you have ever read?

   A. _____   B. _____   C. _____

16. What are the three best nonfiction books you have ever read?

   A. _____   B. _____   C. _____

17. What men or boys from fiction or nonfiction do you remember best?

   _____

18. What women or girls from fiction or nonfiction do you remember best?

   _____

19. What books have you read that you disliked very much? Why?

   _____

20. Check the kinds of things you like to see, read, or hear about. (You may check as many as you wish.)

   ☐ Love stories   ☐ Criminals   ☐ Horses
   ☐ Baseball   ☐ Murder mysteries   ☐ Basketball
   ☐ War stories   ☐ Jokes   ☐ Space travel
   ☐ Mathematics   ☐ Famous people   ☐ Cowboy stories
   ☐ Historical tales   ☐ How to make things   ☐ Travel articles
   ☐ Mythology   ☐ Football   ☐ Encyclopedias
   ☐ Real-life adventures   ☐ Teenagers' problems   ☐ Politics
   ☐ Poetry   ☐ Nature stories   ☐ Health
   ☐ Movie stars   ☐ Scientific experiments

21. What is your favorite subject in school?

   _____

22. What subject do you like least?

   _____

Rubric for a "Musical Poem"

Student's Name   *Date*

Title of Poem

Trait	Score
CONTRIBUTION WHILE WORKING WITH SMALL GROUP	
Gave suggestions (10 points)	_____
Listened to classmates' ideas (10 points)	_____
Respected materials (5 points)	_____
Used indoor voice (5 points)	_____
PERFORMANCE	
"Music" fit the poem's mood (10 points)	_____
Appropriate expression (10 points)	_____
Poise (5 points)	_____
Volume (5 points)	_____
Rate (5 points)	_____
GOOD AUDIENCE MEMBER	
Listened to other groups (5 points)	_____
Gave appropriate response to other groups (5 points)	_____
TOTAL	_____

COMMENTS:

Rubric for Listening to an Advertisement

Student's Name _____   *Date* _____

Product _____

Trait	**Score**
CONTRIBUTION WHILE WORKING WITH SMALL GROUP	
Gave suggestions (10 points)	_____
Listened to classmates' ideas (10 points)	_____
Cooperated while listening (5 points)	_____
Used indoor voice (5 points)	_____
Accurately identified each technique (10 points)	_____
TOTAL	_____

COMMENTS:

Rubric for Indicating Growth in Listening Skills

Student's Name _____   Date _____

Minus sign (−) = never   Plus sign (+) = sometimes
Exclamation sign (!) = most of the time

Grading Period

Competency	1st quarter	2nd quarter	3rd quarter	4th quarter
Listens attentively to teacher	_____	_____	_____	_____
Listens attentively to classmates' presentations	_____	_____	_____	_____
Can follow simple two-step directions	_____	_____	_____	_____
Can restate two-step directions	_____	_____	_____	_____
Shows respect for others in small groups	_____	_____	_____	_____
Makes contributions in group discussions	_____	_____	_____	_____

COMMENTS:

Rubric for a Newscast

Student's Name _____   *Date* _____

Piece of Newscast _____

Trait   **Score**

CONTRIBUTION WHILE WORKING WITH SMALL GROUP

    Gave suggestions (10 points) _____

    Listened to classmates' ideas (10 points) _____

    Researched information (10 points) _____

    Cooperated during taping (5 points) _____

    Used indoor voice (5 points) _____

    Contributed creative ideas (5 points) _____

PERFORMANCE

    Organization (10 points) _____

    Articulation (10 points) _____

    Volume (5 points) _____

    Rate (5 points) _____

    Poise (5 points) _____

GOOD AUDIENCE MEMBER

    Listened to other groups (5 points) _____

    Gave appropriate response to other groups (5 points) _____

TOTAL _____

COMMENTS:

Rubric for a Propaganda Activity

Student's Name _____   *Date* _____

Product _____

Trait	Score
CONTRIBUTION WHILE WORKING WITH SMALL GROUP	
Gave suggestions (10 points)	_____
Listened to classmates' ideas (10 points)	_____
Cooperated while listening (5 points)	_____
Used indoor voice (5 points)	_____
PERFORMANCE	
Clear use of propaganda technique (10 points)	_____
Well articulated (10 points)	_____
Creative advertisement (10 points)	_____
Volume (5 points)	_____
Rate (5 points)	_____
Poise (5 points)	_____
GOOD AUDIENCE MEMBER	
Listened to other groups (5 points)	_____
Gave appropriate response to other groups (5 points)	_____
TOTAL	_____

COMMENTS:

Rubistar Storytelling Rubric

*Student's Name*_____ *Date*_____

CATEGORY	4	3	2	1
Knows the Story	The storyteller knows the story well and has obviously practiced telling the story several times. There is no need for notes and the speaker speaks with confidence.	The storyteller knows the story pretty well and has practiced telling the story once or twice. May need notes once or twice, but the speaker is relatively confident.	The storyteller knows some of the story, but did not appear to have practiced. May need notes 3–4 times, and the speaker ill-at-ease.	The storyteller could not tell the story without using notes.
Speaks Clearly	Speaks clearly and distinctly all (100–95%) the time, and mispronounces no words.	Speaks clearly and distinctly all (100–95%) the time, and mispronounces one word.	Speaks clearly and distinctly most (94–85%) of the time, and mispronounces no more than one word.	Often mumbles or cannot be understood *or* mispronounces more than one word.
Setting	Lots of vivid, descriptive words are used to tell the audience when and where the story takes place.	Some vivid, descriptive words are used to tell the audience when and where the story takes place.	The audience can figure out when and where the story took place, but there isn't much detail (e.g., once upon a time in a land far, far away).	The audience has trouble telling when and where the story takes place.
Characters	The main characters are named and clearly described (through words and/or actions). The audience knows and can describe what the characters look like and how they typically behave.	The main characters are named and described (through words and/or actions). The audience has a fairly good idea of what the characters look like.	The main characters are named. The audience knows very little about the main characters.	It is hard to tell who the main characters are.
Audience Contact	Storyteller looks at and tells the story to all members of the audience.	Storyteller looks at and tells the story to a few people in the audience.	Storyteller looks at and tells the story to 1–2 people in the audience.	Storyteller does not look at or try to involve the audience.
Voice	Always speaks loudly, slowly, and clearly. Is easily understood by all audience members all the time.	Usually speaks loudly, slowly, and clearly. Is easily understood by all audience members almost all the time.	Usually speaks loudly and clearly. Speaks so fast sometimes that audience has trouble understanding.	Speaks too softly or mumbles. The audience often has trouble understanding.

(continued)

CATEGORY	4	3	2	1
Pacing	The story is told slowly where the storyteller wants to create suspense and told quickly when there is a lot of action.	The storyteller usually paces the story well, but one or two parts seem to drag or be rushed.	The storyteller tries to pace the story, but the story seems to drag or be rushed in several places.	The storyteller tells everything at one pace. Does not change the pace to match the story.
Acting/Dialogue	The student uses consistent voices, facial expressions, and movements to make the characters more believable and the story more easily understood.	The student often uses voices, facial expressions, and movements to make the characters more believable and the story more easily understood.	The student tries to use voices, facial expressions, and movements to make the characters more believable and the story more easily understood.	The student tells the story but does not use voices, facial expressions, or movement to make the storytelling more interesting or clear.
Connections/ Transitions	Connections among events, ideas, and feelings in the story are creative, clearly expressed, and appropriate.	Connections among events, ideas, and feelings in the story are clearly expressed and appropriate.	Connections among events, ideas, and feelings in the story are sometimes hard to figure out. More detail or better transitions are needed.	The story seems very disconnected and it is very difficult to figure out the story.
Duration	The storytelling lasts 5–7 minutes.	The storytelling lasts 4 or 8 minutes.	The storytelling lasts 9 minutes.	The storytelling lasts less than 3 minutes or more than 9 minutes.
Listens to Others	Always listens attentively to other storytellers. Is polite and does not appear bored or make distracting gestures or sounds.	Usually listens attentively to other storytellers. Rarely appears bored and never makes distracting gestures or sounds.	Usually listens to other storytellers, but sometimes appears bored. Might once or twice accidentally make a gesture or sound that is distracting.	Does not listen attentively. Tries to distract the storytellers, makes fun of them, or does other things instead of listening.

Source: RubiStar, http://rubistar.4teachers.org. Used with permission.

Modified Rubric for Storytelling

Student's Name _____   *Date* _____

Title/Author of Story _____

Category	**Score**
Knows the story (5 points)	_____
Story in correct sequence (5 points)	_____
Speaks clearly/projects (20 points)	_____
Audience contact (10 points)	_____
Intonation (15 points)	_____
Pacing (10 points)	_____
Use of dialogue (15 points)	_____
Facial expressions (10 points)	_____
Gestures (10 points)	_____
Use of props (5 points)	_____
Appropriate body movements (5 points)	_____
Duration (5 points)	_____
Listens to others (5 points)	_____
TOTAL	_____

COMMENTS:

Rubistar Puppet Show Rubric

Student's Name   Date

CATEGORY	4	3	2	1
Puppet Construction	Puppets were original, creative, and constructed well. No pieces fell off during the performance.	Puppets were original and constructed well. No pieces fell off during the performance.	Puppets were constructed fairly well. No pieces fell off during the performance.	Puppets were not constructed well. Pieces fell off during the performance.
Puppet Manipulation	Puppeteers always manipulated puppets so audience could see them.	Puppeteers usually manipulated puppets so audience could see them.	Puppeteers sometimes manipulated puppets so audience could see them.	Puppeteers rarely manipulated puppets so audience could see them.
Playwriting	Play was creative and really held the audience's interest.	Play was creative and usually held the audience's interest.	Play had several creative elements, but often did not hold the audience's interest.	Play needed more creative elements.
Voice Projection	Voices of puppeteers were always audible to people sitting in the back row.	Voices of puppeteers were usually audible to people sitting in the back row.	Voices of puppeteers were sometimes audible to people sitting in the back row.	Voices of puppeteers were rarely audible to people sitting in the back row.
Accuracy of Story	All important parts of story were included and were accurate.	Almost all important parts of story were included and were accurate.	Quite a few important parts of story were included and were accurate.	Much of the story was left out or was inaccurate.
Expression	Puppeteers' voices showed a lot of expression and emotion.	Puppeteers' voices showed some expression and emotion.	Puppeteers' voices showed a little expression and emotion.	Puppeteers' voices were monotone and not expressive.
Staying in Character	Puppeteers stayed in character throughout the performance.	Puppeteers stayed in character through almost all of the performance.	Puppeteers tried to stay in character through some of the performance.	Puppeteers acted silly or showed off.
Scenery	Scenery was creative, added interest to the play, and did not get in the way of the puppets.	Scenery was creative and did not get in the way of the puppets.	Scenery did not get in the way of the puppets.	Scenery got in the way of the puppets or distracted the audience.

Source: RubiStar, http://rubistar.4teachers.org. Used with permission.

Modified Rubric for a Puppet Show

Student's Name _____   Date _____

Story _____

Category	**Score**
PROCESS	
Puppet construction (5 points)	_____
Cooperated with group (10 points)	_____
PRODUCT	
Puppet manipulation (5 points)	_____
Voice projection (10 points)	_____
Expression (10 points)	_____
Staying in character (10 points)	_____
TOTAL	_____

COMMENTS:

Rubric for Assessment of Presentation Skills

Student's Name _____   *Topic* _____

Total Score _____   *Grading Period*   *1   2   3   4*

Superior = 5   Excellent = 4   Fair = 3   Adequate = 2   Weak = 1

CONTENT

_____ Clarity of purpose   _____ Supporting details

_____ Introduction   _____ Conclusion

_____ Main points   _____ Interesting

PRESENTATION

_____ Rate   _____ Standard English

_____ Volume   _____ Eye contact

VISUAL AIDS

_____ Neatly prepared   _____ Manipulation

_____ Appropriate size   _____ Support topic

COMMENTS:

Storytelling Rubric
Emphasizing Voice Inflection

Student's Name _____

Story _____

Score

APPROPRIATE MATERIAL (15 POINTS)

    Length (2 of 15) _____

    Engaging (5 of 15) _____

    Age appropriate (3 of 15) _____

    Interesting (5 of 15) _____

FACIAL EXPRESSION (13 POINTS) _____

VOICE INFLECTION (50 POINTS)

    Pleasing tone (5 of 50) _____

    Variety of pitch (10 of 50) _____

    Clear diction (10 of 50) _____

    Change for dialogue (10 of 50) _____

    Appropriate dialect (5 of 50) _____

    Variety of rate (10 of 50) _____

APPROPRIATE BODY MOVEMENT (12 POINTS) _____

SPECIAL EFFECTS/PROPS (10 POINTS) _____

TOTAL _____

COMMENTS:

Reading Conference Checklist

Student's Name _____   *Date* _____

Title _____

Type of Material _____

	EXCELLENT	GOOD	OK	NEEDS HELP
WORD RECOGNITION				
Decoding	_____	_____	_____	_____
Use of context clues	_____	_____	_____	_____
Use of structural clues	_____	_____	_____	_____
Use of dictionary	_____	_____	_____	_____
Conceptual connections	_____	_____	_____	_____

	EXCELLENT	GOOD	OK	NEEDS HELP
COMPREHENSION				
Main idea	_____	_____	_____	_____
Supporting details	_____	_____	_____	_____
Relationships	_____	_____	_____	_____
(Cause/effect)	_____	_____	_____	_____
(Compare/contrast)	_____	_____	_____	_____
Description of characters	_____	_____	_____	_____
Sequence of events	_____	_____	_____	_____

LITERARY CONNECTIONS

Retelling summary: _____

Child's opinion of the material: _____

Further responses: _____

Suggestions for future reading: _____

Summary of the conference: _____

Sample Reading Rubric

Student's Name _____   *Date* _____

Activity	Consistent	Inconsistent
Reads and understands all independent books.		
Completes daily and monthly reading.		
Completes literature response log on time.		
Has log that contains high-quality entries.		
Contributes thoughtful comments to literature circles.		
Listens and responds to peer comments in literature circles.		
Completes all assignments on time.		
Has work that shows effort and attempts to achieve quality.		

POINT CREDIT SYSTEM

A—consistent for all areas (7 of 8)

B—consistent for most areas (6 of 8)

C—consistent for many areas (5 of 8)

D—consistent for some areas (4 of 8)

F—consistent for a few areas (3 of 8)

Source: Slightly adapted by permission of Regie Routman: *Invitations: Changing as Teachers and Learners K–12* (Heinemann, a division of Reed Elsevier, Inc., Portsmouth, NH, 1994).

Portfolio Form for Student's Self-Assessment

Name _____ Date _____

Name of Work _____

1. I got my idea from _____

   _____

   _____

2. I got the background information from _____

   _____

   _____

3. The part that was hard to write was _____

   _____

   because _____

   _____

   _____

4. I especially liked this part _____

   _____

   because _____

   _____

   _____

5. I could improve it by _____

   _____

   _____

6. New vocabulary words I used _____

   _____

   _____

Teacher's Comments _____

_____

_____

_____

Teacher's Quarterly Evaluation Form

Name _____

Date _____   *Quarter 1 2 3 4*

1. What was your favorite piece of work this quarter? Explain why.

   _____

   _____

   _____

2. What piece did you like the least? Explain why.

   _____

   _____

   _____

3. Did you make good use of your time? Explain.

   _____

   _____

   _____

4. What things did you learn about yourself as you were writing?

   _____

   _____

   _____

5. Which type of new genre will you attempt next quarter? Why do you want to try it?

   _____

   _____

   _____

6. What one thing would you like most to learn next quarter?

   _____

   _____

   _____

Student's Signature _____

Teacher's Signature _____

Teacher's Portfolio Assessment Rubric

Student's Name _____   Date _____

		EXCELLENT			POOR	
Goals		5	4	3	2	1

WRITING PROCESS	uses various prewriting strategies (brainstorming, webbing, illustrating, etc.)					
	writes a rough draft (ability to put thoughts on paper)					
	revises rough draft (checks details, sequence, clarity, etc.)					
	edits/proofreads (alone, with peers, or with teacher)					
	publishes or shares (final copy or oral reading to classmates or teacher)					
WRITING SKILLS	writes complete sentences					
	uses descriptive words in writing					
	uses correct format when writing paragraphs					
	uses correct format when writing letters					
USAGE	makes subjects and verbs agree					
MECHANICS	punctuates at the end of sentences					
	capitalizes the beginning of sentences					
	uses commas correctly					
	uses quotation marks correctly					
	capitalizes proper nouns in writing					

TEACHER COMMENTS:

_____

Source: Reprinted with permission of the Mid-Del School District, Oklahoma.

Writing Rubric: Holistic Scoring and Student Self-Evaluation

HOLISTIC SCORING

In holistic scoring, written papers are given a quick, general reading for overall content, clarity, organization, flow, and development of thoughts. For teachers who have many papers to grade, this is a time-saving yet effective device to evaluate students' writing. Before using the four-point scale, you must be clear in your own mind what constitutes a 4, 3, 2, 1 grade.

HOLISTIC SCORING FOR STUDENT SELF-EVALUATION

Although holistic scoring was originally developed for teachers, it can be modified to be used by students who have been taught to self-evaluate their own work. It can also be used in a buddy system where peers evaluate one another.

HOLISTIC SCORING RUBRIC USING A FOUR-POINT SCALE

1 = Ineffective Piece: Many problems; not going anywhere.
2 = Ineffective Piece but Salvageable: Has problems but I know how to solve them.
3 = Effective Piece: This works; is well organized, clearly written, and has no mechanical errors.
4 = Most Effective Piece: Includes all components of #3 plus it says something; exemplifies strong writing; moves the reader.

After you have rated your pieces 1, 2, 3, 4, write three reasons for each of the scores. Cite specific examples in the piece to support your reasons.

Rubric for Upper Elementary Grades Writing

Student's Name _____ Date _____

Title of Project _____

Possible Points   **Points You Earned**

1. Separate cover sheet, name, date, title   10   _____

2. Neatly written   10   _____

3. Clearly written sentences   20   _____

4. Well-organized paragraphs   20   _____

5. Clear beginning, middle, and end   20   _____

6. Proofread and edited for errors   20   _____

TOTAL   100   _____

Rubric for Middle Grades Writing Portfolio Assignment

Student's Name   *Date*

Title of Project

Possible Points		**Points You Earned**
1. Portfolio in separate binder with cover sheet, name, date, title	10	
2. Separate table of contents, dividers, drafts, and final copies	10	
3. Typed, double-spaced, neat appearance	10	
4. Content: Written in clear and interesting manner	10	
5. Content: Work attempts to say something important	60	
6. Mechanics: Proofread and edited for errors	50	
TOTAL	150	

Cooperative Learning Self-Assessment Form

Today's date _____

I worked with (names of group members) _____

Name of activity/project _____

Check if the statement fits you

☐ I talked quietly.

☐ I shared materials.

☐ I listened well to others.

☐ I did not demand my own way.

☐ I did my share of the work.

☐ I cleaned up the area.

Today I learned from (name of classmate) _____ the following:

_____

_____

_____

_____

_____

_____

_____

_____

_____

Today I taught (name of classmate) _____ the following:

_____

_____

_____

_____

_____

_____

_____

_____

Signature _____

Teacher's Evaluation Form

Student

Date

Project

	Superior	Good	Adequate	Needs Work
Creative				
Accurate information				
Well organized/attractive				
Indicates research				
Bibliography (correct amount of references)				
Bibliography format correct				
Clearly presented				
Participation in the group				

Additional comments

Discussed with student on this date

Student's Signature

Rubric for Writing Assignment

Student's Name _____   *Date* _____

Title of Project _____

Possible Points   **Points You Earned**

1. Separate cover sheet, name, date, title   5   _____

2. Typed, double-spaced, stapled, neat appearance   5   _____

3. Work says something important   40   _____

4. Written in clear and interesting manner   30   _____

5. Proofread and edited for errors   20   _____

TOTAL   100   _____

Additional Language Arts Websites

TEACHER RESOURCES

www.scils.rutgers.edu/~kvander
Kay Vandergrift's home page. Contains extensive materials on connecting literature across the curriculum as well as lists of multicultural books.

www.kn.pacbell.com/wired/bluewebn
A library of Blue Ribbon learning sites.

www.k12connections.iptv.org
Iowa Public Television's (IPTV) website for distance learning.

www.learner.org
A site of professional development resources.

http://edweb.sdsu.edu/webquest/webquest.html
Resource page for using the WebQuest model.

AUTHORS

www.janbrett.com
There are 2,239 pages of fun activities to do with Jan Brett's books.

www.ipl.org/div/kidspace
Part of the Internet Public Library; offers links to author websites, as well as other literature links.

www.snowcrest.net/kidpower/authors.html
Lists authors who are willing to visit your school.

www.honors.unr.edu/~fenimore/en297/bohannon/sidewalk.html
Contains information on author Shel Silverstein.

www.acs.ucalgary.ca/~dkbrown/authors.html
An index of authors and illustrators on the Web.

www.cbcbooks.org
Children's Book Council site. Contains links to authors.

GRAMMAR AND VOCABULARY

www.grammarnow.com
An e-mail site for proofreading any manuscript.

www.grammarlady.com
Grammar hotline for posting questions.

www.wolinskyweb.com/word.htm
Resource fun with words.

http://webster.commnet.edu/grammar/index.htm
Teaches and reviews grammar.

LITERATURE

www.carolhurst.com
Contains book reviews and activities to use with specific books.

www.acm.org/crossroads
A student magazine containing book reviews. Available in Spanish.

www.ala.org
Contains links to the Caldecott and Newbery Award winners. Click on the "Awards and Scholarships" button.

READING AND WRITING

www.toread.com
A study of the reading process and teaching techniques.

www.cyberkids.com
Online zine accepts student submissions of poetry and fiction.

Word Walls

ABC WORD WALLS TO DO THE FOLLOWING:
- Recognize and write letter forms.
- Demonstrate knowledge of letter–sound correspondence.
- Use initial and final letter cues.
- Introduce the alphabet: List all new words under the appropriate letter of the alphabet.
- Incorporate pictures plus words for emergent readers and writers.

HIGH-FREQUENCY WORD WALLS
- Take words from sight vocabulary lists.
- Add frequently seen words in children's books.
- Include words frequently used by students in their own writing.

CONTENT-AREA WORD WALLS
- List the subjects taught (social studies, science, math, art, etc.).
- Under each subject heading, place words that the children encounter in their reading.

UNIT VOCABULARY
- For each unit taught, create a separate word wall out of butcher-block paper.
- Add new words daily throughout the unit.

References

Abrahamson, R. F. (1980). A plot structure analysis of children's favorite picture books. *The Reading Teacher, 34*(2), 167–170.

Adams, M. J. (1990a). *Beginning to read: Thinking and learning about print.* Cambridge, MA: MIT Press.

After-School Alliance Pool. (2001). *Report #4, July/August 2001 Mott Foundation/JCPenney after school nationwide voters poll report.* Retrieved February 14, 2002, from: www.afterschoolalliance.org.

Allen, R. (2003). The democratic aims of service learning. *Educational Leadership, 60*(6), 51–54.

Allen, V. (1994). Selecting materials for reading instruction of ESL children. In K. Spangenberg-Urbschat & R. Pritchard (eds.), *Kids come in all languages: Reading instruction for ESL students.* Newark, DE: International Reading Association.

Allington, R. (2002a). Accelerating in the wrong direction: Why thirty years of federal testing and accountability hasn't worked yet and what we might do instead. In R. Allington (ed.). *Big brother and the national reading curriculum: How ideology trumped evidence.* Portsmouth, NH: Heinemann.

Allington, R. (2002b). *Big brother and the national reading curriculum: How ideology trumped evidence.* Portsmouth, NH: Heinemann.

Allington, R. (2002c). Troubling times: A short historical perspective. In R. Allington (ed.), *Big brother and the national reading curriculum: How ideology trumped evidence.* Portsmouth, NH: Heinemann.

Alt, M. N. (1997, October). How effective an educational tool is student community service? *NASSP Bulletin: Service Learning: Leaving Footprints on the Planet,* 8–16.

Amiran, E., & Mann, J. (1982). Written composition, grades K–12: Literature synthesis and report. Portland, OR: Northwest Regional Educational Laboratory.

Anderson, R. C., & Pearson, P. D. (1984). A schema-theoretic view of basals. In P. D. Pearson (ed.), *Handbook of reading research.* New York: Longman.

Anderson, R. C., Hiebert, E. H., Scott, J. A., & Wilkinson, I. (1985). *Becoming a nation of readers: The report of the Commission on Reading.* Washington, DC: National Institute of Education, the National Academy of Education.

Anderson, V., & Roit, M. (1996). Linking reading comprehension instruction to language development for language-minority students. *Elementary School Journal, 96*(3), 295–309.

Anderson, W. (1995, July). Learning styles of the various cultures. Class lecture presented in the Education Department at the University of Central Oklahoma, Edmond.

Applebee, A. (1978). *The child's concept of story: Ages 2 to 17.* Chicago: University of Chicago Press.

Applebee, A. (1981). Writing in the secondary school: English and content areas (NCTE Research Report No. 21). Urbana, IL: NCTE.

Applebee, A., Langer, J., & Mullis, J. (1986). The writing report card: Writing achievement in American schools. Princeton, NJ: National Assessment of Educational Progress, Educational Testing Services.

Appleman, D., & Thompson, M. (2002, January). Fighting the toxic status quo: Alfie Kohn on standardized tests and teacher education. *English Education, 34*(2), 95–103.

Armstrong, T. (1996). A holistic approach to attention deficit disorder. *Educational Leadership, 53*(5), 34–36.

Ashton-Warner, S. (1958). *Spinster.* New York: Simon & Schuster.

Ashton-Warner, S. (1963). *Teacher.* New York: Simon & Schuster.

Atkinson, J. W. (1974). Motivational determinants of intellectual performance and cumulative achievement. In J. W. Atkinson & J. O. Raynor (eds.), *Motivation and achievement.* Washington, DC: Winston Publishers.

Atkinson, J. W., & Birch, D. (1978). *An introduction to motivation* (2nd ed.). New York: D. Van Nostrand.

Atwell, N. (1984). Writing and reading literature from the inside out. *Language Arts, 61*(3), 240–252.

Atwell, N. (1998). *In the middle: New understandings about writing, reading and learning* (2nd ed.). Portsmouth, NH: Boynton/Cook.

Atwood, A. (1973). *My own rhythm: An approach to haiku.* New York: Scribner's.

Au, K. H., Mason, J. M., & Scheu, J. A. (1995). *Literacy instruction today.* New York: Harper-Collins.

Baenen, N., Bernholc, A., Dulaney, C., & Banks, K. (1997). Reading Recovery: Long-term progress after three cohorts. *Journal of Education for Students Placed at Risk, 2*(2), 161–181.

Baker, E. (2000, July). Instructional approaches used to integrate literacy and technology. *Reading Online, 4*(1), www.readingonline.org/articles/baker.

Baldwin, J. (1997). If Black English isn't a language, then tell me, what is? Reproduced from a 1997 *New York Times* letter to the editor in "The real Ebonics debate" (T. Perry & L. Delpit, eds.). *Rethinking Schools: An Urban Educational Journal, 12*(1), 16.

Banks, J., & Banks, C. (1993). *Multicultural education: Issues and perspectives* (2nd ed.). Boston: Allyn & Bacon.

Barone, D., & Lovell, J. (1990). Michael the show and tell magician: A journey through literature to self. *Language Arts, 67*(2), 134–143.

Barrow, L. H., & Andrew, B. (1981, April). Activity-oriented science plus language experience approach = science language experience. Paper presented at the meeting of the National Science Teachers' Association, New York.

Barrow, L. H., Kristo, J. V., & Andrew, B. (1984). Building bridges between science and reading. *The Reading Teacher, 38*(2), 188–193.

Baugh, J. (2002). The shot heard from Ann Arbor: Language research and public policy in African America. *Howard Journal of Communication* [Online], *13*(1), 5 pages. Available at: http://web1.epnet.com/citation.asp?tb=1&_ug-dbs+)+In+en%2Dus+sid+F025631A%2D4092%2D97A2%D5D628F6377CE%40sessionmgr3 [2003, March 11].

Bauman, M. L. (1987). Listening, repetition and meaning. *Language Arts, 64*(1), 54–60.

Baumann, J., & Thomas, D. (1997). "If you can pass Momma's tests, then she knows you're getting your education": A case study of support for literacy learning within an African American family. *The Reading Teacher, 51*(2), 108–120.

Baumann, J. F., Hoffman, J. V., Moon, J., & Duffy-Hester, A. M. (1998). Where are teachers' voices in the phonics/whole language debate? Results from a survey of U.S. elementary teachers. *The Reading Teacher, 51*(8), 636–650.

Beall, P. C., & Nipp, S. H. (1979). *Wee sing: Children's songs and fingerplays.* New York: Price Stern Sloan.

Bear, D., Invernizzi, M., Templeton, S., & Johnston, F. (2000). *Words their way: Word study for phonics, vocabulary, and spelling instruction* (2nd ed.). Upper Saddle River, NJ: Prentice Hall/Merrill.

Beck, I., & McKeown, M. G. (1981). Developing questions that promote comprehension: The story map. *Language Arts, 58*(8), 913–918.

Beck, I. L., McKeown, M. G., Hamilton, R. L., & Kucan, L. (1997). *Questioning the author: An approach for enhancing student engagement with text.* Newark, DE: International Reading Association.

Beck, J. (1998, June 13). English the only choice. *Tulsa World,* A17.

Beers, C., & Beers, J. (1981). Three assumptions abut learning to spell. *Language Arts, 58,* 573–580.

Begley, S. (1996, February 19). Your child's brain. *Newsweek,* 55–58.

Begley, S. (1997, August 11). Wombs with a view: For the IQ it's not just genes but prenatal life, too. *Newsweek,* 61.

Bell, L. I. (2002/2003). Strategies that close the gap. *Educational Leadership, 60*(4), 32–34.

Berglund, R., & Johns, J. (1983). A primer on uninterrupted sustained silent reading. *The Reading Teacher, 36*(6), 534–539.

Berkas, T., & Maland, J. (1993). *Excellence in action: The community service learning program.* St. Paul: University of Minnesota, Center for Experiential Education and Service Learning, Department of Vocational and Technical Education.

Berninger, V., Abbott, S., Reed, E., Greep, K., Hooven, C., Sylvester, L., Taylor, J., Clinton, A., & Abbott, R. (1997). Directed reading and writing activities: Aiming intervention to working brain systems. In S. Dollinger & L. DiLalla (eds.), *Prevention and intervention issues across the life span.* Hillsdale, NJ: Erlbaum.

Bernstein, B. (1971). *Class, codes and control.* London: Routledge & Kegan Paul.

Bettelheim, B. (1976). *The uses of enchantment: The meaning and importance of fairy tales.* New York: Random House.

Bianchini, L. (2003). *National Council of Teachers of English, Statement on Visual Literacy: On viewing and visually representing as forms of literacy.* lbianchi@ncte.org.

Bigelow, B. (1989). Discovering Columbus: Rereading the past. *Language Arts, 66*(6), 635–643.

Bing, S. B. (1988). Handwriting: Remediate or circumvent. *Academic Therapy, 23,* 509–514.

Blake, M. (1979, September). SSR revisited. *Teacher,* 95–98.

Blake, M. E. (2000). *Young readers' attitudes.* Unpublished manuscript.

Bloodsworth, J. (1993). *The left-handed writer.* Arlington, VA. (ERIC Document Reproduction Services ED 356494)

Bloom, B. (1981). *All our children learning.* New York: McGraw-Hill.

Bloom, B. (1984). The search for methods of group instruction as effective as one to one tutoring. *Educational Leadership, 41*(8), 4–18.

Bloom, B. (ed.). (1956). *Taxonomy of educational objectives.* New York: David McKay.

Bloom, L. (1991). *Language development from two to three.* New York: Cambridge University Press.

Bloomfield, L. (1933). *Language.* New York: Holt.

Borelli, F. (2001). The school-home connection. *Media and Methods* [Online], *37*(8), 14 pages. Available at: http://web4.epnet.com/citation.asp?tb=1&_ug=dbs+0+fic+1+In+en%2Dus+sid+2D3E8F3E [2003, January 14].

Braddock, R., Lloyd-Jones, R., & Schoer, L. (1963). *Research in written composition.* Champaign, IL: NCTE.

Brandt, R. (1997). On using knowledge about our brain: A conversation with Bob Sylwester. *Educational Leadership, 54*(6), 16–19.

Bransford, J. D., & Johnson, M. K. (1973). Considerations of some problems of comprehension. In W. G. Chase (ed.), *Visual information processing.* New York: Academic Press.

Brisk, M. E. (1998). *Bilingual education: From compensatory to quality schooling.* Mahwah, NJ: Lawrence Erlbaum.

Britton, J. (1973). *The development of writing liabilities.* London: Macmillan.

Britton, J. (1978). The composing process and the functions of writing. In C. Cooper & L. Odell (eds.), *Research on composing: Points of departure.* Urbana, IL: NCTE.

Britton, J. (1986). *Language and learning.* New York: Penguin.

Bromley, K. (1988). *Language arts: Exploring connections.* Boston: Allyn & Bacon.

Brophy, J. (1982). Successful teaching strategies for the inner-city child. *Phi Delta Kappan, 63,* 527–530.

Bross, M. (2003, January 27). Effects of WhizKids on reading scores. Presentation at Southern Nazarene University.

Brown, G., & Ellis, N. (eds.). (1994). *Handbook of spelling: Theory, process and intervention.* New York: John Wiley & Sons.

Brown, R. (1974). A *first language: The early stages.* Cambridge, MA: Harvard University Press.

Bruner, J. (1961a). *The process of education.* Cambridge, MA: Harvard University Press.

Bruner, J. S. (1961b). A *study of thinking.* New York: J. Wiley and Sons.

Bruner, J. (1962). *On knowing.* Cambridge, MA: Harvard University Press.

Bruner, J. S. (1966). *Toward a theory of instruction.* Cambridge, MA: Harvard University Press.

Bruner, J. (1973). Organization of early skilled action. *Child Development, 44,* 1–11.

Bruner, J. S. (1978). The role of dialogue in language acquisition. In A. Sinclair, R. J. Jarvella, & W. M. Levelt (eds.), *The child's conception of language.* New York: Springer-Verlag.

Bruner, J. (1983). *Child's talk: Learning to use language.* New York: W. W. Norton.

Bruner, J. S. (1987). *Making sense: The child's construction of the world.* London: Metheun Publishing Company.

Bruner, J., Jolly, A., & Sylva, K. (1976). *Play: Its role in development and evolution.* London: Penguin Books.

Buchanan, E. (1992). *Spelling for whole language classrooms.* Winnipeg, Canada: Whole Language Consultants Ltd.

Burgess, S. (2003). Shared reading correlates of early reading skills. *Reading Online* [Online]. Available at: www.readingonline.org/articles/burgess/index.html. [2003, February 8].

Burns, P. C., Roe, B. D., & Ross, E. P. (2002). *Teaching reading in today's elementary schools* (8th ed.). Boston: Houghton Mifflin.

Bus, A., Van Izendoorn, M., & Pellegrini, A. (1995). Joint book reading makes for success in learning to read: A meta-analysis on intergenerational transmission of literacy. *Review of Educational Research, 65,* 1–21.

Cadiero-Kaplan, K. (2002). Literacy ideologies: Critically engaging the language arts curriculum. *Language Arts* 79(5), 372–381.

Caine, R., & Caine, G. (1994). *Making connections: Teaching and the human brain.* Palo Alto, CA: Addison-Wesley.

Caldwell, J. (1985). A new look at the old Informal Reading Inventory. *The Reading Teacher, 39*(3), 168–173. [AU: Cite in text or delete.]

Calkins, L. (1983). *Lessons from a child: On the teaching and learning of writing.* Portsmouth, NH: Heinemann.

Calkins, L. (1991). *Living between the lines.* Portsmouth, NH: Heinemann.

Calkins, L. (1994). *The art of teaching writing* (2nd ed.). Portsmouth, NH: Heinemann.

Calkins, L. (2001). *The art of teaching reading.* New York: Longman.

Cambourne, B. (1988). *The whole story: Natural learning and the acquisition of literacy in the classroom.* Jefferson City, MO: Scholastic.

Cambourne, B. (1995). Toward an educationally relevant theory of literacy learning: Twenty years of inquiry. *The Reading Teacher, 49,* 182–192.

Cambourne, B. (2001). What do I do with the rest of the class? The nature of teaching-learning activities. *Language Arts, 79*(2), 124–135.

Cambourne, B. (2002a). The conditions of learning: Is learning natural? *The Reading Teacher, 55*(8), 758–762.

Cambourne, B. (2002b). Holistic, integrated approaches to reading and language arts instruction: The constructivist framework of an instructional theory. In A. E. Farstrup & S. J. Samuels (Eds.), *What research has to say about reading instruction* (pp. 25–47). Newark, DE: The International Reading Association.

Carbo, M. (1997). Reading styles times twenty. *Educational Leadership, 54*(6), 38–42.

Carbo, M., Dunn, R., & Dunn, K. (1986). *Teaching students to read through individual learning styles.* Englewood Cliffs, NJ: Prentice Hall.

Carroll, J. B. (1972). *Language and thought.* Upper Saddle River, NJ: Prentice Hall.

Carter, C. (1997). Why reciprocal teaching? *Educational Leadership, 54*(6), 64–68.

Cazden, C. (1972). *Child language and education.* New York: Holt, Rinehart & Winston.

Cazden, C. (1981). *Language in early childhood education.* Washington, DC: National Association for the Education of Young Children.

Chafe, W. (1988). What good is punctuation? *The Quarterly of the National Writing Project, 10,* 8–11.

Chamot, A., & O'Malley, J. M. (1994). Instructional approaches and teaching procedures. In K. Spangenberg-Urbschat & R. Pritchard (eds.), *Kids come in all languages: Reading instruction for ESL students.* Newark, DE: International Reading Association.

Chandler, K., & the Mapleton Teachers research group (2000). Squaring up to spelling: A teacher-research group surveys parents. *Language Arts, 77,* 224–231.

Checkley, K. (1997). The seventh . . . and eighth. *Educational Leadership, 55*(1), 8–13.

Cheng, K., Magloire, T., Moore, T., & Napier, C. (2001). The impact of clinic-based literacy intervention on language development in inner-city preschool children. *Pediatrics* [Online], *107*, 11 pages. Available at: http://web12. epnet.com/citation.asp?tb=1&_ug=dbs+0+In=en%2Dus+ sid+36BEAOCF%2D16B9%2D44BC%2D9103%2DEE2340 F26324%40sessionmgr [2003, February 14].

Choate, J., & Rakes, T. (1987). The structured listening activity: A model for improving listening comprehension. *The Reading Teacher, 41*(2), 194–200.

Chomsky, N. (1957). *Syntactic structures*. The Hague: Mouton.

Chomsky, N. (1974). *Aspects of the theory of syntax*. Cambridge, MA: Harvard University Press.

Christie, J. (1980). Sentence combining practice. Practical Applications of Research, *PDK Newsletter, 2*(4).

Christie, J., Enz, B., & Vukelich, C. (2003). *Teaching language and literacy* (2nd ed.). Boston: Allyn & Bacon.

Clark, B. (1986). *Optimizing learning: The integrated educational model in the classroom*. Columbus, OH: Merrill.

Claxton, C., & Ralston, Y. (1978). Learning styles: Their impact on teaching and administration (AAE-ERIC Research Paper No. 10). Washington, DC: George Washington University.

Clay, M. (1975). *What did I write?* Portsmouth, NH: Heinemann.

Clay, M. (1979). *Reading: The patterning of complex behavior* (2nd ed.). Auckland, New Zealand: Heinemann.

Clay, M. M. (1985). *The early detection of reading difficulties* (3rd ed.). Portsmouth, NH: Heinemann.

Clay, M. (1990). What is and what might be in evaluation. *Language Arts, 67*(3), 288–298.

Clay, M. (1991). *Becoming literate: The construction of inner control*. Portsmouth, NH: Heinemann.

Coles, G. (2001). Reading taught to the tune of the "scientific hickory stick." *Phi Delta Kappan, 83*(3), 205–214.

Collins, A., Brown, J. S., & Larkin, K. M. (1980). Inferences in text understanding. In R. Spiro, B. Bruce, & W. Brewer (eds.), *Theoretical issues in reading comprehension*. Hillsdale, NJ: Erlbaum.

Collins, J. D., & Stevens, L. M. (1997). Does Reading Recovery really work? *American School Board Journal, 184*(6), 38–39.

Collins, N. L. D., & Shaeffer, M. B. (1997). Look, listen, and learn to read. *Young Children, 52*(5), 65–68.

Comber, B. (1987). Celebrating and analyzing successful teaching. *Language Arts, 64*(2), 182–195.

Cooper, C. (1973). An outline for writing sentence-combination problems. *English Journal, 62*(1), 96–102, 108.

Cordeiro, P., Giacobbe, M., & Cazden, C. (1983). Apostrophes, quotation marks and periods: Learning punctuation in the first grade. *Language Arts, 60*, 323–332.

Cottrell, J. (1987). *Creative drama in the classroom grades 4–6: Teacher's resource book for the theatre arts*. Lincolnwood, IL: National Textbook Company.

Courtney, A. (1985). Profile: Patricia MacLachlan. *Language Arts, 62*(7), 783–787.

Cox, C. (1984). Oral language development and its relationship to reading. In R. A. Thompson & L. L. Smith (eds.), *Reading Research Review*. Minneapolis: Burgess Publisher.

Cudd, E. T., & Roberts, L. (1989). Using writing to enhance content area learning in the primary grades. *The Reading Teacher, 42*(6), 392–404.

Cullinan, B. (1987). Inviting readers to literature. In B. Cullinan (ed.), *Children's literature in the reading program*. Newark, DE: International Reading Association.

Cummins, J. (1989). *Empowering minority students*. Sacramento, CA: CABE.

Cummins, J. (1994). The acquisition of English as a second language. In K. Spangenberg-Urbschat & R. Pritchard (eds.), *Kids come in all languages: Reading instruction for ESL students*. Newark, DE: International Reading Association.

Cunningham, J., & Foster, E. O. (1978). The ivory tower connection: A case study. *The Reading Teacher, 31*(4), 365–369.

Cunningham, J. W. (2002). The National Reading Panel Report [a review]. In R. Allington (ed.), *Big brother and the national reading curriculum: How ideology trumped evidence*. Portsmouth, NH: Heinemann.

Cunningham, P. (1995). *Phonics they use: Words for reading and writing* (2nd ed.). New York: Harper-Collins College Publishers.

Cunningham, P., & Hall, D. (1997). *Month-by-month phonics for first grade*. Greensboro, NC: Carson-Dellosa.

Cunningham, P., & Hall, D. (1998). *Month-by-month phonics for upper grades*. Greensboro, NC: Carson-Dellosa.

Cunningham, P., Hall, D., & Defee, M. (1991). Nonability-grouped, multilevel instruction: A year in a first grade classroom. *The Reading Teacher, 44*, 566–571.

Cunningham, P., Hall, D., & Defee, M. (1998). Nonability-grouped, multilevel instruction: Eight years later. *The Reading Teacher, 52*(8), 652–664.

Daniels, H. (1994). *Literature circles: Voice and choice in the student-centered classroom*. New York: Stenhouse.

Davey, B. (1983). Think aloud: Modeling the cognitive processes of reading comprehension. *Journal of Reading, 27*(1), 44–47.

Davie, J., & Kemp, C. (2002). A comparison of the expressive language opportunities provided by shared book reading and facilitated play for young children with middle to moderate intellectual disabilities. *Educational Psychology, 22*(4), 445–461.

DeCarlo, J. (ed.). (1995). *Perspectives in whole language*. Boston: Allyn & Bacon.

De Fina, A. A. (1992). *Portfolio assessment: Getting started*. New York: Scholastic.

DeKroon, D., Kyte, C., & Johnson, C. (2002). Partner influences on the social pretend play of children with language impairments. *Language, Speech, & Hearing Services in Schools, 33*(4), 253–268.

Delpit, L. (1988). The silenced dialogue: Power and pedagogy in educating other people's children. *Harvard Educational Review, 58*(3), 280–298.

Delpit, L. (1995). *Other people's children: Cultural conflict in the classroom*. New York: The New Press.

Delpit, L. (1997). Ebonics and culturally responsive instruction. In "The real Ebonics debate" (T. Perry & L. Delpit, eds.). *Rethinking Schools: An Urban Education Journal,* 12(1), 6–7.

DeMott, B. (1990). Why we read and write. *Educational Leadership,* 47(6), 6.

Devine, T. (1982). *Listening skills schoolwide: Activities and progress.* Urbana, IL: NCTE.

DeVries, B. A. (2004). *Literacy assessment and intervention for the classroom teacher.* Scottsdale, AZ: Holcomb Hathaway.

Dickinson, D., & McCabe, A. (2001). Bringing it all together: The multiple origins, skills, and environmental supports of early literacy. *Disabilities Research and Practice,* 16(4), 186–202.

Dickinson, D., & Tabors, P. (eds.). (2000). *Beginning literacy with language: Young children learning at home and school.* Baltimore: Paul H. Brooks.

Dickinson, D., & Tabors, P. (2002). Fostering language and literacy in classrooms and homes. *Young Children,* 57(2), 10–18.

DiStefano, P., & Haggerty, P. (1985). Teaching spelling at the elementary level: A realistic perspective. *The Reading Teacher,* 38, 373–377.

Dodd, A. (1988). Demons, dictionaries, and spelling strategies. *English Journal,* 77, 52–53.

Doina, R. (1997). Evaluation of gifted programs. *Gifted Child Today* (Sept./Oct.), 38–40.

Donoghue, M. (1990). *The child and the English language arts* (5th ed.). Dubuque, IA: William C. Brown Co.

Draper, T., Ganong, M., & Goodell, V. (1987). *See how they grow: Concepts in child development and parenting.* Mission Hills, CA: Glencoe.

Dudley-Marling, C., & Murphy, S. (1997). A political critique of remedial reading programs: The example of Reading Recovery. *The Reading Teacher,* 50(6), 460–468.

Dugan, J. (1997). Transactional literature discussions: Engaging students in the appreciation and understanding of literature. *The Reading Teacher,* 51(2), 86–96.

Dunn, R. (1996). *How to implement and supervise a learning styles program.* Alexandria, VA: Association of Supervision and Curriculum Development.

Dunn, R., Beaudry, J., & Klavas, A. (1989). Survey of research on learning styles. *Educational Leadership,* 46(6), 50–58.

Dunn, R., Cavanaugh, D., Eberle, B., & Zenhauser, R. (1982). Hemispheric preference: The newest element of learning style. *The American Biology Teacher,* 44(5), 291–294.

Durkin, D. (1988). A classroom observation study of reading instruction in kindergarten (Technical Report No. 422). Champaign, IL: Center for the Study of Reading.

Early, M., & Barron, R. (1969). Use of the structured overview in mathematics classes. In H. Herber & P. Sanders (eds.), *Research in reading in the content areas: First year report.* Syracuse, NY: Syracuse University.

Edelsky, C. (1986). *Writing in a bilingual program. Habia una vez.* Norwood, NJ: Ablex.

Edwards, S., Maloy, R., & Verock-O'Loughlin, R. E. (2003). *Ways of writing with young kids.* Boston: Allyn & Bacon.

Elbow, P. (1973). *Writing without teachers.* New York: Oxford University Press.

Elbow, P. (1981). *Writing with power.* New York: Oxford University Press.

Eldredge, J. L., & Butterfield, D. (1986). Alternatives to traditional reading instruction. *The Reading Teacher,* 40(1), 32–37.

Elley, W. B., Barham, I. H., & Wyllie, M. (1976). The role of grammar in a secondary English curriculum. *Research in the Teaching of English,* 10, 5–21. Reprinted from *New Zealand Journal of Educational Studies,* May 1975, 10, 26–42.

Emig, J. (1971). *The composing processes of twelfth graders.* Champaign, IL: National Council of Teachers of English.

Erb, T. (2003). Raising non-standardized students to high standards of performance. *Middle School Journal,* 34(4), 4.

Ericson, L., & Juliebo, M. F. (1998). *The phonological awareness handbook for kindergarten and primary teachers.* Newark, DE: International Reading Association.

Ernst-Slavit, G., Moore, M., & Maloney, C. (2002). Changing lives: Teaching English and literature to ESL students. *Journal of Adolescent and Adult Literacy,* 46(2), 116–121.

Evans, K. (1992). Reading aloud: A bridge to independence. *The New Advocate,* 5(1), 47–57.

Ewards, P. (1996). Creating sharing time conversation: Parents and teachers work together. *Language Arts,* 73(1), 344–349.

Faires, J., Nichols, W., & Rickelman, R. (2000). Effects of parental involvement in developing competent readers in first grade. *Reading Psychology,* 21, 195–215.

Family Literacy Organization. (2003). The home literacy environment. Available at: www.famlit.org/research/research.html [2003, February 8].

Farnan, N., Flood, J., & Lapp, D. (1994). Comprehending through reading and writing: Six research-based instructional strategies. In K. Spangenberg-Urbschat & R. Pritchard (eds.), *Kids come in all languages: Reading instruction for ESL students.* Newark, DE: International Reading Association.

Farr, R. C., & Strickland, D. S. (1995). *Treasury of literature.* New York: Harcourt Brace & Company.

Farr, R., & Tone, B. (1998). *Portfolio and performance assessment: Helping students evaluate their progress as readers and writers* (2nd ed.). Fort Worth, TX: Harcourt Brace College Publishers.

Farrell, E. (1989, April). Giving voice to poetry: Oral interpretation in the classroom. Paper presented at the National Council of Teachers of English Meeting, Charleston, SC.

Farris, P. (1991). Views and other views: Handwriting instruction should not become extinct. *Language Arts,* 68, 312–314.

Fashola, O., & Slavin, R. (1997). Promising programs for elementary and middle schools: Evidence of effectiveness and replicability. *Journal of Education for Students Placed at Risk,* 2(3), 251–307.

Feder, J., & Weber, C. (1986). Remedies for reversal. *Academic Therapy*, 22(1), 87–90.

Feeley, J. (1982). Content interests and media preferences of middle graders: Differences in a decade. *Reading World*, 22(1), 11–16.

Feinstein, S. (2003, January). A case for middle school after-school programs in rural America. *Middle School Journal*, 2, 32–37.

Feldhusen, J. (1996). How to identify and develop special talents. *Educational Leadership*, 53(5), 66–69.

Ferguson, P., & Young, T. (1996). Literature talk: Dialogue improvisations and patterned conversations with second language learners. *Language Arts*, 73(8), 597–600.

Fernald, G. (1943). *Remedial techniques in basic school subjects.* New York: McGraw-Hill.

Ferriero, E., & Teberosky, A. (1983). *Writing before schooling.* Portsmouth, NH: Heinemann.

Fiderer, A. (1998). *Practical assessment for literature-based reading classrooms* (1st ed.). New York: Scholastic.

Finders, M., & Hynds, S. (2003). *Literacy lessons: Teaching and learning with middle schools students.* Upper Saddle River, NJ: Merrill/Prentice Hall.

Finn, J. (1998). Parental engagement that makes a difference. *Educational Leadership*, 55(8), 20–24.

Fisher, D., & Frey, N. (2003). Writing instruction for struggling adolescent readers: A gradual release model. *Journal of Adolescent & Adult Literacy*, 45(5), 396–405.

Flanders, N. (1970). *Analyzing teaching behavior.* Reading, MA: Addison-Wesley.

Flower, L., & Hayes, J. (1980). The cognition of discovery: Defining a rhetorical problem. *College, Composition, and Communication*, 31(1), 21–32.

Flower, L., & Hayes, J. R. (1994). The cognition of discovery: Defining a rhetorical problem. In S. Perl (ed.), *Landmark essays on writing process.* Davis, CA: Heragoras Press.

Ford, M. P. (1989–1990). Maximizing literacy opportunities through cross-age groupings. *Reading Today*, 7(3), 14.

Forsythe, S. (1995). It worked! Reader's theatre in second grade. *Language Arts*, 49(3), 264–265.

Fountas, I., & Pinnell, G. (eds.). (1999). *Voices on word matters: Learning about phonics and spelling in the literacy classroom.* Portsmouth, NH: Heinemann.

Fountas, I. C., & Pinnell, G. S. (1996). *Guided Reading.* Portsmouth, NH: Heinemann.

Fowler, D. (1998). Balanced reading instruction in practice. *Educational Leadership*, 55(6), 11–13.

Frager, A., Tway, E., Gandei, L., Hammond, T., Hordie, J., Mohler, P., & Whitt, J. (1987). The uses of free writing in the elementary school. *Oklahoma English Journal*, 2(1), 1–16.

Francis, W. (1964). Revolution in grammar. In H. Allen (ed.), *Readings in applied linguistics.* New York: Appleton-Century-Crofts.

Frazier, D., & Paulson, F. (1992). How portfolios motivate reluctant writers. *Educational Leadership*, 49(5), 62–65.

Freedman, R. (1987). *Lincoln: A photobiography.* New York: Clarion.

Freeman, D., & Freeman, Y. (2001). *Between worlds: Access to second language acquisition.* Portsmouth, NH: Heinemann.

Freshour, F., & Bartholomew, P. (1989). Let's start improving our own listening. *Florida Reading Quarterly*, 25(4), 28–30.

Fries, C. (1952). *The structure of language.* New York: Irvington.

Fry, E. (1977). Fry's readability graph: Clarifications, validity, and extensions to level 17. *Journal of Reading*, 21(3), 242–252.

Fulwiler, T. (1987). *Teaching with writing.* Portsmouth, NH: Boynton/Cook.

Fulwiler, T. (1987a). *The journal book.* Portsmouth, NH: Boynton/Cook.

Furth, H. (1970). *Piaget for teachers.* Englewood Cliffs, NJ: Prentice Hall.

Futrell, M., Gomez, J., & Bedden, D. (2003). Teaching the children of a new America: The challenge of diversity. *Phi Delta Kappan*, 84(5), 381–385.

Galda, L. (1987). Teaching higher order reading skills with literature: Intermediate grades. In B. E. Cullinan (ed.), *Children's literature in the reading program.* Newark, DE: International Reading Association.

Galindo, R. (1997). Language wars: The ideological dimensions of the debates on bilingual education. *Bilingual Research Journal*, 21(2/3), 103–141.

Gallagher, J., Harradine, C., & Coleman, M. (1997). Gifted students in the classroom. *Roper Review*, 19(3), 132–136.

Gambrell, L. (1983). The occurrence of think-time during reading comprehension instruction. *Journal of Educational Research*, 77(3), 77–80.

Gambrell, L. (1985). Reading–writing interaction. *The Reading Teacher*, 38, 512–515.

Garan, E. M. (2002). Beyond the smoke and mirrors: A critique on the National Reading Panel Report on Phonics. In R. Allington (ed.), *Big brother and the national reading curriculum: How ideology trumped evidence.* Portsmouth, NH: Heinemann.

Garcia, E. (1983). Bilingual acquisition and bilingual instruction. In T. H. Escobedo (ed.), *Early childhood bilingual education.* New York: Teacher's College Press.

Garcia, G. (1994). Assessing the literacy development of second-language students: A focus on authentic assessment. In K. Spangenberg-Urbschat & R. Pritchard (eds.), *Kids come in all languages: Reading instruction for ESL students.* Newark, DE: International Reading Association.

Garcia, M., & Verville, K. (1994). Redesigning teaching and learning: The Arizona student assessment program. In S. Valencia, E. Hiebert, & P. Afflerbach (eds.), *Authentic reading assessment: Practices and possibilities.* Newark, DE: International Reading Association.

Gardner, H. (1993). *Frames of mind: The theory of multiple intelligences.* London: Paladin Books.

Garner, W. (1984). Reading is a problem solving process: Psycholinguistic strategies. *The Reading Teacher*, 38(1), 36–39.

Gee, J. (1990). *Social linguistics and literacies: Ideology in discourses.* London: Falmer.

Gee, J. (2001). Seminar presented at the Centre for Expansion of Language and Thinking (CELT): Rejuvenation Conference. Chicago, IL. In Cambourne (2002), The conditions of learning: Is learning natural? *The Reading Teacher,* 55(8), 758–762.

Gentry, J. R. (1984). Developmental aspects of learning to spell. *Academic Therapy,* 20(1), 11–19.

Gentry, J. R. (1987). *Spel . . . is a four-letter word.* Portsmouth, NH: Heinemann.

Gentry, J. R. (2000). A retrospective on invented spelling and a look forward. *The Reading Teacher,* 59(4), 318–332.

Gersten, R., & Dimino, J. (1990). Reading instruction for at-risk students: Implications of current research. *Oregon School Study Council Bulletin,* 33(5).

Glasser, R. (1984). Education and thinking: The role of knowledge. *American Psychologist,* 39(3), 93–104.

Glazer, S. M. (1998). *Assessment is instruction: Reading, writing, spelling, and phonics for all learners.* Norwood, MA: Christopher-Gordon.

Gleason, J. B. (1967, June). Do children imitate? Paper presented at the International Conference on Oral Education of the Deaf, Lexington School for the Deaf, New York.

Goldberg, M. (1989). Portrait of James Gray. *Educational Leadership,* 47(3), 65–68.

Goldman, S. R. & Rakestraw, J A. (2000). Structural aspects of constructing meaning from text. In M. L. Kamil, P. B. Rosenthal, P. D. Pearson, & S. R. Barr (eds.), *Handbook of reading research, Volume III* (pp. 743–770). Mahwah, N. J.: Lawrence Erlbaum.

Gomez, M., Grau, M. E., & Block, M. (1991). Reassessing portfolio assessment: Rhetoric and reality. *Language Arts,* 68, 620–628.

Goodlad, J. (1997). *In praise of education.* New York: Teacher's College Press.

Goodman, K. S. (1967). Reading: A psycholinguistic guessing game. *Journal of the Reading Specialist,* 6(8), 126–135.

Goodman, K. S. (1976). Behind the eye: What happens in reading. In H. Singer & R. Ruddell (eds.), *Theoretical models and processes of reading* (2nd ed.). Newark, DE: International Reading Association.

Goodman, K. S. (1980). Viewpoints . . . from a researcher. *Language Arts,* 57(8), 846–847.

Goodman, K. S. (1986a). Basal readers: A call for action. *Language Arts,* 63(4), 358–363.

Goodman, K. (1986b). *What's whole in whole language?* Portsmouth, NH: Heinemann.

Goodman, K. S. (1992). I didn't found whole language. *The Reading Teacher,* 46(3), 188–199.

Goodman, K. (1996). *Ken Goodman on reading: A common-sense look at the nature of language and the science of reading.* Portsmouth, NH: Heinemann.

Goodman, K., & Freeman, D. (1993). What's simple in simplified language? In M. L. Tickoo (ed.), *Simplification:*

Theory and application. Anthology series 31. (ERIC Document Reproduction Service No. ED 371 578).

Goodman, Y. (1978). Kidwatching: An alternative to testing. *The National Elementary Principal,* 57(2), 41–45.

Goodman, K. & Goodman, Y. (Eds.) (1989). A kid watcher's guide to spelling. In *The whole language evaluation book.* Portsmouth, NH: Heinemann.

Goodman, Y. M. (1980, January). The roots of literacy. Paper presented at the Annual Claremont Reading Conference, Claremont, CA.

Goodman, Y. M. (1989). Roots of the whole-language movement. *The Elementary School Journal,* 90(2), 113–127.

Goodman, Y., & Burke, C. (1988). Reading: Language and psycholinguistic bases. In P. Lamb & R. Arnold (eds.), *Reading foundations and instructional strategies in place.* Katonah, NY: Richard Owens.

Gordon, C. (1985). Modeling inference awareness across the curriculum. *Journal of Reading,* 28(5), 444–447.

Goswami, U., & Bryant, P. (1990). *Phonological skills and learning to read.* Hillsdale, NJ: Erlbaum.

Graham, S. (1992). Issues in handwriting instruction. *Focus on Exceptional Children,* 25, 1–4.

Graham, S. (1999). Handwriting and spelling instruction for students with learning disabilities: A review. *Learning Disabilities Quarterly,* 22, 78–98.

Graham, S., Harris, K., & Chorzempa, B. (2002). Contributions of spelling instruction to the spelling, writing and reading of poor spellers. *Journal of Educational Psychology,* 94(4), 669–686.

Graves, D. (1973). Children's writing: Research directions and hypothesis based upon an examination of the writing processes of seven-year-old children. *Dissertation Abstracts International,* 34, 6255A. Doctoral dissertation, University of New Hampshire.

Graves, D. (1978). We won't let them write. *Language Arts,* 55, 636.

Graves, D. (1989). *Experiment with fiction.* Portsmouth, NH: Heinemann.

Graves, D. (1990, July 27). The process writing model. Paper presented at OKTAWL Conference, Norman, OK.

Graves, D. (1991). *Build a literate class.* Portsmouth, NH: Heinemann.

Graves, D. H. (1994). *A fresh look at writing.* Portsmouth, NH: Heinemann.

Graves, D. (2003). *Writing: Teachers and children at work.* Portsmouth, NH: Heinemann.

Graves, D., & Hansen, J. (1983). The author's chair. *Language Arts,* 60(2), 176–183.

Graves, M. F., Juel, C., & Graves, B. B. (1998). *Teaching reading in the 21st century.* Boston: Allyn & Bacon.

Greenlee, A., Monson, D., & Taylor, B. (1996). The lure of series books: Does it affect appreciation for recommended literature? *The Reading Teacher,* 50(3), 216–225.

Guillaume, A. (1998). Learning with text in the primary grades. *The Reading Teacher,* 51(6), 476–486.

Guthrie, J. T., & McCann, A. D. (1997). Characteristics of classrooms that promote motivations and strategies for learning. In J. T. Guthrie & A. Wigfield (eds.), *Reading engagement: Motivating readers through integrated instruction.* Newark, DE: International Reading Association.

Hahn, J. (1983, May). Organization of a young authors' fair. Paper presented at International Reading Association 28th Annual Convention, Anaheim, CA.

Haley-James, S. (ed.). (1981). *Perspectives on writing in grades 1–8.* Urbana, IL: National Council of Teachers of English.

Halle, T., Kurt-Costes, B., & Mahoney, J. (1997). Family influences on school achievement in low-income, African American children. *Journal of Education Psychology 89*, 527–537.

Halliday, M. (1975). *Learning how to mean: Explorations in the development of language.* London: Edward Arnold Publishers.

Halliday, M. (1976). *System and function in language.* London: Oxford University Press.

Halliday, M. (1977). *Explorations in the functions of language.* New York: Elsevier North-Holland.

Halliday, M. (1978). *Language as a social semiotic: The social interpretation of language and meaning.* Baltimore: University Park Press.

Halliday, M. (1982). Three aspects of children's language development: Learning language, learning through language, learning about language. In Y. Goodman, N. Haussler, & D. Strickland (eds.), *Oral and written language development research: Impact on the schools.* Urbana, IL: National Council of Teachers of English.

Hamilton, M., & Weiss, M. (1993). Children as storytellers: Teaching the basic tools. *School Library Journal, 39*(4), 30–33.

Hancock, L. (1996, February 19). Why do schools flunk biology? *Newsweek,* 58–61.

Hansen, J. (1987). *When writers read.* Portsmouth, NH: Heinemann.

Harrison, S. (1981). Open letter from a left-handed teacher: Some sinistrial ideas on the teaching of handwriting. *Teaching Exceptional Children, 13,* 116–120.

Harste, J. (1990). Jerry Harste speaks on reading and writing. *The Reading Teacher, 43*(4), 316–318.

Harwayne, S. (1992). *Lasting impressions: Weaving literature into the writing workshop.* Portsmouth, NH: Heinemann.

Hauchildt, P., & McMahon, S. (1996). Reconceptualizing "resistant" learners and rethinking instruction: Risking a trip to the swamp. *Language Arts, 73*(8), 576–596.

Heath, S. (1983). *Ways with words: Language, life and work in communities and classrooms.* New York: Cambridge University Press.

Heath, S. B. (1998). Working through language. In S. Hoyle & C. Adger (Eds.), *Kids Talk: Strategic language use in later childhood.* New York: Oxford University Press, pp. 217–240.

Heath, S. B. (2002) A lot of talk about nothing. In B. M. Power & R. S. Hubbard (Eds.), *Language development: A reader for teachers* (pp. 74–79) (2nd ed.). Upper Saddle River, NJ: Merrill Prentice Hall.

Health, S. B., & McLaughlin, M. W., eds. (1993). *Identity and inner-city youth: Beyond ethnicity and classrooms.* New York: Teachers College Press.

Heath, S. B., Soep, E., & Roach, A. (1998). Living the arts through language and learning: A report on Community-Based Youth Organizations. In *Americans for the Arts Monographs, 27,* 1–20.

Heilman, A. W. (1998). *Phonics in proper perspective* (8th ed.). Upper Saddle River, NJ: Merrill.

Henderson, A. (1988). Parents are a school's best friend. *Phi Delta Kappan, 70,* 148–153.

Henderson, E. (1985). *Teaching spelling.* Boston: Houghton Mifflin.

Henkel, J. (2002). Finding activities for kids after school. *FDA Consumer, 36*(3), 33.

Hennings, D. (1989). *Communication in action: Teaching the language arts.* Boston: Houghton Mifflin.

Herman, P. A. (1984, December). Incidental learning of word meanings from expository texts that systematically vary text features. Paper presented at the National Reading Conference, St. Petersburg, FL.

Hessong, R., & Weeks, T. (1987). *Introduction to education.* New York: Macmillan.

Hickman, J. (1984). Research currents: Researching children's responses to literature. *Language Arts, 61*(3), 278–284.

Hiebert, E. H., & Fisher, C. W. (1990). Whole language: Three themes for the future. *Educational Leadership, 47*(6), 62–64.

Hiebert, E. (2002). Standards, assessment and text difficulty. In A. E. Farstrup & S. J. Samuels (Eds.), *What research has to say about reading instruction* (pp. 337–369). Newark: DE: The International Reading Association.

Higgins, N., & Hess, L. (1999). Using electronic books to promote vocabulary development. *Journal of Research on Computing in Education* [Online], *34*(4), 6 pages. Available at: http://web22.epnet.com/com/citation.asp?tb=1&_ug=d bs+0+In+en%2Dus+sid+BE3D29A6%DF611%2D44CF%2 DBB89%2DD9D82810DF69%40 sessionmgr [2003, March 11].

Hill, B., Ruptic, C., & Norwick, L. (1998). *Classroom-based assessment.* Norwood, MA: Christopher-Gordon.

Hillocks, G. (1986). *Research on written composition.* Urbana, IL: ERIC Clearinghouse on Reading and Communication Skills.

Hillocks, G., & Smith, M. W. (1991). Grammar and usage. In J. Flood, J. M. Jensen, D. Lapp, & J. R. Squire (eds.), *Handbook of research on teaching the English language arts.* New York: Macmillan.

Hipple, M. (1985). Journal writing in kindergarten. *Language Arts, 62*(3), 255–261.

Ho, E. S., & Williams, J. (1996). Effects of parental involvement of eighth grade achievement. *Sociology of Education, 69*(2), 126–141.

Ho, B. (2002). Application of participatory action research to family school intervention. *School Psychology Review,*

31(1), 106–122. Available at: http://ehostvgw8.epmet. com/fulltext.asp?resultSetItR00000001&hitNum-8& booleanTer [2002, June 22].

Hodges, R. (1991a). The conventions of writing. In J. Flood, J. M. Jensen, D. Lapp, & J. R. Squire (eds.), *Handbook of research on teaching the English language arts.* New York: Macmillan.

Hodges, R. (1991b). Smart spelling. *Instructor, 100*(7), 69–70.

Hodgin, J., & Wooliscroft, C. (1997). Eric learns to read: Learning styles at work. *Educational Leadership, 54*(6), 43–45.

Hoffman, J. V., McCarthey, S. J., Elliott, B., Bayles, D. L., Price, D. P., Ferree, A., & Abbott, J. A. (1998). The literature-based basals in first-grade classrooms: Savior, Satan, or same-old, same-old? *Reading Research Quarterly, 33*(2), 168–197.

Holdaway, D. (1979). *The foundations of literacy.* New York: Scholastic.

Holdaway, D. (1991). Shared book experience: Teaching reading using favorite books. In C. Kamii, E. Ferreiro, F. Siegrist, H. Sinclair, B. Cuttings, J. Milligan, M. Manning, G. Manning, B. Lewis, R. Long, & B. Engle (eds.), *Early literacy: A constructivist foundation for whole language.* Washington, DC: National Education Association.

Hoover-Dempsey, D., & Sandler, H. (1997). Why do parents become involved in their children's education? *Review of Education Research, 67*, 3–42.

Hoover, M. R. (1997). Ebonics: Myth and realities. In "The real Ebonics debate" (T. Perry & L. Delpit, eds.). *Rethinking Schools: An Urban Education Journal, 12*(1), 17.

Hopkins, L. (1972). *Pass the poetry, please!* New York: Citation Press.

Howell, H. (1978). Write on, you sinistrials! *Language Arts, 55*, 852–856.

Hoyt, L. (2000). *Snapshots: Literacy minilessons up close.* Portsmouth, NH: Heinemann.

Huck, C. (1987). *Children's literature in the elementary school* (4th ed.). New York: Harcourt Brace College Publishers.

Huck, C., Hepler, S., & Hickman, J. (1993). *Children's literature in the elementary school* (5th ed.). New York: Harcourt Brace Jovanovich.

Huck, C., Hepler, S., Hickman, J. & Kiefer, B. (2001). *Children's literature in the elementary school* (7th ed.) Boston: McGraw Hill.

Hunt, L. C. (1970). The effect of self-selection, interest, and motivation upon independent, instructional, and frustration levels. *The Reading Teacher, 24*(2), 146–154.

Inhelder, B., & Piaget, J. (1964). *The early growth of logic in the child.* New York: Norton and Co.

International Reading Association. (1996). Young adults' choices for 1996. *Journal of Adolescent & Adult Literacy, 40*(3), 201–208.

International Reading Association. (1997). The role of phonics in reading instruction: A position statement of the International Reading Association. *Indiana Reading Journal, 29*(3), 23–26.

International Reading Association. (1997/1998a, December/January). Ideas for administrators: Shining examples. *Reading Today, 15*(3), 10.

International Reading Association. (1997/ 1998b, December/January). Parents and reading: Reading to young children: Statistics to consider. *Reading Today, 15*(3), 25.

International Reading Association & National Association for the Education of Young Children. (1998, July). Learning to read and write: Developmentally appropriate practices for young children. *Young Children, 53*(6), 30–46.

International Reading Association (1998). Convention tackles the big issues. *Reading Today, 15*(6), 20.

International Reading Association. (1999). *Using multiple methods of beginning reading instruction.* Newark, DE: International Reading Association.

International Reading Association. (2002). *What is evidenced-based reading instruction?* Newark, DE: International Reading Association.

Irujo, S. (1989, May). Do you know why they all talk at once? Thoughts on cultural differences between Hispanics and Anglos. *Equity and Choice,* 14–18.

Jacka, B. (1985). The teaching of defined concepts: A test of Gagne and Briggs' model of instructional design. *Journal of Educational Research, 78*(4), 224–227.

Jalongo, M. R. (1983). Bibliotherapy: Literature to promote socioemotional growth. *The Reading Teacher, 36*(8), 796–803.

Jalongo, M. (2000). *Early childhood language arts* (2nd ed.). Boston: Allyn & Bacon.

Janeczko, P. (1983). *Poetspeak: In their work, about their work.* New York: Bradbury Press.

Jarolimek, J., & Foster, C. (1985). *Teaching and learning in the elementary school.* New York: MacMillan.

Jensen, J. M., & Roser, N. L. (1990). Are there really 3 R's? *Educational Leadership, 47*(6), 7–12.

Jett-Simpson, M. (1981). Writing stories using model structures: The circle story. *Language Arts, 58*(3), 293–300.

Johns, J., & Ellis, D. (1976). Reading: Children tell it like it is. *Reading World, 16*, 115–128.

Johns, J. (1997). *Basic reading inventory—preprimer to grade eight* (7th ed.). Dubuque, IA: Kendall/Hunt Publishing Company.

Johnson, D. D. (1992). *I can't sit still.* Santa Cruz, CA: ETR Associates.

Johnson, D., & Johnson, R. (1987). *Learning together and alone: Cooperative, competitive and individualistic learning* (2nd ed.). Englewood Cliffs, NJ: Prentice Hall.

Johnson, D. D., & Pearson, P. D. (1984). *Teaching reading vocabulary* (2nd ed.). New York: Holt, Rinehart & Winston.

Johnson, D., Pittelman, S., & Heinlich, J. (1986). Semantic mapping. *The Reading Teacher, 39*(8), 778–783.

Johnston, K. (1989). Parents and reading: A U. K. perspective. *The Reading Teacher, 72*(6), 332–357.

Jones, I. (2002). Social relationships, peer collaboration and children's oral language. *Educational Psychology, 22*(1), 63–73.

Jones, K., & Ongtooguk, P. (2002, March). Equity for Alaska natives: Can high stakes testing bridge the chasm between ideals and realities? *Phi Delta Kappan, 83*(7), 494–503.

Joseph, L. (1998/1999). Word boxes help children with learning disabilities identify and spell words. *The Reading Teacher, 52*(4), 348–356.

Joyce, B., & Weil, M. (1980). Models of teaching. Englewood Cliffs, NJ: Prentice Hall.

Kagan, J. (1965). Impulsive and reflective children: Significance of conceptual tempo. In J. Krumboltz (ed.), *Learning and the education process.* Chicago: Rand McNally.

Kagan, J. (1987). Cognitive style and instructional preferences: Some influences. *Educational Forum, 51*(4), 393–403.

Kagan, J., & Kagan, N. (1970). Individual variation in cognitive process. In P. H. Mussen (ed.), *Carmichael's manual of child psychology: Vol. 1.* New York: Wiley and Co.

Kantrowitz, B., & Wingert, P. (1985, April 17). How kids learn. *Newsweek,* 50–57.

Kaufman, D. (2000). *Conferences and conversations: Listening to the literate classroom.* Portsmouth, NH: Heinemann.

Kaufman, D. (2001). Organizing and managing the language arts workshop: A matter of motion. *Language Arts, 79*(2), 114–123.

Kaufman, F. (1998). Reading report encouraging: Report supports variety of methods, bilingual education. *The Council Chronicle.* The NCTE 7(5), 1, 6.

Kaufman, M. (2002). Putting it all together: From one first-grade teacher to another. *The Reading Teacher, 55*(8), 722–726.

Kear, D., & Yellin, D. (1978, October). Oral language strategies for vocabulary development. Paper presented at SWIRA meeting, Little Rock, AR.

Kehoe, B., & Mixon, V. (1997). *Children and the Internet.* Upper Saddle River, NJ: Prentice Hall.

Kellough, R., & Roberts, P. (1991). *A resource guide for elementary school teaching: Planning for competence* (2nd ed.). New York: Macmillan.

Kemper, D., Nathan, R., & Sebranek, P. (1995). *Writers express: A handbook for young writers, thinkers, and learners.* Burlington, WI: Write Source.

Kennedy, K., Higgins, K., & Pierce, T. (2002). Collaborative partnerships among teachers of students who are gifted and have learning disabilities. *Intervention in School and Clinic* [Online], 38(1), 12 pages. Available at: http://web16.epnet.com/citation.asp?_ug=dis+I+In+en%2Dus+sid+B54AB61D%2D4B77%2D92CC%2D61C22E152CEF%40sessionmgr3%2 [2003, March 3].

Kilpatrick, W. (1993). The moral power of good stories and a selection of great books for children and teens. *American Educator: The Professional Journal of the American Federation for Teachers,* 17(2), 24–35.

King, B. (2003, January 27). After-school tutoring for at-risk students. Paper presented at Southern Nazarene University, Bethany, OK.

King, M. (1989). Speech to writing: Children's growth in writing potential. In J. Gason (ed.), *Reading and writing connections.* Boston: Allyn & Bacon.

Kintsch, W. (1998). *Comprehension: A paradigm for cognition.* Cambridge, UK: Cambridge University Press.

Kluth, P., & Darmody-Lathan, J. (2003). Beyond sight words: Literacy opportunities for students with autism. *The Reading Teacher, 56*(6), 532–534.

Koch, K. (1970). *Wishes, lies, and dreams.* New York: Chelsea House Publishers.

Koch, K. (1973). *Rose, where did you get that red?: Teaching great poetry to children.* New York: Random House.

Koenke, K. (1996). Handwriting instruction: What do we know? *Reading Teacher,* 40(2), 214–216.

Kohl, H. (1967). *36 children.* New York: Signet Press.

Kohn, A. (2000). *The case against standardized testing: Raising the scores, ruining the schools.* San Francisco: Jossey-Bass.

Kong, A., & Fitch, E. (2002/2003). Using book club to engage culturally and linguistically diverse learners in reading, writing, and talking. *The Reading Teacher, 56*(4), 352–362.

Koskinen, P., Blum, I., Bisson, S., Phillips, S., Creamer, T., & Baker, T. (1999). Shared reading books and audiotapes: Supporting diverse students in school and at home. *The Reading Teacher, 52*(5), 430–444.

Koste, V. (1988). *Dramatic play in childhood.* Lanham, MD: University Press of America.

Kozol, J. (1967). *Death at an early age.* Boston: Houghton Mifflin.

Kozol, J. (1991). *Savage inequalities: Children in America's schools.* New York: Crown Publishers.

Krashen, S. (1981). *Second language acquisition and second language learning.* Oxford: Pergamon Press.

Krashen, S. (1982). *Principles and practice in second language acquisition.* New York: Pergamon Press.

Krashen, S. (1985). *The input-hypothesis: Issues and implication.* New York: Longman.

Krashen, S. (1989). *Language acquisition and language education.* Englewood Cliffs, NJ: Prentice Hall.

Krashen, S. (1991). Bilingual education: A focus on current research. In *National Clearinghouse for Bilingual Education, vol. 3.* Washington, DC.

Krashen, S. (1993). *The power of reading: Insights from the research.* Englewood, CO: Libraries Unlimited.

LaBerge, D., & Samuels, S. J. (1985). Toward a theory of automatic information processing in reading. In H. Singer & R. Ruddell (eds.), *Theoretical models and processes of reading.* Newark, DE: International Reading Association.

Labov, W. (1985). The logic of non-standard English. In P. P. Giglioli (ed.), *Language and social context.* New York: Viking Press.

Laminack, L. (1991). *Learning with Zachery*. Portsmouth, NH: Heinemann.

Lamme, L. (1979). Handwriting in an early childhood curriculum. *Young Children*, 20–27.

Lamme, L. (1984). *Growing up writing: Sharing with your children the joys of good writing*. Washington, DC: Acropolis Books.

Lamme, L. L. (1987). Children's literature: The natural way to learn to read. In B. E. Cullinan (ed.), *Children's literature in the reading program*. Newark, DE: International Reading Association.

Lamme, L. (1989). Authorship: A key facet of whole language. *The Reading Teacher, 42*, 704–710.

Lapp, D., & Flood, J. (1994). Integrating the curriculum: The steps. *The Reading Teacher 47*, 416–419.

Lapp, D., Flood, J., & Farnan, N. (1996). *Content area reading and writing instructional strategies* (2nd ed.). Boston: Allyn & Bacon.

Lass, R. (1984). *Phonology: An introduction to basic concepts*. New York: Cambridge University Press.

Laughlin, M., & Latrobe, K. (1990). *Reader's theatre for children: Scripts and script development*. Englewood, CO: Litran's Unlimited.

Lee, D., & Rubin, J. (1979). *Children and language*. Belmont, CA: Wadsworth.

Lemberger, N. (1997). *Bilingual education: Teachers' narratives*. Mahwah, NJ: Lawrence Erlbaum.

Lenneberg, E. (1967). *Biological foundations of language*. New York: John Wiley & Sons.

Leu, D. J. (1997). Exploring literacy on the Internet: Caity's question: Literacy as deixis on the Internet. *The Reading Teacher, 51*(1), 62–67.

Leu, D. J. (2000). Literacy and technology: Deictic consequences in literacy education in an information age. In M. L. Kamil, P. B. Mosenthal, P. D. Pearson, & R. Barr (Eds.), *Handbook of reading research*, Volume III (pp. 743–770). Mahwah, NJ: Lawrence Erlbaum.

Leu, D. (2001). Internet Project: Preparing students for new literacies in a global village. *The Reading Teacher, 54*(6), 568–572.

Leu, D. (2002). Internet Workshop: Making time for literacy. *The Reading Teacher, 55*(5), 466–472.

Leu, D., & Kinzer, C. (2003). *Effective literacy instruction: Implementing best practice* (5th ed.). Upper Saddle River, NJ: Merrill/Prentice Hall.

Leu, D. J., & Leu, D. D. (2000). *Teaching with the Internet: Lessons from the classroom*, (3rd ed.). Norwood, MA: Christopher–Gordon.

Levin, J. (1986). Four cognitive principles of learning-strategy innovation. *Educational Psychologist, 21*(1–2), 3–17.

LeVine, J. (2002). Writing letters to support literacy. *The Reading Teacher, 56*(3), 232–234.

Levy, J. (1982). Children think with whole brains. In *Student learning styles and brain behavior*. Reston, VA: National Association of Secondary School Principals.

Lewis, A. (2002, November). A horse called NCLB. *Phi Delta Kappan, 84*(3), 179–180.

Lewis, R., & Morris, J. (1998). Communities for children. *Educational Leadership, 55*(8), 34–36.

Linderman, E., & Linderman, M. (1984). *Arts and crafts for the classroom* (2nd ed.). New York: Macmillan.

Lindfors, J. (1987). *Children's language and learning* (2nd ed.). Englewood Cliffs, NJ: Prentice Hall.

Loban, W. (1963). *The language of elementary school children (Reading Research Report #1)*. Champaign, IL: National Council of Teachers of English.

Lomax, R. G., & McGee, L. M. (1987). Young children's concepts about print and reading. *Reading Research Quarterly, 22*(2), 237–256.

Love, F. (1996). Communication with parents: What beginning teachers can do. *College Student Journal, 30*(4), 440–445. Available at: http://ehostvgw*epnet.com/get_sml.asp?booleanTerm=School%20home%20relationships.

Lyon, G. R. (1998). Why reading is not a natural process. *Educational Leadership, 55*(6), 14–18.

MacLean, M. (1985, April). Writing to learn about literature. Paper presented at National Council of Teachers of English, Houston, TX.

Madden, N., Livingston, M., & Cummings, N. (1995). *Facilitator's manual for success for all/roots and wings*. Baltimore: Johns Hopkins University, Center for Research on the Education of Students Placed at Risk.

Mandler, J. M., & Johnson, N. S. (1977). Remembrance of things parsed: Story structure and recall. *Cognitive Psychology, 9*(1), 111–151.

Manning, M., Manning, G., & Long, R. (1994). *Theme immersion inquiry-based curriculum in elementary and middle schools*. Portsmouth, NH: Heinemann.

Manning, M., Manning, P., & Hughes, D. (1987). Journals in first grade: What children write. *Reading Teacher, 41*(3), 311–315.

Manzo, A. V. (1968). Improving reading comprehension through reciprocal questioning. Unpublished doctoral dissertation, Syracuse University, NY.

Manzo, A. V. (1969). The ReQuest procedure. *Journal of Reading, 13*(3), 123–126.

Manzo, A., Manzo, U., & Estes, T. (2000). *Content area literacy* (3rd ed.). New York: John Wiley & Sons.

Marlow, L., & Reese, D. (1992). Strategies for using literature with at-risk readers. *Reading Improvement, 29*(2), 130–132.

Marshall, N. (1983). Using story grammar to assess reading comprehension. *The Reading Teacher, 36*(7), 616–619.

Martinez, M., Roser, N., & Strecker, S. (1998/1999). "I never thought I could be a star": A reader's theatre ticket to fluency. *The Reading Teacher, 52*(4), 326–334.

Marzano, R. (1992). *A different kind of classroom: Thinking with dimensions of learning*. Alexandria, VA: Association of Supervision and Curriculum Development.

McCarthy, B. (1997). A tale of four learners: 4MAT's learning styles. *Educational Leadership, 54*(6), 46–53.

McCaslin, N. (1990). *Creative drama in the classroom* (5th ed.). New York: Longman.

McCaslin, N. (1996). *Creative drama in the classroom* (6th ed.). New York: Longman.

McClure, E. F. (1977). *Aspects of code-switching in the discourse of bilingual Mexican-American children.* (Technical Report No. 44). Urbana, IL: Center for the Study of Reading.

McCormick, L., & Schiefelbusch, R. L. (1984). *Early language intervention.* Columbus, OH: Charles E. Merrill.

McCracken, R. (1971). Initiating sustained silent reading. *Journal of Reading, 14*(8), 521–524, 582–583.

McGee, L., & Richgels, D. J. (1985). Teaching expository text structure to elementary students. *The Reading Teacher, 38*(8), 739–748.

McInerney, D., & McInerney, V. (1998). The goals of schooling in culturally diverse classrooms. *The Clearinghouse, 71*(6), 363–366.

McKay, D. (1972). The structure of words and syllables: Evidence from errors in speech. *Cognitive Psychology, 3,* 210–227.

McKenna, E. (1997). Gender differences in reading attitudes. Unpublished master's thesis, Kean College of New Jersey, ED 407653.

McKenna, M. C., & Robinson, R. D. (1990). Content literacy: A definition and implications. *Journal of Reading, 34*(3), 184–186.

McKenna, M., Kear, D., & Ellsworth, R. (1995). Children's attitudes toward reading: A national survey. *Reading Research Quarterly, 30*(4), 934–956.

McMackin, M. C. (1993). The parent's role in literacy development. *Childhood Education, 69*(3), 142–145.

McNeil, D. (1970). *The acquisition of language.* New York: Harper & Row.

McQuade, F. (1980). Examining a grammar course: The rational and the result. *English Journal, 69,* 26–30.

McQuillas, J., & Au, J. (2001). The effect of print access on reading frequency. *Reading Psychology, 22,* 225–248.

Meier, D. (2002, November). Standardization versus standards. *Phi Delta Kappan, 84*(3), 190–198.

Meinbach, A. M., Rothlein, L., & Fredricks, A. (1995). *The complete guide to thematic units: Creating the integrated curriculum.* Norwood, MA: Christopher-Gordon.

Mellon, J. (1969). *Transformational sentence combining: Method of enhancing the development of syntactic fluency in English composition* (Research Report No. 10). Urbana, IL: NCTE.

Mendelsohn, A., Mogilner, L., Dreyer, B., Forman, J., Weinstein, S., Broderick, M., Cheng, K., Magloire, T., Moore, T., & Napier, C. (2001). The impact of clinic-based literacy intervention on language development in inner-city preschool children. *Pediatrics* [Online], 107, 11 pages. Available at: http://web12.epnet.com/citation.asp?tb=1&_ug=dbs+0+In=en%2Dus+sid+36BEAOCF%2D16B9%2D44BC%2D9103%2DEE2340F26324%40sessionmgr [2003, February 14].

Menyuk, P. (1988). *Language development: Knowledge and use.* Glenview, IL: Scott Foresman.

Mersereau, I., Glover, M., & Cherland, M. (1989). Dancing on the edge. *Language Arts, 66*(2), 28–32.

Metsala, J., Brody, G., Stoneman, Z., & McCoy, J. (1995/1996). How caregivers support literacy development of Head Start graduates in a rural setting. *The Reading Teacher, 49*(4), 340–342.

Meyer, B. J. F. (1975). *The organization of prose and its effect in memory.* Amsterdam: North-Holland.

Meyer, B., & Freedle, R. (1979). *The effects of different discourse types on recall.* Princeton, NJ: Educational Testing Service.

Meyers, R. (2002). Captives of the script: Killing us softly with phonics. *Language Arts, 79*(6), 452–461.

Mickelson, N. (1989). Point/counterpoint: The value of basal readers. *Reading Today, 7*(1), 18.

Micklos, J. (Ed.). Young authors create "Techno Books." *Reading Today, 20*(3), p. 10.

Miles, S. (1991). *Adoption literature for children and young adults: An annotated bibliography.* Westport, CT: Greenwood Press.

Miller, I. (1985). *Semantics and syntax: Parallels and connections.* New York: Cambridge University Press.

Miller, W. H. (1995). *Alternative assessment techniques for reading & writing.* West Nyack, NY: The Center for Applied Research in Education.

Miller, W. (2000). *Strategies for developing emergent literacy.* Boston: McGraw-Hill.

Moats, L. C. (1995). *Spelling: Development, disability and instruction.* Baltimore: York Press.

Moffett, J. (1968). *Teaching the universe of discourse.* Boston: Houghton Mifflin.

Moffett, J., & Wagner, B. (1983). *Student-centered language arts and reading, K–13* (3rd ed.). Boston: Houghton Mifflin.

Moffett, J., & Wagner, B. (1991). *Student-centered language arts* (4th ed.). Boston: Houghton Mifflin.

Monahan, J., & Hinson, B. (eds.). (1988). *New directions in reading instruction.* Newark, DE: International Reading Association.

Moore, D. W., & Moore, S. A. (1986). Possible sentences. In E. K. Dishner, T. W. Bean, J. E. Readence, & D. W. Moore (eds.), *Reading in the content areas* (2nd ed.). Dubuque, IA: Kendall/Hunt.

Moore, S. (1986). Curse you, cursive writing. *Reading Research and Instruction, 25*(2), 139–141.

Moore, S. (1995). Focus on research: Questions for research into reading-writing relationships and text structure knowledge. *Language Arts, 72*(8), 598–606.

Moran, B., & Steinfirst, S. (1985). Why Johnny (and Jane) read whodunits in series. *School Library Journal, 31*(7), 113–117.

Morgan, N., & Saxton, J. (1988). Enriching language through drama. *Language Arts, 65*(1), 34–50.

Morine, H., & Morine, G. (1975). *Discovery: A challenge to teachers.* Englewood Cliffs, NJ: Prentice Hall.

Morrow, L. M. (1985). Reading and retelling stories: Strategies for emergent readers. *The Reading Teacher, 38*(9), 870–875.

Morrow, L. M. (1999). Where do we go from here in early literacy research and practice. *Issues in Education* [Online], 7 pages. Available at: http:web4.epnet.com/citation.asp?tb=1&_ug=dbs+0+In+en%2Dus+sid+11531C61%2D7BI [2003, February 3].

Moustafa, M. (1997). *Beyond traditional phonics: Research discoveries and reading instruction.* Portsmouth, NH: Heinemann.

Mundi, S. (1989). Rent-a-Reader. *Learning, 17*(5), 70.

Murray, D. (1978). Internal revision: A process of discovery. In C. Cooper & L. Odell (eds.), *Research on composing: Points of departure.* Urbana, IL: NCTE.

Murray, D. (1985). *A writer teaches reading* (2nd ed.). Boston: Houghton Mifflin.

Murray, D. (1990). *Write to learn* (3rd ed.). New York: Holt, Rinehart & Winston.

NAEP Facts. (1996). National Center for Education Statistics. Washington, DC: U. S. Department of Education, p. 1.

Nagy, W. E., & Scott, J. A. (1990). Word schemas: Expectations about the form and meaning of words. *Cognition and Instruction, 7,* 105–127.

National Assessment of Educational Progress. (1996, March). NAEP 1994 reading report card: Findings from the National Assessment of Educational Progress. Available at: www.nces.ed.gov/NAEP/y25flk/rrcexec.shtml [1998, July 15].

National Assessment of Educational Progress (NAEP) (2001). *The nation's report card: Fourth-grade reading 2000.* Washington, DC: U. S. Department of Education.

National Center for Education Statistics (2000). Dropout rates in the United States: 2000, pages 1–2. Available at http://nces.ed.gov [March 12, 2003].

National Center for Family Literacy (1998). Research: Literacy facts and figures, 1–59. Available at: www.famlit.org. (2003, February 2).

National Center for Family Literacy. (2003). The home literacy environment. Available at: www.famlit.org/research/research.html [2003, February 8].

Neill, S. B. (1982). *Teaching writing: Problems and solutions.* Arlington, VA: American Association of School Administrators. (ERIC Document 191 007).

Newkirk, T. (1978). Grammar instruction and writing: What we don't know. *English Journal, 67,* 48–54.

News of the profession: The city that reads. (1997/1998, December/January). *Reading Today, 15*(3), 27.

Nilsen, D., & Nilsen, A. (1978). *Language play: An introduction to linguistics.* Rowley, MA: Newbury House Publishers.

Noguchi, R. (1991). *Grammar and the teaching of writing: Limits and possibilities.* Urbana, IL: National Council of Teachers of English.

Norton, D. (1989). *The effective teaching of language arts* (1st ed.). Columbus, OH: Merrill.

Norton, D. E. (1990). Teaching multicultural literature in the reading curriculum. *The Reading Teacher, 44*(1), 28–40.

Norton, D. (1997). *The effective teaching of language arts* (5th ed.). Columbus, OH: Merrill.

Oetting, J., & McDonald, J. (2002). Methods for characterizing participants' non-mainstream dialect use in child language research. *Journal of Speech and Language & Hearing Research* [Online], *45*(3), 19 pages. Available at: http://web1.epnet.com/citation.asp?tb=1%_ug=dbs+I+In+en%2Dus+sid+650AC4B5%2D381A%2D405F%2DA95D%2DB4510FEDDE9A%40Sessionmgr

Ogbu, J. (1978). *Minority education and caste.* New York: Academic Press.

Ogbu, J. (1985). Research currents: Cultural-ecological influences on minority school learning. *Language Arts, 62*(8), 860–869.

Ogbu, J., & Simons, H. [AU: Change initial to "J"?](1994). *Cultural models of literacy: A comparative study.* Berkeley, CA: National Center for the Study of Writing and Literacy.

Oglan, G. (2003). *Write, right, rite.* Boston: Allyn & Bacon.

Ogle, D. M. (1986). K-W-L. A teaching model that develops active reading of expository text. *The Reading Teacher, 39*(7), 564–570.

O'Gorman-Hughes, C. (2002). Toys and materials as setting events for the social interaction of preschool children with special needs. *Educational Psychology, 22*(4), 429–445.

O'Halloran, S. (1988). An experienced teacher tells how. In J. Hancock & S. Hill (eds.), *Literature-based reading programs at work.* Portsmouth, NH: Heinemann.

Ohanian, S. (1999). *One size fits few: The folly of educational standards.* Portsmouth, NH: Heinemann.

O'Hare, F. (1973). *Sentence combining: Improving student writing without formal grammar instruction* (Research Report No. 15). Urbana, IL: NCTE.

Oklahoma State Department of Education. (1993). *Regulations for gifted and talented education.* Oklahoma City, OK: Oklahoma State Department of Education.

Oklahoma State Department of Education (2002). *Priority Academic Student Skills (PASS).* Oklahoma City, OK: Oklahoma State Department of Education.

Olson, M., Gee, I., & Forester, N. (1989). Magazines in the classroom: Beyond recreational reading. *The Journal of Reading, 32*(8), 708–713.

O'Neil, W. (1997). If Ebonics isn't language, then tell me, what is? In "The real Ebonics debate" (T. Perry & L. Delpit, eds.). *Rethinking Schools: An Urban Education Journal, 12*(1), 17.

Organization for Economic Co-operation and Development and Statistics Canada (1998, July 13). Literacy, economy, and society: Results of the first international adult literacy survey, 1995. Available at: http://nces.ed.gov/pubsearch/index.html [1998, July 15].

Ornstein, R. (1977). *The psychology of consciousness.* New York: Harcourt Brace Jovanovich.

Overstad, B. (1981). *Bibliotherapy: Books to help young children.* St. Paul, MN: Toys 'n Things Press.

Palincsar, A. S., & Brown, A. L. (1986). Interactive teaching to promote independent learning from text. *The Reading Teacher, 39*(8), 771–777.

Pantier, T. (1998). *A comparison of writing performance of fifth grade students using the process writing approach and the Shurley Method*. Unpublished doctoral dissertation. Oklahoma State University, Stillwater.

Paris, S. G., Lipson, M. Y., & Wixson, K. K. (1983). Becoming a strategic reader. *Contemporary Educational Psychology, 8*(3), 293–316.

Parks, S., & Black, H. (1990). *Organizing thinking: Graphic organizers*. Pacific Grove, CA: Critical Thinking Press and Software.

Payne, R. (2001). *A framework for understanding poverty*. Highlands, TX: aha! Process.

Pavonetti, L. M., Brimmer, K. M., & Cipielewski, J. E. (2002–2003). Accelerated Reader: What are the lasting effects on the reading habits of middle school students exposed to Accelerated Reader in elementary grades? *Journal of Adolescent & Adult Literacy, 46*(4), 300–311.

Pearson, P. D. (1985). Changing the face of reading comprehension instruction. *The Reading Teacher, 38*(8), 724–738.

Pearson, P. D., & Fielding, L. (1982). Research update: Listening comprehension. *Language Arts, 59*(6), 617–629.

Pearson, P. D., & Johnson, D. D. (1985). *Teaching reading comprehension*. New York: Holt, Rinehart & Winston.

Pearson, P. D., Roehler, L. R., Dole, J. A., & Duffy, G. G. (1992). Developing expertise in reading comprehension. In S. J. Samuels & A. E. Farstrup (eds.), *What research has to say about reading instruction* (2nd ed.). Newark, DE: International Reading Association.

Peck, M., Askov, E., & Fairchild, S. (1980). Another decade of research in handwriting: Progress and prospect in the 1970s. *Journal of Education Research, 73*, 283–298.

Peek, D. (1998). *Report portfolio: The Accelerated Reader*. Wisconsin Rapids: Advantage Systems.

Pennock, C. (1984). Choral reading of poetry improves reading fluency. *Highway One, 7*(3), 21–22.

Peregoy, S., & Boyle, O. (1997). *Reading, writing and learning in ESL: A resource book for K–12 teachers*. New York: Longman.

Perrine, L. (1962). *Poetry: Theory and practice*. New York: Harcourt Brace Jovanovich.

Perry, T. (1997). "I'on know why they be trippin.'" In "The real Ebonics debate" (T. Perry & L. Delpit, eds.). *Rethinking Schools: An Urban Education Journal, 12*(1), 3–4.

Piaget, J. (1952). *The origin of intelligence in children*. New York: International Universities Press.

Piaget, J. (1959). *The language and thought of the child* (A. Gabain, trans.). London: Routledge & Kegan Paul.

Piaget, J. (1964). *The psychology of intelligence*. Boston: Routledge and Kegan Paul.

Piaget, J. (1965). *The language and thought of the child*. New York: Meridian Books.

Piaget, J. (1967). Language and thought from the genetic point of view. In D. Elkind (ed.), *Six psychological studies* (A. Tenzer, trans.). New York: Random House.

Piaget, J. (1983). Piaget's theory. In W. Kessen (Ed.), *Handbook of Child Psychology*, Vol. 1, 103–128. New York: Wiley.

Piazza, C. (1999). *Multiple forms of literacy: Teaching literacy and the other arts*. Upper Saddle River, NJ: Merrill.

Piccolo, J. A. (1987). Expository text structure: Teaching and learning strategies. *The Reading Teacher, 40*(9), 838–847.

Pines, M. (1981, September). The civilizing of Genie. *Psychology Today*, 28–34.

Pinnell, G. (1984). Communication in small group settings. *Theory into Practice, 23*(3), 246–254.

Pinnell, G. (1985). Ways to look at the functions of children's language. In A. Jaggar & M. T. Smith-Burke (eds.), *Observing the language learner*. Newark, DE: International Reading Association.

Pinnell, G. S. (1988). *Success of children at risk in a program that combines writing and reading* (Technical Report No. 417). Champaign, IL: Center for the Study of Reading.

Pinnell, G., & Jaggar, A. (1992). Oral language: Speaking and listening in the classroom. In J. Flood et al. (eds.), *Handbook of research in teaching the English language arts*. New York: Macmillan.

Pinnell, G. S., DeFord, D. E., & Lyons, C. A. (1988). *Reading Recovery: Early intervention for at-risk first graders*. Arlington, VA: Educational Research Service.

Pinnell, G. S., Fried, M. D., & Estice, R. M. (1990). Reading Recovery: Learning how to make a difference. *The Reading Teacher, 43*(4), 282–295.

Pixton, W. (1978). *Some conventions of standard written English* (2nd ed.). Dubuque, IA: Kendall/Hunt.

Pogrow, S. (1990). Challenging at-risk students: Findings from the HOTS program. *Phi Delta Kappan, 71*(5), 389–397.

Polette, N. (1986). *Reader's theatre from fairy tales, fantasy and myth*. St. Louis, MO: Book Lures.

Pool, C. (1997). Maximizing learning: A conversation with Renate Nummela Cain. *Educational Leadership, 54*(6), 11–15.

Pooley, R. (1957). *Teaching English grammar*. New York: Appleton-Century-Crofts.

Pransky, K., & Bailey, F. (2002/2003). To meet your students where they are, first you have to find them: Working with culturally and linguistically diverse at-risk students. *The Reading Teacher, 56*(4), 370–383.

Pressley, M. (2002). *Reading instruction that works: The case for balanced teaching*. (2nd ed.). New York: Guilford Press.

Purcell-Gates, V. (2000). Family literacy. In M. L. Kamil, P. B. Mosenthal, P. D. Pearson, & R. Barr (Eds.), *Handbook of Reading Research*, Volume III (pp. 853–870). Mahwah, NJ: Lawrence Erlbaum Associates, Publishers.

Raphael, T. (1982). Teaching questioning–answer strategies for children. *The Reading Teacher, 36*(2), 186–191.

Raphael, T. E. (1984). Teaching learners about sources of information for answering comprehension questions. *Journal of Reading, 27*(4), 303–311.

Raphael, T. E. (1986). Teaching question–answer relationships, revisited. *The Reading Teacher, 39*(5), 516–522.

Rasinski, T. V. (1989). Reading and the empowerment of parents. *The Reading Teacher, 43*(3), 226–231.

Rasinski, T., & Padak, N. (2000). *Effective reading strategies: Teaching children who find reading difficult.* Upper Saddle River, NJ: Merrill.

Read, C. (1986). *Children's creative spelling.* London: Routledge & Kegan Paul.

Reis, S., & Renzulli, J. (1992). Using curriculum compacting to challenge the above-average. *Educational Leadership, 49*(2), 51–57.

Reis, S., Gentry, M., & Park, S. (1996). Extending the pedagogy of gifted education to all students. [Online]. (1998). Available at: www.eskimo.com/~user/zbrief.html.

Reising, B., & Perry, J. (2001). Oral language and the Black dialect speaker. *Clearing House* [Online], 75(2), 2 pages. Available at: http://web20.epnet.com/citation.asp?tb=1&_ug=dis+)+In+en%2Dus+sid+9E8F232C%2D6DD2%2D489B%2DB01EED139435%40sessionmgr [2002, November 19].

Renzulli, J. (1994). *Schools for talent development: A comprehensive plan for total school improvement.* Mansfield Center, CT: Creative Learning Press.

Renzulli, J. (1994/1995). Teachers as talent scouts. *Educational Leadership, 52*(4), 75–81.

Renzulli, J. (2002). Expanding the conception of giftedness to include co-cognitive traits and to promote social capital. *Phi Delta Kappan, 84*(1), 33–40.

Renzulli, J., & Reis, S. (1985). *The schoolwide enrichment model.* Mansfield Center, CT: Creative Learning Press.

Renzulli, J., & Smith, L. H. (1978). *A guidebook for developing individualized educational programs for gifted and talented students.* Mansfield Center, CT: Creative Learning Press.

Reutzel, D. R. (1985). Story maps improve comprehension. *The Reading Teacher, 38*(4), 400–404.

Reutzel, D. R (1989). Point/counterpoint: The value of basal readers. *Reading Today, 7*(1), 18.

Reutzel, D. R. (1999a). A balanced reading approach: Spotlight on theory. In J. Baltas & S. Shafer (eds.), *Guide to balanced reading: 3–6—Making it work for you!* New York: Scholastic.

Reutzel, D. R. (1999b). On balanced reading. *The Reading Teacher, 52*(4), 2–4.

Reutzel, D., & Cooter, R. (1991). Organizing for effective instruction: The reading workshop. *The Reading Teacher, 44*(8), 548–554.

Reutzel, D. R., & Cooter, R. B. (2003). *Strategies for reading assessment and instruction: Helping every child succeed* (2nd ed.). Upper Saddle River, NJ: Merrill.

Reutzel, D. R., & Fawson, P. (1990). Traveling tales: Connecting parents and children through writing. *The Reading Teacher, 44*, 545–554.

Reutzel, D. R., & Hollingsworth, P. M. (1988). Whole language and the practitioner. *Academic Therapy, 23*(4), 405–415. [AU: 416 meant?]

Rhodes, L., & Dudley-Marling, C. (1996). *Readers and writers with a difference* (2nd ed.). Portsmouth, NH: Heinemann.

Rhoten, L., & Yellin, D. (1993). Bookbinding: Promoting authorship in emerging readers. In C. Collins (ed.), *Teaching the language arts.* Boston: Allyn & Bacon.

Rice, J. (1987). The futility of the spelling grind. *The Forum, 23*, 163–172, 409–419.

Richards, J. C., & Anderson, N. A. (2003). What do I See? What do I Think? What do I Wonder? (STW): A visual literacy strategy to help emergent readers focus on storybook illustrations. *The Reading Teacher, 56*(5), 442–443.

Richmond, P. (1970). *An introduction to Piaget.* New York: Basic Books.

Rickards, D., & Cheek, E. (1999). *Designing rubrics for K–6 classroom assessment.* Norwood, MA: Christopher-Gordon.

Rickford, J. (1997a). Holding on to a language of our own. In "The real Ebonics debate" (T. Perry & L. Delpit, eds.). *Rethinking Schools: An Urban Education Journal, 12*(1), 12–13.

Rickford, J. (1997b, December). Suite for Ebony and phonics. *Discover Magazine,* pp. 82–87.

Rief, L. (1990). Finding the value in evaluation: Self-assessment in a middle school classroom. *Educational Leadership, 47*(6), 24–29.

Rief, L. (1999). *Vision and voice: Extending the literacy spectrum.* Portsmouth, NH: Heinemann.

Riefer, D. (1987). Is backward reading an effective proofreading strategy? ERIC Document ED 281 175.

Riesman, D. (1961). *The lonely crowd.* New Haven, CT: Yale University Press.

Rogoff, B. (1990). *Apprenticeship in thinking: Cognitive development in social context.* New York: Oxford University Press.

Rollin, L. W. (1985). Exploring Earthsea: A sixth grade literature project. *Children's Literature in Education, 16*(4), 195–202.

Rollock, B. (1988). *Black authors and illustrators of children's books.* New York: Garland.

Rolon, C. A. (2002/2003). Educating Latino students. *Educational Leadership, 60*(4), 40–43.

Rose, L., & Gallup, A. (1998). The 30th annual Phi Delta Kappa/Gallup poll on the public's attitudes toward public schools. *Phi Delta Kappan, 80*(1), 41–58.

Rose, L. C., & Gallup, A. M. (2002). The 34th annual Phi Delta Kappa/Gallup Poll of the public's attitude toward the public schools. *Phi Delta Kappan, 84*(1), 41–56.

Rosen, L. M. (1987). Developing corrections in student writing: Alternative to the error hunt. *English Journal, 76*(3), 62–69.

Rosenblatt, L. M. (1978). *The reader, the text, the poem: The transactional theory of literary work.* Carbondale: Southern Illinois University Press.

Rosenblatt, L. (1989). Writing and reading: The transactional theory. In J. Mason (ed.), *Reading and writing connections.* Boston: Allyn & Bacon.

Rosenblatt, L. M. (1994). The transactional theory of reading and writing. In R. B. Ruddell, M. R. Ruddell, & H. Singer (eds.), *Theoretical models and processes of reading* (4th ed.). Newark, DE: International Reading Association.

Rosenshine, B., Meister, C., & Chapman, S. (1996). Teaching students to generate questions: A review of the intervention studies. *Review of Educational Research, 66*, 181–221.

Rosenthal, R., & Jacobson, L. (1968). *Pygmalion in the classroom.* New York: Holt, Rinehart & Winston.

Roser, N., Hoffman, J., & Farest, C. (1990, April). Language, literature and at-risk children. *The Reading Teacher, 43*(8), 554–559.

Ross, C. (1995). If they read Nancy Drew, so what?: Series book readers talk back. *Library and Information Science Research, 17*(3), 201–236.

Ross, R. (1996). *Storyteller.* Little Rock, AR: August House Publishers.

Ross, S. M., Smith, L. J., & Casey, J. P. (1997). Preventing early school failure: Impacts of Success for All on standardized test outcomes, minority group performance, and school effectiveness. *Journal of Education for Students Placed at Risk, 2*(1), 29–53.

Ross, S. M., Smith, L. J., Madden, N. A., & Slavin, R. E. (1997). Improving the academic success of disadvantaged children: An examination of Success for All. *Psychology in the Schools, 34*(2), 171–180.

Rotherman, K. (1987). Guided investigation. *School Science Review, 68*(2), 631–634.

Routman, R. (1991). *Invitations.* Portsmouth, NH: Heinemann.

Routman, R. (1996). *Literacy at the crossroads: Crucial talk about reading, writing and other teaching dilemmas.* Portsmouth, NH: Heinemann.

Ruddell, R., & Unrau, N. J. (1994). Reading as a meaning-construction process: The reader, the text, and the teacher. In R. B. Ruddell, M. R. Ruddell, & H. Singer (eds.), *Theoretical models and processes of reading* (4th ed.). Newark, DE: International Reading Association.

Rumberger, R., & Larsen, K. (1998). Toward explaining differences in educational achievement among Mexican-American language-minority students. *Sociology of Education, 71*(1), 68–92.

Rumelhart, D. E. (1980). Schemata: The building blocks of cognition. In R. Spiro, B. Bruce, & W. Brewer (eds.), *Theoretical issues in reading comprehension.* Hillsdale, NJ: Erlbaum.

Rupley, W., Logan, J., & Nichols, W. (1998/1999). Vocabulary instruction in a balanced reading program. *The Reading Teacher, 52*(4), 336–346.

Rush, K. (1999). Caregiver-child interactions and early literacy development of preschool children from low-income environments. *Topics in Early Childhood Special Education* [Online], 19, 20 pages. Available at: http://web4.epnet.com/citation.asp? tb=1&ug=dbs+0+In+en%2Dus+sid+11531C61%2D7BI [2003, February 3].

Ryan, M. (1989, July 23). We can turn our schools around. *Gainesville Sun, Parade Magazine,* pp. 10–11.

Ryan, R., Connell, J., & Deci, E. (1985). A motivational analysis of self-determination and self-regulation in education. In C. Ames & R. Ames (eds.), *Research on motivation in education: The classroom milieu.* New York: Academic Press.

Saccardi, M. C. (1996). Predictable books: Gateways to a lifetime of reading (teaching reading). *The Reading Teacher, 49*(7), 588–590.

Salinger, T. (1988). *Language arts and literacy for young children.* Columbus, OH: Merrill.

Sampson, M. (2002, March). Confirming a K-W-L: Considering the source. *The Reading Teacher, 55*(6), 528–532.

Sapir, E. (1921). *Language: An introduction to speech.* New York: Harcourt Brace Jovanovich.

Sapon-Shevin, M. (1994/1995). Why gifted students belong in inclusive schools. *Educational Leadership, 52*(4), 64–67.

Sarafino, E., & Armstrong, J. (1986). *Child and adolescent development* (2nd ed.). St. Paul, MN: West Publishing Co.

Savage, J. (1998). *Teaching reading and writing: Combining skills, strategies and literacy* (2nd ed.). Boston: McGraw-Hill.

Schifini, A. (1994). Language, literacy, and content instruction: Strategies for teachers. In K. Spangenberg-Urbschat & R. Pritchard (eds.), *Kids come in all languages: Reading instruction for ESL students.* Newark, DE: International Reading Association.

Schirmer, B., Casbon, J., & Twiss, L. (1996). Diverse learners in the classroom. *The Reading Teacher, 49*(5), 412–414.

Searfoss, L. W., & Dishner, E. K. (1977). Improving comprehension through the ReQuest procedure. *Reading Education: A Journal for Australian Teachers, 2*, 22–25.

Searfoss, L., Readence, J., & Mallette, M. (2001). *Helping children learn to read.* (4th ed.) Boston: Allyn and Bacon.

Sebesta, S., Calder, J., & Cleland, L. N. (1981). Story structure in children's book choices. Paper presented at the Conference on Language Arts in the Elementary School, Portland, OR.

Sebranek, P., Meyer, V., & Kemper, D. (1995). *Write source 2000: A guide to writing, thinking, and learning* (3rd ed.). Burlington, WI: Write Source.

Seely, A. (1995). *Integrated thematic units.* Westminster, CA: Teacher Created Materials.

Seuling, B. (1984). *How to write a children's book and get it published.* New York: Charles Scribner's Sons.

Shanahan, T., & Shanahan, S. (1997). Character perspective charting: Helping children to develop a more complete conception of story. *The Reading Teacher, 50*(8), 668–677.

Sheldon, S. (2002). Parents' social networks and beliefs as predictors of parent involvement. *The Elementary School Journal, 102*(4), 301–316.

Shima, K., & Gsovski, B. (1996). Making a way for Diana. *Educational Leadership, 53*(5), 37–40.

Short, K., & Kauffman, G. (1995). "So what do I do?" The role of the teacher in literature circles. In N. Roser & M. Martinez (eds.), *Book talk and beyond.* Newark, DE: International Reading Association.

Short, K., & Klassen, C. (1993). Literature circles: Hearing children's voices. In B. Cullinan (ed.), *Children's voices: Talk in the classroom.* Newark, DE: International Reading Association.

Short, K., Harste, J., & Burke, C. (1996a). *Creating classrooms for authors: The reading-writing connection* (2nd ed.). Portsmouth, NH: Heinemann.

Short, K., Harste, J., & Burke, C. (1996b). *Creating classrooms for authors and inquirers* (2nd ed.). Portsmouth, NH: Heinemann.

Shurley, B., & Wetsell, R. K. (1989). *The Shurley method: English made easy.* Cabot, AR: Shurley Instructional Materials.

Shurley, B., & Wetsell, R. K. (1997). *Shurley method English made easy* (Information Packet Booklet). Cabot, AR: Shurley Instructional Materials.

Shuy, R. (1987). Research currents: Dialogue as the heart of learning. *Language Arts, 64,* 890–897.

Sigmon, C. M. (1997). *Implementing the 4-Blocks Literacy Model.* Greensboro, NC: Carson-Dellosa.

Silvaroli, N. (2001). *Classroom reading inventory* (9th ed.). Dubuque, IA: Wm. C. Brown Publishers.

Sinatra, R. (1991). Integrating whole language with the learning of text structure. *Journal of Reading, 34*(6), 424–433.

Singer, J. L. (1973). *The child's world of make-believe: Experimental studies of imaginative play.* New York: Academic Press.

Skinner, B. (1957). *Verbal behavior.* Englewood Cliffs, NJ: Prentice Hall.

Slavin, R. (1996). Neverstreaming: Preventing learning disabilities. *Educational Leadership, 53*(5), 4–7.

Slavin, R. (2002, February). Mounting evidence supports achievement effects of Success for All. *Phi Delta Kappan, 83*(6), 469–471.

Slavin, R., & Madden, N. (1989). What works for students at risk: A research synthesis. *Educational Leadership, 46*(5), 4–13.

Slavin, R., Kerweitt, N., & Madden, N. (1989). *Effective programs for students at risk.* Boston: Allyn & Bacon.

Slavin, R., Madden, N., Dolan, L., & Wasik, B. (1996). *Every child every school: Success for All.* Thousand Oaks, CA: Corwin Press.

Slavin, R., Madden, N., Dolan, L., Wasik, B., Ross, S., Smith, L., & Dianda, M. (1997) Success for All: A summary of research. *Journal of Education for Students Placed at Risk, 1*(1), 41–76.

Smith, D., Stenner, A. J., Horabin, I., & Smith, M. (1989). *The lexile scale in theory and practice: Final report.* Washington, DC: Metametrics. (ERIC Document Reproduction Service No. ED307577)

Smith, E. (1997). What is Black English? What is Ebonics? In "The real Ebonics debate" (T. Perry & L. Delpit, eds.). *Rethinking Schools: An Urban Education Journal, 12*(1), 14–15.

Smith, F. (1975). *Comprehension and learning.* New York: Holt.

Smith, F. (1977). The uses of language. *Language Arts, 54,* 638–644.

Smith, F. (1982a). *Understanding reading* (3rd ed.). New York: Holt, Rinehart & Winston.

Smith, F. (1982b). The unspeakable habit. *Language Arts, 59*(6), 550–554.

Smith, F. (1988). *Understanding reading* (4th ed.). Hillsdale, NJ: Lawrence Erlbaum Associates.

Smith, F. (1997). *Reading without nonsense* (3rd ed.). New York: Teacher's College Press.

Smith, M. (1986). Grammar and the manipulation of syntax. In G. Hillocks (ed.), *Research on written composition.* Urbana, IL: ERIC Clearinghouse of Reading and Communication Skills.

Smith, M. (2002). *The effects of rhyme rime connection training on second grade reading performance.* Unpublished doctoral dissertation. Oklahoma State University, Stillwater.

Smith, M., & Bean, T. W. (1983). Four strategies that develop children's story comprehension and writing. *The Reading Teacher, 37*(3), 295–301.

Smith, P. (1988). A fresh start with a reception class. In J. Hancock & S. Hill (eds.), *Literature-based reading programs at work.* Portsmouth, NH: Heinemann.

Smitherman, G. (1997). Black English/Ebonics: What it be like? In "The real Ebonics debate" (T. Perry & L. Delpit, eds.). *Rethinking Schools: An Urban Education Journal, 12*(1), 14–15.

Smolin, L. I., & Lawless, K. A. (2003). Becoming literate in the technological age: New responsibilities and tools for teachers. *The Reading Teacher, 56*(5), 570–577.

Snow, C. E. (1983). Literacy and language: Relationships during the preschool years. *Harvard Educational Review, 53*(2), 165–189.

Sommers, N. (1994). Revision strategies of student writers and experienced adult writers. In S. Perl (ed.), *Landmark essays on writing process.* Davis, CA: Heragoras Press.

Sowers, S. (1985). The story and the "all about" book. In J. Hansen, T. Newkirk, & D. Graves (eds.), *Breaking ground: Teachers relate reading and writing in the elementary school.* Portsmouth, NH: Heinemann.

Spandel, V., & Stiggins, R. (1990). *Creating writers: Linking assessment and writing instruction.* New York: Longman.

Spiegel, D. (1996). The role of trust in reader-response groups. *Language Arts, 73*(5), 332–339.

Spigner-Littles, D. (1992). *Learning styles of African-American (Black) students.* Oklahoma City, OK: Oklahoma State Department of Education.

Spring, J. (1988). *Conflicts of interest: The politics of American education.* New York: Longman.

Stahl, S. L., & Miller, P. D. (1989). Whole language and language experiences approaches for beginning reading: A quantitative research synthesis. *Review of Educational Research, 59*(1), 87–116.

Starko, A. (1986). *It's about time.* Mansfield Center, CT: Creative Learning Press.

Staton, J. (1980). Writing and counseling: Using a dialogue journal. *Language Arts, 57,* 514–518.

Stauffer, R. G. (1969). *Directing reading maturity as a cognitive process.* New York: Harper & Row.

Stauffer, R. (1980). *The language experience approach to the teaching of reading.* New York: Harper & Row.

Stein, N. L., & Glenn, C. G. (1979). An analysis of story comprehension in elementary school children. In R. O. Freedle (ed.), *New directions in discourse processing* (Vol. 2). Norwood, NJ: Ablex.

Sternberg, R. (1997). What does it mean to be smart? *Educational Leadership, 54*(6), 20–25.

Stevens, W. (1985, March 15). Black and standard English held diverging more. *New York Times,* sec. 1, p. 14.

Stewig, J. (1981). Choral speaking: Who has the time? Why take the time? *Childhood Education, 57,* 25–29.

Stiggins, R. (2002, June). Assessment crisis: The absence of assessment for learning. *Phi Delta Kappan, 83*(10), 758–765.

Stiggins, R., & Conklin, N. (1992). *In teachers' hands: Investigating the practice of classroom assessment.* New York: State University of New York Press.

Stoll, D. R. (ed.). (1997). *Magazines for kids and teens* (2nd ed.). Glassboro, NJ, & Newark, DE: Educational Press Association of America & International Reading Association.

Stoodt, B. (1988). *Teaching language arts.* New York: Harper & Row.

Strickland, D. (1987). Literature: Key element in the language and reading program. In B. E. Cullinan (ed.), *Children's literature in the reading program.* Newark, DE: International Reading Association.

Strickland, D., & Cullinan, B. (1990) The Afterword. In M. Adams (ed.), *Beginning to read: Thinking and learning about print,* 425–433. Cambridge, MA: MIT Press.

Strickland, D. S., & Morrow, L. M. (1990). Family literacy: Sharing good books (emerging readers and writers). *The Reading Teacher, 43*(7), 518–519.

Strickland, D., Dillon, R., Funkhouser, L., Glick, M., & Rogers, C. (1989). Research currents: Classroom dialogue during literature response groups. *Language Arts, 66*(5), 192–205.

Strickland, D. S., Dillon, R. M., Funkhouser, L., Glick, M., & Rogers, C. (1990). Research currents: Classroom dialogue during literature response groups. *Language Arts, 66*(2), 192–200.

Strong, W. (1993). *Sentence combining: A composing book* (3rd ed.). New York: McGraw-Hill.

Strother, D. (1987). Practical applications of research on listening. *Phi Delta Kappan, 68,* 625–628.

Sullivan, P. (1998). The PTA's National Standards. *Educational Leadership, 55*(8), 43–44.

Sullivan, P. L. (2003). CONNECTing IEP objectives to general curriculum and instruction. *Middle School Journal, 34*(4), 47–52.

Sutherland, Z., & Livingston, M. C. (1984). *The Scott Foresman anthology of children's literature.* Glenview, IL: Scott Foresman & Company.

Taba, H. (1967). *Teacher's handbook for elementary social studies.* Reading, MA: Addison-Wesley.

Tashjian, V. A. (1974). *With a deep sea smile.* Boston: Little, Brown & Company.

Taylor, D. (1983). *Family literacy.* Portsmouth, NH: Heinemann.

Teale, W., & Sulzby, E. (1989). Emergent literacy: New perspectives. In D. S. Strickland & L. M. Morrow (eds.), *Emerging literacy: Young children learn to read and write.* Newark, DE: International Reading Association.

Temple, C., Nathan, R., Burris, N., & Temple, F. (1988). *The beginnings of writing* (2nd ed.). Boston: Allyn & Bacon.

Templeton, S., & Morris, D. (1999). Questions teachers ask about spelling. *Reading Research Quarterly, 34,* 102–112.

Tharp, R. G., & Gallimore, R. (1989). *Rousing minds to life: Teaching, learning, and schooling in social context.* New York: Cambridge University Press.

Thomas, K. (1985). Early reading as a social interaction process. *Language Arts, 62*(5), 469–475.

Thompson, B. (1984, December 23). Children's books need careful review. *The News & Courier,* Charleston, SC.

Thompson, R. A. (1971). Summarizing research pertaining to individualized reading. (ERIC Document Reproduction Service, No. ED 065 836).

Thurber, D. (1987). *D'Nealian handwriting: Grades K–8.* Glenview, IL: Scott Foresman.

Tiedt, I. (1970). Exploring poetry patterns. *English Education, 47*(8), 1083–1084.

Tierney, R. J. (1990). Redefining reading comprehension. *Educational Leadership, 47*(6), 37–42.

Tierney, R., & Pearson, P. D. (1983). Toward a composing model of reading. *Language Arts, 60*(5), 568–589.

Tierney, R. J., & Readence, J. E. (2000). *Reading strategies and practices: A compendium* (5th ed.). Boston: Allyn & Bacon.

Tierney, R., Johnson, P., Moore, D., & Valencia, S. (2000). How will literacy be assessed in the next millennium? *Reading Research Quarterly, 35*(2), 244–250.

Tomlinson, C. A. (2000). Reconcilable differences? Standards-based teaching and differentiation. *Educational Leadership, 58*(1), 6–11.

Tompkins, G. (1990). *Teaching writing: Balancing process and product.* Columbus, OH: Merrill.

Tompkins, G. (1997). *Literacy for the 21st century: A balanced approach.* Upper Saddle River, NJ: Merrill.

Tompkins, G. (2002). *Language arts: Content and teaching strategies* (5th ed.). Upper Saddle River, NJ: Merrill.

Tompkins, G. (2003). *Literacy for the 21st century: Teaching reading and writing in pre-kindergarten through grade 4* (3rd ed.). Upper Saddle River, NJ: Merrill/Prentice Hall.

Tompkins, G., & McGee, L. (1983). Launching non-standard speakers into standard English. *Language Arts, 60*(4), 463–469.

Tough, J. (1984). How young children develop and use language. In D. Fontana (ed.), *The education of the young child.* Oxford: Basil Blackwell Publishers.

Tough, J. (1985). *Listening to children talk.* London: SCDC Publications.

Trelease, J. (1995). *The new read-aloud handbook* (2nd ed.). New York: Penguin Books.

Trelease, J. (2001). *The read-aloud handbook* (5th ed.). New York: Penguin Books.

Trousdale, A. (1990). Interactive storytelling: Scaffolding children's early narratives. *Language Arts, 67*(2), 164–173.

Tunnell, M. O., & Jacobs, J. S. (1989). Using "real" books: Research findings on literature-based reading instruction. *The Reading Teacher, 42*(7), 470–477.

Tway, E. (1984). *Time for writing in the elementary school.* Urbana, IL: National Council of Teachers of English.

U.S. Department of Education. (1996). National Assessment of Educational Progress. Office of Educational Research and Improvement. Washington, DC: U.S. Government Printing Office.

U.S. Department of Education. (2001). National household education survey. *National Center for Education Statistics* [Online]. Available at: http://NCES.org [2003, February 8].

U.S. Department of Education, National Center for Education Statistics. (2001). *The condition of education 2001* (NCED 2001-072). Washington, DC: U.S. Government Printing Office.

Uresti, R., Goertz, J., & Bernal, E. (2002). Maximizing achievement for potentially gifted and talented and regular minority students in the primary classroom. *Roeper*

Vacca, J. L., Vacca, R. T., Gove, M. K., Burkey, L. C., Lenhart, L. A., & McKeon, C. A. (2003). *Reading and learning to read* (5th ed.). Boston: Allyn and Bacon.

Vacca, R. T. (2002). From efficient decoders to strategic readers, *Educational leadership, 60*(3), 6–11.

Vacca, R. (2002). Making a difference in adolescents' school lives: Visible and invisible aspects of content area reading. In A. E. Farstrup & S. J. Samuels (Eds.), *What research has to say about reading instruction* (pp. 184–204). Newark: DE: The International Reading Association.

Vacca, R. T., & Vacca, J. L. (2002). *Content area reading* (7th ed.). Boston: Allyn & Bacon.

Vail, N., & Papenfuss, J. (1989). *Daily oral language. Level 1–12.* Evanston, IL: McDougal, Littell.

Valdes, G. (1990). Unrealistic rhetoric and realistic reform in education: A critical perspective. In H. Romo (ed.), *Latinos and Blacks in the cities.* Austin: University of Texas Press.

Valdes-Fallis, G. (1978). *Code switching and the classroom teacher: Language in education theory and practice 4.* Arlington, VA: Center for Applied Linguistics.

Valencia, S. (1990). A portfolio approach to classroom reading assessment: The whys, whats, and hows. *The Reading Teacher, 43,* 338–340.

Van Allen, R. (1973). The Language Experience Approach. In R. Karlin (ed.), *Perspectives on elementary reading: Principles and strategies of teaching.* New York: Harcourt Brace Jovanovich.

Van Anderson, T. (nondated). Cultural behavior of Asians. Oklahoma City, OK: Oklahoma State Department of Education.

van den Broek, P., Risden, K., Fletcher, C., & Thurlow, R. (1996). A "landscape" view of reading: Fluctuating patterns of activation and the construction of a stable memory representation. In B. K. Britton & A. C. Graesser (eds.), *Models of understanding text.* Mahwah, NJ: Lawrence Erlbaum.

Veatch, J. (1992). Whole language and its predecessors. *Journal of Reading Education, 18,* 69–77.

Venezky, R. L. (1998). As alternative perspective on Success for All. In K. K. Wong (Ed.) *Advances in educational policy* (pp. 145–165). Greenwich, CT: JAI Press.

Vermette, P. (1998). *Making cooperative learning work.* Upper Saddle River, NJ: Merrill.

Viadero, D. (1996). Culture clash. *Education Week, 15*(29), 10 pages. Available at: http://web7.epnet.com/citation.asp?tb=1&_ugdbs+0+In+en%2Dus+sid+FCE8CCD4%2DI [2003, May 19].

Villegas, A., & Lucas, T. (2002, January/February). Preparing culturally responsive teachers: Rethinking the curriculum. *Journal of Teacher Education,* 20–32.

Vinacke, W. E. (1974). *The psychology of thinking* (2nd ed.). New York: McGraw-Hill.

Vitale, B. (1982). *Unicorns are real: A right-brained approach to learning.* Rolling Hills Estates, CA: Jalmar Press.

Vizyak, L. (1997). Using a literacy portfolio in first grade. In R. B. Wiener & J. H. Cohen (eds.), *Literacy portfolios: Using assessment to guide instruction.* Columbus, OH: Merrill.

Vygotsky, L. (1976). *Thought and language* (E. Hanfmann & G. Vaka, eds. and trans.). Cambridge, MA: MIT Press.

Vygotsky, L. (1978a). *Mind and society: The development of psychological processes.* Cambridge, MA: Harvard University Press.

Vygotsky, L. (1978b). *Mind in society: Development of higher psychological processes.* Cambridge, MA: MIT Press.

Walker, B. (2000). *Diagnostic teaching of reading* (4th ed.). Upper Saddle River, NJ: Merrill/Prentice Hall.

Wardhaugh, R. (1972). The study of language. In R. Hodges & E. Rudorf (eds.), *Language and learning to read.* Boston: Houghton Mifflin Co.

Watson, D. J. (1989). Defining and describing whole language. *The Elementary School Journal, 90*(2), 129–141.

Weaver, C. (1994). *Reading process and practice: From socio-linguistics to whole language* (2nd ed.). Portsmouth, NH: Heinemann.

Weaver, C. (1996). *Teaching grammar in context.* Portsmouth, NH: Boynton/Cook Publishers.

Weaver, C. (2002). *Reading process and practice* (3rd ed.). Portsmouth, NH: Heinemann.

Weiner, B. (1972). *Theories of motivation.* Chicago: Rand McNally.

Weir, B. (1989). A research base for prekindergarten literacy programs. *The Reading Teacher, 42*(6), 456–460.

Wells, G. (ed.). (1981). *Learning through interaction: The study of language development.* London: Cambridge University Press.

Wells, G. (1986). *The meaning makers: Children learning language and using language to learn.* Portsmouth, NH: Heinemann.

Wells, G. (1990). Creating the conditions to encourage literate thinking. *Educational Leadership, 47*(6), 13–17.

Welty, E. (1983). *One writer's beginnings.* New York: Warner Books.

Whaley, J. (1981). Grammars and reading instruction. *Language Arts, 34*(7), 762–765.

Wharton-McDonald, Pressley, M., Rankin, J., Mistretta, J., Yokoi, L. & Ettenberger, S. (1997). Effective primary-grades literacy instruction = balanced literacy instruction. *The Reading Teacher, 50*(6), 518–521.

White, J. H., Vaughn, J. L., & Rorie, I. L. (1986). Picture of a classroom where reading is for real. *The Reading Teacher, 40*(1), 84–86.

Whorf, B. (1956). *Language, thought, and reality.* Cambridge, MA: MIT Press.

Wigfield, A., & Asher, S. R. (1984). Social and motivational influences on reading. In P. D. Pearson, R. Barr, M. L. Kamil, & P. Mosenthal (eds.), *Handbook of research on reading* (pp. 423–452). New York: Longman.

Wigginton, E. (1986). *Sometimes a shining moment: The Foxfire experience.* Garden City, NY: Doubleday.

Wilde, S. (1996). A speller's bill of rights. *Primary Voices K–6, 4*(1), 7–10.

Wilde, S. (1997). *What's a schwa sound anyway? A holistic guide to phonetics, phonics, and spelling.* Portsmouth, NH: Heinemann.

Williams, C. (1997). *An examination of the effects of Shurley English on the writing performance of fourth grade students.* Unpublished doctoral dissertation. Oklahoma State University, Stillwater.

Wilwerth, J. (1979, December 19). Ginny and Gracie go to school: Kennedy twins. *Time,* p. 119.

Wineburg, S. (1997). T. S. Eliot, collaboration and the quandaries of assessment in a rapidly changing world. *Phi Delta Kappan, 79*(1), 59–65.

Winn, D. (1988). Develop listening skills as part of the curriculum. *The Reading Teacher, 42*(2), 144–148.

Withers, C. (1948). *A rocket in my pocket.* New York: Scholastic Book Services.

Wixson, K. K., & Lipson, M. Y. (2000). *Reading diagnosis and remediation.* Glenview, IL: Scott Foresman.

Wolf, J. L. & Health, S. B. (1999). When resolution comes in stages: How drama makes good use of conflict. In B. J. Wagner (Ed.), *Building moral communities through educational drama* (pp. 91–112) Stamford, CT: Ablex.

Wong, H., & Wong, R. (1991). *The first days of school: How to be an effective teacher.* Sunnyvale, CA: Harry K. Wong.

Woods, W. (1986). The evolution of nineteenth century grammar teaching. *Rhetoric Review, 5*(1), 4–20.

Wray, D., & Lewis, M. (1997). *Extending literacy: Children reading and writing non-fiction.* New York: Routledge.

Yellin, D. (1980). The Black English controversy: Implications from the Ann Arbor case. *Journal of Reading, 24*(2), 150–154.

Yellin, D. (1983a). *Integrating elementary language arts.* Dubuque, IA: Eddie Bowers Publishing Co.

Yellin, D. (1983b). Left brain, right brain, super brain: The holistic mode. *Reading World, 23*(1), 36–43.

Yellin, D. (1985). *Integrating the elementary language arts.* Dubuque, IA: Eddie Bowers Publishers.

Yellin, D. (1988). My pen pal goes to college: A functional approach to literacy learning. *The Writer's Slate, 4*(1), 1–8.

Yellin, D. (1991). Will evaluation kill whole language? *Kansas Journal of Reading, 7,* 49–54.

Yellin, D., & Blake, M. (1994). *Integrating the language arts: A holistic approach.* New York: HarperCollins.

Zarillo, J. (1989). Teachers' interpretations of literature-based reading. *The Reading Teacher, 43*(1), 22–28.

Zellman, G., & Waterman, J. (1998). Education—parent participation. *Journal of Educational Research, 91*(6), 370–381.

Zorfass, J., & Copel, H. (1995). The I-search: Guiding students toward relevant research. *Educational Leadership, 53*(1), 48–51.

Zutell, J. (1996). The directed spelling thinking activity (DSTA): Providing an effective balance in word study instruction. *The Reading Teacher, 50*(2), 98–108.

Index

Writing Rubric: Holistic Scoring and Student Self-Evaluation

HOLISTIC SCORING

In holistic scoring, written papers are given a quick, general reading for overall content, clarity, organization, flow, and development of thoughts. For teachers who have many papers to grade, this is a time-saving yet effective device to evaluate students' writing. Before using the four-point scale, you must be clear in your own mind what constitutes a 4, 3, 2, 1 grade.

HOLISTIC SCORING FOR STUDENT SELF-EVALUATION

Although holistic scoring was originally developed for teachers, it can be modified to be used by students who have been taught to self-evaluate their own work. It can also be used in a buddy system where peers evaluate one another.

HOLISTIC SCORING RUBRIC USING A FOUR-POINT SCALE

1 = Ineffective Piece: Many problems; not going anywhere.
2 = Ineffective Piece but Salvageable: Has problems but I know how to solve them.
3 = Effective Piece: This works; is well organized, clearly written, and has no mechanical errors.
4 = Most Effective Piece: Includes all components of #3 plus it says something; exemplifies strong writing; moves the reader.

After you have rated your pieces 1, 2, 3, 4, write three reasons for each of the scores. Cite specific examples in the piece to support your reasons.

_____

_____

_____

_____

_____

_____

_____

_____

_____

_____

_____

_____

_____

_____

Rubric for Upper Elementary Grades Writing

Student's Name   *Date*

Title of Project

Possible Points   **Points You Earned**

1. Separate cover sheet, name, date, title   10   _____

2. Neatly written   10   _____

3. Clearly written sentences   20   _____

4. Well-organized paragraphs   20   _____

5. Clear beginning, middle, and end   20   _____

6. Proofread and edited for errors   20   _____

TOTAL   100   _____